D0073750

Z52.5 .M52 O43124 2008

O'Leary, Timothy J.,

Microsoft Office Word
2007   c2008.

2007 10 12

The O'Leary Series

Microsoft® Office
Word 2007

Introductory Edition

DATE DUE	
SEP 2 9 2008	
SEP 2 3 2008	
NOV 3 0 2009	

DISCARDED
NO LONGER THE
PROPERTY OF GBC

BRODART.   Cat. No. 23-221

GEORGE BROWN COLLEGE
CASA LOMA LIBRARY LEARNING COMMONS

The O'Leary Series

Computing Concepts

- *Computing Essentials 2007* Introductory & Complete Editions
- *Computing Essentials 2008* Introductory & Complete Editions

Microsoft® Office Applications

- *Microsoft® Office Word 2007* Brief & Introductory Editions
- *Microsoft® Office Excel 2007* Brief & Introductory Editions
- *Microsoft® Office Access 2007* Brief & Introductory Editions
- *Microsoft® Office PowerPoint 2007* Brief Edition

The O'Leary Series

Microsoft® Office Word 2007

Introductory Edition

Timothy J. O'Leary

Arizona State University

Linda I. O'Leary

GEORGE BROWN COLLEGE
CASA LOMA LIBRARY LEARNING COMMONS

 **McGraw-Hill**
Higher Education

Boston   Burr Ridge, IL   Dubuque, IA   New York   San Francisco   St. Louis
Bangkok   Bogotá   Caracas   Kuala Lumpur   Lisbon   London   Madrid   Mexico City
Milan   Montreal   New Delhi   Santiago   Seoul   Singapore   Sydney   Taipei   Toronto

The McGraw·Hill Companies

McGraw-Hill
Higher Education

THE O'LEARY SERIES MICROSOFT® OFFICE WORD 2007 INTRODUCTORY EDITION

Published by McGraw-Hill, a business unit of The McGraw-Hill Companies, Inc., 1221 Avenue of the Americas, New York, NY, 10020. Copyright © 2008 by The McGraw-Hill Companies, Inc. All rights reserved. No part of this publication may be reproduced or distributed in any form or by any means, or stored in a database or retrieval system, without the prior written consent of The McGraw-Hill Companies, Inc., including, but not limited to, in any network or other electronic storage or transmission, or broadcast for distance learning.

Some ancillaries, including electronic and print components, may not be available to customers outside the United States.

This book is printed on acid-free paper.

1 2 3 4 5 6 7 8 9 0 QPD/QPD 0 9 8 7

ISBN 978-0-07-329450-6
MHID 0-07-329450-0

Vice President/Editor in Chief: *Elizabeth Haefele*
Vice President/Director of Marketing: *John E. Biernat*
Developmental editor: *Kelly L. Delso*
Marketing manager: *Sarah Wood*
Lead media producer: *Damian Moshak*
Media producer: *Benjamin Curless*
Director, Editing/Design/Production: *Jess Ann Kosic*
Project manager: *Marlena Pechan*
Production supervisor: *Jason I. Huls*
Designer: *Srdjan Savanovic*
Senior photo research coordinator: *Jeremy Cheshareck*
Typeface: *10.5/13 New Aster*
Compositor: *Laserwords Private Limited*
Printer: *Quebecor World Dubuque Inc.*

Library of Congress Cataloging-in-Publication Data

O'Leary, Timothy J., 1947-
    Microsoft Office Word 2007 / Timothy J. O'Leary, Linda I. O'Leary.—Introductory ed.
        p. cm.—(The O'Leary series)
    Includes index.
    ISBN-13: 978-0-07-329450-6 (acid-free paper)
    ISBN-10: 0-07-329450-0 (acid-free paper)
    1. Microsoft Word. 2. Word processing. I. O'Leary, Linda I. II. Title.
Z52.5.M52O458 2008b
005.52—dc22
                                                                        2007025546

www.mhhe.com

Brief Contents

Detailed Contents

ix

Acknowledgments

We would like to extend our thanks to the professors who took time out of their busy schedules to provide us with the feedback necessary to develop the 2007 Edition of this text. The following professors offered valuable suggestions on revising the text:

Adida Awan, Savannah State University

Jacqueline Bakal, Felician College

Chet Barney, Southern Utah University

Bruce W. Bryant, University of Arkansas Community College Morrilton

Kelly D. Carter, Mercer University

Cesar Augusto Casas, St. Thomas Aquinas College

Sally Clements, St. Thomas Aquinas College

Donna N. Dunn, Beaufort County Community College

Donna Ehrhart, Genesee Community College

Saiid Ganjalizadeh, The Catholic University of America

Dr. Jayanta Ghosh, Florida Community College

Carol Grazette, Medgar Evers College/CUNY

Susan Gundy, University of Illinois at Springfield

Greg R. Hodge, Northwestern Michigan College

Christopher M. J. Hopper, Bellevue Community College

Ginny Kansas, Southwestern College

Robert Kemmerer, Los Angeles Mission College

Diana I. Kline, University of Louisville

Linda Klisto, Broward Community College North Campus

Nanette Lareau, University of Arkansas Community College Morrilton

Deborah Layton, Eastern Oklahoma State College

Keming Liu, Medgar Evers College/CUNY

J. Gay Mills, Amarillo College

Kim Moorning, Medgar Evers College/CUNY

Dr. Belinda J. Moses, University of Phoenix/Baker College/Wayne County Community College

Lois Ann O'Neal, Rogers State University

Andrew Perry, Springfield College

Michael Philipp, Greenville Technical College

Julie Piper, Bucks County Community College

Brenda Price, Bucks County Community College

Thali N. Rajashekhara, Camden County College

Dr. Marcel Marie Robles, Eastern Kentucky University

Jose (Joe) Sainz, Naugatuck Valley Community College

Pamela J. Silvers, Asheville-Buncombe Technical Community College

Glenna Stites, Johnson County Community College

Joyce Thompson, Lehigh Carbon Community College

Michelle G. Vlaich-Lee, Greenville Technical College

Mary A. Walthall, St. Petersburg College

We would like to thank those who took the time to help us develop the manuscript and ensure accuracy through pain-staking edits: Brenda Nielsen of Mesa Community College–Red Mountain, Rajiv Narayana of SunTech Info-Labs, and Craig Leonard.

Our thanks also go to Linda Mehlinger of Morgan State University for all her work on creating the PowerPoint presentations to accompany the text. We are grateful to Harry Knight of Franklin University, the author of the Instructor's manual and Testbank, for his careful revision of these valuable resource materials and creation of online quizzing materials.

Finally, we would like to thank team members from McGraw-Hill, whose renewed commitment, direction, and support have infused the team with the excitement of a new project. Leading the team from McGraw-Hill are Sarah Wood, Marketing Manager; and Developmental Editors Kelly Delso and Alaina Grayson.

The production staff is headed by Marlena Pechan, Project Manager, whose planning and attention to detail have made it possible for us to successfully meet a very challenging schedule; Srdjan Savanovic, Designer; Jason Huls, Production Supervisor; Ben Curless, Media Producer; Jeremy Cheshareck, Photo Researcher; and Betsy Blumenthal, copyeditor—team members whom we can depend on to do a great job.

Preface

The 20th century brought us the dawn of the digital information age and unprecedented changes in information technology. There is no indication that this rapid rate of change will be slowing—it may even be increasing. As we begin the 21st century, computer literacy is undoubtedly becoming a prerequisite in whatever career you choose.

The goal of the O'Leary Series is to provide you with the necessary skills to efficiently use these applications. Equally important is the goal to provide a foundation for students to readily and easily learn to use future versions of this software. This series does this by providing detailed step-by-step instructions combined with careful selection and presentation of essential concepts.

Times are changing, technology is changing, and this text is changing too. As students of today, you are different from those of yesterday. You put much effort toward the things that interest you and the things that are relevant to you. Your efforts directed at learning application programs and exploring the Web seem, at times, limitless.

On the other hand, students often can be shortsighted, thinking that learning the skills to use the application is the only objective. The mission of the series is to build upon and extend this interest by not only teaching the specific application skills but by introducing the concepts that are common to all applications, providing students with the confidence, knowledge, and ability to easily learn the next generation of applications.

Instructor's Resource CD-ROM

The **Instructor's Resource CD-ROM** contains a computerized Test Bank, an Instructor's Manual, and PowerPoint Presentation Slides. Features of the Instructor's Resource are described below.

- **Instructor's Manual CD-ROM** The Instructor's Manual, authored by Harry Knight of Franklin University, contains lab objectives, concepts, outlines, lecture notes, and command summaries. Also included are answers to all end-of-chapter material, tips for covering difficult materials, additional exercises, and a schedule showing how much time is required to cover text material.

- **Computerized Test Bank** The test bank, authored by Harry Knight, contains over 1,300 multiple choice, true/false, and discussion questions. Each question will be accompanied by the correct answer, the level of learning difficulty, and corresponding page references. Our flexible EZ Test software allows you to easily generate custom exams.

- **PowerPoint Presentation Slides**   The presentation slides, authored by Linda Mehlinger of Morgan State University, include lab objectives, concepts, outlines, text figures, and speaker's notes. Also included are bullets to illustrate key terms and FAQs.

Online Learning Center/Web Site

Found at **www.mhhe.com/oleary,** this site provides additional learning and instructional tools to enhance the comprehension of the text. The OLC/Web Site is divided into these three areas:

- **Information Center**   Contains core information about the text, supplements, and the authors.

- **Instructor Center**   Offers instructional materials, downloads, and other relevant links for professors.

- **Student Center**   Contains data files, chapter competencies, chapter concepts, self-quizzes, flashcards, additional Web links, and more.

Simnet Assessment for Office Applications

Simnet Assessment for Office Applications provides a way for you to test students' software skills in a simulated environment. Simnet is available for Microsoft Office 2007 and provides flexibility for you in your applications course by offering:

Pre-testing options

Post-testing options

Course placement testing

Diagnostic capabilities to reinforce skills

Web delivery of test

MCAS preparation exams

Learning verification reports

For more information on skills assessment software, please contact your local sales representative, or visit us at **www.mhhe.com**.

O'Leary Series

The O'Leary Application Series for Microsoft Office is available separately or packaged with *Computing Essentials*. The O'Leary Application Series offers a step-by-step approach to learning computer applications and is available in both brief and introductory versions. The introductory books are MCAS Certified and prepare students for the Microsoft Certified Applications Specialist exam.

Computing Concepts

Computing Essentials 2008 offers a unique, visual orientation that gives students a basic understanding of computing concepts. *Computing Essentials* encourages "active" learning with exercises, explorations, visual illustrations, and inclusion of screen shots and numbered steps. While combining the "active" learning style with current topics and technology, this text provides an accurate snapshot of computing trends. When bundled with software application lab manuals, students are given a complete representation of the fundamental issues surrounding the personal computing environment.

GUIDE TO THE O'LEARY SERIES

The O'Leary Series is full of features designed to make learning productive and hassle free. On the following pages you will see the kind of engaging, helpful pedagogical features that have helped countless students master Microsoft Office Applications.

EASY-TO-FOLLOW INTRODUCTORY MATERIALS

INTRODUCTION TO MICROSOFT OFFICE 2007

Each text in the O'Leary Series opens with an Introduction to Office 2007, providing a complete overview of this version of the Microsoft Office Suite.

What Is the 2007 Microsoft Office System?

Microsoft's 2007 Microsoft Office System is a comprehensive, integrated system of programs, servers, and services designed to solve a wide array of business needs. Although the programs can be used individually, they are designed to work together seamlessly, making it easy to connect people and organizations to information, business processes, and each other. The applications include tools used to create, discuss, communicate, and manage projects. If you share a lot of documents with other people, these features facilitate access to common documents. This version has an entirely new user interface that is designed to make it easier to perform tasks and help users more quickly take advantage of all the features in the applications. In addition, the communication and collaboration features and integration with the World Wide Web have been expanded and refined.

The 2007 Microsoft Office System is packaged in several different combinations of programs or suites. The major programs and a brief description are provided in the following table.

Program	Description
Word 2007	Word Processor program used to create text-based documents
Excel 2007	Spreadsheet program used to analyze numerical data
Access 2007	Database manager used to organize, manage, and display a database
PowerPoint 2007	Graphics presentation program used to create presentation materials
Outlook 2007	Desktop information manager and messaging client
InfoPath 2007	Used to create XML forms and documents
OneNote 2007	Note-taking and information organization tools
Publisher 2007	Tools to create and distribute publications for print, Web, and e-mail
Visio 2007	Diagramming and data visualization tools
SharePoint Designer 2007	Web site development and management for SharePoint servers
Project 2007	Project management tools
Groove 2007	Collaboration program that enables teams to work together

The four main components of Microsoft Office 2007—Word, Excel, Access, and PowerPoint—are the applications you will learn about in this series of labs. They are described in more detail in the following sections.

I2   Introduction to Microsoft Office 2007   www.mhhe.com/oleary
Word 2007

Overview of Microsoft Office Word 20[...]

What Is Word Processing?

Office Word 2007 is a word processing software application whose p[...] is to help you create any type of written communication. A word pro[...] can be used to manipulate text data to produce a letter, a report, a [...] an e-mail message, or any other type of correspondence. Text data [...] letter, number, or symbol that you can type on a keyboard. The grou[...] the text data to form words, sentences, paragraphs, and pages [...] results in the creation of a document. Through a word processor, y[...] create, modify, store, retrieve, and print part or all of a document.

Word processors are one of the most widely used application software programs. Putting your thoughts in writing, from the simplest note to the most complex book, is a time-consuming process. Even more time-consuming is the task of editing and retyping the document to make it better. Word processors make errors nearly nonexistent—not because they are not made, but because they are easy to correct. Word processors let you throw away the correction fluid, scissors, paste, and erasers. Now, with a few keystrokes, you can easily correct errors, move paragraphs, and reprint your document.

Word 2007 Features

Word 2007 excels in its ability to change or edit a document. Editing involves correcting spelling, grammar, and sentence-structure errors. In addition, you can easily revise or update existing text by inserting or deleting text. For example, a document that lists prices can easily be updated to reflect new prices. A document that details procedures can be revised by deleting old procedures and inserting new ones. This is especially helpful when a document is used repeatedly. Rather than recreating the whole document, you change only the parts that need to be revised.

Revision also includes the rearrangement of selected areas of text. For example, while writing a report, you may decide to change the location of a single word or several paragraphs or pages of text. You can do it easily by cutting or removing selected text from one location, then pasting or placing the selected text in another location. The selection also can be copied from one document to another.

To help you produce a perfect document, Word 2007 includes many additional support features. The AutoCorrect feature checks the spelling and grammar in a document as text is entered. Many common errors are corrected automatically for you. Others are identified and a correction suggested. A thesaurus can be used to display alternative words that have a meaning similar or opposite to a word you entered. A Find and Replace feature can be used to quickly locate specified text and replace it with other text throughout a document. In addition, Word 2007 includes a

WD0.1

INTRODUCTION TO WORD 2007

Each text in the O'Leary Series also provides an overview of the specific application features.

ENGAGING LAB INTRODUCTIONS

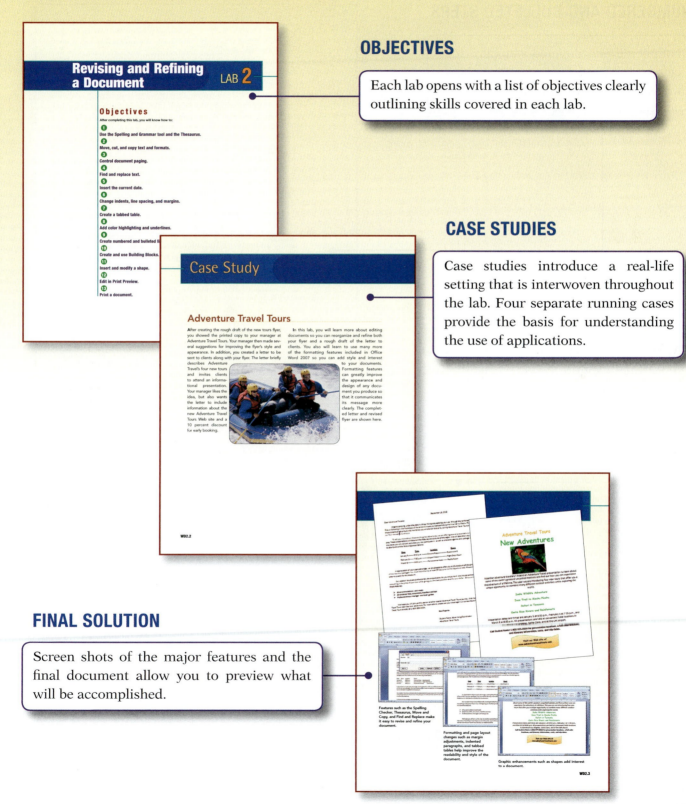

OBJECTIVES

Each lab opens with a list of objectives clearly outlining skills covered in each lab.

CASE STUDIES

Case studies introduce a real-life setting that is interwoven throughout the lab. Four separate running cases provide the basis for understanding the use of applications.

FINAL SOLUTION

Screen shots of the major features and the final document allow you to preview what will be accomplished.

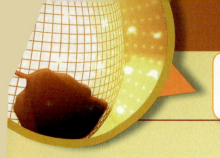

STEP-BY-STEP INSTRUCTION

NUMBERED AND BULLETED STEPS

Numbered and bulleted steps provide clear step-by-step instructions on how to complete a task, or series of tasks.

All steps and bullets appear in the left-hand margin, making it easy not to miss a step.

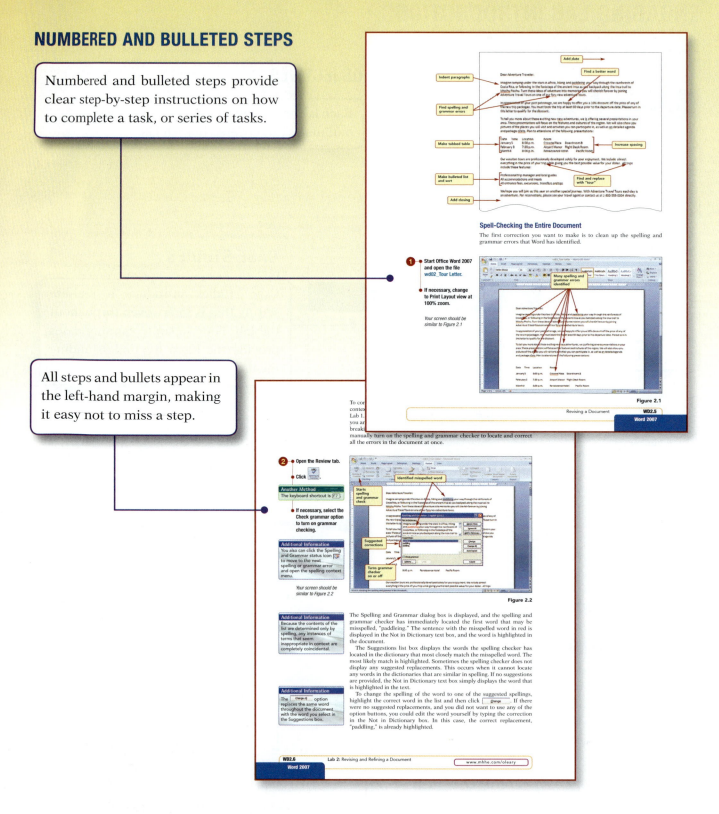

AND EASY-TO-FOLLOW DESIGN

TABLES

Tables provide quick summaries of concepts and procedures for specific tasks.

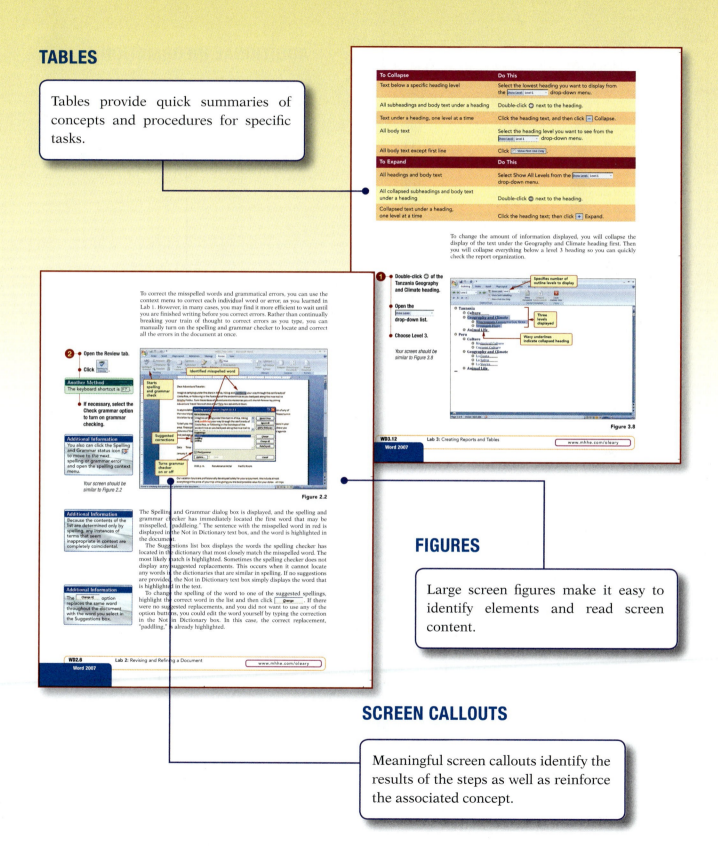

Figure 2.2

Figure 3.8

FIGURES

Large screen figures make it easy to identify elements and read screen content.

SCREEN CALLOUTS

Meaningful screen callouts identify the results of the steps as well as reinforce the associated concept.

SUPPORTIVE MARGIN NOTES

ADDITIONAL INFORMATION

Additional Information offers brief asides with expanded coverage of content.

ANOTHER METHOD

Another Method offers additional ways to perform a procedure.

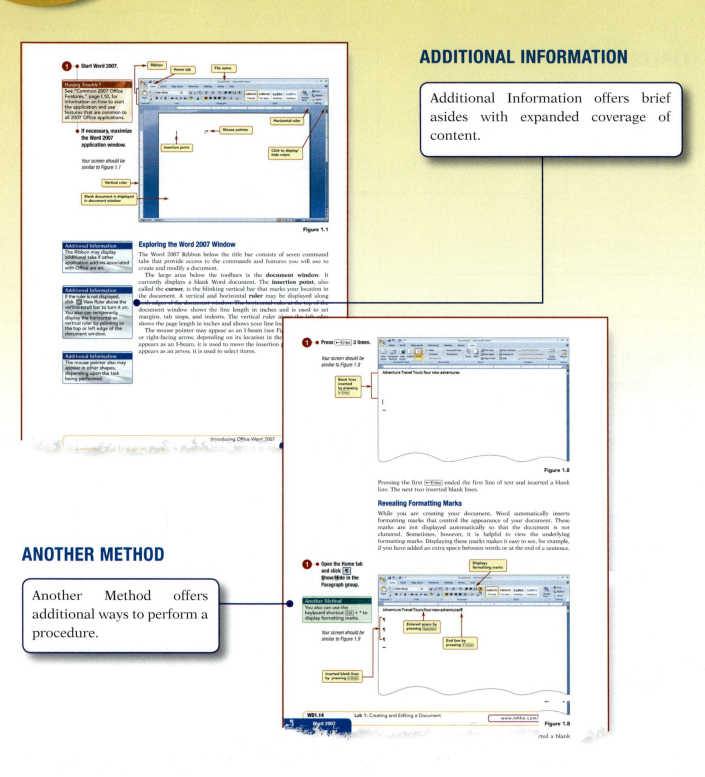

SUPPORTIVE MARGIN NOTES (CONTINUED)

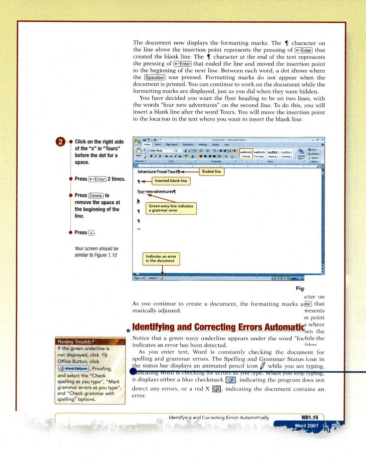

HAVING TROUBLE

Having Trouble helps resolve potential problems as students work through each lab.

MORE ABOUT

New to this edition, the More About icon directs students to the More About appendix found at the end of the book. Without interrupting the flow of the text, this appendix provides additional coverage required to meet MCAS certification.

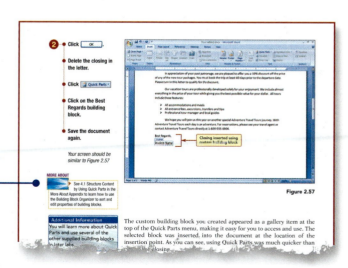

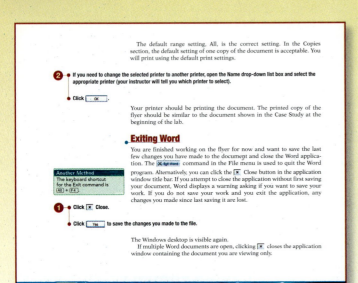

The default range setting, All, is the correct setting. In the Copies section, the default setting of one copy of the document is acceptable. You will print using the default print settings.

2 ● If you need to change the selected printer to another printer, open the Name drop-down list box and select the appropriate printer (your instructor will tell you which printer to select).

● Click [OK].

Your printer should be printing the document. The printed copy of the flyer should be similar to the document shown in the Case Study at the beginning of the lab.

Exiting Word

You are finished working on the flyer for now and want to save the last few changes you have made to the document and close the Word application. The [Exit Word] command in the File menu is used to quit the Word program. Alternatively, you can click the [X] Close button in the application window title bar. If you attempt to close the application without first saving your document, Word displays a warning asking if you want to save your work. If you do not save your work and you exit the application, any changes you made since last saving it are lost.

Another Method
The keyboard shortcut for the Exit command is [Alt] + [F4].

1 ● Click [X] Close.

● Click [Yes] to save the changes you made to the file.

The Windows desktop is visible again.
If multiple Word documents are open, clicking [X] closes the application window containing the document you are viewing only.

Focus on Careers

EXPLORE YOUR CAREER OPTIONS

Food Service Manager
Have you noticed flyers around your campus advertising job positions? Many of these jobs are in the food service industry. Food service managers are traditionally responsible for overseeing the kitchen and dining room. However, these positions increasingly involve administrative tasks, including recruiting new employees. As a food service manager, your position would likely include creating newspaper notices and flyers to attract new staff. These flyers should be eye-catching and error-free. The typical salary range of a food service manager is $34,000 to $41,700. Demand for skilled food service managers is expected to increase through 2010.

Exiting Word | **WD1.71**
Word 2007

FOCUS ON CAREERS

Focus on Careers provides an example of how the material covered may be applied in the "real world."

Each lab highlights a specific career, ranging from forensic science technician to food services manager, and presents job responsibilities and salary ranges for each.

Case Study

Adventure Travel Tours

Adventure Travel Tours provides information on their tours in a variety of forms. Travel brochures, for instance, contain basic tour information in a promotional format and are designed to entice potential clients to sign up for a tour. More detailed regional information packets are given to people who have already signed up for a tour, so they can prepare for their vacation. These packets include facts about each region's climate, geography, and culture. Additional informational formats include pages on Adventure Travel's Web site and scheduled group presentations.

Part of your responsibility as advertising coordinator is to gather the information that Adventure Travel will publicize about each regional tour. Specifically, you have been asked to provide background information for two of the new tours: the Tanzania Safari and the Machu Picchu trail. Because this information is used in a variety of formats, your research needs to be easily adapted. You will therefore present your facts in the form of a general report on Tanzania and Peru.

In this lab, you will learn to use many of the features of Office Word 2007 that make it easy to create an attractive and well-organized report. A portion of the completed report is shown here.

CONTINUING CASE STUDIES

Within each series application, the same Case Study is used to illustrate concepts and procedures.

WD3.2

AND INTEGRATION

WORKING TOGETHER LABS

At the completion of the brief and introductory texts, a final lab demonstrates the integration of Microsoft Office applications. Each Working Together lab also includes end-of-chapter materials.

Working Together 1: Word 2007 and Your Web Browser

Case Study

Adventure Travel Tours

The Adventure Travel Tours Web site is used to promote its products and broaden its audience of customers. In addition to the obvious marketing and sales potential, it provides an avenue for interaction between the company and the customer to improve customer service. The company also uses the Web site to provide articles of interest to customers. The articles, which include topics such as travel background information and descriptions, changes on a monthly basis as an added incentive for readers to return to the site.

You want to use the flyer you developed to promote the new tours and presentations on the Web

site. To do this, you will use Word 2007's Web-editing features that help you create a Web page quickly and easily. While using the Web-editing features, you will be working with Word and with a Web browser application. This capability of all 2007 Microsoft Office applications to work together and with other applications makes it easy to share and exchange information between applications. Your completed Web pages are shown here.

Note: The Working Together tutorial is designed to show how two applications work together and to present a basic introduction to creating Web pages.

WDWT1.1

Lab Exercises

rating system
★ Easy
★★ Moderate
★★★ Difficult

step-by-step

Adding a New Web Page ★

1. You want to continue working on the Web pages about the new tour presentations for the Adventure Travel Web site. Your next step is to create links from each location on the Presentation Locations Web page to information about each location's presentation date and times. Your completed Web page for the Los Angeles area should be similar to the one shown here.

   a. In Word, open the Web page file Tour Locations you created in this lab.
   b. Open the document wdwt_LosAngeles. Save the document as a Web page to the ATT Web Page folder with the file name LosAngeles and a page title of Los Angeles Presentation Information.
   c. Change the page color to a gradient fill effect of your choice. Change the first title line to the Title style and the second title line to a Heading 1 style. Change the title lines to a color of your choice.
   d. Increase the font size of the table to 12 points. Add color to the table headings. Enhance the Web page with any features you feel are appropriate.
   e. Two lines below the table, add the text Contact [your name] at (909) 555-1212 for more information. Apply the Emphasis style to this line and increase the font size to 14 points.
   f. On the Tour Locations page, create a link from the Los Angeles text to the Los Angeles page. Test the link.
   g. Resave both Web pages and preview them in your browser. Print the Los Angeles Web page.
   h. Exit the browser and Word.

Lab Exercises **WDWT1.19**
Word 2007

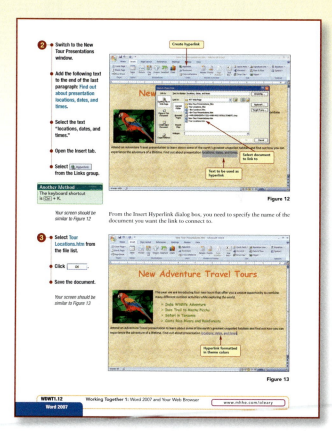

2. ● Switch to the New Tour Presentations window.
   ● Add the following text to the end of the last paragraph: **Find out about presentation locations, dates, and times.**
   ● Select the text "locations, dates, and times."
   ● Open the Insert tab.
   ● Select ▣ Hyperlink from the Links group.

Another Method
The keyboard shortcut is Ctrl + K.

Your screen should be similar to Figure 12

Figure 12

From the Insert Hyperlink dialog box, you need to specify the name of the document you want the link to connect to.

3. ● Select Tour Locations.htm from the file list.
   ● Click OK.
   ● Save the document.

Your screen should be similar to Figure 13

Figure 13

WDWT1.12   Working Together 1: Word 2007 and Your Web Browser   www.mhhe.com/oleary
Word 2007

REINFORCED CONCEPTS

CONCEPT PREVIEW

Concept Previews provide an overview to the concepts that will be presented throughout the lab.

Concept Preview

The following concepts will be introduced in this lab:

1. **Grammar Checker** The grammar checker advises you of incorrect grammar as you create and edit a document, and proposes possible corrections.

2. **Spelling Checker** The spelling checker advises you of misspelled words as you create and edit a document, and proposes possible corrections.

3. **AutoCorrect** The AutoCorrect feature makes some basic assumptions about the text you are typing and, based on these assumptions, automatically corrects the entry.

4. **Word Wrap** The word wrap feature automatically decides where to end a line and wrap text to the next line based on the margin settings.

5. **Font and Font Size** Font, also commonly referred to as a typeface, is a set of characters with a specific design that has one or more font sizes.

6. **Alignment** Alignment is the positioning of text on a line between the margins or indents. There are four types of paragraph alignment: left, centered, right, and justified.

7. **Graphics** A graphic is a nontext element or object such as a drawing or picture that can be added to a document.

Introducing Office Word 2007

Adventure Travel Tours has recently upgraded their computer systems at all locations across the country. As part of the upgrade, they have installed the latest version of the Microsoft Office 2007 suite of applications. You are very excited to see how this new and powerful application can help you create professional letters and reports as well as eye-catching flyers and newsletters.

Starting Office Word 2007

...on Microsoft Office Word 2007 ...nd presentations.

CONCEPT BOXES

Concept boxes appear throughout the lab providing clear, concise explanations and serving as a valuable study aid.

3 • Click outside the menu to close it.

• Open the spelling context menu for "lern" and choose "learn".

The spelling is corrected, and the spelling indicator in the status bar indicates that the document is free of errors.

Using Word Wrap

Now you will continue entering more of the paragraph. As you type, when the text gets close to the right margin, do not press ⏎Enter to move to the next line. Word will automatically wrap words to the next line as needed.

Concept 4

Word Wrap

4 The word wrap feature automatically decides where to end a line and wrap text to the next line based on the margin settings. This feature saves time when entering text because you do not need to press ⏎Enter at the end of a full line to begin a new line. The only time you need to press ⏎Enter is to end a paragraph, to insert blank lines, or to create a short line such as a salutation. In addition, if you change the margins or insert or delete text on a line, the program automatically readjusts the text on the line to fit within the new margin settings. Word wrap is common to all word processors.

Enter the following text to complete the sentence.

1 • Press End to move to the end of the line.

www.mhhe.com/oleary

CONCEPT SUMMARIES

The Concept Summary offers a visual summary of the concepts presented throughout the lab.

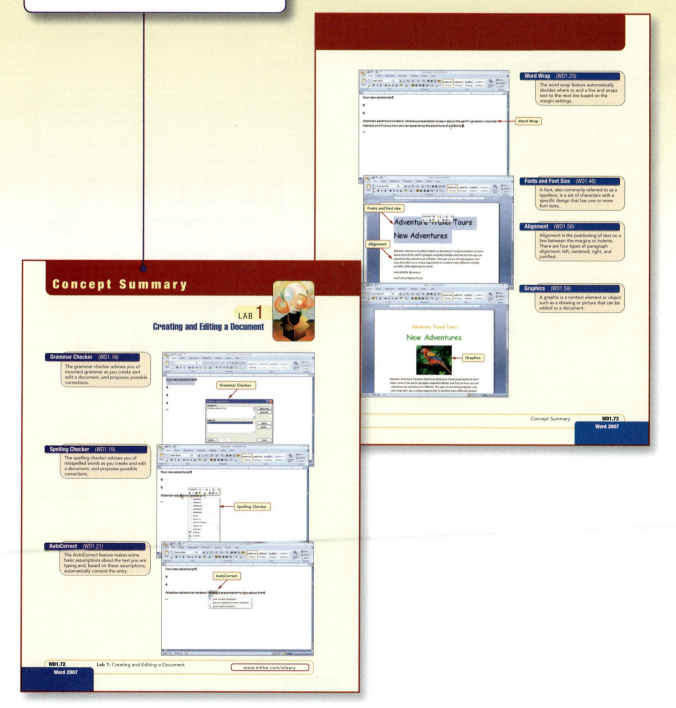

LAB REVIEW

KEY TERMS

Includes a list of all bolded terms with page references.

COMMAND SUMMARY

Command Summaries provide a table of commands, shortcuts and their associated action for all commands used in the lab.

END-OF-CHAPTER MATERIALS

Lab Exercises reinforce the terminology and concepts presented in the lab through Screen Identification, Matching, Multiple Choice, True/False, and Fill-In questions.

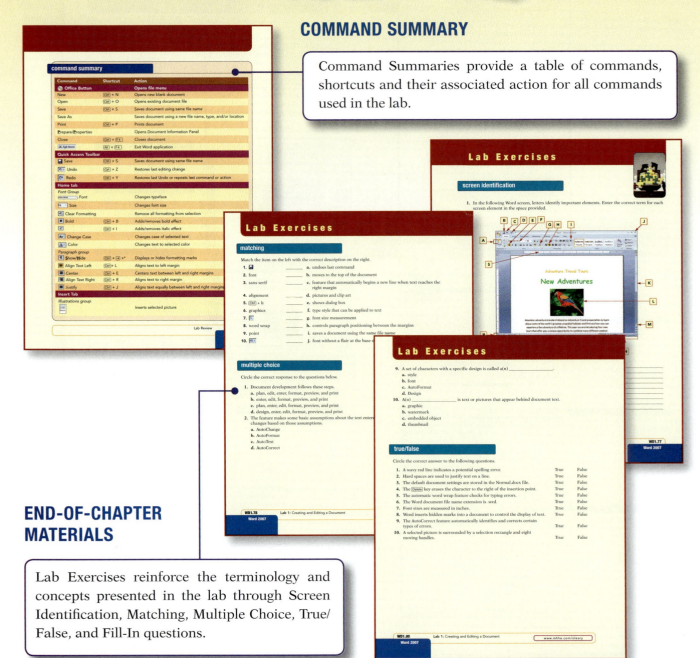

AND SKILL DEVELOPMENT

LAB EXERCISES

Lab Exercises provide hands-on practice and develop critical-thinking skills through step-by-step and on-your-own practice exercises. Many cases in the practice exercises tie to a running case used in another application lab. This helps demonstrate the use of the four applications across a common case setting. For example, the Adventure Tours case used in Word is continued in practice exercises in Excel, Access, and PowerPoint.

ON YOUR OWN

STEP-BY-STEP

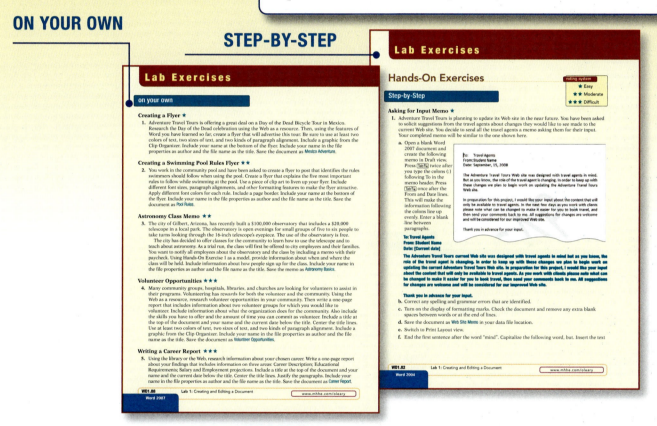

RATING SYSTEM

These exercises have a rating system from easy to difficult and test your ability to apply the knowledge you have gained in each lab. Exercises that build off of previous exercises are noted with a Continuing Exercises icon.

END-OF-BOOK RESOURCES

COMPREHENSIVE COMMAND SUMMARY

Provides a table of commands, shortcuts, and their associated action for all commands used throughout each text in the O'Leary Series.

2007 Word Brief Command Summary

Command	Shortcut	Action
Office Button		**Opens File menu**
New	Ctrl + N	Opens new document
Open	Ctrl + O	Opens existing document file
Save	Ctrl + S, 🖫	Saves document using same file name
Save As	F12	Saves document using a new file name, type, and/or location
Save as/Save As type/ Web Page		Saves file as a Web page document
Print	Ctrl + P	Specify print settings before printing document
Print/Print Preview		Displays document as it will appear when printed
Print/Quick Print		Prints document using default printer settings
Prepare/Properties		Opens Document Information Panel
Close	Ctrl + F4	Closes document
Word Options /Proofing		Changes settings associated with Spelling and Grammar checking
Word Options /Advanced/ Mark formatting inconsistencies		Checks for formatting inconsistencies
Exit Word	Alt + F4 , ×	Closes the Word application
Quick Access Toolbar		
🖫 Save		Saves document using same file name
↶ Undo	Ctrl + Z	Restores last editing change
↷ Redo	Ctrl + Y	Restores last Undo or repeats last command or action
Home tab		
Clipboard Group		
✂ Cut	Ctrl + X	Cuts selection to Clipboard
📋 Copy	Ctrl + C	Copies selection to Clipboard
📋	Ctrl + V	Pastes item from Clipboard
🖌 Format Painter		Copies format to selection

2007 Word Brief Command Summary — **WDCS.1**

Word 2007

Glossary of Key Terms

GLOSSARY

Bolded terms found throughout each text in the O'Leary Series are defined in the glossary.

active window The window containing the insertion point and that will be affected by any changes you make.

alignment How text is positioned on a line between the margins or indents. There are four types of paragraph alignment: left, centered, right, and justified.

antonym A word with the opposite meaning.

author The process of creating a Web page.

AutoCorrect A feature that makes basic assumptions about the text you are typing and automatically corrects the entry.

bibliography A listing of source references that appears at the end of the document.

browser A program that connects you to remote computers and displays the Web pages you request.

building blocks Document fragments that include text and formatting and that can be easily inserted into a document.

bulleted list Displays items that logically fall out from a paragraph into a list, with items preceded by bullets.

caption A title or explanation for a table, picture, or graph.

case sensitive The capability to distinguish between uppercase and lowercase characters.

cell The intersection of a column and row where data are entered in a table.

character formatting Formatting features such as bold and color that affect the selected characters only.

citations Parenthetical source references that give credit for specific information included in a document.

Click and Type A feature available in Print Layout and Web Layout views that is used to quickly insert text, graphics, and other items in

a blank area of a document, avoiding the need to enter blank lines.

clip art Professionally drawn graphics.

control A graphic element that is a container for information or objects.

cross-reference A reference in one part of a document related to information in another part.

cursor The blinking vertical bar that shows you where the next character you type will appear. Also called the insertion point.

custom dictionary A dictionary of terms you have entered that are not in the main dictionary of the spelling checker.

default The initial Word document settings that can be changed to customize documents.

destination The location to which text is moved or copied.

Document Map A feature that displays the headings in the document in the navigation window.

document properties Details about a document that describe or identify it and are saved with the document content.

document theme A predefined set of formatting choices that can be applied to an entire document in one simple step.

document window The area of the application window that displays the contents of the open document.

drag and drop A mouse procedure that moves or copies a selection to a new location.

drawing layer The layer above or below the text layer where floating objects are inserted.

drawing object A simple object consisting of shapes such as lines and boxes.

edit The process of changing and correcting existing text in a document.

Glossary of Key Terms — **WDG.1**

Word 2007

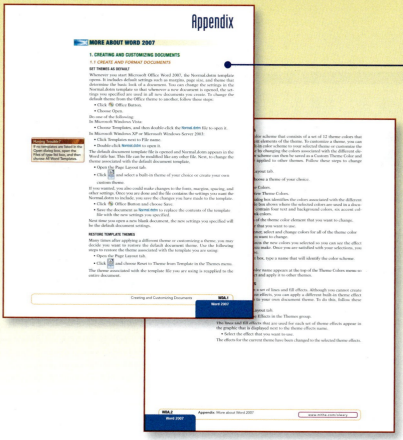

MORE ABOUT APPENDICES

A More About appendix appears at the end of the brief and introductory texts. This appendix offers students additional coverage needed to meet MCAS requirements. Skills pertaining to additional MCAS coverage are denoted by a More About icon in the margins of the text.

REFERENCE 1 - DATA FILE LIST

The Data File List is a reference guide that helps organize data and solution files. It identifies the names of the original and saved files.

REFERENCE 2 - MCAS CERTIFICATION GUIDE

Links all MCAS objectives to text content and end-of-lab exercises. You will always know which MCAS objectives are being covered. Introductory texts are MCAS certified.

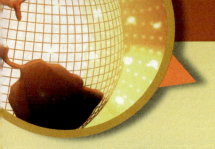

ONLINE LEARNING CENTER (OLC)

www.mhhe.com/oleary

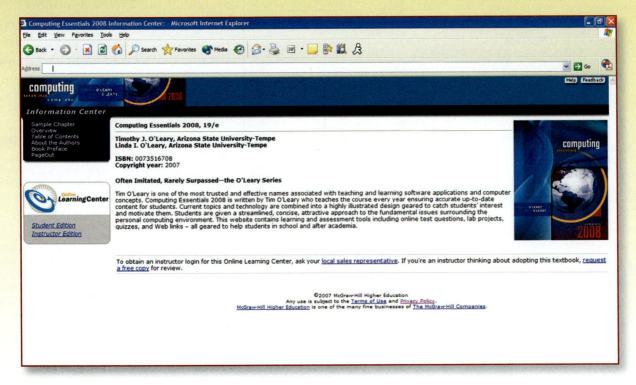

The Online Learning Center follows The O'Leary Series lab by lab, offering all kinds of supplementary help for you. OLC features include:

- Learning Objectives
- Student Data Files
- Chapter Competencies
- Chapter Concepts
- Self-Grading Quizzes
- Additional Web Links

ABOUT THE AUTHORS

Tim and Linda O'Leary live in the American Southwest and spend much of their time engaging instructors and students in conversation about learning. In fact, they have been talking about learning for over 25 years. Something in those early conversations convinced them to write a book, to bring their interest in the learning process to the printed page. Today, they are as concerned as ever about learning, about technology, and about the challenges of presenting material in new ways, in terms of both content and method of delivery.

A powerful and creative team, Tim combines his 25 years of classroom teaching experience with Linda's background as a consultant and corporate trainer. Tim has taught courses at Stark Technical College in Canton, Ohio, and at Rochester Institute of Technology in upstate New York, and is currently a professor at Arizona State University in Tempe, Arizona. Linda offered her expertise at ASU for several years as an academic advisor. She also presented and developed materials for major corporations such as Motorola, Intel, Honeywell, and AT&T, as well as various community colleges in the Phoenix area.

Tim and Linda have talked to and taught numerous students, all of them with a desire to learn something about computers and applications that make their lives easier, more interesting, and more productive.

Each new edition of an O'Leary text, supplement, or learning aid has benefited from these students and their instructors who daily stand in front of them (or over their shoulders). The O'Leary Series is no exception.

DEDICATION

We dedicate this edition to Nicole and Katie who have brought love and joy to our lives.

Introduction to Microsoft Office 2007

Objectives

After completing the Introduction to Microsoft Office 2007, you should be able to:

1 Describe the 2007 Microsoft Office System.

2 Describe the Office 2007 applications.

3 Start an Office 2007 application.

4 Recognize the basic application features.

5 Use menus, context menus, and shortcut keys.

6 Use the Ribbon, dialog boxes, and task panes.

7 Use Office Help.

8 Exit an Office 2007 application.

What Is the 2007 Microsoft Office System?

Microsoft's 2007 Microsoft Office System is a comprehensive, integrated system of programs, servers, and services designed to solve a wide array of business needs. Although the programs can be used individually, they are designed to work together seamlessly, making it easy to connect people and organizations to information, business processes, and each other. The applications include tools used to create, discuss, communicate, and manage projects. If you share a lot of documents with other people, these features facilitate access to common documents. This version has an entirely new user interface that is designed to make it easier to perform tasks and help users more quickly take advantage of all the features in the applications. In addition, the communication and collaboration features and integration with the World Wide Web have been expanded and refined.

The 2007 Microsoft Office System is packaged in several different combinations of programs or suites. The major programs and a brief description are provided in the following table.

Program	Description
Word 2007	Word Processor program used to create text-based documents
Excel 2007	Spreadsheet program used to analyze numerical data
Access 2007	Database manager used to organize, manage, and display a database
PowerPoint 2007	Graphics presentation program used to create presentation materials
Outlook 2007	Desktop information manager and messaging client
InfoPath 2007	Used to create XML forms and documents
OneNote 2007	Note-taking and information organization tools
Publisher 2007	Tools to create and distribute publications for print, Web, and e-mail
Visio 2007	Diagramming and data visualization tools
SharePoint Designer 2007	Web site development and management for SharePoint servers
Project 2007	Project management tools
Groove 2007	Collaboration program that enables teams to work together

The four main components of Microsoft Office 2007—Word, Excel, Access, and PowerPoint—are the applications you will learn about in this series of labs. They are described in more detail in the following sections.

Introduction to Microsoft Office 2007

www.mhhe.com/oleary

Word 2007

Word 2007 is a word processing software application whose purpose is to help you create text-based documents. Word processors are one of the most flexible and widely used application software programs. A word processor can be used to manipulate text data to produce a letter, a report, a memo, an e-mail message, or any other type of correspondence.

Two documents you will produce in the first two Word 2007 labs, a letter and flyer, are shown here.

A letter containing a tabbed table, indented paragraphs, and text enhancements is quickly created using basic Word features.

September 15, 2008

Dear Adventure Traveler:

Imagine camping under the stars in Africa, hiking and paddling your way through the rainforests of Costa Rica, or following in the footsteps of the ancient Inca as you backpack along the Inca trail to Machu Picchu. Turn these dreams of adventure into memories you will cherish forever by joining Adventure Travel Tours on one of our four new adventure tours.

To tell you more about these exciting new adventures, we are offering several presentations in your area. These presentations will focus on the features and cultures of the region. We will also show you pictures of the places you will visit and activities you can partici... to attend one of the following presentations:

Date	Time	
January 5	8:00 p.m.	Cro
February 3	7:30 p.m.	Air
March 8	8:00 p.m.	Res

In appreciation of your past patronage, we ... of the new tour packages. You must book the trip at ... letter to qualify for the discount.

Our vacation tours are professionally devel... everything in the price of your tour while giving you ... these features:

➢ All accommodations and meals
➢ All entrance fees, excursions, transfers and ...
➢ Professional tour manager and local guides ...

We hope you will join us this year on anoth... Travel Tours each day is an adventure. For reservati... Travel Tours directly at 1-800-555-0004.

Adventure Travel Tours
New Adventures

Attention adventure travelers! Attend an Adventure Travel presentation to learn about some of the earth's greatest unspoiled habitats and find out how you can experience the adventure of a lifetime. This year we are introducing four new tours that offer you a unique opportunity to combine many different outdoor activities while exploring the world.

India Wildlife Adventure

Inca Trail to Machu Picchu

Safari in Tanzania

Costa Rica Rivers and Rainforests

Presentation dates and times are January 5 at 8:00 p.m., February 3 at 7:30 p.m., and March 8 at 8:00 p.m. All presentations are held at convenient hotel locations in downtown Los Angeles, Santa Clara, and at the LAX airport.

Call Student Name 1-800-555-0004 for presentation locations, a full color brochure, and itinerary information, costs, and trip dates.

Visit our Web site at
www.adventuretraveltours.com

A flyer incorporating many visual enhancements such as colored text, varied text styles, and graphic elements is both eye-catching and informative.

What Is the 2007 Microsoft Office System?　　　　　I.3

Word 2007

The beauty of a word processor is that you can make changes or corrections as you are typing. Want to change a report from single spacing to double spacing? Alter the width of the margins? Delete some paragraphs and add others from yet another document? A word processor allows you to do all these things with ease.

Word 2007 includes many group collaboration features to help streamline how documents are developed and changed by group members. You also can create and send e-mail messages directly from within Word using all its features to create and edit the message. In addition, you can send an entire document as your e-mail message, allowing the recipient to edit the document directly without having to open or save an attachment.

Word 2007 is closely integrated with the World Wide Web, detecting when you type a Web address and automatically converting it to a hyperlink. You also can create your own hyperlinks to locations within documents, or to other documents, including those at external locations such as a Web site or file server. It also includes features that help you quickly create Web pages and blog entries.

Excel 2007

Excel 2007 is an electronic worksheet that is used to organize, manipulate, and graph numeric data. Once used almost exclusively by accountants, worksheets are now widely used by nearly every profession. Marketing professionals record and evaluate sales trends. Teachers record grades and calculate final grades. Personal trainers record the progress of their clients.

Excel 2007 includes many features that not only help you create a well-designed worksheet, but one that produces accurate results. Formatting features include visual enhancements such as varied text styles, colors, and graphics. Other features help you enter complex formulas and identify and correct formula errors. You also can produce a visual display of data in the form of graphs or charts. As the values in the worksheet change, charts referencing those values automatically adjust to reflect the changes.

Excel 2007 also includes many advanced features and tools that help you perform what-if analysis and create different scenarios. And like all Office 2007 applications, it is easy to incorporate data created in one application into another. Two worksheets you will produce in Labs 2 and 3 of Excel 2007 are shown on the next page.

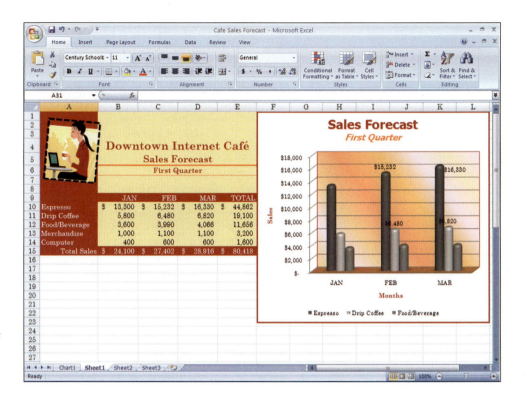

A worksheet showing the quarterly sales forecast containing a graphic, text enhancements, and a chart of the data is quickly created using basic Excel 2007 features.

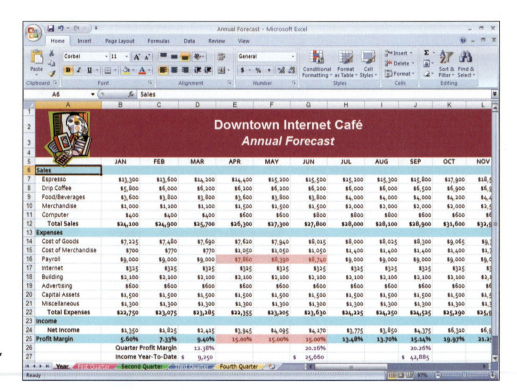

A large worksheet incorporating more complex formulas, visual enhancements such as colored text, varied text styles, and graphic elements is both informative and attractive.

What Is the 2007 Microsoft Office System?   I.5

Word 2007

You will see how easy it is to analyze data and make projections using what-if analysis and what-if graphing in Lab 3 and to incorporate Excel data in a Word document as shown in the following figures.

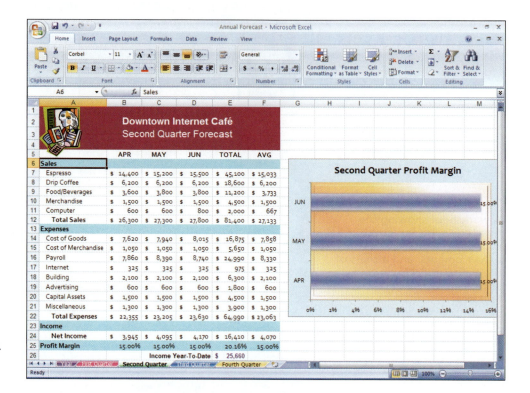

Changes you make in worksheet data while performing what-if analysis are automatically reflected in charts that reference that data.

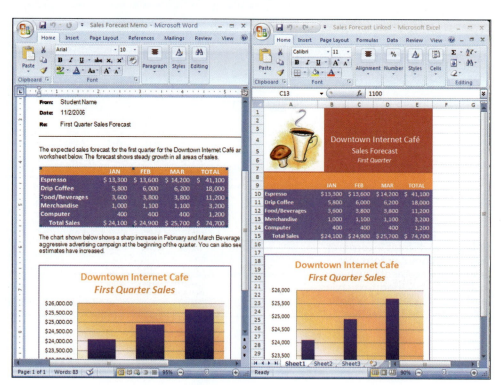

Worksheet data and charts can be copied and linked to other Office documents such as a Word document.

Access 2007

Access 2007 is a relational database management application that is used to create and analyze a database. A database is a collection of related data. In a relational database, the most widely used database structure, data is organized in linked tables. Tables consist of columns (called *fields*) and rows (called *records*). The tables are related or linked to one another by a common field. Relational databases allow you to create smaller and more manageable database tables, since you can combine and extract data between tables.

The program provides tools to enter, edit, and retrieve data from the database as well as to analyze the database and produce reports of the output. One of the main advantages of a computerized database is the ability to quickly add, delete, and locate specific records. Records also can be easily rearranged or sorted according to different fields of data, resulting in multiple table arrangements that provide more meaningful information for different purposes. Creation of forms makes it easier to enter and edit data as well. In the Access labs, you will create and organize the database table shown below.

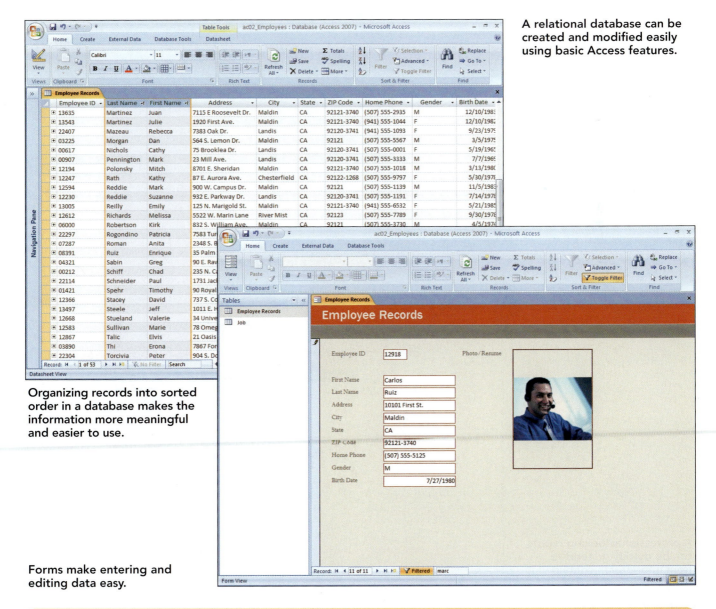

A relational database can be created and modified easily using basic Access features.

Organizing records into sorted order in a database makes the information more meaningful and easier to use.

Forms make entering and editing data easy.

What Is the 2007 Microsoft Office System?   I.7

Word 2007

Another feature is the ability to analyze the data in a table and perform calculations on different fields of data. Additionally, you can ask questions or query the table to find only certain records that meet specific conditions to be used in the analysis. Information that was once costly and time-consuming to get is now quickly and readily available. This information can then be quickly printed out in the form of reports ranging from simple listings to complex, professional-looking reports in different layout styles, or with titles, headings, subtotals, or totals.

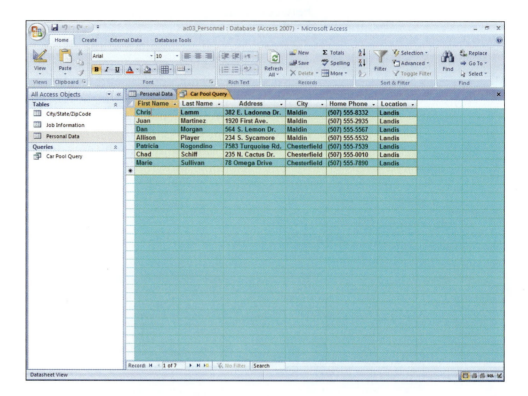

A database can be queried to locate and display only specified information.

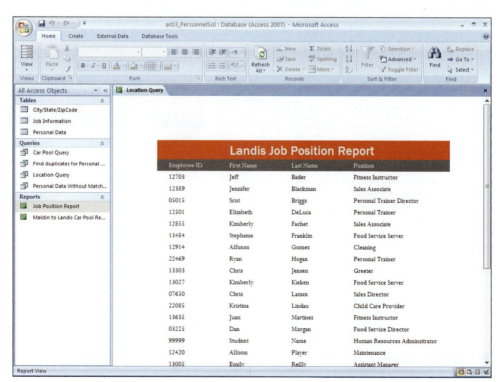

A professional-looking report can be quickly generated from information contained in a database.

www.mhhe.com/oleary

PowerPoint 2007

PowerPoint 2007 is a graphics presentation program designed to help you produce a high-quality presentation that is both interesting to the audience and effective in its ability to convey your message. A presentation can be as simple as overhead transparencies or as sophisticated as an on-screen electronic display. In the first two PowerPoint labs, you will create and organize the presentation shown below.

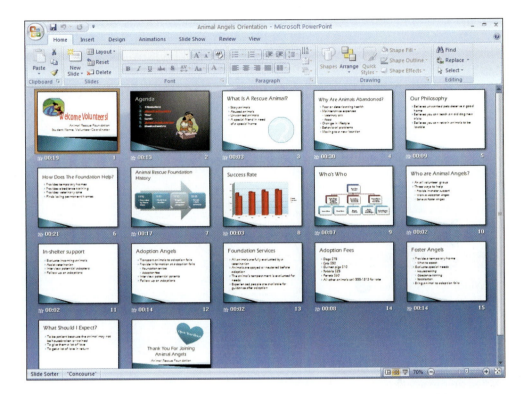

A presentation consists of a series of pages or "slides" presenting the information you want to convey in an organized and attractive manner.

When running an on-screen presentation, each slide of the presentation is displayed full-screen on your computer monitor or projected onto a screen.

Common Office 2007 Interface Features

Additional Information

Please read the Before You Begin and Instructional Conventions sections in the Overview of Microsoft Office Word 2007 (WDO.3) before starting this section.

Now that you know a little about each of the applications in Microsoft Office 2007, we will take a look at some of the interface features that are common to all Office 2007 applications. This is a hands-on section that will introduce you to the features and allow you to get a feel for how Office 2007 works. Although Word 2007 will be used to demonstrate how the features work, only common **user interface** features, a set of graphical images that represent various features, will be addressed. These features include using the File menu, Ribbon, Quick Access Toolbar, task panes, and Office Help, and starting and exiting an application. The features that are specific to each application will be introduced individually in each application text.

Starting an Office 2007 Application

There are several ways to start a Office 2007 application. The two most common methods are by using the Start menu or by clicking a desktop shortcut for the program if it is available. If you use the Start menu, the steps will vary slightly depending on the version of Windows you are using.

1 ● Click **start** to display the Start menu.

Having Trouble?

In Windows Vista, click ●

● **Choose Microsoft Office Word 2007.**

Having Trouble?

If you do not see the program name on the Start menu, select All Programs, select Microsoft Office, and then choose Microsoft Office Word 2007.

OR

1 ● Double-click the shortcut on the desktop.

2 ● If necessary, click ▭ Maximize in the title bar to maximize the window.

Your screen should be similar to Figure 1

Having Trouble?

Your screen may look slightly different based on your Windows operating system settings.

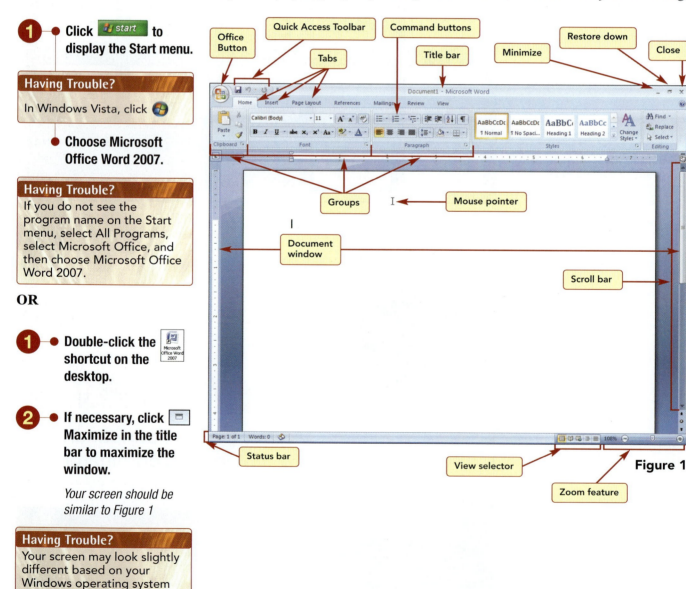

Figure 1

Additional Information

Application windows can be sized, moved, and otherwise manipulated like any other windows on the desktop.

Additional Information

Because the Ribbon can adapt to the screen resolution and orientation, your Ribbon may look slightly different.

The Word 2007 program is started and displayed in a window on the desktop. The application window title bar displays the file name followed by the program name, Microsoft Word. The right end of the title bar displays the ⬚ Minimize, ⬚ Restore Down, and ⬚ Close buttons. They perform the same functions and operate in the same way as all Windows versions.

Below the title bar is the **Ribbon**, which provides a centralized area that makes it easy to find ways to work in your document. The Ribbon has three basic parts: tabs, groups, and commands. **Tabs** are used to divide the Ribbon into major activity areas. Each tab is then organized into **groups** that contain related items. The related items are commands that consist of command buttons, a box to enter information, or a menu. As you use the Office applications, you will see that the Ribbon contains many of the same groups and commands across the applications. You also will see that many of the groups and commands are specific to an application.

The upper left area of the window's title bar displays the ⬚ Office Button and the Quick Access Toolbar. Clicking ⬚ Office Button opens the File menu of commands that allows you to work *with* your document, unlike the Ribbon that allows you to work *in* your document. For example, it includes commands to open, save, and print files. The **Quick Access Toolbar** (QAT) provides quick access to frequently used commands. By default, it includes the ⬚ Save, ⬚ Undo, and ⬚ Redo buttons, commands that Microsoft considers to be crucial. It is always available and is a customizable toolbar to which you can add your own favorite buttons.

The large center area of the program window is the **document window** where open application files are displayed. Currently, there is a blank Word document open. In Word, the mouse pointer appears as I when positioned in the document window and as a ⬚ when it can be used to select items.

On the right of the document window is a vertical scroll bar. A **scroll bar** is used with a mouse to bring additional lines of information into view in a window. The vertical scroll bar is used to move up or down. A horizontal scroll bar is also displayed when needed and moves side to side in the window. At the bottom of the window is the **status bar**, a view selector, and a document zoom feature. Similar information and features are displayed in this area for different Office applications. You will learn how these features work in each individual application.

Using the File Menu

Clicking the ⬚ Office Button opens the File menu of commands that are used to work with files.

1 Click 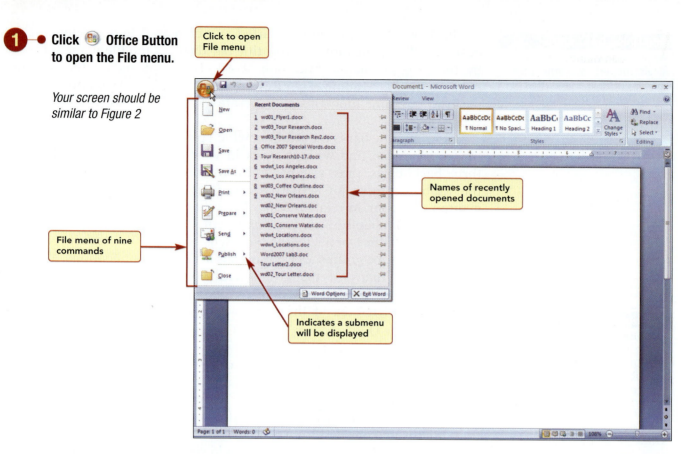 **Office Button to open the File menu.**

Click to open File menu

Your screen should be similar to Figure 2

Names of recently opened documents

File menu of nine commands

Indicates a submenu will be displayed

Figure 2

Additional Information

Clicking the pin next to a file name pins the file and permanently keeps the file name in the recently used list until it is unpinned.

The menu lists nine commands that are used to perform tasks associated with files. Notice that each command displays an underlined letter. This identifies the letter you can type to choose the command. Five commands display a ▶, which indicates the command includes a submenu of options. The right side of the command list currently displays the names of recently opened files (your list will display different file names). The default program setting displays a maximum of 17 file names. Once the maximum number of files is listed, when a new file is opened, the oldest is dropped from the list.

Once the File menu is open, you can select a command from the menu by pointing to it. A colored highlight bar, called the **selection cursor**, appears over the selected command.

 **Point to the Open command.**

Your screen should be similar to Figure 3

Selected command is highlighted with the selection cursor

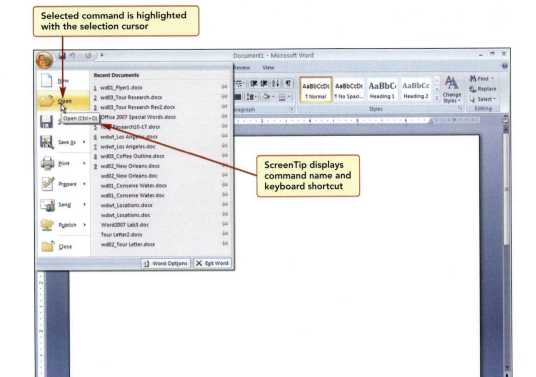

ScreenTip displays command name and keyboard shortcut

Figure 3

A **ScreenTip**, also called a **tooltip**, briefly appears displaying the command name and the keyboard shortcut, Ctrl + O. The keyboard shortcut can be used to execute this command without opening the menu. In this case, if you hold down the Ctrl key while typing the letter O, you will access the Open command without having to open the File menu first. ScreenTips also often include a brief description of the action a command performs.

Next you will select a command that will display a submenu of options.

3 • **Point to the Prepare command.**

• **Point to the Mark as Final submenu option.**

Your screen should be similar to Figure 4

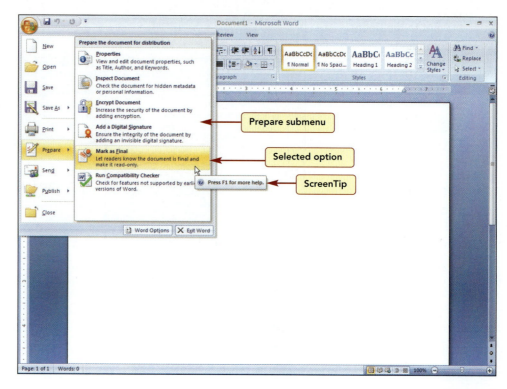

Figure 4

The submenu lists the six Prepare command submenu options and the Mark as Final option is selected. A ScreenTip provides information about how to get help on this feature. You will learn about using Help shortly.

4 • **Point to the Print command.**

• **Point to the ▸ of the Print command.**

Your screen should be similar to Figure 5

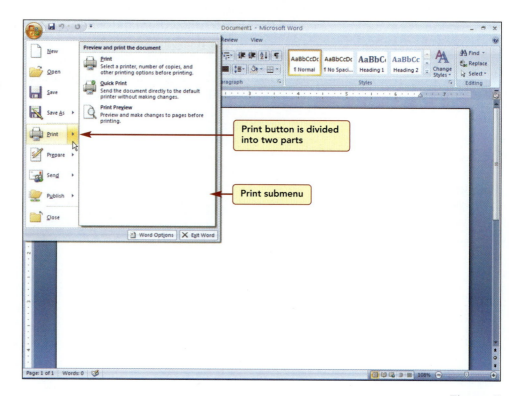

Figure 5

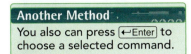

Another Method
You also can use the directional keys to move up, down, left, or right within the menu.

Another Method
You also can press ⏎Enter to choose a selected command.

5 ● **Click the Print command.**

Your screen should be similar to Figure 6

So far you have only selected commands; you have not chosen them. To choose a command, you click on it. When the command is chosen, the associated action is performed. Notice the Print command is divided into two parts. Clicking the Print section on the left will choose the command and open the Print dialog box. Clicking ⌐ in the right section has no effect.

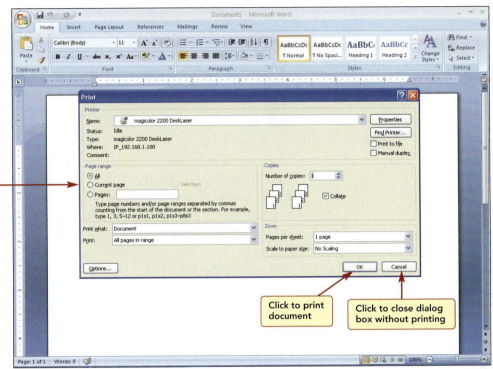

Print dialog box is used to specify print settings

Click to print document

Click to close dialog box without printing

Figure 6

In the Print dialog box, you would specify the print settings and click OK to actually print a document. In this case, you will cancel the action and continue to explore other features of the Office 2007 application.

6 ● **Click** Cancel **.**

Another Method
You also can press Esc to cancel an action.

Using Context Menus

Another way to access some commands is to use a context menu. A **context menu** is opened by right-clicking on an item on the screen. This menu is context sensitive, meaning it displays only those commands relevant to the item. For example, right-clicking on the Quick Access Toolbar will display the commands associated with using the Quick Access Toolbar only. You will use this method to move the Quick Access Toolbar.

1 Point to the Quick Access Toolbar and right-click.

Another Method

You also can click 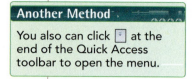 at the end of the Quick Access toolbar to open the menu.

● Click the Show Quick Access Toolbar below the Ribbon option.

Your screen should be similar to Figure 7

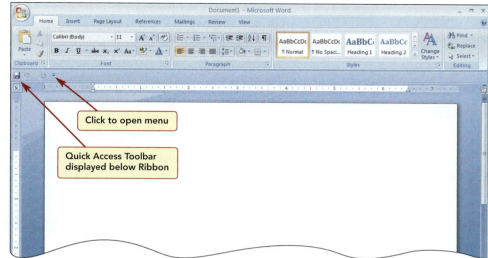

Click to open menu

Quick Access Toolbar displayed below Ribbon

Figure 7

The Quick Access Toolbar is now displayed full size below the Ribbon. This is useful if you have many buttons on the toolbar; however, it takes up document viewing space. You will return it to its compact size using the toolbar's drop-down menu.

2 Click 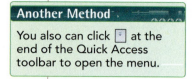 on the right end of the Quick Access Toolbar.

● Choose Show Above the Ribbon.

Your screen should be similar to Figure 8

Quick Access Toolbar displayed above Ribbon again

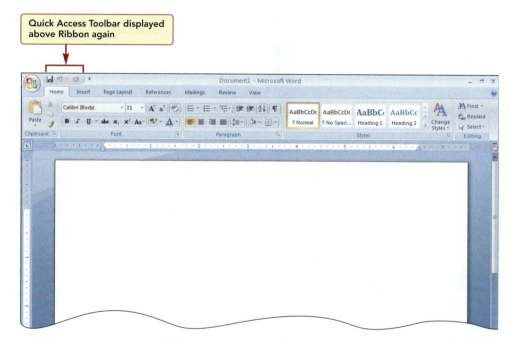

Figure 8

MORE ABOUT

▶ See the More About appendix to learn how to customize the Quick Access Toolbar.

The Quick Access Toolbar is displayed above the Ribbon again. The toolbar's drop-down menu contains a list of commands that are often added to the toolbar. Clicking on the command selects it and adds it to the toolbar.

Using the Ribbon

The Ribbon displays tabs that organize similar features into groups. In Word, there are seven tabs displayed. To save space, some tabs, called **contextual** or **on-demand tabs**, are displayed only as needed. For example, when you are working with a picture, the Picture Tools tab appears. The contextual nature of this feature keeps the work area uncluttered when the feature is not needed and provides ready access to it when it is needed.

Opening Tabs

The Home tab is open when you first start the application or open a file. It consists of five groups: Clipboard, Font, Paragraph, Styles, and Editing. Each group contains command buttons that when clicked on perform their associated action or display a list of additional commands. The commands in the Home tab help you perform actions related to creating the content of your document.

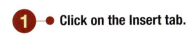

1 ● **Click on the Insert tab.**

Additional Information
The open tab appears highlighted.

Your screen should be similar to Figure 9

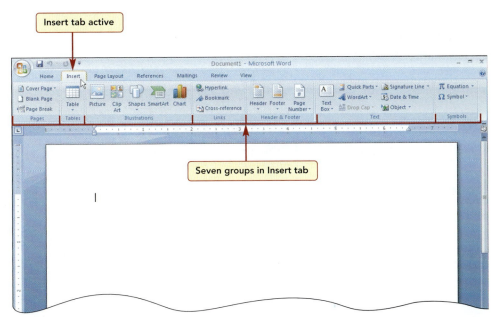

Insert tab active

Seven groups in Insert tab

Figure 9

This Insert tab is now the active tab. It contains seven groups whose commands have to do with inserting items into a document.

2 ● **Click on each of the other tabs, ending with the View tab, to see their groups and commands.**

Your screen should be similar to Figure 10

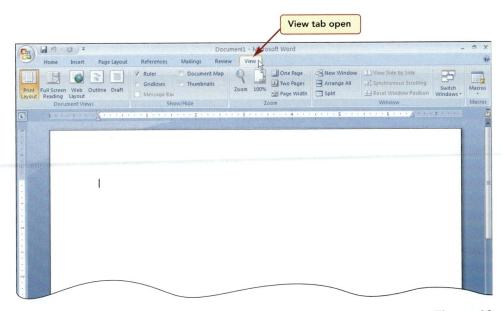

View tab open

Figure 10

Each tab relates to a type of activity; for example, the View tab commands perform activities related to viewing the document. Within each tab, similar commands are grouped together to make finding the commands you want to use much easier.

Displaying Super Tooltips

Many command buttons immediately perform the associated action when you click on them. The buttons are graphic representations of the action they perform. To help you find out what a button does, you can display the button's ScreenTip.

1

- Open the Home tab.

- Point to the upper part of the ▢ button in the Clipboard group.

- Point to the lower part of the Paste button in the Clipboard group.

- Point to ✎ Format Painter in the Clipboard group.

Your screen should be similar to Figure 11

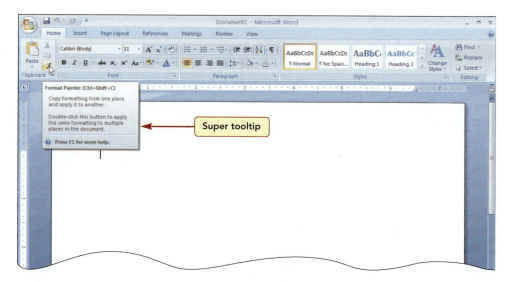

Figure 11

Additional Information
Not all commands have shortcut keys.

Additional Information
You will learn about using Help shortly.

Both parts of the Paste button display tooltips containing the button name, the shortcut key combination, Ctrl + V, and a brief description of what the button does. Pointing to ✎ Format Painter displays a **super tooltip** that provides more detailed information about the command. Super tooltips may even display information such as procedures or illustrations. You can find out what the feature does without having to look it up in Help. If a feature has a Help article, you can automatically access it by pressing F1 while the super tooltip is displayed.

Using Galleries and Lists

Many commands in the groups appear as a **gallery** that displays small graphics that represent the result of applying a command. For example, in the Styles group, the command buttons to apply different formatting styles to text display examples of how the text would look if formatted using that command. These are called **in-Ribbon galleries** because they appear directly in the Ribbon. Other commands include multiple options that appear in **drop-down galleries** or drop-down lists that are accessed by clicking the ▾ button on the right side of the command button. To see an example of a drop-down gallery, you will open the ☰▾ Bullets drop-down gallery.

1 ● Click ⏷ in the ☰⏷ Bullets button.

Your screen should be similar to Figure 12

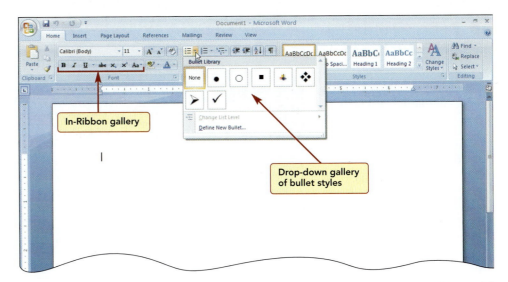

In-Ribbon gallery

Drop-down gallery of bullet styles

Figure 12

A drop-down gallery of different bullets is displayed. The drop-down gallery will disappear when you make a selection or click on any other area of the window. To see an example of a drop-down list, you will open the [11 ⏷] Font Size drop-down list.

2 ● Click outside the Bullet gallery to clear it.

● Click ⏷ in the [11 ⏷] Font Size button.

Your screen should be similar to Figure 13

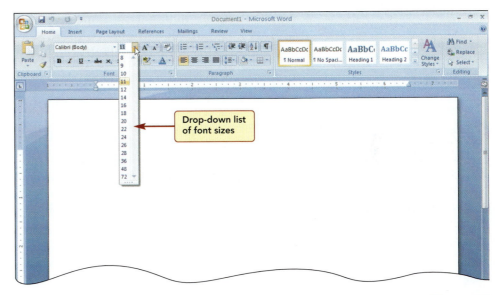

Drop-down list of font sizes

Figure 13

If you click on the button itself, not the ⏷ section of the button, the associated command is performed.

Using the Dialog Box Launcher

Because there is not enough space, only the most used commands are displayed in the Ribbon. If there are more commands available, a ⧉ button, called the **dialog box launcher**, is displayed in the lower-right corner of the group. Clicking ⧉ opens a dialog box or **task pane** of additional options.

1 ● **Click outside the Font size list to clear it.**

● **Point to the ▣ of the Paragraph group to see the tooltip.**

● **Click ▣ of the Paragraph group.**

Your screen should be similar to Figure 14

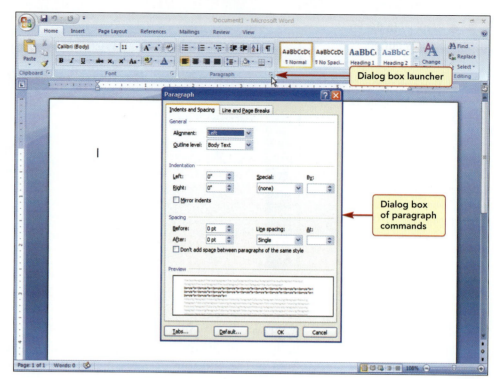

Figure 14

The Paragraph dialog box appears. It provides access to the more advanced paragraph settings features. Selecting options from the dialog box and clicking [OK] will close the dialog box and apply the settings as specified. To cancel the dialog box, you can click [Cancel] or ✕ in the dialog box title bar.

2 ● **Click [Cancel] to close the dialog box.**

● **Click ▣ in the Clipboard group.**

Your screen should be similar to Figure 15

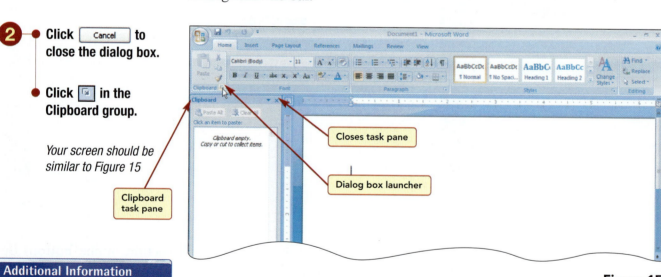

Figure 15

Additional Information

You will learn about using dialog boxes, task panes, and the Clipboard as they are used in the labs.

A task pane is open that contains features associated with the Clipboard. Unlike dialog boxes, task panes remain open until you close them. This allows you to make multiple selections from the task pane while continuing to work on other areas of your document.

3 ● **Click ✕ in the upper-right corner of the task pane to close it.**

Using Access Key Shortcuts

Another way to use commands on the Ribbon is to display the access key shortcuts by pressing the [Alt] key and then typing the letter for the feature you want to use. Every Ribbon tab, group, and command has an access key.

1 ● Press [Alt].

Another Method
You also can press [F10] to display the access keys.

Your screen should be similar to Figure 16

Access keys appear in KeyTips

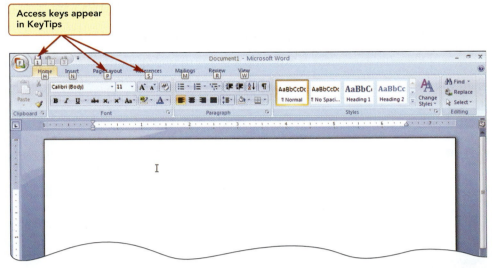

Figure 16

The letters are displayed in **KeyTips** over each available feature. Now typing a letter will access that feature. Then, depending on which letter you pressed, additional KeyTips may appear. To use a Ribbon command, press the key of the tab first, then the group, and then continue pressing letters until you press the letter of the specific command you want to use. You will use KeyTips to display the Paragraph dialog box again.

2 ● Type the letter **H** to access the Home tab.

● Type the letters **PG** to access the Paragraph group and open the dialog box.

Your screen should be similar to Figure 17

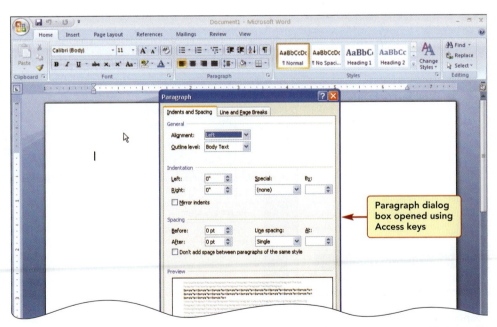

Paragraph dialog box opened using Access keys

Figure 17

Three keystrokes opened the Paragraph dialog box.

Another Method

You also can press F6 to change the focus from the Ribbon to the document area to the View Toolbar.

Another Method

You also can use the keyboard shortcut Ctrl + F1 to minimize and redisplay the Ribbon.

Once the Access key feature is on, you can also use the ← or → directional key to move from one tab to another, and the ↓ key to move from a tab to a group and the ↑ key to move from a group to a tab. You can use all four directional keys to move among the commands in a Ribbon. Tab and ⇧Shift + Tab also can be used to move right or left. Once a command is selected, you can press Spacebar or ←Enter to activate it.

Minimizing the Ribbon

Sometimes you may not want to see the entire Ribbon so that more space is available in the document area. You can minimize the Ribbon by double-clicking the active tab.

1 ● Click ✕ to close the Paragraph dialog box.

● Double-click the Home tab.

Another Method

You also can choose Minimize the Ribbon from the Quick Access Toolbar menu.

Your screen should be similar to Figure 18

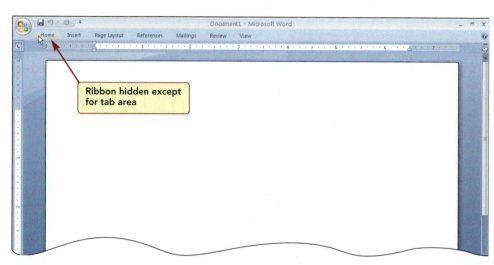

Ribbon hidden except for tab area

Figure 18

Now, the only part of the Ribbon that is visible is the tab area. This allows you to quickly reopen the Ribbon and, at the same time, open the selected tab.

2 ● Double-click the Insert tab.

Your screen should be similar to Figure 19

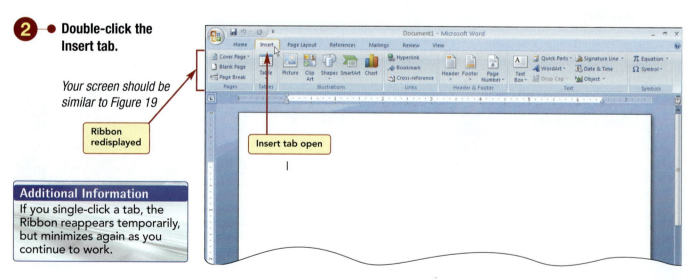

Ribbon redisplayed

Insert tab open

Additional Information

If you single-click a tab, the Ribbon reappears temporarily, but minimizes again as you continue to work.

Figure 19

The full Ribbon reappears and the Insert tab is open and ready for use.

Using the Mini Toolbar

Another method of accessing commands is through the Mini toolbar. The **Mini toolbar** appears automatically when you select text in a document and provides commands that are used to format (enhance) text. It also appears along with the context menu when you right-click an item in a document. Both the Mini toolbar and context menus are designed to make it more efficient to execute commands.

You can see what these features look like by right-clicking in a blank area of the document window.

1 ● **Right-click the blank document window space.**

Your screen should be similar to Figure 20

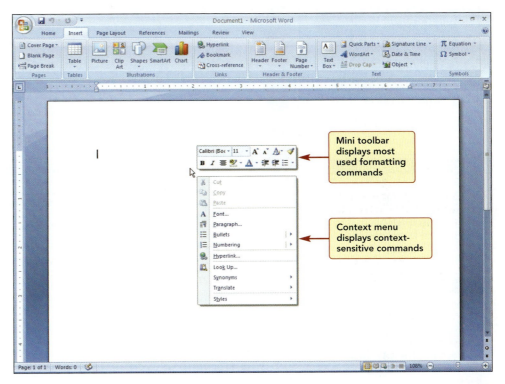

Figure 20

The Mini toolbar displays the most frequently used formatting commands. For example, when the Home tab is closed, you can use the commands in the Mini toolbar to quickly change selected text without having to reopen the Home tab to access the command. When the Mini toolbar appears automatically, it is faded so that it does not interfere with what you are doing, but changes to solid (as it is here) when you point at it.

The context menu below the Mini toolbar displays a variety of commands that are quicker to access than locating the command on the Ribbon. The commands that appear on this menu change depending on what you are doing at the time.

Using Office Help

Another Method
You also can press F1 to access Help.

Notice the ⊚ in the upper-right corner of the Ribbon. This button is used to access the Microsoft Help system. The Help button is always visible even when the Ribbon is hidden. Because you are using the Office Word 2007 application, Office Word Help will be accessed.

1 Click 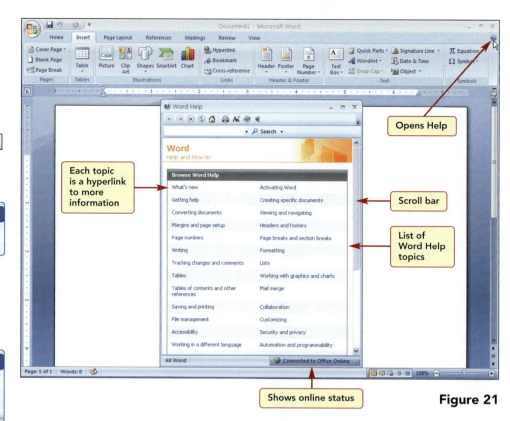 Microsoft Office Word Help.

● If a Table of Contents list is displayed along the left side of the Help window, click 📖 in the Help window toolbar to close it.

Additional Information

You will learn about using the Table of Contents shortly.

Your screen should be similar to Figure 21

Additional Information

Clicking the scroll arrows scrolls the text in the window line by line, and dragging the scroll bar up or down moves to a general location within the window area.

Additional Information

Because Help is an online feature, the information is frequently updated. Your screens may display slightly different information than those shown in the figures in this lab.

Having Trouble?

In addition to being connected to the Internet, the feature to show content from the Internet must be selected. If necessary, click the ⚫ Offline button at the bottom of the Help window and choose Show content from Office Online.

Figure 21

The Microsoft Word Help feature is opened and displayed in a separate window. The Help window on your screen will probably be a different size and arrangement than in Figure 21. Depending on the size of your Help window, you may need to scroll the window to see all the Help information provided.

It displays a listing of Help topics. If you are connected to the Internet, the Microsoft Office Online Web site is accessed and help information from this site is displayed in the window. If you are not connected, the offline help information that is provided with the application and stored on your computer is located and displayed. Generally, the listing of topics is similar but fewer in number.

Selecting Help Topics

There are several ways you can get help. The first is to select a topic from the listing displayed in the Help window. Each topic is a **hyperlink** or connection to the information located on the Online site or in Help on your computer. When you point to the hyperlink, it appears underlined and the mouse pointer appears as 👆. Clicking the hyperlink accesses and displays the information associated with the hyperlink.

1 ● **Click "Getting help."**

Your screen should be similar to Figure 22

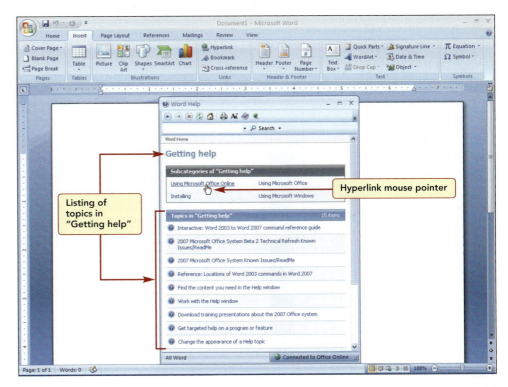

Figure 22

A listing of topics about getting help is displayed. You will get help on using Microsoft Office and the Ribbon.

2 ● **Click "Using Microsoft Office."**

● **Click "Use the Ribbon."**

Your screen should be similar to Figure 23

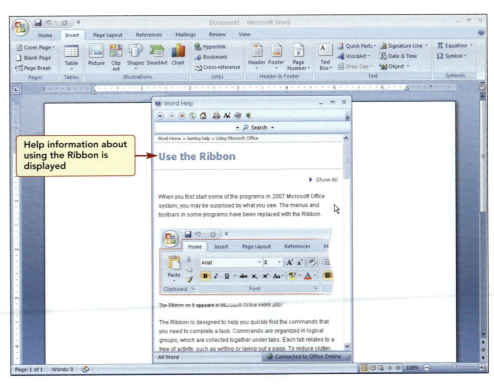

Figure 23

The information on the selected topic is displayed in the window.

3 ● Use the scroll bar to scroll the Help window to read the information about the Ribbon.

● Display the "In this article" section of the window.

Your screen should be similar to Figure 24

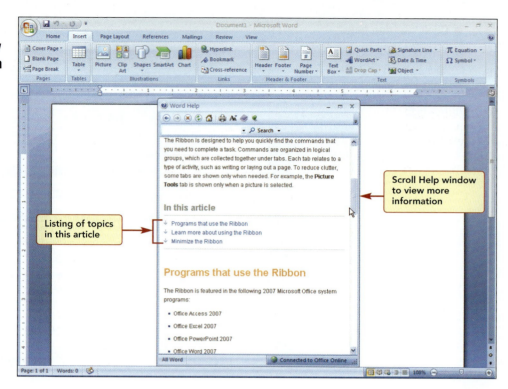

Figure 24

Additional Information
In Windows Vista, an unopened topic heading is preceded with + .

This area of the Help window provides a table of contents listing of the information in this window. Clicking on a link will take you directly to that location in the Help window. As you are reading the information in the window, you will see many topics preceded with ▶. This indicates the information in the topic is not displayed. Clicking on the topic heading displays the information about the topic.

4 ● Click "Learn more about using the Ribbon."

● Click "Microsoft Office Word 2007."

● If necessary, scroll the window to see all the information on this topic.

Your screen should be similar to Figure 25

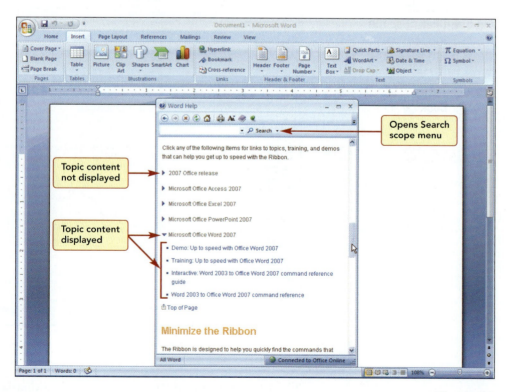

Figure 25

The information on the selected subtopic is displayed. Clicking the table of contents link jumped directly to this section of the window, saving you time by not having to scroll. The ▶ preceding the subtopic has changed to ▼, indicating the subtopic content is displayed.

You can continue to click on the subtopic headings to display the information about each topic individually. Likewise, clicking on an expanded topic hides the information. Additionally you can click ▶ Show All located at the top of the window to display all the available topic information and ▼ Hide All to hide all expanded information.

Additional Information

In Windows Vista, these buttons are ⊞ Show All and ⊟ Hide All.

Searching Help Topics

Another method to find Help information is to conduct a search by entering a sentence or question you want help on in the Search text box of the Help window. Although you also can simply enter a word in the Search box, the best results occur when you type a phrase, complete sentence, or question. A very specific search with 2–7 words will return the most accurate results.

When searching, you can specify the scope of the search by selecting from the Search scope drop-down menu. The broadest scope for a search, All Word, is preselected. You will narrow the scope to search Word Help only.

1 ● Open the 🔍 Search ▾ drop-down list.

● Click "Word Help."

● Click in the Search text box to display the insertion point.

● Type **What is the Ribbon**.

● Click 🔍 Search ▾ .

Additional Information

You also could press ⏎Enter to start the search.

Your screen should be similar to Figure 26

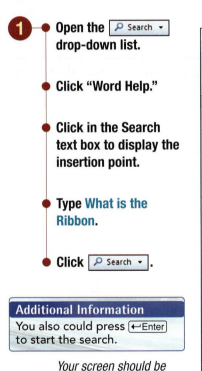

Figure 26

The first 25 located results of the top 100 are displayed in a window. There are four pages of results. The results are shown in order of relevance, with the most likely matches at the top of the list. Now you can continue to locate the information you need by selecting from the topic links provided. To see the next page of results, you can click Next or ➡ or click the specific page number you want to see from the Page count area. To see the previous page of results, click ⬅ .

Topics preceded with  indicate the window will display the related Help topic. Those preceded with a ▨ indicate a tutorial about the topic is available from the Microsoft Training Web site.

2 ● **Click "Use the Ribbon."**

Your screen should be similar to Figure 27

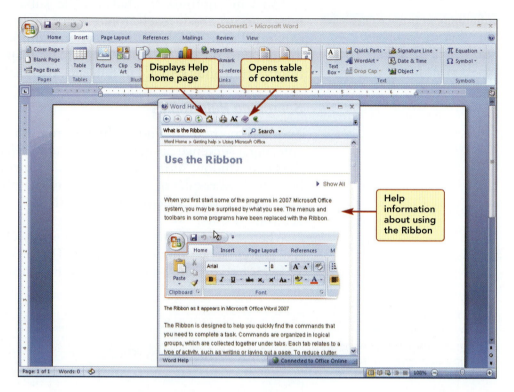

Figure 27

The same Help information you saw previously is displayed.

Using the Help Table of Contents

A third source of help is to use the Help table of contents. Using this method allows you to browse the entire list of Help topics to locate topics of interest to you.

1 ● Click  **Home in the Help window toolbar to return to the opening Help window.**

● Click ▼ **Show Table of Contents from the Help window toolbar.**

Additional Information

You also could click ◀ Back in the Help window toolbar to return to the previous page, page by page.

Your screen should be similar to Figure 28

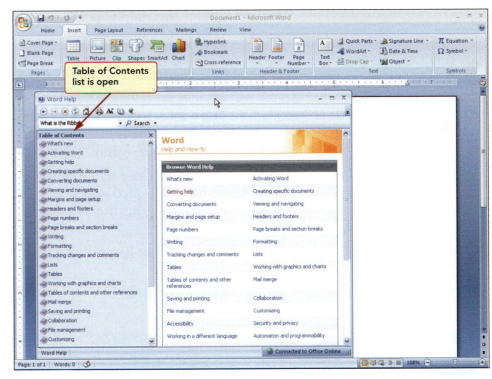

Figure 28

Additional Information

Pointing to an item in the Table of Contents displays a ScreenTip of the entire topic heading.

The entire Word Help Table of Contents is displayed in a pane on the left side of the Help window. Clicking on an item preceded with a 📖 Closed Book icon opens a chapter, which expands to display additional chapters or topics. The 📖 Open Book icon identifies those chapters that are open. Clicking on an item preceded with ❓ displays the specific Help information.

2 ● Click "Getting help" to open this chapter.

● Click "Using Microsoft Office."

● Scroll the table of contents list and click "Use the Ribbon."

Your screen should be similar to Figure 29

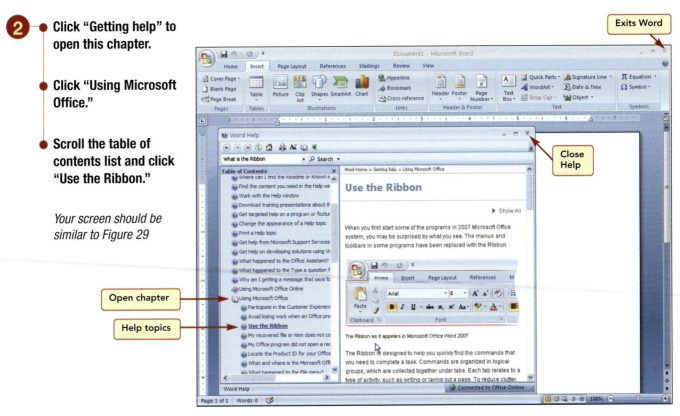

Figure 29

The right side of the Help window displays the same Help information about the Ribbon. To close a chapter, click the ⬜ icon.

3 ● Click ⬜ to close the Using Microsoft Office chapter.

● Click ⬜ Hide Table of Contents in the Help window toolbar to hide the table of contents list again.

Exiting an Office 2007 Application

Now you are ready to close the Help window and exit the Word program. The ☒ Close button located on the right end of the window title bar can be used to exit most application windows.

1 ● Click ☒ Close in the Help window title bar to close the Help window.

● Click ☒ Close in the Word window title bar to exit Word.

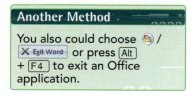

Another Method

You also could choose 🔵 / ☒ Exit Word or press [Alt] + [F4] to exit an Office application.

The program window is closed and the desktop is visible again.

Lab Review

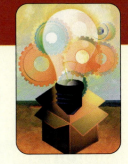

Introduction to Microsoft Office 2007

command summary

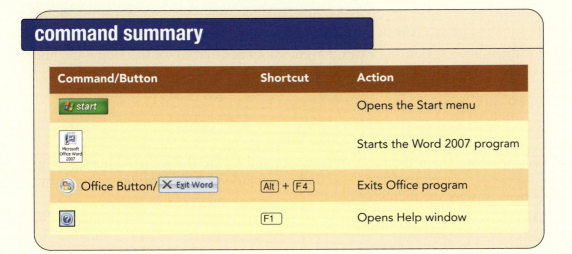

Command/Button	Shortcut	Action
start		Opens the Start menu
Microsoft Office Word 2007		Starts the Word 2007 program
Office Button/ ✕ Exit Word	Alt + F4	Exits Office program
	F1	Opens Help window

Lab Exercises

step-by-step

Using an Office Application ★

1. All Office 2007 applications have a common user interface. You will explore the Excel 2007 application and use many of the same features you learned about while using Word 2007 in this lab.

   a. Use the Start menu or a shortcut icon on your desktop to start Office Excel 2007.

   b. What shape is the mouse pointer when positioned in the document window area? _____

   c. Excel has _____ tabs. Which tabs are not the same as in Word?
   _____

   d. Open the Formulas tab. How many groups are in the Formulas tab? _____

   e. Which tab contains the group to work with charts? _____

   f. From the Home tab, click the Number group dialog box launcher. What is the name of the dialog box that opens? How many number categories are there? _____ Close the dialog box.

   g. Display ToolTips for the following buttons located in the Alignment group of the Home tab and identify what action they perform.

   ▤ _____

   ▤ _____

   ▤ _____

   h. Open the Excel Help window. Open the table of contents and locate the topic "What's new in Microsoft Office Excel 2007?" Open this topic and find information on the number of rows and columns in a worksheet. Answer the following questions:

   How many rows are in a worksheet? _____

   How many columns are in a worksheet? _____

   What are the letters of the last column? _____

   i. Close the table of contents. Close the Help window. Exit Excel.

on your own

Exploring Microsoft Help ★

1. In addition to the Help information you used in this lab, Office 2007 Online Help also includes many interactive tutorials. Selecting a Help topic that starts a tutorial will open the browser program on your computer. Both audio and written instructions are provided. You will use one of these tutorials to learn more about using Word 2007.

   Start Word 2007. Open Help and open the topic "What's New?" Click on the topic "Up to speed with Word 2007." Follow the directions in your browser to run the tutorial. When you are done, close the browser window, close Help, and exit Word 2007.

Overview of Microsoft Office Word 2007

What Is Word Processing?

Office Word 2007 is a word processing software application whose purpose is to help you create any type of written communication. A word processor can be used to manipulate text data to produce a letter, a report, a memo, an e-mail message, or any other type of correspondence. Text data is any letter, number, or symbol that you can type on a keyboard. The grouping of the text data to form words, sentences, paragraphs, and pages of text results in the creation of a document. Through a word processor, you can create, modify, store, retrieve, and print part or all of a document.

Word processors are one of the most widely used application software programs. Putting your thoughts in writing, from the simplest note to the most complex book, is a time-consuming process. Even more time-consuming is the task of editing and retyping the document to make it better. Word processors make errors nearly nonexistent—not because they are not made, but because they are easy to correct. Word processors let you throw away the correction fluid, scissors, paste, and erasers. Now, with a few keystrokes, you can easily correct errors, move paragraphs, and reprint your document.

Word 2007 Features

Word 2007 excels in its ability to change or edit a document. Editing involves correcting spelling, grammar, and sentence-structure errors. In addition, you can easily revise or update existing text by inserting or deleting text. For example, a document that lists prices can easily be updated to reflect new prices. A document that details procedures can be revised by deleting old procedures and inserting new ones. This is especially helpful when a document is used repeatedly. Rather than recreating the whole document, you change only the parts that need to be revised.

Revision also includes the rearrangement of selected areas of text. For example, while writing a report, you may decide to change the location of a single word or several paragraphs or pages of text. You can do it easily by cutting or removing selected text from one location, then pasting or placing the selected text in another location. The selection also can be copied from one document to another.

To help you produce a perfect document, Word 2007 includes many additional support features. The AutoCorrect feature checks the spelling and grammar in a document as text is entered. Many common errors are corrected automatically for you. Others are identified and a correction suggested. A thesaurus can be used to display alternative words that have a meaning similar or opposite to a word you entered. A Find and Replace feature can be used to quickly locate specified text and replace it with other text throughout a document. In addition, Word 2007 includes a variety of tools that automate the process of many common tasks, such as creating tables, form letters, and columns.

You also can easily control the appearance or format of the document. Formatting includes such operations as changing the line spacing and margin widths, adding page numbers, and displaying page headers and footers. You also can quickly change how your text is aligned with the left or right margin. For example, text can be centered between the margins, or justified—evenly aligned on both the left and right margins. Perhaps the most noticeable formatting feature is the ability to apply different fonts (type styles and sizes) and text appearance changes such as bold, italics, and color to all or selected portions of the document. Additionally, you can add color shading behind individual pieces of text or entire paragraphs and pages to add emphasis.

To make formatting even easier, Word 2007 includes Document Themes and Quick Styles. Document Themes apply a consistent font, color, and line effect to an entire document. Quick Styles apply the selected style design to a selection of text. Further, Word 2007 includes a variety of built-in preformatted content that help you quickly produce modern-looking, professional documents. Among these are galleries of cover page designs, pull quotes, and header and footer designs. While selecting many of these design choices, a visual live preview is displayed, making it easy to see how the design would look in your document. In addition, you can select from a wide variety of templates to help you get started on creating many common types of documents such as flyers, calendars, faxes, newsletters, and memos.

To further enhance your documents, you can insert many different types of graphic elements. These include drawing objects, SmartArt, charts, pictures, and clip art. The drawing tools supplied with Word 2007 can be used to create your own drawings, or you can select from over 100 adjustable shapes and modify them to your needs. All drawings can be further enhanced with 3-D effects, shadows, colors, and textures. SmartArt graphics allow you to create a visual representation of your information. They include many different layouts such as a process or cycle that are designed to help you communicate an idea. Once created, you can quickly enhance them using a Quick Style. Charts can be inserted to illustrate and compare data. Complex pictures can be inserted in documents by scanning your own, using supplied or purchased clip art, or downloading images from the World Wide Web. Additionally, you can produce fancy text effects using the WordArt tool.

Word 2007 is closely integrated with the World Wide Web. It detects when you are typing a Web address and converts it to a hyperlink automatically for you. You also can create your own hyperlinks to locations within documents, or to other documents, including those at external locations such as a Web site or file server. Word's many Web-editing features help you quickly create a Web page. Frames can be created to make your Web site easier for users to navigate. Pictures, graphic elements, animated graphics, sound, and movies can all be used to increase the impact of your Web pages.

Group collaboration on projects is common in industry today. Word 2007 includes many features to help streamline how documents are developed and changed by group members. A discussion feature allows multiple people to insert remarks in the same document without having to route the document to each person or reconcile multiple reviewers' comments. You can easily consolidate all changes and comments from different reviewers in one simple step and accept or reject changes as needed.

You also can create and send an entire document by e-mail or Internet Fax service directly from within Word 2007, using all its features to create and edit the message.

Case Study for Office Word 2007 Labs

As a recent college graduate, you have accepted a job as advertising coordinator for Adventure Travel Tours, a specialty travel company that organizes active adventure vacations. The company is headquartered in Los Angeles and has locations in other major cities throughout the country. Your duties include the creation of brochures, flyers, form letters, news releases, advertisements, and a monthly newsletter, all of which promote Adventure Travel's programs. You are also responsible for working on the company Web site.

Brief Version

Lab 1: Adventure Travel Tours has developed four new tours for the upcoming year and needs to promote them, partly through informative presentations held throughout the country. Your first job as advertising coordinator is to create a flyer advertising the four new tours and the presentations about them.

Lab 2: Your next project is to create a letter to be sent to past clients. The letter briefly describes Adventure Travel's four new tours and invites clients to attend an informational presentation.

Lab 3: Part of your responsibility as advertising coordinator is to gather background information about the various tour locations. You will write a report that includes a cover page, table of contents list, and footnotes, providing information about Tanzania and Peru for two of the new tours.

Working Together: Adventure Travel Tours has a company Web site. You will convert the flyer you developed to promote the new tours and presentations to be used on the Web site.

Before You Begin

To the Student

The following assumptions have been made:

- Microsoft Office Word 2007 has been properly installed on your computer system.
- You have the data files needed to complete the series of Word 2007 labs and practice exercises. These may be supplied by your instructor and are also available at the online learning center Web site found at www.mhhe.com/oleary.
- You are already familiar with how to use Microsoft Windows XP or Vista and a mouse.

To the Instructor

A complete installation of Microsoft Office 2007 is required in which all components are available to students while completing the labs. In several labs, an online connection to the Web is needed to fully access a feature.

Please be aware that the following settings are assumed to be in effect for the Office Word 2007 program. These assumptions are necessary so that the screens and directions in the labs are accurate. These settings are made using Office Button/ Word Options in the categories shown below. Features are on when there is a check mark in the check box.

Popular

- The Mini Toolbar feature is selected.
- Always use ClearType is on.
- The Live Preview feature is enabled.
- The color scheme is set to blue.
- Show feature descriptions in ScreenTips is selected.
- Language is set to English (US).

Display

- Show white space between pages in Print Layout view is on.
- Show highlighter marks is on.
- Show document tooltips on hover is on.
- Print drawings created in Word is on.

Proofing

- In the AutoCorrect Options dialog box, all options are on in both the AutoCorrect and AutoFormat tabs. In the AutoFormat as you type tab, all options are on except: Bold and italic with real formatting, Built-in Heading styles, and Define styles based on your formatting.
- Ignore words in Uppercase is on.
- Ignore words that contain numbers is on.
- Ignore Internet and file addresses is on.
- Flag repeated words is on.
- Check spelling as you type is on.
- Check grammar as you type is on.
- Check grammar with spelling is on.

Advanced/Editing options

- Typing replaces selected text is on.
- When selecting, automatically select entire word is on.
- Allow text to be dragged and dropped is on.
- Use Ctrl+Click to follow hyperlink is on.
- Use smart paragraph selection is on.
- Use smart cursoring is on.
- Keep track of formatting is on.
- Mark Formatting Inconsistencies is off.
- Enable Click and type is on.

Advanced/Cut, Copy, and Paste

- The four Pasting options are set to their default settings.
- The Insert/paste pictures as option is set to In line with text.
- Keep bullets and numbers when pasting text with Keep Text Only option is on.
- Show Paste Options button is on.
- Use smart cut and paste is on.

Advanced/Show document content

- Show drawings and text boxes on screen is on.
- Show text animation is on.
- Show Smart Tags is on.

Advanced/Display

- Show 17 Recent Documents.
- Show all windows in the Taskbar is on.
- Show shortcut keys in ScreenTips is on.
- Show horizontal and vertical scroll bars is on.
- Show vertical ruler in Print Layout view is on.

Additionally, the following assumptions are made:

- The feature to access Online Help is on. (From the Help window, open the Connection Status menu and choose Show Content from Office Online.)
- All default settings for the Normal document template are in effect.
- All figures in the text reflect the use of a display monitor set at 1024 by 768 and the Windows XP opearting system. If other monitor settings are used, there may be more or fewer lines of information displayed in the windows than in the figures. If the Windows Vista operating system is used, some features may look slightly different.

Instructional Conventions

Hands-on instructions you are to perform appear as a sequence of numbered steps. Within each step, a series of bullets identifies the specific actions that must be performed. Step numbering begins over within each topic heading throughout the lab. Four types of marginal notes appear throughout the labs. Another Method notes provide alternate ways of performing the same command. Having Trouble? notes provide advice or cautions for steps that may cause problems. Additional Information notes provide more information about a topic. More About notes refer you to the More About Word 2007 appendix for additional information about related features.

Commands

Commands that are initiated using a command button and the mouse appear following the word "Click." The icon (and the icon name if the icon does not include text) is displayed following "Click." If there is another way to perform the same action, it appears in an Another Method margin note when the action is first introduced as shown in Example A.

When a feature has already been covered and you are more familiar with using the application, commands will appear as shown in Example B.

Example A

1 — • Select the list of four tours.

　　• Open the Home tab.

　　• Click **B** Bold in the Font group.

Another Method
The keyboard shortcut is
`Ctrl`+B.

Example B

1 ● Select the list of four tours.

● Click **B** Bold in the Font group of the Home tab.

OR

1 ● Bold the list of four tours.

File Names and Information to Type

Plain blue text identifies file names you need to select or enter. Information you are asked to type appears in blue and bold. (See Example C.)

Example C

1 ● Open the document wd01_Flyer.

● Type Adventure Travel presents four new trips.

Office Button

Clicking Office Button opens the File menu of commands. File menu commands that you are to use by clicking on the menu option appear following the word "Choose." Items that are to be selected (highlighted) will follow the word "Select" and will appear in black text. You can select items with the mouse or directional keys. Initially these commands will appear as in Example A. As you become more familiar with the application, commands will appear as shown in Example B.

Example A

1 ● Click Office Button.

● Choose Open.

● Select My Documents from the Look In drop-down menu.

● Select Flyer1.docx.

● Click Open .

Example B

1 ● Choose Open from the File menu.

● Choose Flyer1.docx.

Creating and Editing a Document

LAB 1

Objectives

After completing this lab, you will know how to:

1 Develop a document as well as enter and edit text.

2 Insert and delete text and blank lines.

3 Use spelling and grammar checking.

4 Use AutoCorrect.

5 Set file properties.

6 Save, close, and open files.

7 Select text.

8 Undo and redo changes.

9 Change fonts and type sizes.

10 Bold and color text.

11 Change alignment.

12 Insert and size pictures.

13 Add page borders and watermarks.

14 Print a document.

Case Study

Adventure Travel Tours

As a recent college graduate, you have accepted a job as advertising coordinator for Adventure Travel Tours, a specialty travel company that organizes active adventure vacations. The company is headquartered in Los Angeles and has locations in other major cities throughout the country. You are responsible for coordination of the advertising program for all locations. This includes the creation of many kinds of promotional materials: brochures, flyers, form letters, news releases, advertisements, and a monthly newsletter. You are also responsible for creating Web pages for the company Web site.

Adventure Travel is very excited about four new tours planned for the upcoming year. They want to promote

them through informative presentations held throughout the country. Your first job as advertising coordinator will be to create a flyer advertising the four new tours and the presentations about them. The flyer will be modified according to the location of the presentation.

The software tool you will use to create the flyer is the word processing application Microsoft Office Word 2007. It helps you create documents such as letters, reports, and research papers. In this lab, you will learn how to enter, edit, and print a document while you create the flyer (shown right) to be distributed in a mailing to Adventure Travel Tours clients.

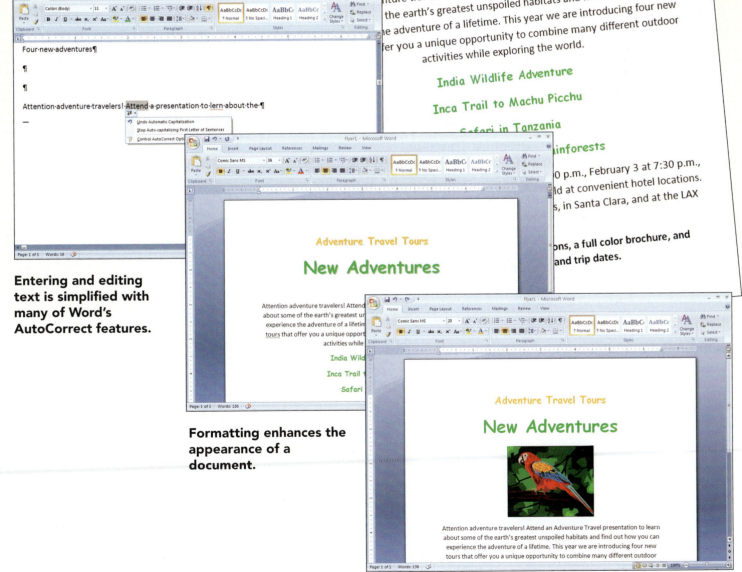

Entering and editing text is simplified with many of Word's AutoCorrect features.

Formatting enhances the appearance of a document.

Pictures add visual interest to a document.

Concept Preview

The following concepts will be introduced in this lab:

1 **Grammar Checker** The grammar checker advises you of incorrect grammar as you create and edit a document, and proposes possible corrections.

2 **Spelling Checker** The spelling checker advises you of misspelled words as you create and edit a document, and proposes possible corrections.

3 **AutoCorrect** The AutoCorrect feature makes some basic assumptions about the text you are typing and, based on these assumptions, automatically corrects the entry.

4 **Word Wrap** The word wrap feature automatically decides where to end a line and wrap text to the next line based on the margin settings.

5 **Font and Font Size** Font, also commonly referred to as a typeface, is a set of characters with a specific design that has one or more font sizes.

6 **Alignment** Alignment is the positioning of text on a line between the margins or indents. There are four types of paragraph alignment: left, centered, right, and justified.

7 **Graphics** A graphic is a nontext element or object such as a drawing or picture that can be added to a document.

Introducing Office Word 2007

Adventure Travel Tours has recently upgraded their computer systems at all locations across the country. As part of the upgrade, they have installed the latest version of the Microsoft Office 2007 suite of applications. You are very excited to see how this new and powerful application can help you create professional letters and reports as well as eye-catching flyers and newsletters.

Starting Office Word 2007

You will use the word processing application Microsoft Office Word 2007 to create a flyer promoting the new tours and presentations.

1 ● **Start Word 2007.**

Having Trouble?

See "Common 2007 Office Features," page I.10, for information on how to start the application and use features that are common to all Office 2007 applications.

● **If necessary, maximize the Word 2007 application window.**

Your screen should be similar to Figure 1.1

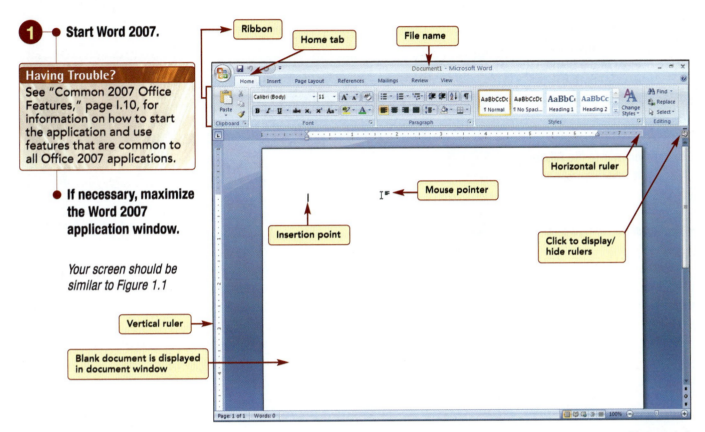

Figure 1.1

Additional Information

The Ribbon may display additional tabs if other application add-ins associated with Office are on.

Additional Information

If the ruler is not displayed, click ⌗ View Ruler above the vertical scroll bar to turn it on. You also can temporarily display the horizontal or vertical ruler by pointing to the top or left edge of the document window.

Additional Information

The mouse pointer also may appear in other shapes, depending upon the task being performed.

Exploring the Word 2007 Window

The Word 2007 Ribbon below the title bar consists of seven command tabs that provide access to the commands and features you will use to create and modify a document.

The large area below the toolbars is the **document window**. It currently displays a blank Word document. The **insertion point**, also called the **cursor**, is the blinking vertical bar that marks your location in the document. A vertical and horizontal **ruler** may be displayed along both edges of the document window. The horizontal ruler at the top of the document window shows the line length in inches and is used to set margins, tab stops, and indents. The vertical ruler along the left edge shows the page length in inches and shows your line location on the page.

The mouse pointer may appear as an I-beam (see Figure 1.1) or a left- or right-facing arrow, depending on its location in the window. When it appears as an I-beam, it is used to move the insertion point, and when it appears as an arrow, it is used to select items.

1 ● Move the mouse pointer into the left edge of the blank document to see it appear as ⇗.

● Move the mouse pointer to the Ribbon to see it appear as ⇘.

Your screen should be similar to Figure 1.2

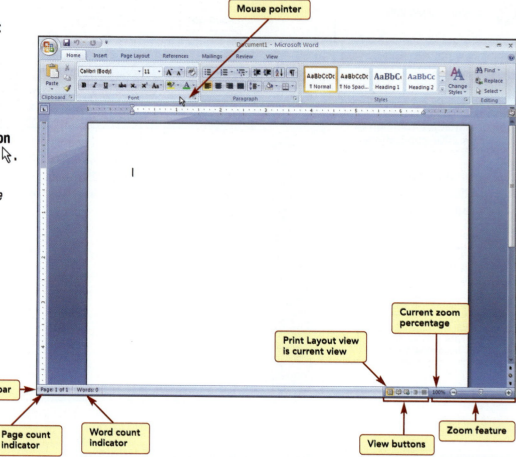

Mouse pointer

Current zoom percentage

Print Layout view is current view

Status bar

Page count indicator

Word count indicator

View buttons

Zoom feature

Figure 1.2

Viewing and Zooming a Document

The status bar at the bottom of the window displays the page and word count indicators. The page indicator identifies the page of text that is displayed onscreen of the total number of pages in the document. The word count indicator displays the number of words in a document. When you first start Word, a new blank document consisting of a single page and zero words is opened.

The right end of the status bar displays five buttons that are used to change the document view and a document zoom feature. Word includes

Additional Information

You also can change views using commands in the Document Views group of the View tab.

several views that are used for different purposes. The different document views are described in the table below.

Document View	Button	Effect on Text
Print Layout		Shows how the text and objects will appear on the printed page. This is the view to use when adjusting margins, working in columns, drawing objects, and placing graphics.
Full Screen Reading		Shows the document only, without Ribbon, status bar, or any other features. Useful for viewing and reading large documents. Use to review a document and add comments and highlighting.
Web Layout		Shows the document as it will appear when viewed in a Web browser. Use this view when creating Web pages or documents that will be displayed on the screen only.
Outline		Shows the structure of the document. This is the view to use to plan and reorganize text in a document.
Draft		Shows text formatting and simple layout of the page. This is the best view to use when typing, editing, and formatting text.

Additional Information

Pointing to the items on the status bar displays a ScreenTip that identifies the feature.

Additional Information

If you have a mouse with a scroll wheel, you can use it to zoom in or out by holding down Ctrl while turning the wheel forward or backward.

Print Layout view is the view you see when first starting Word or opening a document. You can tell which view is in use by looking at the view buttons. The button for the view that is in use appears highlighted.

The document zoom feature is used to change the amount of information displayed in the document window by "zooming in" to get a close-up view or "zooming out" to see more of the document at a reduced view. The default display, 100 percent, shows the characters the same size they will be when printed. You can increase the onscreen character size up to five times the normal display (500 percent) or reduce the character size to 10 percent. The zoom setting for each view is set independently and remains in effect until changed to another zoom setting.

You will "zoom out" on the document to see the entire page so you can better see the default document settings.

1 ● **Drag the Zoom Slider to the left to reduce the zoom until the entire page is visible.**

Your screen should be similar to Figure 1.3

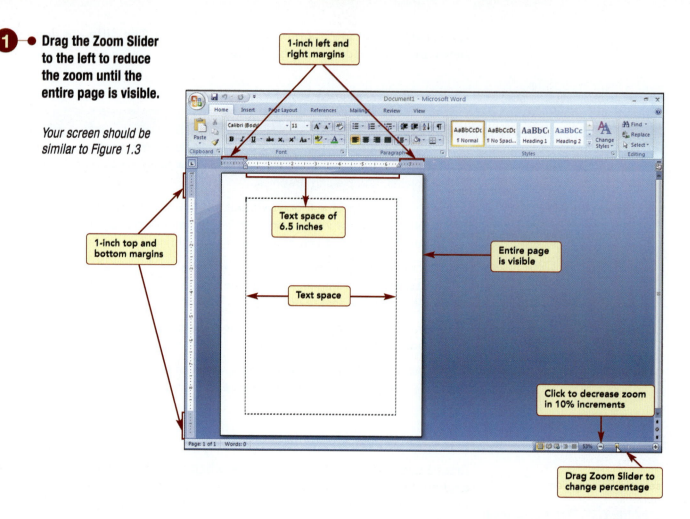

- 1-inch left and right margins
- Text space of 6.5 inches
- 1-inch top and bottom margins
- Text space
- Entire page is visible
- Click to decrease zoom in 10% increments
- Drag Zoom Slider to change percentage

Figure 1.3

Additional Information

You also can click the ⊖ or ⊕ on the Zoom Slider to increase or decrease the zoom percentage by 10 percent increments.

At this zoom percentage, the entire page is displayed and all four edges of the paper are visible. It is like a blank piece of paper that already has many predefined settings. These settings, called **default** settings, are generally the most commonly used settings. The default document settings are stored in the Normal.dotm template file. A **template** is a document that contains many predefined settings that is used as the basis for the document you are creating. The Normal.dotm file is automatically opened whenever you start Word 2007. The default settings include a standard paper-size setting of 8.5 by 11 inches, 1-inch top and bottom margins, and 1-inch left and right margins.

You can verify many of the default document settings by looking at the information displayed in the rulers. The shaded area of the ruler identifies the margins and the white area identifies the text space. The text space occupies 6.5 inches of the page. Knowing that the default page size is 8.5 inches wide, this leaves 2 inches for margins: 1 inch for equal-sized left and right margins. The vertical ruler shows the entire page length is 11 inches with 1-inch top and bottom margins, leaving 9 inches of text space.

You will use Draft view to create the flyer about this year's new tours. You will use the View tab to change both the view and the Zoom percentage.

2
- Open the View tab.
- From the Document Views group, click [Draft] .
- If necessary, click [ ] to display the ruler.
- From the Zoom group, click [Zoom] to open the Zoom dialog box.

Additional Information
Pointing to the items on the Ribbon displays a ScreenTip that identifies the feature.

Your screen should be similar to Figure 1.4

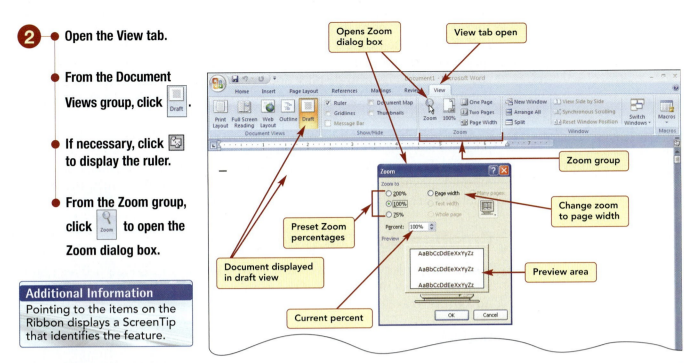

Figure 1.4

Additional Information
The Preview area shows the effects on the screen as you select different zoom options.

From the Zoom dialog box, you can choose from several preset zoom percentages, or set a precise percentage using the Percent scroll box. You want to zoom the window so that the full page width spans the document window. The page width is the area of the paper where the text is displayed.

3
- Choose Page width.
- Click [OK].

Another method
You also could use [Page Width] in the Zoom group to change to page width.

Your screen should be similar to Figure 1.5

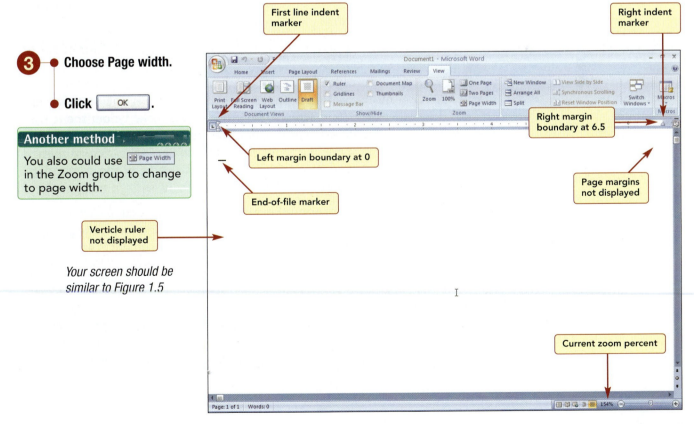

Figure 1.5

Increasing the zoom to page width increases the magnification to 154% and displays the full text area in the document window. In Draft view, the margins and the edges of the page are not displayed. This allows more space on the screen to display document content. This view also displays the **end-of-file marker**, the solid horizontal line that marks the last-used line in a document.

Additional Information
The vertical ruler is not displayed in Draft view.

The ruler also displays other default settings. The symbol ▽ at the zero position is the first-line indent marker and marks the location of the left paragraph indent. The △ symbol on the right end of the ruler line at the 6.5-inch position marks the right paragraph indent. Currently, the indent locations are the same as the left and right margin settings.

Creating New Documents

Your first project with Adventure Travel Tours is to create a flyer about four new tours. You will use the blank document to create the flyer for Adventure Travel Tours.

Developing a Document

The development of a document follows several steps: plan, enter, edit, format, and preview and print.

Step	Description
Plan	The first step in the development of a document is to understand the purpose of the document and to plan what your document should say.
Enter	After planning the document, you enter the content of the document by typing the text using the keyboard. Text also can be entered using the handwriting feature.
Edit	Making changes to your document is called **editing**. While typing, you probably will make typing and spelling errors that need to be corrected. This is one type of editing. Another is to revise the content that you have entered to make it clearer, or to add or delete information.
Format	Enhancing the appearance of the document to make it more readable or attractive is called **formatting**. This is usually performed when the document is near completion, after all editing and revising have been done. It includes many features such as boldfaced text, italics, and bulleted lists.
Preview and Print	The last step is to preview and print the document. When previewing, you check the document's overall appearance and make any final changes before printing.

You will find that you will generally follow these steps in the order listed above for your first draft of a document. However, you will probably retrace steps such as editing and formatting as the final document is developed.

During the planning phase, you spoke with your manager regarding the purpose of the flyer and the content in general. The primary purpose of the flyer is to promote the new tours. A secondary purpose is to advertise the company in general.

You plan to include specific information about the new tours in the flyer as well as general information about Adventure Travel Tours. The content also needs to include information about the upcoming new tour presentations. Finally, you want to include information about the Adventure Travel Web site.

Entering Text

Now that you understand the purpose of the flyer and have a general idea of the content, you are ready to enter the text.

Text is entered using the keyboard. As you type, you will probably make simple typing errors that you want to correct. Word includes many features that make entering text and correcting errors much easier. These features include checking for spelling and grammar errors, auto correction, and word wrap. You will see how these features work while entering the title and first paragraph of the flyer.

Typing Text

To enter text in a new document, simply begin typing the text. The first line of the flyer will contain the text "Adventure Travel Tours New Adventures." As you begin to enter this line of text, include the intentional error identified in italic.

1 ● **Type Adventure Traveel (do not press space after typing the last letter).**

Your screen should be similar to Figure 1.6

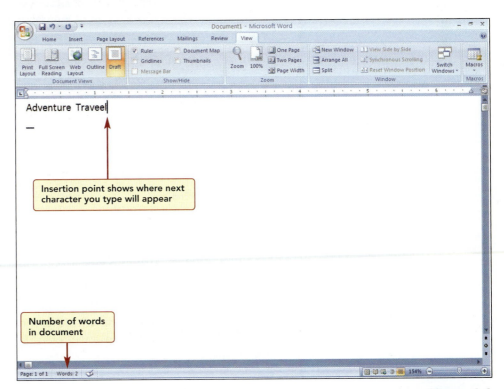

Insertion point shows where next character you type will appear

Number of words in document

Figure 1.6

Additional Information

The status bar also can display additional information such as the horizontal position of the insertion point on the line and the line number. To customize the status bar, right-click the status bar and select the features you want displayed from the status bar context menu.

Notice that, as you type, the insertion point moves to the right and the character appears to the left of the insertion point. The location of the insertion point shows where the next character will appear as you type. Also, the status bar now tells you that there are two words in the document.

Moving through Text

After text is entered into a document, you need to know how to move around within the text to correct errors or make changes. You see you have made a typing error by typing an extra e in the word travel. To correct this error, you first need to move the insertion point back to the correct position on the line. The keyboard or mouse can be used to move through the text in the document window. Depending on what you are doing, one method may be more efficient than another. For example, if your hands are already on the keyboard as you are entering text, it may be quicker to use the keyboard rather than take your hands off to use the mouse.

You use the mouse to move the insertion point to a specific location in a document simply by clicking on the location. When you can use the mouse to move the insertion point, it is shaped as an I-beam. However, when the mouse pointer is positioned in the unmarked area to the left of a line (the left margin), it changes to an arrow ⇗. When the mouse is in this area, it can be used to highlight (select) text.

Additional Information

You will learn about selecting text using this feature shortly.

You use the arrow keys located on the numeric keypad or the directional keypad to move the insertion point in a document. The keyboard directional keys are described in the following table.

Key	Movement
→	One character to right
←	One character to left
↑	One line up
↓	One line down
Ctrl + →	One word to right
Ctrl + ←	One word to left
Home	Beginning of line
End	End of line

1 ● Press ← or position the I-beam between the e and I and click.

The insertion point is positioned between the e and l.

Holding down a directional key or key combination moves quickly in the direction indicated, saving multiple presses of the key. Many of the Word insertion point movement keys can be held down to execute multiple moves.

Using Backspace and Delete

Removing typing entries to change or correct them is one of the basic editing tasks. Corrections may be made in many ways. Two of the most important editing keys are the [Backspace] key and the [Delete] key. The [Backspace] key removes a character or space to the left of the insertion point. It is particularly useful when you are moving from right to left (backward) along a line of text. The [Delete] key removes the character or space to the right of the insertion point and is most useful when moving from left to right along a line.

You will correct the error and continue typing the first line.

Additional Information

You can use the directional keys on the numeric keypad or the dedicated directional keypad area. If using the numeric keypad, make sure the Num Lock feature is off; otherwise, numbers will be entered in the document. The Num Lock indicator light above the keypad is lit when on. Press [Num Lock] to turn it off.

1 ● Press [Backspace] to remove the extra e.

● Press [→] or click at the end of the line.

● Press [Spacebar].

● Type Tours four new adventures and correct any typing errors as you make them using [Backspace] or [Delete].

Your screen should be similar to Figure 1.7

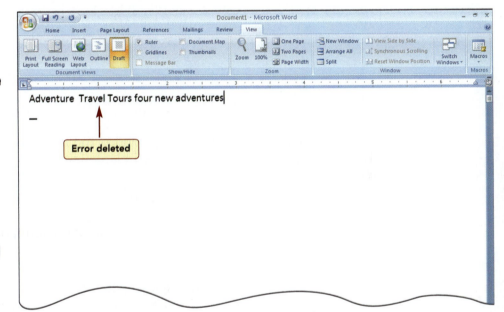

Error deleted

Figure 1.7

Ending a Line and Inserting Blank Lines

Now you are ready to complete the first line of the announcement. To end a line and begin another line, you simply press [←Enter]. The insertion point moves to the beginning of the next line. If you press [←Enter] at the beginning of a line, a blank line is inserted into the document. If the insertion point is in the middle of a line of text and you press [←Enter], all the text to the right of the insertion point moves to the beginning of the next line.

1 ● **Press** ⏎ Enter **3 times.**

Your screen should be similar to Figure 1.8

Blank lines inserted by pressing ⏎ Enter

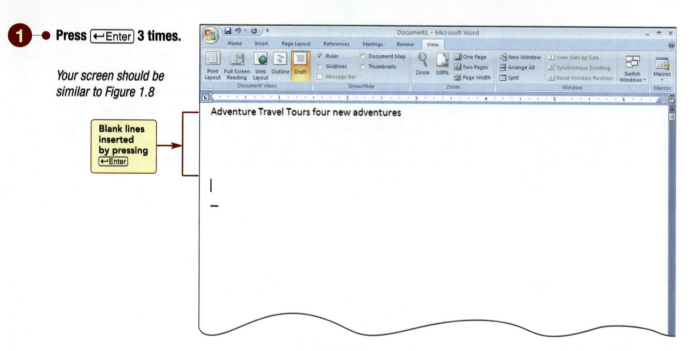

Adventure Travel Tours four new adventures

Figure 1.8

Pressing the first ⏎ Enter ended the first line of text and inserted a blank line. The next two inserted blank lines.

Revealing Formatting Marks

While you are creating your document, Word automatically inserts formatting marks that control the appearance of your document. These marks are not displayed automatically so that the document is not cluttered. Sometimes, however, it is helpful to view the underlying formatting marks. Displaying these marks makes it easy to see, for example, if you have added an extra space between words or at the end of a sentence.

1 ● **Open the Home tab and click** ¶ **Show/Hide in the Paragraph group.**

Another Method
You also can use the keyboard shortcut Ctrl + * to display formatting marks.

Your screen should be similar to Figure 1.9

Inserted blank lines by pressing ⏎ Enter

Displays formatting marks

Entered space by pressing Spacebar

End line by pressing ⏎ Enter

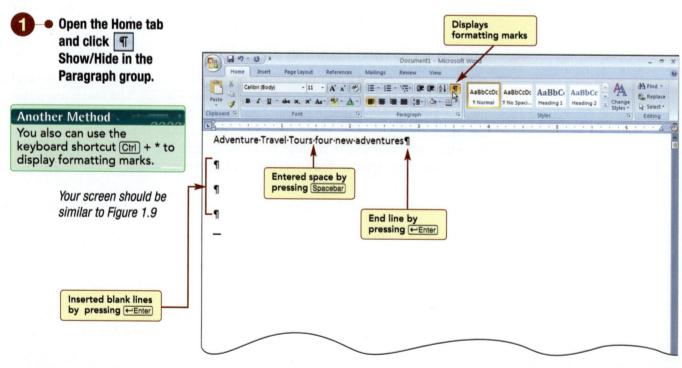

Adventure·Travel·Tours·four·new·adventures¶
¶
¶
¶

Figure 1.9

The document now displays the formatting marks. The ¶ character on the line above the insertion point represents the pressing of ←Enter that created the blank line. The ¶ character at the end of the text represents the pressing of ←Enter that ended the line and moved the insertion point to the beginning of the next line. Between each word, a dot shows where the Spacebar was pressed. Formatting marks do not appear when the document is printed. You can continue to work on the document while the formatting marks are displayed, just as you did when they were hidden.

You have decided you want the flyer heading to be on two lines, with the words "four new adventures" on the second line. To do this, you will insert a blank line after the word Tours. You will move the insertion point to the location in the text where you want to insert the blank line.

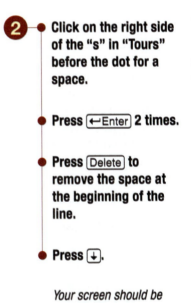

2 ● **Click on the right side of the "s" in "Tours" before the dot for a space.**

● **Press ←Enter 2 times.**

● **Press Delete to remove the space at the beginning of the line.**

● **Press ↓.**

Your screen should be similar to Figure 1.10

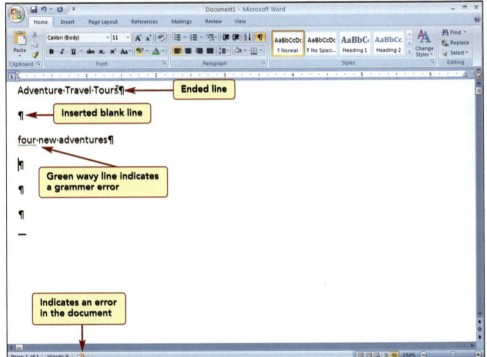

Figure 1.10

As you continue to create a document, the formatting marks are automatically adjusted.

Identifying and Correcting Errors Automatically

Having Trouble?
If the green underline is not displayed, click 🄑 Office Button, click 📄 Word Options , Proofing, and select the "Check spelling as you type", "Mark grammar errors as you type", and "Check grammar with spelling" options.

Notice that a green wavy underline appears under the word "four." This indicates an error has been detected.

As you enter text, Word is constantly checking the document for spelling and grammar errors. The Spelling and Grammar Status icon in the status bar displays an animated pencil icon 🖉 while you are typing, indicating Word is checking for errors as you type. When you stop typing, it displays either a blue checkmark 🗹 , indicating the program does not detect any errors, or a red X 🗷 , indicating the document contains an error.

In many cases, Word will automatically correct errors for you. In other cases, it identifies the error by underlining it. The different colors and designs of underlines indicate the type of error that has been identified. In addition to identifying the error, Word provides suggestions as to the possible correction needed.

Checking Grammar

In addition to the green wavy line under "four," the Spelling and Grammar Status icon appears as [icon] in the status bar. This indicates that a spelling or grammar error has been located. The green wavy underline below the error indicates it is a grammar error.

Concept 1

Grammar Checker

1 The **grammar checker** advises you of incorrect grammar as you create and edit a document, and proposes possible corrections. Grammar checking occurs after you enter punctuation or end a line. If grammatical errors in subject-verb agreements, verb forms, capitalization, or commonly confused words, to name a few, are detected, they are identified with a wavy green line. You can correct the grammatical error by editing it or you can open the context menu for the identified error and display a suggested correction. Because not all identified grammatical errors are actual errors, you need to use discretion when correcting the errors.

---

1 ● **Right-click the word "four" to open the context menu.**

Having Trouble?
Review context menus in the "Common Office 2007 Features" section (page I.15). If the wrong context menu appears, you probably did not have the I-beam positioned on the error with the green wavy line. Press [Esc] or click outside the menu to cancel it and try again.

Your screen should be similar to Figure 1.11

Additional Information
A dimmed menu option means it is currently unavailable.

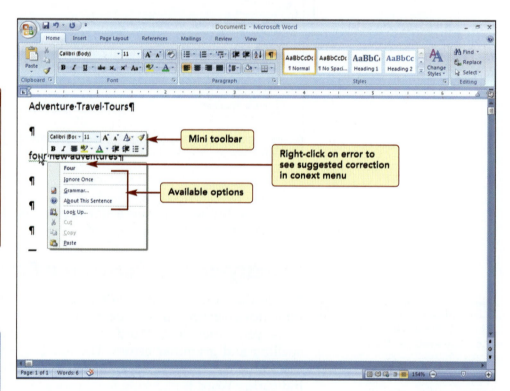

Figure 1.11

Additional Information
You will learn about using the Mini toolbar shortly.

The Word Mini toolbar and a context menu containing commands related to the grammar error are displayed. The first item on the menu is the suggested correction, "Four." The grammar checker indicates you should capitalize the first letter of the word because it appears to be the beginning of a sentence. It also includes four available commands that are relevant to the item, described below.

Command	Effect
Ignore Once	Instructs Word to ignore the grammatical error in this sentence.
Grammar	Opens the grammar checker and displays an explanation of the error.
About This Sentence	Provides help about the grammatical error.
Look up	Looks up word in dictionary.

To make this correction, you could simply choose the correction from the menu and the correction would be inserted into the document. Although, in this case, you can readily identify the reason for the error, sometimes the reason is not so obvious. In those cases, you can open the grammar checker to find out more information.

2 ● **Choose Grammar.**

Your screen should be similar to Figure 1.12

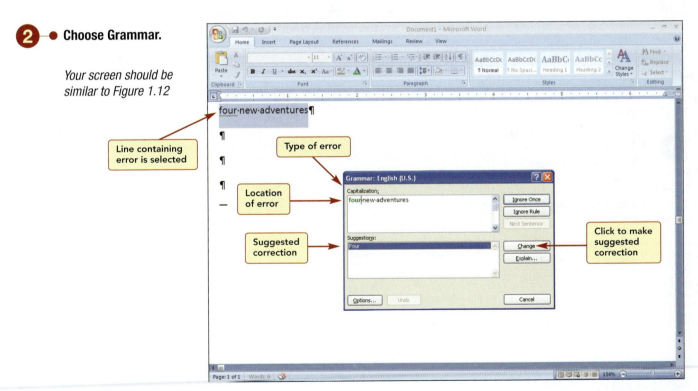

Line containing error is selected

Type of error

Location of error

Suggested correction

Click to make suggested correction

Figure 1.12

The Grammar dialog box identifies the type and location of the grammatical error in the upper text box and the suggested correction in the Suggestions box. The line in the document containing the error is also highlighted (selected) to make it easy for you to see the location of the error. You will make the suggested change.

3 • Click [Change].

• **Move to the blank line at the end of the document.**

Additional Information

Moving the insertion point using the keyboard or mouse deselects or removes the highlight from text that is selected.

Your screen should be similar to Figure 1.13

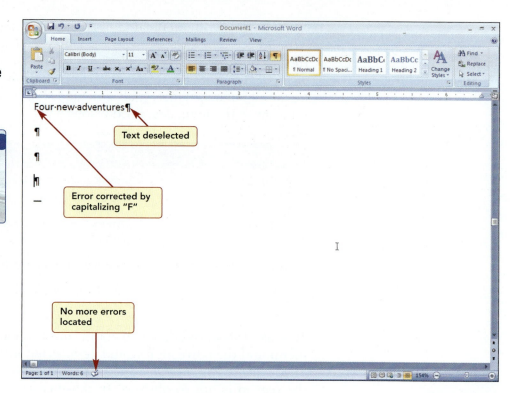

Figure 1.13

The error is corrected, the wavy green line is removed, and the Spelling and Grammar Status icon returns to .

Checking Spelling

Now you are ready to type the text for the first paragraph of the flyer.
    Enter the following text, including the intentional spelling errors.

1 • **Type Attention adventire travellars!**

• **Press** [Spacebar].

Your screen should be similar to Figure 1.14

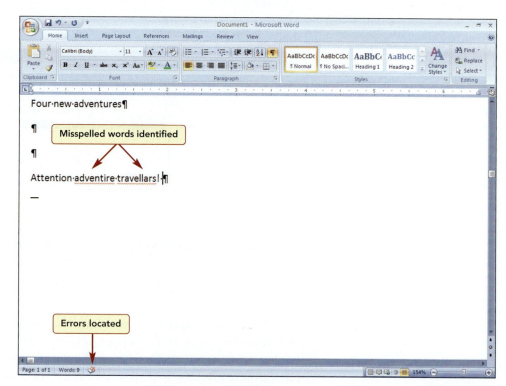

Figure 1.14

As soon as you complete a word by entering a space, the program checks the word for spelling accuracy.

Concept 2

Spelling Checker

2 The **spelling checker** advises you of misspelled words as you create and edit a document, and proposes possible corrections. The spelling checker compares each word you type to a **main dictionary** of words supplied with the program. The main dictionary includes most common words. If the word does not appear in the main dictionary, it then checks the **custom dictionary**. The custom dictionary consists of a list of words such as proper names, technical terms, and so on, that are not in the main dictionary and that you want the spelling checker to accept as correct. Adding words to the custom dictionary prevents the flagging as incorrect of specialized words that you commonly use. Word shares custom dictionaries with other Microsoft Office applications such as PowerPoint.

If the word does not appear in either dictionary, the program identifies it as misspelled by displaying a red wavy line below the word. You can then correct the misspelled word by editing it. Alternatively, you can display a list of suggested spelling corrections for that word and select the correct spelling from the list to replace the misspelled word in the document.

Word automatically identified the two words "adventire travellars" as misspelled by underlining them with a wavy red line. The quickest way to correct a misspelled word is to select the correct spelling from a list of suggested spelling corrections displayed on the context menu.

2 ● Right-click on "adventire" to display the context menu.

Another Method

You also can position the insertion point on the item you want to display a context menu for and press ⇧Shift + F10 to open the menu.

Your screen should be similar to Figure 1.15

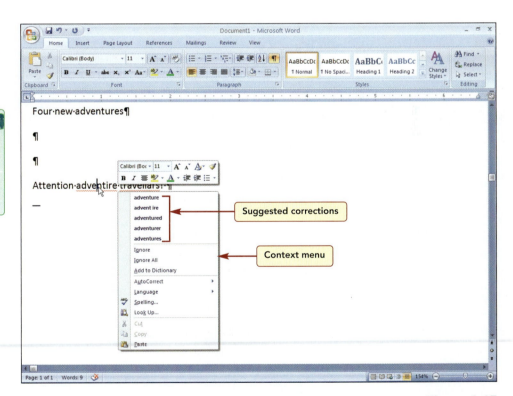

Figure 1.15

A context menu containing suggested correct spellings is displayed. The context menu also includes several related menu options, described in the following table.

Option	Effect
Ignore	Instructs word to ignore the misspelling of this word for this occurrence only.
Ignore All	Instructs Word to ignore the misspelling of this word throughout the rest of this session.
Add to Dictionary	Adds the word to the custom dictionary list. When a word is added to the custom dictionary, Word will always accept that spelling as correct.
AutoCorrect	Adds the word to the AutoCorrect list so Word can correct misspellings of it automatically as you type.
Language	Sets the language format, such as French, English, or German, to apply to the word.
Spelling	Starts the spell-checking program to check the entire document. You will learn about this feature in Lab 2.
Look Up	Searches reference tools to locate similar words and definitions.

Sometimes there are no suggested replacements because Word cannot locate any words in its dictionary that are similar in spelling; or the suggestions are not correct. If this occurs, you need to edit the word manually. In this case, the first suggestion is correct.

3 ● Choose "adventure".

● Correct the spelling for "travellars".

Your screen should be similar to Figure 1.16

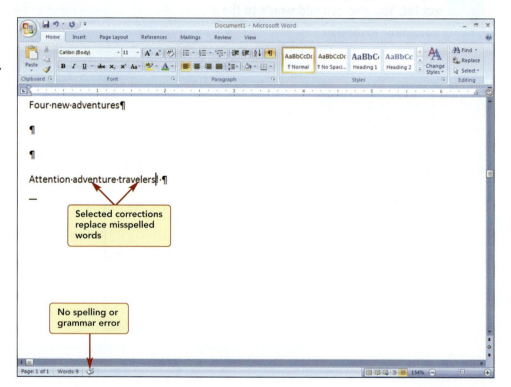

Selected corrections replace misspelled words

No spelling or grammar error

Figure 1.16

The spelling corrections you selected replace the misspelled words in the document. The Spelling and Grammar status icon returns to [✓], indicating that, as far as Word is able to detect, the document is free from errors.

Using AutoCorrect

As you have seen, as soon as you complete a word by entering a space or punctuation, the program checks the word for grammar and spelling accuracy. Also, when you complete a sentence and start another, additional checks are made. Many spelling and grammar corrections are made automatically for you as you type. This is part of the AutoCorrect feature of Word.

Concept 3

AutoCorrect

3 The AutoCorrect feature makes some basic assumptions about the text you are typing and, based on these assumptions, automatically corrects the entry. The AutoCorrect feature automatically inserts proper capitalization at the beginning of sentences and in the names of days of the week. It also will change to lowercase letters any words that were incorrectly capitalized because of the accidental use of the ⬆Shift key. In addition, it also corrects many common typing and spelling errors automatically.

One way the program automatically makes corrections is by looking for certain types of errors. For example, if two capital letters appear at the beginning of a word, Word changes the second capital letter to a lowercase letter. If a lowercase letter appears at the beginning of a sentence, Word capitalizes the first letter of the first word. If the name of a day begins with a lowercase letter, Word capitalizes the first letter. When Spelling Checker provides a single suggested spelling correction for the word, the program will automatically replace the incorrect spelling with the suggested replacement.

Another way the program makes corrections is by checking all entries against a built-in list of AutoCorrect entries. If it finds the entry on the list, the program automatically replaces the error with the correction. For example, the typing error "withthe" is automatically changed to "with the" because the error is on the AutoCorrect list. You also can add words to the AutoCorrect list that you want to be automatically corrected.

Enter the following text, including the errors (identified in italics).

1 ● **Press End to move to the end of the line.**

● **Type attend a presentaation to lern aboutthe**

● **Press Spacebar.**

Your screen should be similar to Figure 1.17

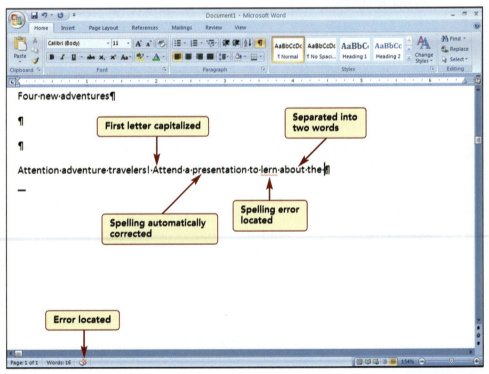

Figure 1.17

Having Trouble?
The "Capitalize first letter of sentences" and "Replace text as you type" AutoCorrect features must be on. Use 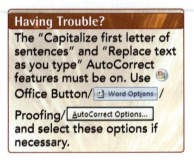 Office Button/ Word Options / Proofing/ AutoCorrect Options... and select these options if necessary.

MORE ABOUT

 See 1.4 Personalize Office Word 2007, Customize Autocorrect Options in the More About appendix to learn how to customize the AutoCorrect feature.

The first letter of the word "attend" was automatically capitalized because, as you were typing, the program determined that it is the first word in a sentence. In a similar manner, it corrected the spelling of "presentation" and separated the words "about the" with a space. The AutoCorrect feature corrected the spelling of "presentation" because it was the only suggested correction for the word supplied by the Spelling Checker. The word "lern" was not corrected because there are several suggested spelling corrections.

When you rest the mouse pointer near text that has been corrected automatically or move the insertion point onto the word, a small blue box appears under the first character of the word. The blue box changes to the AutoCorrect Options button when you point directly to it.

2 ● **Point to the word "Attend" to display the blue box.**

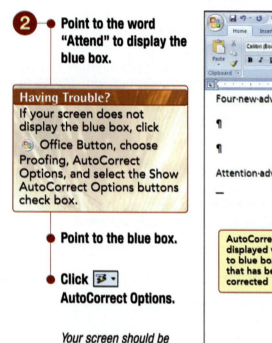

Having Trouble?

If your screen does not display the blue box, click Office Button, choose Proofing, AutoCorrect Options, and select the Show AutoCorrect Options buttons check box.

● **Point to the blue box.**

● **Click** ● **AutoCorrect Options.**

Your screen should be similar to Figure 1.18

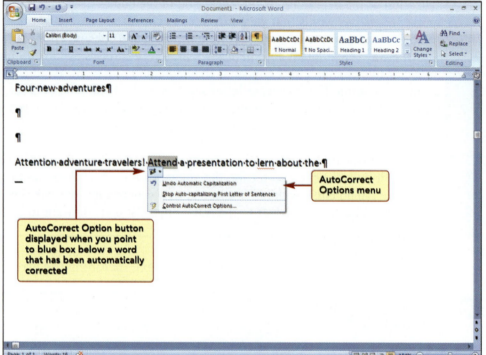

Figure 1.18

Another Method

Use ● Office Button/ Word Options /Proofing/ AutoCorrect Options/ Exceptions to add a word to the exceptions list.

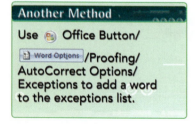

Each time Word uses the AutoCorrect feature, the AutoCorrect Options button is available. The AutoCorrect Options menu allows you to undo the AutoCorrection or to permanently disable the AutoCorrection for the remainder of your document. The Control AutoCorrect Options command is used to change the settings for this feature. In some cases, you may want to exclude a word from automatic correction. You can do this by adding the word to the exceptions list so the feature will be disabled for that word. If you use Backspace to delete an automatic correction and then type it again the way you want it to appear, the word will be automatically added to the exceptions list.

You want to keep all the AutoCorrections that were made and correct the spelling for "lern".

3 ● Click outside the menu to close it.

● Open the spelling context menu for "lern" and choose "learn".

The spelling is corrected, and the spelling indicator in the status bar indicates that the document is free of errors.

Using Word Wrap

Now you will continue entering more of the paragraph. As you type, when the text gets close to the right margin, do not press [←Enter] to move to the next line. Word will automatically wrap words to the next line as needed.

Concept 4

Word Wrap

4 The **word wrap** feature automatically decides where to end a line and wrap text to the next line based on the margin settings. This feature saves time when entering text because you do not need to press [←Enter] at the end of a full line to begin a new line. The only time you need to press [←Enter] is to end a paragraph, to insert blank lines, or to create a short line such as a salutation. In addition, if you change the margins or insert or delete text on a line, the program automatically readjusts the text on the line to fit within the new margin settings. Word wrap is common to all word processors.

Enter the following text to complete the sentence.

1 ● Press [End] to move to the end of the line.

● Type **earth's greatest unspoiled habitats and find out how you can experience the adventure of a lifetime.**

● Correct any spelling or grammar errors that are identified.

Your screen should be similar to Figure 1.19

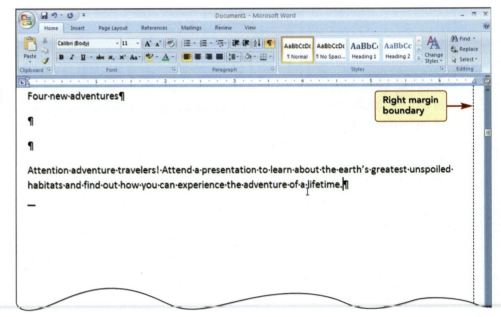

Figure 1.19

Additional Information
Generally, when using a word processor, separate sentences with one space after a period rather than two spaces, which was common when typewriters were used.

The program has wrapped the text that would overlap the right margin to the beginning of the next line.

You have a meeting you need to attend in a few minutes and want to continue working on the document when you get back. You decide to add your name and the current date to the document. As you type the first four characters of the month, Word will recognize the entry as a month and display a ScreenTip suggesting the remainder of the month. You can insert the suggested month by pressing ←Enter. Then enter a space to continue the date and another ScreenTip will appear with the complete date. Press ←Enter again to insert it.

Additional Information
You can continue typing to ignore the date suggestion.

2 ● Move to the end of the sentence and press ←Enter twice.

● Type your name.

● Press ←Enter.

● Type the current date beginning with the month and when the ScreenTips appear for the month and the complete date, press ←Enter to insert them.

● Press ←Enter twice.

● Click ¶ Show/Hide to turn off the display of formatting marks.

Your screen should be similar to Figure 1.20

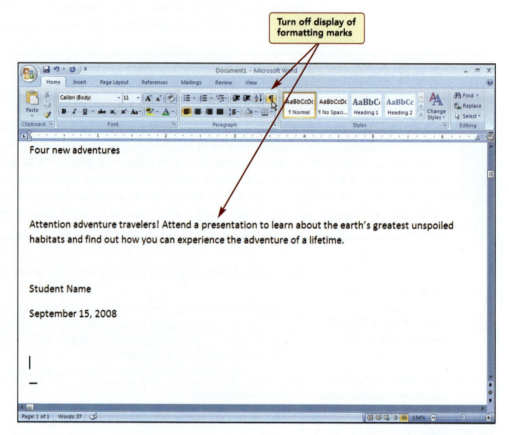

Turn off display of formatting marks

Four new adventures

Attention adventure travelers! Attend a presentation to learn about the earth's greatest unspoiled habitats and find out how you can experience the adventure of a lifetime.

Student Name

September 15, 2008

Figure 1.20

As you have seen, in many editing situations, it is helpful to display the formatting marks. However, for normal entry of text, you will probably not need the marks displayed. Now that you know how to turn this feature on and off, you can use it whenever you want when entering and editing text.

Specifying Document Properties

In addition to the content of the document that you create, Word automatically includes details about the document that describe or identify it called **document properties**. Document properties include details such as title, author name, subject, and keywords that identify the document's topic or contents. Some of these properties are automatically generated. These include statistics such as the number of words in the file and general information such as the date the document was created and last modified. Others such as author name and keywords are properties that you can specify. By specifying relevant information as document properties, you can easily organize, identify, and search for your documents later.

Modifying Document Properties

You will look at the document properties that are automatically included and add documentation to identify you as the author, and specify a document title and keywords to describe the document.

1
- Click 🏛 Office Button.

- Point to Prepare to select it and click on Properties in the submenu to choose it.

Your screen should be similar to Figure 1.21

Document information panel

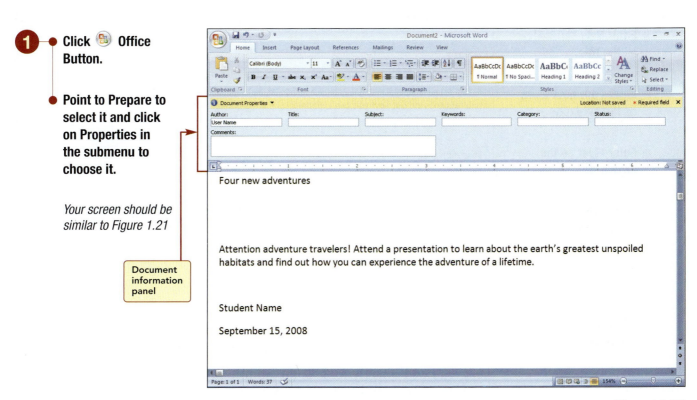

Figure 1.21

MORE ABOUT

▶ See Personalize User Name and Initials in the 1.4 Personalize Office Word 2007 section of the More About appendix to learn how to personalize your copy of Word to include your name and initials.

The Document Information Panel opens and displays the standard properties associated with the document. Most of these properties are blank waiting for you to specify your own information. The Author property may display the user name that is associated with the copy of Word you are using. You will change the author name to your name and add information to fill in the other standard properties.

2 ● If necessary, select the existing text in the Author text box by triple-clicking on it.

Additional Information
You will learn all about selecting text shortly.

● Type **your name** in the Author text box.

● Enter **New Tours Flyer** as the title.

● Enter **Four new tours** as the subject.

● Enter **Flyer** as the keyword.

● Enter **Advertising** as the category.

● Enter **First Draft** as the status.

Your screen should be similar to Figure 1.22

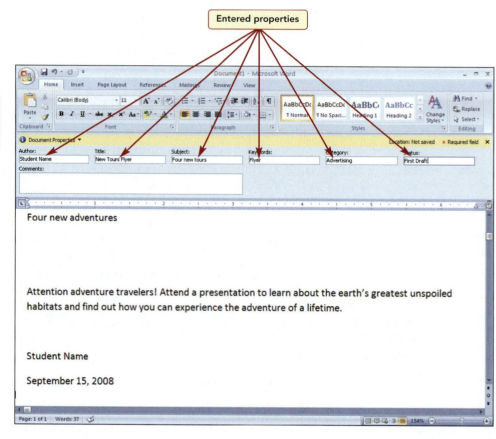

Figure 1.22

Next, you will quickly look at the additional information that is stored as document properties.

3 **Click** Document Properties ▼ **and choose Advanced Properties from the menu.**

Your screen should be similar to Figure 1.23

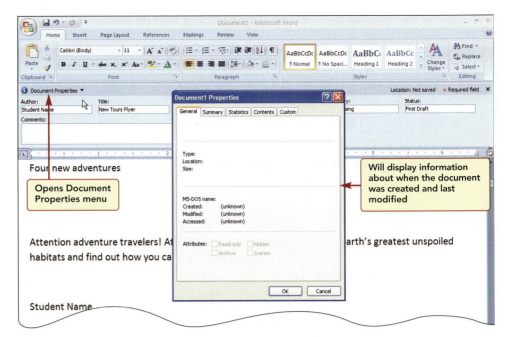

Figure 1.23

The General tab displays file system information about the type, location, and size of the document as well as information about when the document was created and modified. This information is automatically generated by the program. Because your document has not been saved yet, this information is blank. Next you will look at the document statistics.

4 **Open the Statistics tab.**

Your screen should be similar to Figure 1.24

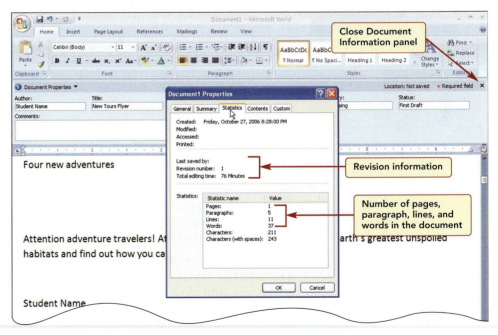

Figure 1.24

This tab includes revision information that identifies who last saved the document, the revision number, and the total editing time in minutes. The Statistics table shows the number of pages, words, lines, paragraphs, and so forth that are in the document. This information also is automatically generated and cannot be changed. The remaining three tabs—Contents, Custom, and Summary—include additional document property information.

You have added all the properties to the document that are needed at this time.

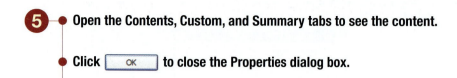

5 ● Open the Contents, Custom, and Summary tabs to see the content.

● Click OK to close the Properties dialog box.

● Click ⊠ to close the Document Information Panel.

Once the standard document properties are specified, you can use them to identify and locate documents. You also can use the automatically updated properties for the same purpose. For example, you can search for all files created by a specified user or on a certain date.

Saving, Closing, and Opening Files

Before leaving to attend your meeting, you want to save your work to a file. As you enter and edit text to create a new document, the changes you make are immediately displayed onscreen and are stored in your computer's memory. However, they are not permanently stored until you save your work to a file on a disk. After a document has been saved as a file, it can be closed and opened again at a later time to be edited further.

As a backup against the accidental loss of work from power failure or other mishap, Word includes an AutoRecover feature. When this feature is on, as you work you may see a pulsing disk icon briefly appear in the status bar. This icon indicates that the program is saving your work to a temporary recovery file. The time interval between automatic saving can be set to any period you specify; the default is every 10 minutes. After a problem has occurred, when you restart the program, the recovery file is automatically opened containing all changes you made up to the last time it was saved by AutoRecover. You then need to save the recovery file. If you do not save it, it is deleted when closed. AutoRecover is a great feature for recovering lost work but should not be used in place of regularly saving your work.

Additional Information

Use ⊞ Office Button/
⊞ Word Options /Save/
Save AutoRecover
Information to set the
AutoRecovery options.

Saving a File

You will save the work you have done so far on the flyer. You can use the Save or Save As command on the ⊞ Office Button File menu to save files.

The Save command or the 🖫 Save button on the Quick Access Toolbar will save the active file using the same file name by replacing the contents of the existing disk file with the document as it appears on your screen. The Save As command is used to save a file using a new file name or to a new location. This leaves the original file unchanged. When you create a new document, you can use either of the Save commands to save your work to a file on the disk. It is especially important to save a new document very soon after you create it because the AutoRecover feature does not work until a file name has been specified.

 Click  **Save in the Quick Access Toolbar.**

Another Method

The keyboard shortcut is Ctrl + S.

Your screen should be similar to Figure 1.25

Having Trouble?

In Windows Vista, the Save As dialog box layout will be different; however, the same information is displayed.

Additional Information

Depending on the dialog box view, the files may be displayed differently and file details such as the size, type, and date modified may be listed.

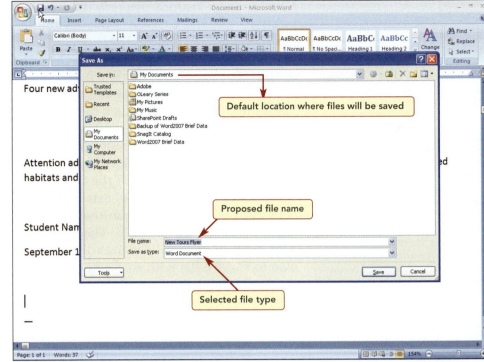

Figure 1.25

MORE ABOUT

▶ See Set a Default Save Location in the 1.4 Personalize Office Word 2007 section of the More About appendix to learn how to change the default save location.

The Save As dialog box is used to specify the location where you will save the file and the file name. The Save In drop-down list box displays the default folder as the location where the file will be saved, and the File Name text box displays the proposed file name. The file list box displays the names of any Word documents in the default location. Only Word-type documents are listed, because Word Document is the specified file type in the Save as Type list box.

First you need to change the location where the file will be saved to the location where you save your files.

2 ● **Open the Save In drop-down list box.**

● **Select the location where you want to save your file.**

Your screen should be similar to Figure 1.26

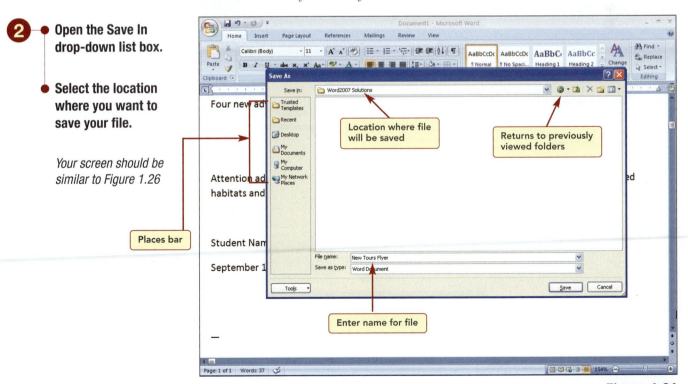

Figure 1.26

MORE ABOUT

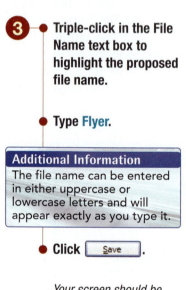 In addition to the .docx file type, Word documents also can be saved in several different file formats that have different file extensions depending upon the format. See Save to Appropriate Formats in the More About appendix.

Additional Information

Windows files can have up to 256 characters in the file name. Names can contain letters, numbers, and spaces; however, the symbols \, /, ?, :, *, ", <, and > cannot be used. The file name can be entered in either uppercase or lowercase letters and will appear exactly as you type it.

MORE ABOUT

See Use the Compatibility Checker in the 6.1 Prepare Documents for Sharing section of the More About appendix to learn how to identify document features that are not supported by previous versions.

Now the large list box displays the names of all Word files, if any, at that location. You also can select the location to save your file from the Places bar along the left side of the dialog box. The icons bring up a list of recently accessed files and folders (My Recent Documents), the contents of the My Documents folder, items on the Windows desktop, and the locations on your computer or on a network. You also can click the ⊙ ▾ button in the toolbar to return to folders that were previously opened.

Next, you need to enter a file name and specify the file type. The File Name box displays the default file name, consisting of the first few words from the document. The Save as Type box displays "Word Document" as the default format in which the file will be saved. Word 2007 documents are identified by the file extension .docx. The file type you select determines the file extension that will be automatically added to the file name when the file is saved. The default extension .docx saves the file in XML format. Previous versions of Word used the .doc file extension. If you plan to share a file with someone using Word 2003 or earlier, you can save the document using the .doc file type; however, some features may be lost. Otherwise, if you save it as a .docx file type, the recipient may not be able to view all features.

You will change the file name to Flyer and use the default document type (.docx).

3 • Triple-click in the File Name text box to highlight the proposed file name.

• Type **Flyer**.

Additional Information

The file name can be entered in either uppercase or lowercase letters and will appear exactly as you type it.

• Click ⟨ Save ⟩ .

Your screen should be similar to Figure 1.27

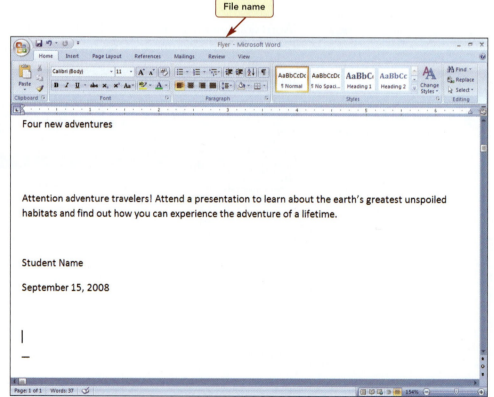

File name

Four new adventures

Attention adventure travelers! Attend a presentation to learn about the earth's greatest unspoiled habitats and find out how you can experience the adventure of a lifetime.

Student Name

September 15, 2008

Figure 1.27

The document is saved as Flyer.docx at the location you selected, and the new file name is displayed in the Word title bar.

Closing a File

Finally, you want to close the document while you attend your meeting.

1 ● Click ▣ **Office Button and choose Close.**

Another Method
The keyboard shortcut is Ctrl + F4.

Additional Information
Do not click ✕ Close in the window title bar as this closes the application.

Your screen should be similar to Figure 1.28

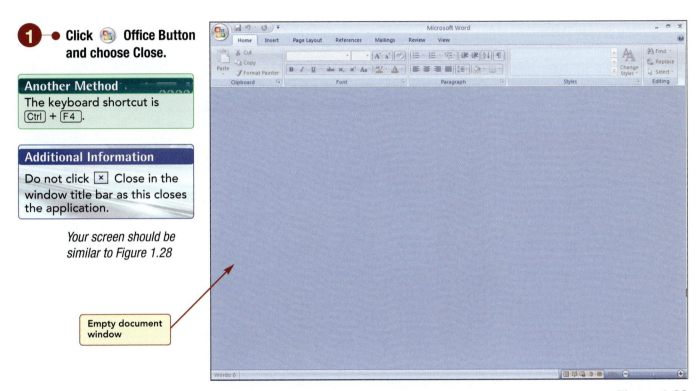

Empty document window

Figure 1.28

Now the Word window displays an empty document window. Because you did not make any changes to the document since saving it, the document window closed immediately. If you had made additional changes, the program would ask whether you wanted to save the file before closing it. This prevents the accidental closing of a file that has not been saved first.

Opening a File

Additional Information
To open a new blank document, click ▣ Office Button, choose New, and choose Blank Document from the Blank Document dialog box.

You asked your assistant to enter the remaining information in the flyer for you while you attended the meeting. Upon your return, you find a note from your assistant on your desk. The note explains that he had a little trouble entering the information and tells you that he saved the revised file as Flyer1. You want to open the file and continue working on the flyer.

1 ● Click 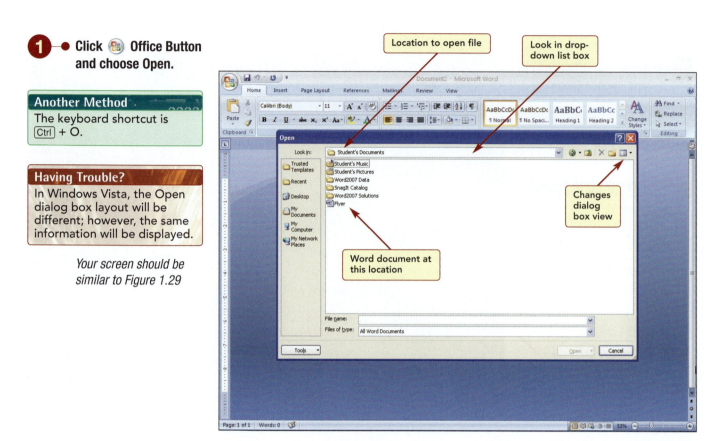 Office Button and choose Open.

Another Method
The keyboard shortcut is Ctrl + O.

Having Trouble?
In Windows Vista, the Open dialog box layout will be different; however, the same information will be displayed.

Your screen should be similar to Figure 1.29

Location to open file

Look in drop-down list box

Changes dialog box view

Word document at this location

Figure 1.29

Additional Information
You can display a preview of the first page of a selected file by choosing Preview from the Views menu.

In the Open dialog box, you specify the location and name of the file you want to open. The current location is the location you last used when you saved the flyer document. As in the Save As dialog box, the Look In drop-down list box displays folders and document files at this location. You will need to change the location to the location containing your data files.

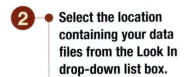

② ● Select the location containing your data files from the Look In drop-down list box.

● Select wd01_Flyer1.

Having Trouble?
Click on the file name to select it. Depending on your Window's settings, your files may display file extensions and additional information.

● Open the ⊞ ▾ Views drop-down list.

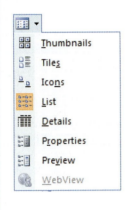

● Choose Properties.

Your screen should be similar to Figure 1.30

Having Trouble?
In Windows Vista, open the Organize drop-down list and choose Properties.

Additional Information
Pointing to a file name displays document property information in a ScreenTip about the type of file, author, title, date modified, and size.

Properties of selected file

Click to open selected file

Figure 1.30

The document properties for the selected file are displayed in the right pane of the dialog box. You will return the view to the list of file names and open this file.

3 ● Open the 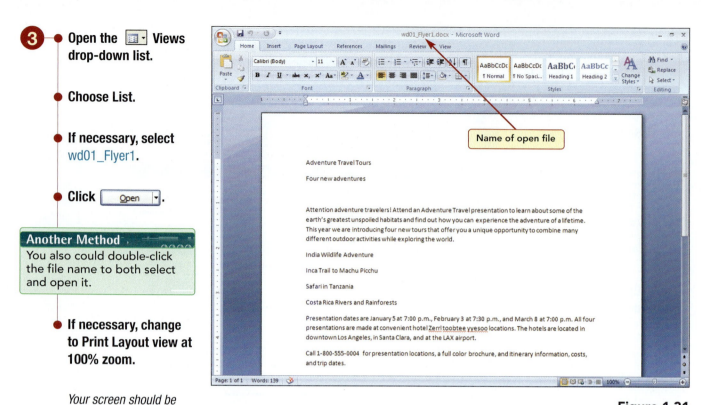 Views drop-down list.

● Choose List.

● If necessary, select wd01_Flyer1.

● Click Open ▾.

Another Method

You also could double-click the file name to both select and open it.

● If necessary, change to Print Layout view at 100% zoom.

Your screen should be similar to Figure 1.31

Figure 1.31

The file is opened and displayed in the document window. This file contains the additional content you asked your assistant to add to the flyer.

Navigating a Document

As documents increase in size, they cannot be easily viewed in their entirety in the document window and much time can be spent moving to different locations in the document. Word includes many features that make it easy to move around in a large document. The basic method is to scroll through a document using the scroll bar or keyboard. Another method is to move directly to a page or other identifiable item in the document, such as a table. You also can quickly return to a previous location, or browse through a document to a previous page or item.

Other features that help move through a large document include searching the document to locate specific items and using the Document Map or a table of contents. You will learn about many of these features in later labs.

Scrolling a Document

Now that more information has been added to the document, the document window is no longer large enough to display the entire document. To bring additional text into view in the window, you can scroll

01341/0268361

Additional Information

If you have a mouse with a scroll wheel, you can use it to scroll a document vertically.

the document using either the scroll bars or the keyboard. Again, both methods are useful, depending on what you are doing. The tables below explain the mouse and keyboard techniques that can be used to scroll a document.

Mouse	Action
Click ▼	Moves down line by line.
Click ▲	Moves up line by line.
Click above/below scroll box	Moves up/down window by window.
Drag scroll box	Moves up/down quickly through document.
Click ⬆	Moves to top of previous page.
Click ⬇	Moves to top of next page.
Click ⊙ Select Browse Object	Changes how you want the ⬆ and ⬇ buttons to browse through a document, such as by table or graphic. The default setting is by page.

Key	Action
↓	Down line by line
↑	Up line by line
Page Up	Top of window
Page Down	Bottom of window
Ctrl + Home	Beginning of document
Ctrl + End	End of document

Additional Information

You also can scroll the document window horizontally using the horizontal scroll bar or the ← and → keys.

You will use the vertical scroll bar to view the text at the bottom of the flyer. When you use the scroll bar to scroll, the insertion point does not move. To move the insertion point, you must click in a location in the window.

GEORGE BROWN COLLEGE
CASA LOMA LIBRARY LEARNING COMMONS

1 • Click  in the vertical scroll bar 12 times.

• Click anywhere in the last line to move the insertion point.

Your screen should be similar to Figure 1.32

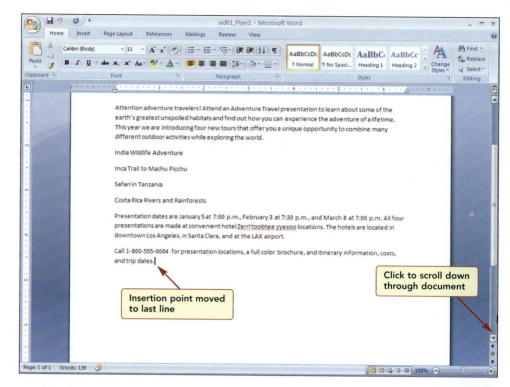

Figure 1.32

Having Trouble?

If your screen scrolls differently, this is a function of the type of monitor you are using.

The text at the beginning of the flyer has scrolled off the top of the document window, and the text at the bottom of the flyer is now displayed.

You also can scroll the document using the keyboard. While scrolling using the keyboard, the insertion point also moves. The insertion point attempts to maintain its position in a line as you scroll up and down through the document. In a large document, scrolling line by line can take a while. You will now try out several of the mouse and keyboard scrolling features that move by larger jumps.

2 • Hold down ⬆ for several seconds until the insertion point is on the first line of the flyer.

• Click below the scroll box in the scroll bar.

• Drag the scroll box to the top of the scroll bar.

• Press Ctrl + End.

Your screen should be similar to Figure 1.33

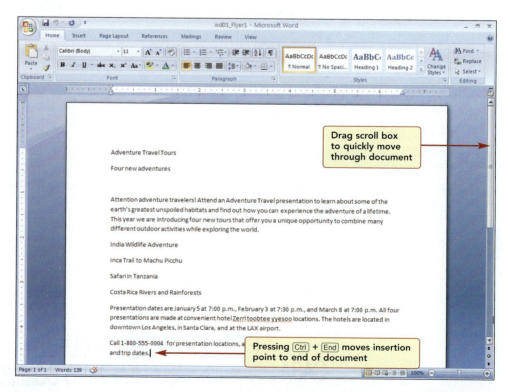

Figure 1.33

WD1.36

Word 2007

Lab 1: Creating and Editing a Document

www.mhhe.com/oleary

The insertion point is now at the end of the document. Using these features makes scrolling a large document much more efficient. Remember that when scrolling using the mouse, if you want to start working at that location, you must click at the new location to move the insertion point.

Editing Documents

While entering text and creating a document, you will find that you will want to edit or make changes and corrections to the document. Although many of the errors are identified and corrections are made automatically for you, others must be made manually. You learned how to use the [Backspace] and [Delete] keys earlier to correct errors. But deleting characters one at a time can be time consuming. Now you will learn about several additional editing features that make editing your work more efficient.

After entering the text of a document, you should proofread it for accuracy and completeness and edit the document as needed. After looking over the flyer, you have identified several errors that need to be corrected and changes you want to make to the content. The changes you want to make are shown below.

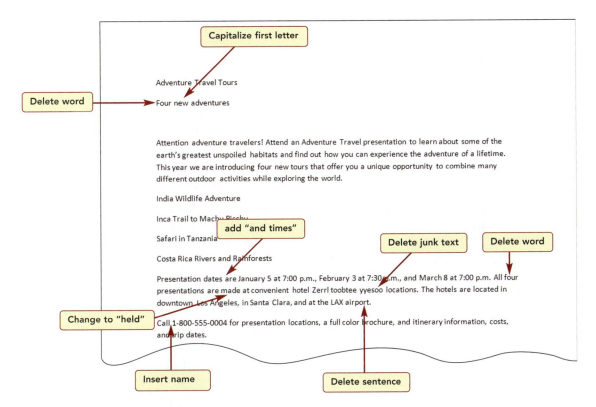

Inserting Text

As you check the document, you see that the first sentence of the paragraph below the list of trips is incorrect. It should read: "Presentation dates and times are . . . " The sentence is missing the words "and times." In addition, you want to change the word "made" to "held" in the following sentence. These words can easily be entered into the sentence without retyping the entire line. This is because Word uses **Insert mode** to allow new characters to be inserted into the existing text by moving the existing text to the right to make space for the new characters. You will insert the words "and times" after the word "dates" in the first sentence.

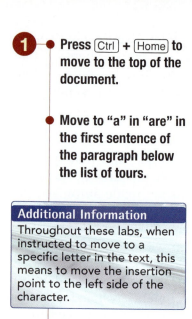

1 ● Press [Ctrl] + [Home] to move to the top of the document.

● Move to "a" in "are" in the first sentence of the paragraph below the list of tours.

Additional Information

Throughout these labs, when instructed to move to a specific letter in the text, this means to move the insertion point to the left side of the character.

● Type **and times**.

● Press [Spacebar].

Your screen should be similar to Figure 1.34

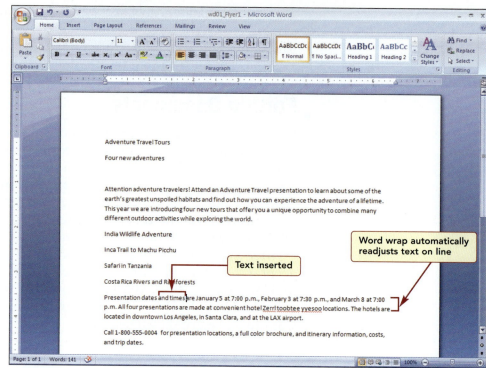

Figure 1.34

The inserted text pushes the existing text on the line to the right, and the word wrap feature automatically readjusts the text on the line to fit within the margin settings.

Selecting and Replacing Text

In the second sentence, you want to change the word "made" to "held." You could delete this word and type in the new word, or you can select the text and type the new text. Text that is selected is highlighted.

To select text using the mouse, first move the insertion point to the beginning or end of the text to be selected, and then drag to highlight the text you want selected. You can select as little as a single letter or as much as the entire document. You can quickly select a standard block of text. Standard blocks include a sentence, paragraph, page, tabular column, rectangular portion of text, or the entire document. The following tables summarize the mouse and keyboard techniques used to select standard blocks.

Additional Information

You can replace existing text using Overtype mode, in which each character you type replaces an existing character. This feature is turned on using [icon] Office

Button/ [icon] Word Options
/Advanced/Use overtype mode.

To Select	Mouse
Word	Double-click in the word.
Sentence	Press [Ctrl] and click within the sentence.
Line	Click to the left of a line when the mouse pointer is 🖱.
Multiple lines	Drag up or down to the left of a line when the mouse pointer is 🖱.
Paragraph	Triple-click on the paragraph or double-click to the left of the paragraph when the mouse pointer is 🖱.
Multiple paragraphs	Drag to the left of the paragraphs when the mouse pointer is 🖱.
Document	Triple-click or press [Ctrl] and click to the left of the text when the mouse pointer is 🖱.

To Select	Keyboard
Next space or character	[⇧Shift] + [→]
Previous space or character	[⇧Shift] + [←]
Next word	[Ctrl] + [⇧Shift] + [→]
Previous word	[Ctrl] + [⇧Shift] + [←]
Text going backward to beginning of paragraph	[Ctrl] + [⇧Shift] + [↑]
Text going forward to end of paragraph	[Ctrl] + [⇧Shift] + [↓]
Entire document	[Ctrl] + A

To remove highlighting to deselect text, simply click anywhere in the document or press any directional key.

1 ● Double click on "made".

Your screen should be similar to Figure 1.35

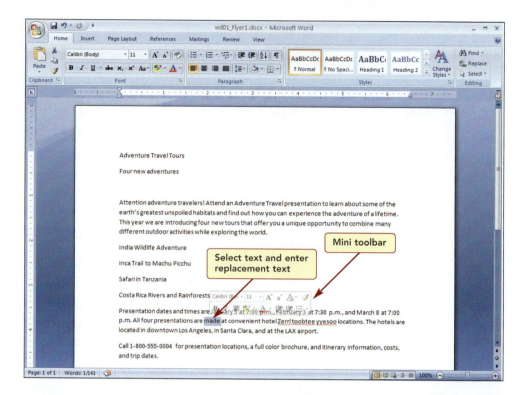

Figure 1.35

Text that is selected can be modified using many different Word features. The Mini toolbar appears automatically when text is selected and the mouse pointer is pointing to the selection. You will learn about using this feature shortly. In this case, you want to replace the selected text with new text.

2 ● Type held.

Your screen should be similar to Figure 1.36

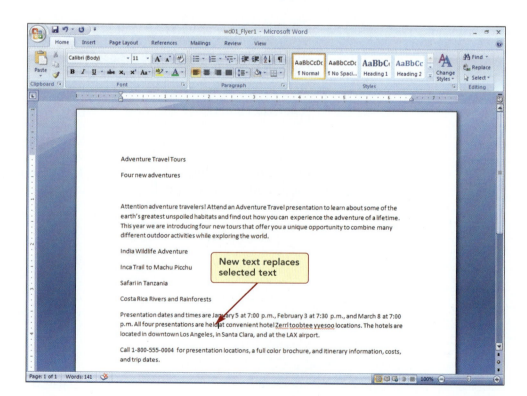

Figure 1.36

As soon as you began typing, the selected text was automatically deleted. The new text was inserted in the line just like any other text.

Deleting a Word

Additional Information
The Ctrl + Backspace key combination deletes text to the left of the insertion point to the beginning of the next group of characters.

You next want to delete the word "four" from the same sentence. The Ctrl + Delete key combination deletes text to the right of the insertion point to the beginning of the next group of characters. In order to delete an entire word, you must position the insertion point at the beginning of the word.

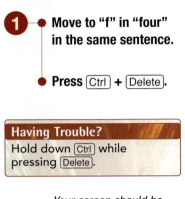

- **Move to "f" in "four" in the same sentence.**

- **Press Ctrl + Delete.**

Having Trouble?
Hold down Ctrl while pressing Delete.

Your screen should be similar to Figure 1.37

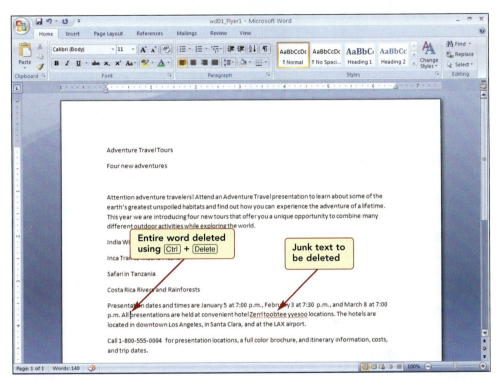

Figure 1.37

The word "four" has been deleted.

Selecting and Deleting Text

As you continue proofreading the flyer, you see that the end of this sentence contains a section of junk characters. To remove these characters, you could use Delete and Backspace to delete each character individually, or Ctrl + Delete or Ctrl + Backspace to delete each word or group of characters. This is very slow, however. Several characters, words, or lines of text can be deleted at once by first selecting the text and then pressing Delete.

The section of characters you want to remove follows the word "hotel" in the second line of the paragraph below the list of trips. You also decide to delete the entire last sentence of the paragraph.

1 ● Move to "Z" (following the word "hotel").

● Drag to the right until all the text including the space before the word "locations" is highlighted.

Having Trouble?
Hold down the left mouse button while moving the mouse to drag.

Additional Information
When you start dragging over a word, the entire word including the space after it is automatically selected.

● Press [Delete].

● Hold down [Ctrl] and click anywhere in the third sentence of the paragraph below the list of trips.

● Press [Delete].

Your screen should be similar to Figure 1.38

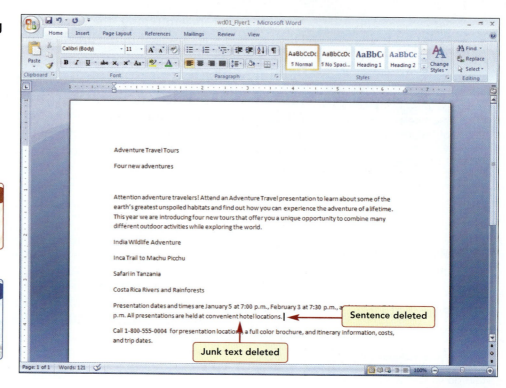

Figure 1.38

The selected junk text and the complete sentence were removed from the flyer.

Undoing Editing Changes

After removing the sentence, you decide it may be necessary after all. To quickly restore this sentence, you can use ↺ Undo to reverse your last action or command.

1 Click  Undo in the Quick Access Toolbar.

Another Method
The keyboard shortcut is Ctrl + Z.

Your screen should be similar to Figure 1.39

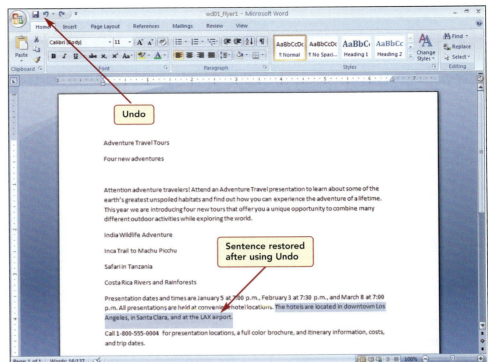

Figure 1.39

Undo returns your last deletion and restores it to its original location in the text, regardless of the current insertion point location. Notice that the Undo button includes a drop-down list button. Clicking this button displays a list of the most recent actions that can be reversed, with the most recent action at the top of the list. When you select an action from the drop-down list, you also undo all actions above it in the list.

2 Open the  Undo drop-down list.

● **Choose Delete Word.**

Your screen should be similar to Figure 1.40

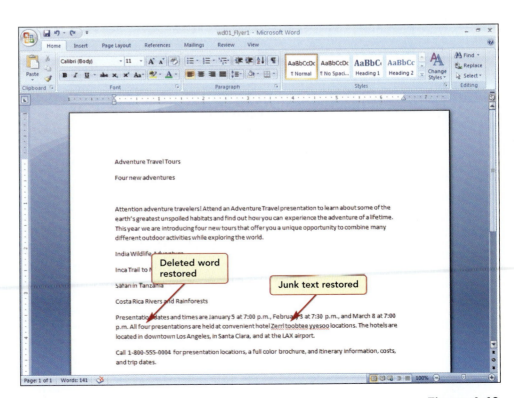

Figure 1.40

The junk characters and the word "four" are restored. Immediately after you undo an action, the 🔄 Redo button is available so you can restore the action you just undid. You will restore your corrections and then save the changes you have made to the document to a new file.

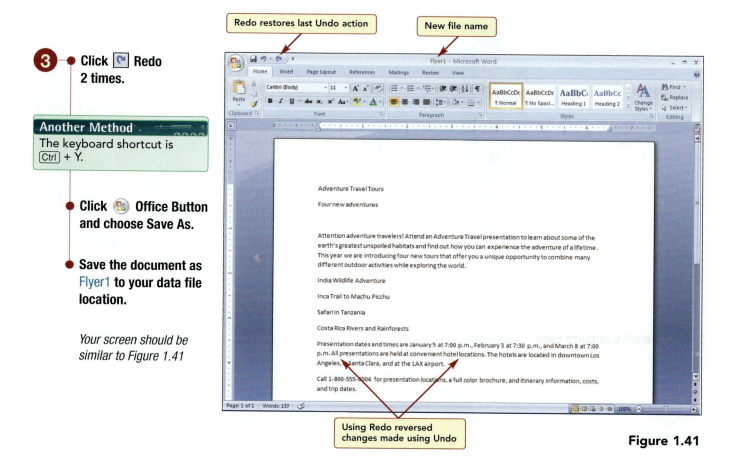

3 ● **Click** 🔄 **Redo 2 times.**

Another Method
The keyboard shortcut is
Ctrl + Y.

● **Click** 📄 **Office Button and choose Save As.**

● **Save the document as Flyer1 to your data file location.**

Your screen should be similar to Figure 1.41

Redo restores last Undo action

New file name

Using Redo reversed changes made using Undo

Figure 1.41

Repeatedly using the 🔄 Undo or 🔄 Redo buttons performs the actions in the list one by one. So that you can see what action will be performed, these button's ScreenTips identify the action.

The new file name, Flyer1, is displayed in the window title bar. The original document file, wd01_Flyer 1 is unchanged.

Changing Case

You also want to delete the word "Four" from the second line of the flyer title and capitalize the first letter of each word. Although you could change the case individually for the words, you can quickly change both using the Change Case command in the Font group.

1 • Move the insertion point to the beginning of the word "Four".

• Press Ctrl + Delete.

• Click in the left margin to select the entire title line.

• From the Font group, click Aa▾ Change Case.

Your screen should be similar to Figure 1.42

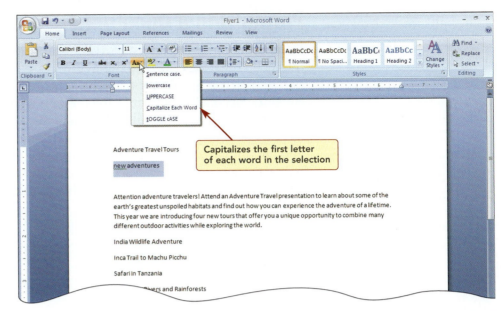

Capitalizes the first letter of each word in the selection

Figure 1.42

The Change Case drop-down menu allows you to change the case of selected words and sentences to the desired case without having to make the change manually. You want both words in the title to be capitalized.

2 • Select Capitalize Each Word.

• Click anywhere to deselect the title line.

Your screen should be similar to Figure 1.43

First letters capitalized

Figure 1.43

Additional Information
You also can use ⇧Shift + F3 to cycle through and apply the different change case options.

The first letter of each word in the title is now capitalized and the highlight is removed from the text.

Formatting a Document

Because this document is a flyer, you want it to be easy to read and interesting to look at. Applying different formatting to characters and paragraphs can greatly enhance the appearance of the document. **Character formatting** consists of formatting features that affect the selected characters only. This includes changing the character style and size, applying effects such as bold and italics to characters, changing the character spacing, and adding animated text effects. **Paragraph formatting** features affect an entire paragraph. A paragraph consists of all text up to and including the paragraph mark. Paragraph formatting features include how the paragraph is positioned or aligned between the margins, paragraph indentation, spacing above and below a paragraph, and line spacing within a paragraph.

Changing Fonts and Font Sizes

The first formatting change you want to make is to use different fonts and font sizes in the flyer.

Concept 5

Font and Font Size

5   A **font**, also commonly referred to as a **typeface**, is a set of characters with a specific design. The designs have names such as Times New Roman and Courier. Using fonts as a design element can add interest to your document and give readers visual cues to help them find information quickly.

Two basic types of fonts are serif and sans serif. **Serif fonts** have a flair at the base of each letter that visually leads the reader to the next letter. Two common serif fonts are Roman and Times New Roman. Serif fonts generally are used for text in paragraphs. **Sans serif fonts** do not have a flair at the base of each letter. Arial and Helvetica are two common sans serif fonts. Because sans serif fonts have a clean look, they are often used for headings in documents. A good practice is to use only two types of fonts in a document, one for text and one for headings. Using too many different font styles can make your document look cluttered and unprofessional.

Each font has one or more sizes. **Font size** is the height and width of the character and is commonly measured in points, abbreviated "pt." One point equals about 1/72 inch, and text in most documents is 10 pt or 12 pt.

Several common fonts in different sizes are shown in the table below.

Font Name	Font Type	Font Size
Arial	Sans serif	This is 10 pt. This is 16 pt.
Courier New	Serif	This is 10 pt. This is 16 pt.
Times New Roman	Serif	This is 10 pt. This is 16 pt.

To change the font before typing the text, use the command and then type. All text will appear in the specified setting until another font setting is selected. To change a font setting for existing text, select the text you want to change and then use the command. If you want to apply font formatting to a word, simply move the insertion point to the word and the formatting is automatically applied to the entire word.

First you want to increase the font size of all the text in the flyer to make it easier to read. Currently, you can see from the Font Size button in the Font group that the font size is 11 points.

1 ● **Triple-click in the left margin when the mouse pointer is 𝄎 to select the entire document.**

Having Trouble?
The left margin is the white space to the left of the text.

Another Method
The keyboard shortcut is Ctrl + A.

● **From the Font group, open the** 11 ▾ **Font Size drop-down list.**

Another Method
The keyboard shortcut is Ctrl + ⇧Shift + P.

Your screen should be similar to Figure 1.44

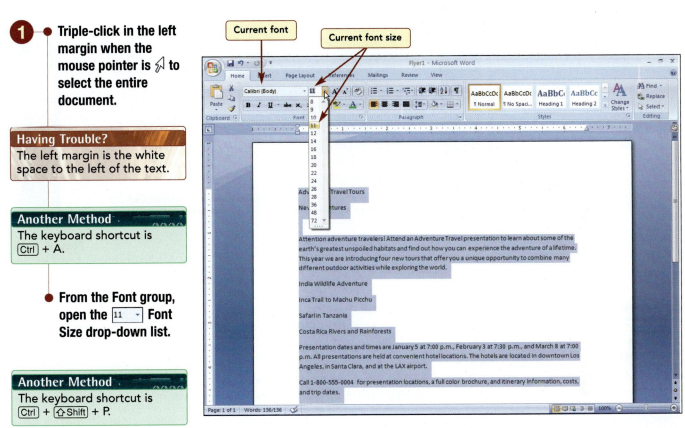

Figure 1.44

The current (default) font size of 11 is selected. You will increase the font size to 14 points. As you point to the size options, the selected text in the document displays how it will appear if chosen. This is the **Live Preview** feature of Word.

● **Point to several different point sizes in the list to see the Live Preview.**

● **Click 14 to choose it.**

Your screen should be similar to Figure 1.45

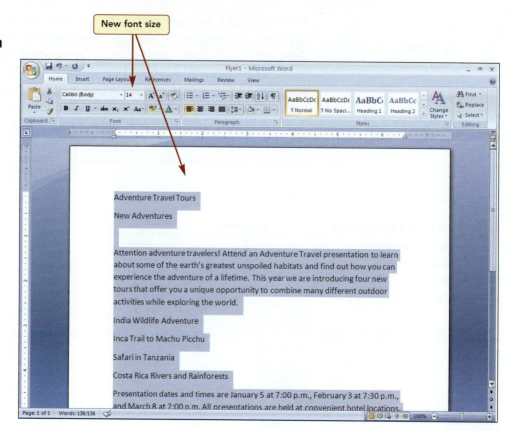

New font size

Figure 1.45

Additional Information

If a selection includes text of various sizes, the Font Size button will be blank.

The font size of all text in the document has increased to 14 points, making the text much easier to read. The Font Size button displays the new point size setting for the text at the location of the insertion point.

Next you will change the font and size of the two title lines. First you will change the font to Comic Sans MS and then you will increase the font size.

Many of the formatting commands are on the Mini toolbar that appears whenever you select text. The Mini toolbar appears dimmed until you point to it. This is so it is not distracting as you are using features that are not available on the Mini toolbar. To use the Mini toolbar, just point to it to make it solid and choose command buttons just as you would from the Ribbon.

3 • Select the two title lines and point to the Mini toolbar.

• Open the [Calibri (Boc ▾] Font drop-down menu in the Mini toolbar.

• Choose Comic Sans MS.

Additional Information
Font names are listed in alphabetical order.

Having Trouble?
If this font is not available on your computer, choose a similar font.

Your screen should be similar to Figure 1.46

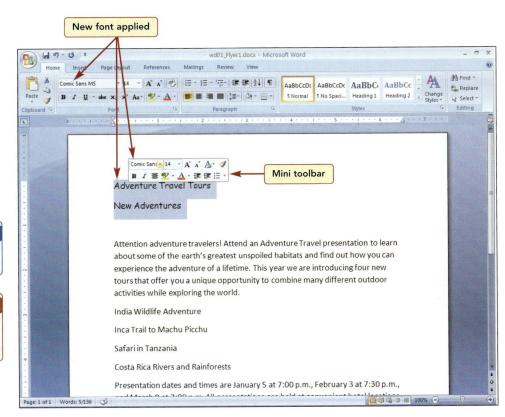

Figure 1.46

Using the Mini toolbar to apply the formats is a quick and convenient alternative to using the Ribbon. Next, you will change the font size.

4 • Open the [14 ▾] Size drop-down menu in the Mini toolbar.

• Choose 36.

Your screen should be similar to Figure 1.47

Figure 1.47

The selected font and size have been applied to the selection, making the title lines much more interesting and eye-catching. The Font and Font Size buttons reflect the settings in use in the selection. As you look at the title lines, you decide the font size of the first title line is too large. You will reduce it to 20 points.

5 ● **Select the first title line.**

● **Choose 20 points from the [36 ▾] Font Size drop-down menu.**

Your screen should be similar to Figure 1.48

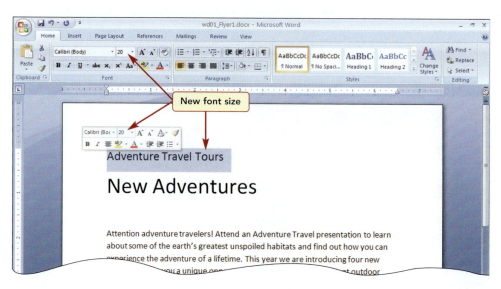

Figure 1.48

Finally, you want to change the font of the list of four tours.

6 ● **Select the list of four tours.**

● **Use [Calibri (Body) ▾] Font in the Mini toolbar to change the font to Comic Sans MS.**

Additional Information
Theme fonts and recently used fonts appear at the top of the list. You will learn about themes in Lab 3.

● **Click anywhere on the highlighted text to deselect it.**

● **Reduce the zoom so the entire page is visible.**

Your screen should be similar to Figure 1.49

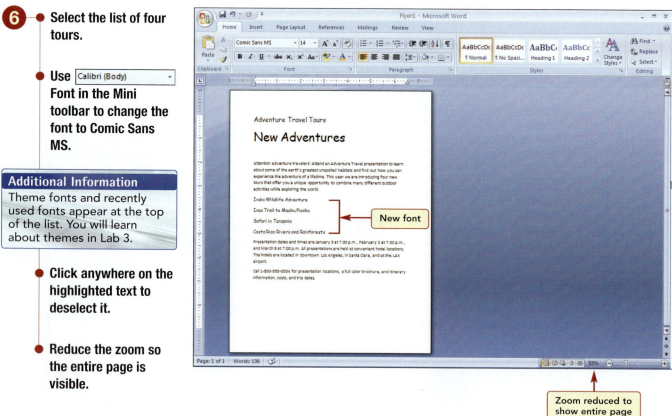

Figure 1.49

The changes you have made to the font and font size have made the flyer somewhat more interesting. However, you want to further enhance the document.

Applying Character Effects

Next you want to liven up the flyer by adding character effects such as color and bold to selected areas. The table below describes some of the effects and their uses.

Format	Example	Use
Bold, italic	**Bold** *Italic*	Adds emphasis.
Underline	<u>Underline</u>	Adds emphasis.
Strikethrough	~~Strikethrough~~	Indicates words to be deleted.
Double strikethrough	~~Double Strikethrough~~	Indicates words to be deleted.
Superscript	"To be or not to be."[1]	Used in footnotes and formulas.
Subscript	H_2O	Used in formulas.
Shadow	Shadow	Adds distinction to titles and headings.
Outline	Outline	Adds distinction to titles and headings.
Emboss	Emboss	Adds distinction to titles and headings.
Engrave	Engrave	Adds distinction to titles and headings.
Small caps	SMALL CAPS	Adds emphasis when case is not important.
All caps	ALL CAPS	Adds emphasis when case is not important.
Hidden		Prevents selected text from displaying or printing. Hidden text can be viewed by displaying formatting marks.
Color	Color Color Color	Adds interest

Additional Information
You will learn about background colors in Lab 2.

First you will add color and bold to the top title line. The default font color setting is Automatic. This setting automatically determines when to use black or white text. Black text is used on a light background and white text on a dark background.

1 • Return the zoom to 100%.

• Select the first title line and point to the Mini toolbar.

• Open the  Font Color drop-down list on the Mini toolbar.

• Click ▮ Orange from the Standard Colors bar.

Additional Information
A ScreenTip displays the name of the color when selected.

• Click **B** Bold on the Mini Toolbar.

Another Method
The keyboard shortcut is Ctrl + B.

• Click on the title line to clear the selection.

Your screen should be similar to Figure 1.50

Figure 1.50

The buttons reflect the settings associated with the text at the insertion point. The Font Color button appears in the last selected color. This color can be quickly applied to other selections now simply by clicking the button.

Next you will add color and bold to several other areas of the flyer.

2 • **Select the second title line.**

• **Using the Mini toolbar, change the font color to green and add bold.**

• **Select the list of four trips.**

• **Click** ⬛ **Font Color to change the color to green.**

Additional Information

The currently selected font color can be applied to the selection simply by clicking the button.

• **Click** **B** **Bold,** *I* **Italic.**

• **Click** *I* **Italic again to remove the italic effect.**

Additional Information

Many formatting commands are toggle commands. This means the feature can be turned on and off simply by clicking on the command button.

• **Apply bold, italic, and orange font color to the last sentence of the flyer.**

• **Click in the document to deselect the text.**

Your screen should be similar to Figure 1.51

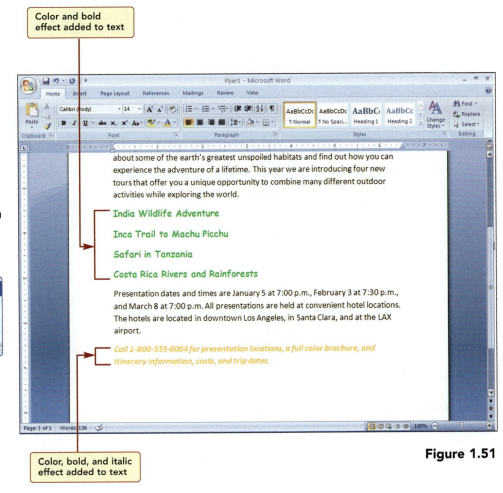

Color and bold effect added to text

Color, bold, and italic effect added to text

Figure 1.51

The character formatting effects you added to the flyer make it much more interesting.

The next formatting change you want to make is to add a shadow to the title lines. Since the Ribbon does not display a button for this feature, you need to open the Font dialog box to access this feature.

3 ● **Select both title lines.**

● **Click ◨ in the bottom-right corner of the Font group to open the Font dialog box.**

Your screen should be similar to Figure 1.52

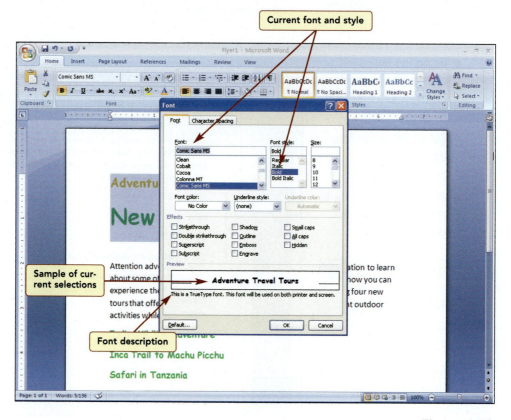

Figure 1.52

The Font dialog box contains all of the Font commands in the Font group and more. Using the Dialog Box Launcher to open a dialog box allows you to access the more-advanced or less-used features of a group. The font and font style used in the selected text are identified in the list boxes. However, because the selection includes two different font sizes, the font size is not identified.

The Preview box displays an example of the currently selected font setting. Notice the description of the font below the Preview box. It states that the selected font is a TrueType font. **TrueType** fonts are fonts that are automatically installed when you install Windows. They appear onscreen exactly as they will appear when printed. Some fonts are printer fonts, which are available only on your printer and may look different onscreen than when printed. Courier is an example of a printer font.

You will add a shadow to the selected lines.

4 ● **Choose Shadow.**

● **Click** ⬚OK⬚.

Your screen should be similar to Figure 1.53

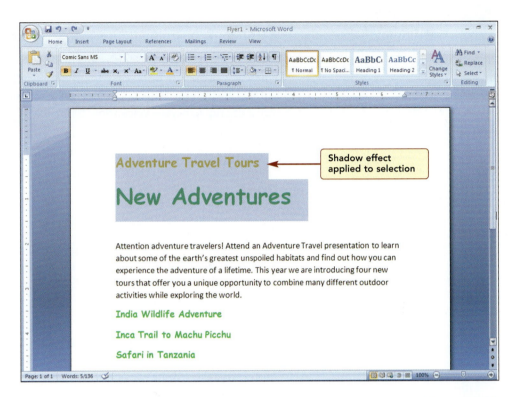

Figure 1.53

A shadow effect has been applied to all text in the selection.

Setting Paragraph Alignment

The final formatting change you want to make is to change the paragraph alignment.

Concept 6

6 **Alignment** is the positioning of text on a line between the margins or indents. There are four types of paragraph alignment: left, centered, right, and justified. The alignment settings affect entire paragraphs and are described in the table below.

Alignment		Effect on Text Alignment
	Left	Aligns text against the left margin of the page, leaving the right margin ragged or uneven. This is the most commonly used paragraph alignment type and therefore the default setting in all word processing software packages.
	Center	Centers each line of text between the left and right margins. Center alignment is used mostly for headings or centering graphics on a page.
	Right	Aligns text against the right margin, leaving the left margin ragged. Use right alignment when you want text to line up on the outside of a page, such as a chapter title or a header.
	Justify	Aligns text against the right and left margins and evenly spaces out the words by inserting extra spaces, called soft spaces, that adjust automatically whenever additions or deletions are made to the text. Newspapers commonly use justified alignment so the columns of text are even.

The commands to change paragraph alignment are available in the Paragraph dialog box. However, it is much faster to use the keyboard shortcuts or command buttons in the Paragraph group shown below.

Alignment	Keyboard Shortcut	Button
Left	Ctrl + L	☰
Center	Ctrl + E	☰
Right	Ctrl + R	☰
Justify	Ctrl + J	☰

You want to change the alignment of all paragraphs in the flyer from the default of left-aligned to centered.

1 • Triple-click in the left margin to select the entire document.

• Click ☰ Center in the Mini toolbar.

Another Method

You also can use ☰ in the Paragraph group of the Home tab or in the Paragraph dialog box.

• Reduce the zoom so the entire page is visible.

Your screen should be similar to Figure 1.54

Additional Information

In addition to using the Zoom feature, you can use [ ] One Page in the Zoom group of the View tab.

Additional Information

The alignment settings also can be specified before typing in new text. As you type, the text is aligned according to your selection until the alignment setting is changed to another setting.

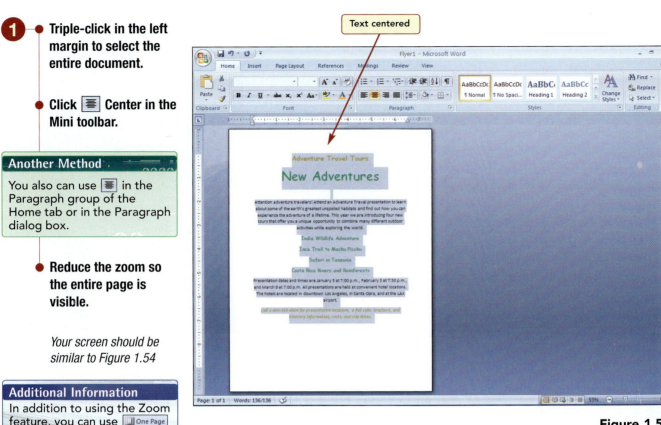

Text centered

Figure 1.54

Each line of text is centered evenly between the left and right page margins.

Clearing Formats

As you look at the entire flyer, you decide the last line is overformatted. You think it would look better if it did not include italics and color. Since it has been a while since you applied these formats, using Undo also would remove many other changes that you want to keep. Instead, you will quickly clear all formatting from the selection and then apply only those you want.

1
- Select the last sentence.

- Click  Clear Formatting.

Your screen should be similar to Figure 1.55

Clears all formatting from selection

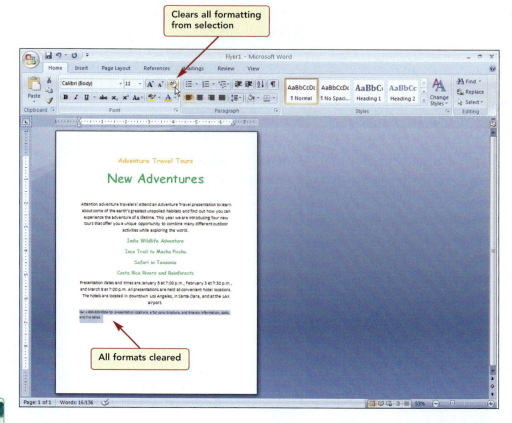

All formats cleared

Figure 1.55

Another Method
Instead of clearing all formats, you could simply reselect the command button to remove the formats that you did not want or select another format to replace it.

All formatting associated with the selection, including text alignment and font size, has been removed and the text appears in the default document font and size.

2
- Format the last sentence to bold, centered, and a font size of 14.

- Click 🖫 Save in the Quick Access Toolbar to save the file using the same file name.

The formatting of the last sentence looks much better now. As you are working on a document, it is a good idea to save your document frequently to prevent the accidental loss of work from a power outage or other mishap. While AutoRecover is a great feature for recovering lost work, it should not be used in place of regularly saving your work.

Working with Graphics

Finally, you want to add a graphic to the flyer to add interest.

Concept 7

Graphics

7 A **graphic** is a nontext element or object such as a drawing or picture that can be added to a document. An **object** is an item that can be sized, moved, and manipulated.

A graphic can be a simple **drawing object** consisting of shapes such as lines and boxes. A drawing object is part of your Word document. A **picture** is an illustration such as a graphic illustration or a scanned photograph. Pictures are graphics that were created using another program and are inserted in your Word document as **embedded objects**. An embedded object becomes part of the Word document and can be opened and edited from within the Word document using the **source program**, the program in which it was created. Any changes made to the embedded object are not made to the original picture file because they are independent. Several examples of drawing objects and pictures are shown below.

Drawing object

Graphic illustration

Photograph

Add graphics to your documents to help the reader understand concepts, to add interest, and to make your document stand out from others.

Inserting a Picture

Picture files can be obtained from a variety of sources. Many simple drawings called **clip art** are available in the Clip Organizer, a Microsoft Office tool that arranges and catalogs clip art and other media files stored on the computer's hard disk. Additionally, you can access Microsoft's Clip Art and Media Web site for even more graphics.

Digital images created using a digital camera are one of the most common types of graphic files. You also can create picture files using a scanner to convert any printed document, including photographs, to an electronic format. Most images that are scanned and inserted into documents are stored as Windows bitmap files (.bmp). All types of pictures, including clip art, photographs, and other types of images, can be found on the Internet. These files are commonly stored as .jpg or .pcx files. Keep in mind that any images you locate on the Internet may be copyrighted and should only be used with permission. You also can purchase CDs containing graphics for your use.

You want to add a picture to the flyer below the two title lines. You will move to the location in the document where you want to insert a photograph of a lion you recently received from a client. The photograph has been saved as a picture image.

Additional Information
You also can scan a picture and insert it directly into a Word document without saving it as a file first.

1 ● **Change the zoom to 100%.**

Additional Information
In addition to using the Zoom feature, you can click 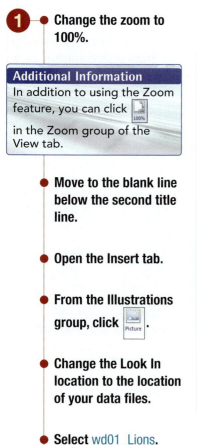 in the Zoom group of the View tab.

● **Move to the blank line below the second title line.**

● **Open the Insert tab.**

● **From the Illustrations group, click** [Picture].

● **Change the Look In location to the location of your data files.**

● **Select** wd01_Lions.

● **Click** [Insert ▾].

Your screen should be similar to Figure 1.56

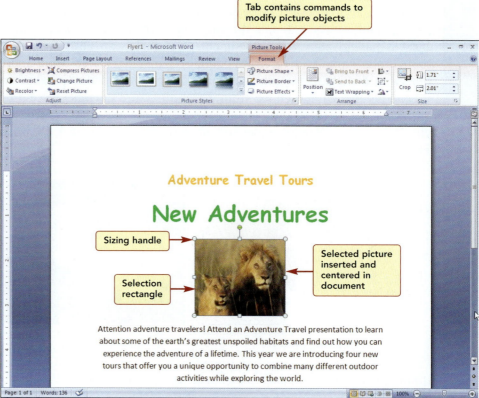

Figure 1.56

The picture is inserted in the document at the location of the insertion point. It is centered because the paragraph in which it was placed is centered. Notice the picture is surrounded by a **selection rectangle** and four circles and four squares, called **sizing handles**, indicating it is a selected object and can now be deleted, sized, moved, or modified. A Picture Tools tab automatically appears and can be used to modify the selected picture object.

Although you like the picture of the lions that you might see on one of the tours, you want to check the Clip Art Gallery to see if a picture of a tiger or parrot would be better.

Additional Information
You will learn more about the Picture Tools tab features in later labs.

2

- **Click to the right side of the graphic to deselect it.**

- **Open the Insert tab.**

- **From the Illustrations group, click** 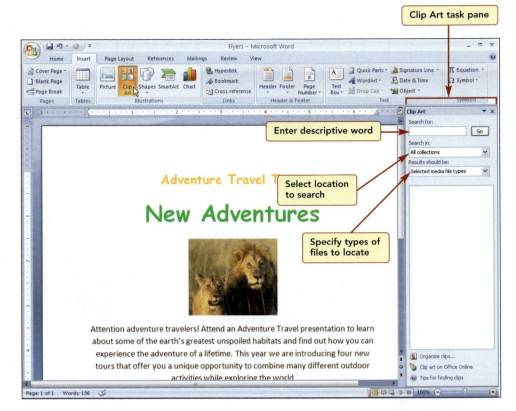.

Your screen should be similar to Figure 1.57

Figure 1.57

The Clip Art task pane appears in which you can enter a word or phrase that is representative of the type of picture you want to locate. You also can specify the locations to search and the type of media files, such as clip art, movies, photographs, or sound, to display in the results. You want to find clip art and photographs of animals.

3 • If necessary, select any existing text in the Search For text box.

• Type animals.

• If All Collections is not displayed in the Search In text box, select Everywhere from the drop-down list.

• Open the Results Should Be drop-down list, select Clip Art and Photographs, and deselect all other options.

Having Trouble?
Click the box next to an option to select or deselect (clear the checkmark).

• Click [Go].

Your screen should be similar to Figure 1.58

Having Trouble?
Your Clip Art task pane may display different pictures than shown in Figure 1.58.

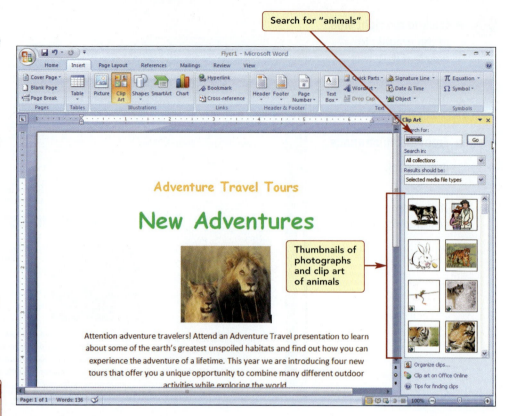

Search for "animals"

Thumbnails of photographs and clip art of animals

Figure 1.58

The program searches all locations on your computer and, if you have an Internet connection established, Microsoft's Clip Art and Media Web site for clip art and graphics that match your search term. The Results area displays **thumbnails**, miniature representations of pictures, of all located graphics. The pictures stored on your computer in the Microsoft Clip Organizer appear first in the results list, followed by the Office Online clip art.

Pointing to a thumbnail displays a ScreenTip containing the keywords associated with the picture and information about the picture properties. It also displays a drop-down list bar that accesses the item's context menu.

4 ● **Scroll the list to view additional images.**

● **Point to any thumbnail to see a ScreenTip.**

Your screen should be similar to Figure 1.59

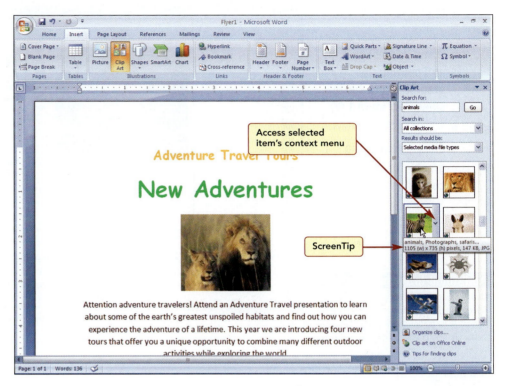

Figure 1.59

Each graphic has several keywords associated with it. All the displayed graphics include the keyword "animals." Because so many pictures were located, you decide to narrow your search to display pictures with keywords of "animals" and "parrots" only. Additionally, because it is sometimes difficult to see the graphic, you can preview it in a larger size.

5 ● Add a comma after the word "animals" in the Search For text box and then type parrots.

● Click Go .

● Scroll the results area and point to the graphic of the parrot shown in Figure 1.60.

● Click ⌄ next to the graphic to open the context menu.

● Choose Preview/Properties.

Additional Information

If you cannot find the picture of the parrot shown in Figure 1.60, it is provided with the files downloaded for the lab. Use 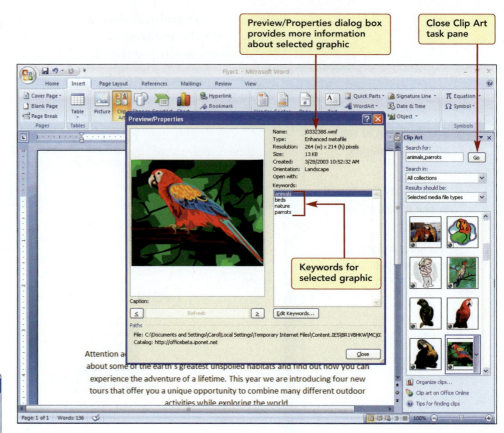 to insert it into the flyer.

Your screen should be similar to Figure 1.60

Preview/Properties dialog box provides more information about selected graphic

Close Clip Art task pane

Keywords for selected graphic

Figure 1.60

Because the search term is more specific, fewer results are displayed. The Preview/Properties dialog box displays the selected graphic larger so it is easier to see. It also displays more information about the properties associated with the graphic, including the keywords used to identify the graphic. You think this looks like a good choice and will insert it into the document.

6 • Click [Close] to close the dialog box.

• Click on the graphic to insert it in the document.

Another Method
You also could choose Insert from the thumbnail's context menu.

• Click [×] in the Clip Art task pane title bar to close it.

Your screen should be similar to Figure 1.61

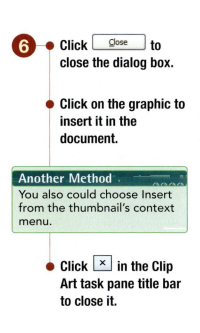

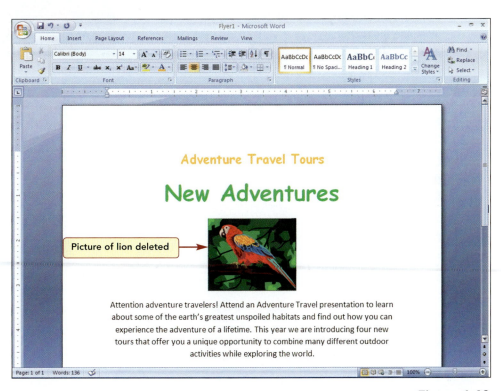

Figure 1.61

The clip art graphic is inserted next to the lion picture.

Deleting a Graphic

There are now two graphics in the flyer. You decide to use the parrot graphic and need to remove the picture of the lion. To do this, you select the graphic and delete it.

1 • Click on the lion graphic.

• Press [Delete].

Your screen should be similar to Figure 1.62

Figure 1.62

The lion graphic is removed.

Sizing a Graphic

Usually, when a graphic is inserted, its size will need to be adjusted. A graphic object can be manipulated in many ways. You can change its size; add captions, borders, or shading; or move it to another location. A graphic object can be moved anywhere on the page, including in the margins or on top of or below other objects, including text. The only places you cannot place a graphic object are into a footnote, endnote, or caption.

In this case, you want to increase the picture's size. To size a graphic, you select it and drag the sizing handles to increase or decrease the size of the object. The mouse pointer changes to ⬉ when pointing to a handle. The direction of the arrow indicates the direction in which you can drag to size the graphic. You want to increase the image to approximately 3 inches wide by 2.5 inches high.

Additional Information

A selected graphic object can be moved by dragging it to the new location.

Another Method

You also can size a picture to an exact measurement using commands in the Size group of the Picture Tools tab.

1 ● Click on the graphic to select it.

● Point to the lower-right corner handle.

Additional Information

Dragging a corner handle maintains the original proportions of the graphic.

● With the pointer as a ⬉, drag outward from the picture to increase the size to approximately 2.5 inches wide by 2 inches high (use the ruler as a guide and refer to Figure 1.63).

● Click anywhere in the document to deselect the graphic.

● Click 💾 Save.

Your screen should be similar to Figure 1.63

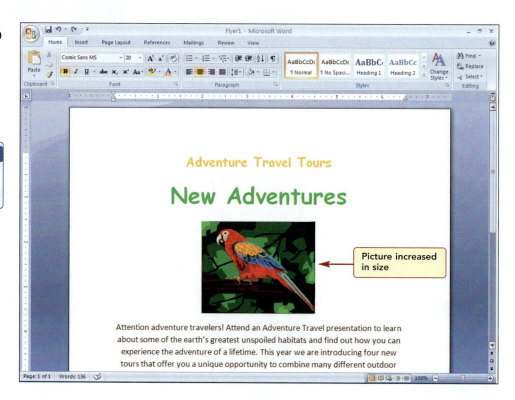

Figure 1.63

Enhancing the Page

The final changes you want to make to the flyer for now are to add a border line around the entire page and to add a watermark in the page background. Borders can add interest and emphasis to various parts of your document, including entire pages, selected text, tables, graphic objects, and pictures. **Watermarks** are text or pictures that appear behind document text. They often add interest or identify the document status, such as marking a document as a Draft. Both page borders and watermarks are features that affect an entire page and are found in the Page Layout tab.

Adding a Page Border

You want to add a decorative border around the entire page to enclose the text and enhance the appearance of the flyer.

1 • Open the Page Layout tab.

• Click ⬚ Page Borders in the Page Background group.

Your screen should be similar to Figure 1.64

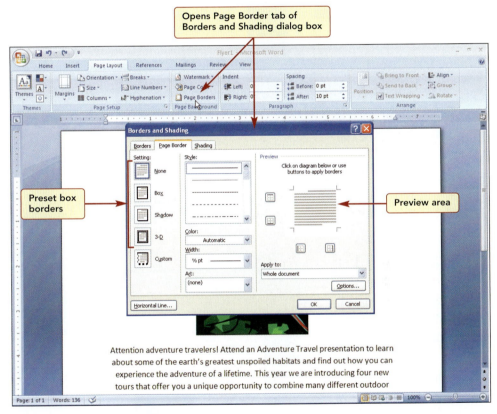

Opens Page Border tab of Borders and Shading dialog box

Preset box borders

Preview area

Figure 1.64

Additional Information
There are also a variety of graphical borders available in the Art list box.

Additional Information
You will learn about creating custom borders in later labs.

From the Page Borders tab of the Borders and Shading dialog box, you first select either a preset box border or a custom border. Then you specify the style, color, weight, and location of the border. A page border can be applied to all pages in a document, to pages in selected parts of a document, to the first page only, or to all pages except the first.

You want to create a box border around the entire page of text. As you specify the border settings, the Preview area will reflect your selections.

2 • Choose Box from the Settings area.

• Scroll the Style list box and select

• Open the Color palette and select Orange, Accent 6.

• From the Width drop-down list box, select 3 pt.

Having Trouble?

Use the None option to remove all border lines, or remove individual lines by selecting the border location again.

Your screen should be similar to Figure 1.65

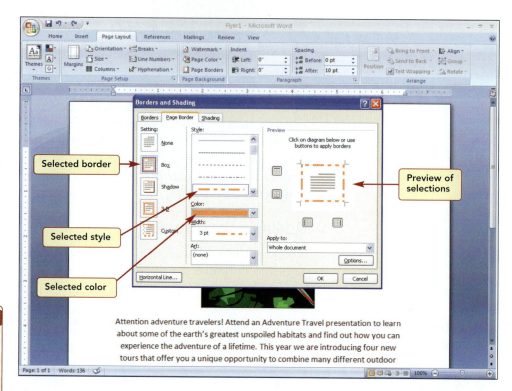

Figure 1.65

The Preview area shows how the box page border will appear in the style, color, and point size you selected. The default selection of Document, as to what part of the document to apply the border, is acceptable because the document is only one page long.

3 • Click OK .

• Reduce the zoom to display the entire page.

Your screen should be similar to Figure 1.66

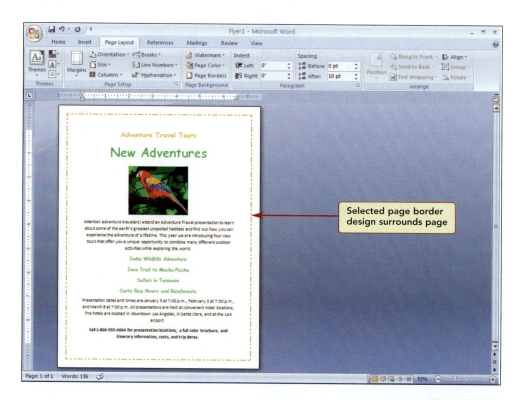

Figure 1.66

The specified page border appears in the middle of the margin space around the entire page.

Adding a Watermark

Finally, you want to add a watermark to the background of the flyer identifying the document as a draft. You can insert a predesigned watermark from a gallery of watermark text, or you can insert a watermark with custom text.

1 ● Click  from the Page Background group.

● Scroll the Watermark gallery and choose the **Draft1** design from the **Disclaimers** section.

Additional Information
Choose Remove Watermark from the ⬛ Watermark ▾ menu to remove a watermark.

Your screen should be similar to Figure 1.67

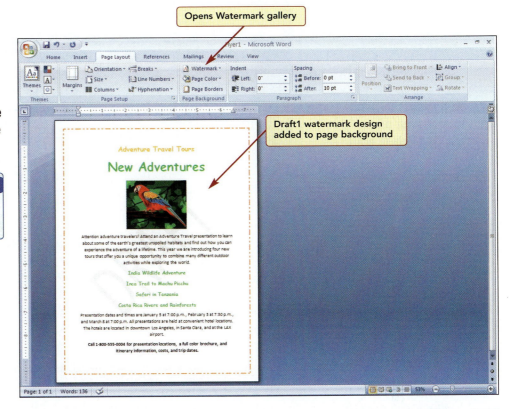

Figure 1.67

The DRAFT watermark appears diagonally across the background of the page. The entire page is displayed as it will appear when printed. The flyer looks good and does not appear to need any further modifications immediately.

Additional Information
You can only see watermarks in Print Layout view and Full Screen Reading view or in a printed document.

Printing a Document

Although you still plan to make several formatting changes to the document, you want to give a copy of the flyer to the manager to get feedback regarding the content and layout.

First you need to add your name to the flyer and to the document properties and check the print settings.

1 ● Increase the zoom to 100%.

● Scroll to the bottom of the flyer.

● Add your name at before the phone number in the last sentence of the flyer.

● Replace Student Name with your name in the document properties.

● If necessary, make sure your printer is on and ready to print.

● Click ● Office Button and choose Print.

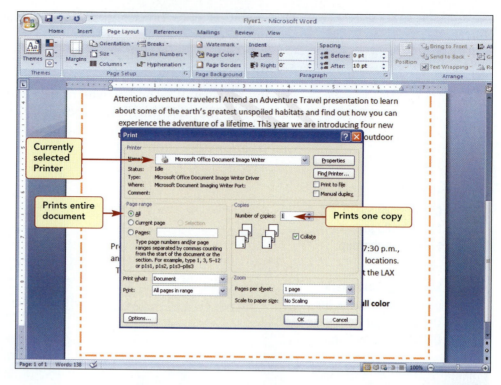

Figure 1.68

Another Method
The keyboard shortcut for the Print command is Ctrl + P.

Additional Information
You also can use Quick Print on the Print submenu to print the active document immediately using the current print settings.

Your screen should be similar to Figure 1.68

From the Print dialog box, you need to specify the printer you will be using and the document settings. The printer that is currently selected is displayed in the Name drop-down list box in the Printer section of the dialog box.

The Page Range area of the Print dialog box lets you specify how much of the document you want printed. The range options are described in the following table:

Option	Action
All	Prints entire document.
Current page	Prints selected page or page the insertion point is on.
Pages	Prints pages you specify by typing page numbers in the dialog box.
Selection	Prints selected text only.

Note: Please consult your instructor for printing procedures that may differ from the following directions.

The default range setting, All, is the correct setting. In the Copies section, the default setting of one copy of the document is acceptable. You will print using the default print settings.

2 • If you need to change the selected printer to another printer, open the Name drop-down list box and select the appropriate printer (your instructor will tell you which printer to select).

• Click [OK].

Your printer should be printing the document. The printed copy of the flyer should be similar to the document shown in the Case Study at the beginning of the lab.

Exiting Word

You are finished working on the flyer for now and want to save the last few changes you have made to the document and close the Word application. The [✕ Exit Word] command in the File menu is used to quit the Word program. Alternatively, you can click the [✕] Close button in the application window title bar. If you attempt to close the application without first saving your document, Word displays a warning asking if you want to save your work. If you do not save your work and you exit the application, any changes you made since last saving it are lost.

Another Method
The keyboard shortcut for the Exit command is [Alt] + [F4].

1 • Click [✕] Close.

• Click [Yes] to save the changes you made to the file.

The Windows desktop is visible again.

If multiple Word documents are open, clicking [✕] closes the application window containing the document you are viewing only.

Focus on Careers

EXPLORE YOUR CAREER OPTIONS

Food Service Manager
Have you noticed flyers around your campus advertising job positions? Many of these jobs are in the food service industry. Food service managers are traditionally responsible for overseeing the kitchen and dining room. However, these positions increasingly involve administrative tasks, including recruiting new

employees. As a food service manager, your position would likely include creating newspaper notices and flyers to attract new staff. These flyers should be eye-catching and error-free. The typical salary range of a food service manager is $34,000 to $41,700. Demand for skilled food service managers is expected to increase through 2010.

Concept Summary

LAB 1

Creating and Editing a Document

Grammar Checker (WD1.16)

The grammar checker advises you of incorrect grammar as you create and edit a document, and proposes possible corrections.

Spelling Checker (WD1.19)

The spelling checker advises you of misspelled words as you create and edit a document, and proposes possible corrections.

AutoCorrect (WD1.21)

The AutoCorrect feature makes some basic assumptions about the text you are typing and, based on these assumptions, automatically corrects the entry.

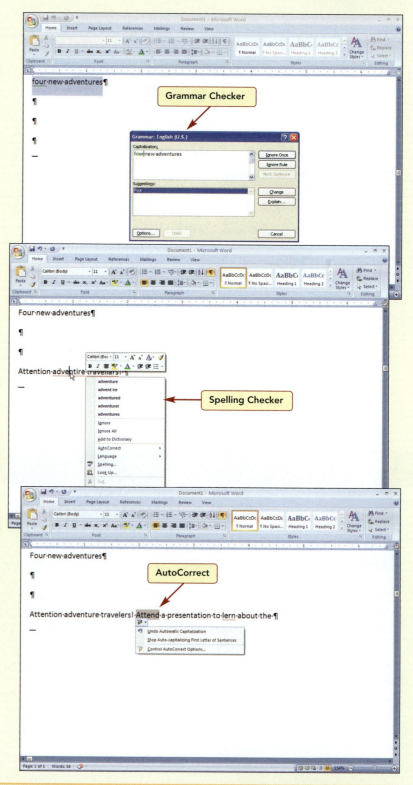

Word Wrap (WD1.23)

The word wrap feature automatically decides where to end a line and wraps text to the next line based on the margin settings.

Font and Font Size (WD1.46)

A font, also commonly referred to as a typeface, is a set of characters with a specific design that has one or more font sizes.

Alignment (WD1.56)

Alignment is the positioning of text on a line between the margins or indents. There are four types of paragraph alignment: left, centered, right, and justified.

Graphics (WD1.59)

A graphic is a nontext element or object such as a drawing or picture that can be added to a document.

Lab Review

key terms

alignment WD1.56
AutoCorrect WD1.21
character formatting WD1.46
clip art WD1.59
cursor WD1.5
custom dictionary WD1.19
default WD1.8
document properties WD1.25
document window WD1.5
drawing object WD1.59
edit WD1.10
embedded object WD1.59
end-of-file marker WD1.10

font WD1.46
font size WD1.46
format WD1.10
grammar checker WD1.16
graphic WD1.59
Insert mode WD1.37
insertion point WD1.5
Live Preview WD1.47
main dictionary WD1.19
object WD1.59
paragraph formatting WD1.46
picture WD1.59
ruler WD1.5

sans serif font WD1.46
selection rectangle WD1.60
serif font WD1.46
sizing handles WD1.60
soft space WD1.56
source program WD1.59
spelling checker WD1.19
template WD1.8
thumbnail WD1.62
TrueType WD1.54
typeface WD1.46
watermark WD1.67
word wrap WD1.23

MCAS skills

The Microsoft Certified Applications Specialist (MCAS) certification program is designed to measure your proficiency in performing basic tasks using the Office 2007 applications. Getting certified demonstrates that you have the skills and provides a valuable industry credential for employment. See Reference 2 MCAS Certification Guide for a complete list of the skills that were covered in Lab 1.

WD1.74
Word 2007
Lab 1: Creating and Editing a Document
www.mhhe.com/oleary

command summary

Command	Shortcut	Action
Office Button		**Opens File menu**
New	Ctrl + N	Opens new blank document
Open	Ctrl + O	Opens existing document file
Save	Ctrl + S	Saves document using same file name
Save As	F12	Saves document using a new file name, type, and/or location
Print	Ctrl + P	Prints document
Prepare/Properties		Opens Document Information Panel
Close	Ctrl + F4	Closes document
X Exit Word	Alt + F4	Exit Word application
Quick Access Toolbar		
Save	Ctrl + S	Saves document using same file name
Undo	Ctrl + Z	Restores last editing change
Redo	Ctrl + Y	Restores last Undo or repeats last command or action
Home tab		
Font Group		
Calibri (Body) Font		Changes typeface
11 Size		Changes font size
Clear Formatting		Removes all formatting from selection
B Bold	Ctrl + B	Adds/removes bold effect
I Italic	Ctrl + I	Adds/removes italic effect
Aa˅ Change Case		Changes case of selected text
A˅ Color		Changes text to selected color
Paragraph group		
¶ Show/Hide	Ctrl + → +*	Displays or hides formatting marks
Align Text Left	Ctrl + L	Aligns text to left margin
Center	Ctrl + E	Centers text between left and right margins
Align Text Right	Ctrl + R	Aligns text to right margin
Justify	Ctrl + J	Aligns text equally between left and right margins
Insert Tab		
Illustrations group		
Picture		Inserts selected picture

command summary (continued)

Command	Shortcut	Action
Clip Art		Accesses Clip Organizer and inserts selected clip
Page Layout Tab		
Page Background group		
Watermark ▾		Inserts ghosted text behind page content
Page Borders		Adds a border around page
Review Tab		
Proofing group		
ABC Spelling & Grammar		Opens Spelling and Grammar dialog box
View Tab		
Document Views group		
Print Layout	▤	Shows how text and objects will appear on printed page
Full Screen Reading	▤	Displays document only, without application features
Web Layout	▤	Shows document as it will appear when viewed in a Web browser
Outline	▤	Shows structure of document
Draft	▤	Shows text formatting and simple layout of page
Show/Hide group		
☑ Ruler	▤	Displays/hides ruler
Zoom group		
Zoom		Opens Zoom dialog box
100%		Zooms document to 100% of normal size
One Page		Zooms document so an entire page fits in window
Page Width		Zooms document so width of page matches width of window

screen identification

1. In the following Word screen, letters identify important elements. Enter the correct term for each screen element in the space provided.

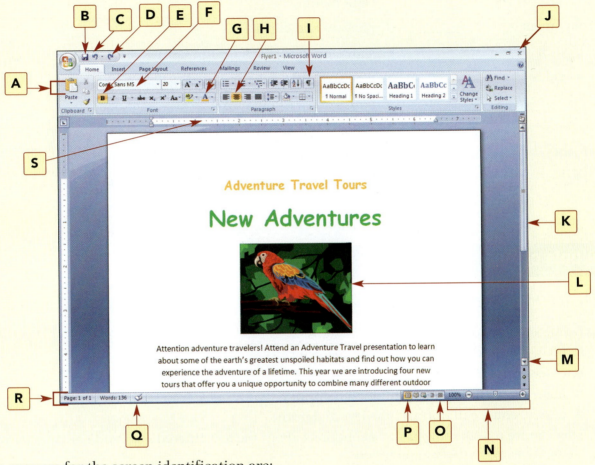

Possible answers for the screen identification are:

Scrolls down	Zoom	A. _____	K. _____
Draft view	Center	B. _____	L. _____
Tab mark	Spelling and grammar	C. _____	M. _____
Ribbon	status icon	D. _____	N. _____
Save	Redo	E. _____	O. _____
Print Layout view	Bold	F. _____	P. _____
Font color	Status bar	G. _____	Q. _____
Font	Scroll bar	H. _____	R. _____
Undo	Graphic	I. _____	S. _____
Show/Hide	Paragraph mark	J. _____	
Close	Ruler		

Lab Exercises

matching

Match the item on the left with the correct description on the right.

1. 🖫   _____   **a.** undoes last command

2. font   _____   **b.** moves to the top of the document

3. sans serif   _____   **c.** feature that automatically begins a new line when text reaches the right margin

4. alignment   _____   **d.** pictures and clip art

5. Ctrl + h   _____   **e.** shows dialog box

6. graphics   _____   **f.** type style that can be applied to text

7. ▣   _____   **g.** font size measurement

8. word wrap   _____   **h.** controls paragraph positioning between the margins

9. point   _____   **i.** saves a document using the same file name

10. ↺▾   _____   **j.** font without a flair at the base of each letter

multiple choice

Circle the correct response to the questions below.

1. Document development follows these steps.
   a. plan, edit, enter, format, preview, and print
   b. enter, edit, format, preview, and print
   c. plan, enter, edit, format, preview, and print
   d. design, enter, edit, format, preview, and print

2. This feature makes some basic assumptions about the text entered and automatically makes changes based on those assumptions.
   a. AutoChange
   b. AutoFormat
   c. AutoText
   d. AutoCorrect

3. Words that are not contained in the main dictionary can be added to the _____ dictionary.
   a. custom
   b. additional
   c. supplemental
   d. user defined

4. A(n) _____ is a nontext element or object that can be added to a document.
   a. illustration
   b. picture
   c. drawing
   d. all of the above

5. When text is evenly aligned on both margins, it is _____.
   a. center aligned
   b. justified
   c. left aligned
   d. right aligned

6. Words that may be spelled incorrectly in a document are indicated by a _____.
   a. green wavy line
   b. red wavy line
   c. blue wavy line
   d. purple dotted underline

7. Font sizes are measured in _____.
   a. inches
   b. points
   c. bits
   d. pieces

8. The _____ feature shows how various formatting choices would look on selected text.
   a. Actual Preview
   b. Real Preview
   c. Active Preview
   d. Live Preview

9. A set of characters with a specific design is called a(n) _____.
   a. style
   b. font
   c. AutoFormat
   d. Design

10. A(n) _____ is text or pictures that appear behind document text.
    a. graphic
    b. watermark
    c. embedded object
    d. thumbnail

true/false

Circle the correct answer to the following questions.

1.	A wavy red line indicates a potential spelling error.	True	False
2.	Hard spaces are used to justify text on a line.	True	False
3.	The default document settings are stored in the Normal.docx file.	True	False
4.	The [Delete] key erases the character to the right of the insertion point.	True	False
5.	The automatic word wrap feature checks for typing errors.	True	False
6.	The Word document file name extension is .wrd.	True	False
7.	Font sizes are measured in inches.	True	False
8.	Word inserts hidden marks into a document to control the display of text.	True	False
9.	The AutoCorrect feature automatically identifies and corrects certain types of errors.	True	False
10.	A selected picture is surrounded by a selection rectangle and eight moving handles.	True	False

fill-in

Complete the following statements by filling in the blanks with the correct terms.

1. The default document settings are stored in the _____ template file.

2. A small blue box appearing under a word or character indicates that the _____ feature was applied.

3. The _____ feature displays each page of your document in a reduced size so you can see the page layout.

4. To size a graphic evenly, click and drag the _____ in one corner of the graphic.

5. It is good practice to use only _____ types of fonts in a document.

6. Word 2007 documents are identified by the _____ file extension.

7. The _____ at the top of the window contains commands that are organized into related groups.

8. Use _____ when you want to keep your existing document with the original name and make a copy with a new name.

9. A _____ is a miniature representation of all located graphics in the Clip Art task pane.

10. The _____ feature shows how your formatting choices will appear on selected text.

Hands-On Exercises

rating system

★ Easy

★★ Moderate

★★★ Difficult

Step-by-Step

Asking for Input Memo ★

1. Adventure Travel Tours is planning to update its Web site in the near future. You have been asked to solicit suggestions from the travel agents about changes they would like to see made to the current Web site. You decide to send all the travel agents a memo asking them for their input. Your completed memo will be similar to the one shown here.

    a. Open a blank Word 2007 document and create the following memo in Draft view. Press [Tab⇆] twice after you type the colon (:) following To in the memo header. Press [Tab⇆] once after the From and Date lines. This will make the information following the colons line up evenly. Enter a blank line between paragraphs.

    To: Travel Agents
    From: Student Name
    From:Student Name
    Date: September, 15, 2008

    The Adventure Travel Tours Web site was designed with travel agents in mind. But as you know, the role of the travel agent is changing. In order to keep up with these changes we plan to begin work on updating the Adventure Travel Tours Web site.

    In preparation for this project, I would like your input about the content that will only be available to travel agents. In the next few days as you work with clients please note what can be changed to make it easier for you to book travel, and then send your comments back to me. All suggestions for changes are welcome and will be considered for our improved Web site.

    Thank you in advance for your input.

    To: Travel Agents
    From: Student Name
    Date: [Current date]

    The Adventure Travel Tours current Web site was designed with travel agents in mind but as you know, the role of the travel agent is changing. In order to keep up with these changes we plan to begin work on updating the current Adventure Travel Tours Web site. In preparation for this project, I would like your input about the content that will only be available to travel agents. As you work with clients please note what can be changed to make it easier for you to book travel, then send your comments back to me. All suggestions for changes are welcome and will be considered for our improved Web site.

    Thank you in advance for your input.

    b. Correct any spelling and grammar errors that are identified.

    c. Turn on the display of formatting marks. Check the document and remove any extra blank spaces between words or at the end of lines.

    d. Save the document as Web Site Memo in your data file location.

    e. Switch to Print Layout view.

f. End the first sentence after the word "mind". Capitalize the following word, but. Insert the text "In the next few days" before the word "As," in the fifth sentence. Change the "A" in As to lower case. Delete the word "current" from the first and third sentences.

g. Start a new paragraph beginning with the third sentence.

h. Change the font size for the entire memo to 14 pt and the alignment of the body of the memo to justified.

i. Turn off the display of formatting marks.

j. Add an ASAP watermark.

k. Include your name in the document properties as author and the file name as the title.

l. Save the document again and print the document.

Promoting Celebrate Bikes Sunday ★★

2. You are the program coordinator for the city of Westbrook's Parks and Recreation Department. In next week's newspaper, you plan to run an article to promote bike riding in the community through the Celebrate Bikes Sunday event. Your completed article will be similar to the one shown here.

a. Enter the following information in a new Word 2007 document. Leave a blank line between paragraphs.

Celebrate Bicycling!

May is traditionally National Bike Month, so take out your bicycle, tune it up and get a breath of fresh air! And plan to take part in Celebrate Bikes Sunday on 5/8 to learn about the benefits of bike riding.

Businesses and organizations participating in the event are all "related to biking in Westbrook and most of them are involved in the development of the trail system" says event director Mary Jo Miller.

As part of the activities on this day, the Westbrook Parks and Recreation Department is sponsoring a bike ride from the West Avenue YMCA to the Main Street Park beginning at 11am.

At the end of the bike ride, the riders are encouraged to stay for the fun and informative activates in the park. Activities include a bike safety program, entertainment, and food booths. The Safe Route to School program will work with parents and children to find the safest route to either walk or bike to school.

Celebrate Bicycling!

May is National Bike Month, so take out your bicycle, tune it up, and get a breath of fresh air! And plan to take part in Celebrate Bicycling Sunday on *May 8th* to learn about the benefits of bike riding and bicycle safety.

Businesses and organizations participating in the event are all "related to biking in Westbrook and most of them are involved in the development of the trail system" says event director Mary Jo Miller.

As part of the activities on this day, the Westbrook parks and Recreation Department is sponsoring a bike ride from the West Avenue YMCA to the Main Street Park. The ride begins at *11 am*.

At the end of the bike ride, stay for the fun and informative activities in the park. Activities include a bike safety program, entertainment, and food booths. The Safe Route to School program will work with parents and children to find the safest route to either walk or bike to school.

Registration is free and available by calling *(603) 555-1313*, visiting the YMCA during regular business hours or beginning at 10am on Sunday at the YMCA.

Student Name
September, 15, 2008

Registration is free and available by calling (603) 555-1313, visiting the YMCA during regular business hours or beginning at 10am on Sunday at the YMCA.

b. Correct any spelling or grammar errors. Save the document as Bike Event.

c. Turn on the display of formatting marks. Check the document and remove any extra blank spaces between words or at the end of lines.

d. In Print Layout view, center the title. Change the title font to Broadway (or a font of your choice), 16 pt, and red font color.

e. In the first paragraph, delete the word "traditionally" and change the number 5/8 to "May 8th." Add the text "and bicycle safety" to the end of the second sentence in this paragraph.

f. End the first sentence in paragraph 3 after the word "Park". Change the following sentence to "The ride begins at 11 am."

g. Delete the phrase "the riders are encouraged to" from the first sentence of the fourth paragraph.

h. Add italics, bold, and red font color to the date in the first paragraph, the time in the third paragraph, and the phone number in the last paragraph.

i. Justify the paragraphs.

j. Increase the font size of the paragraphs to 12 pt.

k. Below the title, insert a clip art graphic of your choice of a child riding a bike by searching on the keyword "bike" or use the graphic file wd01_Child on Bike. Center it and adjust the size of the graphic appropriately. Add a blank line above and below the graphic.

l. Add your name and the current date on separate lines several lines below the last line. Left-align both lines. Turn off the display of formatting marks.

m. Review the document and, if necessary, adjust the size of the graphic to fit the document on a single page.

n. Include your name in the file properties as author and the file name as the title.

o. Save the document again. Print the document.

Creating a Grand Opening Flyer ★★

3. The Downtown Internet Cafe is planning a grand re-opening celebration. The cafe combines the relaxed atmosphere of a coffee house with the fun of using the Internet. You want to create a flyer about the celebration that you can give to customers and also post in the window of other local businesses about the celebration. Your completed flyer will be similar to the one shown here.

a. Open a new Word document and enter the following text, pressing ⏎Enter where indicated.

Grand Re-Opening Celebration ⏎Enter (2 times)

Downtown Internet Cafe ⏎Enter (2 times)

Your newly remodeled neighborhood coffee shop ⏎Enter (2 times)

Stop on by and enjoy an excellent dark Italian Roast coffee, premium loose teas, blended drinks and quality light fare of sandwiches, pitas and salads. ⏎Enter (2 times)

Starting Friday, September 1st and continuing all week through Sunday, September 10th we will take 15 percent off all cappuccino and blended drinks. Plus take $2.00 off any sandwich order. ⏎Enter (2 times)

So enjoy a drink and use our free wifi service to get online with the fastest connection in the neighborhood! ⏎Enter
(3 times)

2314 Telegraph Avenue ⏎Enter

Cafe Hours: Sunday - Thursday 8:00 a.m. to 9:00 p.m. Friday and Saturday 8:00 a.m. to 12:00 a.m. ⏎Enter

b. Correct any spelling and grammar errors that are identified.

c. Save the document as Grand Re-Opening.

d. Type **Join Us for Live Entertainment!** after the location and hours. Use the Undo feature to remove this sentence.

e. Turn on the display of formatting marks. Center the entire document.

f. Capitalize each word of the third line. Replace the word percent with the % symbol. Change the case of the text "free wifi" to uppercase. Delete the following word, "service."

g. Change the first line to a font color of blue, font type of Arial Black or a font of your choice, and size of 24 pt.

h. Change the second line to a font color of purple, font type of Arial or a font of your choice, and size of 36 pt.

i. Change the third line to a font color of dark red and a font size of 16 pt. Change the last two lines (address and hours) to a font color of dark red.

j. Increase the font size of the three paragraphs to 14 points.

k. Insert the graphic file wd01_coffee (from your data files) on the middle blank line below the third title line. Size the graphic to be approximately 2 by 2¼ inches using the ruler as a guide.

l. Add a page border of your choice to the flyer.

m. Add your name and the current date, left-aligned, on one line, below the last line. Turn off the display of formatting marks.

n. If necessary, reduce the size of the graphic so the entire flyer fits on one page.

o. Include your name in the file properties as author and the file name as the title. Save and print the flyer.

Grand Re-Opening Celebration
Downtown Internet Café
Your Newly Remodeled Neighborhood Coffee Shop

Stop on by and enjoy an excellent dark Italian Roast coffee, premium loose teas, blended drinks and quality light fare of sandwiches, pitas and salads.

Starting Friday, September 1st and continuing all week through Sunday, September 10th we will take 15% off all cappuccino and blended drinks. Plus take $2.00 off any sandwich order.

So enjoy a drink and use our FREE WIFI to get online with the fastest connection in the neighborhood!

2314 Telegraph Avenue
Café Hours: Sunday – Thursday 8:00a.m. to 9:00p.m. Friday and Saturday 8:00a.m. to 12:00a.m.

Student Name-Date

Preparing a Lecture on Note-Taking Skills ★★★

4. You teach a college survival skills class and have recently read about the results of a survey conducted by the Pilot Pen Company of America about note-taking skills. The survey of 500 teenagers found that students typically begin taking classroom notes by sixth grade and that only half had been taught how to take classroom notes. It also found that those students trained in note-taking earned better grades. Note-taking becomes increasingly important in high school and is essential in college. Lecture notes are a key component for mastering material. In response to the survey, the pen manufacturer came up with 10 tips for better note-taking. You started a document of these tips that you plan to use to supplement your lecture on this topic. You will continue to revise and format the document. The revised document will be similar to the one shown here.

Tips for Taking Better Classroom Notes

Be Ready

Review your assigned reading and previous notes you've taken before class. Bring plenty of paper and a sharpened pencil, an erasable pen or a pen that won't skip or smudge. Write the class name, date and that day's topic at the top the page.

Write Legibly

Print if your handwriting is poor. Use a pencil or erasable pen if you cross out material a lot so that your notes are easier to read. Take notes in one-liners rather than paragraph form. Skip a line between ideas to make it easier to find information when you're studying for a test.

Use Wide Margins

Leave a wide margin on one side of your paper so you'll have space to write your own thoughts and call attention to key material. Draw arrows or stars beside important information like dates, names and events. If you miss getting a date, name, number or other fact, make a mark in the margin so you'll remember to come back to it.

Fill in Gaps

Check with a classmate or your teacher after class to get any missing names, dates, facts or other information you could not write down.

Mark Questionable Material

Jot down a "?" in the margin beside something you disagree with or do not think you recorded correctly. When appropriate, ask your teacher, classmate, or refer to your textbook, for clarification.

Student Name

Date

a. Open the Word document wd01_Note Taking Skills.

b. Correct any spelling and grammar errors that are identified. Save the document as Note Taking Skills.

c. Switch to Draft view. Turn off the display of formatting marks. Change the font of the title line to a font of your choice, 18 pt. Center and add color of your choice to the title line.

d. In the Be Ready tip, delete the word "lots". In the Write Legibly tip, delete the word "cursive" and add the words "an erasable" before the word "pen." Change the tip heading "Margins" to "Use Wide Margins."

e. Above the Mark Questionable Material tip, insert the following tip:

Fill in Gaps

Check with a classmate or your teacher after class to get any missing names, dates, facts or other information you could not write down.

f. Change the tip heading lines font to Lucida Sans with a font size of 16 pt and a color of your choice.

g. Change the alignment of the paragraphs to justified. Use Undo Changes to return the alignment to left. Use Redo Changes to return the paragraphs to justified again.

h. Insert a clip art graphic of your choice (search on "pencil") below the title. Size it appropriately and center it.

i. Add your name and the current date, centered, on separate lines two lines below the last line.

j. Include your name in the file properties as author and the document title as the title. Save the document. Print the document.

Writing an Article on the History of Ice Cream ★★★

5. Each month the town's free paper prints a fun article on the history of something people are familiar with but might not know anything about. You researched the topic online and found the information you needed about the history of ice cream from the International Dairy Foods Association's Web site at www.idfa.org/facts/icmonth/page7.cfm. You started writing the article a few days ago and just need to continue the article by adding a few more details. Then you need to edit and format the text and include a graphic to enhance the appearance of the article. Your completed article will be similar to the one shown here.

a. Open the file named wd01_History of Ice Cream.

b. Correct any spelling and grammar errors. (Hint: Click 🔲 in the status bar to move to each error.) Save the document as Ice Cream History.

c. Enter the following headings at the location shown in parentheses.

History of Ice Cream (above first paragraph)

The Evolution of Ice Cream (above second paragraph)

Ice Cream in America (above third paragraph)

d. Center the article title. Change the font to Impact with a point size of 24. Add a color of your choice to the title.

e. Change the other two headings to bold with a type size of 14 pt. Center the heads. Use the same color as in the title for the heads.

f. Change the alignment of the first paragraph to justified.

g. Add a blank line below the main title of the article and insert the picture wd01_Ice Cream (from your data files) at this location.

h. Size the picture to be 2 inches wide (use the ruler as a guide). Center it below the title.

i. Add a Draft watermark.

j. Add your name and the current date below the last line of the article. View the whole page and, if necessary, reduce the size of the graphic so the entire article fits on one page.

k. Include your name in the file properties as author and the document title as the title. Save the document again. Print the document.

History of Ice Cream

Ice cream probably began as snow and ice flavored with honey and nectar. Alexander the Great, King Solomon and Nero Claudius Caesar were known to have enjoyed this treat. Although the origin of ice cream has been traced back as far as the second century B.C., a specific date is not known and no one inventor has been indisputably credited with its discovery.

The Evolution of Ice Cream

It is thought that the recipe for ice cream evolved from a recipe that was bought back to Italy by Marco Polo when he returned from the Far East over a thousand years later. This recipe closely resembled our current day sherbet. Sometime in the 16th century, ice cream, similar to what we have today, appeared in both Italy and England. However, only royalty and wealthy enjoyed this treat until 1660 when ice cream was made available to the general public at *Café Procope*, the first café in Paris.

Ice Cream in America

It took a while before ice cream made its way to the New World. A letter written in 1744 by a guest of Maryland Governor William Bladen describes ice cream and the first advertisement for ice cream appeared in the *New York Gazette* on May 12, 1777. President George Washington was particularly fond of ice cream and inventory records from his Mount Vernon estate included two pewter pots used to make ice cream. Both Presidents Thomas Jefferson and James Madison were also known to have served ice cream during important presidential events.

This desert continued to be enjoyed mostly by the elite until insulated ice houses were invented in early 1800. Finally, in 1851 Jacob Fussell, a Baltimore milk dealer, began to manufacture and provide ice cream to the public. Technological innovations, such as steam power, mechanical refrigeration, the homogenizer, electric power and motors and motorized delivery vehicles, were use to manufacture ice cream soon making ice cream a major an industry in America.

Student Name – Current Date

Lab Exercises

on your own

Creating a Flyer ★

1. Adventure Travel Tours is offering a great deal on a Day of the Dead Bicycle Tour in Mexico. Research the Day of the Dead celebration using the Web as a resource. Then, using the features of Word you have learned so far, create a flyer that will advertise this tour. Be sure to use at least two colors of text, two sizes of text, and two kinds of paragraph alignment. Include a graphic from the Clip Organizer. Include your name at the bottom of the flyer. Include your name in the file properties as author and the file name as the title. Save the document as Mexico Adventure.

Creating a Swimming Pool Rules Flyer ★★

2. You work in the community pool and have been asked to create a flyer to post that identifies the rules swimmers should follow when using the pool. Create a flyer that explains the five most important rules to follow while swimming at the pool. Use a piece of clip art to liven up your flyer. Include different font sizes, paragraph alignments, and other formatting features to make the flyer attractive. Apply different font colors for each rule. Include a page border. Include your name at the bottom of the flyer. Include your name in the file properties as author and the file name as the title. Save the document as Pool Rules.

Astronomy Class Memo ★★

3. The city of Gilbert, Arizona, has recently built a $100,000 observatory that includes a $20,000 telescope in a local park. The observatory is open evenings for small groups of five to six people to take turns looking through the 16-inch telescope's eyepiece. The use of the observatory is free.

    The city has decided to offer classes for the community to learn how to use the telescope and to teach about astronomy. As a trial run, the class will first be offered to city employees and their families. You want to notify all employees about the observatory and the class by including a memo with their paycheck. Using Step-by-Step Exercise 1 as a model, provide information about when and where the class will be held. Include information about how people sign up for the class. Include your name in the file properties as author and the file name as the title. Save the memo as Astronomy Basics.

Volunteer Opportunities ★★★

4. Many community groups, hospitals, libraries, and churches are looking for volunteers to assist in their programs. Volunteering has rewards for both the volunteer and the community. Using the Web as a resource, research volunteer opportunities in your community. Then write a one-page report that includes information about two volunteer groups for which you would like to volunteer. Include information about what the organization does for the community. Also include the skills you have to offer and the amount of time you can commit as volunteer. Include a title at the top of the document and your name and the current date below the title. Center the title lines. Use at least two colors of text, two sizes of text, and two kinds of paragraph alignment. Include a graphic from the Clip Organizer. Include your name in the file properties as author and the file name as the title. Save the document as Volunteer Opportunities.

Writing a Career Report ★★★

5. Using the library or the Web, research information about your chosen career. Write a one-page report about your findings that includes information on three areas: Career Description; Educational Requirements; Salary and Employment projections. Include a title at the top of the document and your name and the current date below the title. Center the title lines. Justify the paragraphs. Include your name in the file properties as author and the file name as the title. Save the document as Career Report.

Revising and Refining a Document

Objectives

After completing this lab, you will know how to:

1 Use the Spelling and Grammar tool and the Thesaurus.

2 Move, cut, and copy text and formats.

3 Control document paging.

4 Find and replace text.

5 Insert the current date.

6 Change indents, line spacing, and margins.

7 Create a tabbed table.

8 Add color highlighting and underlines.

9 Create numbered and bulleted lists.

10 Create and use Building Blocks.

11 Insert and modify a shape.

12 Edit in Print Preview.

13 Print a document.

Case Study

Adventure Travel Tours

After creating the rough draft of the new tours flyer, you showed the printed copy to your manager at Adventure Travel Tours. Your manager then made several suggestions for improving the flyer's style and appearance. In addition, you created a letter to be sent to clients along with your flyer. The letter briefly describes Adventure Travel's four new tours and invites clients to attend an informational presentation. Your manager likes the idea, but also wants the letter to include information about the new Adventure Travel Tours Web site and a 10 percent discount for early booking.

In this lab, you will learn more about editing documents so you can reorganize and refine both your flyer and a rough draft of the letter to clients. You also will learn to use many more of the formatting features included in Office Word 2007 so you can add style and interest to your documents. Formatting features can greatly improve the appearance and design of any document you produce so that it communicates its message more clearly. The completed letter and revised flyer are shown here.

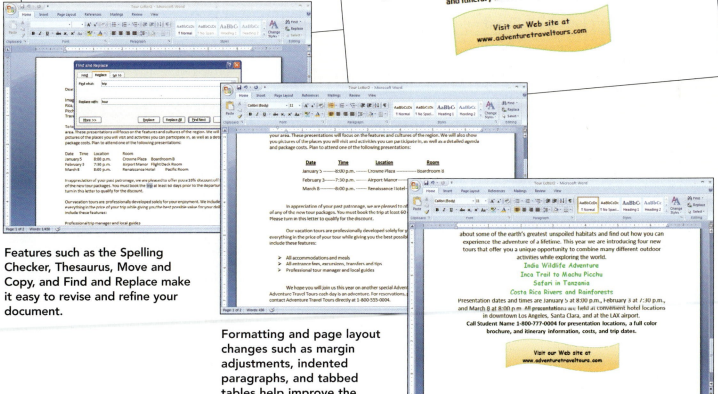

Features such as the Spelling Checker, Thesaurus, Move and Copy, and Find and Replace make it easy to revise and refine your document.

Formatting and page layout changes such as margin adjustments, indented paragraphs, and tabbed tables help improve the readability and style of the document.

Graphic enhancements such as shapes add interest to a document.

Concept Preview

Revising a Document

After speaking with the manager about the letter's content, you planned the basic topics that need to be included in the letter: to advertise the new tours, invite clients to the presentations, describe the early-booking discount, and promote the new Web site. You quickly entered the text for the letter, saved it as Tour Letter, and printed out a hard copy. As you are reading the document again, you mark up the printout with the changes and corrections you want to make. The marked-up copy is shown here.

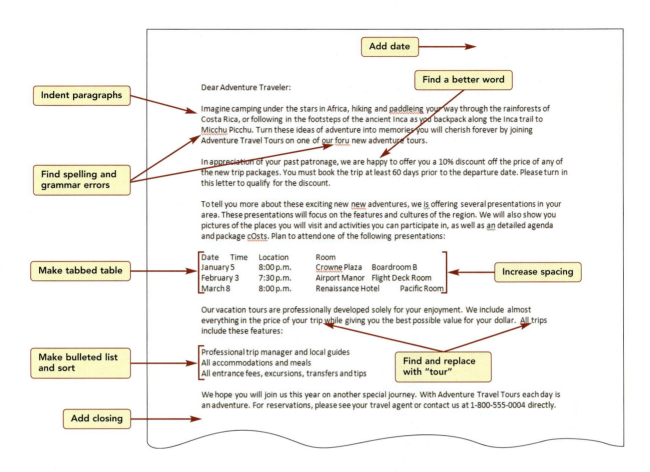

Add date

Find a better word

Indent paragraphs

Dear Adventure Traveler:

Imagine camping under the stars in Africa, hiking and paddleing your way through the rainforests of Costa Rica, or following in the footsteps of the ancient Inca as you backpack along the Inca trail to Micchu Picchu. Turn these ideas of adventure into memories you will cherish forever by joining Adventure Travel Tours on one of our foru new adventure tours.

Find spelling and grammar errors

In appreciation of your past patronage, we are happy to offer you a 10% discount off the price of any of the new trip packages. You must book the trip at least 60 days prior to the departure date. Please turn in this letter to qualify for the discount.

To tell you more about these exciting new new adventures, we is offering several presentations in your area. These presentations will focus on the features and cultures of the region. We will also show you pictures of the places you will visit and activities you can participate in, as well as an detailed agenda and package cOsts. Plan to attend one of the following presentations:

Make tabbed table

Increase spacing

Date   Time   Location   Room
January 5   8:00 p.m.   Crowne Plaza   Boardroom B
February 3   7:30 p.m.   Airport Manor   Flight Deck Room
March 8   8:00 p.m.   Renaissance Hotel   Pacific Room

Our vacation tours are professionally developed solely for your enjoyment. We include almost everything in the price of your trip while giving you the best possible value for your dollar. All trips include these features:

Make bulleted list and sort

Professional trip manager and local guides
All accommodations and meals
All entrance fees, excursions, transfers and tips

Find and replace with "tour"

We hope you will join us this year on another special journey. With Adventure Travel Tours each day is an adventure. For reservations, please see your travel agent or contact us at 1-800-555-0004 directly.

Add closing

Spell-Checking the Entire Document

The first correction you want to make is to clean up the spelling and grammar errors that Word has identified.

1 • **Start Office Word 2007 and open the file** wd02_Tour Letter.

• **If necessary, change to Print Layout view at 100% zoom.**

Your screen should be similar to Figure 2.1

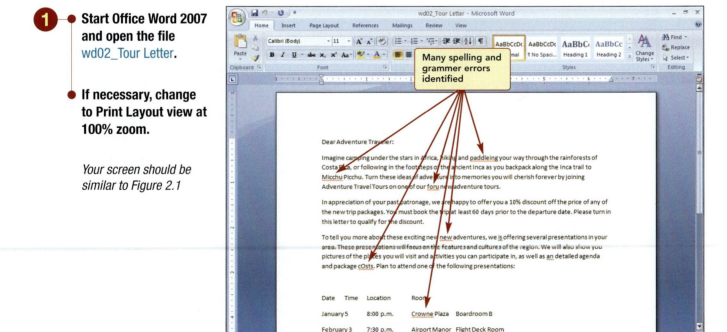

Many spelling and grammer errors identified

Figure 2.1

To correct the misspelled words and grammatical errors, you can use the context menu to correct each individual word or error, as you learned in Lab 1. However, in many cases, you may find it more efficient to wait until you are finished writing before you correct errors. Rather than continually breaking your train of thought to correct errors as you type, you can manually turn on the spelling and grammar checker to locate and correct all the errors in the document at once.

2 ● **Open the Review tab.**

● **Click** 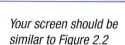 **.**

Another Method

The keyboard shortcut is F7.

● **If necessary, select the Check grammar option to turn on grammar checking.**

Additional Information

You also can click the Spelling and Grammar status icon 📖 to move to the next spelling or grammar error and open the spelling context menu.

Your screen should be similar to Figure 2.2

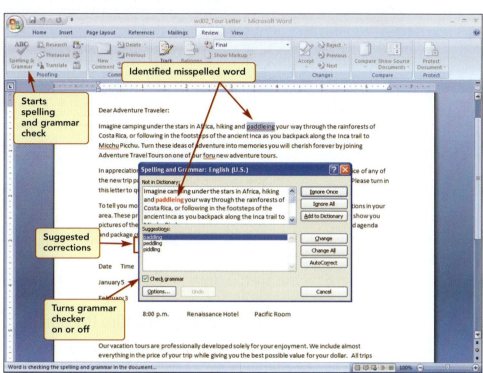

Figure 2.2

Additional Information

Because the contents of the list are determined only by spelling, any instances of terms that seem inappropriate in context are completely coincidental.

The Spelling and Grammar dialog box is displayed, and the spelling and grammar checker has immediately located the first word that may be misspelled, "paddleing." The sentence with the misspelled word in red is displayed in the Not in Dictionary text box, and the word is highlighted in the document.

The Suggestions list box displays the words the spelling checker has located in the dictionary that most closely match the misspelled word. The most likely match is highlighted. Sometimes the spelling checker does not display any suggested replacements. This occurs when it cannot locate any words in the dictionaries that are similar in spelling. If no suggestions are provided, the Not in Dictionary text box simply displays the word that is highlighted in the text.

Additional Information

The [Change All] option replaces the same word throughout the document with the word you select in the Suggestions box.

To change the spelling of the word to one of the suggested spellings, highlight the correct word in the list and then click [Change]. If there were no suggested replacements, and you did not want to use any of the option buttons, you could edit the word yourself by typing the correction in the Not in Dictionary box. In this case, the correct replacement, "paddling," is already highlighted.

3 ● Click [Change].

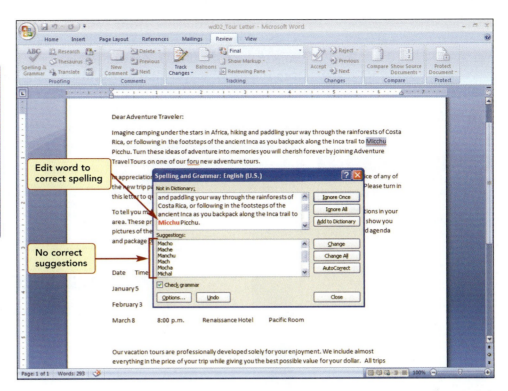

Additional Information

On your own computer system, you would want to add words to the custom dictionary that you use frequently and that are not included in the standard dictionary so they will be accepted when typed correctly and offered as a suggested replacement when not typed correctly.

Your screen should be similar to Figure 2.3

Figure 2.3

The spelling checker replaces the misspelled word with the selected suggested replacement and moves on to locate the next error. This time the error is the name of the Inca ruins at Machu Picchu. "Micchu" is the incorrect spelling for this word; there is no correct suggestion, however, because the word is not found in the dictionary. You will correct the spelling of the word by editing it in the Not in Dictionary text box.

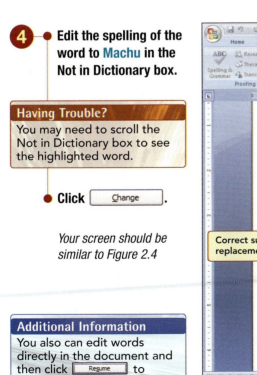

4 ● Edit the spelling of the word to **Machu** in the **Not in Dictionary box.**

Having Trouble?

You may need to scroll the Not in Dictionary box to see the highlighted word.

● Click [Change].

Your screen should be similar to Figure 2.4

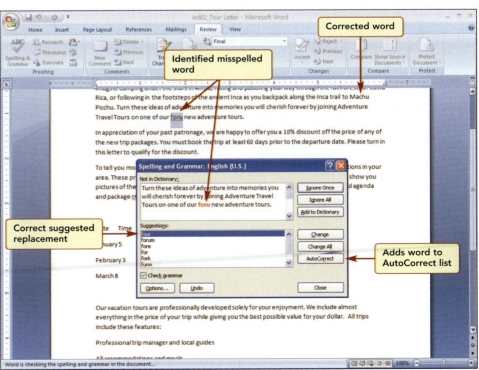

Additional Information

You also can edit words directly in the document and then click [Resume] to continue using the Spelling and Grammar Checker.

Figure 2.4

The next located error, "foru," is a typing error that you make frequently when typing the word four. The correct spelling is selected in the Suggestions list box. You want to change it to the suggested word and add it to the list of words that are automatically corrected.

5 • **Click** [AutoCorrect] .

Having Trouble?

If a dialog box appears telling you an AutoCorrect entry already exists for this word, simply click [Yes] to continue.

Your screen should be similar to Figure 2.5

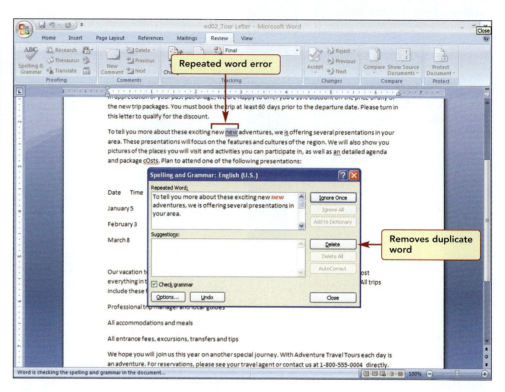

Figure 2.5

The word is corrected in the document. Because you also added it to the AutoCorrect list, in the future whenever you type this word incorrectly as "foru," it will automatically be changed to "four." The next five errors that will be identified and their causes are shown in the following table

Identified Error	Cause	Action	Result
new	Repeated word	Delete	duplicate word "new" is deleted
we is	Subject-verb disagreement	Change	we are
cOsts	Inconsistent capitalization	Change	costs
an detailed	Grammatical error	Change	a
Crowne	Spelling error	Ignore Once	accepts the word as correct for this occurrence only

6 • Respond to the spelling and grammar checker by taking the actions in the table above for the five identified errors.

• Click [OK] in response to the message telling you that the spelling and grammar check is complete.

• Move to the top of the document.

Your screen should be similar to Figure 2.6

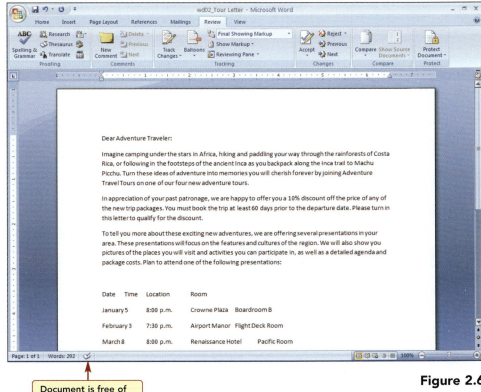

Document is free of spelling and grammar errors

Figure 2.6

Using the Thesaurus

The next text change you want to make is to find a more descriptive word for "ideas" in the first paragraph and "happy" in the second paragraph. To help find a similar word, you will use the thesaurus tool.

Concept 1

Thesaurus

1   Word's **thesaurus** is a reference tool that provides synonyms, antonyms, and related words for a selected word or phrase. **Synonyms** are words with a similar meaning, such as "cheerful" and "happy." **Antonyms** are words with an opposite meaning, such as "cheerful" and "sad." Related words are words that are variations of the same word, such as "cheerful" and "cheer." The thesaurus can help to liven up your documents by adding interest and variety to your text.

First you need to identify the word you want looked up by moving the insertion point onto the word. Then you use the thesaurus to suggest alternative words. The quickest way to get synonyms is to use the context menu for the word you want to replace.

1 • **Right-click on the word "ideas" (first paragraph, second sentence) to display the context menu.**

• **Select Synonyms on the Context menu.**

Having Trouble?
Simply point to the menu option to select it.

Additional Information
Whenever you right-click an item, both the context menu and Mini toolbar are displayed.

Your screen should be similar to Figure 2.7

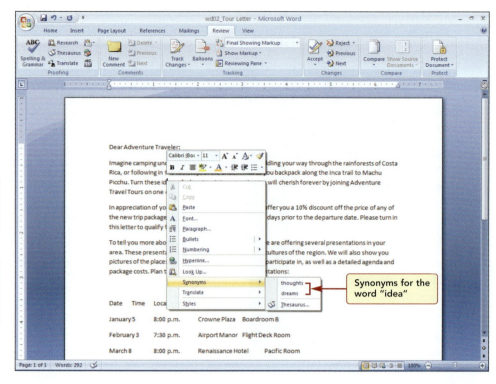

Figure 2.7

The Synonyms submenu lists two words with similar meanings. You decide to replace "ideas" with "dreams." Then you will look for a synonym for "happy." You will use the Research pane to locate synonyms this time.

2 • **Choose "dreams".**

• **Click on the word "happy" (first sentence, second paragraph).**

• **Click**  **Thesaurus in the Proofing group.**

Another Method
The keyboard equivalent is ⇧Shift + F7.

Your screen should be similar to Figure 2.8

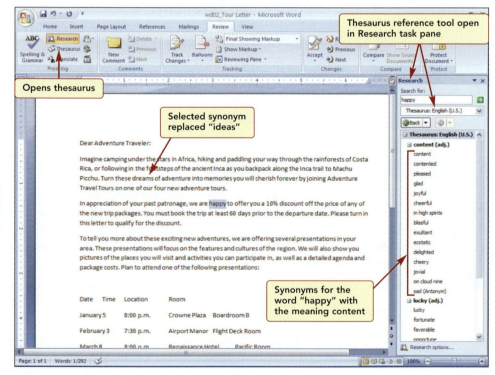

Figure 2.8

The thesaurus opens in the Research task pane and the word the insertion point is on is displayed in the Search For text box. The list box displays words that have similar meanings for the word "happy" with a meaning of "content (adj)." The best choice from this list is "pleased." To see whether any other words are closer in meaning, you will look up synonyms for the word "pleased."

3 ● **Choose "pleased".**

Additional Information
You also can choose Look Up from the word's drop-down menu to look up synonyms for the word.

Your screen should be similar to Figure 2.9

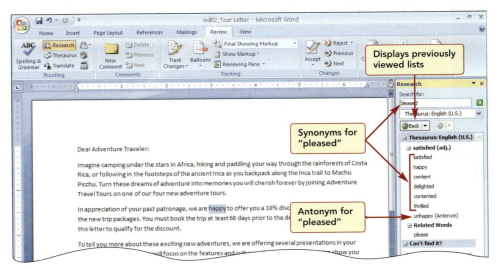

Figure 2.9

The word "pleased" is the new search term, and the list displays synonyms, as well as an antonym, for this word. You decide to use "pleased" and will return to the previous list and insert the word into the document.

4 ● **Click 🔙Back ▼ to display the list for the word "happy."**

● **Open the "pleased" synonym drop-down menu.**

● **Choose Insert.**

● **Close the Research task pane.**

● **Move to the top of the document and save the revised document as Tour Letter2 to the appropriate data file location.**

Your screen should be similar to Figure 2.10

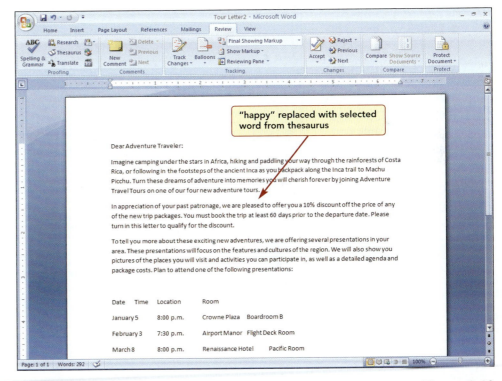

Figure 2.10

The word "happy" is replaced with the selected word from the thesaurus.

Moving and Copying Selections

After looking over the letter, you decide to add the company name in several other locations and to change the order of paragraphs. To make these changes quickly, you can move and copy selections.

Concept 2

Move and Copy

2 Text and graphic selections can be moved or copied to new locations in a document or between documents, saving you time by not having to recreate the same information. A selection that is moved is cut from its original location, called the **source**, and inserted at a new location, called the **destination**. A selection that is copied leaves the original in the source and inserts a duplicate at the destination.

When a selection is cut or copied, the selection is stored in the **system Clipboard**, a temporary Windows storage area in memory. It is also stored in the **Office Clipboard**. The system Clipboard holds only the last cut or copied item, whereas the Office Clipboard can store up to 24 items that have been cut or copied. This feature allows you to insert multiple items from various Office documents and paste all or part of the collection of items into another document.

Using Copy and Paste

You want to include the company name in the last paragraph of the letter in two places. Because the name has already been entered in the first paragraph, you will copy it instead of typing the name again.

1 • Select "Adventure Travel Tours" (first paragraph, last sentence).

• Click 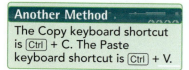 Copy in the Clipboard group of the Home tab.

• Move to the beginning of the word "journey" (last paragraph, first sentence).

• Click [Paste] in the Clipboard group.

Another Method

The Copy keyboard shortcut is [Ctrl] + C. The Paste keyboard shortcut is [Ctrl] + V.

Your screen should be similar to Figure 2.11

Additional Information

Using the [Paste] button or keyboard shortcut inserts the system Clipboard contents, not the Office Clipboard contents. You will learn about using the Office Clipboard in Lab 3.

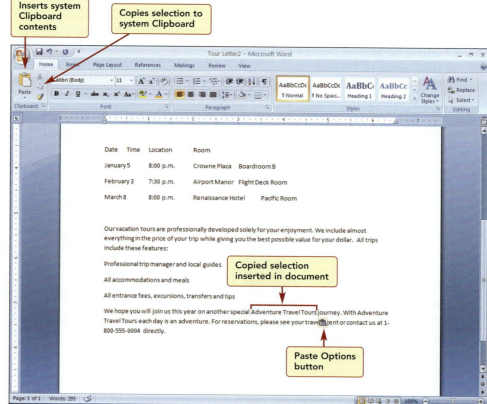

Figure 2.11

The copied selection is inserted at the location you specified. The Paste Options button appears automatically whenever a selection is pasted. It is used to control the format of the pasted item.

2 ● **Click the** 📋 **Paste Options button.**

Your screen should be similar to Figure 2.12

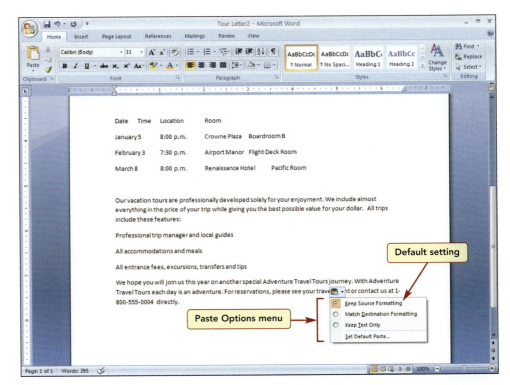

Figure 2.12

The Paste options are used to specify whether to insert the item with the same formatting that it had in the source, to change it to the formatting of the surrounding destination text, or to insert text only (from a selection that is a combination of text and graphics). The default, to keep the formatting from the source, is appropriate. The last option is used to change the default paste formatting setting to another.

Next, you want to insert the company name in place of the word "us" in the last sentence of the letter.

3 ● **Click outside the menu to close it.**

● **Select "us" (last sentence).**

● **Right-click on the selection and choose Paste from the context menu.**

Your screen should be similar to Figure 2.13

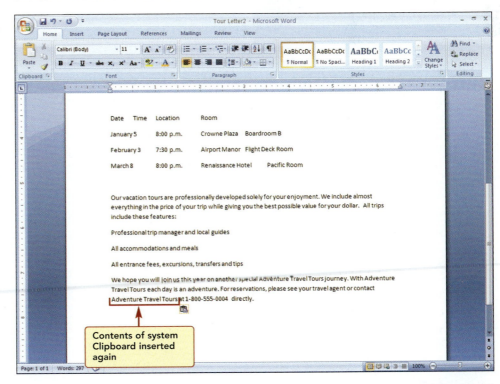

Figure 2.13

The selected text was deleted and replaced with the contents of the system Clipboard. The system Clipboard contents remain in the Clipboard until another item is copied or cut, allowing you to paste the same item multiple times.

Using Cut and Paste

You want the paragraph about the 10 percent discount (second paragraph) to follow the list of presentation dates. To do this, you will move the paragraph from its current location to the new location. The Cut and Paste commands in the Clipboard group of the Home tab are used to move selections. You will use the context menu to select the Cut command.

1 ● Select the second paragraph.

Having Trouble?
Double-click in the margin space to the left of the paragraph to select it.

● Click ✄ Cut in the Clipboard group.

Another Method •
The Cut keyboard shortcut is Ctrl + X. You also can choose Cut from the context menu.

Your screen should be similar to Figure 2.14

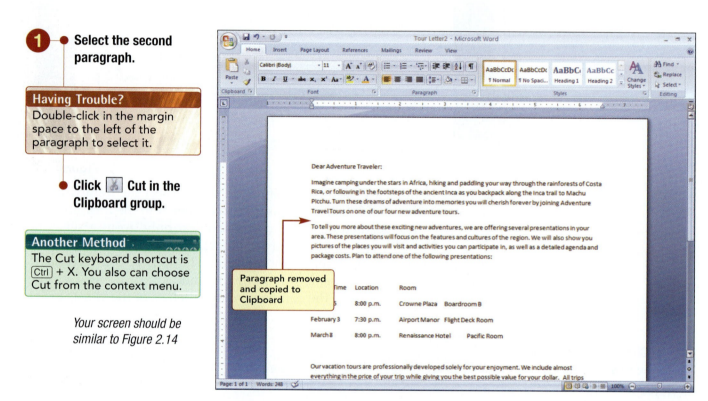

Paragraph removed and copied to Clipboard

Figure 2.14

The selected paragraph is removed from the source and copied to the Clipboard. Next, you need to move the insertion point to the location where the text will be inserted and paste the text into the document from the Clipboard.

2 ● Move to the beginning of the paragraph below the list of presentation dates.

● Press [Ctrl] + V.

● If necessary, scroll down to view the pasted paragraph.

Your screen should be similar to Figure 2.15

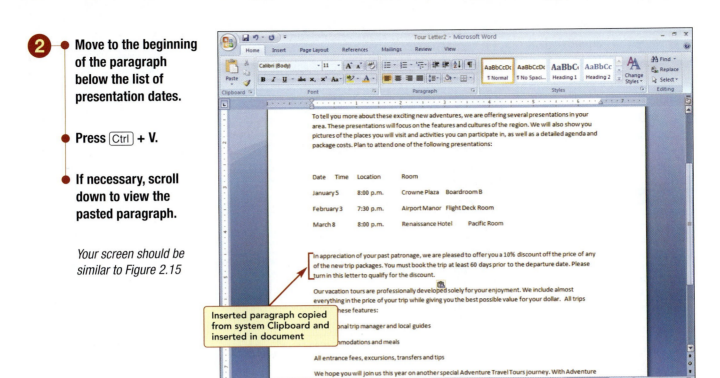

Inserted paragraph copied from system Clipboard and inserted in document

Figure 2.15

The cut paragraph is reentered into the document at the insertion point location. That was much quicker than retyping the whole paragraph!

Using Drag and Drop

Finally, you also decide to move the word "directly" in the last paragraph so that the sentence reads " . . . contact Adventure Travel Tours directly at 1-800-555-0004." Rather than use Cut and Paste to move this text, you will use the **drag-and-drop** editing feature. This feature is most useful for copying or moving short distances in a document.

To use drag and drop to move a selection, point to the selection and drag it to the location where you want the selection inserted. The mouse pointer appears as ⬚ as you drag, and a temporary insertion point shows you where the text will be placed when you release the mouse button.

Additional Information
You also can use drag and drop to copy a selection by holding down [Ctrl] while dragging. The mouse pointer shape is ⬚.

1 ● Select "directly" (last word in last paragraph).

● Drag the selection to before "at" in the same sentence.

Additional Information

You also can move or copy a selection by holding down the right mouse button while dragging.
    When you release the mouse button, a context menu appears with the available move and copy options.

Your screen should be similar to Figure 2.16

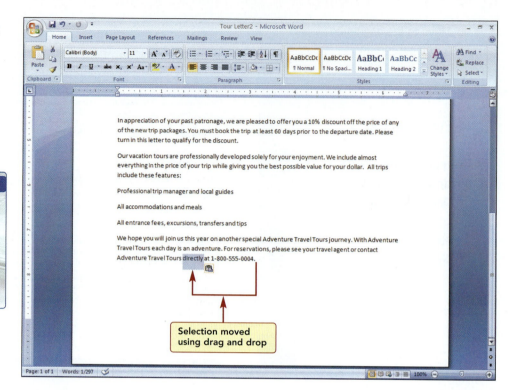

Figure 2.16

The selection is moved to the new location.

Copying between Documents

You plan to include the flyer with the letter to be mailed to clients. To do this, you will open the flyer document and copy it into the letter document file. Because all Office 2007 applications allow you to open and use multiple files at the same time, this is a very simple procedure.

1 ● Move to the top of the document.

● Click  Save.

● Open the wd02_Flyer2 document.

Additional Information

Sometimes you may want to open several files at once. To do this, you can select multiple files from the Open dialog box by holding down [Ctrl] while clicking on each file name. If the files are adjacent, you can click the first file name, hold down [⇧ Shift], and click on the name of the last file.

Your screen should be similar to Figure 2.17

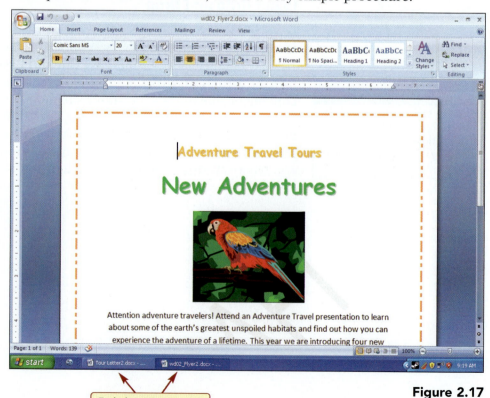

Figure 2.17

Lab 2: Revising and Refining a Document

www.mhhe.com/oleary

Additional Information

You also can switch quickly from one window to the other using ⊞ in the Window group or by clicking the button for each open document window in the taskbar.

The flyer document is opened and displayed in a separate Word 2007 application window. You made a few changes to the flyer that your supervisor suggested. You would like to see both documents in the window at the same time. This makes it easy to compare documents or to move or copy information between documents.

2 ● Open the View tab.

● Click ⊞ View Side by Side in the Window group.

Having Trouble?

Do not be concerned if your windows are reversed.

● Reduce the Zoom to 75%.

● Scroll to the bottom of the wd02_Flyer2 window and replace Student Name with your name.

Your screen should be similar to Figure 2.18

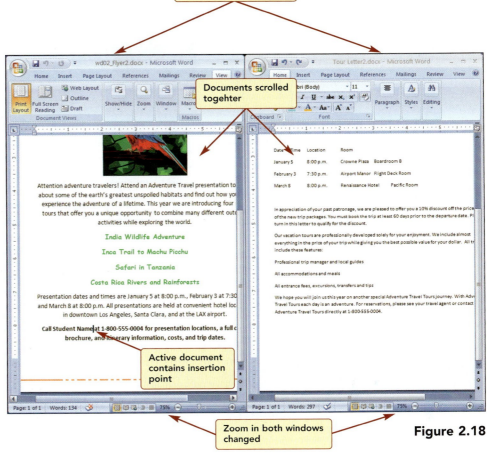

Figure 2.18

Additional Information

Using ⊞ Arrange All arranges all open windows horizontally on the screen.

Now, the two Word application windows are arranged side by side on the screen. The flyer contains the insertion point, which indicates that it is the **active window**, or the window in which you can work. Simply clicking on the other document makes it active. Because the windows are side by side and there is less horizontal space in each window, the Ribbon groups are compressed. To access commands in these groups, simply click on the group button and the group commands appear.

Did you notice when you scrolled the document that both documents scrolled together? This is because the windows are **synchronized**, meaning both windows will act the same. When synchronized, the documents in both windows will scroll together so you can compare text easily. If you are not comparing text, this feature can be turned off so that they scroll independently.

3 • Click [Window] to display the Window group commands.

• Click **Synchronous Scrolling** to turn off this feature.

• Scroll to the top of the wd02_Flyer2 document.

Your screen should be similar to Figure 2.19

Click to open group

Maximize window

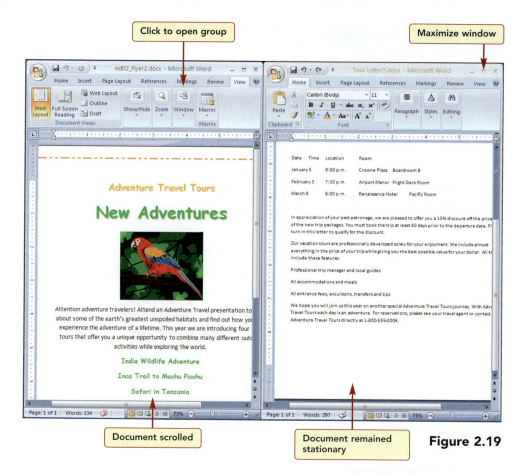

Document scrolled

Document remained stationary

Figure 2.19

The flyer document scrolled while the letter document remained stationary. Next you will copy the entire flyer to the bottom of the letter document using drag and drop. To copy between documents using drag and drop, hold down the right mouse button while dragging. When you release the button, a context menu appears where you specify the action you want to perform. If you drag using the left mouse button, the selection is moved by default.

4 ● Click in the Tour Letter2 window to make it active and press Ctrl + End to move to the last (blank) line of the document.

● Click in the Flyer2 window to make it active and drag in the left margin to select the entire flyer.

● Right-drag the selection to the blank line at the end of the letter.

● Release the mouse button and choose Copy Here from the context menu.

● Click ☐ Maximize in the Tour Letter2 title bar to maximize the application window.

● Scroll the window to see the bottom of page one and the top of page two.

Your screen should be similar to Figure 2.20

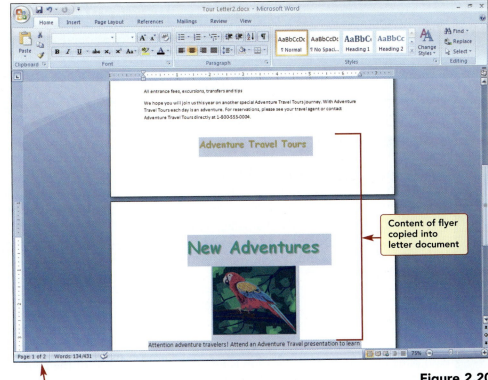

Content of flyer copied into letter document

Document consists of two pages

Figure 2.20

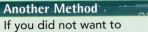

Another Method

If you did not want to arrange windows, you could just copy the selection in the active window, click on the taskbar button of the other open window to make it active, and then paste the selection in the document.

The letter now consists of two pages. Notice the status bar shows the insertion point location is on page 1 of 2 pages.

Controlling Document Paging

As text and graphics are added to a document, Word automatically starts a new page when text extends beyond the bottom margin setting. The beginning of a new page is identified by a page break.

Concept 3

Page Break

3 A **page break** marks the point at which one page ends and another begins. Two types of page breaks can be used in a document: soft page breaks and hard page breaks. As you fill a page with text or graphics, Word inserts a **soft page break** automatically when the bottom margin is reached and starts a new page. As you add or remove text from a page, Word automatically readjusts the placement of the soft page break.

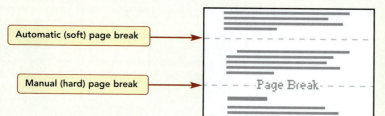

Many times, however, you may want to force a page break to occur at a specific location. To do this you can manually insert a **hard page break**. This action instructs Word to begin a new page regardless of the amount of text on the previous page. When a hard page break is used, its location is never moved regardless of the changes that are made to the amount of text on the preceding page. All soft page breaks that precede or follow a hard page break continue to adjust automatically. Sometimes you may find that you have to remove the hard page break and reenter it at another location as you edit the document.

In Print Layout view, the page break is identified by a space between pages. However you cannot tell if it is a hard or soft page break. You will switch back to Draft view to see the soft page break that was entered in the document. Also notice that images are not shown in Draft view.

1 • **Click in the document to deselect the flyer text.**

• **Switch to Draft view at 100% zoom.**

• **If necessary, scroll the document to see the soft page break line.**

Your screen should be similar to Figure 2.21

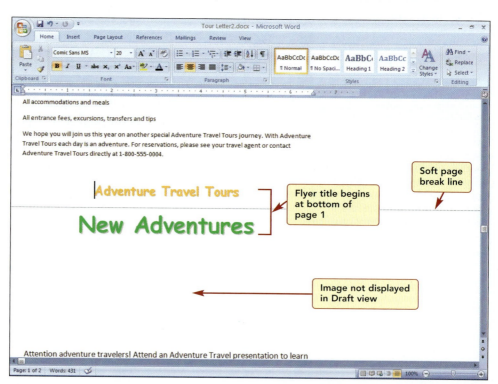

Figure 2.21

To show where one page ends and another begins, Word displays a dotted line across the page to mark the soft page break.

Inserting a Hard Page Break

Many times, the location of the soft page break is not appropriate. In this case, the location of the soft page break displays the flyer title on the bottom of page 1 and the remaining portion of the flyer on page 2. Because you want the entire flyer to print on a page by itself, you will manually insert a hard page break above the flyer title.

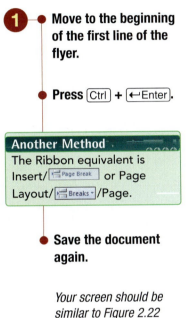

1 ● **Move to the beginning of the first line of the flyer.**

● **Press** Ctrl + ← Enter.

Another Method
The Ribbon equivalent is Insert/ Page Break or Page Layout/ Breaks /Page.

● **Save the document again.**

Your screen should be similar to Figure 2.22

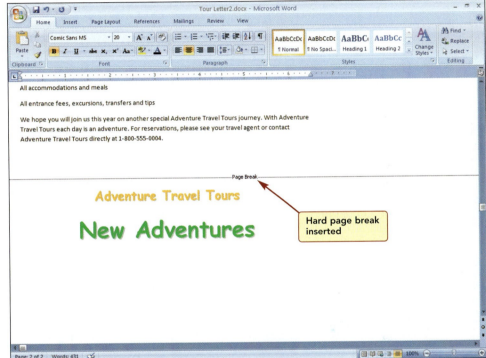

Figure 2.22

Additional Information
To remove a hard page break, simply select the hard page break line and press Delete.

A dotted line and the words "Page Break" appear across the page above the flyer title, indicating that a hard page break was entered at that position.

Finding and Replacing Text

As you continue proofing the letter, you notice that the word "trip" is used frequently. You think that the letter would read better if the word "tour" was used in place of "trip" in some instances. To do this, you will use the Find and Replace feature.

Concept 4

Find and Replace

4 To make editing easier, you can use the Find and Replace feature to find text in a document and replace it with other text as directed. For example, suppose you created a lengthy document describing the type of clothing and equipment needed to set up a world-class home gym, and then you decided to change "sneakers" to "athletic shoes." Instead of deleting every occurrence of "sneakers" and typing "athletic shoes," you can use the Find and Replace feature to perform the task automatically.

You also can find and replace occurrences of special formatting, such as replacing bold text with italicized text, as well as find and replace formatting marks. Additionally, special characters and symbols, such as an arrow or copyright symbol, can be easily located or replaced. This feature is fast and accurate; however, use care when replacing so that you do not replace unintended matches.

Finding Text

First, you will use the Find command to locate all occurrences of the word "trip" in the document.

1 ● **Switch to Print Layout view at 100% zoom.**

● **Move the insertion point to the top of the document.**

> **Another Method**
> Reminder: Use Ctrl + Home to quickly move to the top of the document.

● **Click** 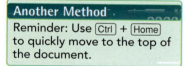 **in the Editing group.**

> **Another Method**
> The keyboard shortcut is Ctrl + F. You also can open the Find and Replace dialog box by clicking the  Select Browse Object button in the vertical scroll bar and selecting Find from the menu.

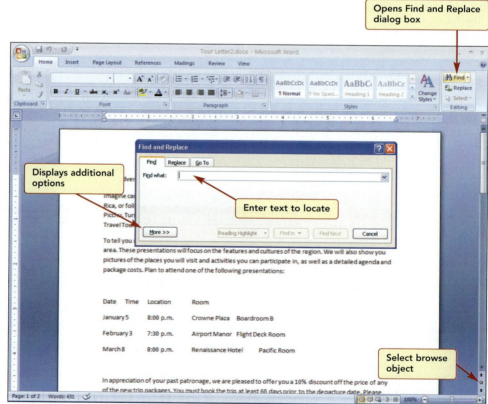

Your screen should be similar to Figure 2.23

Figure 2.23

The Find tab of the Find and Replace dialog box is used to define the information you want to locate. In the Find What text box, you enter the text you want to locate. In addition, you can use the search options to refine the search.

2 ● Click  .

Your screen should be similar to Figure 2.24

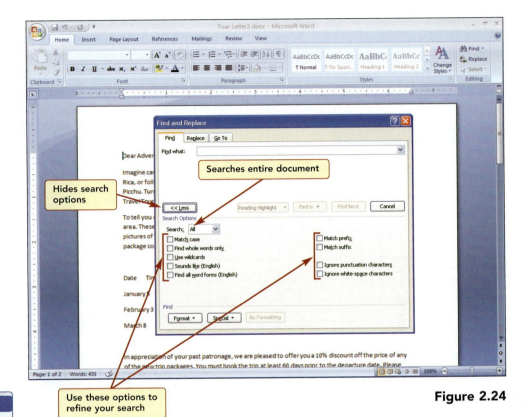

Figure 2.24

Additional Information

Clicking [Format ▾] is used to search for specific formatting such as bold. Clicking [Special ▾] is used to search for special characters and document elements.

The search options can be combined in many ways to help you find and replace text in documents. They are described in the table below.

Option	Effect on Text
Match case	Finds only those words in which the capitalization matches the text you typed.
Find whole words only	Finds matches that are whole words and not part of a larger word. For example, finds "cat" only and not "catastrophe" too.
Use wildcards	Fine-tunes a search; for example, c?t finds "cat" and "cot" (one-character matches), while c*t finds "cat" and "court" (searches for one or more characters).
Sounds like (English)	Finds words that sound like the word you type; very helpful if you do not know the correct spelling of the word you want to find.
Find all word forms (English)	Finds and replaces all forms of a word; for example, "buy" will replace "purchase," and "bought" will replace "purchased."

When you enter the text to find, you can type everything lowercase, because the Match Case option is not selected and the search will not be **case sensitive**. This means that lowercase letters will match both upper- and lowercase letters in the text. To further control the search, you can specify to match prefixes or suffixes. Because these are not selected, a letter or group of letters added at the beginning or end of a word to form another word will not affect the search. For example, the search will find "quick" or "quickly". Finally punctuation and white spaces will be ignored when searching the document unless these options are selected.

Also notice that the Search option default setting is All, which means Word will search the entire document, including headers and footers. You also can choose to search Up to the top of the document or Down to the end of the document from your current location in the document. These options search in the direction specified but exclude the headers, footers, footnotes, and comments from the area to search. Because you want to search the entire document, All is the appropriate setting. You will hide the search options again and begin the search.

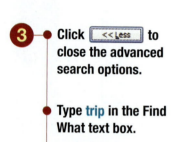

Additional Information

You will learn about headers, footers, footnotes, and comments in later labs.

3 ● Click [<< Less] to close the advanced search options.

● Type **trip** in the Find What text box.

● Click [Find Next].

Your screen should be similar to Figure 2.25

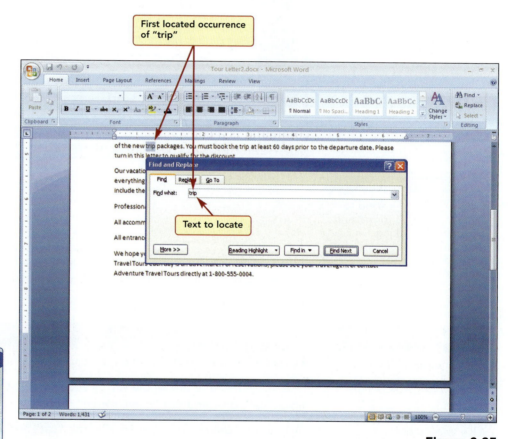

Figure 2.25

Additional Information

If you use the Up or Down options and the search does not begin at the top of the document, when Word reaches the beginning or end of the document, it asks if you want to continue searching from the end or beginning of the document. You also can highlight text to restrict the search to a selection.

Word searches for all occurrences of the text to find beginning at the insertion point, locates the first occurrence of the word "trip," and highlights it in the document.

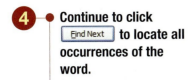

4 ● Continue to click Find Next to locate all occurrences of the word.

Additional Information
The Find and Replace dialog box automatically moves out of the way to show the located text.

● Click OK when Word indicates the entire document has been searched.

Your screen should be similar to Figure 2.26

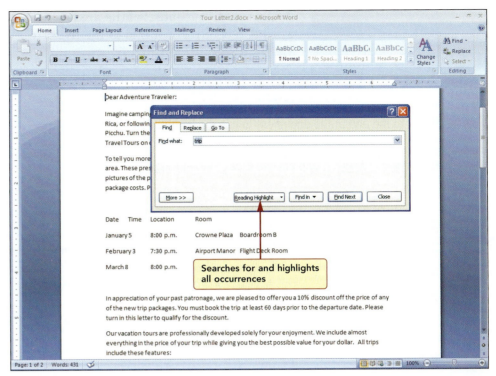

Searches for and highlights all occurrences

Figure 2.26

The word "trip" is used six times in the document. Using the Find command is a convenient way to quickly navigate through a document to locate and move to specified information.

To better see all located words, you will highlight them using the Reading Highlight feature.

5 ● Click Reading Highlight.

● Choose Highlight All.

● If necessary, scroll the document to view the first five highlighted words.

Your screen should be similar to Figure 2.27

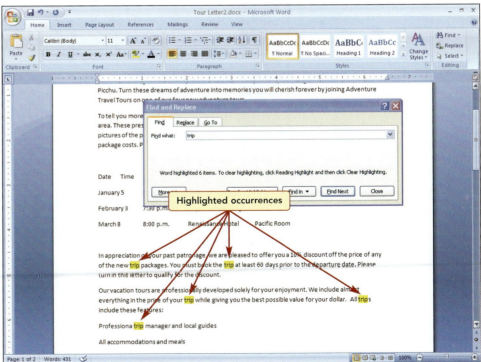

Word highlighted 6 items. To clear highlighting, click Reading Highlight and then click Clear Highlighting.

Highlighted occurrences

Figure 2.27

Additional Information

The highlight color is determined by the currently selected color in 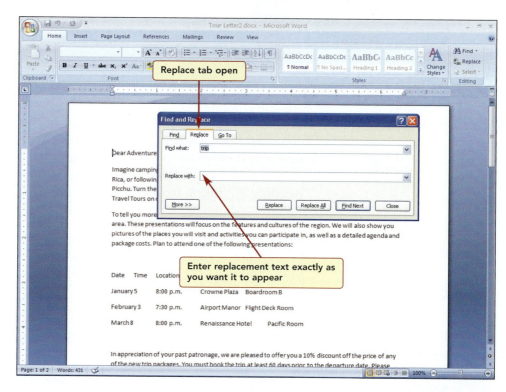 Text Highlight.

The first five located words are highlighted in yellow. The last use of the word trip is in the last line of the flyer. You will move to that location, and then you will turn off highlights.

6 ● Scroll to the end of the document to see the highlighted word.

● Click Reading Highlight ▾ and choose Clear Highlighting.

Replacing Text

You decide to replace several occurrences of the word "trip" in the letter with "tour" where appropriate. You will use the Replace feature to specify the text to enter as the replacement text.

1 ● Move to the top of the document.

● Open the Replace tab.

Your screen should be similar to Figure 2.28

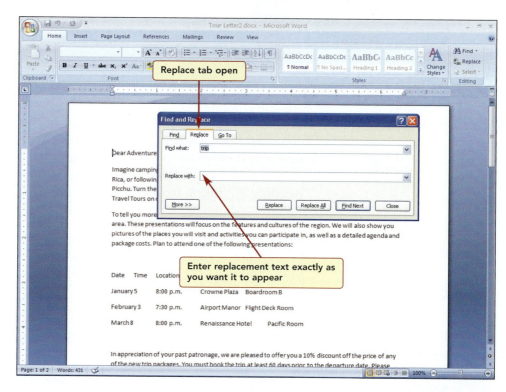

Figure 2.28

The Replace tab includes a Replace with text box in which you enter the replacement text. This text must be entered exactly as you want it to appear in your document. You want to find and replace the first occurrence of the word "trip" with "tour."

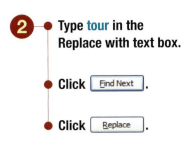

2 • Type **tour** in the Replace with text box.

• Click [Find Next].

• Click [Replace].

Your screen should be similar to Figure 2.29

First located word "trip" replaced by "tour"

Second located occurrence of word "trip"

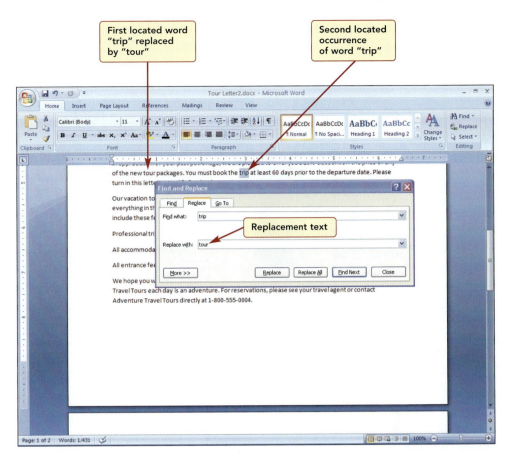

Replacement text

Figure 2.29

Word replaced the first located word with "tour" and has highlighted the second occurrence of the word "trip." You do not want to replace this occurrence of the word. You will continue the search without replacing the highlighted text.

3 ● Click [Find Next] to skip this occurrence and locate the next occurrence.

● Replace the next located occurrence.

● Continue to review the document, replacing all other occurrences of the word "trip" with "tour," except on the final line of the flyer.

● Click [Find Next].

● Click [OK] to close the information dialog box.

● Click [Close] to close the Find and Replace dialog box.

Your screen should be similar to Figure 2.30

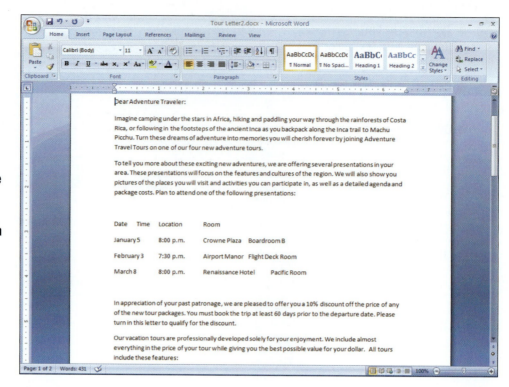

Figure 2.30

When using the Find and Replace feature, if you wanted to change all the occurrences of the located text, it is much faster to use [Replace All]. Exercise care when using this option, however, because the search text you specify might be part of another word and you may accidentally replace text you want to keep. If this happens, you could use Undo to reverse the action.

Inserting the Current Date

The last text change you need to make is to add the date to the letter. The Date and Time command on the Insert tab inserts the current date as maintained by your computer system into your document at the location of the insertion point. You want to enter the date on the first line of the letter, five lines above the salutation.

1 • If necessary, move to the "D" in "Dear" at the top of the letter.

• Press ←Enter 2 times to insert two blank lines.

• Move to the first blank line.

• Click ⑤ Date & Time in the Text group of the Insert tab.

Your screen should be similar to Figure 2.31

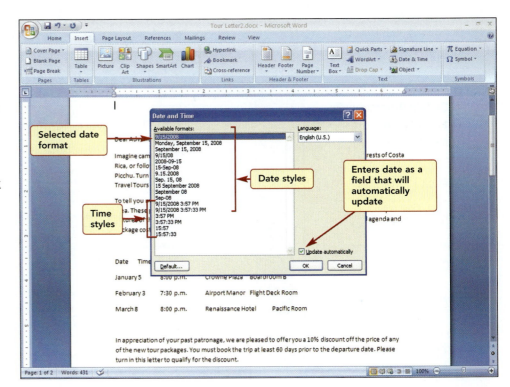

Selected date format

Date styles

Enters date as a field that will automatically update

Time styles

Figure 2.31

Additional Information

The current time also can be inserted into a document using the same procedure.

From the Date and Time dialog box, you select the style in which you want the date displayed in your document. The Available Formats list box displays the format styles for the current date and time. You want to display the date in the format Month XX, 2XXX, the third format setting in the list.

You also want the date to be updated automatically whenever the letter is opened or printed. You use the Update Automatically option to do this, which enters the date as a field.

Concept 5

Field

5 A **field** is a placeholder that instructs Word to insert information into a document. The **field code** contains the directions as to the type of information to insert or action to perform. Field codes appear between curly brackets {}, also called braces. The information that is displayed as a result of the field code is called the **field result**. Many field codes are automatically inserted when you use certain commands; others you can create and insert yourself. Many fields update automatically when the document changes. Using fields makes it easier and faster to perform many common or repetitive tasks.

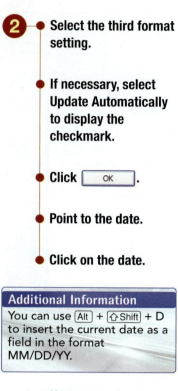

2 Select the third format setting.

● If necessary, select **Update Automatically** to display the checkmark.

● Click [OK].

● Point to the date.

● Click on the date.

Additional Information

You can use [Alt] + [⇧ Shift] + D to insert the current date as a field in the format MM/DD/YY.

Your screen should be similar to Figure 2.32

Having Trouble?

The date on your screen will reflect the current date on your system. If your date is not shaded, this is because the setting for this feature is off in your program.

Additional Information

To show or remove field shading, choose 🅑 Office Button/[🅑 Word Options]/Advanced and then select Never, Always, or When Selected from the Field Shading box.

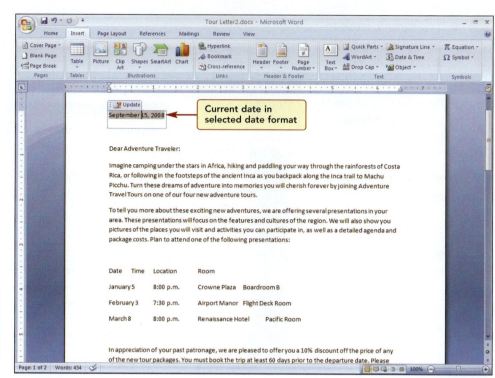

Figure 2.32

The current date is entered in the document in the format you selected. When you point to a field, the entire entry is shaded to identify the entry as a field. When the insertion point is positioned in a field entry, the entire entry is highlighted, indicating it is selected and can be modified.

The date is the field result. You will display the field code to see the underlying instructions.

3 • Right-click on the date and choose Toggle Field Codes from the context menu.

Another Method
The keyboard shortcut is
⇧Shift + F9 .

Your screen should be similar to Figure 2.33

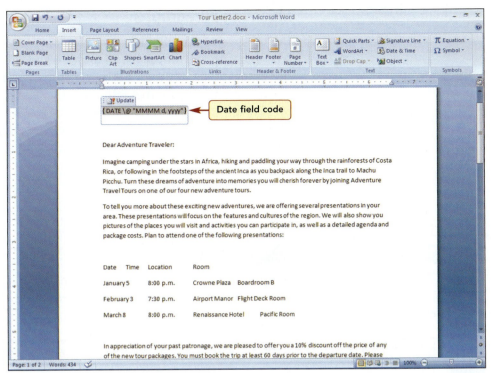

Date field code

Figure 2.33

Additional Information
You can press Alt + F9 to show or hide field codes for all fields in a document.

The field code includes the field name, DATE, followed by the field properties, in this case the date format instructions. Whenever this document is printed, Word will print the current system date using this format.

4 • Press ⇧Shift + F9 to display the field result again.

• Save the document.

Modifying Page Layout

Next the manager has suggested that you make several changes to improve the overall appearance of the letter and flyer. Two common page layout features are paragraph settings, such as indents and line spacing, and page margin settings. Other page layout features include page background colors, themes, and vertical alignment and orientation of text on a page.

Additional Information
You will be learning about these other page layout features in future labs.

To give the document more interest, you can indent paragraphs, use tabs to create tabular columns of data, and change the line spacing. These formatting features are all paragraph formats that affect the entire selected paragraph.

Indenting Paragraphs

Business letters typically use a block layout style or a modified block style with indented paragraphs. In a block style, all parts of the letter, including the date, inside address, all paragraphs in the body, and closing lines, are evenly aligned with the left margin. The block layout style has a very formal appearance. The modified block style, on the other hand, has a more casual appearance. In this style, certain elements such as the date, all paragraphs in the body, and the closing lines are indented from the left margin.

Concept 6
Indents

6 To help your reader find information quickly, you can **indent** paragraphs from the margins. Indenting paragraphs sets them off from the rest of the document. There are four types of indents, and their effects are described below.

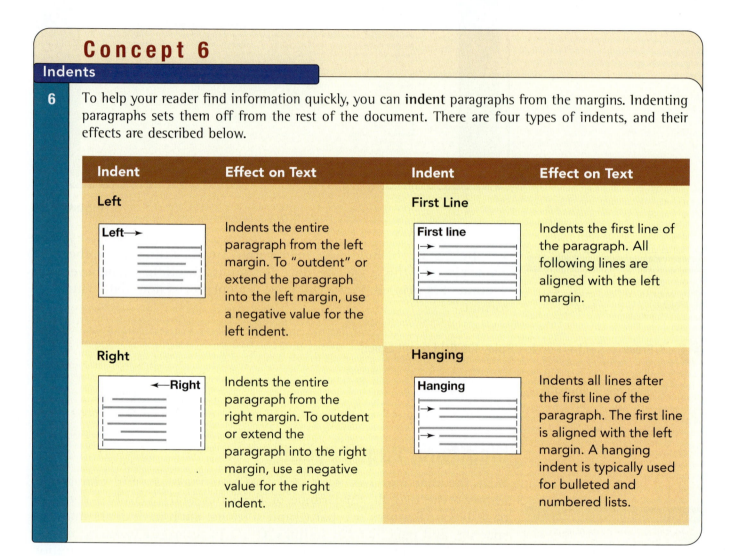

Indent	Effect on Text	Indent	Effect on Text
Left	Indents the entire paragraph from the left margin. To "outdent" or extend the paragraph into the left margin, use a negative value for the left indent.	**First Line**	Indents the first line of the paragraph. All following lines are aligned with the left margin.
Right	Indents the entire paragraph from the right margin. To outdent or extend the paragraph into the right margin, use a negative value for the right indent.	**Hanging**	Indents all lines after the first line of the paragraph. The first line is aligned with the left margin. A hanging indent is typically used for bulleted and numbered lists.

You want to change the letter style from the block paragraph style to the modified block style. You will begin by indenting the first line of the first paragraph. The quickest way to indent the first line of a paragraph is to press Tab⇆ when the insertion point is positioned at the beginning of the first line. Pressing Tab⇆ indents the first line of the paragraph to the first tab stop from the left margin. A tab stop is a marked location on the horizontal ruler that indicates how far to indent text each time the Tab⇆ key is pressed. The default tab stops are every 0.5 inch.

1 ● **Change the zoom to Page Width.**

Another Method

Click on the Zoom percentage in the status bar to open the Zoom dialog box.

● **Move to the beginning of the first paragraph.**

● **Press** Tab.

Another Method

You can also open the Indents and Spacing tab of the Paragraph dialog box and choose Special/First Line/By 0.5.

Your screen should be similar to Figure 2.34

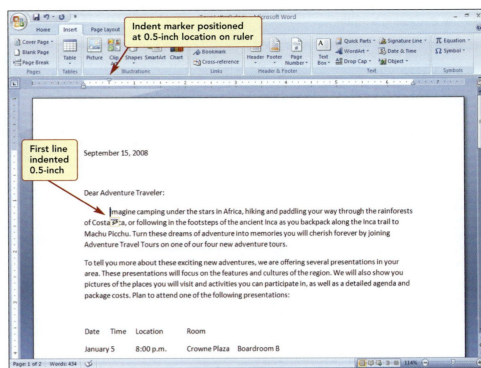

Figure 2.34

Additional Information

To indent an entire paragraph, click in front of any line except the first line and press Tab.

The first line of the paragraph indents a half inch from the left margin. The text in the paragraph wraps as needed, and the text on the following line begins at the left margin. Notice that the First Line Indent marker on the ruler moved to the 0.5-inch position. This marker controls the location of the first line of text in the paragraph.

If the insertion point was positioned anywhere else within the line of text, pressing Tab would move the text to the right of the insertion point to the next tab stop and the indent marker would not move.

You can indent the remaining paragraphs individually, or you can select the paragraphs and indent them simultaneously by dragging the upper indent marker on the ruler.

2 ● Beginning with the second paragraph, select the remaining text on page 1.

● Drag the First Line Indent marker on the ruler to the 0.5-inch position.

Additional Information

A ScreenTip identifies the First Line Indent marker when you point to it.

Your screen should be similar to Figure 2.35

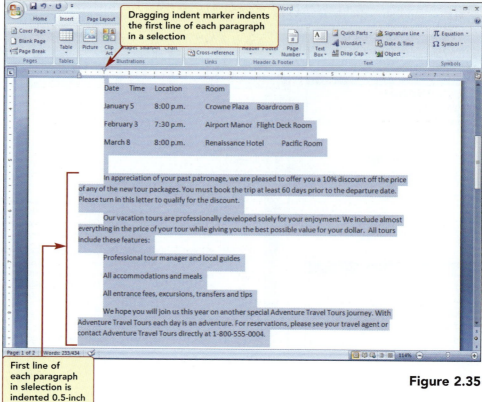

Figure 2.35

The first line of each paragraph in the selection is indented. Notice that each line of the presentation date and time information and the list of tour features also are indented. This is because Word considers each line a separate paragraph (each line ends with a paragraph mark.) You decide to further indent the date and time information to the 1-inch position.

3 ● Select the line of table headings and the three lines of data.

● Drag the First Line Indent marker on the ruler to the 1-inch position.

Having Trouble?

If the selection does not move to the 1-inch position, repeat dragging the First Line Indent marker to the 1-inch position.

Your screen should be similar to Figure 2.36

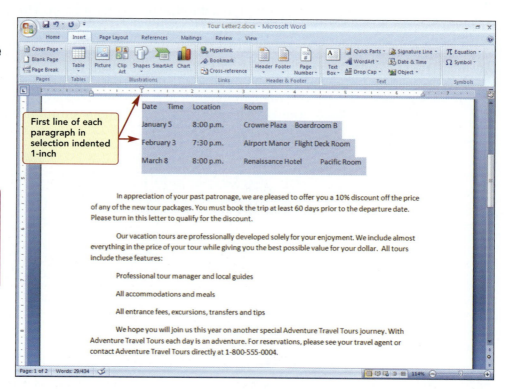

Figure 2.36

1

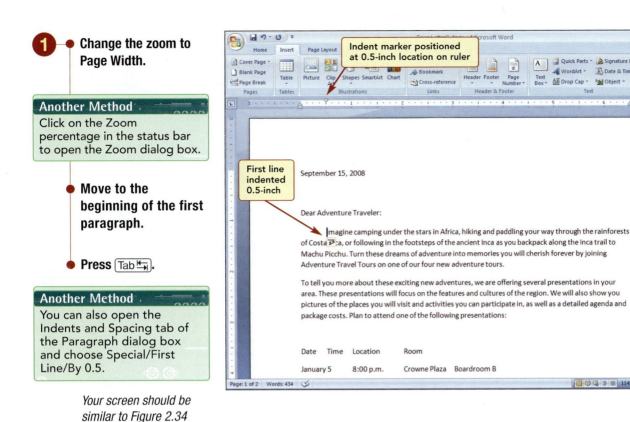

Setting Tab Stops

Additional Information

The default tab stops are visible on the ruler as light vertical lines below the numbers.

Next you want to improve the appearance of the list of presentation times and dates. The date and time information was entered using the [Tab ⇆] key to separate the different columns of information. However, because the default tab stops are set at every 0.5 inch, the columns are not properly aligned. You want to reformat this information to appear as a tabbed table of information so that it is easier to read, as shown below.

Date	Time	Location	Room
January 5 ----- 7:00 p.m -----------		Town Center Hotel -------	Room 284B
February 3 ---- 7:30 p.m ----------		Airport Manor -------------	Conference Room A
March 8 ------- 7:00 p.m ----------		Country Inn----------------	Mountainside Room

To improve the appearance of the information, you will set manual **tab stops** that will align the information in evenly spaced columns. You also can select from five different types of tab stops that control how characters are positioned or aligned with the tab stop. The following table explains the five tab types, the tab marks that appear in the tab alignment selector box (on the left end of the horizontal ruler), and the effects on the text.

To align the information, you will set three left tab stops at the 2-inch, 3-inch, and 4.5-inch positions. You can quickly specify manual tab stop locations and types using the ruler. To select a type of tab stop, click the tab alignment selector box to cycle through the types. Then, to specify where to place the selected tab stop type, click on the location in the ruler. As you specify the new tab stop settings, the table information will align to the new settings.

Tab Type	Tab Mark	Effects on Text	Example
Left	⌊	Extends text to right from tab stop	left
Center	⊥	Aligns text centered on tab stop	center
Right	⌋	Extends text to left from tab stop	right
Decimal	⊾	Aligns text with decimal point	35.78
Bar	⌶	Draws a vertical line through text at tab stop	

1

- If necessary, select the line of table headings and the three lines of information.

- If necessary, click the tab alignment selector box until the left tab icon 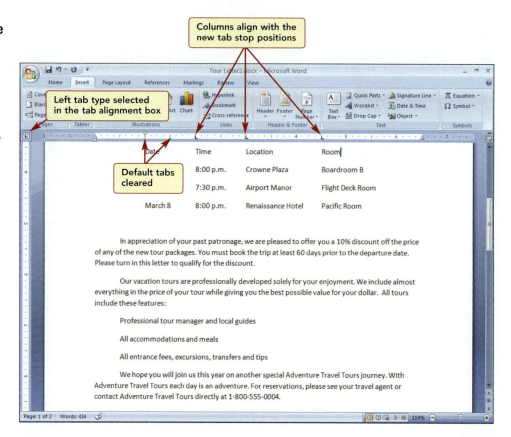 appears.

- Click on the 2-inch position on the ruler.

- Click on the 3-inch and the 4.5-inch positions on the ruler.

- Click anywhere in the table to deselect it.

Your screen should be similar to Figure 2.37

Figure 2.37

The three tabbed columns appropriately align with the new tab stops. All default tabs to the left of the manual tab stops are cleared. After looking at the columns, you decide the column headings would look better centered over the columns of information. To make this change, you will remove the three left tab stops for the heading line and then add three center tab stops.

Manual tab stops can be removed by dragging the tab stop up or down off the ruler. They also can be moved by dragging them left or right along the ruler. In addition the Tabs dialog box can be used to make these same changes. You will first drag a tab stop off the ruler to remove it and then you will use the Tabs dialog box to clear the remaining tab stops.

2 ● Move to anywhere in the table heading line.

● Drag the 2-inch tab stop mark off the ruler.

● Double-click any tab stop to open the Tabs dialog box.

● Click [Clear All] to remove the remaining two tab stops.

● Click [OK].

● Click the tab alignment selector box until the center tab icon appears.

● Set center tab stops at the 1.25-inch, 2.25-inch, 3.5-inch, and 5-inch positions.

Your screen should be similar to Figure 2.38

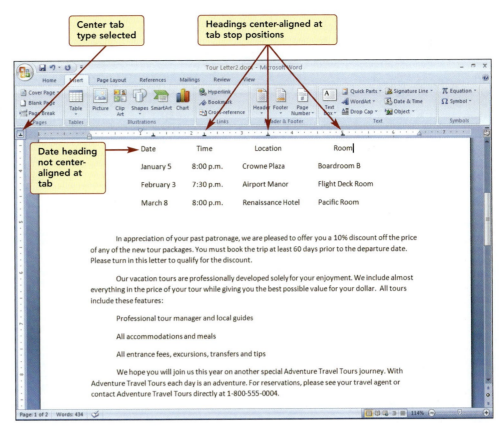

Figure 2.38

The Time, Location, and Room headings are appropriately centered on the tab stops. However, the Date heading still needs to be indented to the 1.25-inch tab stop position by pressing (Tab).

3 ● If necessary, move to the "D" in "Date."

● Press [Tab⇥].

Your screen should be similar to Figure 2.39

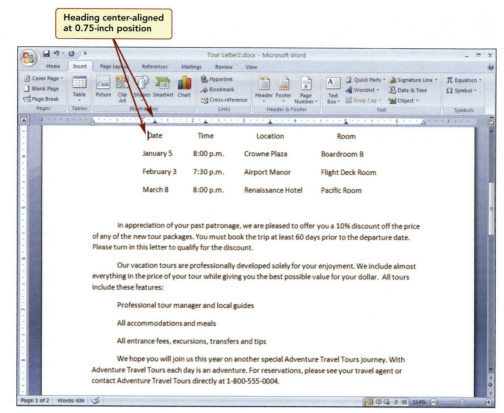

Figure 2.39

As you can see, setting different types of tab stops is helpful for aligning text or numeric information vertically in columns. Using tab stops ensures that the text will indent to the same set location. Setting manual tab stops instead of pressing [Tab⇥] or [Spacebar] repeatedly is a more professional way to format a document, as well as faster and more accurate. It also makes editing easier because you can change the tab stop settings for several paragraphs at once.

Adding Leader Characters

To make the presentation times and location information even easier to read, you will add leader characters before each of the tab stops. **Leader characters** are solid, dotted, or dashed lines that fill the blank space between tab stops. They help the reader's eye move across the blank space between the information aligned at the tab stops. To do this, you use the Tabs dialog box.

1 • Select the three lines of presentation information, excluding the heading line.

• Double-click any tab stop on the ruler.

Another Method

You could also open the Paragraph dialog box and choose [Tabs...].

Your screen should be similar to Figure 2.40

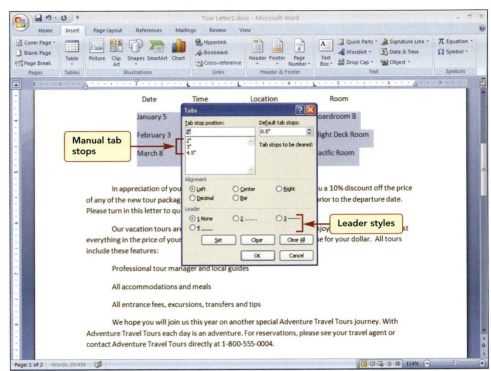

Figure 2.40

Additional Information

The Tabs dialog box can be used to set more precise tab stops than can be set using the ruler.

Notice that the Tabs dialog box displays the manual tabs you set on the ruler. You also can set tab stops using the Tabs dialog box by entering the tab positions in the text box and selecting the tab alignment. You also can clear an individual tab stop by selecting the tab stop position from the list and clicking [Clear].

The 2-inch tab stop appears in the Tab stop position text box, indicating it is the tab stop that will be affected by your actions. The Leader setting is None for the 2-inch tab stop. You can select from three styles of leader characters. You will use the third leader style, a series of dashed lines. The leader characters fill the empty space to the left of the tab stop. Each tab stop must have the leader style individually set.

2 • Select the  leader style.

• Click [Set].

• Select the 3-inch tab stop setting from the Tab Stop Position list box.

• Select .

• Click [Set].

• In a similar manner, set the tab leader for the 4.5-inch tab.

• Click [OK].

• Click in the table to deselect the text.

Your screen should be similar to Figure 2.41

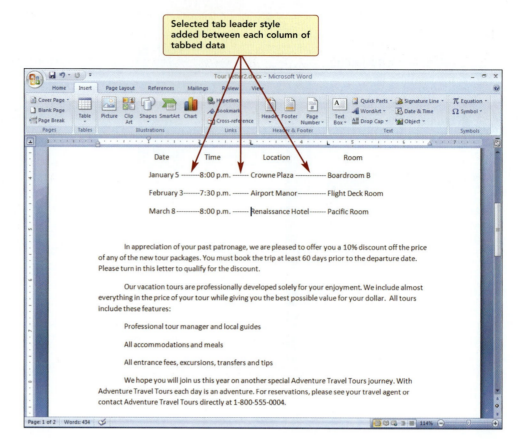

Figure 2.41

The selected leader style has been added to the blank space between each column of tabbed text.

Changing Line Spacing

You decide you want to adjust the spacing above and below the table as well as between the lines in the table to help make the table stand out from the other text in the letter.

Concept 7

7 Adjusting the **line spacing**, or the vertical space between lines of text, helps set off areas of text from others and when increased makes it easier to read and edit text. If a line contains a character or object, such as a graphic, that is larger than the surrounding text, the spacing for that line is automatically adjusted. Additional line spacing settings are described in the table below.

Spacing	Effect
Single	Accommodates the largest font in that line, plus a small amount of extra space; the amount of extra space varies with the font that is used.
1.5 lines	Spacing is one and a half times that of single line spacing.
Double (2.0)	Spacing is twice that of single line spacing.
At least	Uses a value specified in points as the minimum line spacing that is needed to fit the largest font or graphic on the line.
Exactly	Uses a value specified in points as a fixed line spacing amount that is not adjusted, making all lines evenly spaced. Graphics or text that is too large will appear clipped.
Multiple	Uses a percentage value to increase or decrease the spacing from single spacing. For example, 1.3 will increase the spacing by 33 percent.

The default line spacing for a Word 2007 document is set to multiple with a 15 percent increase (1.15) over single spacing.

In addition to changing line spacing within paragraphs, you also can change the spacing before or after paragraphs. The default paragraph spacing adds a small amount of space (10 pt) after a paragraph and no extra space before a paragraph.

The 📑 command in the Paragraph group of the Home tab can be used to specify standard spacing settings, such as double and triple spacing. It also lets you turn on or off the extra spacing between paragraphs. You want to look at the line spacing settings and make the adjustments from the Paragraph dialog box.

1 ● Select the table including the blank lines above and below it.

● Open the [icon] Line Spacing drop-down menu in the Paragraph group of the Home tab.

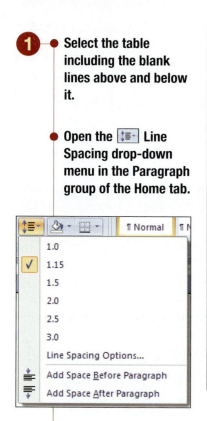

● Choose Line Spacing Options.

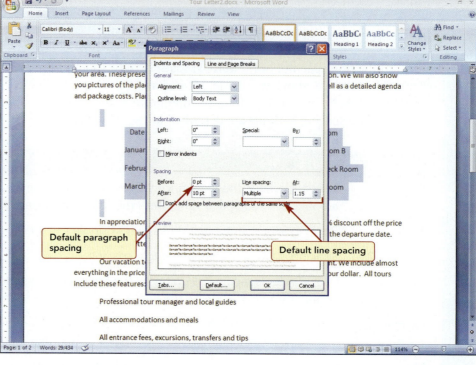

Figure 2.42

Another Method

You also could click [icon] in the Paragraph group to open the Paragraph dialog box to access this feature.

Another Method

You also can use [Ctrl] + # to change the line spacing to the number specified.

Your screen should be similar to Figure 2.42

The default document line spacing setting, multiple at 1.15, before paragraph spacing of 0 pt, and after paragraph spacing of 10 pt are displayed in the Spacing section of the dialog box. You want to decrease the spacing between each line of the table. Because Word considers each line of the table and the blank lines above and below it as separate paragraphs, you can decrease the space after paragraph setting to achieve this effect. You will also change the line spacing to single to remove the 15 percent spacing increase. As you make these changes, the Preview box will show you a sample of the effect they will have on the text.

2 • Select Single from the Line Spacing drop-down menu.

• Click the down scroll button of the After box to decrease the spacing to 6 pt.

• Click [OK].

Your screen should be similar to Figure 2.43

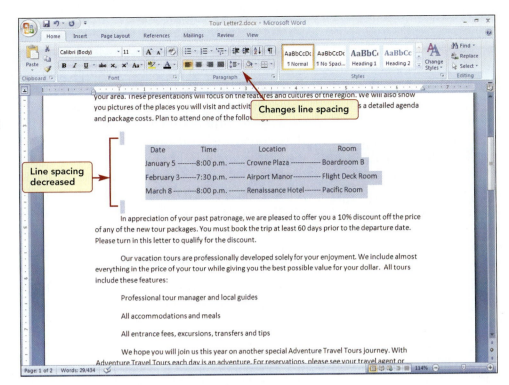

Figure 2.43

The change in line and paragraph spacing improves the appearance of the table and makes the information stand out more from the other text in the letter. You think this same change also would be effective in the list of tour features.

3 • Select the list of three tour features.

• Change the line spacing to Single.

• Select the first two items in the feature list and change the space after paragraph to 6 pt.

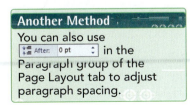

Another Method
You can also use ⬚ After: 0 pt in the Paragraph group of the Page Layout tab to adjust paragraph spacing.

Your screen should be similar to Figure 2.44

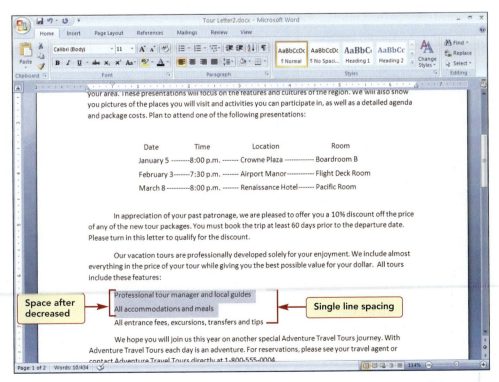

Figure 2.44

More Character Formatting

As you look at the letter, you still feel that the table of presentation dates and times does not stand out enough. You can add emphasis to information in your documents by formatting specific characters or words. Applying color shading or highlighting behind text is commonly used to identify areas of text that you want to stand out. It is frequently used to mark text that you want to locate easily as you are revising a document. Italics, underlines, and bold are other character formats that add emphasis and draw the reader's attention to important items. Word applies character formatting to the entire selection or to the entire word at the insertion point. You can apply formatting to a portion of a word by selecting the area to be formatted first.

Additional Information

When you use highlights in a document you plan to print in black and white, select a light color so the text is visible.

Adding Color Highlighting

First, you want to see how a color highlight behind the tabbed table of presentation times and locations would look.

1
- **Click anywhere in the table.**

- **Open the** 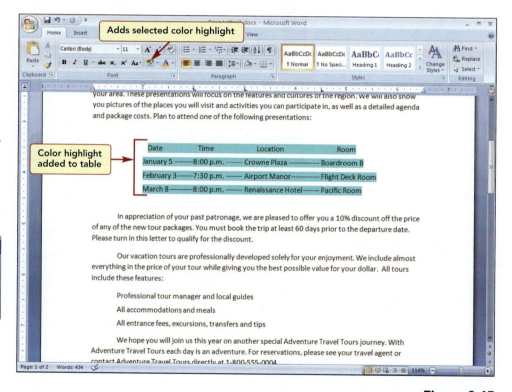 **Text Highlight Color drop-down list in the Font group of the Home tab.**

- **Select the turquoise color from the color palette.**

Additional Information

The mouse pointer appears as ⟋ when positioned on text, indicating the highlighting feature is on.

- **Select the entire presentation locations table.**

Another Method

You also can select the area you want to highlight first and then click ✏ to select and apply a color.

- **Click** ✏ **or press [Esc] to turn off the highlighting feature.**

Your screen should be similar to Figure 2.45

Figure 2.45

Although the highlight makes the table stand out, it does not look good.

Underlining Text

Instead, you decide to bold and underline the headings. The default underline style is a single black line. In addition, Word includes 15 other types of underlines.

1 • Click 🔄 **Undo.**

• **Select the table heading line.**

• Click **B** **Bold from the Mini toolbar.**

• Click **U** ▾ **Underline from the Font group.**

Your screen should be similar to Figure 2.46

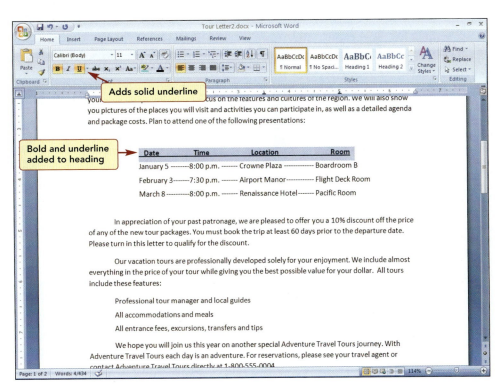

Figure 2.46

All the words are bold, and a single black underline has been added below the entire selection. You decide you want the underline to appear under each word only and to stand out more. To do this, you will select another underline style and apply the underline to the word individually. When the insertion point is positioned on a word, the selected underline style is applied to the entire word.

2 ● Click ⤺ Undo to remove the underline.

● Click on the "Room" heading in the table.

● Open the U · Underline drop-down menu.

● Point to the dotted underline style to see the Live Preview.

Your screen should be similar to Figure 2.47

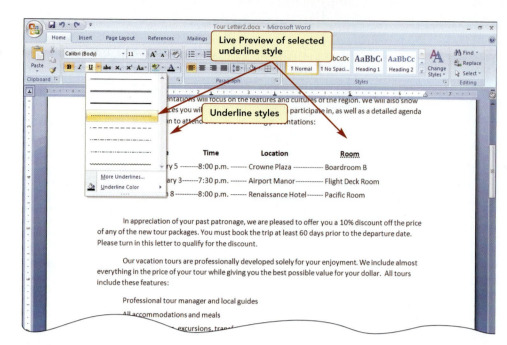

Figure 2.47

The eight most popular underline styles are listed in the menu. Using More Underlines will open the Font dialog box, where you can select other styles, clear underlining from a selection using the None option, or select the Words Only option to display a single underline below words in the selection only, not under the spaces between words. Live Preview shows you how the selection will appear in the document.

3 ● Select several other underline styles and see how they appear in the Live Preview.

● Click the double underline style.

Additional Information
Using the keyboard shortcut Ctrl + U adds the default single underline style.

Your screen should be similar to Figure 2.48

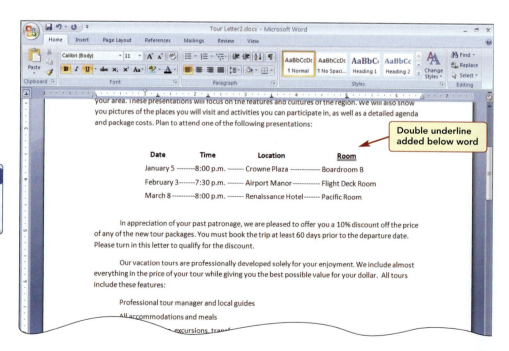

Figure 2.48

The selected word is underlined using the double underline style.

Copying Formats with Format Painter

You want to quickly apply the same formats to the other headings. To do this, you can use the **Format Painter**. This feature applies the formats associated with the current selection to new selections. If the selection is a paragraph (including the paragraph mark), the formatting is applied to the entire paragraph. If the selection is a character, the format is applied to a character, word, or selection you specify.

Additional Information

When Format Painter is on, the mouse pointer appears as ⬛I.

To use this feature, move the insertion point to the text whose formats you want to copy and click the ⬛ Format Painter button. Then select the text to which you want the formats applied. The format is automatically applied to an entire word simply by clicking on the word. To apply the format to more or less text, you must select the area.

1 ● If necessary, click on the "Room" heading.

● Double-click ⬛ Format Painter in the Clipboard group.

● Click on the Date, Time, and Location headings.

● Click ⬛ to turn off Format Painter.

Another Method

You can press [Esc] to turn off Format Painter.

● Save the document again.

Your screen should be similar to Figure 2.49

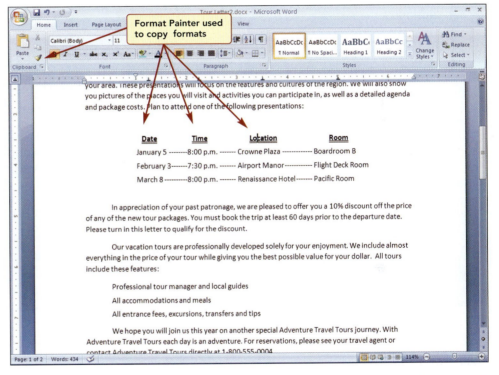

Figure 2.49

Creating Lists

Additional Information

A list can be used whenever you present three or more related pieces of information.

The next change you want to make is to display the three lines of information about tour features as an itemized list so that they stand out better from the surrounding text.

Concept 8

Bulleted and Numbered Lists

8 Whenever possible, add bullets or numbers before items in a list to organize information and to make your writing clear and easy to read. Word includes many basic bullet, a dot or other symbol, and number formats from which you can select. Additionally, there are many picture bullets available. If none of the predesigned bullet or number formats suits your needs, you also can create your own customized designs.

Use a **bulleted list** when you have several items in a paragraph that logically make a list. A bulleted list displays one of several styles of bullets before each item in the list. You can select from several types of symbols to use as bullets and you can change the color, size, and position of the bullet.

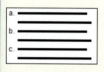

Use a **numbered list** when you want to convey a sequence of events, such as a procedure that has to follow in a certain order. A numbered list displays numbers or letters before the text. Word automatically increments the number or letter as you start a new paragraph. You can select from several different numbering schemes to create your numbered lists.

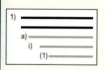

Use an **outline numbered list** to display multiple outline levels that show a hierarchical structure of the items in the list. There can be up to nine levels.

Numbering a List

Because both bullet and number formats will indent the items automatically when applied, you first need to remove the indent from the three tour features. Then you will try a numbered list format to see how it looks.

①

Select the three tour features.

● **Drag the First Line Indent marker on the ruler back to the margin boundary.**

● **Right-click on the selection and select Numbering from the menu.**

Another Method

The Ribbon equivalent is 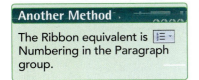 Numbering in the Paragraph group.

Your screen should be similar to Figure 2.50

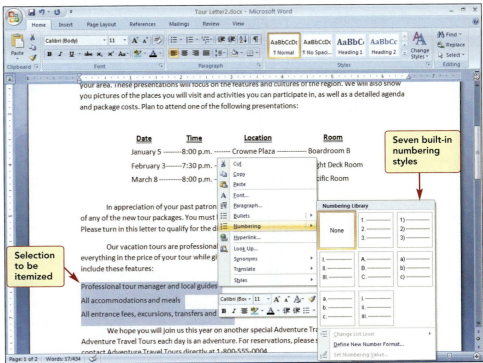

Figure 2.50

The Numbering gallery displays examples of seven built-in numbered list formats in the Numbering Library category. The None option is used to remove an existing numbering format. Numbers followed by periods is the default style that is applied when clicking [icon] Numbering in the Paragraph group. However, if another style has been used since starting Word, the last-used numbering format is inserted.

The numbering gallery also may include a Recently Used category if this feature has already been used since Word 2007 was started. If the document contains another numbered list, the gallery will display the used number style in a Document Number Formats category.

The three options at the bottom of the menu are used to change the indent level of the items, to customize the appearance of the built-in formats, and to set a start number for the list (1 is the default). For example, you could indent the list more, change the color of the numbers, and start numbering with 3 instead of 1.

You will use the second number format that has a number followed by a parenthesis.

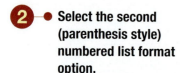

2 ● **Select the second (parenthesis style) numbered list format option.**

Your screen should be similar to Figure 2.51

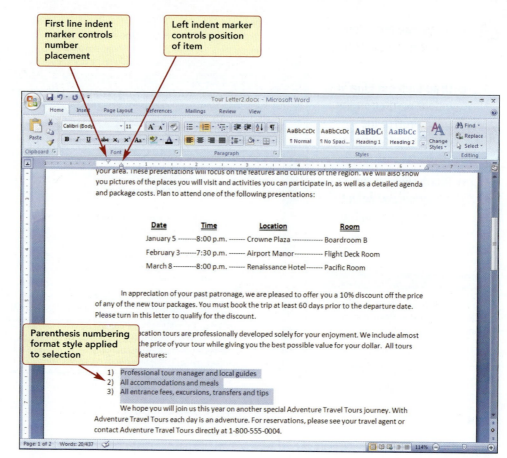

Figure 2.51

Lab 2: Revising and Refining a Document

www.mhhe.com/oleary

Additional Information

You also can create bulleted and numbered lists as you type. To create a bulleted list, type an asterisk (*) followed by a space, and then type the text. To create a numbered list, type a number, type a period followed by a space, and then type the text. When you press ⏎Enter, Word automatically creates a list and adds numbers or bullets to the next line. To turn off the list, press ⏎Enter twice.

A number is inserted at the 0.25-inch position before each line, and the text following the number is indented to the 0.5-inch position. In an itemized list, the First Line Indent marker on the ruler controls the position of the number or bullet, and the Left Indent marker controls the position of the item following the number or bullet. The Left Indent marker creates a hanging indent. If the text following each bullet were longer than a line, the text on the following lines would also be indented to the 0.5-inch position. Additionally, the extra space between the lines was removed because the feature that adds space between paragraphs of the same style was automatically turned off.

Bulleting a List

After looking at the list, you decide it really would be more appropriate if it were a bulleted list instead of a numbered list. The solid round bullet format is the default when clicking ⊞ ▾ Bullets. However, if another style was previously used since starting Word 2007, that style is inserted. The bullet submenu is divided into the same three groups as the Numbering submenu and has similar options.

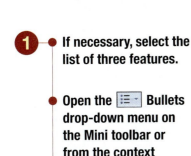

1 ● If necessary, select the list of three features.

● Open the ▤▾ Bullets drop-down menu on the Mini toolbar or from the context menu.

Another Method

You also can use ▤▾ Bullets in the Paragraph group of the Home tab.

● Choose the ➤ bullet format.

Your screen should be similar to Figure 2.52

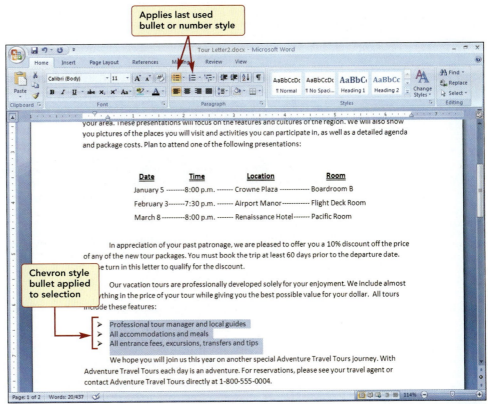

Applies last used bullet or number style

your area. These presentations will focus on the features and cultures of the region. We will also show you pictures of the places you will visit and activities you can participate in, as well as a detailed agenda and package costs. Plan to attend one of the following presentations:

Date	Time	Location	Room
January 5 --------8:00 p.m. ------- Crowne Plaza ------------- Boardroom B
February 3-------7:30 p.m. ------- Airport Manor------------ Flight Deck Room
March 8 ----------8:00 p.m. ------- Renaissance Hotel-------- Pacific Room

In appreciation of your past patronage, we are pleased to offer you a 10% discount off the price of any of the new tour packages. You must book the trip at least 60 days prior to the departure date. ...e turn in this letter to qualify for the discount.

Chevron style bullet applied to selection

Our vacation tours are professionally developed solely for your enjoyment. We include almost ...ything in the price of your tour while giving you the best possible value for your dollar. All tours ...clude these features:

➤ Professional tour manager and local guides
➤ All accommodations and meals
➤ All entrance fees, excursions, transfers and tips

We hope you will join us this year on another special Adventure Travel Tours journey. With Adventure Travel Tours each day is an adventure. For reservations, please see your travel agent or contact Adventure Travel Tours directly at 1-800-555-0004.

Page: 1 of 2   Words: 20/437

Figure 2.52

Additional Information

To remove bullets or numbers, select the text, open the ▤▾ drop-down menu, and select None, or click ▤▾ again.

The selected bullet format is applied to the selection.

Sorting a List

As you look at the bulleted list, you decide you want the three items to appear in alphabetical order. To make this change quickly, you can sort the list.

Concept 9

9   Word can quickly arrange or **sort** text, numbers, or data in lists or tables in alphabetical, numeric, or date order based on the first character in each paragraph. The sort order can be ascending (A to Z, 0 to 9, or earliest to latest date) or descending (Z to A, 9 to 0, or latest to earliest date). The following table describes the rules that are used when sorting.

Sort by	Rules
Text	First, items beginning with punctuation marks or symbols (such as !, #, $, %, or &) are sorted.
	Second, items beginning with numbers are sorted. Dates are treated as three-digit numbers.
	Third, items beginning with letters are sorted.
Numbers	All characters except numbers are ignored. The numbers can be in any location in a paragraph.
Date	Valid date separators include hyphens, forward slashes (/), commas, and periods. Colons (:) are valid time separators. If unable to recognize a date or time, Word places the item at the beginning or end of the list (depending on whether you are sorting in ascending or descending order).
Field results	If an entire field (such as a last name) is the same for two items, Word next evaluates subsequent fields (such as a first name) according to the specified sort options.

When a tie occurs, Word uses the first nonidentical character in each item to determine which item should come first.

You will use the default Sort settings that will sort by text and paragraphs in ascending order.

1
- If necessary, select the entire list.

- Click ⬆⬇ in the Paragraph group.

- Click ☐ OK ☐ to accept the default settings.

- Click on the document to clear the highlight.

- Increase the space after for the third list item to 12 pt.

Your screen should be similar to Figure 2.53

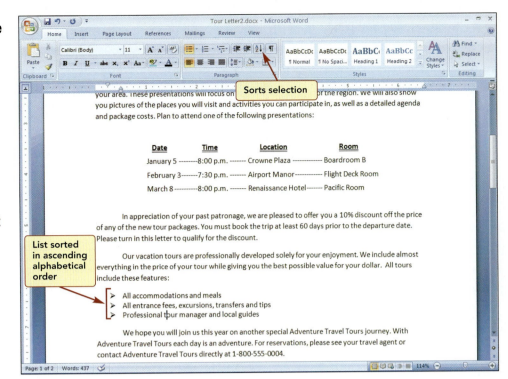

Figure 2.53

The three items in the list now appear in ascending sorted order.

Using Quick Parts

While looking at the letter, you realize that the closing lines have not been added to the document. You can quickly insert text and graphics that you use frequently using the Quick Parts feature. The Quick Parts feature includes reusable pieces of content or document parts, called **building blocks,** that give you a head start in creating content such as page numbers, cover pages, headers and footers, and sidebars. In addition to the supplied building blocks, you also can create your own custom building blocks.

Using Supplied Building Blocks

You will create the closing for the letter using the Author and Company supplied building blocks that get their information from the file's document properties.

1 Move to the first blank line below the last paragraph of the letter.

● Type **Best Regards,**.

● Press ⏎ Enter .

● Open the Insert tab and click 📄 Quick Parts ▾ in the Text group.

● Select Document Property and choose Author from the submenu.

Your screen should be similar to Figure 2.54

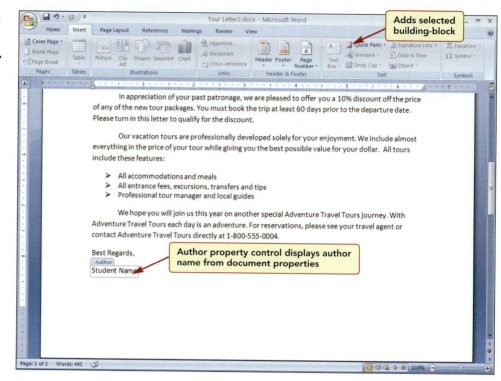

Figure 2.54

Additional Information

If you change the information stored in the Document Information Panel, any property controls in the document using that information also will be updated.

An Author property control containing the name that is currently stored in the file's Author document property is inserted in the document. A **control** is a graphic element that is a container for information or objects. Controls, like fields, appear shaded when you point to them.

You can update or modify the information displayed in a property control by editing the entry. Any changes you make in the property control are automatically updated in the Document Information Panel. You will change the information in the Author property to your name and then continue to create the closing.

2

- Select the text in the Author control and type your name.

- Press → to deselect it.

- Type , Advertising Coordinator following your name.

- Press ←Enter .

- Insert the Company document property control.

- Select the last two lines and remove the space after the paragraphs.

Your screen should be similar to Figure 2.55

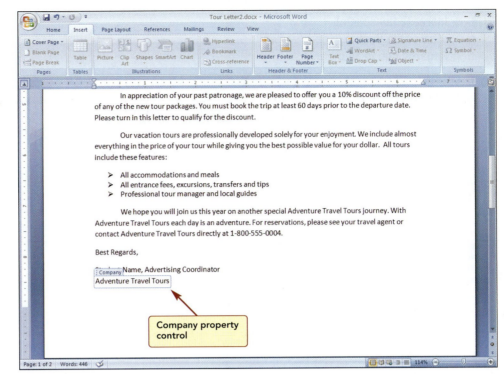

Figure 2.55

The closing is now complete and the document properties now include your name as the author. Using document property controls in a document is particularly helpful when the same controls are used multiple times, as in a contract. Then, when one control is updated or edited, all controls of the same type throughout the document are automatically updated.

Creating a Custom Building Block

In addition to the supplied building blocks, you can create your own. In this case, because you frequently use the same closing when creating correspondence, you will create a building block that you can use to quickly insert this information.

1 ● **Increase the spacing after of the Best Regards line to 18 pt.**

● **Select the entire closing.**

● **Click** [Quick Parts ▾]**.**

● **Choose Save Selection to Quick Part Gallery.**

Another Method
The keyboard shortcut is [Alt] + [F3].

Your screen should be similar to Figure 2.56

Selection will be used as custom building block

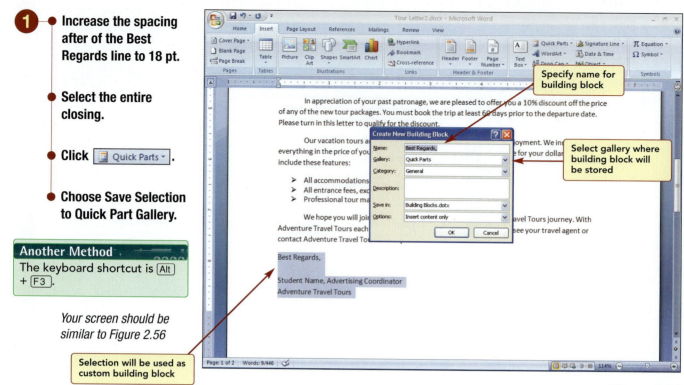

Specify name for building block

Select gallery where building block will be stored

Figure 2.56

In the Create New Building Block dialog box, you define the properties for the building block. This includes entering a unique name for the building block, specifying the gallery where you want the building block stored, and other information that is needed to identify and use the building block.

You will use the proposed name, Best Regards, and store it in the Quick Parts Gallery. All the other default settings for this building block are appropriate. After saving the building block, you will erase the closing you typed in the letter and then reinsert it using the stored Quick Part.

MORE ABOUT
▶ See 4.1 Structure Content by Using Quick Parts in the More About appendix to learn more about saving frequently used data as building blocks.

② Click [OK].

Delete the closing in the letter.

Click [Quick Parts ▾]

Click on the Best Regards building block.

Save the document again.

Your screen should be similar to Figure 2.57

MORE ABOUT

See 4.1 Structure Content by Using Quick Parts in the More About appendix to learn how to use the Building Block Organizer to sort and edit properties of building blocks.

Additional Information

You will learn more about Quick Parts and use several of the other supplied building blocks in later labs.

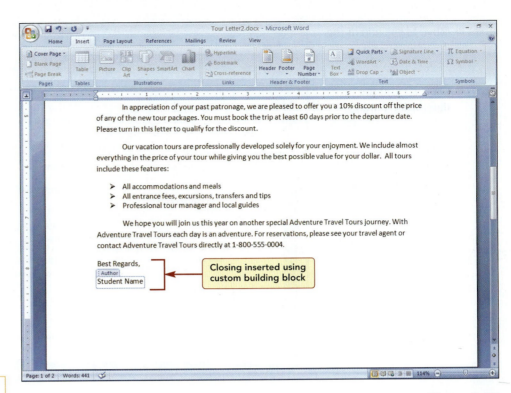

In appreciation of your past patronage, we are pleased to offer you a 10% discount off the price of any of the new tour packages. You must book the trip at least 60 days prior to the departure date. Please turn in this letter to qualify for the discount.

Our vacation tours are professionally developed solely for your enjoyment. We include almost everything in the price of your tour while giving you the best possible value for your dollar. All tours include these features:

➢ All accommodations and meals
➢ All entrance fees, excursions, transfers and tips
➢ Professional tour manager and local guides

We hope you will join us this year on another special Adventure Travel Tours journey. With Adventure Travel Tours each day is an adventure. For reservations, please see your travel agent or contact Adventure Travel Tours directly at 1-800-555-0004.

Best Regards,
Author
Student Name

Closing inserted using custom building block

Figure 2.57

The custom building block you created appeared as a gallery item at the top of the Quick Parts menu, making it easy for you to access and use. The selected block was inserted into the document at the location of the insertion point. As you can see, using Quick Parts was much quicker than typing the closing.

Adding and Modifying Shapes

You also want to add a special graphic to the flyer containing information about the company Web site to catch the reader's attention. To quickly add a shape, you will use one of the ready-made shapes that are supplied with Word. These include basic shapes such as rectangles and circles, a variety of lines, block arrows, flowchart symbols, stars and banners, and callouts. Additional shapes are available in the Clip Organizer. You also can combine shapes to create more complex designs. To see and create shapes, the view needs to be Print Layout view. In Draft view, shapes are not displayed. If you are using Draft view when you begin to create a shape, the view will change automatically to Print Layout view.

Inserting a Shape

You want to add a graphic of a banner to the bottom of the flyer.

1 ● Move to the end of the document.

● Click 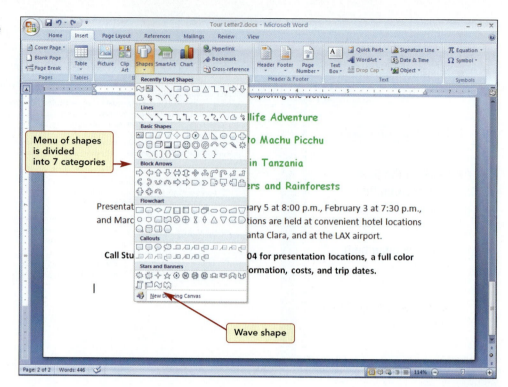 in the Illustrations group.

● From the Stars and Banners group, point to the Wave shape.

Your screen should be similar to Figure 2.58

Figure 2.58

The Shapes menu displays seven categories of shapes. Pointing to a shape displays the shape name in a ScreenTip. The recently selected shapes appear at the top of the menu. You will insert the Wave shape at the end of the flyer.

2 ● Click the Wave shape.

● Click below the last line of the flyer to insert the shape.

● Drag the sizing handles to obtain a shape similar to that shown in Figure 2.59.

Additional Information

To maintain the height and width proportions of a shape, hold down ⇧Shift while you drag.

Your screen should be similar to Figure 2.59

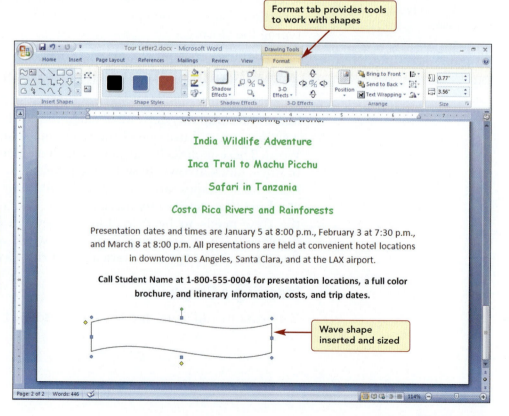

Figure 2.59

Notice the Drawing Tools Format tab is displayed and open so you can continue working with the shape.

Filling the Shape with Color

The shape can be enhanced using many of the features on the Format tab, such as adding a background fill color, gradient, and line color. A **gradient** is a gradual progression of colors and shades, usually from one color to another, or from one shade to another of the same color.

As you make your selections, the Live Preview feature will show how they will look.

1 ● Open the [icon] Shape Fill drop-down menu in the Shape Styles group.

● Choose the orange fill color from the standard colors palette.

● Open the [icon] Shape Fill drop-down menu, select Gradient and choose the Linear Up gradient from the Light Variations section (3rd row).

● In the same manner, open the [icon] Shape Outline menu and choose green.

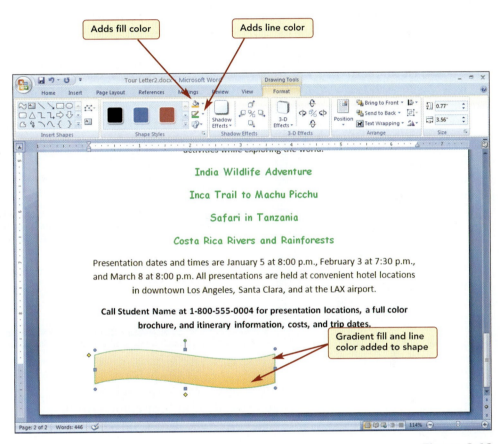

Adds fill color

Adds line color

India Wildlife Adventure

Inca Trail to Machu Picchu

Safari in Tanzania

Costa Rica Rivers and Rainforests

Presentation dates and times are January 5 at 8:00 p.m., February 3 at 7:30 p.m., and March 8 at 8:00 p.m. All presentations are held at convenient hotel locations in downtown Los Angeles, Santa Clara, and at the LAX airport.

Call Student Name at 1-800-555-0004 for presentation locations, a full color brochure, and itinerary information, costs, and trip dates.

Gradient fill and line color added to shape

Figure 2.60

Additional Information

The color and gradient names appear in a ScreenTip as you point to them.

Your screen should be similar to Figure 2.60

Adding Text to a Shape

Next you will add text to the shape. The manager also has asked you to add information about the company's Web site to the flyer. You will include the Web site's address, called a **URL** (Uniform Resource Locator), in the shape. Word automatically recognizes URLs you enter and creates a hyperlink of the entry. A **hyperlink** is a connection to a location in the current document, another document, or a Web site. It allows the reader to jump to the referenced location by clicking on the hyperlink text when reading the document on the screen.

1
- Right-click on the shape to open the context menu.

- Choose Add Text.

- Type **Visit our Web site at www. adventuretraveltours. com** and press ⌷Spacebar⌷.

- If necessary, adjust the shape size to fully display the text.

Your screen should be similar to Figure 2.61

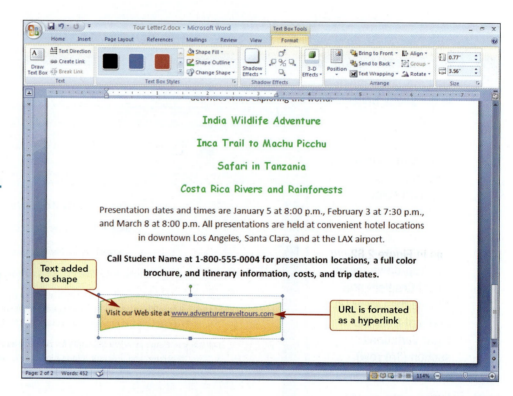

Figure 2.61

The text appears in the selected font settings. The text color is black because the default font color setting is Automatic. This setting will make the text color black if the background fill color is light and white if the fill color is dark.

Removing Hyperlinks

The Web address is automatically formatted in blue and underlined, indicating the entry is a hyperlink. The AutoFormat feature makes certain formatting changes automatically to your document. These formats include formatting a Web address, replacing ordinals (1st) with a superscript (1st) and fractions (1/2) with fraction characters (½), and applying a bulleted list format to a list if you type an asterisk (*) followed by a space at the beginning of a paragraph. These AutoFormat features can be turned off if the corrections are not needed in your document.

Additional Information

You can turn off the AutoFormat feature so the hyperlinks are not created automatically using 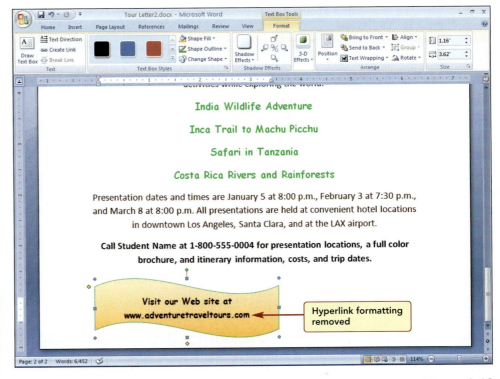 Office Button/[Word Options]/Proofing/AutoCorrectOptions/AutoFormat and clear the Internet and network paths with hyperlinks option.

Because this is a document you plan to print, you do not want the text displayed as a link. Since the hyperlink was created using the AutoFormat feature, you can undo the correction or turn it off using the AutoCorrect Options button.

1 ● Right-click on the hyperlink and choose Remove Hyperlink from the context menu.

● Select the text and using the Mini toolbar, change the font to Comic Sans MS, 12 pt, bold, and centered.

● Adjust the shape size as in Figure 2.62.

Additional Information

A ScreenTip appears when you point to a hyperlink with instructions on how to follow a link.

Another Method

You also could click ↺ Undo to remove the hyperlink AutoFormatting.

Your screen should be similar to Figure 2.62

Figure 2.62

The Web address now appears as normal text.

Moving an Object

Finally, you need to center the shape at the bottom of the flyer. You will do this by dragging the object to the desired location.

1 • **Point to the shape and when the mouse pointer appears as ⤯, drag the shape to the position shown in Figure 2.63.**

• **Click outside the shape to deselect it.**

• **Save the document again.**

Your screen should be similar to Figure 2.63

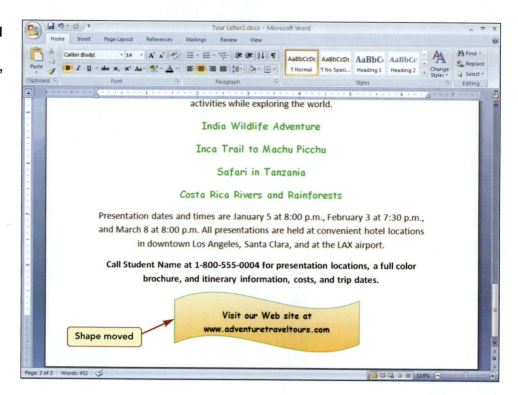

Figure 2.63

The banner complements the colors used in the flyer and adds the needed information about the Web site.

Previewing and Editing Multiple Pages

Next you will preview and make any final changes to the letter and flyer before printing it. When previewing a document, it is often useful to see multiple pages at the same time to check formatting and other items. First, you want to display both pages of your document at the same time in the window.

1
- Move to the top of the document.

- Use the Zoom slider to reduce the zoom to 50%.

Your screen should be similar to Figure 2.64

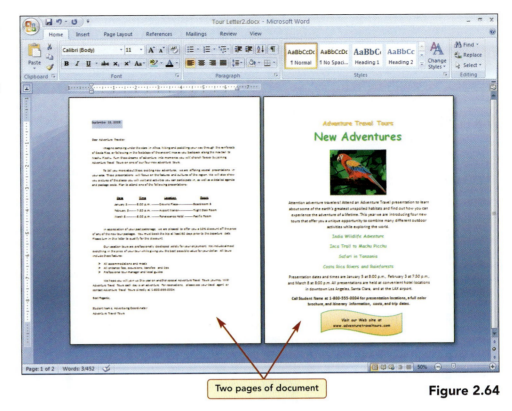

Two pages of document

Figure 2.64

Now that you can see the entire letter, you decide to indent the date and closing to the 3.5-inch tab position. You will select both these items at the same time and then change the indent. To select nonadjacent areas in a document, hold down Ctrl while selecting each additional area.

2
- Select the date.

- Hold down Ctrl and select the closing.

- Drag the upper indent marker to the 3.5-inch position.

Your screen should be similar to Figure 2.65

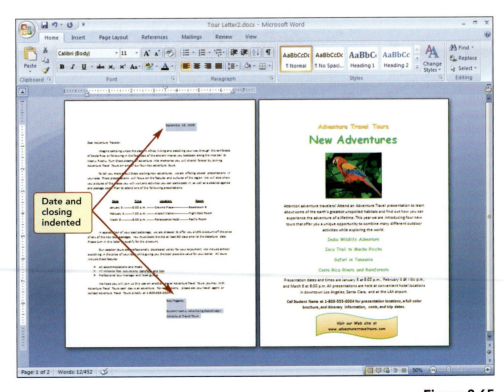

Date and closing indented

Figure 2.65

While looking at the document, you decide to emphasize the list of tour features by adding bold. You also want to decrease the space between the tour names in the flyer.

3
- Select the three bulleted items.

- Click **B** Bold on the Mini toolbar.

- Select the list of four tours in the flyer.

- Decrease the spacing after to 6 pt.

- Click in the list to cear the selection.

Your screen should be similar to Figure 2.66

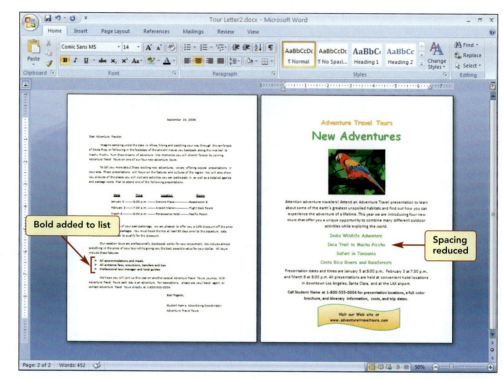

Figure 2.66

Setting Page Margins

Finally, you decide the document may look better if the left and right page margins were narrower.

Concept 10

10 The **page margin** is the blank space around the edge of a page. Generally, the text you enter appears in the printable area inside the margins. However, some items can be positioned in the margin space. You can set different page margin widths to alter the appearance of the document.

Standard single-sided documents have four margins: top, bottom, left, and right. Double-sided documents with facing pages, such as books and magazines, also have four margins: top, bottom, inside, and outside. These documents typically use mirror margins in which the left page is a mirror image of the right page. This means that the inside margins are the same width and the outside margins are the same width. (See the illustrations below.)

You also can set a "gutter" margin that reserves space on the left side of single-sided documents, or on the inside margin of double-sided documents, to accommodate binding. There are also special margin settings for headers and footers. (You will learn about these features in Lab 3.)

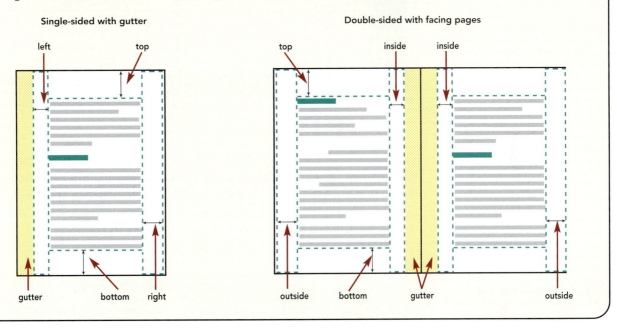

The default document setting for the left and right margins is 1 inch. You would like to see how the document would look if you decreased the size of the right and left margin widths. The Page Setup group is used to change settings associated with the layout of the entire page.

1 ● Open the Page Layout tab.

● Click [Margins] in the Page Setup group.

Your screen should be similar to Figure 2.67

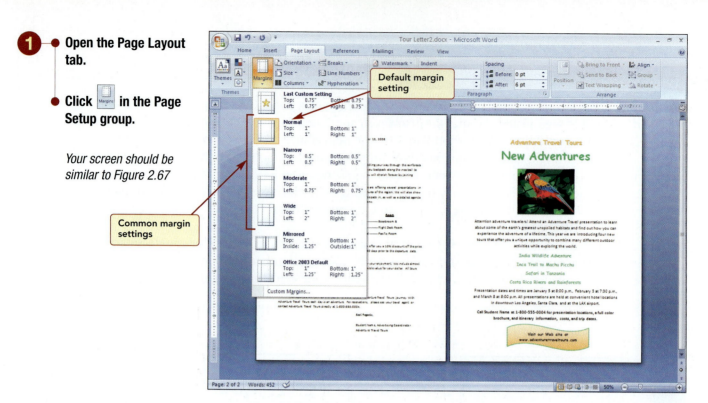

Figure 2.67

The Margins drop-down menu displays several common margin setting options for a single-sided document, including the default setting of Normal. The Mirrored option is used for documents that will be printed double-sided with facing pages, such as a book. Additionally, if you have used a custom margin setting, it also appears in the menu.

You decide to try the Narrow option first.

2 ● Choose Narrow.

Your screen should be similar to Figure 2.68

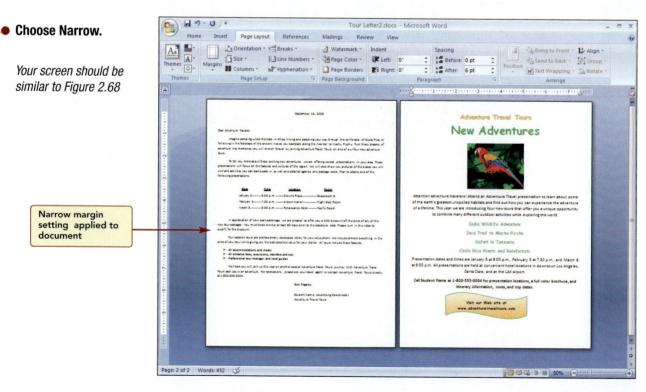

Figure 2.68

Additional Information

Use the custom margins option if you want the new margin settings to be saved for future use.

You do not like how this setting looks at all and will undo the change. Then you will create a custom setting to change this document to 0.8-inch side margins. Custom margin settings are specified using the Custom Margins option on the Margins drop-down menu. You also can double-click on the margin section of the ruler to access this feature.

3 ● **Click** ⟲ **Undo to cancel this change.**

● **Double-click the margin section of the ruler.**

Your screen should be similar to Figure 2.69

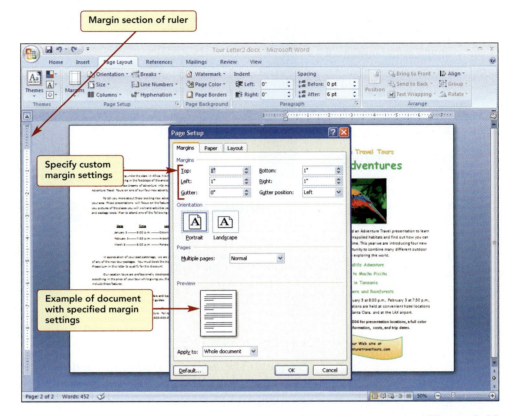

Figure 2.69

The Margins tab of the Page Setup dialog box displays the default margin settings for a single-sided document. The Preview box shows how the current margin settings will appear on a page. New margin settings can be entered by typing the value in the text box, or by clicking the ▲ and ▼ scroll buttons or pressing the ↑ or ↓ keys to increase or decrease the settings by tenths of an inch.

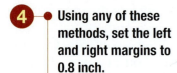

4
- Using any of these methods, set the left and right margins to 0.8 inch.

- Click .

- If necessary, readjust the placement of the shape at the bottom of the flyer.

- Save the document again.

Additional Information

You also can change the margins by dragging the left and right margin boundaries on the ruler.

Your screen should be similar to Figure 2.70

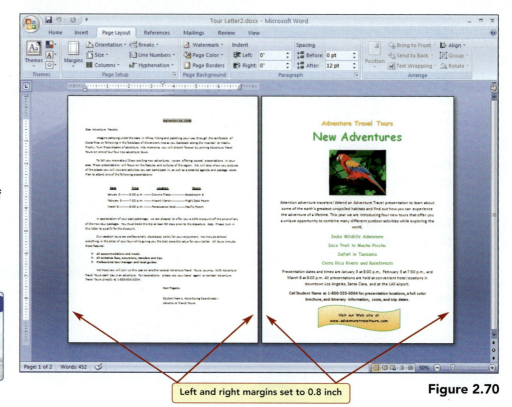

Left and right margins set to 0.8 inch

Figure 2.70

Although the text is difficult to read, you can easily see the layout of the pages and that the margin settings have been changed for both pages. You are happy with the new settings.

Printing the Document

Now that the document has been edited and formatted the way you want, you will print a copy of the document using the default print settings.

Note: If you need to specify a different printer, you will need to use the Print command on the 🔘 Office Button menu.

1 • Click 🔘 **Office Button and choose Print/Quick Print.**

The printed output should be similar to text shown in the Case Study at the beginning of the lab.

2 ● Click ⊠ to close the Tour Letter2 document.

● Click ⊠ Close to close the wd02_Flyer2 document.

Additional Information

Using ⊠ Close both closes the file and exits the application. If you want to keep the application open, use the Close command in the 🔵 Office Button menu.

● If a question dialog box appears about modified styles, click [No].

● If a question dialog box appears about a large amount of text in the Clipboard, click [No].

If you were using your own computer, you would want to save the modified block style so that it would be available the next time you used the application.

Focus on Careers

EXPLORE YOUR CAREER OPTIONS

Assistant Broadcast Producer
Have you wondered who does the background research for a film or television broadcast? Or who is responsible for making sure a film production runs on schedule? Assistant producers are responsible for background research and the daily operations of a shooting schedule. They also may produce written materials for broadcast. These written materials are often compiled from multiple documents and sources. The typical salary range for an assistant broadcast producer is $27,000 to $38,000. Demand for those with relevant training and experience is expected to continue in this competitive job market.

Thesaurus (WD2.9)

Word's Thesaurus is a reference tool that provides synonyms, antonyms, and related words for a selected word or phrase.

Move and Copy (WD2.12)

Text and graphic selections can be moved or copied to new locations in a document or between documents, saving you time by not having to retype the same information.

Page Break (WD2.20)

A page break marks the point at which one page ends and another begins. Two types of page breaks can be used in a document: soft page breaks and hard page breaks.

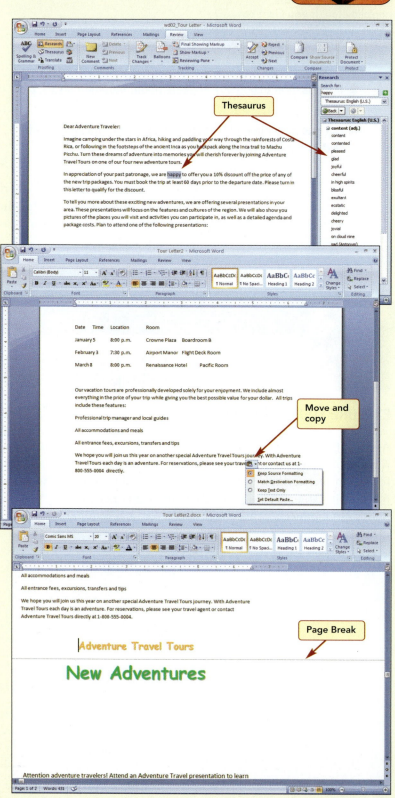

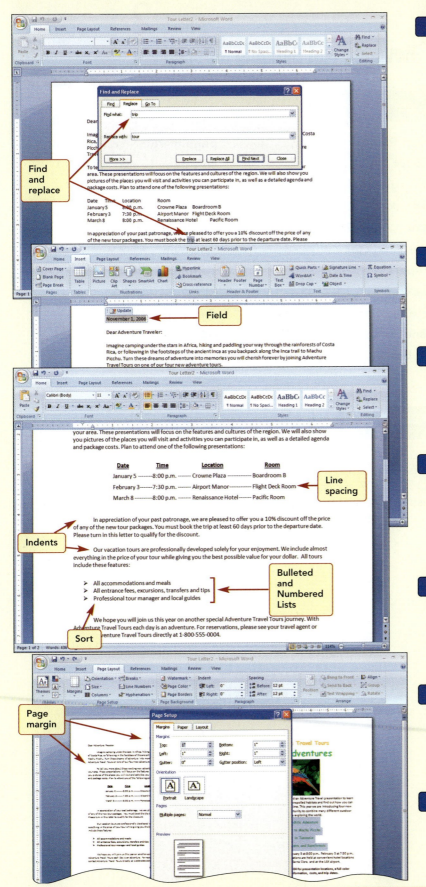

Find and Replace (WD2.22)

To make editing easier, you can use the Find and Replace feature to find text in a document and replace it with other text as directed.

Field (WD2.29)

A field is a placeholder that instructs Word to insert information into a document.

Indents (WD2.32)

To help your reader find information quickly, you can indent paragraphs from the margins. Indenting paragraphs sets them off from the rest of the document.

Line Spacing (WD2.41)

Adjusting the line spacing, or the vertical space between lines of text, helps set off areas of text from others and, when increased, makes it easier to read and edit text.

Bulleted and Numbered Lists (WD2.48)

Whenever possible, add bullets or numbers before items in a list to organize information and make your writing clear and easy to read.

Sort (WD2.52)

Word can quickly arrange or sort text, numbers, or data in lists or tables in alphabetical, numeric, or date order based on the first character in each paragraph.

Page Margin (WD2.65)

The page margin is the blank space around the edge of the page. Standard single-sided documents have four margins: top, bottom, left, and right.

key terms

active window   WD2.17

antonym   WD2.9

building blocks   WD2.53

bulleted list   WD2.48

case sensitive   WD2.24

control   WD2.54

destination   WD2.12

drag and drop   WD2.15

field   WD2.29

field code   WD2.29

field result   WD2.29

Format Painter   WD2.47

gradient   WD2.59

hard page break   WD2.20

hyperlink   WD2.60

indent   WD2.32

leader character   WD2.38

line spacing   WD2.41

numbered list   WD2.48

Office Clipboard   WD2.12

outline numbered list   WD2.48

page break   WD2.20

page margin   WD2.65

soft page break   WD2.20

sort   WD2.52

source   WD2.12

synchronized   WD2.17

synonym   WD2.9

system Clipboard   WD2.12

tab stop   WD2.35

thesaurus   WD2.9

URL   WD2.60

MCAS skills

The Microsoft Certified Applications Specialist (MCAS) certification program is designed to measure your proficiency in performing basic tasks using the Office 2007 applications. Getting certified demonstrates that you have the skills and provides a valuable industry credential for employment. See Reference 2 MCAS Certification Guide for a complete list of the skills that were covered in Lab 2.

command summary

Command	Shortcut	Action
Home tab		
Clipboard group		
✂ Cut	Ctrl + X	Cuts selection to Clipboard
📋 Copy	Ctrl + C	Copies selection to Clipboard
📋 Paste	Ctrl + V	Pastes item from Clipboard
Editing group		
🔍 Find ▾	Ctrl + F	Locates specified text
Replace	Ctrl + H	Locates and replaces specified text
Font group		
U̲ ▾ Underline	Ctrl + U	Underlines selected text with single line
Paragraph group		
Bullets		Creates a bulleted list
Numbering		Creates a numbered list
Sort		Rearranges information in a list in alphabetical order
Increase Indent		Increases indent of paragraph to next tab stop
Line Spacing		Changes spacing between lines of text
▫/ Tabs...		Specifies types and positions of tab stops
▫/Indents and Spacing/ Special/First Line	Tab	Indents first line of paragraph from left margin
▫/Indents and Spacing/ Line Spacing	Ctrl + #	Changes the spacing between lines of text
Insert tab		
Pages group		
Page Break	Ctrl + Enter	Inserts hard page break
Illustrations group		
Shapes		Inserts graphic shapes
Text group		
Quick Parts ▾		Inserts Building Blocks
Date & Time		Inserts current date or time, in selected format

Lab Review

Command	Shortcut	Action
Page Layout tab		
Page Setup group		
Margins		Sets margin sizes
Breaks ▾		Inserts page and section breaks
Review tab		
Proofing group		
ABC Spelling & Grammar	F7	Starts Spelling and Grammar Checker
Thesaurus	⇧Shift + F7	Opens Thesaurus tool
View tab		
Window group		
Arrange All		Arranges all open windows horizontally on the screen
View Side by Side		Displays two document windows side by side to make it easy to compare content

Lab Exercises

matching

Match the item on the left with the correct description on the right.

1. 🖌 _____
2. Tab⇄ _____
3. synonyms _____
4. A/Z↓ _____
5. drag and drop _____
6. field _____
7. soft page break _____
8. Ctrl + ←Enter _____
9. leader character _____
10. line spacing _____

a. indents first line of paragraph

b. mouse procedure that moves or copies a selection to a new location

c. placeholder that instructs Word to insert information into a document

d. automatically starts a new page when a previous page is filled with text

e. arranges selection in sorted order

f. inserts a hard page break

g. words with similar meaning

h. copies formatting to another place

i. vertical space between lines of text

j. solid, dotted, or dashed lines between tab stops

multiple choice

Circle the correct response to the questions below.

1. Word includes preformatted content, called _____, that gives you a head start in creating content such as page numbers, cover pages, headers and footers, and sidebars.
   a. drag and drop
   b. Format Painter
   c. building blocks
   d. AutoContent

2. A _____ marks the point at which one page ends and another begins.
   a. leader character
   b. selection point
   c. field code
   d. page break

3. The _____ is a reference tool that provides synonyms and antonyms.
   a. find and replace feature
   b. research
   c. thesaurus
   d. clipboard

4. The information that is displayed as a result of a field is called _____.
   a. a field code
   b. a field result
   c. a quick part
   d. a wildcard

5. The blank space around the edge of the page is called the _____.
   a. gutter
   b. indent
   c. margin
   d. white space

6. The field _____ contains the directions that identify the type of information to insert.
   a. results
   b. code
   c. placeholder
   d. format

7. To convey a sequence of events in a document, you should consider using a _____.
   a. bulleted list
   b. numbered list
   c. sorted list
   d. paragraph list

8. A _____ is a Web site address.
   a. URL
   b. RUL
   c. WSL
   d. ULR

9. The feature most useful for copying or moving short distances in a document is _____.
   a. drag and drop
   b. drop and drag
   c. move and place
   d. drag and place

10. _____ is a feature that applies the formats associated with a selection to another selection.
   a. Format Painter
   b. Find and Replace
   c. AutoFormat
   d. Format Designer

true/false

Circle the correct answer to the following questions.

1.	The thesaurus identifies synonyms for common words.	True	False
2.	Draft view does not display graphics.	True	False
3.	Indents are used to set paragraphs off from the rest of the text.	True	False
4.	The Find and Replace feature is used to locate misspelled words in a document.	True	False
5.	A sorted list conveys a sequence of events.	True	False
6.	A source is the location from which text is moved or copied.	True	False
7.	Soft page breaks are automatically inserted whenever the text reaches the bottom margin.	True	False
8.	The Clipboard is a permanent storage area.	True	False
9.	The Quick Parts feature can be used to quickly insert text and graphics.	True	False
10.	A hyperlink is a connection to a location in the current document, to another document, or to a Web site.	True	False

fill-in

Complete the following statements by filling in the blanks with the correct terms.

1. Windows that are _____ scroll together.

2. A(n) _____ code instructs Word to insert the current date in the document using the selected format whenever the document is printed.

3. As you add or remove text from a page, Word automatically _____ the placement of the soft page break.

4. Double-sided documents with facing pages typically use _____ margins.

5. _____ are reuseable pieces of content that can be quickly inserted in a document.

6. In a _____ style letter, all parts are aligned with the left margin.

7. _____ and _____ organize information and make your writing clear and easy to read.

8. A _____ is a gradual progression of colors and shades.

9. Two types of page breaks that can be used in a document are _____ and _____.

10. When a selection is moved or copied, the selection is stored in the _____ Clipboard, a temporary Windows storage area in memory.

Hands-On Exercises

step-by-step

Expanding the Note-Taking Skills Handout ★

1. You are continuing to work on the handout to supplement your lecture on note-taking skills and tips. Although the content is nearly complete, there are several more tips you need to add to the document. You also want to rearrange the order of the tips. This handout is also going to be included in the freshman orientation information packet and needs to include formatting to make the document interesting and appealing to students. Your completed document will be similar to the one shown here.

a. Open the file wd02_Note Taking Tips. Spell-check the document.

b. Use the thesaurus to find a better word for "gist" in the first tip.

c. Open the document Note Taking Skills you created in Step-by-Step Exercise 4 in Lab 1. Display the document windows side by side. Copy the tips from the wd02_Note Taking Tips document to the end of the tips in the Note Taking Skills document. Close the wd02_Note Taking Tips document without saving your changes.

Tips for Taking Better Classroom Notes

Be Ready

- Review your assigned reading and previous notes you've taken before class.
- Bring plenty of paper and a sharpened pencil, an erasable pen or a pen that won't skip or smudge.
- Write the class name, date and that day's topic at the top the page.

Write Legibly

- Print if your handwriting is poor. Use a pencil or erasable pen if you cross out material a lot so that your notes are easier to read.
- Take notes in one-liners rather than paragraph form.
- Skip a line between ideas to make it easier to find information when you're studying for a test.

Use Abbreviations

- ❖ Abbreviations let you write more quickly.
- ❖ To abbreviate, condense a word or phrase into initials, or use a symbol. For instance, use b/c for because; w/ for with; w/o for without; and govt for government.
- ❖ Always use the same abbreviations for the same words and phrases so you'll immediately know what they stand for.

Use Wide Margins

- Leave a wide margin on one side of your paper so you'll have space to write your own thoughts and call attention to key material.
- Draw arrows or stars beside important information like dates, names and events.
- If you miss getting a date, name, number or other fact, make a mark in the margin so you'll remember to come back to it.

Fill in Gaps

- ✓ Check with a classmate or your teacher after class to get any missing names, dates, facts or other information you could not write down.

d. Increase the size of the title to 24 points. Use Format Painter to change the format of the new headings to the same as the existing headings.

e. Move the "Use Abbreviations" tip below the "Write Legibly" tip. Move the "Check the Board" tip to below the "Mark Questionable Materials" tip.

f. Change the margins to Moderate. Change the space after paragraphs to 6 points for the entire document. Remove any blank lines between topics.

g. Break the tips under each topic heading into separate bulleted items using bullet styles of your choice. (A bulleted item may be more than one sentence if it contains an explanation or is a continuation of the same tip topic.)

h. Insert a hard page break before the Mark Questionable Materials topic.

i. Left-align your name and the date. Delete your name and replace it using the Author quick part. Replace the date with a date field using a format of your choice.

j. Add the shape "Curved Down Ribbon" from the Stars and Banners category to the bottom of the document.

k. Add the text **Good Notes = Better Grades** to the shape. Bold, center, and size the text to 18 pt. Size the shape to display the text on two lines.

l. Add a fill color to the shape and color to the text to complement the colors you used in the document. Center the shape at the bottom of the document.

m. Add document properties. Save the document as Note Taking Skills2 and print it.

Water Conservation Article ★★

2. Each month, the town newsletter is included with the utility bill. This month the main article is about conserving water. You started the column a few days ago and need to expand the article by adding a few more suggestions. Then you need to edit and format the text and include a graphic to enhance the appearance of the article. Your completed article will be similar to that shown here.

a. Open the document wd02_Water Conservation. Spell and grammar-check the document.

b. Center the title. Change the font to Impact with a point size of 24. Add a color of your choice to the title.

c. Change the three category heads to bold with a type size of 14 pt. Center the heads. Use the same color as in the title for the heads.

d. Change the alignment of the introductory paragraph to justified.

e. Insert the picture wd02_Water Hose (from your data files) below the main title of the article.

f. Size the picture to be 2 inches wide (use the ruler as a guide). Center it below the title.

g. Save the document using the file name Water Conservation Column.

h. Open the document wd02_Conservation Tips. Find and replace all occurrences of "h2o" with "water."

Lab Exercises

i. Display the document windows side by side. Copy the tips from the wd02_Conservation Tips document to the appropriate categories in the wd02_Water Conservation Column document. Close the wd02_Conservation Tips document without saving your changes.

j. Save the document again.

k. Change the line spacing of the tips by decreasing the spacing after to 0 points.

l. Change the top and bottom margins to 0.75 inch. Change the right and left margins to 1 inch.

m. Apply three different bullet styles to the tips under the three categories. Indent the bulleted tips to the 0.5-inch position.

n. Use the thesaurus to find a better word for "biggest" in the first paragraph. Indent the first line of the first paragraph.

o. Two lines below the last group of tips, insert a shape that includes the text **Visit us for more water conservation tips at www.citywaterprogram.com**. Remove the hyperlink formatting. Apply formatting, such as color and bold, of your choice to this line. Fill the shape with a gradient color.

p. Add your full name using the Author quick part and the current date as a date field below the last line of tips.

q. Preview the document and, if necessary, reduce the size of the graphic to make the entire document fit on one page. Print the document.

r. Add document properties. Save and close the document.

How Can I Conserve Water?

Nearly 75% of water used indoors is in the bathroom with baths, showers and toilet flushing account for most of this. If you have a lawn, chances are that this is your main water use. Typically, at least 50% of water consumed by households is used outdoors. The City's Water Conservation Program has many publications that offer suggestions to help you conserve water. Some of these suggestions include:

Personal Use Tips
❖ Take short showers instead of baths
❖ Run dishwashers and clothes washers with full loads only, or adjust water level to load size
❖ Turn the water off when brushing your teeth or shaving
❖ Keep a jug of cold water in the refrigerator instead of letting the tap run until cool

Repair Tips
➤ Install low-flow showerheads or flow restrictors
➤ Repair dripping faucets by replacing washers
➤ Check your toilet for leaks by placing a few drops of food coloring in the tank. If it shows up in the bowl, replace the flapper
➤ Replace older toilets with new low-flow toilets or place a plastic jug filled with water in the tank to displace some of the water
➤ Check for hidden leaks by monitoring your water meter
➤ Insulate your water pipes – you'll get hot water faster and avoid wasting water while it heats up

Outdoor Tips
✓ When washing the car, use soap and water from a bucket. Use a hose with a shut-off nozzle for the final rinse
✓ Plant low-water use and native plants instead of turf
✓ Clean your driveway with a broom, not a hose
✓ Adjust irrigation when the seasons change
✓ Adjust sprinkler so only the lawn is watered, not the sidewalk or street
✓ Don't water on windy days
✓ When mowing, raise the blade level to its highest level. Close cut grass makes the roots work harder, requiring more water

Student Name – Current Date

Visit us for more water conservation tips at www.citywaterprogram.com

Promoting New Fitness Classes ★★

3. The Lifestyle Fitness Club has just started a new series of informal classes for the members and their families. You want to spread the word by creating a flyer for club members to pick up at the front desk. You have created a Word document with the basic information that you want to include in the flyer. Now you just need to make it look better. Your completed flyer will be similar to the one shown here.

a. Open the file wd02_Fitness Fun.

b. Find each occurrence of "class" and replace it with "Class" where appropriate. Be sure to use the match case and whole words only options. Find and replace all occurrences of "mins" with "minutes."

c. Use the spelling and grammar checker to correct the identified errors.

d. Save the document as Fitness Fun Flyer.

e. Change the title font to Gill Sans Ultra Bold (or a font of your choice), 26 pt, and a color of your choice. Center the title.

f. Center the introductory paragraph and set line spacing to 1.5.

g. Use Format Painter to format the "Class Descriptions" heading the same as the title. Reduce the font size to 14 and left align it. Add space before the paragraph.

h. Use Format Painter to increase the font size to 12; add bold and a color highlight to the eight class titles.

i. Delete the class title, description, and scheduling information on the Beginning Ballroom Dance class because you do not have an instructor for this month.

j. Set the margins to Moderate.

k. Use drag and drop to move the Tai Chi class description below the Move to Movies description. Adjust the line spacing as needed between descriptions.

l. Create a tabbed table of the schedule. Add left tab marks at 1.5, 3, and 5 inches. Bold, add color, and underline the words only of the table heads: Day, Class, Time, and Length of Class. Move the tab marker from the 5-inch position to the 4.5-inch position for the entire table. Change the tab at the 3-inch position to a center tab stop at the 3.25-inch position. Add tab leaders of your choice between the columns of data. Add space after the heading line only of the tabbed table.

m. Above the table, add the heading **October Class Schedule**. Format it the same as the "Class Descriptions" heading. Insert a hard page break above the table heading.

n. Add the shape "Explosion 2" from the Stars and Banners section below the Line Dancing description at the bottom of page one. Add the text **Fun for the Whole Family!**. Bold and size the text to 12 pt. Add fill color and font color of your choice to the shape. Size and position the shape appropriately.

o. Delete the Line Dancing class title and description. Delete the hard page break. Move and size the shape to fit at the top right of the flyer title.

p. Add your name using the Author quick part and the current date (as a field) on the last line on the page.

q. Add document properties. Save and print the document.

Orientation Meeting Schedule ★★★

4. The Animal Rescue Foundation is actively seeking volunteers to help with an upcoming conference. You are preparing the information that will appear on the Web site and the flyer that will be distributed to local businesses. Your completed document will be similar to the one shown here.

a. Open a new document and set the left and right page margins to 1.5 inch.

b. On the first line, center the title **ARF Needs You!**. Increase the font to 26 points and apply formats of your choice.

c. Several lines below the title, type the following paragraphs:

The Animal Rescue Foundation needs volunteers to help with our upcoming conference.

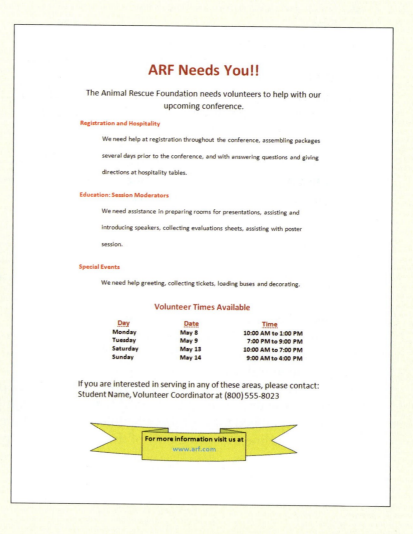

Registration and Hospitality

We need help at registration throughout the meeting, assembling packets several days prior to the meeting, and with answering questions and giving directions at hospitality tables.

Education: Session Moderators

We need help in preparing rooms for presentations, assisting and introducing speakers, collecting evaluation sheets, assisting with poster session.

Special Events

We need help greeting, collecting tickets, loading buses and decorating.

If you are interested in serving in any of these areas, please contact:

[Your Name], Volunteer Coordinator at (800) 555-8023

d. Spell-check the document. Use the thesaurus to find a better word for "help" in the Education: Session Moderators paragraph.

e. Find and replace all occurrences of "meeting" with "conference."

f. Save the document as Conference Volunteers.

g. Center the first line and increase the font size to 14. Add bold and color to the three headings. Indent the paragraphs below each heading 0.5 inch and set the line spacing to double.

h. Below the Special Events topic, enter the title **Volunteer Times Available**. Use the same formatting as the main title with a font size of 14 points.

i. Below this heading, you will create a table. Place center tab stops at 1, 2.5, and 4.25 inches on the ruler. Enter the word **Day** at the first tab stop, **Date** at the second tab stop, and **Time** at the third tab stop.

j. Press ⏎Enter, then clear the tab stops. Create a left tab at 0.75 and 2.25 and a right tab stop at 5. Enter the schedule information shown here into the table.

Monday	May 8	10:00 AM to 1:00 PM
Tuesday	May 9	7:00 PM to 9:00 PM
Saturday	May 13	10:00 AM to 7:00 PM
Sunday	May 14	9:00 AM to 4:00 PM

k. Change the font size of the table headings to 12 points, bold, and the same color as the title. Add an underline style of your choice to the table headings. Bold the text in the remainder of the table. Change the line spacing of the entire table to single with no space after.

l. Create a shape of your choice and add the text **For more information visit us at www.arf.com** using a font size of 12 points and bold. Size the shape appropriately. Remove the hyperlink format from the URL. Add color to the URL. Add a fill color to the shape. Center the shape at the bottom of the page.

m. Add document properties. Save and print the document.

Advertising Weekly Specials ★★★

5. Now that the Downtown Internet Cafe has had its grand re-opening celebration, the owner wants to continue to bring in new and repeat customers by offering weekly specials. You want to create a flyer describing the coffee varieties and specials for the week. Your completed flyer will be similar to the one shown here.

a. Open a new document.

b. Enter the title **Downtown Internet Cafe** on the first line. Change the font to Arial Rounded MT Bold. Add three blank lines.

c. Enter **Italian Market Reserve** on the line followed by two blank lines.

d. On line 7, place a left tab stop at 0.5 and center tabs at 3.25 and 5.75 inches.

e. Enter the word **Coffee** at the first tab stop, **Description** at the second tab stop, and **Cost/Pound** at the third tab stop.

f. On the next line, clear all the tab stops and enter the rest of the information for the table shown in the final document using left tabs at 0.5, 2, and 5.5.

Original	Our Signature Coffee! With Old World charm	$10.49
Decaffeinated	All the original has to offer — decaffeinated natural.	$13.49
Reduced Caffeine	All the original has to offer with half of the caffeine.	$13.49

g. Add tab leaders of your choice between the data in the table. Remove the space after each line in the table.

h. Center the first title line and change the font color to green with a font size of 28 pt.

i. Center the second title line and change it to purple with a font size of 22 pt.

j. Increase the font of the table headings to 14 pt. Add bold, color, and an underline style of your choice to the table headings.

k. Save the document as Weekly Specials.

l. Open the file wd02_Coffee Flyer. Display the document windows side by side. Copy the first two paragraphs and insert them above "Italian Market Reserve" in the new document.

m. Spell-check the document. Use the thesaurus to find better words for "desire" and "giant" in the first paragraph.

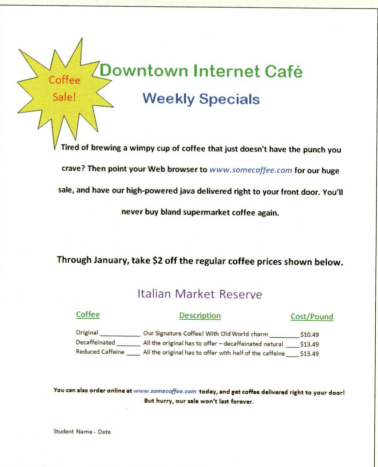

n. Use Find and Replace to replace all occurrences of "java" with "coffee" (except the one following "high-powered").

o. Center the words **Weekly Specials** below the title. Use the same font as the title, change the font size to 24 points, and select a color of your choice.

p. Make the paragraph that begins with "Tired" bold, centered, and 14 pt, and set the line spacing to double. Add blue color to the URL.

q. Increase the font size of the line above "Italian Market Reserve" to 16 pt. Center the text.

r. Copy the remaining paragraph from the wd02_Coffee Flyer document and insert it at the bottom of the new document. Include two blank lines between the table and the paragraph. Close the wd02_Coffee Flyer document.

s. Bold and center the final paragraph. Remove the hyperlink format from the URL. Format the URL as italic and blue.

t. Increase the top, left, and right margins to 1.5 inches.

u. Create the Explosion 1 shape from the Stars and Banners group. Enter and center the text **Coffee Sale!** in red, 22 pt font size within it. Add a fill color. Size the shape appropriately. Move the shape to the left of the pricing table.

v. Adjust the formatting of the document as needed to improve its appearance.

w. Add your name using the Author quick part and the current date (as a field) several lines below the final paragraph.

x. Add document properties. Save and print the document.

Lab Exercises

on your own

Requesting a Reference ★

1. Your first year as a business major is going well and you are looking for a summer internship with a local advertising firm. You have an upcoming interview and want to come prepared with a letter of reference from your last position. Write a business letter directed to your old supervisor, Kevin Westfall, at your former position, R & A Publishing. Use the modified block letter style shown in the lab. Be sure to include the date, a salutation, two paragraphs, a closing, and your name as a signature. Spell-check the document, save the document as Reference Letter, and print it.

Cell Phone Rates ★

2. MyRatePlan.com posts up-to-date rate information on cell phone rates and available minutes at each price break. The company wants you to create the following table of rates for quick reference. Create a tabbed table using the information shown below. Bold and underline the column heads. Add style 2 tab leaders to the table entries. Above the table, write a paragraph explaining the table contents.

	Cingular	NEXTEL	Sprint	T-Mobile	Verizon Wireless
$39.99	450	300-400	300-400	600-1,000	450
$49.99				1,000	
$59.99	900	500-1,000	500-1,000	1,500	900
$79.99	1,350	800-1,400	800-1,400		1,350
$99.99	2,000	1,000-2,000	2,000-1,000	2,500	2,000

Include your name and the date below the table. Save the document as Cell Phone Rates and print the document.

Yard Sale ★ ★

3. Create a flyer to advertise a yard sale you plan for Saturday morning. Include the following features on your flyer:

- Different fonts in different sizes, colors, and styles.
- Bulleted or numbered list.
- Indents.
- A shape with appropriate text.
- A graphic.
- A tabbed table with tab leaders.

Include your name as the contact information. Save the document as Yard Sale Flyer and print it.

Wyoming Relocation ★★

4. You work for the Department of Tourism for the state of Wyoming. You have been asked to produce a relocation packet to aid people planning to move to the state. This packet includes information on state history, the weather, geography, major cities, population statistics, and so forth. Research information on the Web about Wyoming and create a one-page fact sheet of your findings. Your completed project should include an introductory paragraph on relocation, graphics, table with the average weather statistics, a bulleted list of attractions, and shapes. Include your name as the contact and save the file as Wyoming Facts. Print the file.

Downloading Music ★★★

5. Your ethics class is studying the ethics of downloading free music from online sources. Your instructor has divided the class into groups and assigned each group a research project. Your group is to find out about court cases related to copyright infringement. Use the Web to research this topic and write a one-page report on your findings. Include a table of the data you found. Use other features demonstrated in this lab, including shapes, indents, bulleted lists, font colors, and so forth to make your report attractive and easy to read. Be sure to reference your sources on the Web for the data you located. Include your name and the current date below the report. Save the report as Ethics Report and print your report.

Creating Reports and Tables

LAB 3

Objectives

After you have completed this lab, you will know how to:

1 Create and modify an outline.

2 Create a cover page.

3 Apply and customize Document Themes.

4 Apply and customize Quick Styles.

5 Create and update a table of contents and table of figures.

6 Navigate using hyperlink, Document Map, and thumbnails.

7 Add citations and create a bibliography.

8 Add footnotes, captions, and cross-references.

9 Wrap text around graphics.

10 Create and format a simple table.

11 Create and format sections.

12 Add headers, footers, and page numbers.

Adventure Travel Tours

Adventure Travel Tours provides information on their tours in a variety of forms. Travel brochures, for instance, contain basic tour information in a promotional format and are designed to entice potential clients to sign up for a tour. More detailed regional information packets are given to people who have already signed up for a tour, so they can prepare for their vacation. These packets include facts about each region's climate, geography, and culture. Additional informational formats include pages on Adventure Travel's Web site and scheduled group presentations.

Part of your responsibility as advertising coordinator is to

gather the information that Adventure Travel will publicize about each regional tour. Specifically, you have been asked to provide background information for two of the new tours: the Tanzania Safari and the Machu Picchu trail. Because this information is used in a variety of formats, your research needs to be easily adapted. You will therefore present your facts in the form of a general report on Tanzania and Peru.

In this lab, you will learn to use many of the features of Office Word 2007 that make it easy to create an attractive and well-organized report. A portion of the completed report is shown here.

Adventure Travel Tours

Tanzania and Peru

---

region to region, ranging from tropical to arctic. Its varied climate corresponds to the sharpl
contrasting geographical features of seafront, mountains, and rainforests.

La Costa
Occupying the slender area along Peru's western coastline, La Costa, provides a division
between the mountains and sea. Although some of this area is fertile, mostly it is extremely d
and arid. This region's temperature averages approximately 68°F, and it receives almost 2 inc
of rainfall annually. The Andes Mountains prevent greater annual precipitation coming from t
east. Some areas in the south are considered drier than the Sahara. Conversely, there are a few
areas in this region where mountain rivers meet the ocean that are green with life and do not gi
the impression of being in a desert at all.

La Selva
La Selva, a region of tropical rainforest, is the easternmost region in Peru. This region, with the
eastern foot of the Andes Mountains, forms the Amazon Basin, into which numerous rivers flow
The Amazon River begins at the meeting point of the two dominant rivers, the Ucayali and
Marañón. La Selva is extremely wet, with some areas exceeding an annual precipitation of 137
inches. Its wettest season occurs from November to April. The weather here is humid and
extremely hot.

La Sierra
Inland and to the east is the mountainous region called La Sierra, encompassing Peru's share of
the Andes mountain range. The southern portion of this region is prone to volcanic activity, and
some volcanoes are active today. La Sierra is subject to a dry season from May to September,
which is winter in that part of the world. The weath
in some areas during the night. The weath
precipitation. The former Incan capital Cu
the Incas. This region also contains Lake T

Region	An
La Costa	
La Sierra	
La Selva	

Table 1: Peru Climate

---
³ Lake Titicaca is 12,507 feet above sea level.

Table of Contents

American and European ancestry), 15 percent white, and 3 percent other (primarily Black and
Asian). The official language is Spanish, and the predominant religion is Roman Catholic.

Animal Life

Peru is home to many exotic animals, but is particularly known for its
large population of birds. More than 1,700 species can be found,
including parakeets, toucans, and Amazon parrots. Many extremely rare
families of birds also live here. Each geographical region of Peru boasts
its own distinct habitat, and some types of birds cannot
else.

Figure 2: Amazon Parrot

The popular Manu National Park spanning over 4.5 mil
unbroken Peruvian rain forest is alive with several species of monkeys, the oce
boars, iguana, and the anaconda. It is also considered one of the best places in t
the elusive jaguar. Both the squirrel monkey, named for its relatively small size
monkey, which is quite loud vocally, can be spotted throughout the rainforests
many of the Amazon River basins and lakes. Though they are known to be vici
common misconception that they are man-eaters; in fact, they will graciously s
with human swimmers. Also found in the remote Yarapa and Amazon Rivers i
pink dolphin, so named because of its striking pink hue.

Table of Figures
Figure 1: Giraffe in Serengeti...
Table 1: Peru Climate..
Figure 2: Amazon Parrots...

Works Cited
Camerapix, comp. Spectrum Guide to Tanzania. Edison: Hunter, 1992.

Country Studies US. Peru. 2003-2005. 3 November 2006
<http://countrystudies.us/peru/23.htm>.

Wikipedia: The Free Encyclopedia. Tanzania. 5 October 2006. 3 November 2006
<http://en.wikipedia.org/wiki/Tanzania>.

Tables, footnotes, cross-references, and headers and footers are many standard features that are quick and easy to include in a report.

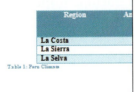

Wrapping text around graphics, adding figure captions, and applying a document theme are among many features that can be used to enhance a report.

A cover page and table of contents listing can be created quickly using Word's built-in features.

A bibliography can be quickly generated from cited sources.

Concept Preview

The following concepts will be introduced in this lab:

1 **Quick Styles** Applying a quick style, a predefined set of formatting characteristics, allows you to quickly apply a whole group of formats to a selection in one simple step.

2 **Document Theme** A document theme is a predefined set of formatting choices that can be applied to an entire document in one simple step.

3 **Table of Contents** A table of contents is a listing of the topic headings that appear in a document and their associated page references.

4 **Citations and Bibliography** Parenthetical source references, called citations, give credit for specific information included in the document. Complete information for citations is included in a bibliography at the end of the report.

5 **Footnote and Endnote** Footnotes and endnotes are used in documented research papers to explain or comment on information in the text, or provide source references for text in the document.

6 **Text Wrapping** You can control the appearance of text around a graphic object by specifying the text wrapping style.

7 **Captions and Cross-References** A caption is a numbered label for a figure, table, picture, or graph. A cross-reference is a reference from one part of a document to related information in another part.

8 **Table** A table is used to organize information into an easy-to-read format of horizontal rows and vertical columns.

9 **Table of Figures** A table of figures is a list of the figures, tables, or equations used in a document and their associated page references.

10 **Header and Footer** A header is a line or several lines of text in the top margin of each page. A footer is a line or several lines of text in the margin space at the bottom of every page.

11 **Section** To format different parts of a document differently, you can divide a document into sections.

Creating and Modifying an Outline

After several days of research, you have gathered many notes from various sources including books, magazines, and the Web. However, the notes are very disorganized and you are having some difficulty getting started writing the report. Often the best way to start is by creating an outline of the main topics.

Word 2007 allows you to create and view document content easily as an outline using Outline view. Outline view shows the hierarchy of topics in a document by displaying the different heading levels indented to represent their level in the document's structure, as shown in the example at right. The

- Tanzania
  - Culture
  - Geography
    - Climate
  - Animal Life
- Peru
  - Culture
    - Historical Culture
      - Machu Picchu
  - Geography and Climate
  - Animal Life

arrangement of headings in a hierarchy of importance quickly shows the relationship between topics. You can use Outline view to help you create a new document or to view and reorganize the topics in an existing document.

Using Outline View

You will use Outline view to help you organize the main topics of the report.

1 ● **Start Office Word 2007.**

● **Click** ▤ **Outline View in the status bar.**

● **If necessary, increase the zoom to 100%.**

Another Method

You also can use ⬚ in the Document Views group of the View tab.

Your screen should be similar to Figure 3.1

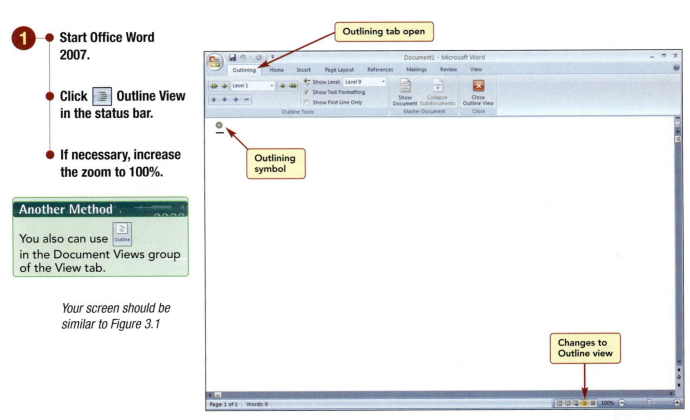

Figure 3.1

The Outlining tab containing buttons that make it easy to create and modify the outline is displayed. Notice the first line of the blank document displays the ⊖ outline symbol. This symbol indicates that the line does not contain subtopics. You will begin by entering the main topic headings for the report.

2 ● Type the following headings, pressing ⏎Enter after each except the last:

Tanzania

Climate

Geography

Animal Life

Peru

Culture

Historical Culture

Machu Picchu

Geography and Climate

Animal Life (do not press ⏎Enter))

● Correct any misspelled words and use Ignore All for any identified proper names.

Your screen should be similar to Figure 3.2

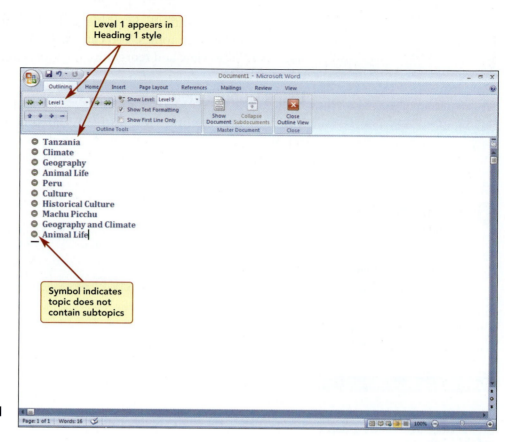

Level 1 appears in Heading 1 style

Symbol indicates topic does not contain subtopics

Figure 3.2

As you create a new document in Outline view, Word automatically applies styles to the text as it is entered in the outline.

1 Applying a **quick style**, a predefined set of formatting characteristics, allows you to quickly apply a whole group of formats to a selection in one simple step. Word includes 75 predefined quick styles. Each quick style is assigned a name. You also can create your own custom styles. Many styles are automatically applied when certain features, such as footnotes, are used. Others must be applied manually to selected text.

Styles can be applied to characters, paragraphs, tables, and lists as described below.

Type of Style	Description
Character	Affects selected text within a paragraph, such as the font and size of text, and bold and italic formats.
Paragraph	Controls all aspects of a paragraph's appearance, such as text alignment, tab stops, and line spacing. It also can include character formatting. The default paragraph quick style is named Normal, which includes character settings of Calibri, 11 pt, and paragraph settings of left indent at 0, 1.15 line spacing, and left alignment. In addition, many paragraph styles are designed to affect specific text elements such as headings, captions, and footnotes.
Table	Provides a consistent look to borders, shading, alignment, and fonts in tables.
List	Applies similar alignment, numbering or bullet characters, and fonts to lists.

Having Trouble?

If your document does not display the styles, click ☑ Show Text Formatting in the Outline Tools group to turn on this feature.

The outline levels are automatically formatted using **heading styles**. They are designed to identify different levels of headings in a document. Heading styles include combinations of fonts, type sizes, color, bold, italics, and spacing. The heading styles used here are those associated with the default document settings. The heading styles and the formats associated with each are shown in the table below:

Heading Level	Appearance
Heading 1	**Cambria, 14 pt, bold, left align, spacing 24 pt before, 0 pt after, blue**
Heading 2	**Cambria, 13 pt, bold, left align, spacing 10 pt before, 0 pt after, blue**
Heading 3	Cambria, 13 pt, left align, spacing 10 pt before, 0 pt after, blue
Heading 4	*Cambria, 11 pt, bold italic, left align, spacing 10 pt before, 0 pt after, blue*

The Outline Level button in the Outlining tab shows that the selected item is a Level 1 heading, which is automatically assigned a Heading 1 style. This style is the largest and most prominent. The Level 2 headings (subheadings) are assigned the Heading 2 style, and so on. Headings give the reader another visual cue about how information is organized in your document.

Changing Outline Levels

Next, you need to arrange the headings by outline levels. As you rearrange the topic headings and subheadings, different heading styles are applied based upon the position or level of the topic within the outline hierarchy. Headings that are level 1 appear as the top level of the outline and appear in a Heading 1 style, level 2 headings appear indented below level 1 headings and appear in a Heading 2 style, and so on.

First you will make the Climate topic heading a subtopic below the main heading of Tanzania. The ➡ Promote and ➡ Demote buttons in the Outline Tools group are used to change outline levels one level at a time.

Additional Information

Clicking 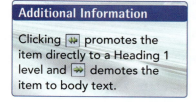 promotes the item directly to a Heading 1 level and ➡ demotes the item to body text.

1 ● **Click on the Climate topic.**

● **Click ➡ Demote in the Outline Tools group.**

Your screen should be similar to Figure 3.3

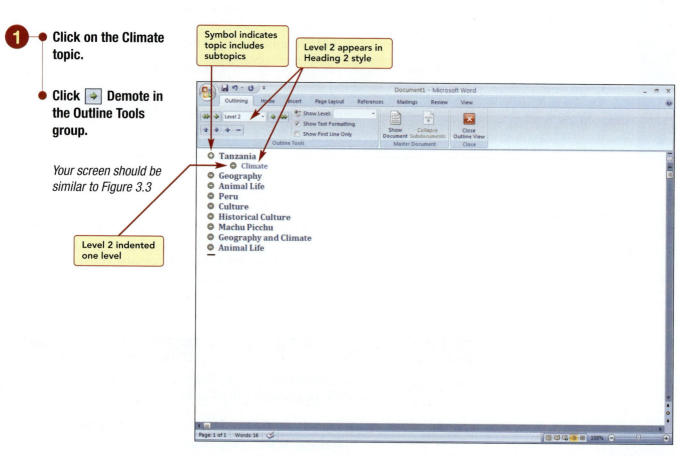

Symbol indicates topic includes subtopics

Level 2 appears in Heading 2 style

Level 2 indented one level

Figure 3.3

The Climate heading has changed to a Heading 2 style and the heading is indented one level to show it is subordinate to the heading above it. The Tanzania heading now displays an outline ⊕ symbol, which indicates the topic heading includes subtopics.

The outline symbols also can be used to select and move the heading to a new location or level within the document. Dragging the outline symbol to the right or left changes the level. To demote a heading to a lower level, drag the symbol to the right; to promote a heading to a higher level, drag the symbol to the left. As you drag the symbol, a vertical solid gray line appears at each outline level to show where the heading will be placed.

2 ● Drag the ⊖ symbol of the Geography heading to the right two levels (Level 3).

Additional Information

The mouse pointer changes to ⊹, indicating that dragging it will move the heading.

● Demote the remaining topics to the heading levels shown below.

Animal Life	Level 2
Culture	Level 2
Historical Culture	Level 3
Machu Picchu	Level 4
Geography and Climate	Level 2
Animal Life	Level 2

Your screen should be similar to Figure 3.4

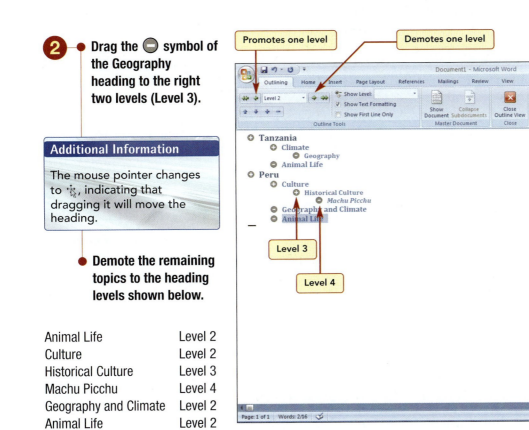

Figure 3.4

Another Method

You also can click ⬆ Move Up and ⬇ Move Down to move a topic or use the keyboard shortcuts Alt + Shift + ↑ or Alt + Shift + ↓.

Moving and Inserting Outline Topics

Next, you want to change the order of topics. To move a heading to a different location, drag the outline symbol up or down. As you drag, a horizontal line shows where the heading will be placed when you release the mouse button. You also realize you forgot to include a heading for Culture under Tanzania and will insert the new topic at the appropriate location in the outline.

1

- Drag the Geography heading up above the Climate heading.

- Promote the Geography heading to a level 2.

- Demote the Climate heading to a level 3.

- Move to the beginning of the Geography heading.

- Press ⏎Enter to insert a blank topic heading.

- Type Culture on the blank heading line.

Your screen should be similar to Figure 3.5

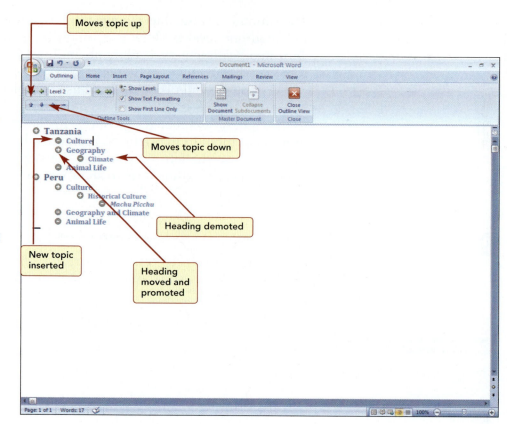

Figure 3.5

When you are satisfied with the organization, you can close Outline view to add detailed body text and graphics.

2

- Click  in the Close group.

- If necessary, set the zoom to 100%.

Another Method
You also could switch directly to another view to close Outline view.

Your screen should be similar to Figure 3.6

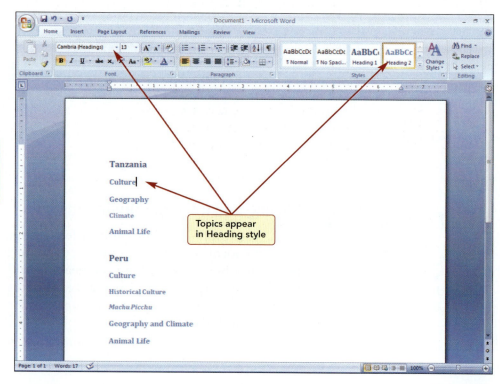

Figure 3.6

The topic headings appear left-aligned on the page in the heading style that was applied to the text as the outline was created. You will learn more about using Styles later in the lab.

Collapsing and Expanding the Outline

You have continued to work on the outline and report organization. Then you entered much of the information for the report and saved it. You will open the document to see the information that has been added to the report.

1 ● **Open the file** **wd03_Tour Research.**

● **Switch to Outline view.**

● **Scroll the window to view the entire document.**

● **Return to the top of the document.**

Your screen should be similar to Figure 3.7

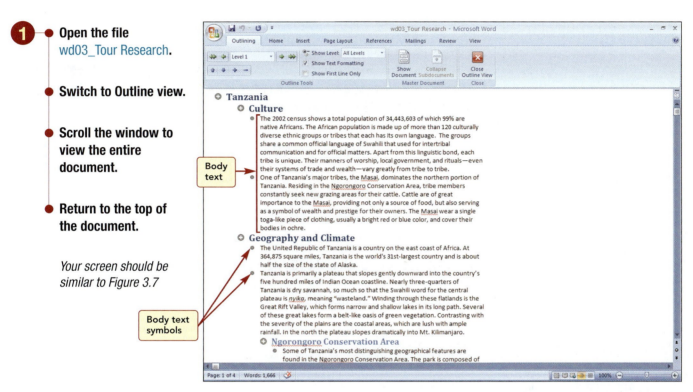

Figure 3.7

The document is displayed as an outline with the topic headings indented appropriately. The body text appears below the appropriate heading. Any text that has not been formatted in a heading style is considered body text and is identified in outline view by the small circles to the left of a paragraph.

In Outline view, you can display as much or as little of the document text as you want. To make it easier to view and reorganize the document's structure, you can "collapse" the document to show just the headings you want. Alternatively, you can "expand" the document to display part of the body text below each heading or the entire body text. You can then easily move the headings around until the order is logical, and the body text will follow the heading. The table below shows how you can collapse and expand the amount of text displayed in Outline view.

To Collapse	Do This
Text below a specific heading level	Select the lowest heading you want to display from the [Show Level: Level 1 ▼] drop-down menu.
All subheadings and body text under a heading	Double-click ⊕ next to the heading.
Text under a heading, one level at a time	Click the heading text, and then click [–] Collapse.
All body text	Select the heading level you want to see from the [Show Level: Level 1 ▼] drop-down menu.
All body text except first line	Click [☐ Show First Line Only].

To Expand	Do This
All headings and body text	Select Show All Levels from the [Show Level: Level 1 ▼] drop-down menu.
All collapsed subheadings and body text under a heading	Double-click ⊖ next to the heading.
Collapsed text under a heading, one level at a time	Click the heading text; then click [+] Expand.

To change the amount of information displayed, you will collapse the display of the text under the Geography and Climate heading first. Then you will collapse everything below a level 3 heading so you can quickly check the report organization.

1 ● Double-click ⊕ of the Tanzania Geography and Climate heading.

● Open the [Show Level: ▼] drop-down list.

● Choose Level 3.

Your screen should be similar to Figure 3.8

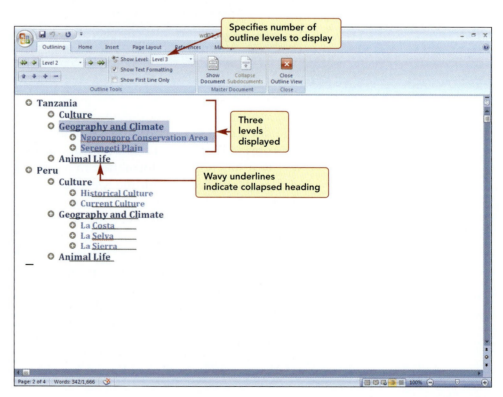

Figure 3.8

Now only the three heading levels are displayed. The wavy line below a heading means the heading includes hidden or collapsed headings or body text.

As you look at the organization of the report, you decide to move the discussion of culture to follow the Geography and Climate section. Moving headings in Outline view quickly selects and moves the entire topic, including subtopics and all body text.

2 ● Drag the Culture heading in the Tanzania section down to above the Animal Life heading in the same section.

● Drag the Culture heading in the Peru section down to above the Animal Life heading in the same section.

● Choose All Levels from the Show Level: Level 3 drop-down list.

● Scroll the report up to see the top of the Peru Culture section on page 3.

● Click in the document to deselect the text.

Your screen should be similar to Figure 3.9

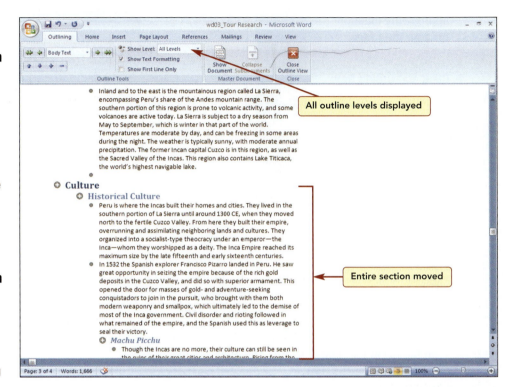

Figure 3.9

The subtopics and body text appear below the heading you moved. When you move or change the level of a heading that includes collapsed subordinate text, the collapsed text also is selected. Any changes you make to the heading, such as moving, copying, or deleting it, also affect the collapsed text.

Saving to a New Folder

Next, you will save the outline and the research document with its changes in a folder that you will use to hold files related to the report. You can create a new folder at the same time you save a file.

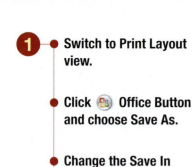

1 • Switch to Print Layout view.

• Click  Office Button and choose Save As.

• Change the Save In location to the appropriate location for your data files.

• Click 📁 Create New Folder.

Another Method
The keyboard shortcut to create a new folder is
[Alt] + 4.

Your screen should be similar to Figure 3.10

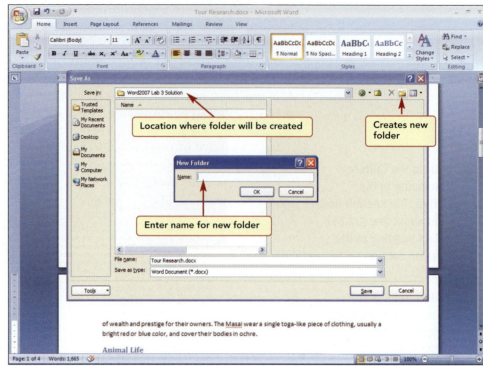

Figure 3.10

Additional Information
See "Saving, Closing, and Opening Files" in Lab 1 for file-naming rules.

In the New Folder dialog box, you enter the folder name. The rules for naming folders are the same as for naming files, except they typically do not include an extension.

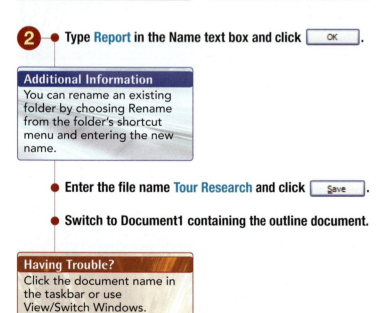

2 • Type **Report** in the Name text box and click [OK].

Additional Information
You can rename an existing folder by choosing Rename from the folder's shortcut menu and entering the new name.

• Enter the file name **Tour Research** and click [Save].

• Switch to Document1 containing the outline document.

Having Trouble?
Click the document name in the taskbar or use View/Switch Windows.

• Save the outline to the Report folder with the file name **Research Outline**.

• Close the **Research Outline** document.

The documents are saved in the newly created folder, Report.

Hiding Spelling and Grammar Errors

As you have been working on the report, you have noticed that many spelling and grammar errors are identified. You want to scroll the document to take a quick look at the types of errors identified. You have noticed that scrolling a larger document in Print Layout view takes more time because the view displays the extra blank (white) space on the page and the space allocated for the headers and footers. You can hide the display of this white space to make it faster to move through the document.

1 ● **Double-click on the blue page separator space between any pages.**

Additional Information
The mouse pointer appears as ⊞ when you can hide the white space.

● **Scroll to see the bottom of page 1 and the top of page 2.**

Additional Information
The page number appears in a ScreenTip as you scroll by dragging the scroll box.

Your screen should be similar to Figure 3.11

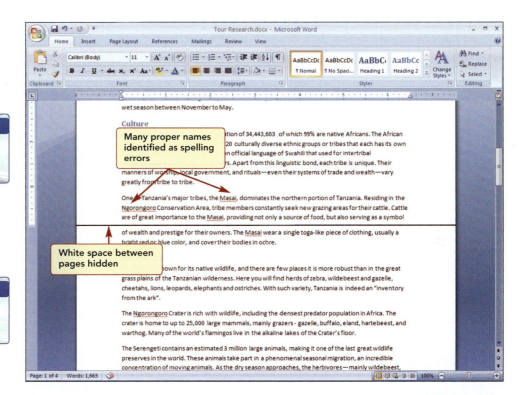

Figure 3.11

Any extra white space is eliminated, making scrolling much faster. As you scrolled the document, you noticed that most of the identified errors are for proper names and words that are not in the dictionary. While working on a document, you can turn off the display of these errors so that they are not distracting.

2 ● Click ⬛ **Office Button.**

● Click 🔲 Word Options .

● **Open the Proofing group.**

Your screen should be similar to Figure 3.12

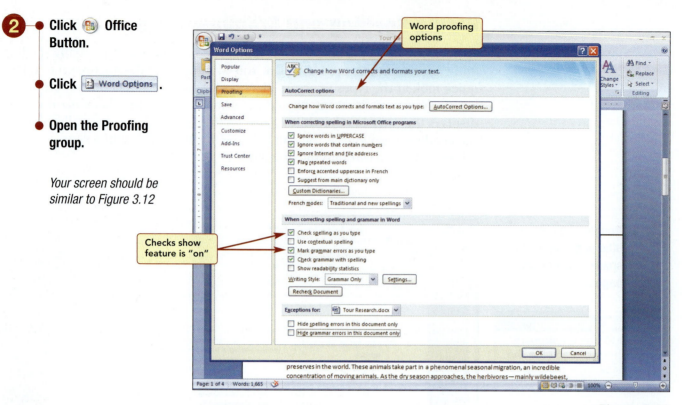

Figure 3.12

The Proofing options are used to change the way the AutoCorrect and Spelling and Grammar features operate. Checkmarks next to options indicate the setting is on. You want to turn off the display of spelling and grammar errors.

3 ● **Select Hide spelling errors in this document only.**

● **Select Hide grammar errors in this document only.**

● Click OK .

● **Double-click on the page separator line to show the white space again.**

Additional Information
The mouse pointer appears as ‡‡‡ when you can show white space.

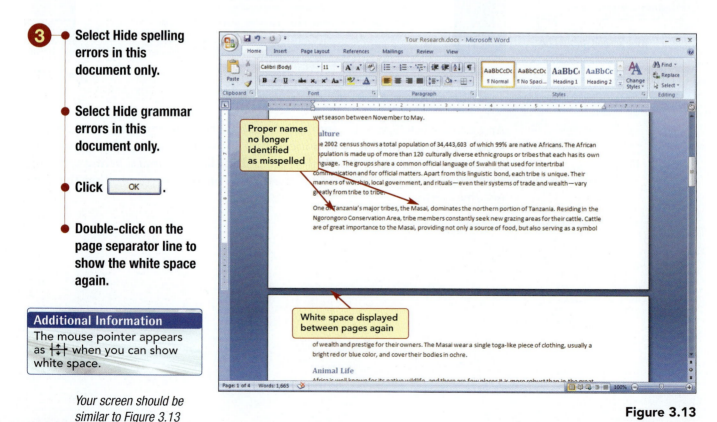

Your screen should be similar to Figure 3.13

Figure 3.13

The red and green wavy lines are no longer displayed. You can still run spelling and grammar checking manually to check errors at any time. The extra blank space at the bottom of page 3 and the header and footer space are displayed again. Now that you know how to use this feature, you can turn it on and off whenever you want.

Creating a Cover Page

Now that you have finished reorganizing the report, you want to add a title or cover page. Generally, this page includes information such as the report title, the name of the author, and the date.

When preparing research reports, two styles of report formatting are commonly used: MLA (Modern Language Association) and APA (American Psychological Association). Although they require the same basic information, they differ in how this information is presented. For example, MLA style does not include a separate title page, but APA style does. The report you will create in this lab will use many of the style requirements of the MLA. However, because this report is not a formal report to be presented at a conference or other academic proceeding, some liberties have been taken with the style to demonstrate Word 2007 features.

Inserting and Modifying a Cover Page

Word 2007 includes many preformatted building blocks that help you quickly create professional-looking documents. The preformatted content includes cover pages, pull quotes, and headers and footers. They are fully formatted and provide spaces where you enter the title, date, and other information. You will use this feature to insert a cover page. Regardless of the location of the insertion point in a document, a cover page is always inserted at the beginning of the document.

1

- Open the Insert tab.

- Choose Cover Page from the Pages group.

- Scroll the gallery and choose the Mod cover page design.

- Change the zoom to display two pages.

Having Trouble?
Use the Zoom slider or Two Pages on the View tab.

Your screen should be similar to Figure 3.14

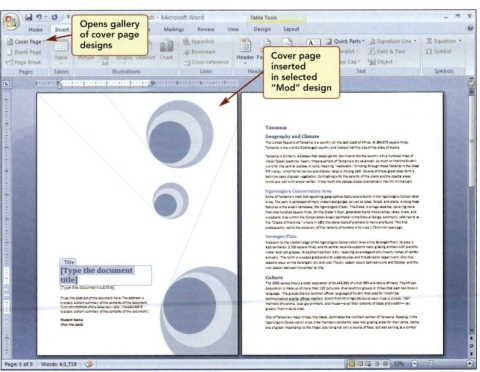

Figure 3.14

A new page is inserted at the beginning of the document with the selected cover page design. After looking at this design, you decide to change it to a more traditional cover page look.

2 ● Click [Cover Page ▾] .

● **Choose the Sideline design.**

Your screen should be similar to Figure 3.15

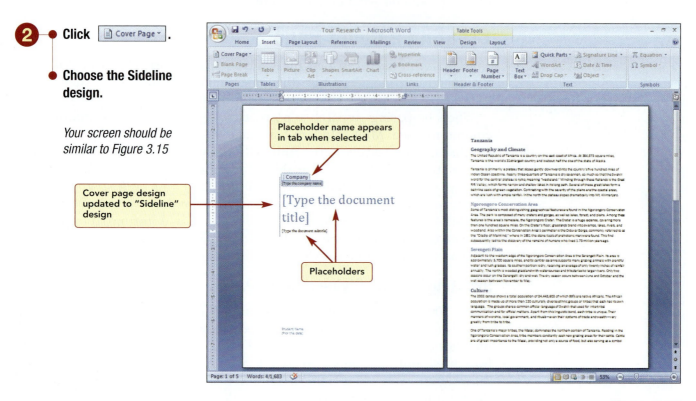

Cover page design updated to "Sideline" design

Placeholder name appears in tab when selected

Placeholders

Figure 3.15

The new cover page design you selected replaces the first cover page you inserted. This design includes a blue vertical line to the left of the sample title information centered on the page. The title text is a larger font size and blue. Additionally, the design includes the author and date information in blue at the bottom of the page. In addition to the design elements, the cover page includes placeholders for the information you need to enter. A **placeholder** is a graphic element that is designed to contain specific types of information. In this case, placeholders identify the content that should be entered to complete the information for the cover page. If the company name and document title have already been entered in the document properties, the placeholders will automatically display this information.

Additional Information

To delete a cover page, choose Remove Current Cover Page from the [Cover Page ▾] menu.

When you click on a placeholder, the placeholder name appears in a tab and the placeholder text is selected and ready to be replaced. You will replace the Company and Title placeholder text.

3 • **Increase the zoom to 80 percent and scroll the page so you can see both the report title and the author and date areas.**

• **Click the Company placeholder and type Adventure Travel Tours.**

• **Click the Title placeholder and type Tanzania and Peru.**

Your screen should be similar to Figure 3.16

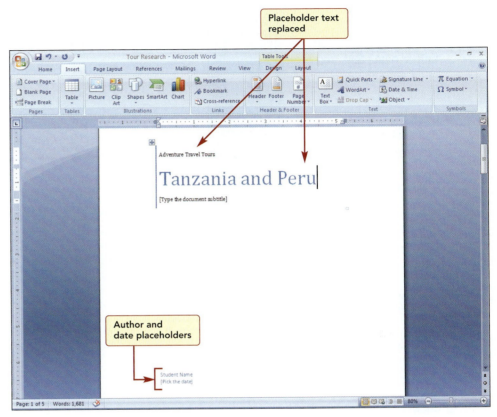

Figure 3.16

The placeholder text was replaced with the text you typed. Additionally, the company name and title information you entered have been automatically added to the document properties.

Finally, you will delete the Subtitle placeholder and add your name as author and the current date. Notice Student Name appears as the Author because this is the name that is stored in the document properties. Since the name is not placeholder text, you will need to select it before replacing it with your name. When you click on the date placeholder, you will use the date picker feature to quickly enter the current date from the pop-up calendar.

4 ● Select the Subtitle placeholder and press Delete twice to delete the contents and then the placeholder.

● Click the Author placeholder, select the author name text, and enter your name.

● Click the Date placeholder and open the drop-down list to display the date-picker calendar.

● Choose Today to display the current date.

Additional Information

You also can click on a specific date in the calendar that you want and use the right and left arrow buttons to scroll through the months.

● Click outside the placeholder.

● Save the document.

Your screen should be similar to Figure 3.17

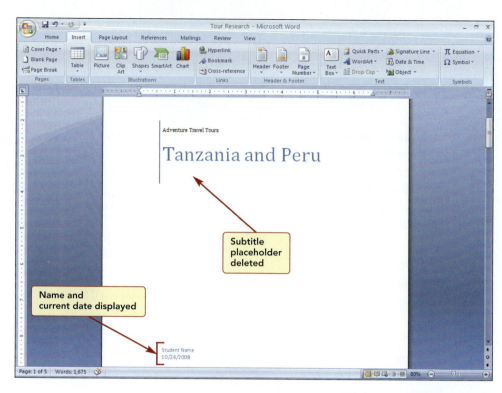

Figure 3.17

The cover page is now complete.

Using Document Themes

Because color and design are important elements of documents, Word includes a collection of built-in document themes.

2 A **document theme** is a predefined set of formatting choices that can be applied to an entire document in one simple step. Word includes 20 named built-in document themes. Each document theme includes three subsets of themes: colors, fonts, and effects. Each color theme consists of 12 colors that are applied to specific elements in a document. Each fonts theme includes different body and heading fonts. Each effects theme includes different lines and fill effects. You also can create your own custom themes by modifying an existing document theme and saving it as a custom theme. The default document (Normal.dotm) uses the Office theme.

Using themes gives your documents a professional and modern look. Because document themes are shared across 2007 Office applications, all your office documents can have the same uniform look.

Applying a Theme

You decide to see how the report would look using a different document theme.

1
● Change the zoom to display two pages.

● Open the Page Layout tab.

● Click [Themes] from the Themes group.

Your screen should be similar to Figure 3.18

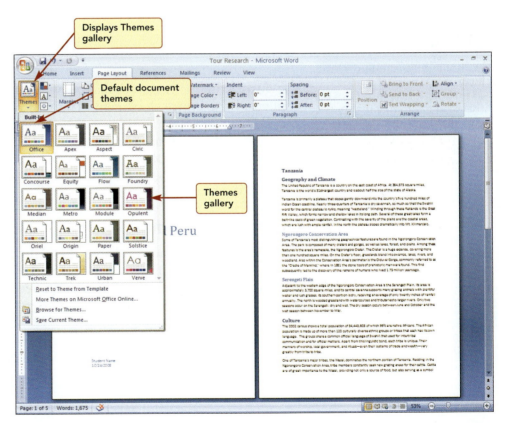

Figure 3.18

A gallery of 20 built-in named themes is displayed. A sample shows the color and font effects included in each theme. The Office theme is highlighted because it is the default theme and is the theme that is used in this document. Pointing to each theme will display a Live Preview of how it will appear in the document.

2 • **Point to several themes to preview them.**

• **Choose the Trek theme.**

Your screen should be similar to Figure 3.19

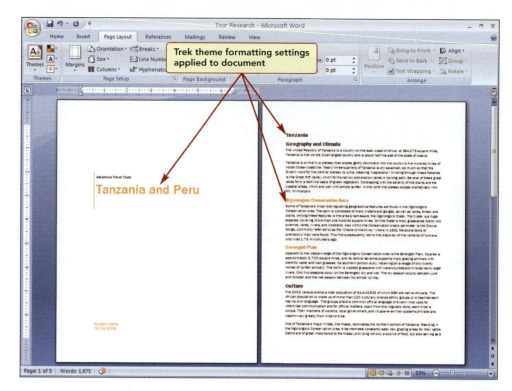

Figure 3.19

Additional Information

If you made manual changes to text, for example, by changing the font and font size of the title as opposed to applying a Title style, these changes are not updated to the new theme design.

The formatting settings associated with the selected theme have been applied to the entire document. The two obvious changes are the color and font changes for the titles and heading levels. The font of all heading styles has changed to Franklin Gothic medium from the default of Cambria. The color associated with the different heading levels also has changed. Additionally, the body text font has changed from Calibri to Franklin Gothic Book.

Customizing a Theme

Sometimes, you cannot find just the right combination of features in a built-in theme. To solve this problem, you can customize a theme by changing the color scheme, fonts, and effects. Although you like much of the Trek theme design, you decide to try customizing the theme by changing the color scheme and fonts.

First you will change the color scheme. Each theme has an associated set of colors that you can change by applying the colors from another theme to the selected theme.

MORE ABOUT

▶ To learn how to customize theme colors, see 1.1 Format Documents in the More About appendix.

1 ● Click ■ Theme Colors.

Additional Information

The colors you see in the ■ Theme Colors button represent the current text and background colors.

Your screen should be similar to Figure 3.20

Current color scheme is selected

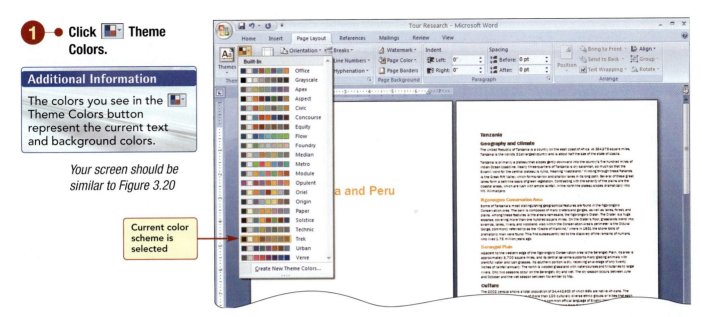

Figure 3.20

The colors used in each of the themes are displayed in the Built-In drop-down list. The set of eight colors that appears next to each theme color name represent the text, background, accent, and hyperlink colors. The Trek color scheme is selected because it is the color scheme currently in use. You want to see how the Concourse color scheme would look.

2 ● Point to several color schemes to preview them.

● Choose the Concourse theme.

Your screen should be similar to Figure 3.21

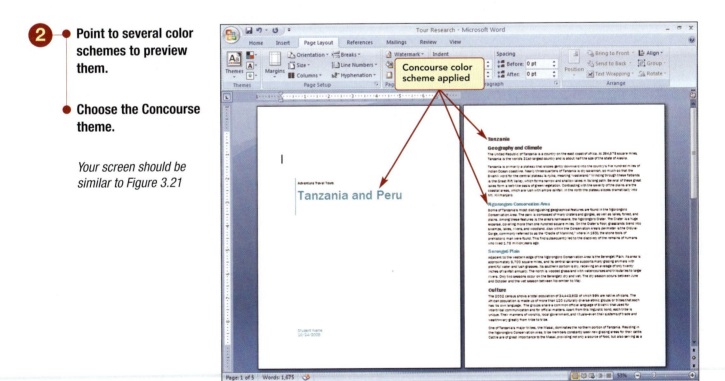

Figure 3.21

The new color scheme has been applied to different elements such as the headings. All other aspects of the Trek theme are unchanged.

Next, you will change the theme fonts. Just like theme colors, you could change fonts by applying fonts from another theme to the selected theme. This time, however, you will specify your own font settings for the selected theme. Each theme contains a heading font and a body text font.

3 ● Click  Theme Fonts.

Additional Information
The name of the heading and body text fonts for each theme appears below the Theme Fonts name in the Theme Fonts gallery.

● Choose Create New Theme Fonts

Your screen should be similar to Figure 3.22

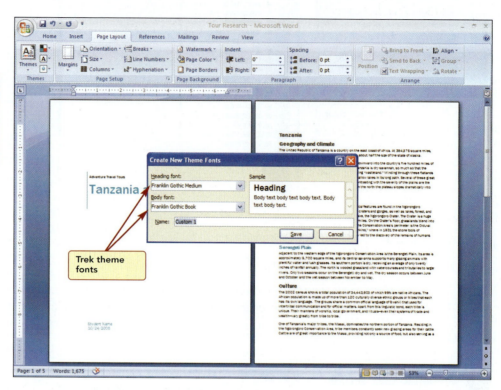

Figure 3.22

The fonts used in the current theme are displayed in the Heading and Body font text boxes. You will change the heading font to Constantia and the body font to Times New Roman.

4 • **From the Heading font drop-down list, select Constantia.**

• **From the Body font drop-down list, select Times New Roman.**

• **Replace the default name with Report Font.**

• **Click** [Save] .

• **Click** [A▾] **Theme Fonts.**

Additional Information

To remove a custom theme font, choose Delete from the Theme Font shortcut menu.

Your screen should be similar to Figure 3.23

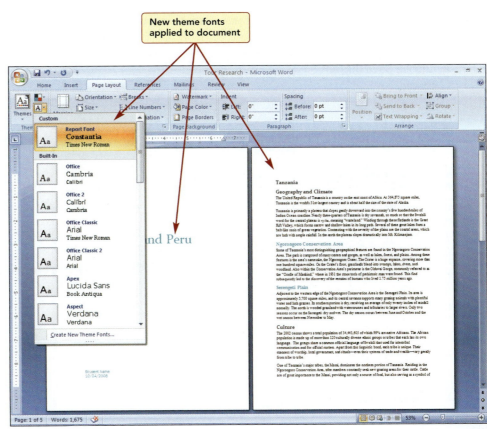

New theme fonts applied to document

Figure 3.23

MORE ABOUT

 To learn how to customize theme effects, see "Change Theme Effects" in the 1.1 Format Documents section of the More About appendix.

The name of the custom theme font appears at the top of the Theme Fonts gallery list and could be applied simply by selecting it from the list. As you add other features to the document, they will be formatted using the customized Trek theme colors and fonts.

Saving a Custom Theme

After making all these changes to the Trek theme, you decide to save the changes as a custom theme. This will make it easy to reapply the same settings to another document in the future.

1 ● Click 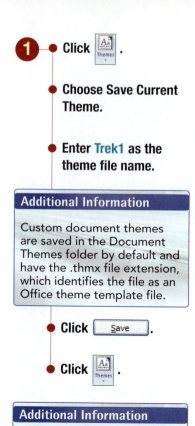.

● Choose Save Current Theme.

● Enter **Trek1** as the theme file name.

Additional Information

Custom document themes are saved in the Document Themes folder by default and have the .thmx file extension, which identifies the file as an Office theme template file.

● Click [Save] .

● Click 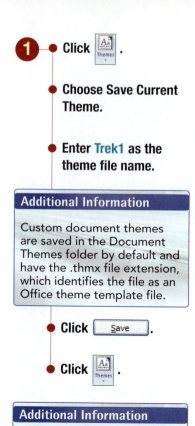.

Additional Information

To remove a custom theme, choose Delete from the theme's shortcut menu.

Your screen should be similar to Figure 3.24

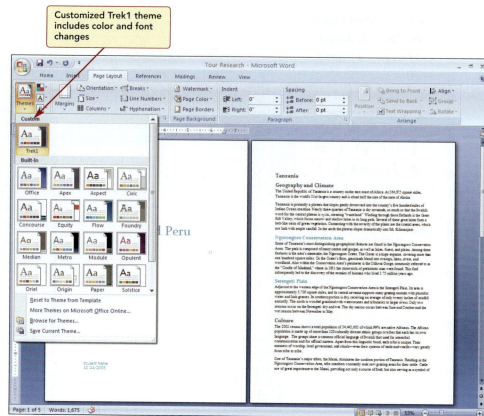

Figure 3.24

Additional Information

You can quickly return a document back to the default style using Reset to Theme from Template on the 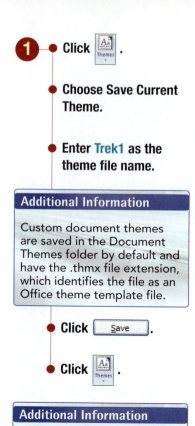 menu.

MORE ABOUT

▶ To learn how to set a theme as a default theme and how to restore template themes, see these topics in the 1.1 Format Documents section of the More About appendix.

The custom theme you created appears at the top of the Themes gallery. Now you can quickly reapply this entire theme in one step to another document, just like the built-in themes.

Inserting a Blank Page

Next you will create a new page to contain a table of contents. You will enter a title for the page and then improve the appearance of the title by applying a style to the title. You want the new page to be inserted above the Tanzania topic heading. Blank pages are inserted above the location of the insertion point.

1 • Move to the blank line above the Tanzania heading at the top of page 2.

• Open the Insert tab and click 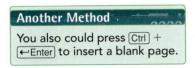 in the Pages group to create a blank page above it.

Another Method

You also could press [Ctrl] + [←Enter] to insert a blank page.

Your screen should be similar to Figure 3.25

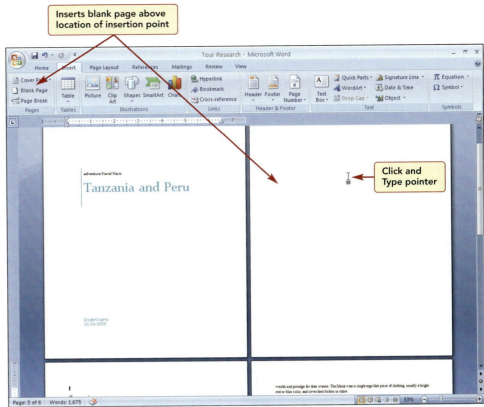

Inserts blank page above location of insertion point

Click and Type pointer

Figure 3.25

A blank page has been inserted in the document.

Using Click and Type

Next you want to enter a title for the table of contents that you plan to display on this page. You will use the **Click and Type** feature to enter this information. This feature, available in Print Layout and Web Layout views, is used to quickly insert text, graphics, and other items in a blank area of a document, avoiding the need to enter blank lines. This feature also applies the paragraph formatting needed to position an item at the location you clicked.

Print Layout view includes formatting "zones" that control the formatting that will be applied. As you move the mouse pointer through the zones, the I-beam pointer displays an icon that indicates the formatting that will be applied when you double-click at that location. This is the Click and Type pointer. The pointer shapes and their associated formatting are described in the table below.

Pointer shape	Formatting applied
	Align left
	Align center
	Align right
	Left indent

To enable the Click and Type pointer, first click on a blank area; then, as you move the mouse pointer, the pointer shape indicates how the item will be formatted. Double-clicking on the location in the page moves the insertion point to that location and applies the formatting to the entry. You will enter the page title, Table of Contents, centered on the page.

1 ● Click at the top of the new page to enable Click and Type.

● Increase the zoom to 100%.

● If necessary, display the ruler.

● Move the mouse pointer from left to right across the blank page and observe the change in the mouse pointer.

● Double-click on the center of the page at the 1-inch vertical ruler position while the mouse pointer is a $\underline{\text{I}}$.

● Type **Table of Contents**.

Your screen should be similar to Figure 3.26

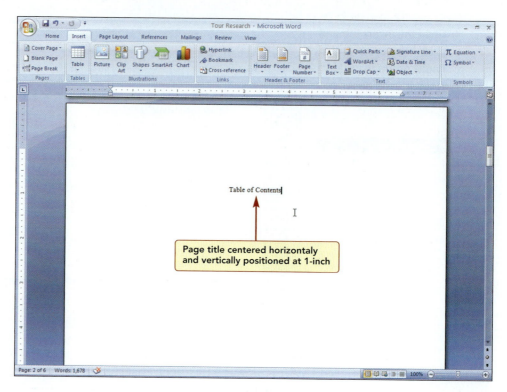

Page title centered horizontaly and vertically positioned at 1-inch

Figure 3.26

In one quick step, the insertion point moves to the location where you clicked and the center format was applied to the text you typed.

Applying a Quick Style

Next, you will improve the appearance of the title by applying a quick style. As you learned when creating the outline, many styles are applied automatically to text. Others can be applied manually by selecting the quick style you want to use from the Styles gallery.

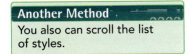

1 Open the Home tab.

If necessary, move to anywhere in the line containing the Table of Contents title.

Click ▾ More in the Styles group to open the Styles gallery.

Another Method
You also can scroll the list of styles.

Your screen should be similar to Figure 3.27

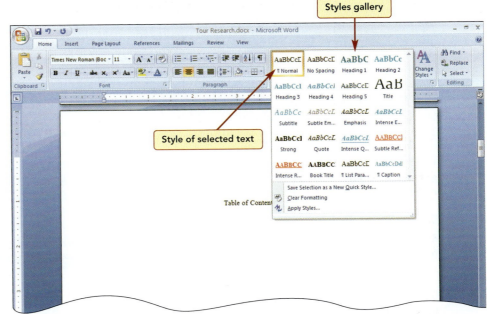

Figure 3.27

The Styles gallery appears with the current style of Normal for the selected text highlighted. Each quick style is named and displays a sample of the style above the name. The formatting of the different styles in the gallery reflects the new theme colors, fonts, and effects. When you point to a style, the document displays a Live Preview of how that style would appear if selected. If it is a paragraph style, the entire table of contents title will be affected. If it is a text style, only the word the insertion point is on will be affected.

2 Point to several quick styles to see how they would look.

Choose Title.

Having Trouble?
If you accidentally apply the wrong style, simply reselect the correct style.

Your screen should be similar to Figure 3.28

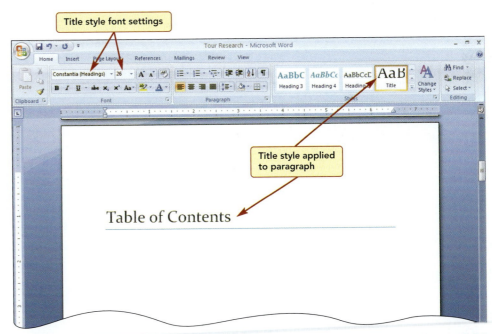

Figure 3.28

Notice that the entire title appears in the selected style. This is because the Title style is a paragraph style, affecting the entire paragraph at the insertion point. The Title style includes font settings of Constantia, 26 pt. in black. It also includes a blue line below the title that is part of the Trek theme effects.

Creating a Custom Quick Style

Although the Title quick style looks good, you decide instead that you want the title to be the same color as the title on the cover page. To do this, you will modify the Title style and then save the modified design as a custom quick style so you can quickly apply the style in the future.

1
- **Right-click on the Table of Contents title and select Styles.**

- **Choose Save selection as a New Quick Style from the submenu.**

- **Click** [Modify...] **from the Create New Style from Formatting dialog box.**

Your screen should be similar to Figure 3.29

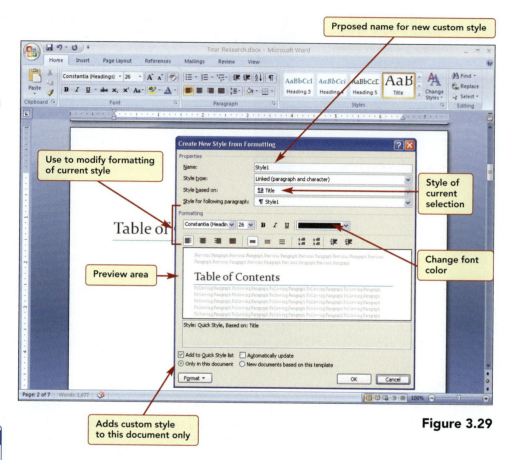

Figure 3.29

Additional Information

If you wanted a custom style to be available in future documents, you would use the New documents based on this template option.

The Create New Style from Formatting dialog box displays the settings associated with the selected text. The only action you need to take is to change the font color and then give the custom style a descriptive name. The options to add the new style to the quick style list for this document only are appropriately selected. The preview area will show you how your selections will look.

1 ● Open the Font Color drop-down menu and choose the Turquoise, Accent 1 theme color.

● In the Name text box, replace the default name with **TOC Title**.

● Click [OK].

Your screen should be similar to Figure 3.30

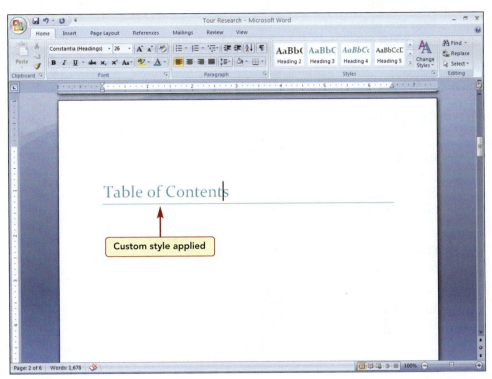

Custom style applied

Figure 3.30

The new TOC Title style is applied to the selection and added to the gallery of quick styles. If you ever need to change a style back to the default document style, you can easily clear the style by moving to the text whose style you want removed and choosing Clear Formatting from the Style gallery or clicking 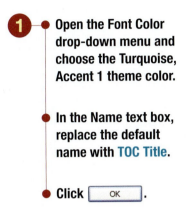 Clear Formatting in the Font group.

Formatting Body Text

The last style change you want to make is to increase the font size of all body text to 12 points. You think this will make the report easier to read.

1 ● **Select and format the body text of the first paragraph below the Tanzania heading to 12 points.**

● **Clear the selection.**

● **Right-click on the paragraph and select Styles from the context menu.**

● **Choose Update Normal to Match Selection.**

Your screen should be similar to Figure 3.31

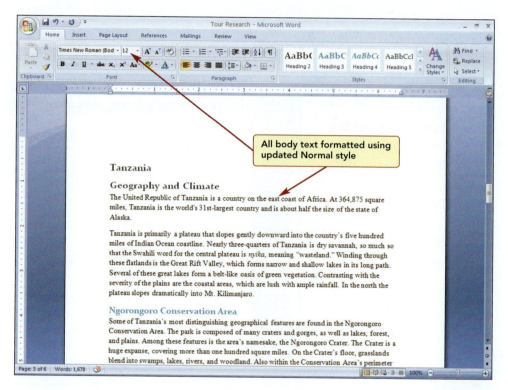

Figure 3.31

MORE ABOUT

To learn how to change all text formatted with one style to another style, see 2.1 Format Text and Paragraphs in the More About appendix.

All body text in the document that uses the Normal style has been immediately updated to the new font size of 12 points.

Creating a Table of Contents

Now you are ready to create the table of contents.

Concept 3

Table of Contents

3   A **table of contents** is a listing of the topic headings that appear in a document and their associated page references (see the sample below). It shows the reader at a glance the topics that are included in the document and makes it easier for the reader to locate information. Word can generate a table of contents automatically after you have applied heading styles to the document headings. To do this, Word first searches the document for headings. Then it formats and inserts the heading entry text into the table of contents. The level of the heading style determines the table of contents level.

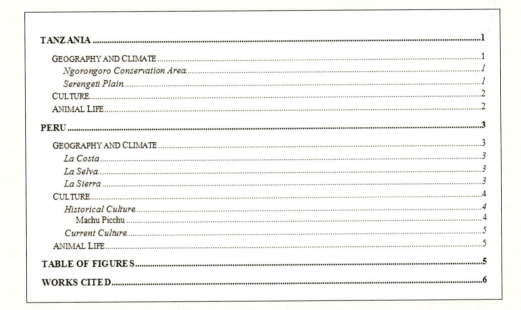

The table of contents that is generated is a field that can be easily updated to reflect changes you may make to the document after the list is generated. Additionally, each entry in the table is a hyperlink to the heading in the document.

Generating a Table of Contents

The report already includes heading styles to identify the different topics in the report. Now, all you need to do is select the style you want to use for the table of contents. You want the table of contents listing to be displayed several lines below the table of contents heading.

Additional Information

MLA and APA styles do not use a table of contents.

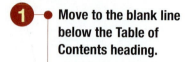

1 ● Move to the blank line below the Table of Contents heading.

● Open the References tab.

● Click 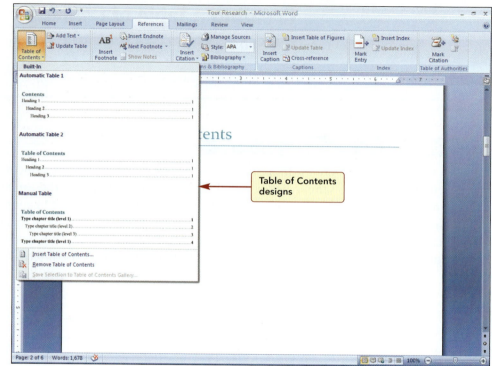 in the Table of Contents group.

Your screen should be similar to Figure 3.32

Table of Contents designs

Figure 3.32

A gallery of three preformatted table of contents styles is displayed. The first two options automatically create a table of contents list using the heading 1–3 styles in the document. The main difference between these two options is that the title used in Automatic Table 1 is Contents and in Automatic Table 2 it is Table of Contents. The third option, Manual Table, creates a table of contents that you can fill out independent of the content in the document.

2 ● Choose Automatic Table 2.

● Scroll upward to see the table of contents.

● Click in the table of contents to select it.

Your screen should be similar to Figure 3.33

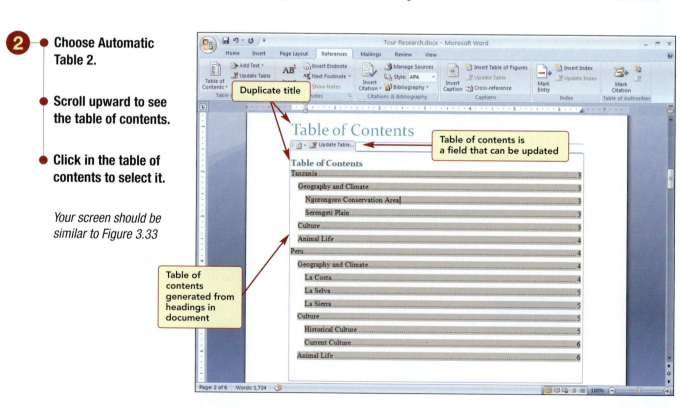

Duplicate title

Table of contents is a field that can be updated

Table of contents generated from headings in document

Figure 3.33

Word searched for headings with the specified styles, sorted them by heading level, referenced their page numbers, and displayed the table of contents using the selected style in the document. The headings that were assigned a Heading 1 style are aligned with the left margin, and subordinate heading levels are indented as appropriate. The table of contents displays the page numbers flush with the right margin with a dotted-line tab leader between the heading entry and the page number. It includes all entries in the document that are formatted with Headings 1, 2, and 3.

The table of contents is a field that is highlighted and enclosed in a box when selected. The field tab provides quick access to the Table of Contents menu by clicking [icon] and the [Update Table...] command button. Because it is a field, the table of contents can be easily updated to reflect changes you may make to the document after the list is generated.

Modifying a Table of Contents

You want the table of contents to include topics formatted with the Heading 4 style also. Additionally, you want to remove the table of contents title that was automatically included with the listing. To do this, you need to modify the table of contents settings.

1 ● **Click**  .

● **Choose Insert Table of Contents.**

Your screen should be similar to Figure 3.34

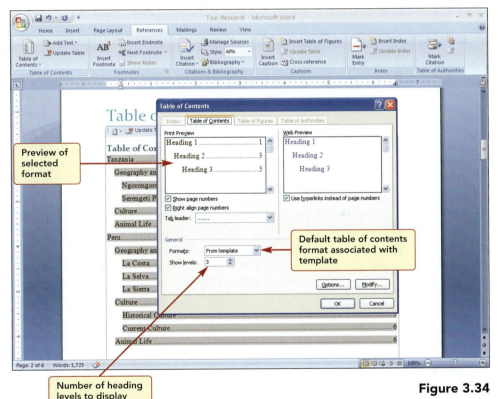

Figure 3.34

Additional Information

You also can create a new table of contents list directly from the Table of Contents dialog box.

MORE ABOUT

You also can add static text to tables of contents. To learn how to do this, see 1.3 Make Documents and Content Easier to Find in the More About appendix.

From the Table of Contents dialog box, you select the format (style) of the table and the number of levels to show. The default style is determined by the Normal template and the number of levels to show is set to three. The two Preview boxes display an example of how the selected format will look in a printed document or in a document when viewed in a Web browser. You will change the format to another and the level to four. You also will remove the duplicate table of contents title. The title is static text that can be removed without affecting the table of contents field.

2 ● **Select Formal from the Formats list.**

● **Specify 4 in the Show Levels box.**

● **Click** OK **.**

● **Click** OK **to replace the current contents list.**

● **Select and delete the table of contents title in the table of contents field.**

Your screen should be similar to Figure 3.35

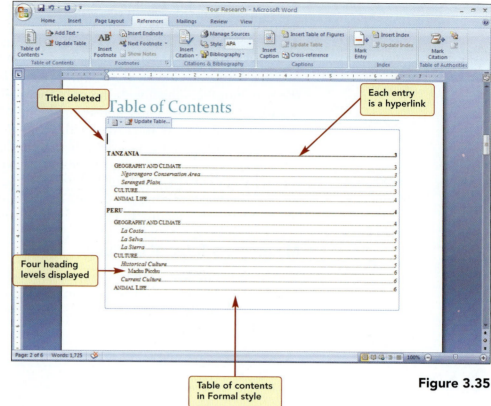

Figure 3.35

The table is regenerated using the new style and the one level 4 heading for Machu Picchu is now displayed in the table of contents.

Additional Information

To remove a table of contents, choose Remove Table of Contents from the menu or from the table of contents field's tab menu.

Navigating a Document

In a large document, locating and moving to an area of text you want to view can take a lot of time. However, after headings have been applied to different areas of a document, there are several features that can make navigation easier. As a help when scrolling by dragging the scroll box, a ScreenTip identifies the topic heading in addition to the page number that will be displayed when you stop dragging the scroll box. If you have generated a table of contents, you can use the table of contents entries to quickly move to different areas. Even more convenient, however, is to use the Navigation window features to jump to a selected location.

Using a Table of Contents Hyperlink

Not only does the table of contents display the location of topic headings in the report, but it also can be used to quickly move to these locations. This is because each entry in the table is a hyperlink to the heading in the document. A hyperlink, as you have learned, is a connection to a location in the current document, another document, or a Web site. To use a hyperlink in Word, hold down Ctrl while clicking on the hyperlink.

Additional Information

Pointing to an entry in a table of contents displays a ScreenTip with directions on how to follow the hyperlink.

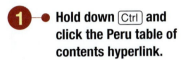 Hold down Ctrl and click the Peru table of contents hyperlink.

Additional Information

The mouse pointer shape changes to a 🖑 when holding down Ctrl and pointing to a hyperlink.

Your screen should be similar to Figure 3.36

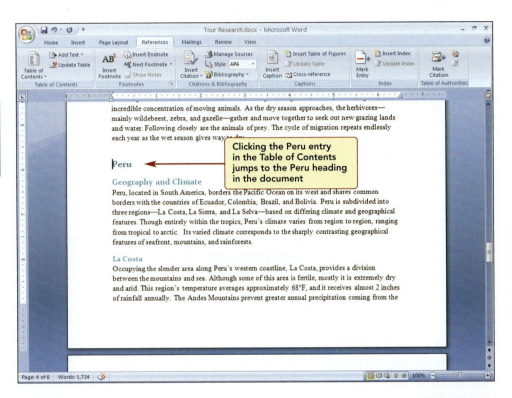

Figure 3.36

The insertion point jumps to the Peru heading in the document. Now, however, the table of contents is no longer visible. If you wanted to move to a different topic, you would need to return to the table of contents page and select another hyperlink.

Using Document Map

Another way to quickly move to different locations in the document is to use the Document Map feature. **Document Map** displays in a separate pane called the **navigation window** a list of the items in a document that have been formatted using a heading style. It is used to quickly navigate through the document by clicking on a heading and keeps track of your location in it.

1 ● Open the View tab.

● Click ☐ Document Map
from the Show/Hide
group.

*Your screen should be
similar to Figure 3.37*

Navigation window
displays Document Map

Turns on/off
Document Map

Document Map
displays all
headings
in document

Current location
in document is
highlighted

Indicates
subordinate
levels are displayed

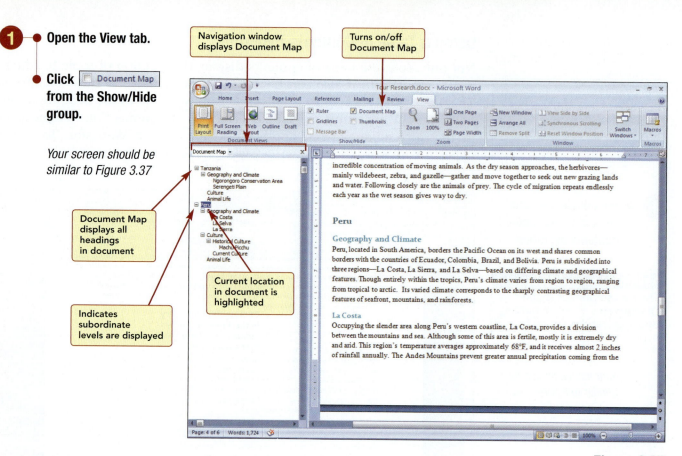

Figure 3.37

Additional Information
The navigation window pane
can be resized by dragging
the divider line between the
panes.

The Document Map opens in the navigation window and displays a list of all
the document headings. When your document does not contain any headings
formatted with heading styles, the program automatically searches the
document for paragraphs that look like headings (for example, short lines
with a larger font size) and displays them in the Document Map. If it cannot
find any such headings, the Document Map is blank.

Notice the ☐ symbol to the left of many of the headings; this symbol
indicates that all subordinate headings are displayed. A ☐ symbol would
indicate that subordinate headings are not displayed. The highlighted
heading shows your location in the document. Clicking on a heading in
the Document Map quickly jumps to that location in the document.

2 ● **Click on Culture (under Peru) in the Document Map.**

● **Click on Tanzania.**

Your screen should be similar to Figure 3.38

Clicking heading in Document Map moves to that location in document

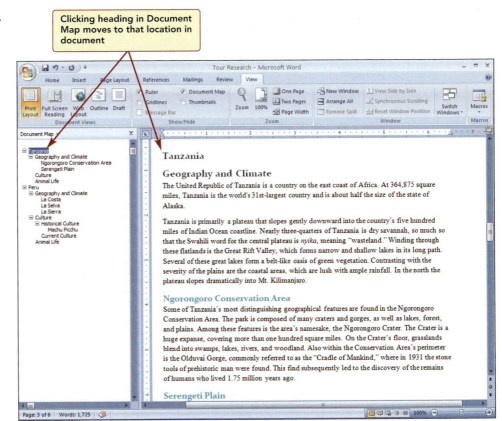

Figure 3.38

You quickly moved from one topic location in the document to another. When using the Document Map, the selected topic appears at the top of the window.

Using Thumbnails

The navigation window also can display **thumbnails**, miniature images of each page in the document. Clicking on a thumbnail moves directly to that page.

1
- Open the [Document Map ▾] drop-down button at the top of the navigation window.

- Choose Thumbnails.

- Scroll the navigation window and click on page 5.

Another Method
You also can click [☐ Thumbnails] in the Show/Hide group.

Your screen should be similar to Figure 3.39

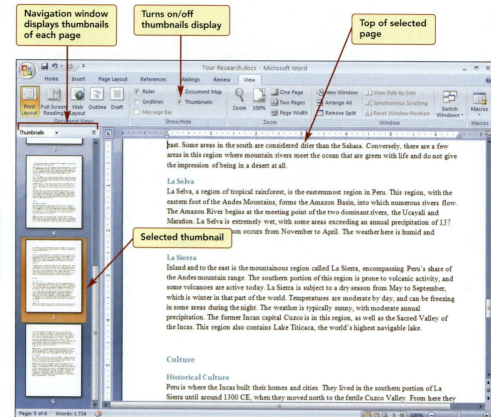

Figure 3.39

The selected page is displayed in the document window and the selected thumbnail is highlighted.

The Document Map and Thumbnails features are available in all views. The navigation window remains open in the view you are using until you close the window or turn off the feature. It must be turned on and off in each view independently.

Note: If you are running short on time to complete this lab, this is an appropriate time to stop. Close the navigation window and save the document. When you begin again, open the saved document and the navigation window.

Including Source References

Documented research papers typically provide credit for the sources of information that were used in developing the document. These sources are cited both within the text of the document and in a bibliography.

4 Parenthetical source references, called **citations**, give credit for specific information included in the document. Complete source information for citations is included in a **bibliography** at the end of the report. Citations and bibliographies must be entered using the appropriate reference style, such as MLA or APA style. Word includes a feature that will automatically format citations and bibliographies according to different reference styles. This saves you the time it would take to learn the style from the documentation manuals, and of entering the citations and bibliographies using the correct format.

As you insert citations, Word asks for the bibliography information for each source. Once a source is created, it is stored in two places: a Master List and a Current List. The Master List is a database of all sources ever created. The Current List includes all of the sources that will be used in the current document. The purpose of the Master List is to save you from retyping and reentering information about sources that you commonly use. This is because you can select and copy sources in your Master List to add them to your Current List.

Word uses the information in the Current List to quickly generate a complete bibliographic list (similar to the sample shown here) of the information for each source according to the selected reference style.

Works Cited

Camerapix, comp. Spectrum Guide to Tanzania. Edison: Hunter, 1992.

Country Studies US. Peru. 2003-2005. 3 November 2006
<http://countrystudies.us/peru/23.htm>.

Wikipedia: The Free Encyclopedia. Tanzania. 5 October 2006. 3 November 2006
<http://en.wikipedia.org/wiki/Tanzania>.

Both citations and bibliography entries are inserted as fields in the document. This means that any changes you may make to the source information is automatically updated in both the citation and the bibliography.

Selecting a Reference Style

You have been following the MLA reference style guidelines for this report and will specify the MLA reference style before you begin inserting citations. You can change the reference style at any point while working on your document and your citations and bibliography will be automatically updated to reflect the new style.

Additional Information

Changing reference styles allows you to repurpose documents to be submitted to a number of publications requiring different reference standards.

1 ● **Open the References tab.**

● **Open the** [Style: APA ▾] **drop-down list in the Citations and Bibliography group.**

● **Choose MLA from the drop-down list.**

Now, as you enter citations and create a bibliography, they will be formatted using the MLA style guidelines.

Creating Citations

Research papers using the MLA style require citations to include the author's last name and a page number or range within parentheses. The first citation that needs to be included in the document is to credit the source of the geography statistics about Tanzania. The source of this information was from the Wikipedia Web site. To create a citation, the bibliography information for the source is entered first.

1 ● **Display the Document Map.**

● **Move to the end of the first paragraph (before the period) of the Tanzania Geography section.**

● **Click** [Insert Citation ▾] **in the Citations and Bibliography group.**

● **Choose Add New Source.**

Your screen should be similar to Figure 3.40

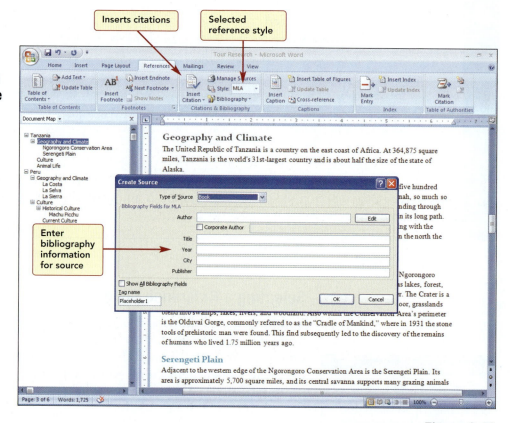

Inserts citations

Selected reference style

Enter bibliography information for source

Figure 3.40

Additional Information
Word includes the capability to search an external library through the Research and Reference pane to locate data and import it with one click. The source information is automatically entered in the Create Source form for you.

In the Create Source dialog box, you first select the type of source, for example, a book, a journal article, or a Web site. Then you enter the bibliography information for the source in the appropriate text boxes for the selected source type.

2 ● Choose Web site as the type of source.

● Enter the following in the appropriate locations to complete the bibliography information for this citation.

Author	Wikipidea
Name of Web Page	Tanzania
Year	2006
Month	October
Day	5
Year Accessed	Enter the current year
Month Accessed	Enter the current month
Day Accessed	Enter the current day
URL	http://en.wikipedia.org/wiki/Tanzania

● Click [OK].

Your screen should be similar to Figure 3.41

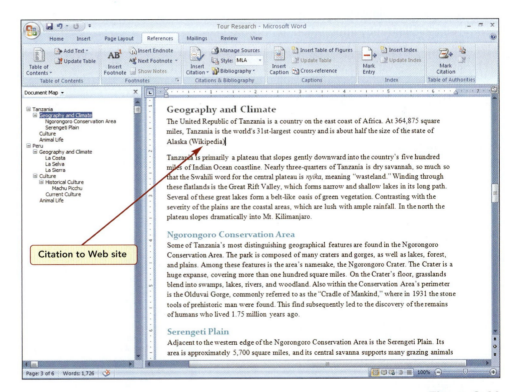

Figure 3.41

Additional Information

You also can create a citation placeholder to mark the place in a document where you need to add a citation. You can then complete the bibliographic information later by editing the citation. The default citation placeholder tag is "Placeholder" followed by a number. You can use the default placeholder tag names or you can enter whatever you want.

The citation is inserted at the location of the insertion point. It is a field that is linked to the source information. The source information is now stored in both the Master List and the Current List.

The next citation is also to the Wikipedia Web site. Once source information has been specified, it is easy to insert the citation again. This is because the Insert Citation drop-down menu displays a brief bibliographic entry for each source in the Current List. You will insert another citation for the same source in the report and then you will add a citation for the quote at the end of the first paragraph of the Tanzania Animal Life topic. This quote was found on page 252 of a book that was compiled by Camerapix Publishers International. Because this citation is to a quote, the page number must be included in the citation. You will enter the source information and then edit the citation to include the page.

3
- Using the Document Map, move to the end of the third sentence (before the period) in the first paragraph of the Tanzania Culture section.

- Click 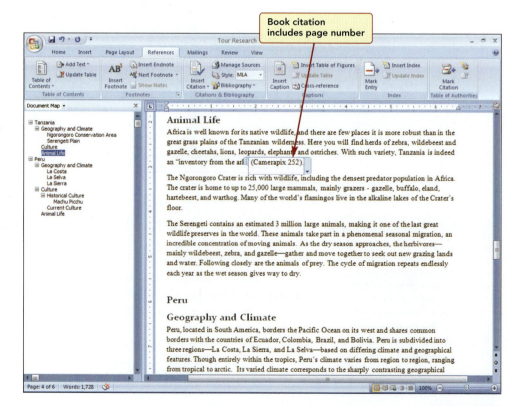 and select the Wikipedia entry from the Citation list.

- Using the Document Map, move to the end of the first paragraph (before the period) of the Tanzania Animal Life section.

- Click [Insert Citation] and choose Add New Source.

- Choose Book as the type of source.

- Enter the following in the appropriate locations to complete the bibliography information for this citation.

Author	**Camerapix, comp.**
Title	**Spectrum Guide to Tanzania**
Year	**1992**
City	**Edison**
Publisher	**Camerapix Publishers International**

- Click [OK].

- Click on the citation and open the drop-down menu.

- Choose Edit Citation.

- Enter 252 as the page number.

- Click [OK].

Your screen should be similar to Figure 3.42

Book citation includes page number

Animal Life

Africa is well known for its native wildlife, and there are few places it is more robust than in the great grass plains of the Tanzanian wilderness. Here you will find herds of zebra, wildebeest and gazelle, cheetahs, lions, leopards, elephants and ostriches. With such variety, Tanzania is indeed an "inventory from the ark" (Camerapix 252).

The Ngorongoro Crater is rich with wildlife, including the densest predator population in Africa. The crater is home to up to 25,000 large mammals, mainly grazers - gazelle, buffalo, eland, hartebeest, and warthog. Many of the world's flamingos live in the alkaline lakes of the Crater's floor.

The Serengeti contains an estimated 3 million large animals, making it one of the last great wildlife preserves in the world. These animals take part in a phenomenal seasonal migration, an incredible concentration of moving animals. As the dry season approaches, the herbivores— mainly wildebeest, zebra, and gazelle—gather and move together to seek out new grazing lands and water. Following closely are the animals of prey. The cycle of migration repeats endlessly each year as the wet season gives way to dry.

Peru

Geography and Climate

Peru, located in South America, borders the Pacific Ocean on its west and shares common borders with the countries of Ecuador, Colombia, Brazil, and Bolivia. Peru is subdivided into three regions—La Costa, La Sierra, and La Selva—based on differing climate and geographical features. Though entirely within the tropics, Peru's climate varies from region to region, ranging from tropical to arctic. Its varied climate corresponds to the sharply contrasting geographical

Figure 3.42

The last citation you will complete for now is to credit the source of the geography statistics about Peru. The source of this information was from the Country Studies Web site. This Web site contains the online versions of books that were published by the Federal Research Division of the Library of Congress as part of the Country Studies/Area Handbook series.

4 ● Using the Document Map, move to the end of the second sentence (before the period) in the first paragraph in the Peru Geography and Climate section.

● Insert a Web site citation using the following source information:

Corporate Author	Country Studies US
Name of Web Page	Peru
Year	2003-2005
Year Accessed	Enter the current year
Month Accessed	Enter the current month
Day Accessed	Enter the current day
URL	http://countrystudies.us/peru/23.htm

Your screen should be similar to Figure 3.43

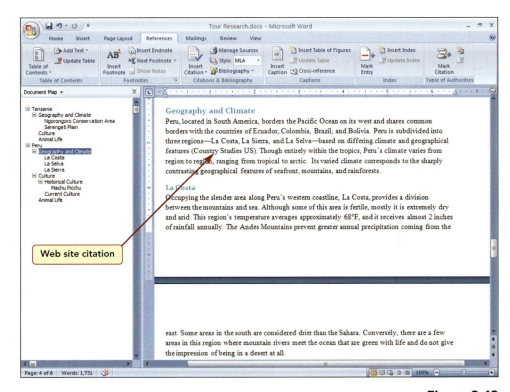

Figure 3.43

Editing a Source

As you look back at the citations you just entered, you realize the author for the Wikipidea Web site should have been entered as a corporate author, not an individual author. Additionally, the Web site name is incomplete. You will quickly return to this citation using the GoTo feature and edit the source.

1 Click 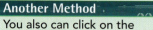 on the Home tab and open the Go To tab.

Another Method
You also can click on the page count indicator in the status bar to open the Go To dialog box.

- Select Field from the Go to What list.

- Click [Previous] three times to search backward through the document.

- Click [Close] when the Wikipidea citation is located.

- Choose Edit Source from the citation's drop-down list.

- Click Corporate Author to move the information in the Author text box to the Corporate Author text box.

- Type :The Free Encyclopedia following Wikipedia in the Author box.

- Click [OK].

- Click [Yes] to update both the Master and Current Lists.

Your screen should be similar to Figure 3.44

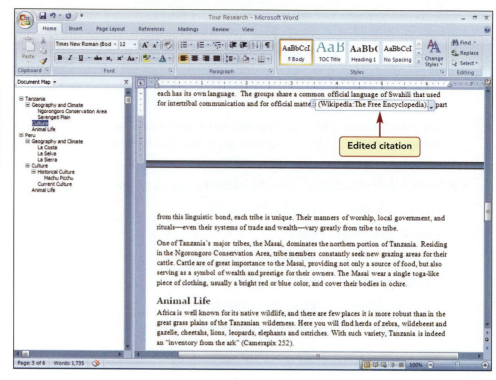

Figure 3.44

The information for the source is now correct and both citations to this source have been updated appropriately.

Including Footnotes

You still have several reference notes you want to include in the report as footnotes to help clarify some information.

Concept 5

Footnote and Endnote

5   Footnotes and endnotes are used in documented research papers to explain or comment on information in the text, or provide source references for text in the document. A **footnote** appears at the bottom of a page containing the material that is being referenced. An **endnote** appears at the end of a document. You can have both footnotes and endnotes in the same document.

Footnotes and endnotes consist of two parts, the **note reference mark** and the **note text**. The default note reference mark is a superscript number appearing in the document at the end of the material being referenced (for example, text). You also can use custom marks consisting of any nonnumeric character or combination of characters, such as an asterisk. The note text for a footnote appears at the bottom of the page on which the reference mark appears. The footnote text is separated from the document text by a horizontal line called the **note separator**. Endnote text appears as a listing at the end of the document.

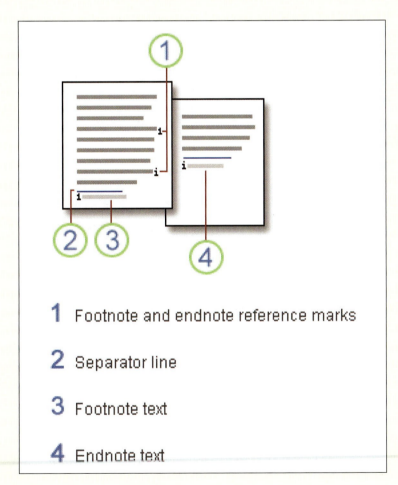

1 Footnote and endnote reference marks

2 Separator line

3 Footnote text

4 Endnote text

Note text can be of any length and formatted just as you would any other text. You also can customize the appearance of the note separators.

Inserting Footnotes in Draft View

The first footnote reference you want to add is the height of Mt. Kilimanjaro. This note will follow the reference to the mountain at the end of the second paragraph in the Geography and Climate section for Tanzania. To identify the location of the footnote number in the document, you position the insertion point at the document location first. You want to create numbered footnotes, so the default settings are acceptable.

1
- Using the Document Map, move to the Tanzania Geography and Climate heading.

- Switch to Draft view.

- Move to the end of the second paragraph.

- Open the References tab.

- Click **AB¹ Insert Footnote** from the Footnotes group.

Another Method

The keyboard shortcut to insert a footnote using the default settings is Alt + Ctrl + F.

Your screen should be similar to Figure 3.45

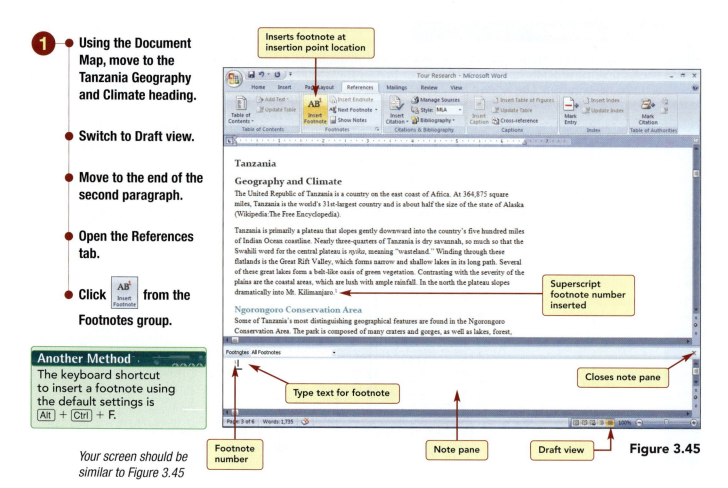

Figure 3.45

The document window is now horizontally divided into upper and lower panes. The report is displayed in the upper pane. The footnote number, 1, appears as a superscript in the document where the insertion point was positioned when the footnote was created. The **note pane** displays the footnote number and the insertion point. This is where you enter the text for the footnote.

When you enter a footnote, you can insert, edit, and format footnotes just like any other text.

2 Type **Mt. Kilimanjaro is 19,340 feet high, making it the fourth tallest mountain in the world.**

Having Trouble?

If you make a typing or spelling error, correct it like any other text in a document.

● Click ☒ to close the note pane.

● Point to note reference mark 1 in the document.

Additional Information

You can hide and display the note pane anytime by using ⏹ or by double-clicking on a note reference mark.

Your screen should be similar to Figure 3.46

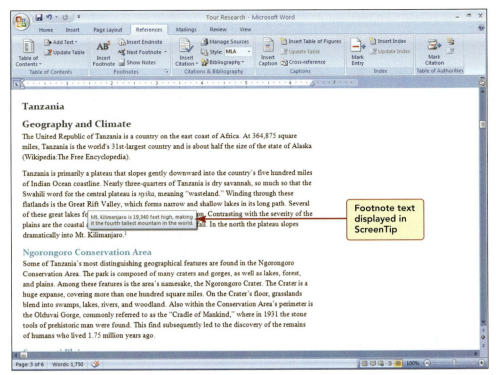

Figure 3.46

In Draft view, the only way to see the footnote text when the footnote pane is not open is in the reference mark's ScreenTip.

Inserting Footnotes in Print Layout View

The second footnote you want to add is in the Geography and Climate section under Peru. You also can insert footnotes in Print Layout view. After using the command to insert a footnote, the footnote number appears in the footnote area at the bottom of the page, ready for you to enter the footnote text. You want to add a note about Lake Titicaca.

1 • Switch to Print Layout view at 100% zoom.

• Using the Document Map, move to the La Sierra heading in the Peru Geography and Climate section.

• Click at the end of the paragraph in the La Sierra section after the word "lake."

• Click .

• Type Lake Titicaca is 12,507 feet above sea level.

Your screen should be similar to Figure 3.47

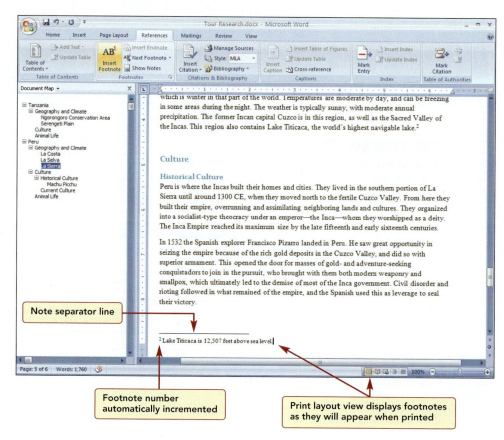

Figure 3.47

Additional Information

A footnote or endnote can be copied or moved by selecting the note reference mark and using Cut or Copy and Paste. You also can use drag and drop to copy or move a note.

Additional Information

In Print Layout view, you also can display the footnote text in a ScreenTip by pointing to the note reference mark.

The footnote number 2 was automatically entered at the location of the insertion point in the text and the footnote text is displayed immediately above the bottom margin separated from the text by the note separator line. Footnotes are always displayed at the bottom of the page containing the footnote reference mark. Print Layout view displays footnotes as they will appear when the document is printed.

Now you realize that you forgot to enter a footnote earlier in the document, on page 2.

2 • **Using the Document Map, move to the Ngorongoro Conservation Area heading.**

• **Move to after the period at the end of the first sentence of the first paragraph, following the word "Area."**

• **Insert the following footnote at this location: The Conservation Area is a national preserve spanning 3,196 square miles.**

• **Save the document.**

Your screen should be similar to Figure 3.48

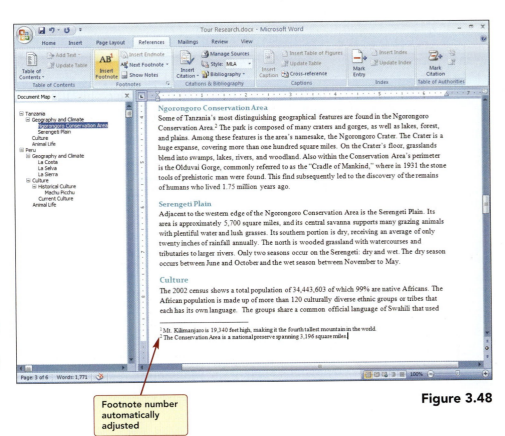

Footnote number automatically adjusted

Figure 3.48

Additional Information
To delete a footnote or endnote, highlight the reference mark and press Delete. The reference mark and associated note text are removed, and the following footnotes are renumbered.

Notice that this footnote is now number 2 in the document. Word automatically adjusted the footnote numbers when the new footnote was inserted.

You are finished entering footnotes for now. Footnotes can quickly be converted to endnotes and vice versa by right-clicking on the note you want to convert and choosing Convert from the context menu.

Formatting Picture Layout

Next you want to add two pictures to the report and you want the text to wrap around the pictures. To do this, you change the text-wrapping layout for the picture.

Text Wrapping

6 You can control the appearance of text around a graphic object by specifying the **text wrapping** style. The text in the paragraph may wrap around the object in many different ways as shown below.

Inline with Text   Square   Tight   Through   Top and Bottom   Behind Text   In Front of Text

When a picture is inserted into a Word document, it is an **inline object**. This means it is positioned directly in the text at the position of the insertion point. It becomes part of the paragraph and any paragraph alignment settings that apply to the paragraph also apply to the picture.

By changing a graphic to a **floating object**, it is inserted into the **drawing layer**, a separate layer from the text that allows graphic objects to be positioned precisely on the page. You can change an inline object to a floating picture by changing the wrapping style of the object.

Wrapping Text around Graphics

You will insert a picture of a giraffe next to the second paragraph on page 2.

1 ● Use the Document Map to move to the Geography and Climate head under Tanzania.

● Close the Navigation window.

● Move to the beginning of the second paragraph.

● Insert the picture wd03_Giraffe from your data files.

● Reduce the size of the picture to approximately 2 by 2 inches.

Additional Information

Dragging the corner handle maintains the original proportions of the picture.

Your screen should be similar to Figure 3.49

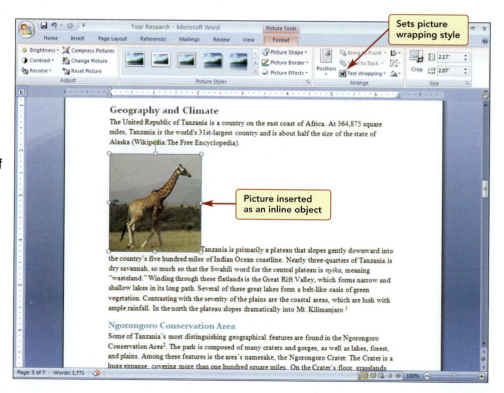

Figure 3.49

The picture has been inserted as an inline object and appears at the beginning of the paragraph like the first text characters of the paragraph. The text continues to the right of the picture. The Picture Tools Format tab is automatically displayed and is used to modify the selected picture object.

You want to change the wrapping style so that the text wraps around the picture. To do this, you will change the wrapping style to Square.

2 • Click ⬛ Text Wrapping ▾ from the Arrange group.

• Choose Square from the submenu.

• If necessary, resize and position the picture until the text wraps around it as in Figure 3.50.

Your screen should be similar to Figure 3.50

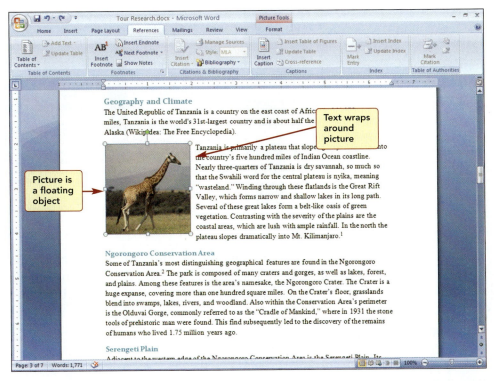

Figure 3.50

Additional Information

Sometimes a floating object is hidden behind another. If this happens, you can press ⌨Tab to cycle forward or ⌨Shift + ⌨Tab to cycle backward through the stacked objects.

The picture is changed to a floating object that can be placed anywhere in the document, including in front of or behind other objects including the text. Because the picture is even with the left margin, the text wraps to the right side of the object. If you moved the picture, because the wrapping style is Square, the text would wrap around the object on all sides.

3 ● **Move the picture to the center of the page to see how the text wraps around it.**

Your screen should be similar to Figure 3.51

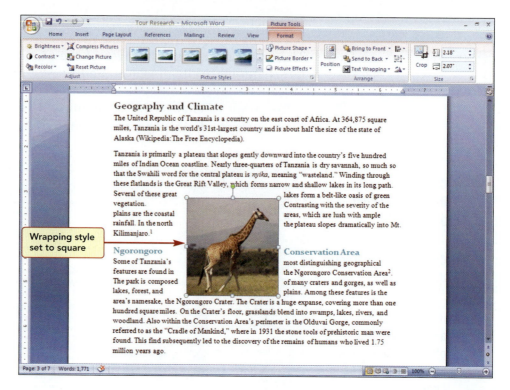

Figure 3.51

The text wraps on all sides of the object, depending on its location in the text. You will align this picture with the left margin again. Then you will add a second picture in the Peru Animal Life section.

4 ● **Move the picture back to the left margin and aligned with the top of the paragraph (see Figure 3.50).**

● **Move to the beginning of the first paragraph in the Peru Animal Life section.**

● **Insert the picture wd03_Parrots to the left of the first paragraph.**

● **Change the wrapping style to Square.**

● **Size and position the picture as in Figure 3.52.**

● **Save the document.**

Your screen should be similar to Figure 3.52

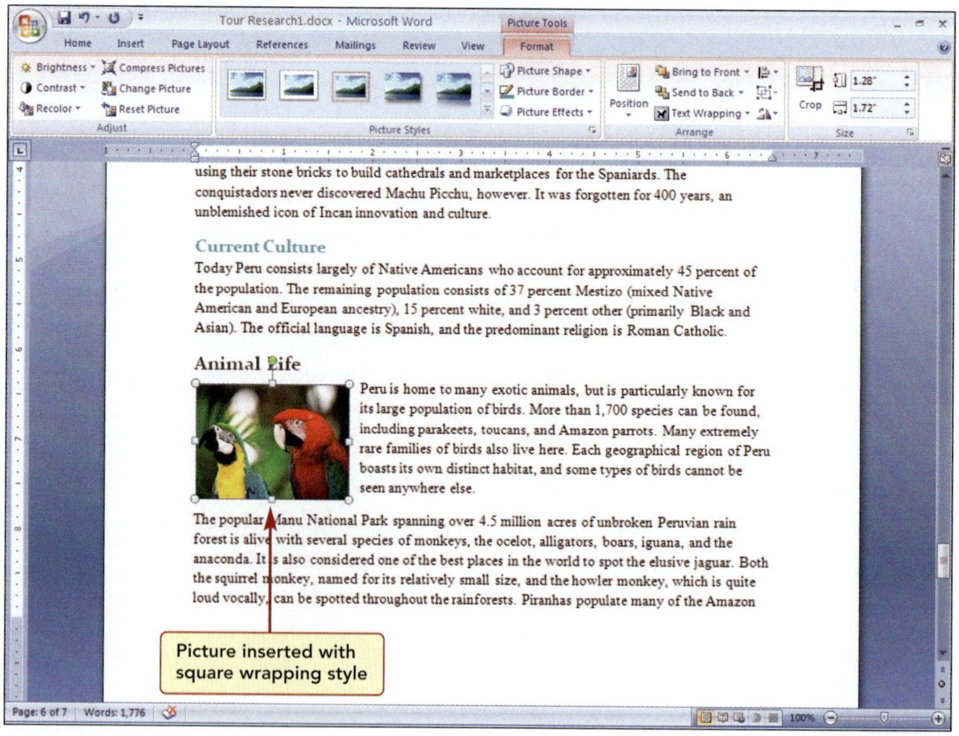

Figure 3.52

Referencing Figures

After figures and other illustrative items have been added to a document, it is helpful to include figure references to identify the items. Figure references include captions and cross-references. If the reader is viewing the document online, the captions and cross-references become hyperlinks to allow the reader to jump around in the document.

Concept 7

Captions and Cross-References

7 Using captions and cross-references in a document identifies items in a document and helps the reader locate information quickly. A **caption** is a numbered label for a figure, table, picture, or graph. Word can automatically add captions to graphic objects as they are inserted, or you can add them manually. The caption label can be changed to reflect the type of object to which it refers, such as a table, chart, or figure. In addition, Word automatically numbers graphic objects and adjusts the numbering when objects of the same type are added or deleted.

A **cross-reference** is a reference from one part of a document to related information in another part. Once you have captions, you also can include cross-references. For example, if you have a graph in one part of the document that you would like to refer to in another section, you can add a cross-reference that tells the reader what page the graph is on. A cross-reference also can be inserted as a hyperlink, allowing you to jump to another location in the same document or in another document.

Adding a Figure Caption

Next, you want to add a caption below the picture of the giraffe.

1 • Select the Giraffe picture in the Tanzania section.

• Open the References tab.

• Click [Insert Caption] .

Your screen should be similar to Figure 3.53

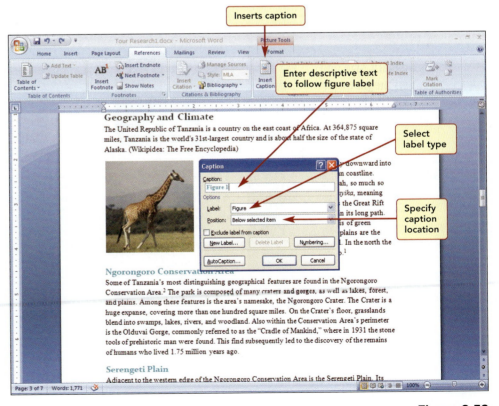

Figure 3.53

The Caption options are described in the following table.

Option	Description
Label	Select from one of three default captions: Table, Figure, or Equation.
Position	Specify the location of the caption, either above or below a selected item. When an item is selected, the Position option is available.
New Label	Create your own captions.
Numbering	Specify the numbering format and starting number for your caption.
AutoCaption	Turns on the automatic insertion of a caption (label and number only) when you insert selected items into your document.

The default caption label is Figure 1. You will use this caption and add additional descriptive text. The default setting of "Below selected item" is also correct.

2 • In the Caption text box, following "Figure 1," type : Giraffe in Serengeti.

• Click [OK].

• If necessary, size and position the picture and caption as in Figure 3.54.

Your screen should be similar to Figure 3.54

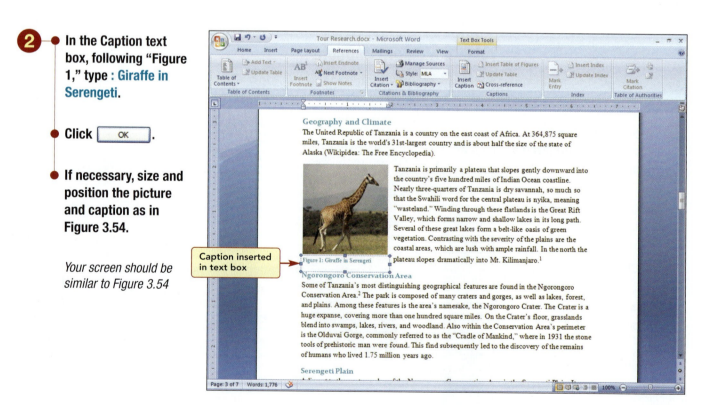

Figure 3.54

Additional Information

Only captions that are associated with floating graphic objects are in text boxes. Otherwise, they are text entries.

Additional Information

You will learn more about text boxes in later labs.

The caption label appears below the figure. It is formatted using the caption style associated with the selected theme. The figure number is a field that will update automatically as you add or delete captions in the document. The caption is contained in a **text box**, a container for text and other graphic objects that can be moved like any other object.

3 • In a similar manner, add a Figure 2: Amazon Parrots caption below the parrot picture.

• Size and position the picture and caption as in Figure 3.55.

Your screen should be similar to Figure 3.55

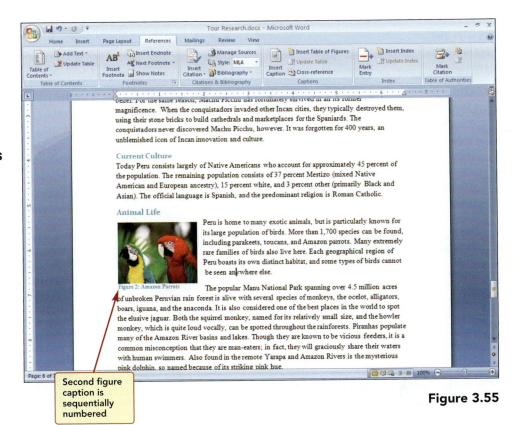

Second figure caption is sequentially numbered

Figure 3.55

Adding a Cross-Reference

In the Animal Life section of the report, you discuss the animals found in the Serengeti. You want to include a cross-reference to the picture at this location. While doing this, you will **split** the document **window** into separate viewing areas so you can see the figure you will reference in one area and the text where you will enter the cross-reference in the other area.

1
- Open the View tab.

- Choose 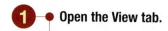 from the Window group.

- Drag the split bar to the position shown in Figure 3.56.

- Click to position the split at that location.

Another Method
You also can drag the split box located above the vertical scroll bar to create a split.

Your screen should be similar to Figure 3.56

Additional Information
You can display the document in different views in each pane. For example, you can display the document in Print Layout view in one pane and Draft view in the other.

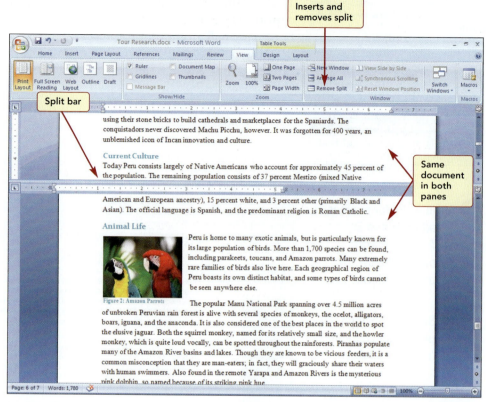

Figure 3.56

The document area is divided into two horizontal sections. Each section is displayed in a pane that can be scrolled and manipulated independently.

Next, you will scroll the document in the panes to display the areas you want to view. While using panes, the insertion point and the ruler are displayed in the active pane or the pane in which you are currently working.

2
- Scroll the upper pane to display the Figure 1 caption below the giraffe picture.

- Scroll the lower pane to display the third paragraph in the Tanzania Animal Life section (page 3, section 2).

Your screen should be similar to Figure 3.57

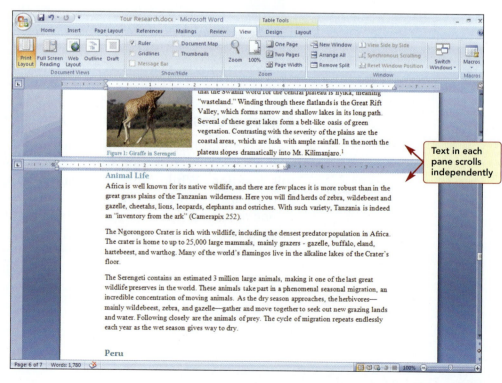

Figure 3.57

The text in each pane scrolls independently. Now you can conveniently see both areas of the document while you enter the cross-reference.

3 • Move to after the word "water" (before the period) in the third paragraph in the Tanzania Animal Life section.

• Press Spacebar.

• Type **(see** and press Spacebar.

• Open the References tab.

• Click Cross-reference from the Captions group.

Your screen should be similar to Figure 3.58

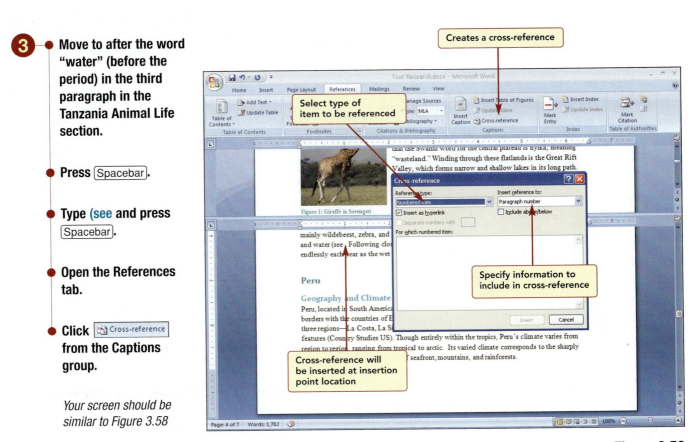

Figure 3.58

In the Cross-reference dialog box, you specify the type of item you are referencing and how you want the reference to appear. You want to reference the giraffe picture, and you want only the label "Figure 1" entered in the document. From the For Which Caption list box, you select the figure you want to reference from the list of all figure captions in the document. Notice that the Insert as Hyperlink option is selected by default. This option creates a hyperlink between the cross-reference and the caption. The default setting is appropriate.

4 ● From the Reference
Type drop-down list
box, select Figure.

● From the Insert
Reference To drop-
down list box, select
Only label and number.

● Click [Insert ▾]

● Click [Close] .

● Type **)**.

● Click on the Figure 1
cross-reference.

*Your screen should be
similar to Figure 3.59*

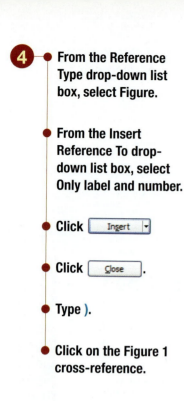

that the Swahili word for the central plateau is nyika, meaning
"wasteland." Winding through these flatlands is the Great Rift
Valley, which forms narrow and shallow lakes in its long path.
Several of these great lakes form a belt-like oasis of green
vegetation. Contrasting with the severity of the plains are the
coastal areas, which are lush with ample rainfall. In the north the
plateau slopes dramatically into Mt. Kilimanjaro.[1]

Figure 1: Giraffe in Serengeti

mainly wildebeest, zebra, and gazelle—gather and move together to seek out new grazing lands
and water (see Figure 1). Following closely are the animals of prey. The cycle of migration
repeats endlessly each year as the wet season gives way to dry.

Peru

Geography and Climate

Peru, located in South America, borders the Pacific Ocean on its west and shares common
borders with the countries of Ecuador, Colombia, Brazil, and Bolivia. Peru is subdivided into
three regions—La Costa, La Sierra, and La Selva—based on differing climate and geographical
features (Country Studies US). Though entirely within the tropics, Peru's climate varies from
region to region, ranging from tropical to arctic. Its varied climate corresponds to the sharply
contrasting geographical features of seafront, mountains, and rainforests.

> Cross-reference is inserted
> as a field and a hyperlink

Page: 4 of 7 | Words: 1,783

Figure 3.59

The cross-reference to Figure 1 is entered into the document as a field.
Therefore, if you insert another picture or item that is cross-referenced,
the captions and cross-references will renumber automatically. If you edit,
delete, or move cross-referenced items, you should manually update the
cross-references using Update Field. When you are working on a long
document with several figures, tables, and graphs, this feature is very
helpful.

Using a Cross-Reference Hyperlink

The cross-reference field is also a hyperlink and, just like a table of
contents field, can be used to jump to the source it references.

1 • Hold down [Ctrl] and click on the Figure 1 cross-reference.

Your screen should be similar to Figure 3.60

Clicking cross-reference jumps to associated figure in document

Double-click to remove split

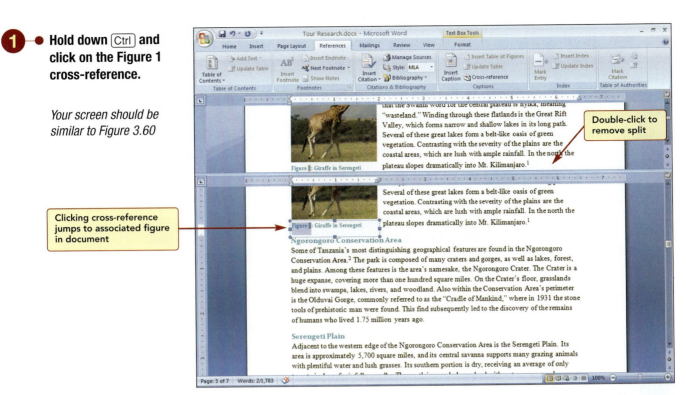

Figure 3.60

The document in the lower pane jumped to the caption beneath the figure. You will clear the split and save the document next.

2 • Double-click on the split bar (above the ruler) to remove the split.

• Save the document.

Another Method
You also can choose Remove Split from the Window group of the View tab or drag the split bar to the top of the document window.

The split is removed and the document window returns to a single pane. As you can see, splitting the document window is most useful for viewing different sections of the document at the same time and allows you to quickly switch between panes to access information in the different sections without having to repeatedly scroll to the areas.

Creating a Simple Table

Next, you want to add a table comparing the rainfall and temperature data for the three regions of Peru.

8 A **table** is used to organize information into an easy-to-read format of horizontal rows and vertical columns. The insertion of a row and column creates a **cell** in which you can enter data or other information. Cells in a table are identified by a letter and number, called a **table reference**. Columns are identified from left to right beginning with the letter A, and rows are numbered from top to bottom beginning with the number 1. The table reference of the top-leftmost cell is A1 because it is in the first column (A) and first row (1) of the table. The second cell in column 2 is cell B2. The fourth cell in column 3 is C4.

A	B	C	D	E
(A1)	Jan	Feb	Mar	Total
East	7 (B2)	7	5	19
West	6	4	7	17
South	8	7 (C4)	9	24
Total	21	18	21	60

Tables are a very effective method for presenting information. The table layout organizes the information for readers and greatly reduces the number of words they have to read to interpret the data. Use tables whenever you can to make your documents easier to read.

The table you want to create will display columns for regions, rainfall, and temperature. The rows will display the data for each region. Your completed table will be similar to the one shown below.

Region	Annual Rainfall (Inches)	Average Temperature (Fahrenheit)
La Costa	2	68
La Sierra	35	54
La Selva	137	80

Inserting a Table

Word includes several methods you can use to create tables. One method will quickly convert text that is arranged in tabular columns into a table. Another uses the Draw Table feature to create any type of table, but is most useful for creating complex tables that contain cells of different heights or a varying number of columns per row. Another method inserts a preformatted table containing sample data that you replace with your data.

The last method, which you will use, creates a simple table consisting of the same number of rows and columns by highlighting boxes in a grid to define the table size.

1 ● Move to the blank line below the paragraph on La Sierra.

● Press ⏎Enter to insert another blank line.

● Open the Insert tab.

● Click Table .

● Point to the boxes in the grid in the drop-down menu to highlight a 3-by-3 section.

Additional Information
The dimensions are reflected at the top of the grid and Live Preview shows you how it will look in the document.

● Click on the lower-right corner of the selection to insert it.

Your screen should be similar to Figure 3.61

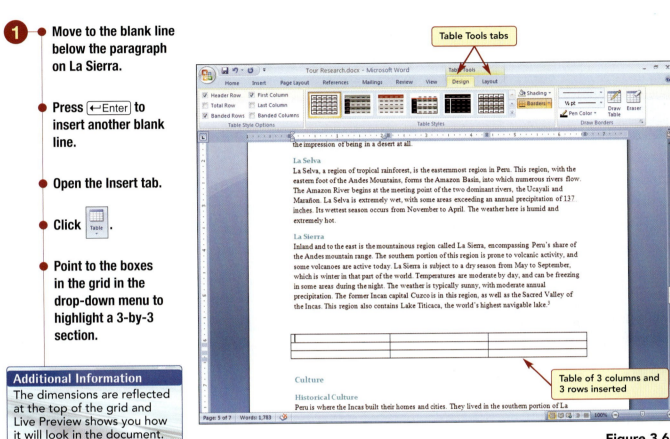

Figure 3.61

A table the full width of the page is drawn. It has equal-sized columns and is surrounded by a black borderline. The Table Tools tab is automatically open and includes a Design tab and a Layout tab that are used to work with the table.

Entering Data in a Table

Now you are ready to enter information in the table. Each cell contains a single line space where you can enter data. You can move from one cell to another by using the arrow keys or by clicking on the cell. The insertion point appears in the cell that is selected. In addition, you can use the keys shown in the table below to move around a table.

To Move to	Press
Next cell in row	[Tab]
Previous cell in row	[Shift] + [Tab]
First cell in row	[Alt] + [Home]
Last cell in row	[Alt] + [End]
First cell in column	[Alt] + [Page Up]
Last cell in column	[Alt] + [Page Down]
Previous row	[↑]
Next row	[↓]

Additional Information

Pressing [Tab] when in the last cell of a row moves to the first cell of the next row.

The mouse pointer also may appear as a solid black arrow when pointing to the table. When it is a ↓, you can click to select the entire column. When it is ↗, you can click to select a cell. You will learn more about this feature shortly.

You will begin by entering the information for La Costa in cells A1 through C1. You can type in the cell as you would anywhere in a normal document.

1 • If necessary, click cell A1 to select it.

• Type **La Costa**.

• Press [Tab].

• In the same manner, type **2** in cell B1 and **68** in cell C1.

• Continue entering the information shown below, using [Tab] to move to the next cell.

Cell	Entry
A2	La Sierra
B2	35
C2	54
A3	La Selva
B3	137
C3	80

Your screen should be similar to Figure 3.62

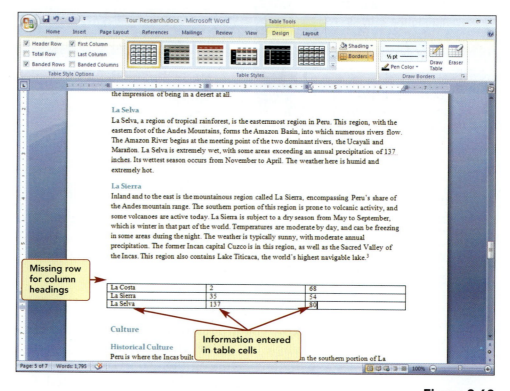

Figure 3.62

Inserting a Row

After looking at the table, you realize you need to include a row above the data to display the descriptive column headings. To add a row, simply click in any cell above or below the location where you want to add the row and then use the appropriate command to insert a row. Once the row is inserted, you will enter the column headings in the cells.

1 ● Move to any cell in row 1.

● Open the Table Tools Layout tab.

● Click **Insert Above** from the Rows & Columns group.

● In cell A1 type **Region**.

● In cell B1 type **Annual Rainfall**.

● Press ⏎Enter to insert a second line in the cell.

● Type **(Inches)**.

● In cell C1 type **Average Temperature** on the first line and **(Fahrenheit)** on the second.

Your screen should be similar to Figure 3.63

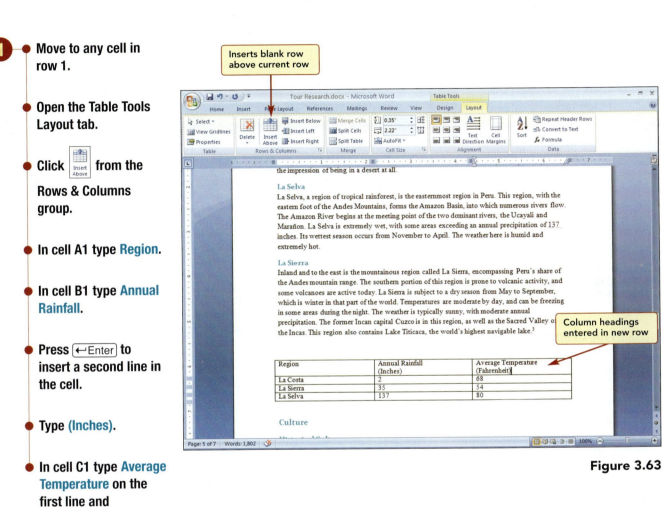

Figure 3.63

Sizing a Table

The table is much wider than it needs to be. To quickly reduce the overall table size, you can drag the resize handle □. This handle appears in the lower-right corner whenever the mouse pointer rests over the table. Once the table is smaller, you will select the entire table by clicking the ⊞ move handle and center it between the margins.

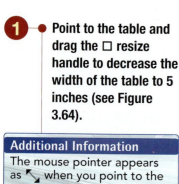

1 • Point to the table and drag the □ resize handle to decrease the width of the table to 5 inches (see Figure 3.64).

Additional Information

The mouse pointer appears as ↖ when you point to the □ resize handle.

• Click ⊞ to select the entire table.

Additional Information

The mouse pointer appears as ⊹ when you point to the ⊞ select handle.

• Click ≡ Center on the Mini toolbar.

Another Method

You also can drag the ⊞ move handle to move the table to any location or click ▤ Center in the Table Properties dialog box.

Your screen should be similar to Figure 3.64

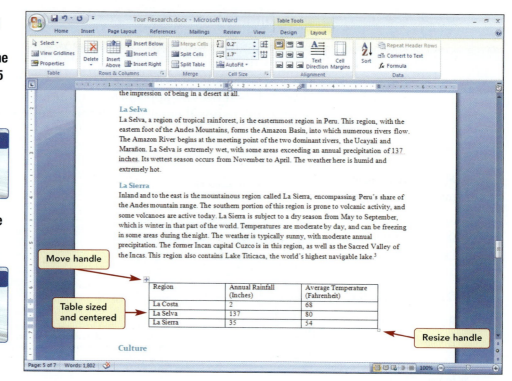

Move handle

Table sized and centered

Resize handle

Figure 3.64

Having Trouble?

See Concept 9: Sort in Lab 2 to review this feature.

Sorting a Table

Next you decide you want the three regions to appear in alphabetical order as they are presented in the report. To make this change quickly, you can **sort** the table. The process is similar to sorting a list.

You will use the default Sort settings that will sort by text and paragraphs in ascending order. Additionally, when sorting a table, the program assumes the first row of the table is a header row and uses the information in that row for you to select the column to sort on. The default is to sort on the first column. In this case, this is acceptable because you want to sort the table by Region.

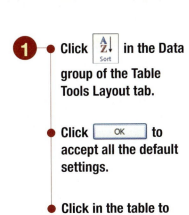

1 • Click 🔤 Sort in the Data group of the Table Tools Layout tab.

• Click OK to accept all the default settings.

• Click in the table to clear the highlight.

Your screen should be similar to Figure 3.65

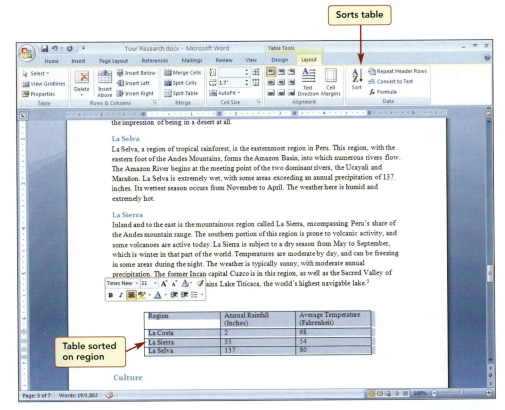

Figure 3.65

The three regions now appear in ascending sort order in the table.

Formatting a Table

To enhance the appearance of the table, you can apply many different formats to the cells. This process is similar to adding formatting to a document, except that the formatting affects the selected cells only or the entire table.

The quickest way to apply formats to a table is to use a table style. This feature includes built-in combinations of formats that consist of different fill or background colors, patterns, borders, fonts, and alignment settings.

1
- Open the Table Tools Design tab.

- Click ▾ More to open the table styles gallery.

Your screen should be similar to Figure 3.66

Additional Information
If a custom style has been saved, it appears in a Custom styles area.

Additional Information
The Table Grid style is the default style.

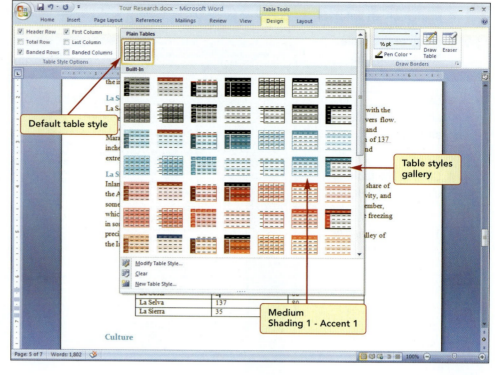

Figure 3.66

From the table styles gallery, you select the table design you want to use. There are 146 Built-in styles. As you point to the style, the style name appears in a ScreenTip and Live Preview shows how it will look.

2
- Point to several styles and look at the Live Preview.

- Choose Medium Shading 1 - Accent 1 (4th row, 6th column).

Your screen should be similar to Figure 3.67

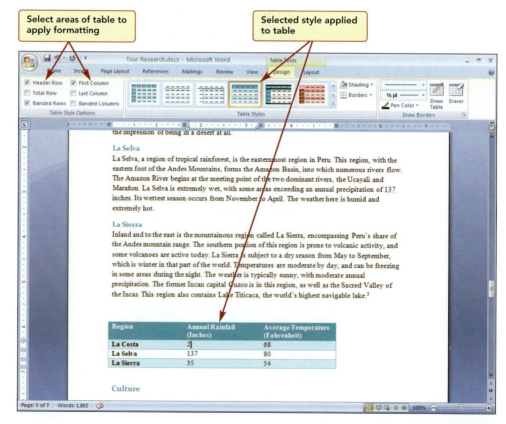

Figure 3.67

The table is reformatted to the new design. It includes a different color background for the heading row and banded shades of color for the table data. In addition, the row heading text is bold and the column heading text is white. Notice that the table is no longer centered; however, the table size was not changed. The table alignment was changed because the new design includes left alignment. Using a table style was much faster than applying these features individually.

Even after applying a table style, you may want to make additional changes. For example, the selected table style applies special formatting to the header row and first column. It also uses a banded row effect for the table data. If you do not want one or all of these features, you can turn them off using the quick styles options. You would like to see how the table would look without some of these features.

3 • Choose ☑ Header Row and ☑ First Column in the Table Style Options group to turn off these features.

• Click ☐ Last Column to turn on this feature.

Your screen should be similar to Figure 3.68

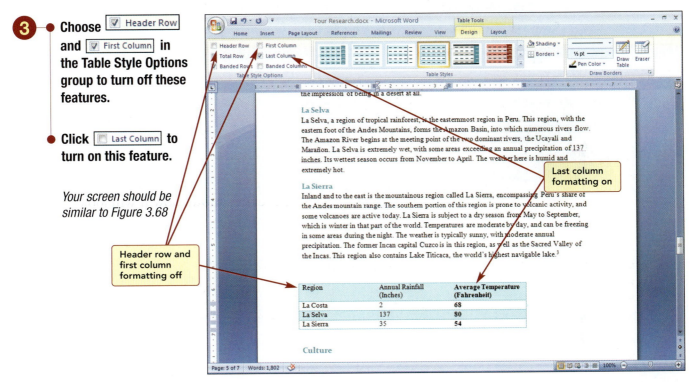

Figure 3.68

Additional Information
The gallery of table styles also reflects the changes in the style options.

The dark blue color background was removed from the table header and the bold effect was removed from the row headings. Bold was added to the last column to emphasize the data. As you can see, the Table Style Options allow you to quickly emphasize different areas of the table. You prefer how the table looked before these changes and will restore these features.

4 ● Choose 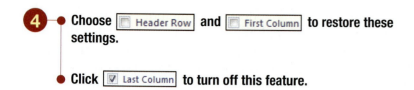 Header Row and First Column to restore these settings.

● Click ☑ Last Column to turn off this feature.

However, there are a few changes you would like to make. As you continue to modify the table, many cells can be selected and changed at the same time. The table below describes the procedures to select information in a table.

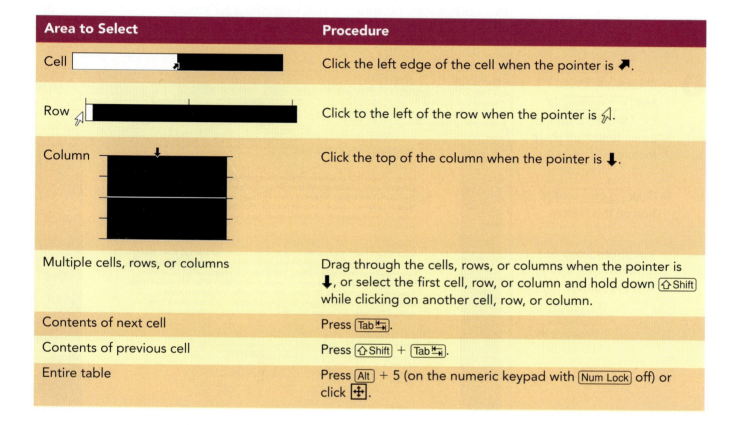

Area to Select	Procedure
Cell	Click the left edge of the cell when the pointer is ➤.
Row	Click to the left of the row when the pointer is ⭜.
Column	Click the top of the column when the pointer is ⬇.
Multiple cells, rows, or columns	Drag through the cells, rows, or columns when the pointer is ⬇, or select the first cell, row, or column and hold down ⇧Shift while clicking on another cell, row, or column.
Contents of next cell	Press Tab↹.
Contents of previous cell	Press ⇧Shift + Tab↹.
Entire table	Press Alt + 5 (on the numeric keypad with Num Lock off) or click ⊞.

You want the entries in the header row (cells A1 through C1), and the table date in cells B2 through C4, to be centered in their cell spaces. You also want to increase the font size of the header text. Finally, you will add a caption below the table.

5 ● Select cells A1 through C1 containing the table headings.

● Open the Table Tools Layout tab.

● Click 🖻 Align Top Center from the Alignment group.

● In the same manner, center cells B2 through C4.

● Select the header row again.

● Click 🅰 Grow in the Mini toolbar.

● Select the table and center it again.

● Add the caption Table 1: Climate below the table.

● Click outside the table to deselect it.

● Insert a blank line below the caption.

● Save the document.

Your screen should be similar to Figure 3.69

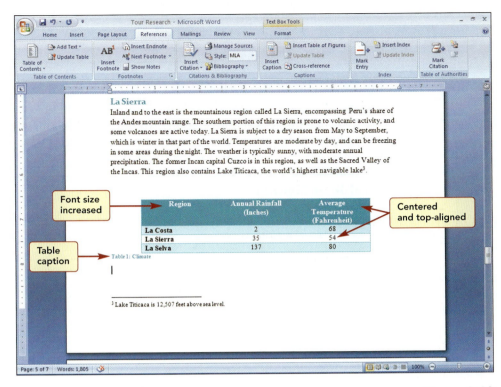

Figure 3.69

Including a Table of Figures

The report is near completion and you want to add a table of figures to the report.

Concept 9

Table of Figures

9 A **table of figures** is a list of the figures, tables, or equations used in a document and their associated page number, similar to how a table of contents lists topic headings. The table of figures is generated from captions that are included in the document and is a field that can be easily updated to reflect changes you may make to the document after the list is generated.

Table of Figures

Additionally, each entry in the table is a separate field that is a hyperlink to the caption in the document. It can then be used to quickly locate specific figures or other items in the document.

The table of figures is typically placed at the end of a long document.

Creating a Table of Figures

Because you have already added captions to several items in the report, creating a table of figures will be a simple process.

1 ● Move to the end of the report.

● Enter the title **Table of Figures** and format it with a Heading 1 style.

● Press ⏎Enter to move to a blank line below the title.

● Open the References tab.

● Click 🔲 Insert Table of Figures in the Captions group.

Your screen should be similar to Figure 3.70

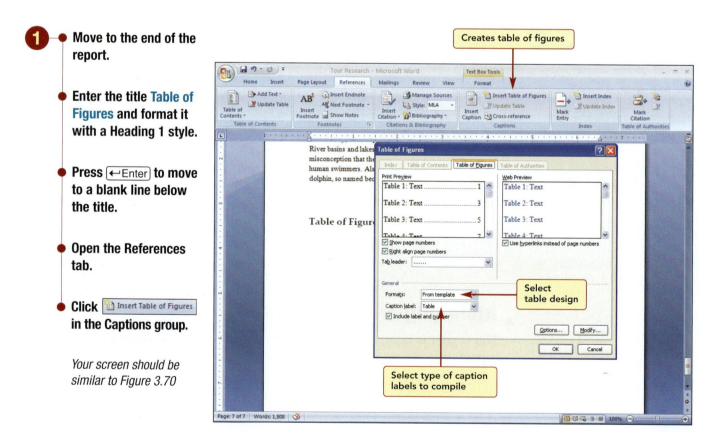

Figure 3.70

The Table of Figures dialog box options are very similar to those in the Table of Contents dialog box. The default options to show and right-align page numbers are appropriate as well as the use of the tab leaders. The Formats box is used to select a design for the table of figures. The default design is the design included in the Normal template and is displayed in the Preview boxes. In the Caption label box, you select the type of caption label you want to compile in the table of figures. The default is to display Table caption labels. You will change the Format to another style and the caption label to compile figures.

2 • **Select Distinctive from the Formats drop-down list.**

• **Choose Figure from the Caption label drop-down list.**

• **Click** OK .

Your screen should be similar to Figure 3.71

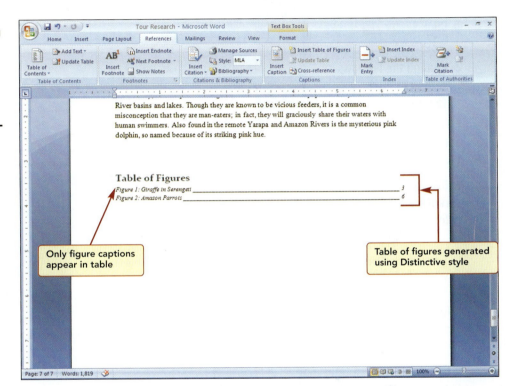

Only figure captions appear in table

Table of figures generated using Distinctive style

Figure 3.71

The program searched for all figure captions in the document and displays them in the table of figures in sorted order by number. The table appears formatted in the selected style.

Modify a Table of Figures

You also want to include the table references in the table of figures. To do this, you could create a second table of figures to display the table references only. Alternatively, you can modify the table of figures to display all types of captions in a single table. You decide, since there are only three captions, to use one table. You also decide that you do not like how the Distinctive format looks and will use the default template formatting instead.

1 • **Click** [Insert Table of Figures] **from the Captions group.**

• **Click** [Options...] .

• **Choose Caption from the Style drop-down list.**

• **Click** [OK] .

• **Change the Formats setting to From Template.**

• **Click** [OK] .

• **Click** [Yes] **to replace the table of figures.**

Your screen should be similar to Figure 3.72

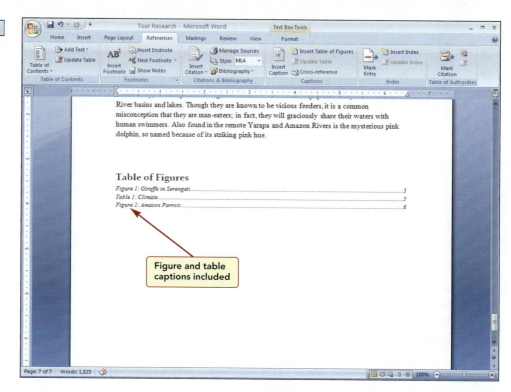

Figure and table captions included

Figure 3.72

The table of figures now includes both table and figure captions using the default template style.

Updating a Table of Figures

You have decided to change the table caption to Peru Climate to make it more descriptive of the table contents. Then you will update the table of figures to reflect this change.

1 ● Use the Table 1: Climate hyperlink in the table of figures to jump to that location in the document.

● Click in the caption before the word Climate, type **Peru**, and press Spacebar.

● Click on the table of figures to select it and click ⊞ Update Table in the Captions group.

● Choose Update entire table and click OK.

Another Method
You also could press F9 to update the table of figures or choose Update table from the table's context menu.

Your screen should be similar to Figure 3.73

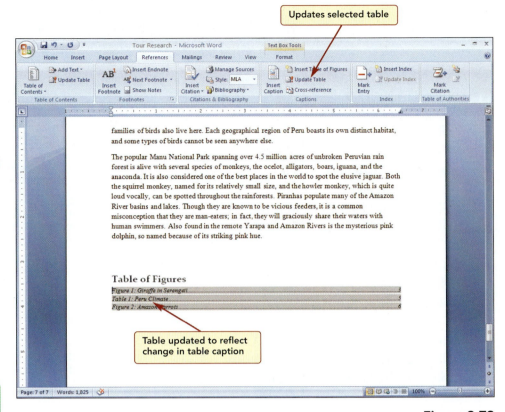

Updates selected table

Table updated to reflect change in table caption

Figure 3.73

MORE ABOUT

► To learn about creating, modifying, and updating a table of authorities and an index, see 4.4 Insert and Format References and Captions in the More About appendix.

The entry for the table is updated in the table of figures to reflect the change you made to the table caption.

Creating a Bibliography

Finally, you are ready to create the bibliography for the report (see Concept 4). Word makes the process of creating a bibliography effortless by automatically generating the bibliography using the selected report style from the source information you entered when creating citations.

Additional Information

Word can automatically generate a complete bibliography that lists all sources associated with the document or an abbreviated bibliography that lists only those sources that have been cited.

Generating the Bibliography

The requirements for formatting a bibliography vary depending on the report style used. You are using the MLA style for this report. This style requires that each work directly referenced in the paper be listed in alphabetical order by author's last name on a separate page with the title "Works Cited."

Because you have already specified the MLA reference style, when the Works Cited bibliography is generated, the entries will automatically appear using the selected reference style.

1 • Insert a new blank page after the table of figures.

• Click **Bibliography ▾** in the Citations and Bibliography group of the References tab.

• Choose the Works Cited option from the gallery.

• If necessary, scroll to the top of the page to see the bibliography.

Your screen should be similar to Figure 3.74

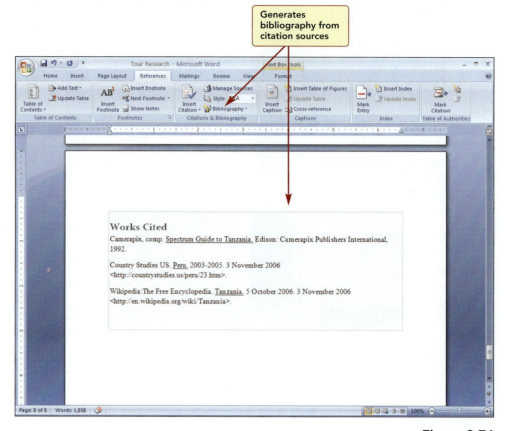

Generates bibliography from citation sources

Figure 3.74

The Works Cited bibliography is formatted using the selected MLA documentation style. The page is labeled with a Works Cited heading and each citation source is listed in ascending alphabetical order.

Updating a Bibliography

Now, as you look at the Works Cited list, you believe you entered the wrong publisher information for the Camerapix source. Even though the bibliography has been generated, it can easily be updated to reflect additions and modifications to the sources. This is because the bibliography is a field that is linked to the sources in the Current List. You will fix the source information and update the bibliography. Rather than return to the citation in the document for this source to edit it, you will use the Source Manager.

1 • **Click** [Manage Sources] **in the Citations & Bibliography group.**

Your screen should be similar to Figure 3.75

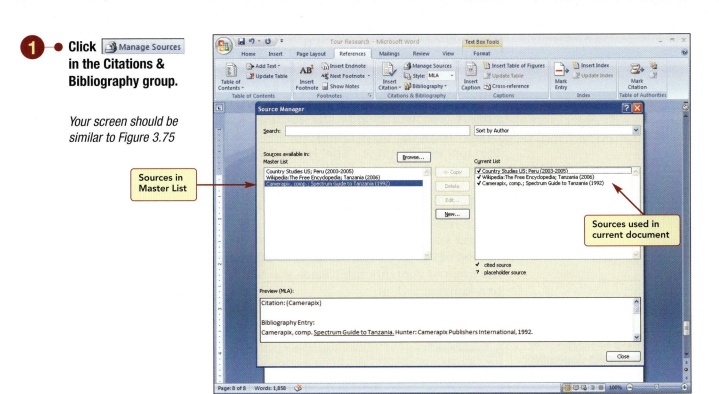

Sources in Master List

Sources used in current document

Figure 3.75

The Source Manager dialog box displays the three sources you entered in both the Master and Current List boxes. It is used to add, copy, delete, and edit sources. Notice that the items in the Current List are preceded with checkmarks. This indicates they have all been cited in the document. All items in the Current List will appear in the bibliography when it is generated. If a source appears in the Master List that you want to appear in the bibliography, you can select it and copy it to the Current List. You need to edit the Camerapix bibliography information.

2 • **Select the Camerapix citation in the Current List box.**

• **Click** [Edit...].

• **Change the Publisher to Hunter.**

• **Click** [OK].

• **Click** [Yes] **to update both lists.**

• **Click** [Close].

• **Select the bibliography and click** [Update Citations and Bibliography] **to update the list.**

Your screen should be similar to Figure 3.76

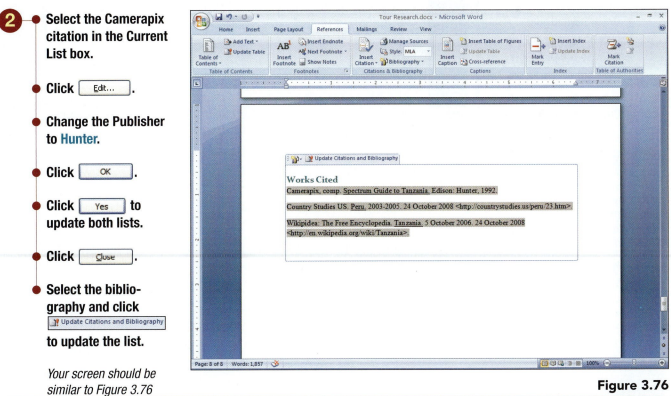

Figure 3.76

The bibliography information for the Camerapix source is now correct and the Works Cited list has been appropriately updated.

Modifying a Bibliography

Finally, you will modify the format of the Works Cited page to more closely meet the MLA requirements. The page title should be centered at the top of the page. The bibliography entries must be formatted as hanging indents—the first line is even with the left margin and subsequent lines of the same work are indented 0.5 inch. MLA formatting for the Works Cited page also requires that it should be double-spaced, as is the entire report.

First you will format the page title. In addition to centering the title at the top of the page, you decide to change the style of the title to the same as the table of contents title. Then you will change the paragraph formatting to a hanging indent.

1
- Move to anywhere in the Works Cited title.

- Choose TOC Title from the Styles group of the Home tab.

- Click ▤ Center.

- Select the three entries in the Works Cited list.

- Drag the hanging indent marker on the ruler to the 0.5-inch position.

- Clear the highlight.

Another Method
You also could choose Hanging from the Special drop-down list of the Paragraph dialog box or press Ctrl + T.

Your screen should be similar to Figure 3.77

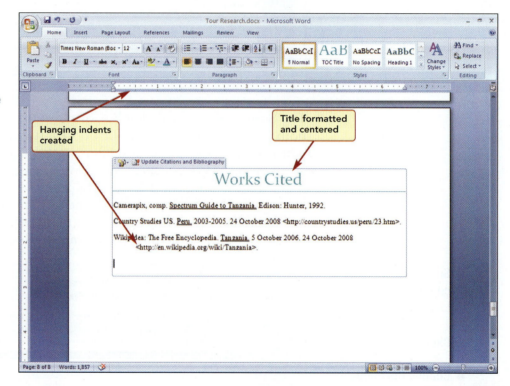

Figure 3.77

Any entries that are longer than one line appear with a hanging indent.

Creating Headers and Footers

Next you want to add information in a header and footer to the report.

Concept 10
Header and Footer

10 Headers and footers provide information that typically appears at the top and bottom of each page in a document and helps the reader locate information in a document. A **header** is a line or several lines of text in the top margin of each page. The header usually contains the title and the section of the document. A **footer** is a line or several lines of text in the margin space at the bottom of every page. The footer usually contains the page number and perhaps the date. Headers and footers also can contain graphics such as a company logo.

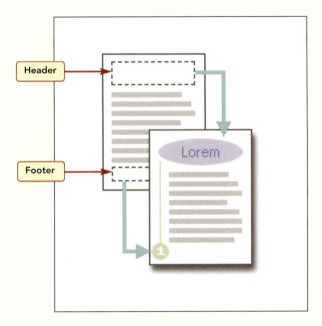

The same header and footer can be used throughout a document, or a different header and footer can be used in different sections of a document. For example, a unique header or footer can be used in one section and a different one in another section. You also can have a unique header or footer on the first page, or omitted entirely from the first page, or use a different header and footer on odd and even pages.

You want to add a header and footer to the entire document except for the first two pages.

Creating Document Sections

Many format and layout settings, including headers and footers, when applied affect an entire document. To apply layout or formatting changes to a portion of a document, you need to create separate sections in the document by inserting section breaks

Concept 11

To format different parts of a document differently, you can divide a document into **sections**. Initially a document is one section. To separate it into different parts, you insert section breaks. The **section break** identifies the end of a section and stores the document format settings associated with that section of the document. Once a document is divided into sections, the following formats can be changed for individual sections: margins, paper size and orientation, paper source for a printer, page borders, vertical alignment, headers and footers, columns, page numbering, line numbering, and footnotes and endnotes.

The three types of section breaks, described below, control the location where the text following a section break begins.

NEXT PAGE
Starts the new section on the next page.

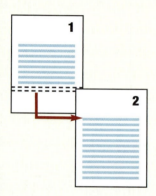

CONTINUOUS
Starts the new section on the same page.

ODD OR EVEN
Starts the new section on the next odd or even numbered page.

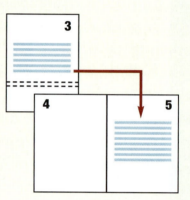

If you delete a section break, the preceding text becomes part of the following section and assumes its section formatting.

Because you do not want headers and footers on the first two pages of the document, you need to divide the document into two sections. You will replace the hard page break that you inserted when creating the table of contents page with a Next Page section break.

1 • Move to the table of contents page.

• Turn on display of paragraph marks.

• Select the hard page break line below the table of contents and press Delete to remove it.

• Open the Page Layout tab.

• Click  from the Page Setup group.

• Choose Next Page from the Section Breaks category.

• If necessary, scroll to see the bottom of the table of contents list.

Your screen should be similar to Figure 3.78

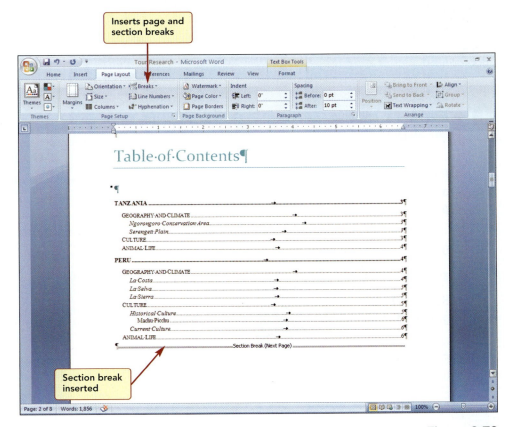

Figure 3.78

MORE ABOUT

 To learn how to delete a section break, see 2.3 Control Pagination in the More About appendix.

A double dotted line and the words "Section Break" identify the type of document break that was inserted. A section break, like a hard page break line, can be deleted.

You also decide to insert another section break at the beginning of the Peru topic. Again you want it to start on a new page.

2 • Move to the Peru topic heading and insert a Next Page section break at that location.

Additional Information

If you do not create a section break first, Word will automatically insert a section break for you if you change the formatting of selected text, such as inserting columns or centering selected text vertically on a page.

The report now contains two section breaks that divide the report into three sections that can each be formatted independently if needed.

Additional Information

MLA style requires that headers and footers be placed 0.5 inch from the top and bottom of the page. This is the default layout for the normal document. Headers are to include the page number preceded by the author's last name, right-aligned.

Using a Predesigned Header

Word includes many features that help you quickly create attractive headers and footers. Among these features are predesigned built-in header and footer designs that include placeholders to help you enter information. You will create a header for the report using this feature.

1 ● **Move to the Tanzania heading on page 3.**

● **Press** Ctrl **+ * to turn off the display of paragraph marks.**

● **Open the Insert tab and click** [Header] **in the Header & Footer group.**

● **From the gallery of header designs, choose Sideline.**

Your screen should be similar to Figure 3.79

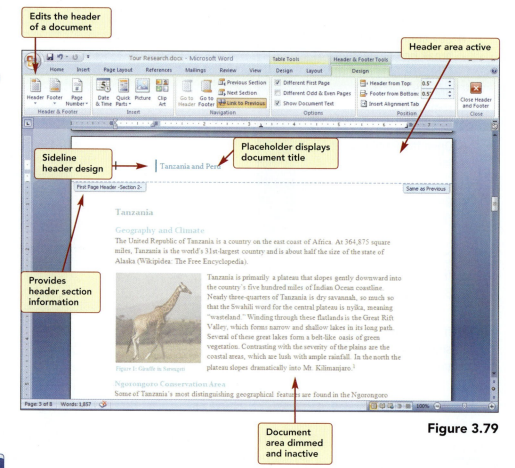

Edits the header of a document

Header area active

Placeholder displays document title

Sideline header design

Provides header section information

Document area dimmed and inactive

Figure 3.79

Additional Information

You can hide the display of the document text while working with headers and footers by deselecting ☑ Show Document Text in the Options group of the Design tab.

MORE ABOUT

You also can insert predesigned headers using the Quick Parts Building Blocks Organizer. To learn how to do this, see 4.1 Structure Content Using Quick Parts in the More About appendix.

The document area dims and the header area, above the dashed line, is active. The Header and Footer Tools Design tab is automatically displayed. Its buttons are used to add items to the header and footer and to navigate between headers and footers.

The Sideline design includes a graphic bar like that used in the cover page and the report title placeholder that displays the title from the document properties in blue. Notice that in addition to the Header and Footer Tools tab, the Table Tools tab is displayed. This is because the design is contained in a table consisting of a single cell that is used to control the placement of items.

Modifying Header Settings

Notice the tab on the left below the dashed line of the header. This tab identifies the section information for each page of the document. Each section has its own header areas that can be formatted differently.

1 ● **Change the zoom to 39%.**

Your screen should be similar to Figure 3.80

Each section includes two types of headers

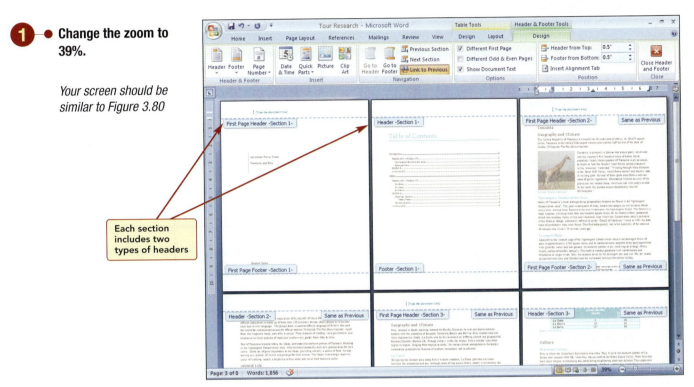

Figure 3.80

Now you can see that each section is made up of two types of headers: "First Page Headers" and running "Headers." Word automatically added first page headers because it detected that the document includes a cover page. This allows you to create a unique header for the first page. Notice the Sidelines design has been inserted only in the "First Page Header" headers and that the headers on the following pages of the same section are blank.

Since it is not necessary to have a separate First Page Header in sections 2 and 3, you will remove them and then insert the Sideline design again for the running headers in the two sections.

2 ● Click [☐ Different First Page] to turn off this feature for Section 2.

● Click [☐ Next Section] to move to the First Page Header of Section 3.

● Click [☐ Different First Page].

● Scroll up to see the top of the window.

● Click in the Header of the first page of section 2.

● Click [Header] in the Header & Footer group and choose Sideline.

Your screen should be similar to Figure 3.81

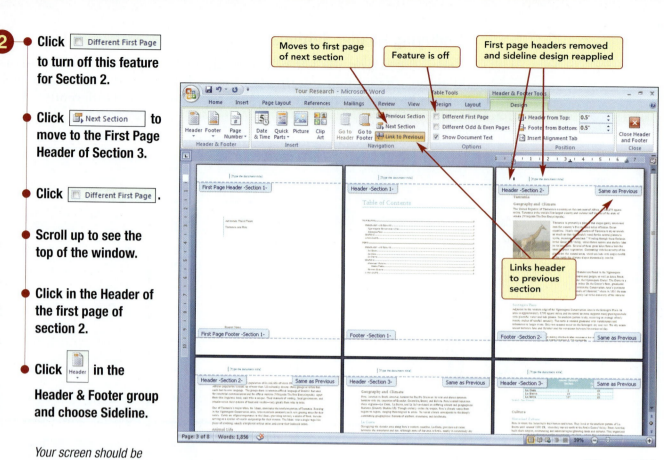

> Moves to first page of next section

> Feature is off

> First page headers removed and sideline design reapplied

> Links header to previous section

Figure 3.81

Now all headers in all sections of the document are formatted using this design. The same design was applied to all sections because the headers are initially linked even though the document is divided into sections. Notice the tab on the right displays "Same as Previous." When this setting is on, the header in the previous sections will have the same settings as the header in the section you are defining. Because you do not want the title or contents pages in section 1 to display information in the header, you will break the connection between sections 1 and 2 by turning off this option. Then you will remove the header from section 1.

3 ● **Click** [Link to Previous].

● **Click** [Previous Section]

● **Click** [Different First Page].

● **Click** [Header] **and choose Remove Header.**

Your screen should be similar to Figure 3.82

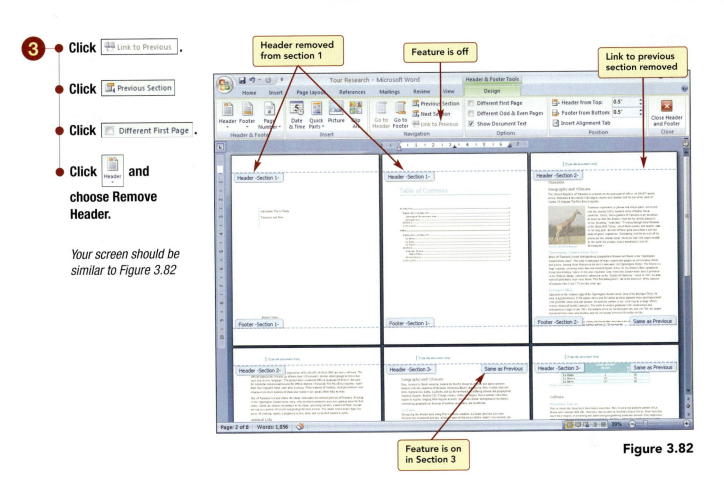

Header removed from section 1

Feature is off

Link to previous section removed

Feature is on in Section 3

Figure 3.82

The header information is removed from Section 1. It is displayed in Section 3 because the Same as Previous option is on for that section. You can tell if the headers are linked because "Same as Previous" appears in a tab below the header area.

Changing Header Content

Instead of the report title, you want to display the section title, Tanzania. To do this, you need to remove the title placeholder and type the section heading. You edit the content of a header as if it were a mini-document.

1 • Click 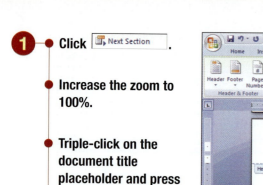 Next Section .

• Increase the zoom to 100%.

• Triple-click on the document title placeholder and press [Delete] to remove it.

• Type **Tanzania**.

Your screen should be similar to Figure 3.83

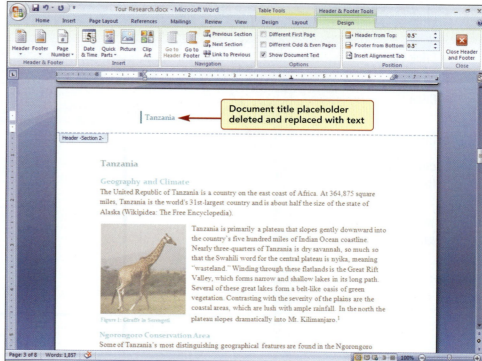

> Document title placeholder deleted and replaced with text

Figure 3.83

Next, you want to add your name right-aligned to the header. To quickly add this information, you will use a Quick Parts entry. Quick Parts insert built-in information automatically for you, such as document and user information.

2 • Click [🔲 Insert Alignment Tab].

• Choose Right and click [OK].

• Click [Quick Parts] in the Insert group.

• Select Document Property and choose Author.

Your screen should be similar to Figure 3.84

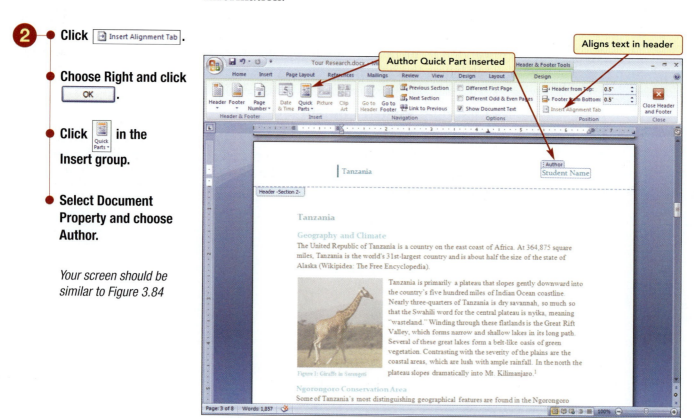

> Author Quick Part inserted

> Aligns text in header

Figure 3.84

Lab 3: Creating Reports and Tables

www.mhhe.com/oleary

The Author placeholder is right-aligned in the header and displays your name because this information is stored in the document properties.

Inserting and Modifying the Date

Finally, you will add an automatic date stamp to display the current date after your name in the header.

1 ● Press Tab, →, and Spacebar to move to the end of the Author placeholder and enter a space.

● Click **Date & Time** in the Insert group.

● If necessary, select **Update Automatically** to turn on this feature.

● Click **OK** to insert the date in the default format.

Your screen should be similar to Figure 3.85

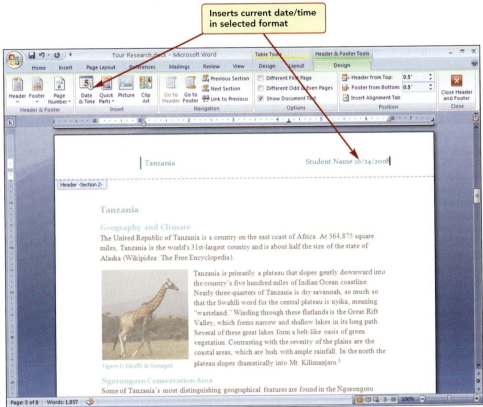

Figure 3.85

The current date is inserted as a field and will update when the system date changes. Instead you decide to change the date to display the date the document was last saved using a Quick Parts entry.

2 ● Select and delete the date placeholder.

● Click 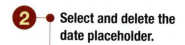 and choose Field.

● Choose Date and Time from the Categories list.

● Choose SaveDate from the Field Names list.

● Choose the M/d/yyyy h:mm am/pm date and time format (10/12/2008 11:09 AM).

● Click [OK].

● Reduce the zoom to 39%.

Your screen should be similar to Figure 3.86

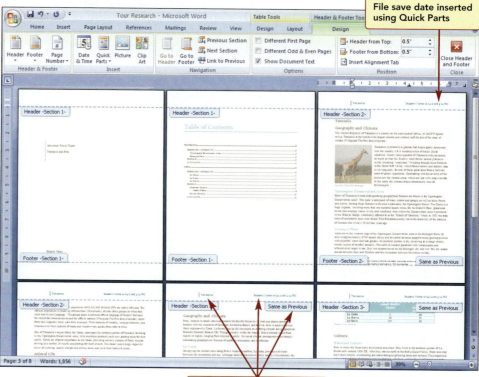

File save date inserted using Quick Parts

Section 3 header same as section 2 because the link to previous section is still on

Figure 3.86

The date and time reflect the date and time the file was last saved. It can be updated when you save the file again. Notice that the same header information is used in Section 3. You want to break the link between the Section 3 header and the Section 2 header so you can change the section title from Tanzania to Peru in the Section 3 header.

3 ● Click on the Section 3 header and click  to break the link.

● Select the text Tanzania and replace it with Peru.

● Scroll up to see the first six pages as in Figure 3.87.

Your screen should be similar to Figure 3.87

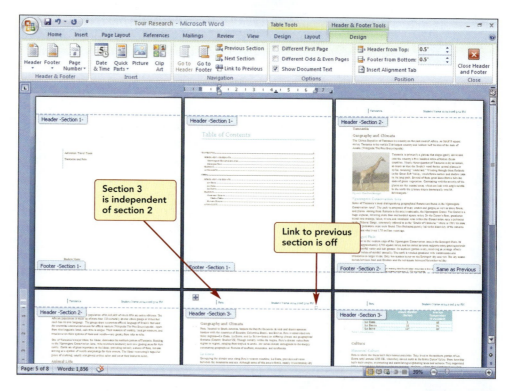

Section 3 is independent of section 2

Link to previous section is off

Figure 3.87

You can now see that the header for Sections 2 and 3 are formatted independently and that Section 1 does not display any header information.

Inserting and Modifying Page Numbers

Next, you will add information to the footer. You want the footer to display the page number, file name, and date. Page numbers can be added to the top, bottom, or side margins of the page. Word includes many built-in page number designs that include formatting and graphic elements to help you quickly create attractive page numbers. You will add the number to the bottom of the page, which inserts it in the footer.

MORE ABOUT

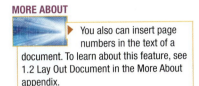 ▶ You also can insert page numbers in the text of a document. To learn about this feature, see 1.2 Lay Out Document in the More About appendix.

1 ● **Click** [Page Number] **from the Header & Footer group.**

● **Select Bottom of Page.**

Additional Information

You also can easily change the built-in designs or create your own custom designs and save them to the gallery using the Save Selection as Page Number option.

● **Scroll the list of page number styles and choose Large Color 3.**

Your screen should be similar to Figure 3.88

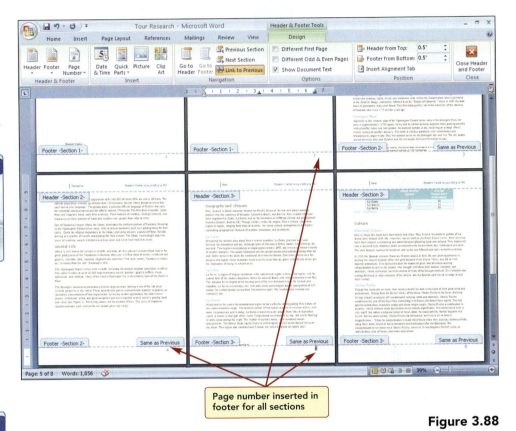

Page number inserted in footer for all sections

Figure 3.88

Additional Information

You also can display different information on odd and even pages for both headers and footers using [☐ Different Odd & Even Pages].

Additional Information

You also can change the format of page numbers from Arabic to Roman Numerals or letters and include chapter numbers.

The footer area is active and the page number appears right-aligned in the selected design in the footer of all sections. The number is a field that updates to reflect the document page. By default, when you insert sections, page numbering continues from the previous section. Because you do not want the title or contents pages in section 1 to display the footer information, you will break the connection between sections 1 and 2 by turning off this option. Then you will remove the footer from section 1 and begin page numbering with section 2.

2 ● Move to the section 2 footer.

● Click 🖳 Link to Previous .

● Move to the footer of section 1.

● Click [Footer] and choose Remove Footer.

● Move to the footer of section 2.

● Click [Page Number] in the Header and Footer group.

● Choose Format Page Numbers.

● Choose Start At.

Additional Information
The default Start At setting begins numbering with 1.

● Click [OK].

● Increase the zoom to 100%.

● Click in the footer area to clear the selection.

Your screen should be similar to Figure 3.89

Additional Information
You also can use [Footer] on the Insert tab or the Header & Footer Tools Design tab to insert a predesigned footer with placeholders for items such as the date and page number.

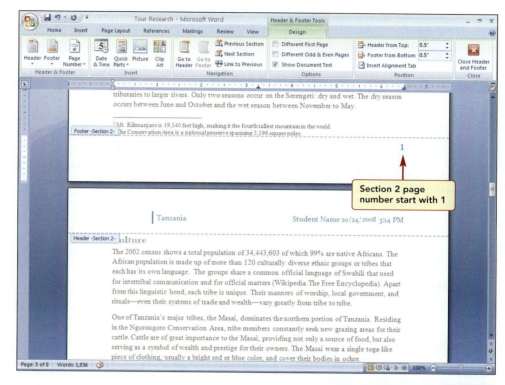

Figure 3.89

The Section 2 footer now displays "1" as the current page number.

Adding the File Name Quick Parts

Next, you will add the file name centered in the footer. To quickly add the file information, you will use a Quick Parts entry. Then you will save the document and update the date field in the header.

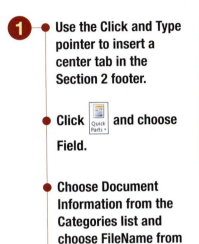

1
- Use the Click and Type pointer to insert a center tab in the Section 2 footer.

- Click  and choose Field.

- Choose Document Information from the Categories list and choose FileName from the Field Names list.

- Click **OK**.

- Save the report.

- Right-click on the date field in the header and choose Update Field from the context menu.

Your screen should be similar to Figure 3.90

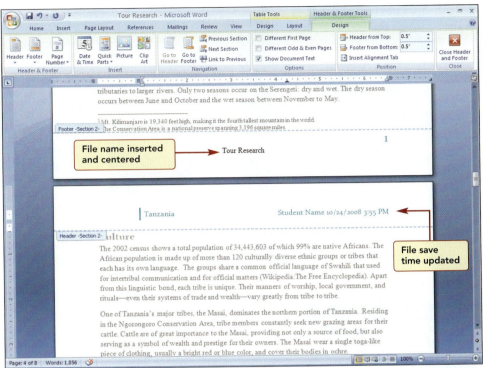

Figure 3.90

The date and time have updated to reflect the last time the file was saved. Likewise, because the file name is also a field, it can be updated if you change the file name to another. Notice the file name is in black font. This is because it was not entered using a design style and formats using the default font color setting.

2 Select the file name and use the Mini toolbar to change the font color to the Turquoise, Accent 1 theme color.

Click [Close Header and Footer].

Another Method
You also can double-click in the document area to make it active again.

Your screen should be similar to Figure 3.91

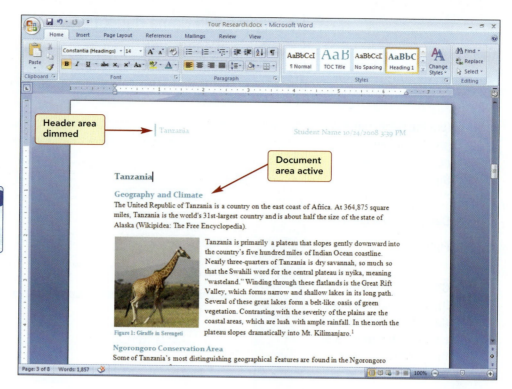

Header area dimmed → Tanzania   Student Name 10/24/2008 3:39 PM

Document area active

Tanzania

Geography and Climate
The United Republic of Tanzania is a country on the east coast of Africa. At 364,875 square miles, Tanzania is the world's 31st-largest country and is about half the size of the state of Alaska (Wikipidea: The Free Encyclopedia).

Tanzania is primarily a plateau that slopes gently downward into the country's five hundred miles of Indian Ocean coastline. Nearly three-quarters of Tanzania is dry savannah, so much so that the Swahili word for the central plateau is nyika, meaning "wasteland." Winding through these flatlands is the Great Rift Valley, which forms narrow and shallow lakes in its long path. Several of these great lakes form a belt-like oasis of green vegetation. Contrasting with the severity of the plains are the coastal areas, which are lush with ample rainfall. In the north the plateau slopes dramatically into Mt. Kilimanjaro.[1]

Figure 1: Giraffe in Serengeti

Ngorongoro Conservation Area
Some of Tanzania's most distinguishing geographical features are found in the Ngorongoro

Page: 3 of 8   Words: 1,857

Figure 3.91

Additional Information
Headers and footers can be removed from the entire document by making the document area active and clicking [Header] or [Footer] on the Insert tab and choosing Remove Header or Remove Footer from the menu.

The document area is active again, and the header and footer text appears dimmed. The header and footer can only be seen in Print Layout view and when the document is printed.

Redisplaying Spelling and Grammar Errors

Now you will turn on the display of spelling and grammar errors again and then spell and grammar check the document.

1

- If necessary, move to the top of page 1 of section 2.

- Choose Office Button/ Word Options /Proofing.

- Clear the checkmark from Hide spelling errors in this document only.

- Clear the checkmark from Hide grammar errors in this document only.

- Click OK.

- Open the Review tab.

- Click Spelling & Grammar in the Proofing group.

- Respond appropriately to any other located errors and choose Ignore All for all proper names, special terms, and abbreviations.

- Click OK to end spelling and grammar checking.

Your screen should be similar to Figure 3.92

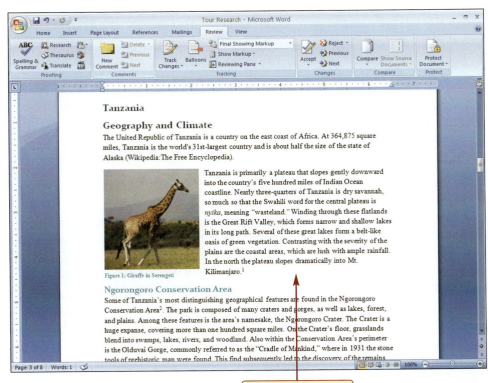

Spelling and grammar errors checked and cleared

Figure 3.92

The Spelling and Grammar Checker first checked the document text for errors, then the footnotes, and finally the headers and footers.

Updating a Table of Contents

You have made many modifications to the report since generating the table of contents, so you want to update the listing. Because the table of contents is a field, if you add or remove headings, rearrange topics, or make other changes that affect the table of contents listing, you can quickly update the table of contents. In this case, you have added pictures, a table, a bibliography, and a table of figures that have affected the paging and content of the document. You will update the table of contents to ensure that the page references are accurate and that any new content is included.

1 ● **Move to the table of contents page.**

● **Click anywhere on the table of contents area.**

● **Click** [Update Table] **in the field tab.**

Another Method

You also can use [Update Table] on the References tab, or choose Update Field from the table of contents context menu, or press **F9** to quickly update a table of contents field.

● **Choose Update entire table.**

● **Click** [OK].

Your screen should be similar to Figure 3.93

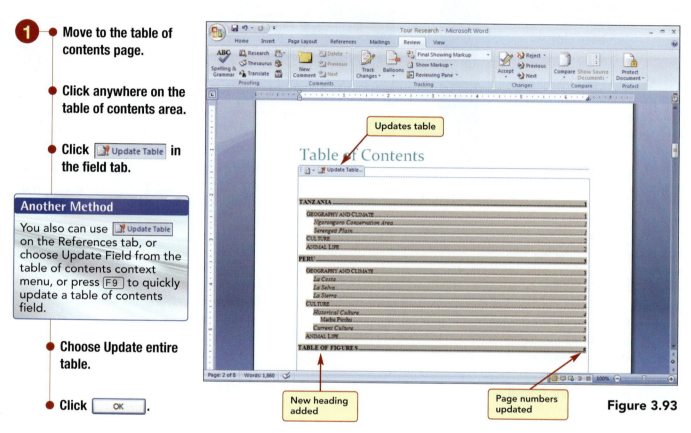

Figure 3.93

The page numbers referenced by each table-of-contents hyperlink have been updated as needed and the Table of Figures heading has been added to the list. However, the Works Cited page is not included. This is because the Works Cited page title is formatted using the TOC Title style, not a heading style. You will add the Works Cited page to the table of contents listing by marking the individual entry.

2 • Move to the Works Cited page title.

• Click ⊟ Add Text ▾ in the Table of Contents group of the References tab.

• Select Level 1 as the level for the heading.

• Click 🗐 Update Table in the Table of Contents group.

• Choose Update entire table.

• Click OK.

• Display the table of contents page.

Your screen should be similar to Figure 3.94

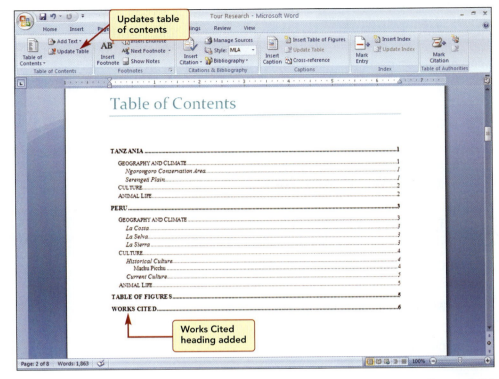

Figure 3.94

The listing now includes a hyperlink to the Works Cited page.

MORE ABOUT

To learn how to update a table of contents with selected text, see 1.3 Make Documents and Content Easier to Find in the More About appendix

Printing Selected Pages

You are now ready to print the report.

1 • Click 🖫 Save.

• Choose 🅾 Office Button/Print/Print Preview.

• Reduce the zoom to display all eight pages.

Your screen should be similar to Figure 3.95

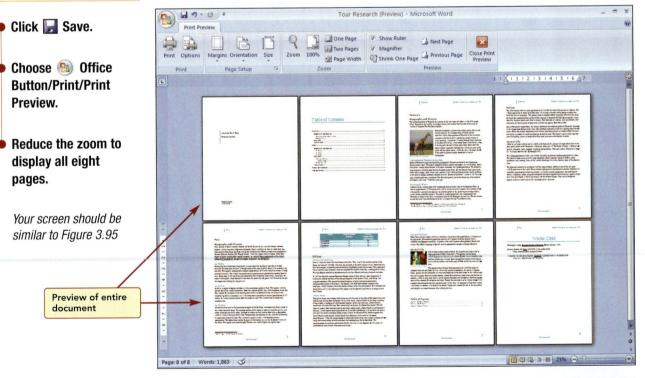

Figure 3.95

You would like to print only the first and second pages in section one, and the sixth, seventh, and eighth pages in section three of the document. To do this, you use the Print dialog box to select the pages you want to print. When printing pages in different sections, the page number and section number (p#s#) must be identified in the page range.

2 • Click 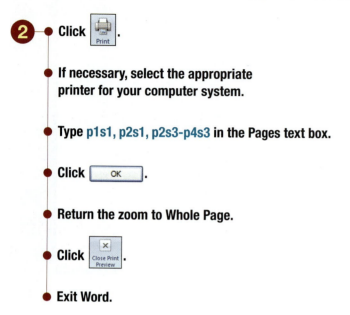 .

• If necessary, select the appropriate printer for your computer system.

• Type p1s1, p2s1, p2s3-p4s3 in the Pages text box.

• Click OK .

• Return the zoom to Whole Page.

• Click Close Print Preview .

• Exit Word.

Your printed output should be similar to that shown in the Case Study at the beginning of the lab.

Focus on Careers

EXPLORE YOUR CAREER OPTIONS

Market Research Analyst
Have you ever wondered who investigates the market for new products? Ever thought about the people who put together phone surveys? Market research analysts are responsible for determining the potential sales for a new product or service. They conduct surveys and compile statistics for clients or their employer. These reports usually include report features like a table of contents, cross-references, headers and footers, and footnotes for references. Market research analysts may hold positions as faculty at a university, work for large organizations, or hold governmental positions. The salary range for an entry-level market research analyst position is $39,300 to $49,400 and demand is high in a strong economy.

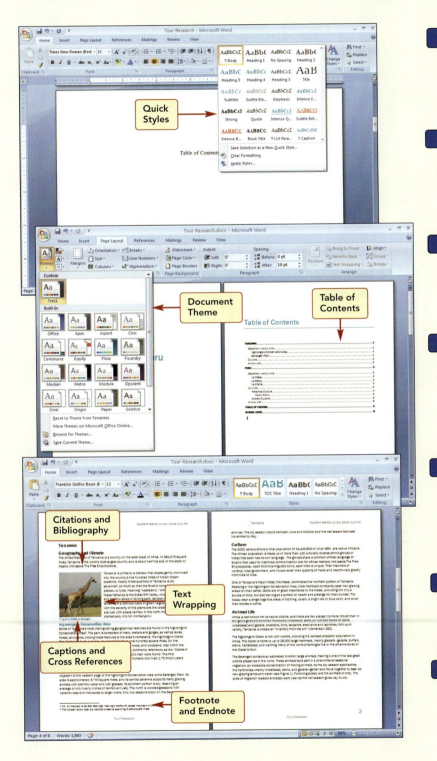

Quick Styles

Document Theme

Table of Contents

Citations and Bibliography

Text Wrapping

Captions and Cross References

Footnote and Endnote

Quick Styles (WD3.7)

Applying a style, a predefined set of formatting characteristics, allows you to quickly apply a whole group of formats in one simple step to a selection.

Document Theme (WD3.21)

A document theme is a predefined set of formatting choices that can be applied to an entire document in one simple step.

Table of Contents (WD3.33)

A table of contents is a listing of the topic headings that appear in a document and their associated page references

Citations and Bibliography (WD3.41)

Parenthetical source references, called citations, give credit for specific information included in the document. Complete source information for citations is included in a bibliography at the end of the report.

Footnote and Endnote (WD3.47)

Footnotes and endnotes are used in documented research papers to explain or comment on information in the text, or provide source references for text in the document.

Text Wrapping (WD3.52)

You can control the appearance of text around a graphic object by specifying the text wrapping style.

Captions and Cross-References (WD3.55)

A caption is a numbered label for a figure, table, picture, or graph. A cross-reference is a reference from one part of a document to related information in another part.

Table (WD3.62)

A table is used to organize information into an easy-to-read format of horizontal rows and vertical columns.

Table of Figures (WD3.72)

A table of figures is a list of the figures, tables, or equations used in a document and their associated page number.

Header and Footer (WD3.79)

A header is a line or several lines of text in the top margin of each page. A footer is a line or several lines of text in the margin space at the bottom of every page.

Section (WD3.80)

To format different parts of a document differently, you can divide a document into sections.

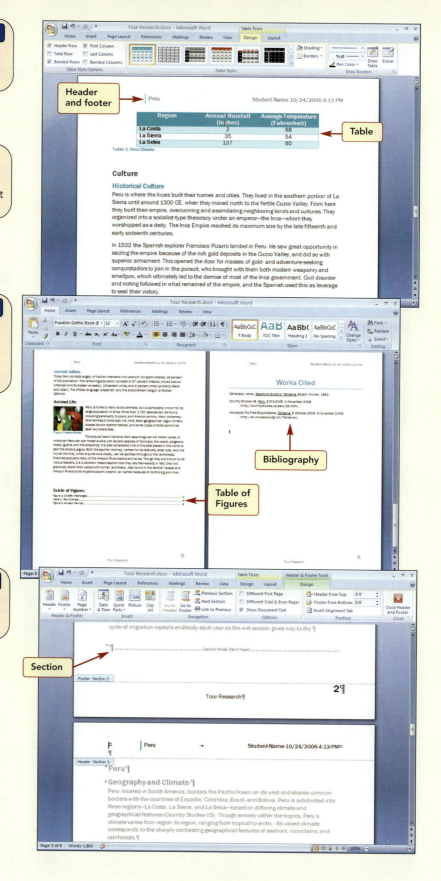

Header and footer

Table

Bibliography

Table of Figures

Section

Lab Review

key terms

bibliography WD3.41
caption WD3.55
cell WD3.62
citations WD3.41
Click and Type WD3.27
cross-reference WD3.55
Document Map WD3.37
document theme WD3.21
drawing layer WD3.52
endnote WD3.47
floating object WD3.52
footer WD3.79

footnote WD3.47
header WD3.79
heading style WD3.7
inline object WD3.52
navigation window WD3.37
note pane WD3.48
note reference mark WD3.47
note separator WD3.47
note text WD3.47
placeholder WD3.18
quick style WD3.7

section WD3.80
section break WD3.80
sort WD3.66
split window WD3.57
table WD3.62
table of contents WD3.33
table of figures WD3.72
table reference WD3.62
text box WD3.57
text wrapping WD3.52
thumbnails WD3.39

MCAS skills

The Microsoft Certified Applications Specialist (MCAS) certification program is designed to measure your proficiency in performing basic tasks using the Office 2007 applications. Getting certified demonstrates that you have the skills and provides a valuable industry credential for employment. See Reference 2 MCAS Certification Guide for a complete list of the skills that were covered in Lab 3.

command summary

Button/Command	Shortcut	Action
Office Button Menu		
Print/Print Preview		Displays document as it will appear when printed
Word Options /Proofing		Changes settings associated with Spelling and Grammar checking
Word Options /Advanced/Mark formatting inconsistencies		Checks for formatting inconsistencies
Home tab		
Font group		
Grow Font		Increases selected font size by increments
Paragraph group		
Sort		Rearranges items in a selection into ascending alphabetical/numerical order
Styles group		
More		Opens Quick Styles gallery
Insert tab		
Pages group		
Cover Page		Inserts a preformatted cover page
Blank Page		Inserts a blank page
Tables group		
Table		Inserts table at insertion point
Header and Footer group		
Header		Inserts predesigned header style
Footer		Inserts predesigned footer style
Page Layout tab		
Themes group		
Themes		Applies selected theme to document
		Changes colors for current theme
		Changes fonts for current theme

command summary

Button/Command	Shortcut	Action
Page Setup group		
Breaks ▾		Inserts page and section breaks
Arrange group		
Text Wrapping ▾		Controls how text wraps around a selected object
References tab		
Table of Contents group		
Table of Contents ▾		Generates a table of contents
Add Text ▾		Adds selected text as an entry in table of contents
Update Table	F9	Updates the table of contents field
Footnotes group		
AB¹ Insert Footnote	Alt + Ctrl + F	Inserts footnote reference at insertion point
Citations & Bibliography group		
Insert Citation ▾		Creates a citation for a reference source
Manage Sources		Displays list of all sources cited
Style: MLA ▾		Sets the style of citations
Bibliography ▾		Creates a bibliography list of sources cited
Captions group		
Insert Caption		Adds a figure caption
Cross-reference		Creates figure cross-references
View tab		
Document Views group		
Outline		Changes to Outlining view
Show/Hide group		
Document Map		Displays or hides Document Map in navigation pane
Thumbnails		Displays or hides thumbnails in navigation pane

Lab Review

Button/Command	Shortcut	Action
Window group		
▦ Split		Divides a document into two horizontal sections
Picture Tools Format tab		
Arrange group		
⊠ Text Wrapping ▾		Specifies how text will wrap around picture
Table Tools Design tab		
Table Style Options group		
☑ Header Row		Turns on/off formats for header row
☑ First Column		Turns on/off formats for first column
☐ Last Column		Turns on/off formats for last column
Table Styles group		
▾ More		Opens Table Styles gallery
Table Tools Layout tab		
Rows & Columns group		
Insert Above		Inserts a new row in table above selected row
Alignment group		
▤ Align top center		Aligns text at top center of cell space
Header & Footer Tools Design tab		
Header & Footer Group		
Page Number ▾		Inserts page number in header or footer
Insert group		
Date & Time		Inserts current date or time in header or footer
Quick Parts ▾ /Document Property		Inserts selected document property into header or footer
Quick Parts ▾ /Field		Inserts selected field Quick Part

command summary

Button/Command	Shortcut	Action
Navigation group		
Go to Footer		Switches to footer area
Next Section		Navigates to next section
Previous Section		Navigates to previous section
Link to Previous		Turns on/off link to header or footer in previous section
Option group		
Different First Page		Specify a unique header and footer for the first page
Position group		
Insert Alignment Tab		Inserts a tab stop to align content in header/footer
Close group		
Close Header and Footer		Closes header/footer area
Outlining tab		
Outline Tools group		
Promote to Heading 1		Promotes selected item to Heading 1 level
Promote	Alt + ⇧Shift + ←	Promotes selected item one level
Level 1 ▾ Outline Level		Choose outline level for selected item
Demote	Alt + ⇧Shift + →	Demotes selected item one level
Demote to body text		Demotes selected item to body text
Move Up	Alt + ⇧Shift + ↑	Moves selected item up
Move Down	Alt + ⇧Shift + ↓	Moves selected item down
Expand	Alt + ⇧Shift + +	Expand the selected item
Collapse	Alt + ⇧Shift + −	Collapse the selected item
Level 9 ▾ Show Level		Choose levels to display in outline
✓ Show Text Formatting		Show the outline as formatted text
Show First Line Only		Shows only the first line of each item
Close Outline View		Closes Outline view and displays last used view

Lab Exercises

matching

Match the item on the left with the correct description on the right.

1. citation _____
2. heading style _____
3. cross-reference _____
4. tight wrap _____
5. Document Map _____
6. section break _____
7. inline image _____
8. Quick Parts _____
9. document theme _____
10. table reference _____

a. combination of fonts, type sizes, bold, and italics used to identify different topic levels in a document

b. inserts built-in pieces of information automatically

c. graphic positioned directly in the text

d. a predefined set of formatting choices

e. letter and number used to identify table cells

f. uses headings to navigate through the document

g. text closely follows contours around a graphic

h. reference from one part of the document to another part

i. instructs Word to end one set of format settings and begin another

j. parenthetical source reference

multiple choice

Circle the correct response to the questions below.

1. A _____ allows you to see two parts of the same document at the same time.
   a. divided window
   b. split window
   c. sectioned window
   d. note pane

2. _____ are lines of text at the top and bottom of a page outside the margin lines.
   a. Characters and paragraphs
   b. Headers and footers
   c. Tables and text wrappers
   d. Styles and sections

3. A(n) _____ displays information in horizontal rows and vertical columns.
   a. Document Map
   b. cell reference
   c. object
   d. table

4. A _____ is inserted automatically when a new page is created in a document.
    a. hard page break
    b. section break
    c. soft page break
    d. page division

5. _____ shows the hierarchy of topics in a document.
    a. Full Screen Reading view
    b. Outline view
    c. Print Layout view
    d. Multiple page view

6. You can control how text appears around a graphic with _____ styles.
    a. sorting
    b. text wrapping
    c. section
    d. caption

7. A(n) _____ is a predesigned set of formats that can be applied to an entire document.
    a. AutoFormat
    b. document theme
    c. style
    d. Quick Part

8. A _____ is a reference from one part of a document to related information in another part of the same document.
    a. citation
    b. caption
    c. heading
    d. cross-reference

9. _____ inserts items in a blank area of a document, avoiding the need to press [↵Enter].
    a. Type and Point
    b. Click and Type
    c. Point and Type
    d. Type and Click

10. A _____ is a line of text that describes the object that appears above it.
    a. citation
    b. cross-reference
    c. caption
    d. footnote

true/false

Circle the correct answer to the following questions.

1. Character styles are a combination of any character formats and paragraph formats that affect all text in a paragraph.   True   False

2. Word automatically applies styles to the text in an outline as it is entered.   True   False

3. Footnotes must be manually renumbered as you move text around in a document.   True   False

4. The navigation window displays the headings in your document.   True   False

5. A document theme is applied to selected characters and paragraphs.   True   False

6. A section break identifies the end of a section and stores the document format settings.   True   False

7. A table of contents hyperlink is used to jump directly to a specific location in a document.   True   False

8. A style is a combination of character formats.   True   False

9. A table of contents and a cross-reference are fields.   True   False

10. Thumbnails are small pictures of each page of a document.   True   False

fill-in

Complete the following statements by filling in the blanks with the correct terms.

1. A _____ identifies the content to be entered in a cover page.

2. A(n) _____ is a set of formats that is assigned a name and can be quickly applied to a document.

3. The _____ for a footnote appears at the bottom of the page on which the reference mark appears.

4. By changing a graphic to a(n) _____, it is inserted into the drawing layer.

5. The intersection of a row and a column creates a(n) _____.

6. A _____ is a small picture of each page of the document.

7. A(n) _____ is a line or several lines of text at the top of each page in a document.

8. A(n) _____ is used to organize information into horizontal rows and vertical columns.

9. Specifying _____ controls how text appears around a graphic object.

10. The _____ is used to move by headings or pages in a document.

Hands-On Exercises

Creating and Modifying an Outline ★

1. You are just starting work on a research report on Internet Spam. To help organize your thoughts, you decide to create an outline of the main topics to be included. Your completed outline will be similar to the one shown here.

   a. Open a new blank document. Switch to Outline view.

   b. The topics you want to discuss are shown below. Enter these topics at the outline level indicated, pressing ⏎Enter at the end of each.

   Why Am I Getting All This Spam? (Level 1)

   Summary (Level 2)

   Introduction (Level 2)

   Major Findings (Level 2)

   Methodology (Level 2)

   Experimental Anti-Spam Measures (Level 3)

   Removal from public accessibility (Level 4)

   Posting in "human-readable" form (Level 4)

   Posting in HTML-obscured form (Level 4)

   Posting in unreadable form (Level 4)

   Changing personal preferences on a Web site (Level 4)

   Tips for Avoiding Spam (Level 3)

   Disguise e-mail addresses (Level 4)

   Use multiple e-mail addresses (Level 4)

   Use long e-mail addresses (Level 4)

   Use a filter (Level 4)

   Results (Level 2)

   Addresses Posted on the Public Web (Level 3)

   Public Postings to USENET Newsgroups (Level 3)

   Consumer Preferences (Level 3)

   Web Discussions (Level 3)

   Domain Name Registration (Level 3)

   Conclusions (Level 2)

   Appendix 1 (Level 2)

   Appendix 2 (Level 2)

   > Student Name   ~ 1 ~   October 30, 2008
   >
   > **Why am I getting all this Spam?**
   > **Summary**
   > **Introduction**
   > **Major Findings**
   > **Methodology**
   > **Tips for Avoiding Spam**
   > *Disguise e-mail addresses*
   > *Use multiple e-mail addresses*
   > *Use a filter*
   > *Use long e-mail addresses*
   > **Experimental Anti-Spam Measures**
   > *Removal from public accessibility*
   > *Posting in "human-readable" form*
   > *Posting in HTML-obscured form*
   > *Changing personal preferences on a Web site*
   > **Results**
   > **Addresses posted on the Public Web**
   > **Public Postings to USENET Newsgroups**
   > **Consumer Preferences**
   > **Web Discussions**
   > **Domain Name Registration**
   > **Mail Server Attacks**
   > **Conclusions**
   > **Appendix 1**
   > **Appendix 2**

   c. Correct any spelling errors.

   d. Move the "Experimental Anti-Spam Measures" topic and all subtopics to below the "Tips for Avoiding Spam" topic. In the "Tips for Avoiding Spam" topic, move "Use long e-mail addresses" to below "Use a filter."

Lab Exercises

e. Change the level of the "Conclusions", "Appendix 1", and "Appendix 2" topics to level 1.

f. Add a new level 3 topic, **Mail Server Attacks**, as the last subtopic under "Results."

g. Delete the "Posting in unreadable form" topic under "Experimental Anti-Spam Measures."

h. Switch to Print Layout view. Remove the space after paragraphs. Change the theme to Aspect.

i. Insert the Blank (Three Columns) built-in header. Use the Author quick part to add your name in the left placeholder. Insert the page number in the middle placeholder using the Current Position page number option and the Tildes design. Enter the current date in the right placeholder using the month xx, xxxx format.

j. Save the outline as Spam Outline in a new folder named Research.

k. Print the outline. Close the file.

Creating a Table ★

2. You work for the Animal Rescue Foundation and are putting together a list of contact information. You would like to display the information in a table. Your completed document will be similar to the one shown here.

a. Open a new document and use Click and Type to enter the title **Animal Rescue Foundation** left-aligned at the top of the document on the first line and **Telephone Contacts** on the second line. Apply the Title style to the first line and the Subtitle style to the second line.

b. Enter the following introductory paragraph left-aligned below the title.

This listing of direct-dial telephone numbers will make it easy for you to contact the ARS department you need. If you are unsure of your party's extension, please dial the main number, (555) 545-0900. You will be greeted by an automated attendant, which will provide you with several options for locating the party with whom you wish to speak.

Animal Rescue Foundation

Telephone Contacts

This listing of direct-dial telephone numbers will make it easy for you to contact the ARS department you need. If you are unsure of your party's extension, please dial the main number, (555) 545-0900. You will be greeted by an automated attendant, which will provide you with several options for locating the party with whom you wish to speak. *

Department	Contact	Telephone Number
Behavior Helpline	Samantha Wilson	555-545-8532
Education Department	Jon Willey	555-545-4722
Job Hotline	Gavin Smith	555-545-8533
Membership & Giving	Mike Miller	555-545-4332
Pet Adoption	Wendy Jones	555-545-0958
Therapeutic Programs	Samantha Wilson	555-545-8532
Volunteer Services	James Thomas	555-545-5873

*If you need operator assistance, simply press "0" at any time.

c. Several lines below the paragraph, insert a simple table with 3 columns and 7 rows. Enter the following information into the table:

Pet Adoption	Wendy Jones	555-545-0958
Behavior Helpline	Samantha Wilson	555-545-8532
Education Department	Jon Willey	555-545-4722
Therapeutic Programs	Samantha Wilson	555-545-8532

Volunteer Services	James Thomas	555-545-5873
Job Hotline	Gavin Smith	555-545-8533
Membership & Giving	Mike Miller	555-545-4332

d. Insert a new row above the first entry and enter the following headings:

| Department | Contact | Telephone Number |

e. Change the sort order of the table so that it is sorted by department in ascending order.

f. Select a document theme and then apply a table style of your choice to the table.

g. Reduce the size the table to just small enough to display the data in each row on a single line. Center the table.

h. Insert the footnote **If you need operator assistance, simply press "0" at any time.** using the * symbol instead of a number. Place the reference mark at the end of the introductory paragraph.

i. Add a footer to the document using the Motion design. Use the Author quick part to display your name left-aligned in the footer.

j. Save the document as ARS Department Contacts.

k. Print the document.

Creating an Informational Sheet ★★

3. You are the manager of Elaina's Cameragraphics, a small camera repair and retail shop. You have fielded many different questions about digital cameras lately and have decided to compile these questions into an informational sheet. Your completed informational sheet will answer your customer's most frequently asked questions about digital technology to help them make an informed choice when buying a new camera. Your completed document will be similar to the one shown here.

a. Open the file wd03_Digital Cameras.

b. Apply the Title style to the main title.

c. Use the Document Map to locate the headings in the document and apply Level 1 headings to them.

d. Create a bulleted list in the Advantages of Digital Cameras section. Change the hanging indent to the 2.25 position and add a left tab at the 0.5 position. Use Format Painter to add bold and underlines to the beginning of each sentence, before the semicolon. Do the same for the Disadvantages of Digital Cameras section.

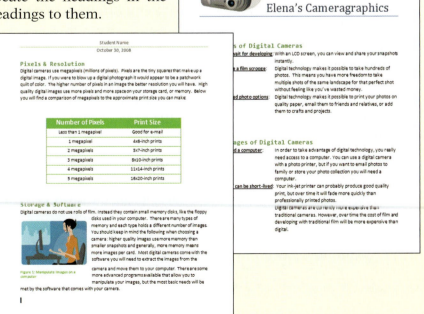

e. Select a document theme of your choice.

f. Use the following information to create a simple table below the paragraph on Pixels & Resolution.

Number of Pixels	Print Size
Less than 1 megapixel	Good for e-mail
1 megapixel	4 × 6-inch prints
2 megapixels	5 × 7-inch prints
3 megapixels	8 × 10-inch prints
4 megapixels	11 × 14-inch prints
5 megapixels	16 × 20-inch prints

g. Remove the space after paragraphs in the table. Apply a table style of your choice. Turn off the first column style effect. Center-align all the text in the table. Increase the font size of the column headings to 16 points. Size the table to the contents and center the table.

h. Insert the wd03_Camera image to the left side of the main title.

i. Insert the wd03_Computer image in front of the Storage & Software paragraph. Use the tight wrapping style and position the graphic to the left of the paragraph. Add the following caption below the graphic: **Figure 1: Manipulate images on a computer**.

j. Insert a hard page break above the Pixels & Resolution section.

k. Insert the Stacks style footer and enter the name of the store followed by the phone number **(555) 977-1650**.

l. Insert the Conservative style header. Replace the document title with your name using the Quick Parts feature. Enter the current date.

m. Make any adjustments to make the information sheet layout look like the one pictured.

n. Save the document as Digital Cameras. Print the document.

Creating a Brochure ★★★

4. Your next project as marketing coordinator at Adventure Travel Tours is to create a brochure promoting three new adventures. You have already started working on the brochure and have added most of the text content. Because this brochure is for clients, you want it to be both factual and attractive. To do this, you plan to enhance the appearance of the document by adding some finishing formatting touches. Additionally, you want to include a table of contents on the second page of the document, several pictures, and a table of tour dates. Your completed brochure will be similar to that shown here.

a. Open the file wd03_ATT Brochure.

b. Create a cover page using the Pinstripes design. Enter the title **Three New Adventures** and subtitle **Kayaking the Blue Waters of Mexico, Hiking the Great Eastern Trail, Alaska Scenic Rail Tour**. Select the current date. Add your name as the Author and **Adventure Travel Tours** as the Company Name.

c. Create a custom document theme that includes custom colors and fonts for the brochure. Add a coordinating color to the title and subtitle on the cover page.

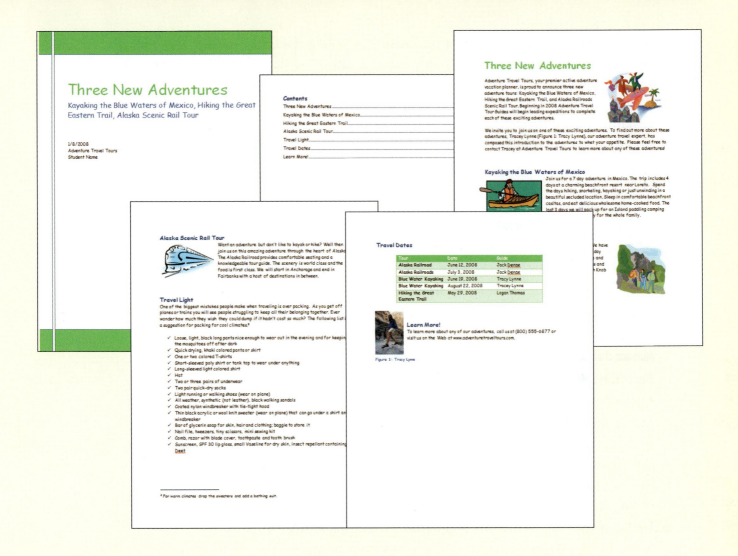

d. Create a custom heading style for the first topic heading line. Apply Heading 1 styles to the following five topic headings.

e. Insert a new page as page 2 and insert a Contents listing.

f. In this step, you will be inserting several graphics. For each of these, size the graphic appropriately. Wrap the text around the picture using a text wrapping style of your choice.

- Insert the graphic wd03_ATT to the right of the first paragraph.
- Insert the graphic wd03_Kayaking to the left of the first paragraph of the "Kayaking the Blue Waters of Mexico" section.
- Insert the graphic wd03_Hiking to the right of the first paragraph of the "Hiking the Great Eastern Trail" section.
- Insert the graphic wd03_Train to the left of the paragraph in the "Alaska Railroads Scenic Rail Tours" section.

- Insert wd03_Tracey to the left of the last paragraph in the last section of the report.

g. Add the caption **Tracy Lynne** below her photograph.

h. In the second paragraph of the "Three New Adventures" section, after the word "Lynne," add a cross-reference, with the figure number and caption, for the photo of Tracey. Use the split window feature to add the cross-reference.

i. Add a bullet style of your choice to the packing list items.

j. At the end of the first sentence in the section "Hiking the Great Eastern Trail," add the following text as a footnote: **The Appalachian Trail is 2,155 miles long.**

k. At the end of the first paragraph in the "Travel Light" section, add the following text as a footnote: **For warm climates drop the sweaters and add a bathing suit.**

l. Add a new section titled **Travel Dates** before the "Learn More!" section. Apply a Heading 1 style to the section heading. Insert a hard page break above this section.

m. Enter the following information in a table:

Tour	Date	Guide
Hiking the Great Eastern Trail	May 29, 2008	Logan Thomas
Alaska Railroad	June 12, 2008	Jack Denae
Blue Water Kayaking	June 19, 2008	Tracey Lynne
Alaska Railroads	July 3, 2008	Jack Denae
Blue Water Kayaking	August 22, 2008	Tracey Lynne

n. Size the table appropriately. Apply formatting of your choice to the new table. Sort the table in ascending sort order by tour. Center the table.

o. Change the heading for the Alaska railroad tour to **Alaska Scenic Rails Tour**. Insert a hard page break above this section.

p. Update the table of contents and adjust formatting as needed.

q. Add a header that includes a right-aligned page number.

r. Save the document as ATT Brochure. Print the report.

Writing a Report ★★★

5. As a senior trainer at Lifestyle Fitness Club, you are responsible for researching new fitness trends and sharing your findings with other trainers and clients. You have written a Beginner's Guide to Yoga for this purpose. Pages two and three contain the body of your report. You still need to add several pictures, footnotes, and citations to the report. Your completed report will be similar to that shown here.

a. Open the file wd03_Yoga Guide.

b. Turn off the display of spelling and grammar errors.

c. Create a cover page using a design of your choice. Include the report title, **Beginner's Guide to Yoga** and your name as the author. Remove any other placeholders.

d. Apply a Heading 1 style to the five topic headings.

e. Create a table of contents on a separate page after the cover page.

f. Insert the graphic wd03_Yoga Pose to the right of the second paragraph in the "What is Yoga" section as shown in the example. Size the graphic appropriately and use the square text wrapping style. Include the figure caption **Yoga emphasizes breathing and meditation** below the graphic.

g. Insert the graphic wd03_History to the left of the first two paragraphs in the "History of Yoga" section as shown in the example. Size the graphic appropriately and use the square text wrapping style. Include the figure caption **Yoga's roots lie in ancient India** below the graphic.

h. Apply a document theme of your choice for the report.

i. In the "History of Yoga" section, move to the end of the second sentence in the first paragraph after the word "poses" and add the following text as a footnote:

Ancient ceramics found in the caves of Mojendro-Daro and Harappa depict recognizable yoga positions.

j. In the "Ashtanga (Power Yoga)" description, move to the end of the second sentence after the word "style" and add the following text as a footnote:

Vinyasa is a flow or sequence of poses.

k. Display the six types of yoga in alphabetical order.

l. Enter citations in the text at the locations specified below using the information in the following four reference sources:

Location	Source
End of second sentence, first paragraph	Sparrowe
End of third paragraph	Wilber
Fifth paragraph, end of third sentence	Iyengar
End of second paragraph	Phillips

Type	Author	Title	Year	City	Publisher
Book	Linda Sparrow	Yoga	2002	New York	Hugh Lautner Levin Associates
Book	B. K. S. Iyengar	Yoga: The Path to Holistic Health	2001	Los Angeles	DK Publishing
Book	Kathy Phillips	The Spirit of Yoga	2002	Los Angeles	Barrons Educational Series
Book	Ken Wilber	The Yoga Tradition: History, Religion, Philosophy and Practice Unabridged	2001	Philadelphia	Hohm Printers

m. At the end of the document, create a table of figures and a Works Cited bibliography. Add a title above the table of figures formatted using the Heading 1 style.

n. Update the table of contents and adjust any formatting as necessary.

o. Use the Alphabet footer design and use the document quick part to add the company name, **Lifestyle Fitness Club**. Do not display the footer on the cover page.

p. Redisplay spelling and grammar errors. Check the document for errors and fix any located errors appropriately.

q. Save the document as Yoga Guide in a new folder named Yoga. Print the report.

on your own

Designing a Flyer ★

1. The Sports Company is introducing a new line of kayaking and equipment. It is holding a weekend promotional event to familiarize the community with paddling equipment. You have already started designing a flyer to advertise the event, but it still needs additional work.

- Open the file wd03_Kayaking Flyer.

- Create the following table of data below the " . . . boat giveaway!" paragraph. Use an appropriate table style.

TIME	EVENT
12:00 p.m.	Freestyle Whitewater Panel Discussion
1:15 p.m.	Kids Canoe Relay Race

1:30 p.m.	Becky Andersen & Brad Ludden Autographed Boats Charity Auction
2:30 p.m.	Drawing for Extrasport Joust Personal Flotation Device
3:00 p.m.	Team Dagger Autograph Session
5:00 p.m.	Free BBQ dinner

- Insert the picture wd03_Kayacking from your data files to the right of the text "Meet Team Dagger." Size and position the graphic appropriately.
- Add a caption below the image.
- Add formatting and styles of your choice to the document.
- Make any editing changes you feel are appropriate.
- Enter your name and the date centered in the footer.
- Save the document as Kayaking Flyer.
- Print the document.

Creating a Report from an Outline ★★

2. You are working on the Downtown Internet Café Web site and want to include information about the characteristics of the different coffee beans. You have created an outline that includes the main characteristics of coffee beans, with examples of different beans that emphasize these characteristics. Expand on the outline by researching the topics in the outline on the Web. Include the following features in your report:

- Open the file wd03_Coffee Outline.
- Create a cover page and table of contents.
- Select a Document theme.
- The body of the report should include at least three footnotes and two cross-referenced images.
- Include three citations. Generate a bibliography of your sources.
- Add page numbers to the report, excluding the title page.
- Include your name, file name, and the date in the footer.
- Save the report as Coffee Report in a new folder. Preview and print the title page, the first page, and the works cited page.

Preparing for a Job Search ★★

3. You are graduating next June and plan to begin your job search early. To prepare for getting a job, locate three sources of information on how to conduct a job search. Use your school's career services department, the library, newspapers, magazine articles, and the Web as possible sources. Begin by creating an outline of the topics you will include in the report. Using the outline, write a brief report about your findings. Include the following features in your report:

- A cover page that displays the report title, your name, and the current date.
- A table of contents page.
- The body of the paper should include at least two levels of headings.
- A minimum of three citations and three footnotes.
- A header that includes your name and page numbers on the top-right corner of every page (excluding the title page).
- At least one picture with a caption and cross-reference.

- A table that compares the jobs you are interested in and a table caption.
- A table of figures that has a formatted title that will appear in the table of contents.
- A bibliography of your reference sources. Format the bibliography appropriately.
- Include a page title and format it to appear in the table of contents.

Save the report as Job Search in a new folder. Print the document.

Writing a Research Paper ★★★

4. Create a brief research report (or use a paper you have written in the past) on a topic of interest to you. The paper must include the following features:

- A cover page that displays the report title, your name, and the current date.
- A table of contents.
- At least two levels of headings and a minimum of three footnotes and three citations.
- At least one picture with a caption and cross-reference.
- A table of information with a caption.
- A table of figures.
- A bibliography page of your reference sources.
- A header and/or footer that displays the page numbers, file name, and date. Do not include this information on the cover page or table of contents page.

Save the document as Research in a new folder. Print the cover page, table of contents page, and the last page of the report.

Researching Virus Hoaxes ★★★

5. There are a lot of real computer viruses that can wreak havoc with your computer. This makes virus hoaxes even more annoying, as they may lead some users to ignore all virus warning messages, leaving them vulnerable to a genuine, destructive virus.

Use the Web as a resource to learn more about virus hoaxes. Write a brief report defining virus hoaxes. Describe three hoaxes, how they are perpetuated, and the effect they could have if the receiver believes the hoax. The report must include the following features:

- A cover page that displays the report title, your name, and the current date.
- A table of contents.
- The body of the paper should include at least two levels of headings and a minimum of two footnotes and three citations.
- At least one picture with a caption and cross-reference.
- A table of information with a caption.
- A table of figures.
- A bibliography page of your reference sources.
- The page numbers, file name, and date in a header and/or footer. Do not include this information on the cover page or table of contents page.

Save the document as Computer Viruses. Print the document.

Working Together 1: Word 2007 and Your Web Browser

Case Study

Adventure Travel Tours

The Adventure Travel Tours Web site is used to promote its products and broaden its audience of customers. In addition to the obvious marketing and sales potential, it provides an avenue for interaction between the company and the customer to improve customer service. The company also uses the Web site to provide articles of interest to customers. The articles, which include topics such as travel background information and descriptions, changes on a monthly basis as an added incentive for readers to return to the site.

You want to use the flyer you developed to promote the new tours and presentations on the Web site. To do this, you will use Word 2007's Web-editing features that help you create a Web page quickly and easily. While using the Web-editing features, you will be working with Word and with a Web browser application. This capability of all 2007 Microsoft Office applications to work together and with other applications makes it easy to share and exchange information between applications. Your completed Web pages are shown here.

Note: The Working Together tutorial is designed to show how two applications work together and to present a basic introduction to creating Web pages.

Saving a Word Document as a Web Page

You want to create a Web page to be used on the company's Web site. A **Web page** is a document that can be used on the World Wide Web (WWW). The Web page you will create will provide information about the tour presentations. Word offers two ways to create or **author** Web pages. One way is to start with a blank Web page and enter text and graphics much as you would a normal document. Another is to quickly convert an existing Word document to a Web page.

Because the tour flyer has already been created as a Word document and contains much of the information you want to use on the Web page, you will convert it to a Web page document. You made a couple of changes to the flyer, giving it a title that is more appropriate for the Web page and removing the banner. You will use the modified version of the flyer as the basis for the Web page.

1 • Start Word 2007.

• Open the file wdwt_Presentations from the appropriate location.

Your screen should be similar to Figure 1

Revised flyer

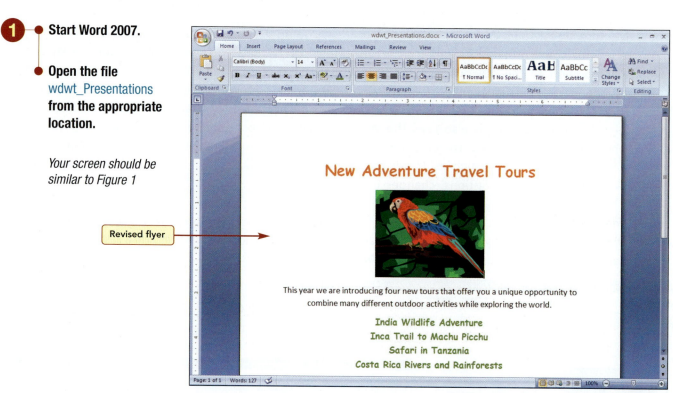

Figure 1

Word converts a document to a Web page by adding HTML coding to the document. **HTML (HyperText Markup Language)** is a programming language used to create Web pages. HTML commands control the display of information on a page, such as font colors and size, and the way an item will be processed. HTML also allows users to click on hyperlinks and jump to other locations on the same page, other pages in the same site, or other sites and locations on the WWW. HTML commands are interpreted by the browser software you are using. A **browser** is a program that connects you to remote computers and displays the Web pages you request.

When a file is converted to a Web page, the HTML coding is added and it is saved to a new file with an .html file extension. You want to save the Web page using the file name New Tour Presentations in a new folder.

2 ● Click 🔵 **Office Button and choose Save as.**

● **If necessary, change the location to save to the appropriate save location.**

● **Create a new folder named** ATT Web Page.

● **Change the file name to** New Tour Presentations.

● **From the Save as Type drop-down list, choose Web Page.**

Your screen should be similar to Figure 2

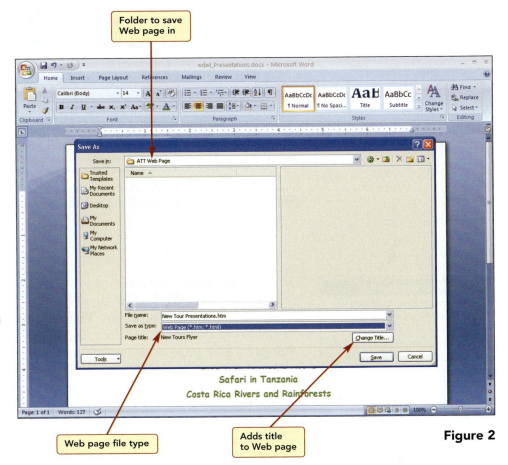

Folder to save Web page in

Web page file type

Adds title to Web page

Figure 2

You also need to provide a title for the page. This is the text that will appear in the title bar of the Web browser when the page is displayed. You want the title to be the same as the file name.

3 ● Click Change Title... .

● Change the title to **New Tour Presentations**.

● Click OK .

● Click Save .

Your screen should be similar to Figure 3

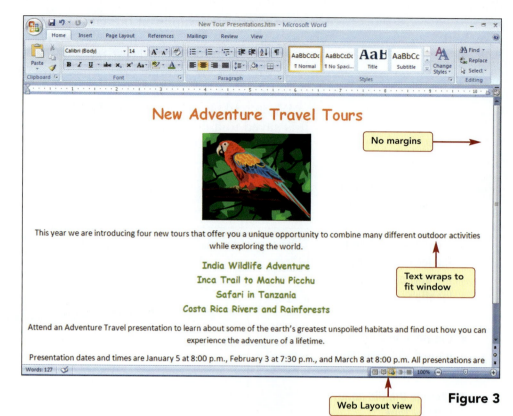

New Adventure Travel Tours

No margins

This year we are introducing four new tours that offer you a unique opportunity to combine many different outdoor activities while exploring the world.

India Wildlife Adventure
Inca Trail to Machu Picchu
Safari in Tanzania
Costa Rica Rivers and Rainforests

Text wraps to fit window

Attend an Adventure Travel presentation to learn about some of the earth's greatest unspoiled habitats and find out how you can experience the adventure of a lifetime.

Presentation dates and times are January 5 at 8:00 p.m., February 3 at 7:30 p.m., and March 8 at 8:00 p.m. All presentations are

Words: 127

Web Layout view

Figure 3

Additional Information

Some formatting features, such as emboss and shadow effects, are not supported by HTML or other Web browsers and are not available when authoring Web pages.

The flyer has been converted to an HTML document and is displayed in Web Layout view. This view displays the document as it will appear if viewed using a Web browser. This document looks very much like a normal Word document. In fact, the only visible difference is the margin settings. A Web page does not include margins. Instead, the text wraps to fit the window space. However, the formatting and features that are supported by HTML, in this case the paragraph and character formatting such as the font style, type size, and color attributes, have been converted to HTML format.

Making Text Changes

Next, you want to change the layout of the Web page so that more information is displayed in the window when the page is viewed in the browser. To do this, you will delete any unnecessary text and change the paragraph alignment to left-aligned.

1
- Delete the last two paragraphs.

- Left-align all the text below the picture.

- Add bullets preceding the list of four tours.

- Increase the font size of the title to 36 points.

- Clear the highlight.

Your screen should be similar to Figure 4

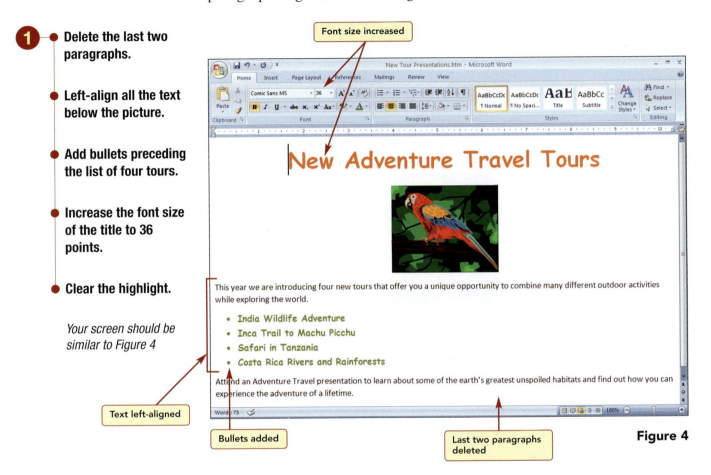

Font size increased

New Adventure Travel Tours

This year we are introducing four new tours that offer you a unique opportunity to combine many different outdoor activities while exploring the world.

- India Wildlife Adventure
- Inca Trail to Machu Picchu
- Safari in Tanzania
- Costa Rica Rivers and Rainforests

Attend an Adventure Travel presentation to learn about some of the earth's greatest unspoiled habitats and find out how you can experience the adventure of a lifetime.

Words: 75

Text left-aligned

Bullets added

Last two paragraphs deleted

Figure 4

Now, all the information is visible within the window.

Changing the Picture Layout

Additional Information

When graphic files are added to a Web page, they are copied to the same folder location as the Web page. The graphic files must always reside in the same location as the HTML document file in which they are used.

Next, you want to move the picture to the left edge of the window and wrap the text to the right around it. Unlike a normal Word document, a Web page document does not have pictures and other graphic elements embedded in it. In an HTML file, each graphic object is stored as a separate file that is accessed and loaded by the browser when the page is loaded. Word creates a link to the object's file in the HTML file. The link is a **tag** that includes the location and file name of the graphic file.

Additionally, graphics are inserted into a Web page document as inline objects. You can change the wrapping style and move, size, and format graphic objects in a Web page just like embedded objects in a Word document.

1 ● Click on the picture to select it.

● Drag the picture to the "T" in "This" at the beginning of the first paragraph.

● From the Picture Tools Format tab, click Text Wrapping ▾ and select Square.

Your screen should be similar to Figure 5

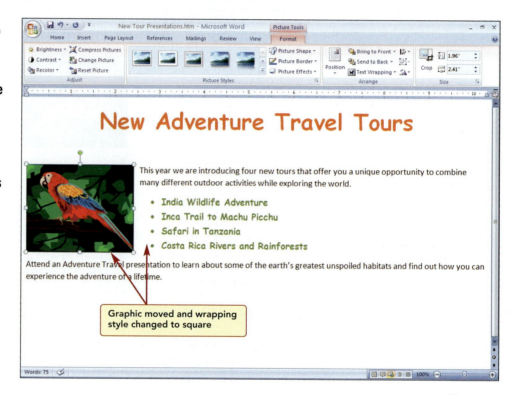

Graphic moved and wrapping style changed to square

Figure 5

Next, you will make a few other adjustments to improve the appearance.

Applying Page Color

Because color and design are important elements of Web pages, you can add a background color to the Web page. You think a light blue may look good.

1 ● Deselect the graphic.

● Open the Page Layout tab.

● Click [Page Color] in the Page Background group.

● Point to several different shades of blue to see how they look in Live Preview.

Additional Information

The gallery of colors associated with the default Office theme is displayed.

Your screen should be similar to Figure 6

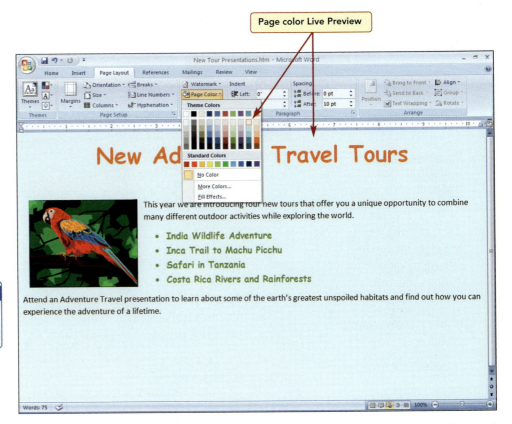

Figure 6

You do not really like how any of these colors look and decide to try a fill effect instead. Fill effects include gradient color, texture, patterns, or pictures. These effects should be used in moderation—you want them to enhance, not detract from, the content. You will try a blue gradient effect first.

2 • Choose Fill Effects.

• Choose One color.

• From the Color1 drop-down list, select Blue, Accent 1, Lighter 40%

• Drag the shade slider closer to the Light side (see Figure 7).

• If necessary, select Horizontal in the Shading styles options.

• Select the top to bottom variant (upper-right square).

Your screen should be similar to Figure 7

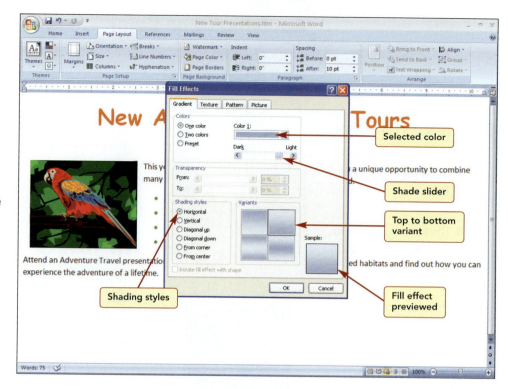

Figure 7

The Sample area shows how your color selections will appear. Now you are ready to apply these settings to the page.

3 • Click [OK].

Your screen should be similar to Figure 8

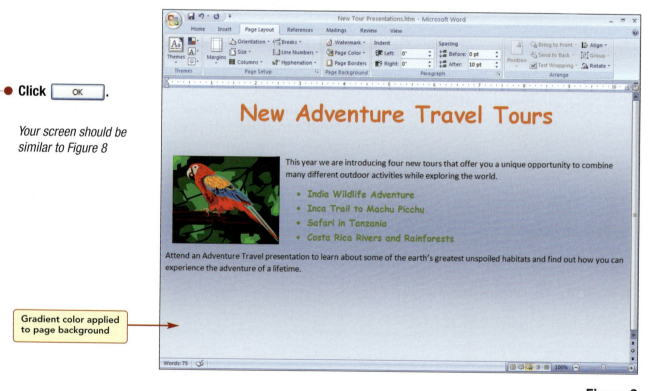

Figure 8

Although adding gradient color shading looks nice, you still are not satisfied. You will try a texture instead.

4 • Click 🎨 Page Color ▾.

• Choose **Fill Effects.**

• Open the **Texture** tab.

• Select the **Stationery** texture (fourth row, fourth column).

Having Trouble?
When you click on a texture, the texture name appears below the list box.

• Click OK.

Your screen should be similar to Figure 9

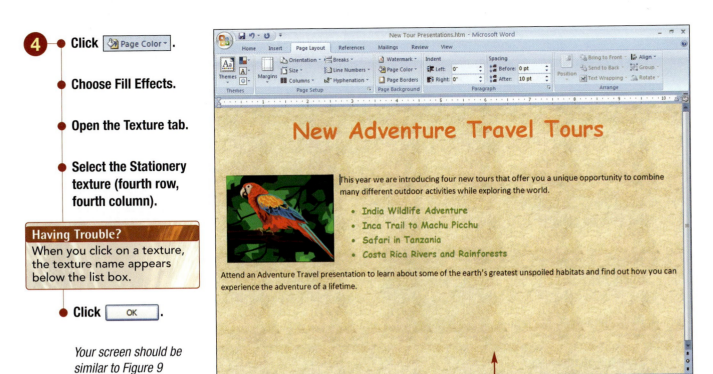

Texture fill effect applied to page background

Figure 9

You like the more natural effect of this background.

Changing Bullet Styles

The last enhancement you want to make is to change the bullet style.

1 • Select the four bulleted items.

• Open the Home tab.

• Open the ▤ ▾ Bullets drop-down gallery.

• Choose ➢ from the Bullet Library.

• Clear the selection.

• Save the changes you have made to the Web page.

Your screen should be similar to Figure 10

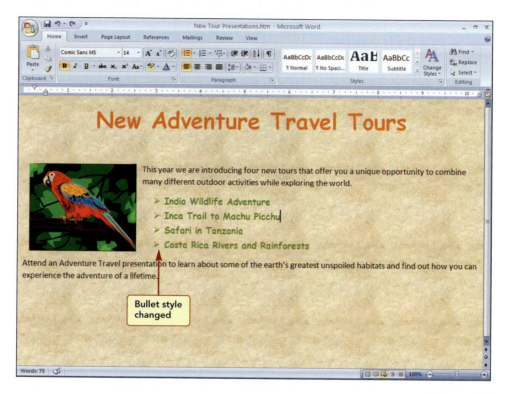

Figure 10

Additional Information

Many more graphic bullets are available in the Web Elements folder of the Clip Organizer.

Creating a Hyperlink

Next, you want to create another Web page that will contain a list of presentation locations. You will then add a hyperlink to this information from the New Tour Presentations page. As you have learned, a hyperlink provides a quick way to jump to other documents, objects, or Web pages. Hyperlinks are the real power of the WWW. You can jump to sites on your own system and network as well as to sites on the Internet and WWW.

The list of tour locations has already been entered as a Word document and saved as a file.

1 ● Open the file **wdwt_Locations**.

● Save the document as a Web page to the ATT Web Page folder with the file name **Tour Locations** and a page title of **Tour Presentation Locations**.

● Apply the same bullet style to this page.

● Apply the Stationery texture background page color.

● Save the page again.

Your screen should be similar to Figure 11

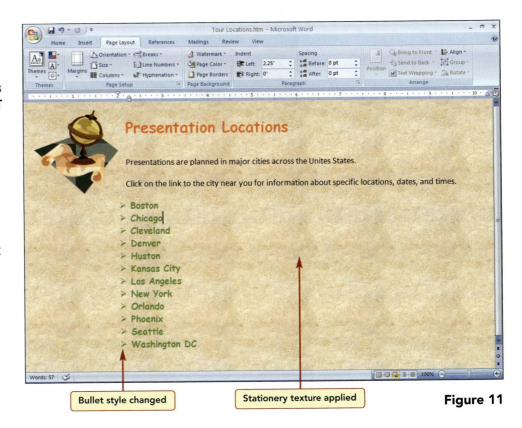

Bullet style changed

Stationery texture applied

Figure 11

Now you are ready to create the hyperlink from the New Tour Presentations page to the Tour Locations page.

2 ● Switch to the New Tour Presentations window.

● Add the following text to the end of the last paragraph: **Find out about presentation locations, dates, and times.**

● Select the text "locations, dates, and times."

● Open the Insert tab.

● Select  from the Links group.

Another Method
The keyboard shortcut is Ctrl + K.

Your screen should be similar to Figure 12

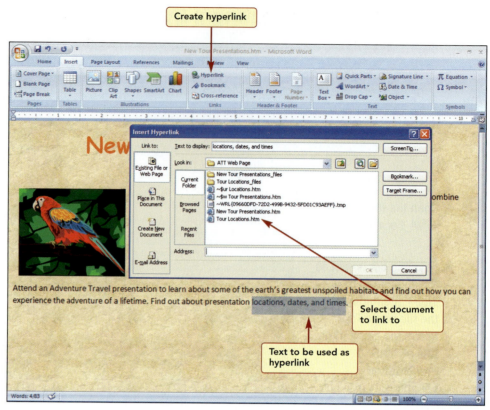

Figure 12

From the Insert Hyperlink dialog box, you need to specify the name of the document you want the link to connect to.

3 ● Select Tour Locations.htm from the file list.

● Click OK.

● Save the document.

Your screen should be similar to Figure 13

Figure 13

The selected text appears as a hyperlink in the design colors specified by the theme.

Next, you will use the hyperlink to display the Presentation Locations document.

4 ● **Hold down** Ctrl **and click the hyperlink.**

Your screen should be similar to Figure 14

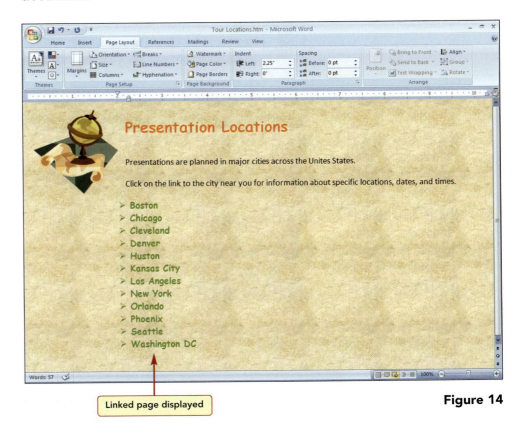

Linked page displayed

Figure 14

Because the Locations document is already open in a window, clicking the hyperlink simply switches to the open Word window and displays the page. You plan to add hyperlinks from each location to information about specific location dates and times at a later time.

Previewing the Page

To see how your Web page will actually look when displayed by your browser, you can preview it.

Note: The following figures will display Internet Explorer 7, If you are using a different browser or a different version of Internet Explorer, your screens will look different. Additionally, you will need to substitute the equivalent procedures for your browser in the following steps.

1 ● **Open your Web browser.**

● **If necessary, maximize the browser window.**

● **Open the Location drop-down menu and change to the location containing the ATT Web Page folder.**

● **Choose** New Tour Presentations.htm **from the ATT Web page folder.**

Your screen should be similar to Figure 15

Location drop-down menu

Web page previewed in browser window

Figure 15

The Web page you created is displayed in the browser window. Sometimes the browser may display a page slightly differently from the way it appears in Web Page view. In this case, the bulleted list overlaps the picture and the last paragraph wraps to the side of the picture. To stop this from happening, you will insert a special text wrapping break that is used in Web pages to separate text around objects.

2 ● Switch to the New Tour Presentation document in the Word 2007 application window.

● Select the bulleted list of tours and drag the left indent marker to the 3.25-inch position on the ruler.

● Move to the beginning of the last paragraph, before the word Attend.

● Click [Breaks] in the Page Setup group of the Page Layout tab.

● Choose Text Wrapping.

● Save the document.

● Turn on the display of formatting marks.

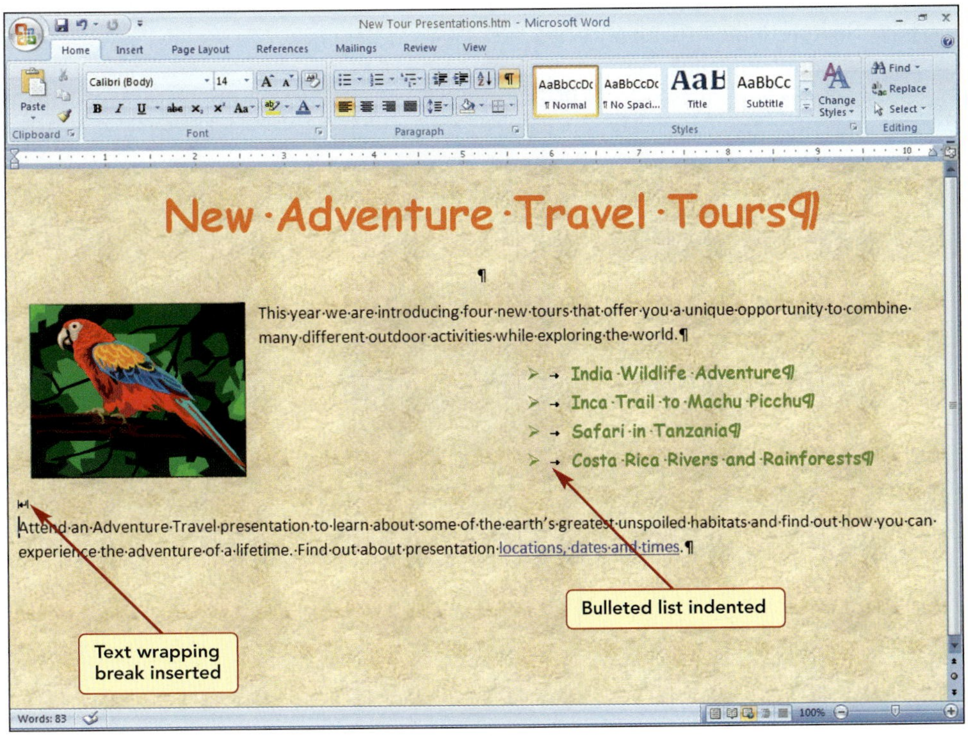

Your screen should be similar to Figure 16

Figure 16

Although the bulleted list does not display as you want it in the Word document, the list wll indent appropriately when viewed in the browser. The text wrapping break that was inserted before the paragraph stopped the text following the break from wrapping around the object. The text wrapping break character |↵| is not visible unless you display formatting marks.

3 ● Switch to the browser window and click the Refresh button to see the revised version of the Web page.

Additional Information

In Internet Explorer 7, the Refresh button is 🔄.

Your screen should be similar to Figure 17

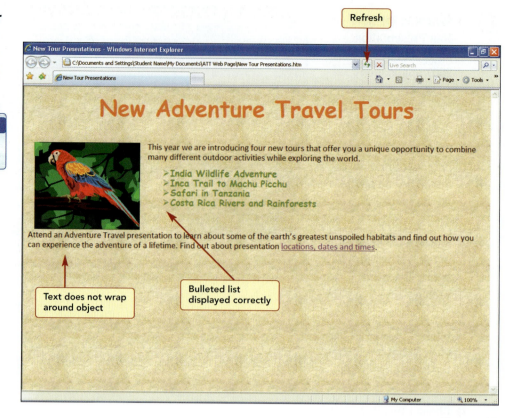

Figure 17

Inserting the text wrapping break stopped the text in the last paragraph from wrapping around the object. Next, you will use the hyperlink to open the Presentation Locations Web page in the browser.

4 • Click on the hyperlink.

• If necessary, open the Tour Presentation Locations tab.

Your screen should be similar to Figure 18

Linked page opened in Browser

Figure 18

This page looks fine and does not need any additional formatting.

5 • Click ☒ in the title bar to exit the browser program.

• Close both documents and exit Word 2007.

Making a Web Page Public

Now that you have created Web pages, you need to make them available on the Internet for others to see them. The steps that you take to make your pages public depend on how you want to share them. There are two main avenues: on your local network or intranet for limited access by people within an organization or on the Internet for access by anyone using the WWW. To make pages available to other people on your network, save your Web pages and related files, such as pictures, to a network location. To make your Web pages available on the WWW, you need to install Web server software on your computer or to locate an Internet service provider that allocates space for Web pages.

Lab Review

key terms

author WDWT1.2	**HTML (HyperText Markup Language)** WDWT1.2	**tag** WDWT1.6
browser WDWT1.3		**Web page** WDWT1.2

MCAS skills

The Microsoft Certified Applications Specialist (MCAS) certification program is designed to measure your proficiency in performing basic tasks using the Office 2007 applications. Getting certified demonstrates that you have the skills and provides a valuable industry credential for employment. See Reference 2 MCAS Certification Guide for a complete list of the skills that were covered in this lab.

command summary

Command	Shortcut	Action
Office Button		
Save/Save as Type/Web Page		Saves file as a Web page document
Insert tab		
Links group		
Hyperlink	Ctrl + K	Inserts hyperlink
Page Layout tab		
Page Setup group		
Breaks /Text Wrapping		Stops text from wrapping around objects in a Web page
Page Background group		
Page Color		Adds selected color to page background
Page Color /Fill Effects		Adds selected color effect to page background

Lab Exercises

rating system

★ Easy

★★ Moderate

★★★ Difficult

step-by-step

Adding a New Web Page ★

1. You want to continue working on the Web pages about the new tour presentations for the Adventure Travel Web site. Your next step is to create links from each location on the Presentation Locations Web page to information about each location's presentation date and times. Your completed Web page for the Los Angeles area should be similar to the one shown here.

   a. In Word, open the Web page file Tour Locations you created in this lab.

   b. Open the document wdwt_LosAngeles. Save the document as a Web page to the ATT Web Page folder with the file name LosAngeles and a page title of **Los Angeles Presentation Information**.

   c. Change the page color to a gradient fill effect of your choice. Change the first title line to the Title style and the second title line to a Heading 1 style. Change the title lines to a color of your choice.

   d. Increase the font size of the table to 12 points. Add color to the table headings. Enhance the Web page with any features you feel are appropriate.

   e. Two lines below the table, add the text **Contact [your name] at (909) 555-1212 for more information.** Apply the Emphasis style to this line and increase the font size to 14 points.

   f. On the Tour Locations page, create a link from the Los Angeles text to the Los Angeles page. Test the link.

   g. Resave both Web pages and preview them in your browser. Print the Los Angeles Web page.

   h. Exit the browser and Word.

Converting a Flyer to a Web Page ★★

2. The Westbrook Parks and Recreation Department has asked you to modify the Celebrate Bikes article you created and convert it into a Web page to add to the Web site. Your completed Web page should be similar to the one shown here.

a. Open the file Bike Event you created in Step-by-Step Exercise 2 in Lab 1.

b. Convert the article to a Web page and save it as Celebrate Bicycling in a new folder. Include an appropriate page title.

c. Apply a page background color effect of your choice.

d. Change the text wrapping style of the graphic to square. Move the graphic to the left of the title. Left-align the title and increase the size of the title to 36 points. Size and position the graphic appropriately.

e. Delete your name and the date from the document. Add **[Your name] at** before the phone number in the last line.

f. Save the Web page. Preview the page in your browser. Adjust the layout as needed. Close your browser. Resave the Web page.

g. Print the Web page.

Advertising on the Web ★★★

3. You would like to advertise the grand re-opening of the Internet Café on the Web. You plan to use the information in the advertisement flyer you created as the basis for the Web pages. Your completed Web pages should be similar to those shown here.

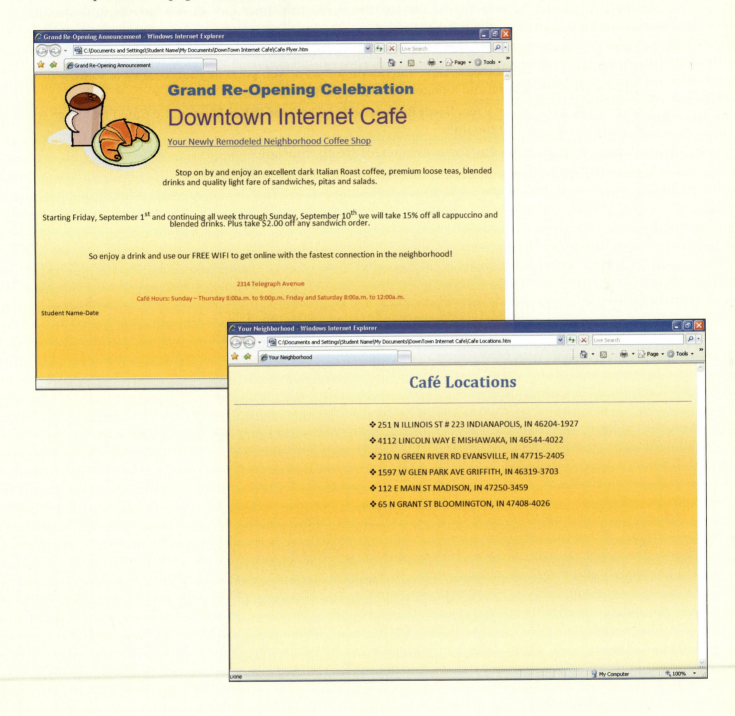

a. Open the file Grand Re-Opening you created in Step-by-Step Exercise 3 in Lab 1. Convert the document to a Web page, add a title of **Grand Re-Opening Announcement**, and save it as Café Flyer in a new folder.

b. Delete the graphic. Insert the image wdwt_Coffee. Change the picture text wrapping style to square. Move the picture to the left of the three title lines, as shown above, and size it appropriately. Left-align the three title lines.

c. Save the changes.

d. Open the file wdwt_Café Locations. Save the document as a Web page to your Web Page folder with the file name Café Locations and a page title of **Your Neighborhood**.

e. Create a link from the text **Your Newly Remodeled Neighborhood Coffee Shop** in the Café Flyer page to the Locations page. Test the link.

f. Enhance the pages with any features you feel are appropriate.

g. Resave the Web pages and preview them in your browser.

h. Print the pages.

Creating a Newsletter

LAB 4

Objectives

After completing this lab, you will know how to:

1 Create and enhance a WordArt object.

2 Research information on the Web.

3 Collect and paste multiple items.

4 Create and use bookmarks.

5 Modify styles.

6 Create newsletter-style columns.

7 Use hyphenation and justification.

8 Create sidebars and text boxes.

9 Add borders and shading to paragraphs.

10 Create, format, and link text boxes.

11 Crop, compress, adjust contrast, adjust brightness, and rotate pictures.

12 Insert custom bullets, symbols, and drop caps.

Adventure Travel Tours

The Adventure Travel Tours manager is very pleased with the research you did on Tanzania and Peru. The company plans to feature tours to these areas in the next few months and wants to provide its clients with much of the information you gathered. A good way to present this type of information is through a monthly newsletter. Newsletters allow businesses to present timely information. Unlike a flyer, whose purpose is to quickly attract attention and provide a small amount of information, a newsletter is designed to provide detailed information. Because newsletters are generally several pages long, you have enough space to paint a picture and tell a story.

After discussing the plans for the upcoming newsletters with the Adventure Travel Tours manager, you have decided to make the African safari in Tanzania the focus of the next month's newsletter. In addition to using several topics from the material in the report on Tanzania, the newsletter will include various tips and facts about the country. You will also include some information about other upcoming tours and events.

In a newsletter, information must be easy to read and, more important, visually appealing. In this lab, you will use the WordArt and desktop publishing tools in Word 2007 to create the newsletter shown on the following page.

Use the WordArt feature to create an attractive headline.

Newsletter-style columns make newsletters easy to read as well as attractive.

Text boxes, graphics, color, and borders enhance the appearance of the newsletter.

Concept Preview

The following concepts will be introduced in this lab:

1 **WordArt** WordArt is used to enhance your documents by changing the shape of text and adding special effects such as 3-D and shadows.

2 **Collect and Paste** Collecting and pasting is the capability of the program to store multiple copied items in the Office Clipboard and then paste one or more of them into another document.

3 **Newsletter-Style Columns** Newsletter-style columns display text so that it flows from the bottom of one column to the top of the next.

4 **Hyphenation** The hyphenation feature inserts a hyphen in long words that fall at the end of a line, splitting the word between lines.

5 **Text Box** A text box is a graphic object that is a container for text or graphics.

6 **Anchor** Each floating graphic in a document is attached to a particular location, such as to a page or a paragraph, by an anchor.

Creating a Newsletter Headline

A newsletter commonly consists of two basic parts: the headline and the body (see the following figure). The headline, also called the nameplate or banner, is the top portion of the newsletter. It generally contains the name, issue or volume number, and publication date. It also may include a company logo, a line that announces the main subject or article included in the newsletter, and a brief table of contents. The body, which is the text of the newsletter, is commonly displayed in a two- or three-column format. Article headings often include subheadings that help organize the newsletter topics. The headline is often visually separated from the body by horizontal lines, called rules. Your sample newsletter will include many of these features.

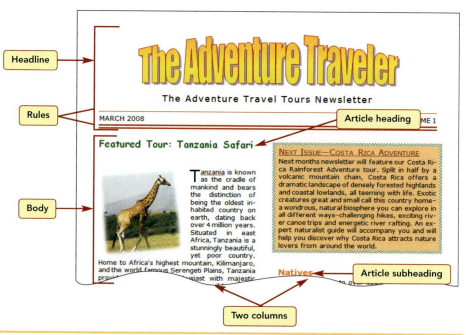

The first thing you want to do is to create a headline for the newsletter. The headline will display the name of the newsletter, "The Adventure Traveler"; the date of publication; and the volume number. The text for the headline has already been entered for you.

1 • **Start Office Word 2007.**

• **If necessary, maximize the Word application window.**

• **To see the headline text, open the file** wd04_Headline.

• **If necessary, change to Print Layout view.**

Your screen should be similar to Figure 4.1

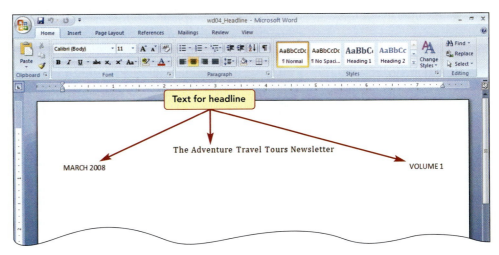

Figure 4.1

Using WordArt

You need to add the newsletter name above the headline text. You will use the WordArt feature to make this name unique and more interesting.

Concept 1

Word Art

1 WordArt is used to enhance your documents by changing the shape of text and adding special effects such as 3-D and shadows. You also can rotate, flip, and skew WordArt text. The text that is added to the document using WordArt is a graphic object that can be edited, sized, or moved to any location in the document. In addition, it can be changed using the Drawing toolbar buttons.

You can use WordArt to add a special touch to your documents. However, you should limit its use to headlines in a newsletter or to a single element in a flyer. You want the WordArt to capture the reader's attention. Here are some examples of WordArt.

You will create a WordArt object consisting of the newsletter name for the headline.

1
- If necessary, move to the blank line above the headline text.

- Open the Insert tab.

- Click  in the Text group.

Your screen should be similar to Figure 4.2

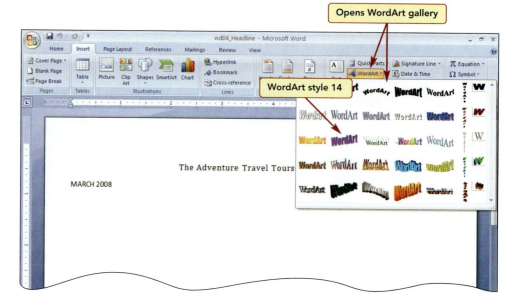

Opens WordArt gallery

WordArt style 14

Figure 4.2

The WordArt gallery displays the 30 WordArt styles or designs from which you can select. The styles consist of a combination of fonts, colors, and shapes and are just a starting point. As you will soon see, you can alter the appearance of the style by selecting a different color or shape and by adding special effects.

2
- Choose WordArt style 14.

Your screen should be similar to Figure 4.3

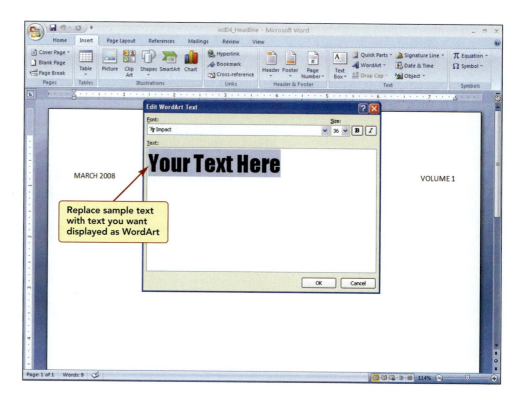

Replace sample text with text you want displayed as WordArt

Figure 4.3

Next, in the Edit WordArt Text dialog box, you need to replace the sample text with the text you want displayed using the selected WordArt design.

3 • Type **The Adventure Traveler.**

• Click [OK].

Your screen should be similar to Figure 4.4

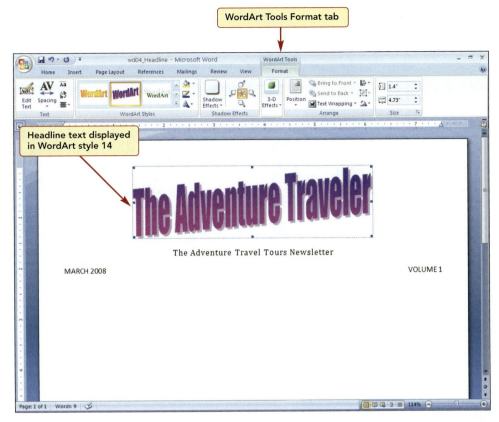

WordArt Tools Format tab

Headline text displayed in WordArt style 14

Figure 4.4

Another Method

To review alternative wrapping styles, refer to Concept 4: Text Wrapping in Lab 3.

Now the words you entered are displayed in the selected WordArt style in the document. When a WordArt object is first inserted in the document, it has a default wrapping style of In Line with Text, assuming the formatting of the line into which it was inserted, in this case, centered.

Changing the WordArt Shape and Size

Now that you can see how the selected style looks in the headline, you decide to change the WordArt shape to another. You can select from 40 different shapes provided in the WordArt palette and apply the shape to the selected object.

Whenever a WordArt object is selected, the WordArt Tools Format tab is displayed and is used to modify the WordArt.

1 ● Click 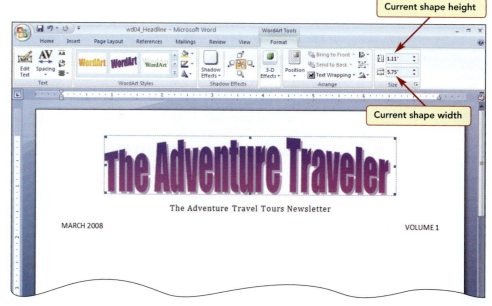 Change WordArt Shape in the WordArt Styles group.

● Select several shapes to see the Live Preview.

● Choose ▬ Inflate Top (third row, first column).

Your screen should be similar to Figure 4.5

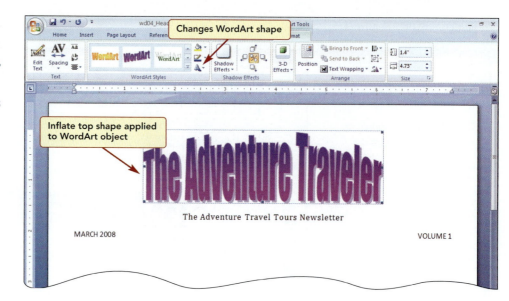

Figure 4.5

The selected shape is applied to the WordArt object. You also want the WordArt object to extend the full width of the text space between the margins. To do this, you will increase its width.

2 ● Drag the sizing handles of the WordArt shape to adjust the size to be similar to the shape in Figure 4.6.

Another Method
You also can adjust the size to exact measurements using ▭ 0.71″ ⬍ Shape Height and ▭ 4.16″ ⬍ Shape Width in the Size group.

Your screen should be similar to Figure 4.6

Figure 4.6

The WordArt is now narrower and longer and the ▭ 1.11″ ⬍ Shape Height and ▭ 5.75″ ⬍ Shape Width buttons in the Size group reflect the current object size settings you established by dragging the sizing handles.

Changing the WordArt Fill and Line Color

Next you want to change the color of the WordArt characters. You can easily do this using some of the special effects options that can be applied to graphic objects.

Special drawing effects such as shadows and 3-D effects can easily be added to text and graphics, including WordArt objects, to enhance the appearance of your document. When you draw an object, a border automatically appears around it. You can change the thickness and color of the border. You also can fill a drawing object with a solid color, a gradient color, texture, or a picture. Adding shadows or 3-D effects gives depth to an object.

Use these effects in moderation. You want to capture the reader's interest with your graphics but not detract from your message.

1 ● Open the 🖉 ▾ Shape Fill color gallery in the WordArt Styles group.

● Select Gradient and choose More Gradients.

Your screen should be similar to Figure 4.7

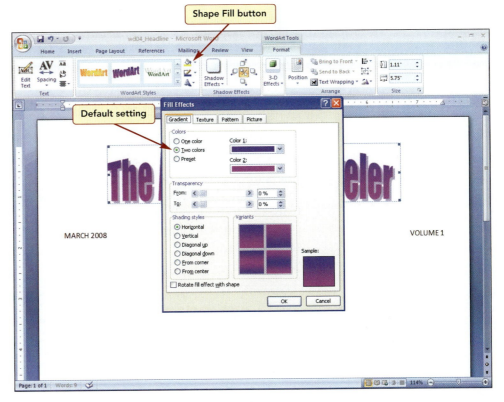

Figure 4.7

Additional Information
You will learn more about setting transparency shortly.

The default color setting for the selected WordArt design style is a two-color gradient fill set to 0 percent transparency. When set, the transparency option makes the selected fill color less opaque, allowing any underlying color to bleed through. When set to zero, the color is solid or opaque. You want to change the WordArt color to an orange and yellow color combination.

2 ● **Select Orange (from the Standard colors) for Color 1 and Yellow for Color 2.**

Your screen should be similar to Figure 4.8

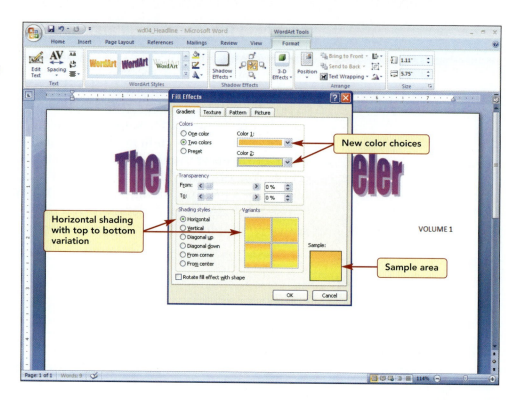

Figure 4.8

The sample area shows how your color selections will appear. You think the default shading style of horizontal with the shading variation setting from top to bottom looks good.

Next, you will change the line color to coordinate with your new color selections and make the line weight heavier.

3 ● **Click** [OK] **.**

● **Open the**  **Shape Outline drop-down menu in the WordArt Styles group.**

● **Select Dark Red from the Color gallery.**

● **Open the** ⬛ **Shape Outline drop-down menu, select Weight, and choose 1 pt.**

Your screen should be similar to Figure 4.9

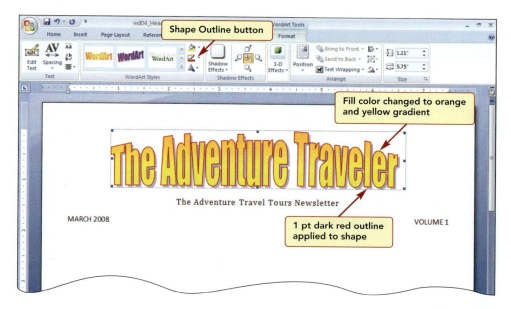

Figure 4.9

The selected gradient fill, line color, and weight changes are applied to the WordArt shape.

Modifying Character Spacing

Finally, you want to change the spacing of the characters in the WordArt object to be closer together. The character spacing for WordArt objects can be changed from the normal spacing (set at 100 percent) to closer together or wider apart. A larger percent value increases the spacing and a smaller percent value decreases the spacing. In addition, kerning can be specified. **Kerning** alters the spacing between particular pairs of letters to improve the appearance of the text. You want to condense the spacing between characters as much as possible.

1 ● Click  in the Text group.

● Choose Very Tight.

Your screen should be similar to Figure 4.10

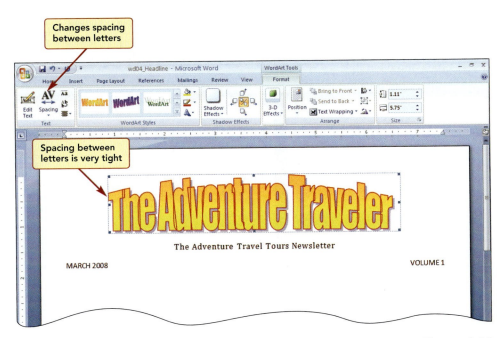

Figure 4.10

You do not like how the overlapping of the characters looks, and instead decide to increase the spacing slightly.

2 ● Click  and choose Tight.

Your screen should be similar to Figure 4.11

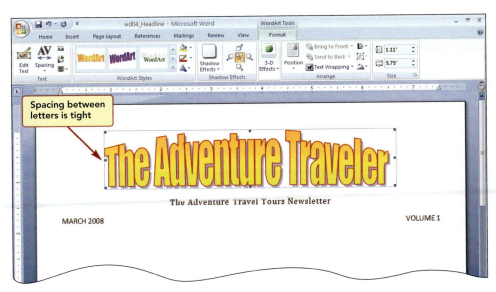

Figure 4.11

Now that the WordArt object is complete, the headline subtitle below it looks very small. You will make the font size larger and stretch the text to expand the character spacing.

3

- **Select the subtitle line of text below the newsletter title.**

- **Increase the font size to 14.**

- **Open the Font dialog box and open the Character Spacing tab.**

Your screen should be similar to Figure 4.12

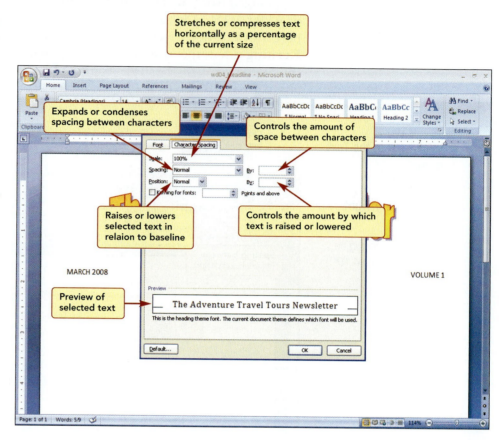

Stretches or compresses text horizontally as a percentage of the current size

Expands or condenses spacing between characters

Controls the amount of space between characters

Raises or lowers selected text in relaion to baseline

Controls the amount by which text is raised or lowered

Preview of selected text

Figure 4.12

The Character Spacing tab is used to expand or condense the space between characters by a specified amount. You also can kern characters above a specified point size. Expanding or condensing characters changes the space by an equal amount regardless of the font design. You also can specify the amount of space by which you want to expand or condense the spacing. The default spacing setting is Normal at 1 point. The preview area shows how the spacing changes will look on the selection as they are made.

4 ● From the Spacing drop-down list, choose **Expanded**.

● Increase the By amount to 1.5 pt.

● Click [OK].

● Click on the subtitle line to deselect it.

Your screen should be similar to Figure 4.13

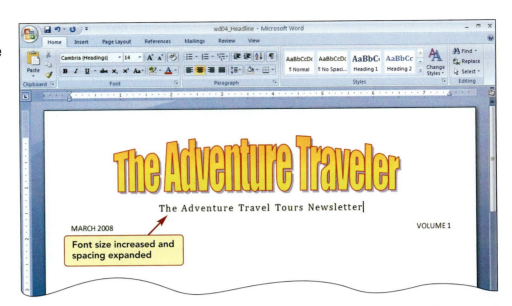

Font size increased and spacing expanded

Figure 4.13

The spacing between characters has increased, making the headline subtitle more prominent.

Creating Horizontal Rules

Next you want the newsletter's issue identification information, which in this newsletter is the publication date and issue number, to be displayed between two horizontal lines or rules. Rules can be added to any side of a selected paragraph or object.

1 ● Move to anywhere within the line of text containing the publication date and volume number.

● Open the [▦ ▾] Border drop-down menu.

● Choose Borders and Shading.

Your screen should be similar to Figure 4.14

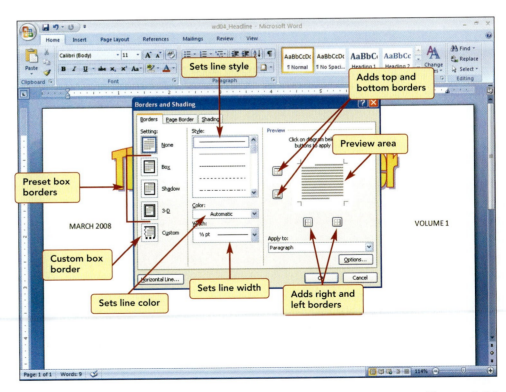

Sets line style

Adds top and bottom borders

Preview area

Preset box borders

Custom box border

Sets line color

Sets line width

Adds right and left borders

Figure 4.14

From the Borders and Shading dialog box, you can specify the style, color, weight, and location of the border. You can apply either a preset box border by selecting from the Setting options, or a custom border. You want to create a custom border that will display a 1.5-point single-line border in dark red above the text and a 3-point double-line border in dark red below the text. As you specify the line settings, the Preview area will reflect your selections.

2 ● Click ▤ Custom.

● From the Width drop-down list box, choose 1½ pt.

● Open the Color palette and choose Dark Red.

● Click ▦ Top Border in the Preview area.

Your screen should be similar to Figure 4.15

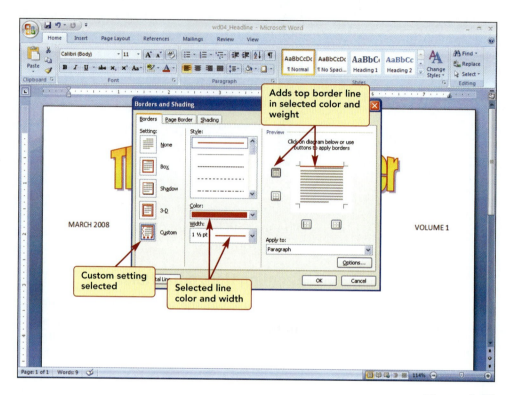

Figure 4.15

The Preview area of the dialog box shows how a top border line using the settings you specified will appear. Next you will add a double-line bottom border.

3 ● From the Style list box, choose  .

● From the Width drop-down list, choose 3 pt.

● From the Color drop-down list, choose Dark Red.

● Click ⊞ Bottom Border in the Preview area.

Having Trouble?
Use the None option to remove all border lines, or remove individual lines by selecting the border location again.

● Click [OK] .

● Save the headline document as Newsletter Headline to your solution file location.

Your screen should be similar to Figure 4.16

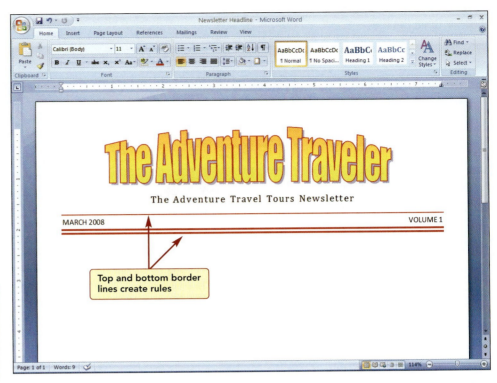

Figure 4.16

The horizontal lines extend between the margins above and below the text in the color, style, and point size you specified. The newsletter headline is now complete and can be used with any newsletter.

Another Method
You can also create a single horizontal line by typing - three times and pressing [←Enter] and a double line by typing = three times and pressing [←Enter].

Researching Information on the Web

You have created a file of facts about Tanzania and still need to add the Tanzania Embassy address and Web site to the document. You will get this information using the Research task pane to access the Web.

Note: You need an Internet connection and the Online Services feature must be activated. Click [🔍 Research options...] in the Research task pane and select the services you want to access. If you do not have this feature available, type the information shown in Figure 4.19 and skip to step 4.

1 • Open the file **wd04_Tanzania Facts.**

• Open the Review tab.

• Click in the Proofing group.

• Click in the Search for box and, if necessary, select and delete any existing text.

• Type **US embassies** in the Search for text box.

• Open the reference drop-down menu and choose MSN Search.

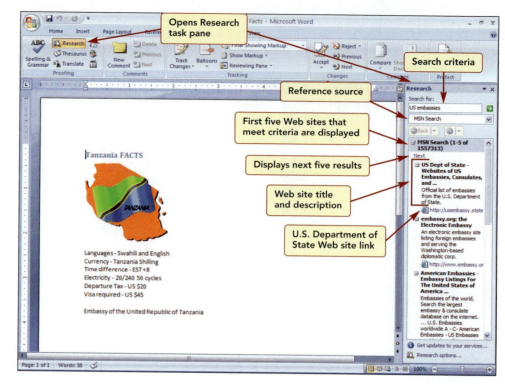

Figure 4.17

Additional Information

Click ⊐ to hide or ⊐ to show the detail information about a located Web site.

Your screen should be similar to Figure 4.17

More About

The 🔍 Research options... command in the Research task pane is used to verify and change research options. To learn about this feature, see 1.4 Personalize Word in the More About appendix.

The results area of the Research task pane displays the first five Web sites that meet your search criteria. Each result includes a link to the Web site. You will locate a Web site that looks like it will have the information you need and then click on the link to that site.

2 • If necessary, scroll the results list to locate "US Dept of State – Websites of US Embassies . . .".

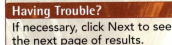

Having Trouble?
If necessary, click Next to see the next page of results.

• Click the http:// usembassy.state. gov link.

• If necessary, maximize your browser window.

Having Trouble?
If this Web site is not available, select a link to another located site to find this information.

Your screen should be similar to Figure 4.18

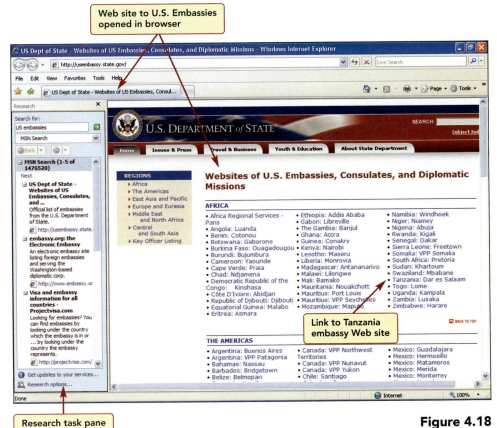

Figure 4.18

The Web site opens for the selected page. If your browser is Internet Explorer, the Research task pane is displayed along the left side of the screen to allow you to select and view other sites. This Web page displays a list of all embassies by continent. You will locate the Tanzania embassy information and then copy the address from the Web page to the Word document.

3
- Click the Tanzania: Dar es Salaam link in the Africa category.

- Select (highlight) the site address to the Web page in the Address bar.

- Press [Ctrl] + C to copy it to the Clipboard.

- Close all browser windows.

- Move to the last line in the document and press [Ctrl] + V to paste the Web address.

- Delete the / at the end of the Web address.

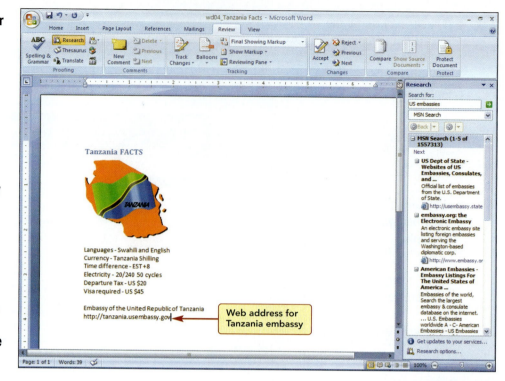

Figure 4.19

Your screen should be similar to Figure 4.19

You quickly located and inserted the information into the document that you needed about the Tanzania embassy.

4
- Close the Research task pane.

- Save the document as Tanzania Facts to your solution file location.

Assembling the Newsletter from a Variety of Sources

Now that your research is complete, you are ready to assemble the newsletter. Following your manager's suggestions, you modified the report you wrote about Tanzania and Costa Rica by shortening the topic coverage and dividing the topics into several brief articles to be used in this and future newsletters. You saved the articles on different topics in separate files.

In this month's newsletter, you will use the articles about the African Safari. You also have two other short topics to include in this month's newsletter saved in separate files. You will open all of the documents and then combine the articles to create the content for the newsletter.

- Open the file wd04_ Newsletter Articles.

- If necessary, change the view to Print Layout and the zoom to 100%.

- Scroll through the text to view the contents of the document.

- Open the files wd04_ Be an Adventure Traveler and wd04_ Costa Rica Adventure.

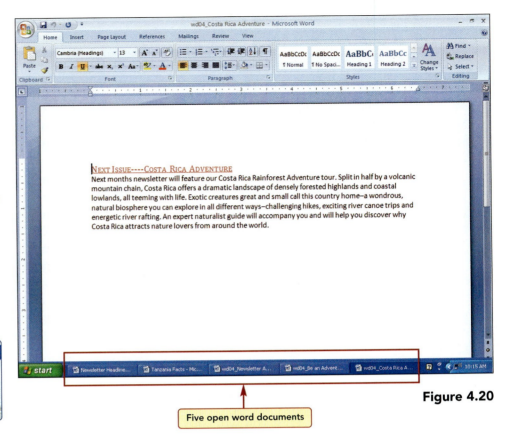

Additional Information
Hold down Ctrl while selecting multiple file names to open multiple files at the same time.

Having Trouble?
The wd04_Costa Rica Adventure document may be displayed depending upon the order in which you opened the files.

Having Trouble?
Your screen may show taskbar buttons in a group if the Properties settings of the taskbar have been changed.

Your screen should be similar to Figure 4.20

Five open word documents

Figure 4.20

You now have five open Word documents. The content of the last opened document is displayed.

Using the Office Clipboard

You want to copy the newsletter banner into the document containing the lead article about the African Safari. In addition, you want to copy the information from the other three documents—Tanzania Facts, Costa Rica Adventure, and Be an Adventure Traveler—into this same file containing the lead article. You can copy and paste the selections one after the other, or you can use the Office Clipboard to collect multiple items and paste them into the document as needed.

Concept 2

Collect and Paste

2   **Collecting and pasting** is the capability of the program to store multiple copied items in the Office Clipboard and then paste one or more of them into another document. For example, you could copy a chart from Excel, then switch to Word and copy a paragraph, then switch to PowerPoint and paste the two stored items into a slide in one easy step. This saves you from having to switch back and forth between documents and applications.

The Office Clipboard and the system Clipboard are similar but separate features. The major difference is that the Office Clipboard can hold up to 24 items, whereas the system Clipboard holds only a single item. When the Office Clipboard feature is closed, any cut or copied item is copied to both the system and Office Clipboards. The next cut or copied item replaces the existing item in both Clipboards. When the Office Clipboard is open, each successive cut or copied item is added to the Office Clipboard, while it replaces the last item stored in the system Clipboard. When you use the Office Clipboard, you can select the items in any order to paste from any of the items stored.

The Office Clipboard is available for all Office 2007 applications and non-Office programs if the Cut, Copy, and Paste commands are available. You can copy from any program that provides copy and cut capabilities, but you can only paste into Word, Excel, Access, PowerPoint, and Outlook.

Copying Multiple Objects to the Office Clipboard

First you will copy the headline to the Office Clipboard. You will open the Office Clipboard before copying the item so you can see the item as it is added to the clipboard list.

1 • Switch to the Newsletter Headline document window.

• Click ⬛ in the Clipboard group to open the Clipboard dialog box.

Your screen should be similar to Figure 4.21

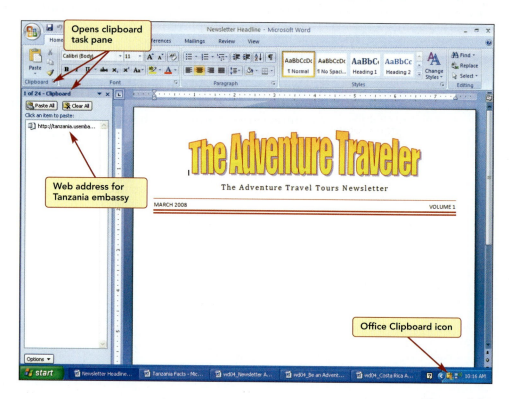

Figure 4.21

Having Trouble?

If you typed the embassy address instead of copying it from the Web page, it will not appear in the Clipboard task pane.

Additional Information

The Office Clipboard is automatically activated if you copy or cut two different items consecutively in the same program; if you copy one item, paste the item, and then copy another item in the same program; or if you copy one item twice in succession.

2 ● Click ⬚ Select ▾ in the Editing group of the Home tab and choose Select All to select the entire document.

● Click ⬚ Copy.

Another Method

You also can use Ctrl + A to select the entire document and Ctrl + C to copy the selection to the Clipboard.

Your screen should be similar to Figure 4.22

The Clipboard task pane is displayed automatically when the Office Clipboard is opened. The task pane is used to view the items in the Office Clipboard and to select and paste items into other documents. The task pane displays an entry for the Embassy address that was added to the Office Clipboard when you copied it. The entry includes an icon representing the source Office program of the item and a portion of the copied text or a thumbnail of a copied graphic.

The ⬚ Office Clipboard icon appears in the status area of the system taskbar to show that the Clipboard is active. It also briefly displays a ScreenTip showing the number of items collected out of a possible 24 items as each selection is copied or when you point to it.

Next, you will copy the headline document to the Clipboard.

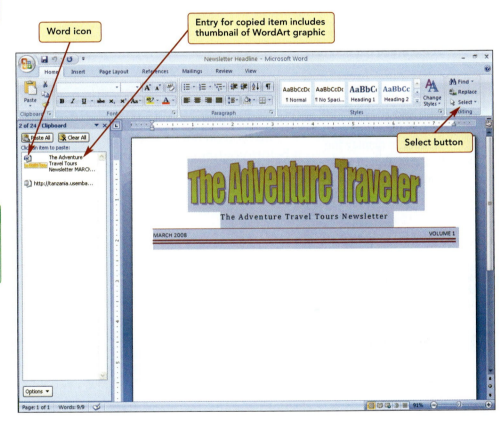

Figure 4.22

The copied item is added to the Office Clipboard and an entry for the item is displayed in the Clipboard task pane. The last-copied item appears at the top of the list of entries. This entry is preceded with a Word icon because the source program is Word 2007.

Next, you will copy the contents of the other three documents into the Office Clipboard. When the Office Clipboard is open in the Clipboard task pane in one program or document, the Clipboard task pane does not automatically appear when you switch to another program or document. However, it is still active and will continue to store copied items.

Additional Information

You also can open the Office Clipboard without displaying the Clipboard task pane by turning on the Collect Without Showing Office Clipboard option from the Options menu on the Clipboard task pane.

3 ● Switch to the wd04_ Be an Adventure Traveler document.

● Select the entire document.

● Click 📋 Copy.

● In a similar manner, copy the entire contents of the Tanzania Facts and wd04_Costa Rica Adventure documents to the Office Clipboard.

● Double-click 📋 Clipboard in the status area of the system taskbar to display the Office Clipboard task pane.

Your screen should be similar to Figure 4.23

Having Trouble?
If the embassy address is not displayed, skip step 4.

4 ● Point to the http:// tanzania . . . entry and click the ▾ drop-down list button.

Another Method
You also can right-click on the item to open the shortcut menu.

● Choose Delete from the menu.

Your screen should be similar to Figure 4.24

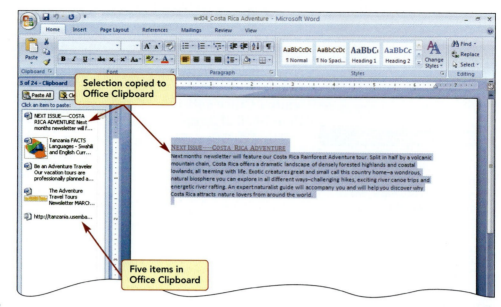

Figure 4.23

The Office Clipboard now contains five items. The most recently added item is displayed at the top of the list.

Since you do not need the Tanzania embassy address item, you will delete it before continuing.

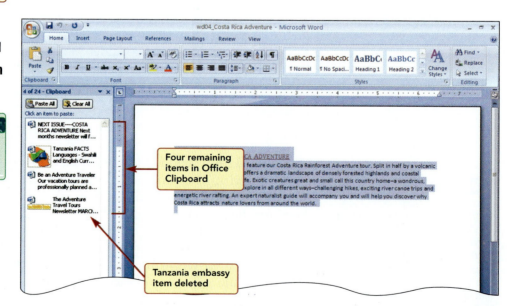

Figure 4.24

There are now four items in the Office Clipboard. Next, you will close files that you no longer need.

5 Close the following files: **wd04_Costa Rica Adventure, Tanzania Facts, wd04_Be an Adventure Traveler, and Newsletter Headline.**

Pasting Multiple Objects from the Office Clipboard

Now you are ready to paste the items into the main article document. You want to paste the headline first.

1 If necessary, move to the beginning of the **Featured Tour** heading at the top of the **wd04_Newsletter Articles** document.

● Display the Clipboard task pane.

● Click on the newsletter headline item to paste it into the top of the document.

Another Method
You also could choose Paste from the item's menu.

More About
To learn more about using the Office Clipboard, see 2.2 Manipulate Text in the More About appendix.

Your screen should be similar to Figure 4.25

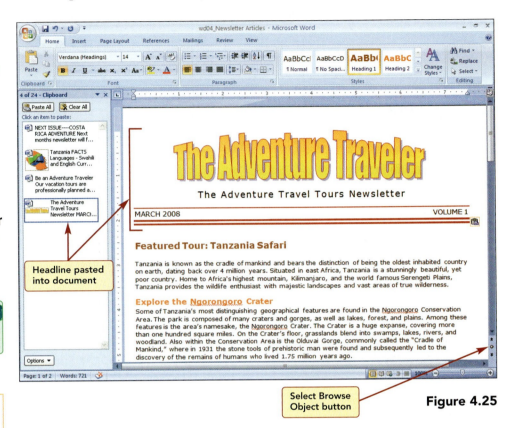

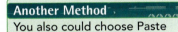
Headline pasted into document

Select Browse Object button

Figure 4.25

Next, you want to insert the Be an Adventure Traveler content before the article about Animal Life. A quick way to move to specific elements in a document is to use the ⊙ Select Browse Object feature and select the type of object by which you want to browse through the document. Then you use the Browse Objects scroll buttons to move to the next or previous located element of the specified type.

2

- Click 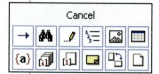 Select Browse Object (at the bottom of the vertical scroll bar).

- Click ⧉ Browse by Heading from the object menu.

- Click ⏷ Next Heading 3 times (in the scroll bar) to move to the Animal Life heading.

- Paste the Be an Adventure Traveler . . . item from the Office Clipboard.

Your screen should be similar to Figure 4.26

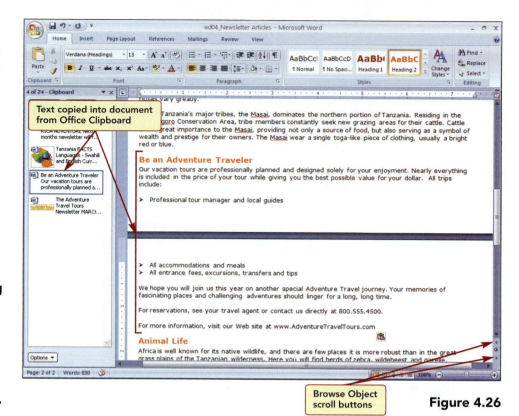

Text copied into document from Office Clipboard

Browse Object scroll buttons

Figure 4.26

Now you will insert the Costa Rica Adventure text above the Natives section in the document. Because you last specified Heading as the element to go to, you can quickly scroll the document by headings using the Browse Objects scroll buttons. These buttons scroll based on the last selected element type.

3 Click ⬆ Previous Heading 2 times (in the scroll bar) to move to the Natives heading on page 1.

● Paste the NEXT ISSUE----COSTA . . . item from the Office Clipboard.

● Close the Clipboard task pane.

● Save the document as March Newsletter to your data file location.

● Change the zoom so that the two pages of the newsletter are displayed.

Your screen should be similar to Figure 4.27

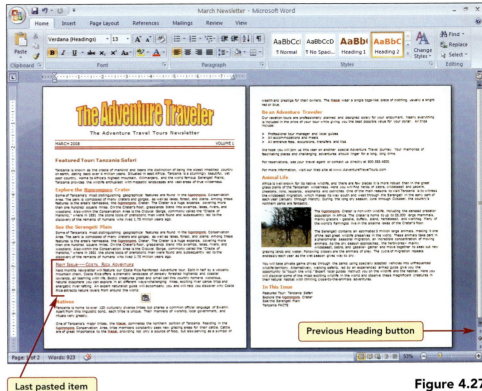

Last pasted item

Previous Heading button

Figure 4.27

This document uses the Aspect theme. The body text has been sized to 10 points and does not include extra spacing. The copied content was pasted into the March Newsletter document using the destination document style.

Adding a Bookmark

As you look at the newsletter, you feel it would benefit greatly from the addition of a picture near the top of the document. You know that one of the guides has several pictures that would be suitable. Until you get the pictures, however, you want to add a reminder in the document to do this. But you do not want the reminder to display or affect the layout of the document.

To do this, you will create a bookmark for the reminder. A **bookmark** is a link that identifies a location or a selection of text that you name. Then, instead of scrolling through the document to locate the text, you can quickly go to it by selecting the bookmark from the list of bookmarks stored with the document. A bookmark name must begin with a letter and cannot contain spaces. It also can include numbers and special characters such as underscores, which are commonly used to separate words.

1
- Change the zoom to 100%.

- Move to the beginning of the first paragraph of the newsletter.

- Click 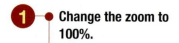 in the Links group of the Insert tab.

- Type Add_picture_ here in the Bookmark name text box.

Your screen should be similar to Figure 4.28

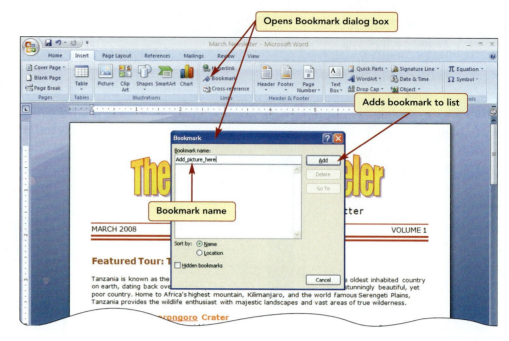

Opens Bookmark dialog box

Adds bookmark to list

Bookmark name

Figure 4.28

Then, to complete the bookmark, you add it to the list. The bookmark text is hidden and does not affect the layout of the document. Once a bookmark is created, you can select the bookmark name from the Bookmark list and go directly to that location.

2
- Click Add.

- Press Ctrl + End to move to the end of the document.

- Click 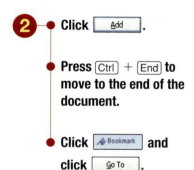 Bookmark and click Go To.

Your screen should be similar to Figure 4.29

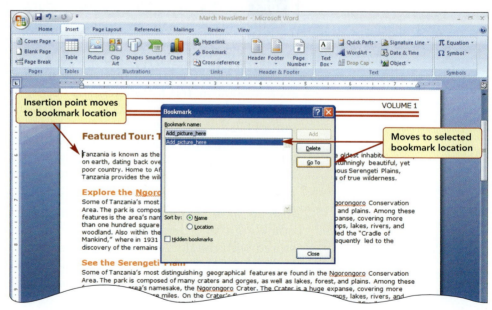

Insertion point moves to bookmark location

Moves to selected bookmark location

Figure 4.29

The insertion point moves to the bookmark location. If there were several bookmarks saved with the document, you would need to select the bookmark name from the list before using Go To.

3
- Click Close.

Creating a New Style

The next change you want to make is to the headline of the lead story. You want the headline to stand out more than the Heading 1 style currently applied to it. You decide to create a new style just for use in the newsletter. Because you do not want to modify the current Heading 1 style, you will first remove the formatting and then create a unique style.

1 Select the headline Featured Tour: Tanzania Safari.

Click Clear Formatting in the Font group of the Home tab.

Format the line to Comic Sans MS font, size 16 pt, bold, and Dark Green, Accent 4 color.

Add space before the paragraph.

Having Trouble?
To add space before the paragraph, click Line Spacing.

Your screen should be similar to Figure 4.30

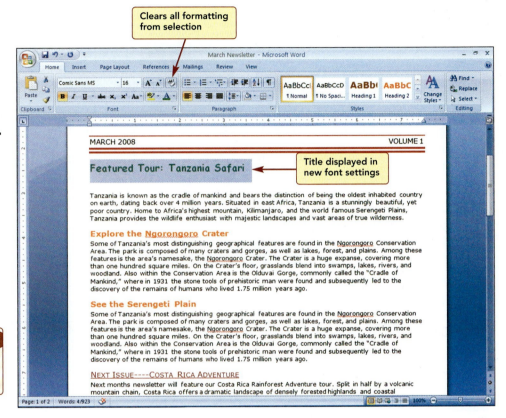

Clears all formatting from selection

Title displayed in new font settings

Figure 4.30

Rather than have to recreate this combination of formats for the newsletter heading each time you want to use it, you will save it as a quick style. This process is similar to modifying an existing style, except that it creates an entirely new style without the underlying elements associated with an existing style.

2
- Right-click on the selection, select Styles, and choose Save Selection as a New Quick Style.

- Type **Newsletter Heading 1** in the name box and click ⟨ OK ⟩.

- Apply the Newsletter Heading 1 style to the Be an Adventure Traveler heading and to the In This Issue heading.

- Click 🔲 in the Styles group to display the Styles pane.

- Point to Newsletter Heading 1 in the Styles pane.

Your screen should be similar to Figure 4.31

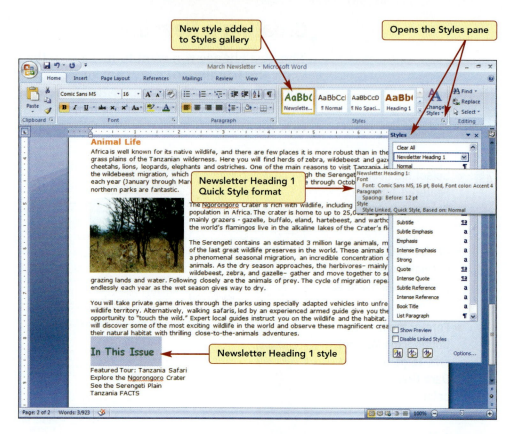

Figure 4.31

The Styles pane lists all available styles in the document. Pointing to a style reveals the formatting associated with the selected style. If you click one of the styles, the style will be applied to the selected text.

3
- Close the Styles pane.

Creating Newsletter-Style Columns

Now you are ready to format the newsletter to display in newsletter-style columns.

Concept 3

Newsletter-Style Columns

3 Newsletter-style columns display text so that it flows from the bottom of one column to the top of the next. The default document setting is one column the full width of the margins, so the text appears to flow continuously from one page to the next. On occasion, the layout for your document may call for two or more columns on a page.

Newspapers, magazines, and newsletters are common applications for newsletter-style columns. The optimum column width for reading comfort is 4.5 inches. In a newsletter, narrow columns help the reader read the articles more quickly, and you as the writer can fit information on a page in a visually pleasing arrangement. Note, however, that if you use more than four columns on an $8^1/_2$-by-11-inch page, the columns will be too narrow and the page will look messy.

Applying a Two-Column Layout

You want the newsletter to have two columns of text on the first page. Word includes five preset column formats: three with evenly spaced columns and two with unevenly spaced columns. You will use the two evenly spaced preset column layout.

When you change the format of a document to display multiple columns, the entire document changes to the new format. To affect only a portion of a document, you need to divide the document into sections. Because you do not want the headline to appear in column format, you will add a section break below the headline.

1 Move to the beginning of the first heading, **Featured Tour: Tanzania Safari.**

● Click [Breaks] in the Page setup group of the Page Layout tab and choose **Continuous.**

Having Trouble?
Refer to Lab 3, Concept 2, to review section breaks.

● Click [Columns] in the Page Setup group and choose **Two.**

● Reduce the zoom so that two pages are displayed.

Having Trouble?
Do not be concerned if the text in your columns wraps differently than in Figure 4.32. This is a function of the selected printer on your system.

Your screen should be similar to Figure 4.32

Splits text into two or more columns

Adds page, section, or column breaks

Section continuing headline is one-column format

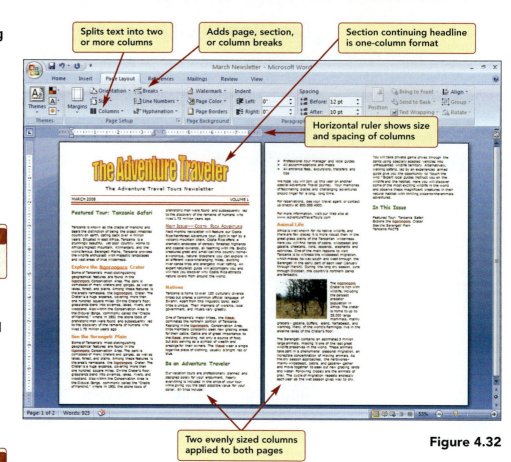

Horizontal ruler shows size and spacing of columns

Two evenly sized columns applied to both pages

Figure 4.32

Each page is displayed as two evenly sized newsletter-style columns separated by 0.5 inch of blank space. The text at the bottom of the first column continues at the top of the second column. The column markers on the horizontal ruler above a page show the size and spacing of each column.

Based on the number of columns you specify and your document's left and right margin settings, Word automatically calculates the size of the columns and the spacing between them.

Applying a Three-Column Layout

Next, you would like the second page of the newsletter to be in three-column format. You want a second page to begin at the Be an Adventure Traveler heading. To force a new page and section, you will insert a New Page section break. Then you will format the section to three columns.

1 • Move to the beginning of the Be an Adventure Traveler heading.

• Click [Breaks ▾] on the Page Layout tab and choose Next Page.

• Click [Columns ▾] and choose Three.

Your screen should be similar to Figure 4.33

Additional Information

If you select the area of the text to be affected before setting the format to columns, Word automatically inserts a continuous section break at the beginning (and end, if necessary) of your selection.

Three equal-width columns with 0.5-inch space between columns

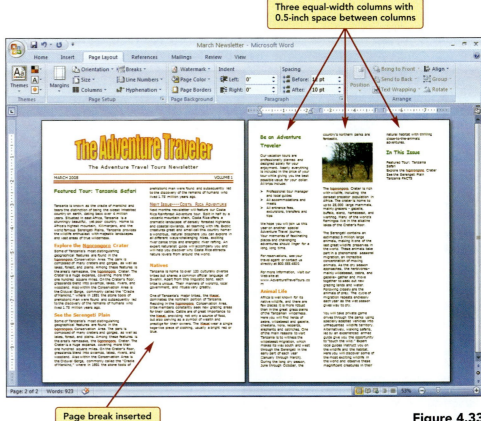

Page break inserted

Figure 4.33

The text following the page break appears in three equally sized columns separated by 0.5 inch of blank space.

Sizing Columns

While the default width of 0.5 inch between the columns looks fine for the first page, it seems too wide for the three columns on the second page. You want to reduce the space between these columns to 0.3 inch and maintain equal column widths.

1 • Click [Columns ▾] and choose More Columns.

Your screen should be similar to Figure 4.34

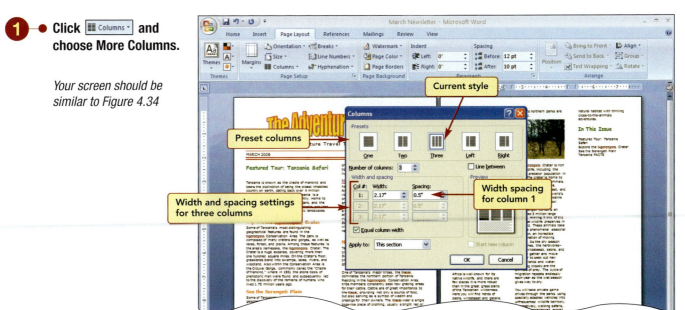

Current style

Preset columns

Width and spacing settings for three columns

Width spacing for column 1

Figure 4.34

The Columns dialog box allows you to choose from the five preset columns, to specify up to 14 columns, and to modify the column width and spacing settings. The setting to create equal-sized columns is selected because this is the default associated with the preset three-column layout currently in use.

2
- In the Width and spacing section of the dialog box, reduce Spacing to 0.3" for column 1.

- Click OK.

- Increase the zoom to 100%.

- Save the document.

Another Method
You also can adjust the column size and spacing between columns by dragging the column marker in the ruler.

Your screen should be similar to Figure 4.35

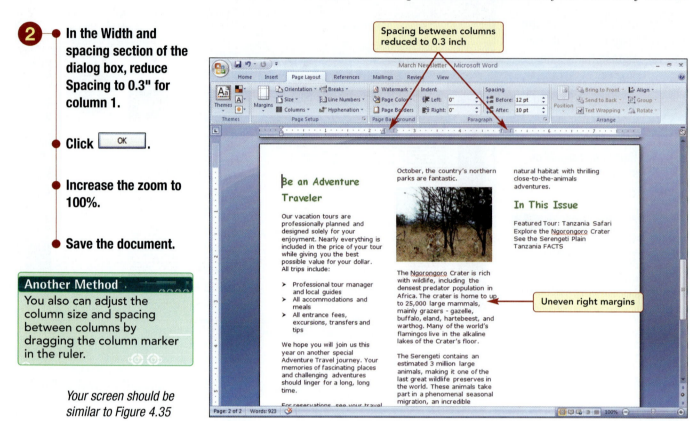

Figure 4.35

The columns are equally sized with 0.3 inch between them. Now, because the columns are wider, more text can be displayed on each line.

Using Hyphenation and Justification

Now that the layout is in columns, you notice that the lines have very uneven right margins. On lines of text where there are several short words, wrapping the text to the next line is not a problem. However, when long words are wrapped to the next line, a large gap is left on the previous line. To help solve this problem, you will hyphenate the document.

Concept 4

Hyphenation

4 The **hyphenation** feature inserts a hyphen in long words that fall at the end of a line, splitting the word between lines. Because Word automatically moves long words that fall at the end of a line to the beginning of the next line, uneven right margins or large gaps of white space commonly occur in a document. Using hyphenation reduces the amount of white space and makes line lengths more even, thereby improving the appearance of a document. The program inserts **optional hyphens**, which break the word only if it appears at the end of a line. Then, as you edit the document, the hyphenation is adjusted appropriately.

1 ● Click [Hyphenation ▼] in the Page Setup group of the Page Layout tab and choose Automatic.

Your screen should be similar to Figure 4.36

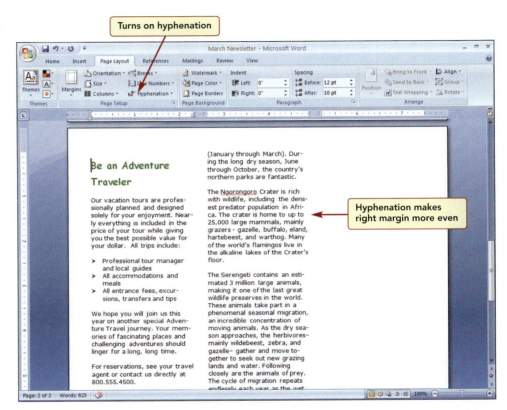

Turns on hyphenation

Hyphenation makes right margin more even

Figure 4.36

Word has examined each line and determined where it is possible to hyphenate a word. Although hyphenating the newsletter has made the column margins less uneven, you want to refine the default hyphenation settings to see if you can make the columns more even. To do this, you adjust the size of the **hyphenation zone,** an unmarked space along the right margin that controls the amount of white space in addition to the margin that Word will allow at the end of a line. Making the hyphenation zone narrower (a smaller number) reduces the unevenness of lines by hyphenating more words, while making the zone wider (a larger number) hyphenates fewer words.

2 Click  and choose Hyphenation Options.

Your screen should be similar to Figure 4.37

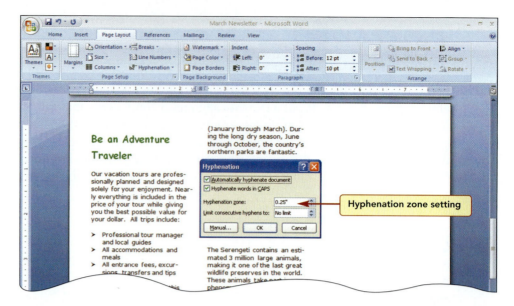

Figure 4.37

Additional Information

Use the [Manual...] button only if you want to be able to accept, reject, or change the proposed hyphenation of each word that Word is considering hyphenating.

From the Hyphenation dialog box, you can select the Automatically Hyphenate Document option, which lets Word set hyphenation for the entire document. You also can specify whether words appearing in all capital letters should be hyphenated. Finally, you can change the size of the hyphenation zone.

3 Reduce the hyphenation zone setting to 0.1".

Click [OK].

Your screen should be similar to Figure 4.38

Having Trouble?

Depending on your printer, different words may be hyphenated.

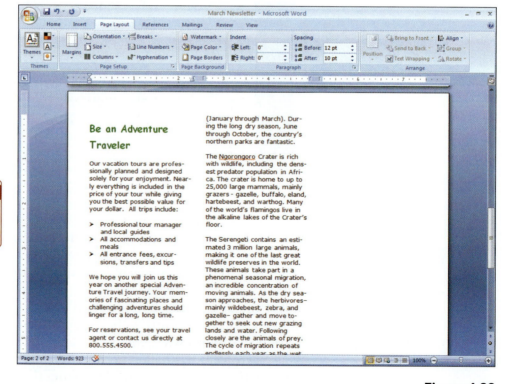

Figure 4.38

Word reexamined the document and adjusted the hyphenation on any lines affected by the smaller hyphenation zone. Word generally proposes accurate hyphenation. If you do not agree with how a word is hyphenated after it has been done, you can select the word and hyphenate it manually.

To further improve the appearance of the columns, you decide to change the text alignment to justified.

4 ● Select all the text that is formatted in columns.

● Click ▤ Justify in the Home tab.

● Scroll the document to check the layout.

● To improve the appearance of the heading Be an Adventure Traveler, change the heading alignment to left-aligned.

● Save the document.

Your screen should be similar to Figure 4.39

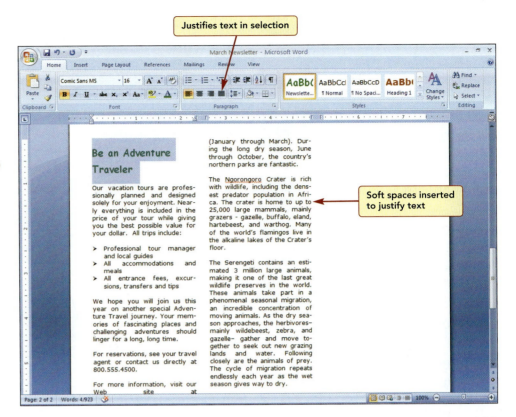

Justifies text in selection

Soft spaces inserted to justify text

Figure 4.39

All full lines now end with the right edge of each column. To do this, soft spaces were inserted between words to push the text to the right edge of each column. The soft spaces adjust automatically whenever additions or deletions are made to the text.

Creating Sidebars

You would like to set the Next Issue----Costa Rica Adventure article on the first page of the newsletter apart from the rest of the newsletter articles by adding a border and shading to the paragraph. An article you want to keep separate from other articles or information, and that highlights an article next to it, is called a **sidebar.** You can use a sidebar for such things as a list of contributors, addresses or contact information, a small self-contained story, a preview of the next issue, or a calendar or schedule.

Adding Borders and Shading to Paragraphs

One way to create a sidebar is to add a border around the article and shading behind the text. First you will add the border around the article. To do this, you first select the text you want to include in the sidebar.

When text is formatted into columns, you can use the mouse to move and select text just as in a document formatted with a single column. When you drag to select text in column layout, however, the selection moves from the bottom of one column to the top of the next.

1. **Move to the Next Issue----Costa Rica Adventure heading (on the first page).**

- **Select the text from the heading to the end of the paragraph.**

- **Open the ▦▾ Border drop-down list and choose Borders and Shading.**

- **Choose Box and select ⟨〰〰〰〰〰〰⟩ style and the color Green, Accent 4.**

- **Open the Shading tab.**

- **Open the Fill color gallery and choose Orange, Accent 1, Lighter 60%.**

- **Click ⟨ OK ⟩.**

- **Click on the selection to deselect it.**

Your screen should be similar to Figure 4.40

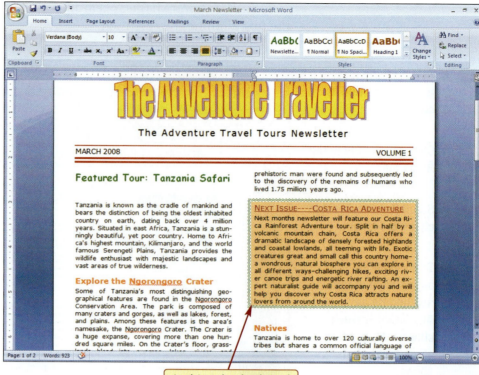

Applying a box border and fill color creates a side bar

Figure 4.40

The box border and shading background set off this article from the others on the page.

Creating Text Boxes

Next, you want to add the information about the Tanzania Facts to the newsletter. You also would like to make this information stand out by displaying it as a sidebar.

Another way to display information as a sidebar is to insert it in a text box.

5   A **text box** is a graphic object that is a container for text or graphics. Because text boxes are graphic objects, you can place them on the page as you would a picture or WordArt, and move and resize them. You also can add drawing features to text boxes to enhance their appearance.

When using newsletter-style columns, the text scrolls from the bottom of one column to the top of the next. If you want your newsletter to have specific objects in fixed places on the page, it is best to use text boxes and link those that need to flow from one page to the next. When you link text boxes together, the large articles will automatically flow into the correct text boxes on the other pages in the newsletter. Text that is contained in a single text box or linked text boxes is called a **story**.

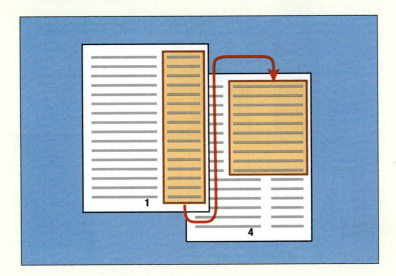

Generally, the first page of a newsletter should contain the beginnings of a main article and a secondary article, a sidebar with the newsletter contents, and perhaps a quote pulled from the article to capture the interest of someone just skimming the first page. The remainders of the articles are usually found on another page.

You will create a text box on the last page to hold the Tanzania facts information.

1 • Move to the top of the second column on page 2.

• Click [Text Box] on the Insert tab.

• Choose Simple Text Box from the gallery.

Your screen should be similar to Figure 4.41

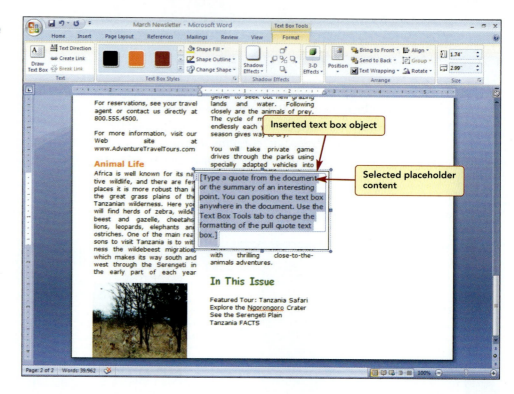

Inserted text box object

Selected placeholder content

[Type a quote from the document or the summary of an interesting point. You can position the text box anywhere in the document. Use the Text Box Tools tab to change the formatting of the pull quote text box.]

Figure 4.41

Having Trouble?

Do not be concerned if your text box is in a different location than shown in Figure 4.41. You will move it next.

A text box object has been inserted into page two of the document. The text box contains placeholder text of instructions on how to proceed. The placeholder content is already selected, ready for you to enter the replacement information. You will copy the Tanzania Facts information directly from the Clipboard into the text box.

2 • Display the Clipboard task pane.

• Click the Tanzania FACTS . . . item to insert it in the text box.

• Click 🌂 Clear All to clear the contents of the Office Clipboard.

Additional Information
The system Clipboard is cleared also.

• Close the Clipboard task pane.

• Move the text box to the top of the third column.

Your screen should be similar to Figure 4.42

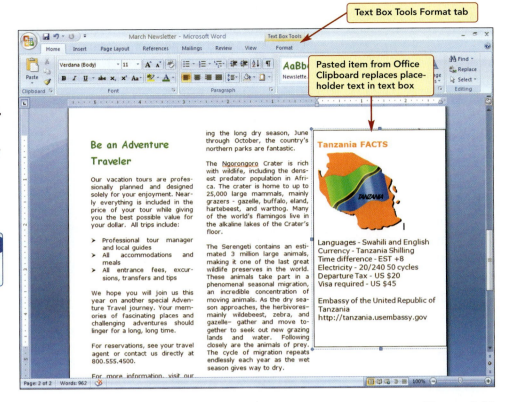

Figure 4.42

The text is pasted into the text box and the box automatically increased in size to display the entire article content. In addition, the Text Box Tools Format tab is automatically displayed, ready for you to add features to enhance the appearance of the box.

The text box is a graphic object and is considered one graphic element (see figure below). When you move or size it, all the objects within the text box move and size as a single unit. However, you can still format the text and objects individually within the text box.

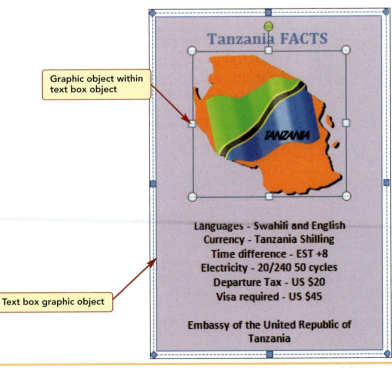

Additionally, text boxes are inserted as floating objects with the text wrapping style set to In Front of Text. You will change the wrapping style to Square so that the text wraps around the object when new items are inserted or the object is moved.

Formatting a Text Box

The text was inserted in the text box using the Normal style font size of 11 points. You will reduce the font size and enhance the appearance of the text and text box next.

1 ● Reduce the text size (excluding the heading) to 9 points and bold the text.

● Delete the last blank line in the text box.

● Click **Shape Fill** in the Text Box Styles group on the Text Box Tools Format tab.

● Select Dark Green, Accent 4, Lighter 60%.

● Click **Shape Outline** and select Orange, Accent 1.

● Reduce the size of the map graphic object as in Figure 4.43.

Your screen should be similar to Figure 4.43

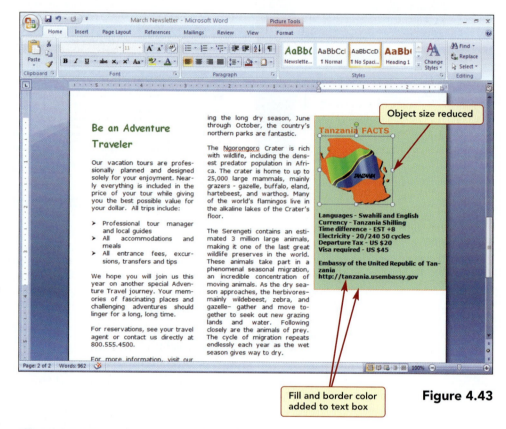

Figure 4.43

The color fill and outline add much interest to the text box. You will finish formatting the text box by centering the contents and sizing it to the column width. Finally, you will change the wrapping style to square.

2 Select and center the entire contents of the text box.

- Size and position the text box as in Figure 4.44.

- Click 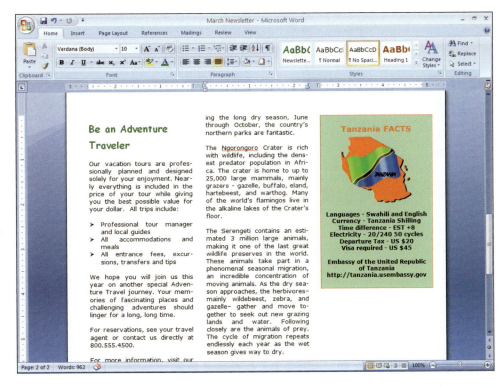 Text Wrapping from the Arrange group on the Text Box Tools Format tab and choose Square.

- Deselect the text box.

Your screen should be similar to Figure 4.44

Figure 4.44

More About

To learn about formatting quoted material, see 2.1 Format Text and Paragraphs in the More About appendix. To learn about inserting pull quotes, see 3.3 Format Text Graphically in the More About appendix.

Additional Information

Because sidebars commonly occupy the entire side or width of a page, many of the sidebar designs are full width or height text boxes.

It has taken quite a few steps to format the text box. In addition to the plain text box design, Word includes many preformatted text boxes that are specifically designed as containers for sidebars or quotes. You will use one of these to display the listing of newsletter contents. Then you will move it to the first page of the newsletter.

3 ● Move to the In This Issue heading at the bottom of page 2.

● Select and cut the heading and the four lines of text that follow.

Having Trouble?

Do not be concerned as objects move around and overlap in the document as you add and delete items. You will fix the newsletter layout shortly.

● Click [Text Box] on the Insert tab.

● Choose Annual Sidebar from the gallery.

● Paste the cut selection into the text box.

● Reduce the size of the text box to just large enough to display the text.

● Move the text box to the bottom of page 1 and resize it to fit the width of the page as shown in Figure 4.45.

● Right-align the content of the text box.

● Click outside the text box to deselect it.

Your screen should be similar to Figure 4.45

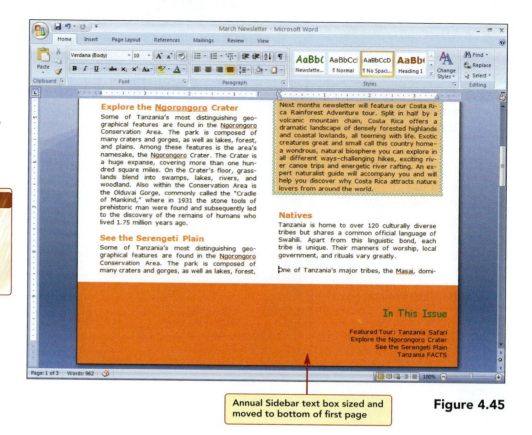

Annual Sidebar text box sized and moved to bottom of first page

Figure 4.45

Now you would like to see the effects your changes have made to the layout and design of your newsletter.

4 — Save the document again.

● Reduce the zoom to display all pages.

Your screen should be similar to Figure 4.46

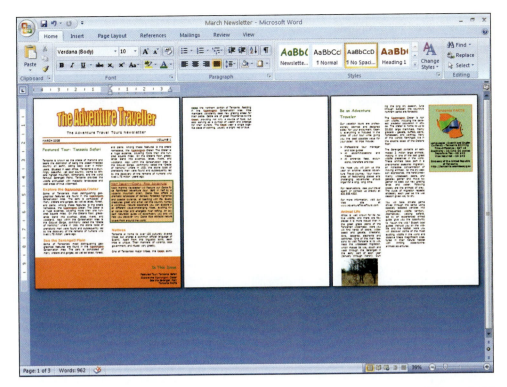

Figure 4.46

The document now consists of three pages. This is because, as you added elements to the first page of the newsletter, some text moved to the second page, and a page break forced the third page. Because you still want to add a picture to the first page, even more of the text will be pushed to the second page.

Linking Text Boxes

To fix this and to reduce the document back to two pages, you will rearrange elements and create a linked text box to control the flow of the text between the newsletter pages. As you look at the layout, you decide to create a linked text box for the two topics about the Ngorongoro Crater and the Serengeti Plain.

1 Change the zoom to 100%.

- Move to the heading **Explore the Ngorongoro Crater** and select the text through the end of the **See the Serengeti Plain** article.

- Click [Text Box] and choose **Draw Text Box**.

Your screen should be similar to Figure 4.47

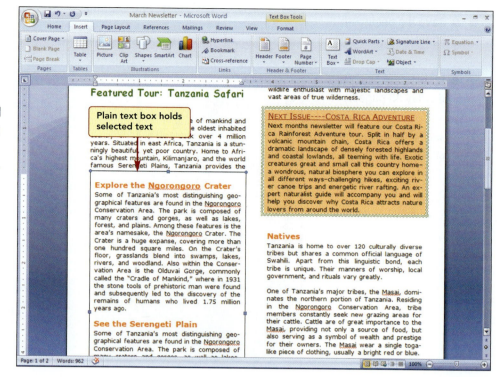

Figure 4.47

The Draw Text Box automatically creates a plain text box to contain the selection. Next, you will quickly format the text box by selecting a text box style.

2 Open the Text Box Styles gallery in the Text Box styles group on the Text Box Tools Format tab.

- Choose [ ] **Linear Up Gradient – Accent 4** style.

- Reduce the length of the text box until only the first article is displayed in it.

Your screen should be similar to Figure 4.48

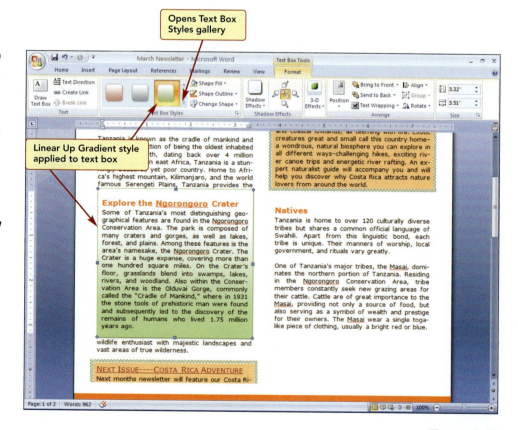

Figure 4.48

Using a text box style quickly applies a combination of color, line, and shape effects to a text box. Now you will create the second text box where you want the remainder of the story to be displayed. You will use the Draw Text Box option again to create this text box. However, because you will not preselect content to go in the text box, you will need to create the text box shape manually.

3 ● **Move to anywhere on the last page.**

● **Click** [Text Box] **and choose Draw Text Box.**

Additional Information

The mouse pointer appears as + to show it is ready to draw.

● **Drag down and to the right to create a text box.**

● **Size and position the text box as shown in Figure 4.49.**

● **Apply the same text box style to this box.**

Your screen should be similar to Figure 4.49

Having Trouble?

See Concept 6: Text Wrapping in Lab 3 to review this feature.

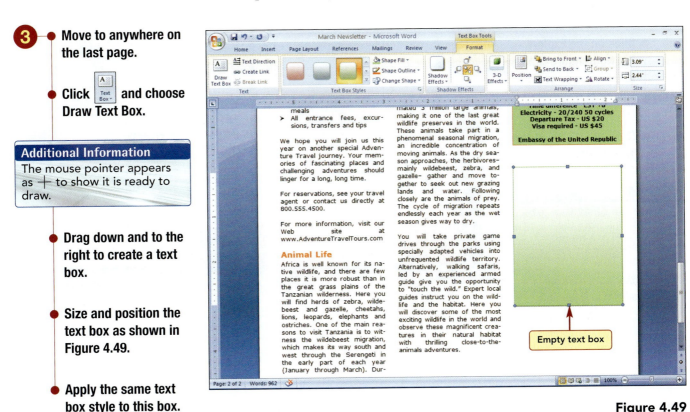

Figure 4.49

You will change the wrapping style to Square so that text will wrap around the object. Then you will create a link between the two text boxes so that the overflow information from the first text box will flow into the empty text box. The text boxes to which you link must be empty—they cannot contain text.

To make it easier to see what happens as you link the boxes, you will change the zoom to display all the pages again.

4
- Change the text wrapping to Square.

- Reduce the zoom percentage to display two pages.

- Click on the Explore the Ngorongoro Crater text box on page 1 to select it.

- Click [Create Link] in the Text group.

Another Method
You also can select Create Text Box Link from the object's shortcut menu.

Your screen should be similar to Figure 4.50

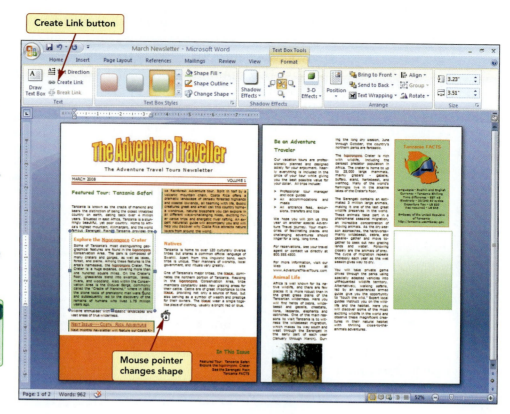

Figure 4.50

The mouse pointer changes to a 🖑, which indicates there is text that is not showing that can flow into another text box. The next step is to link the boxes.

5
- Click on the blank text box on page 2.

Additional Information
The mouse pointer changes to a 🖑 to indicate that the text will be poured into the text box.

Your screen should be similar to Figure 4.51

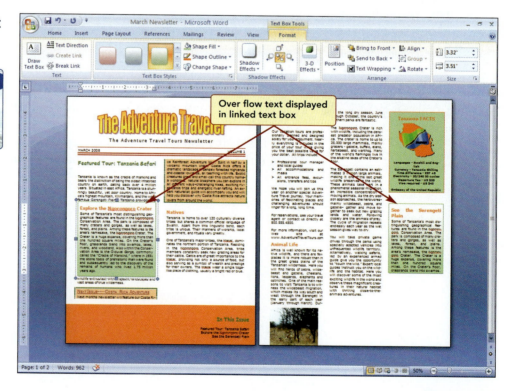

Figure 4.51

The overflow text from the first text box flows into the linked text box.

6 • Increase the zoom to 100%.

• Select the text box on page 2 and adjust the width of the text box to the column width and the height to fully display the text.

Having Trouble?

As you size and position objects, others may move. You will make final adjustments to the layout of the newsletter shortly.

• Left-align the title in the text box.

• Deselect the text box.

• Save the newsletter again.

Your screen should be similar to Figure 4.52

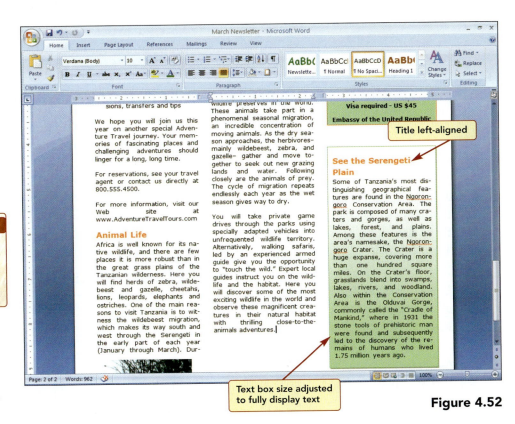

Figure 4.52

You also want the Be an Adventure Traveler article to be in a text box.

7 • Select the Be an Adventure Traveler article.

• Create a text box using Draw Text Box.

• Apply the Diagonal Gradient, Accent 1 text box style.

• Change the wrapping style to Square.

Your screen should be similar to Figure 4.53

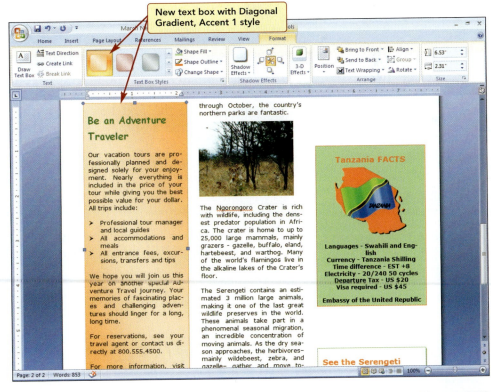

Figure 4.53

Although you like how the article appears in the text box, you feel it does not draw enough attention to the reservation and Web site information at the end of the article.

Use Building Blocks Organizer to Create a Sidebar

To make this information more visible, you decide to include this information in a separate sidebar. You will use the Building Blocks Organizer to insert this sidebar.

1
- Select and cut the last two sentences of the Be an Adventure Traveler article.

- Delete the blank line at the bottom of the box.

- Click outside the text box anywhere on page 3.

- Open the [Quick Parts ▾] menu in the Text group of the Insert tab and choose Building Blocks Organizer.

- If necessary, double click on the Gallery heading to sort the items by gallery.

- Scroll to see the Text Boxes gallery items and choose Sticky Quote.

Your screen should be similar to Figure 4.54

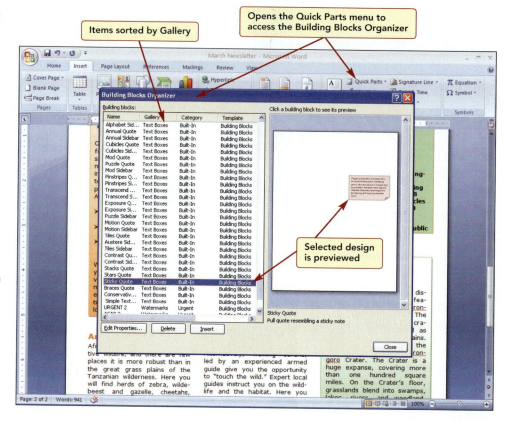

Figure 4.54

The names of all the text box designs are listed and the preview area displays the selected design.

2 Click .

- Paste the text into the text box.

- Move the text box to the bottom of column 3 as shown in Figure 4.55.

- Change the text box style to Diagonal Gradient, Accent 1.

- Replace the words "us directly" with your name.

- Center the text in the text box and size it to fit within the column width and display all the content as in Figure 4.55.

Your screen should be similar to Figure 4.55

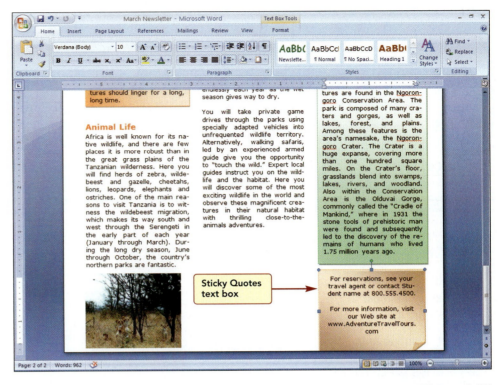

Figure 4.55

The Sticky Quotes text box now makes the reservations and contact information much more prominent.

Formatting Illustrations

Now you are ready to work on the pictures in the newsletter. You want to improve the appearance of the lion picture and insert a new picture on the first page.

The picture of the lions in the Animal Life section is dark and includes a lot of unneeded background. Word includes a wide variety of tools that you can use to improve the format of pictures, including cropping, scaling, and rotating images and adjusting the contrast and brightness. You will try out several of these features to see if you can improve this picture.

Cropping and Compressing a Picture

The first change you want to make is to **crop,** or trim vertical or horizontal edges of the picture, to eliminate all but the main group of lions. When the cropping feature is on, the selected object is surrounded with cropping handles.

More About

To learn more about formatting pictures, see 3.2 Format Illustrations in the More About appendix.

Cropping handles

Dragging the side cropping handle inward removes picture content from the sides and dragging a corner cropping handle removes content from the adjoining sides. To crop equally from all four sides at once, hold down Ctrl while dragging the corner cropping handle. To crop eqally on two sides at once, hold down Ctrl while dragging the center side cropping handle.

1 ● Select the lion picture and move it to a blank space on page 2.

● Click [Crop] in the Size group of the Picture Tools Format tab.

Additional Information

The mouse pointer appears as ⯐ when it is used to crop a picture.

● Crop the picture to appear similar to Figure 4.56 by

  ● Pointing to the upper-left corner of the photo and, when the mouse changes to a ⌐ , dragging inward to remove the excess background above and to the left side of the group of lions.

  ● Dragging the right center side cropping handle inward to remove the excess background on the right side of the lions.

  ● Cropping the bottom of the graphic slightly to remove some of the foreground.

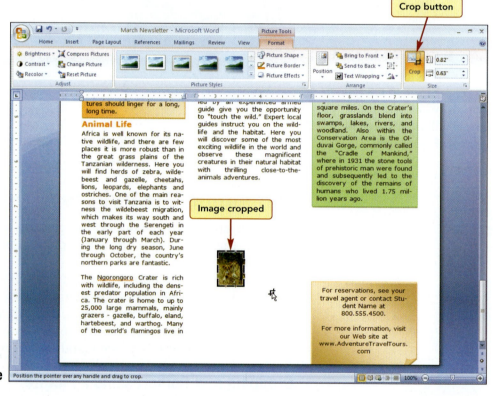

Figure 4.56

Having Trouble?

To undo a crop, click [Reset Picture] in the Adjust group to restore the picture to the original size or use ↺ Undo.

Your screen should be similar to Figure 4.56

Another Method

You can crop to an exact dimension by opening the Size dialog box and specifying exact measurements in the Crop From section.

The extra background has been eliminated, which allows you to focus on the lions. Next, you will increase the size of the picture. You want to maintain the proportion of the picture and keep the center of the object in the same place as you increase the size. To do this, hold down both Ctrl and ⇧ Shift as you drag the sizing handle.

2 • Click  to turn off this feature.

• Move the picture to the location shown in Figure 4.57.

• Hold down Ctrl and Shift as you drag a corner sizing handle to increase the picture size as in Figure 4.57.

• Reposition the picture as in Figure 4.57.

Your screen should be similar to Figure 4.57

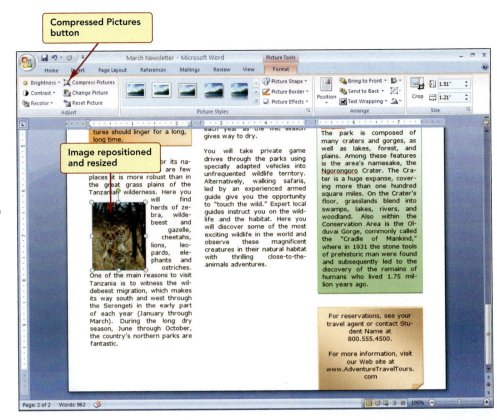

Figure 4.57

Once a picture has been cropped and the file saved, it cannot be restored to its original size. Cropping visually reduces the size of a picture; however, the cropped parts are not removed from the file until you compress the picture.

3 • Click ⌷ Compress Pictures in the Adjust group.

• Click OK to compress the picture.

Additional Information
If there were several pictures in the document, all would be compressed unless you chose the Apply to selected picture option.

Although no change is visible, the excess picture parts have been removed from the file. This helps reduce the overall file size.

Adjusting Contrast and Brightness

Next, you want to adjust the contrast and brightness of the picture. Adjusting the contrast increases the difference between the darkest and lightest areas of the picture. Adjusting the brightness changes a picture's relative lightness.

1 ● **Click** [☀ Brightness ▾] **and choose +10%.**

● **Click** [◑ Contrast ▾] **and choose +20%.**

Your screen should be similar to Figure 4.58

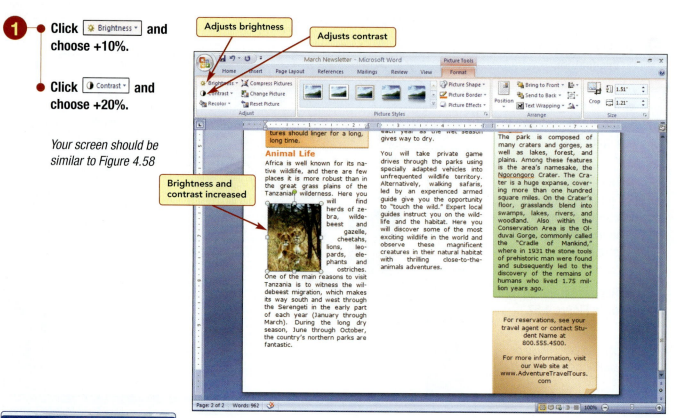

Adjusts brightness

Adjusts contrast

Brightness and contrast increased

Figure 4.58

Additional Information
You can fine-tune brightness and contrast using the Picture Corrections Options command and setting an exact value.

The changes in contrast and brightness make the animals in the picture much more visible.

The last change you want to make to the picture is to attach the picture to the section of text where it is positioned in the paragraph so that it moves when the text moves.

6 Each floating graphic in a document is attached to a particular location such as to a page or a paragraph by an **anchor**. This is because floating graphics are placed in a separate graphics layer. Without the anchor, the graphic would not maintain its location in the document. When you position a floating graphic, the graphic is automatically anchored relative to wherever you positioned it. For example, if you positioned it in a paragraph, it is anchored to the beginning of the paragraph.

If you add or remove text and the anchor moves to another page, the graphic moves with it because the graphic and its anchor must be on the same page. The anchor does not attach the graphic to any particular location in the paragraph. To keep the graphic with a specific section of text, you need to select the Move object with text option in the Advanced Layout dialog box.

Anchors are not visible unless you display paragraph marks and the object is selected. If you move the graphic, the anchor will move to the associated paragraph. If, because of changes you make to the text, the anchor is not associated with the correct paragraph, it can be moved by dragging it. The object may or may not move depending on whether it has been positioned relative to the paragraph or the page. If you move the anchor to another page, the graphic moves with it.

Floating graphics are positioned horizontally relative to the column and vertically relative to the paragraph by default. You can change the position with respect to various features such as margins, page, or paragraph. You also can specify an absolute vertical and or horizontal position by manually entering an exact distance. These settings show up automatically if you drag the graphic to a location in the page, but can be easily changed. Further, you can specify the distance between the text and the edge of the graphic for most wrapping styles. You also can lock an anchor so that it cannot be moved. These settings are available in the Advanced Layout dialog box.

Many times in a newsletter-type publication, it is best to put all elements into separate text boxes. This is because you can place them wherever you want them and you can easily control their size, shape, and appearance. Additionally, when moving selected blocks of text, any floating graphics that are anchored to the paragraphs in the selection are affected, and consequently they may move unexpectedly to different locations.

2 ● Click 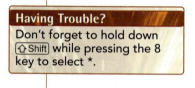 **and choose More Layout Options.**

● **Choose Move object with text in the Picture Position tab of the Advanced Layout dialog box.**

● **Click** OK **.**

● **Insert a blank line above the Animal Life heading.**

● **Select the graphic and press** Ctrl **+ * to display paragraph marks.**

Having Trouble?
Don't forget to hold down ⇧Shift while pressing the 8 key to select *.

● **Save the document.**

Your screen should be similar to Figure 4.59

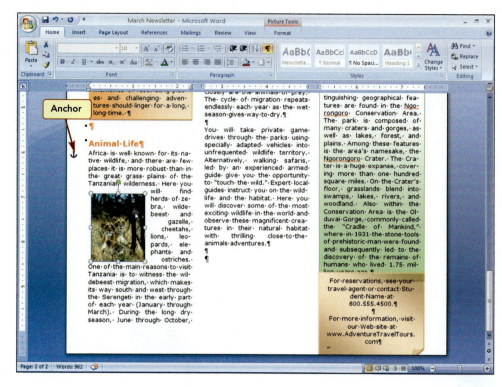

Figure 4.59

The insertion of the blank line above the paragraph moved all content below it down one line. Because you enabled the feature to move with text, the picture also moved relative to the text to which it is associated. Otherwise it would have remained stationary while the surrounding text moved because it was positioned horizontally relative the column and vertically relative to the paragraph.

The anchor for the selected graphic appears at the top of the paragraph in which the graphic is positioned.

Deleting a Bookmark

Next, you want to insert a picture where you added a Bookmark reminder to include it. To go to the location where you want to add the picture, you will use the Bookmark and then delete it because you will no longer need it.

1

- Press [Ctrl] + * to hide paragraph marks.

- Click  on the Insert tab and click ⟨ Go To ⟩.

- Click ⟨ Delete ⟩ to remove the bookmark and click ⟨ Close ⟩.

- Insert the picture wd04_Giraffe from your data file location.

- Change the wrapping style to Square.

- Size and position the picture as in Figure 4.60.

- Adjust the contrast and brightness as needed.

Your screen should be similar to Figure 4.60

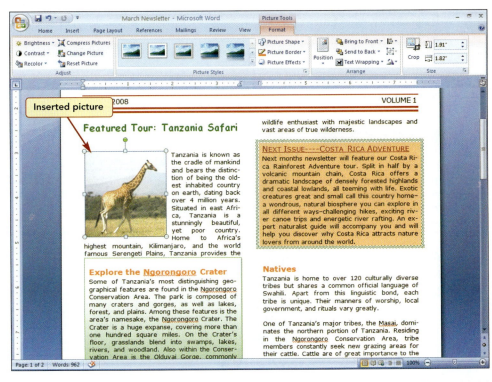

Figure 4.60

Additional Information

Holding down [⇧Shift] while using the rotate handle rotates the object in 15-degree increments.

Rotating a Picture

Next, you want to enhance the picture by rotating it and adding a picture style. Rotating a picture changes the angle of the picture. You can rotate an object by 90 degrees left or right or flip it vertically or horizontally, using the ⟨▣▾⟩ Rotate command in the Arrange group of the Picture Tools Format tab. You also can specify the exact degree of rotation in the Size dialog box. Finally, you can use the 🟢 rotate handle for the selected object, which allows you to rotate the object to any degree in any direction.

1

- If necessary, select the picture.

- Drag the rotate handle to the left slightly.

Additional Information

The mouse pointer appears as ⟳ when positioned on the rotate handle and Live Preview shows how the object will look as you rotate it.

- Add the Soft Edge Rectangle picture style to the picture.

Your screen should be similar to Figure 4.61

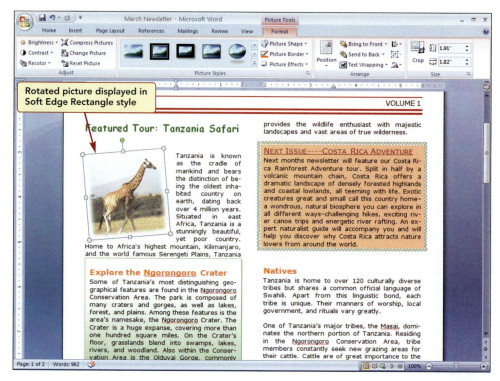

Figure 4.61

You like the added interest the angle and picture style effect add to the newsletter.

Finalizing the Newsletter

You are almost finished with the newsletter. You have added many objects to the newsletter and have not been concerned about the newsletter layout. Now that you are finished adding objects, you can focus on the overall layout of the newsletter. You also will make a few additional formatting changes to enhance the appearance.

Refining the Layout and Position of Graphics

Now you need to check the newsletter layout and move text and graphic elements around on the page until the newsletter has an orderly, yet interesting appearance.

1 ● Reduce the zoom to display both pages of the newsletter.

Having Trouble?
Do not be concerned if your newsletter shows objects in different locations than in Figure 4.62.

Your screen should be similar to Figure 4.62

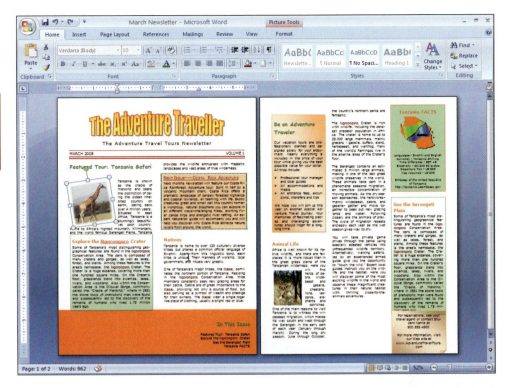

Figure 4.62

Many of the objects are in locations that do not look good. You need to select the objects and place them where they fit and look best on the page.

2 ● Position and size the graphic elements so your newsletter is similar to that shown in Figure 4.63.

Having Trouble?
If the objects are moving around strangely, display paragraph marks and check and adjust the anchor locations as needed.

● Save the file.

Your screen should be similar to Figure 4.63

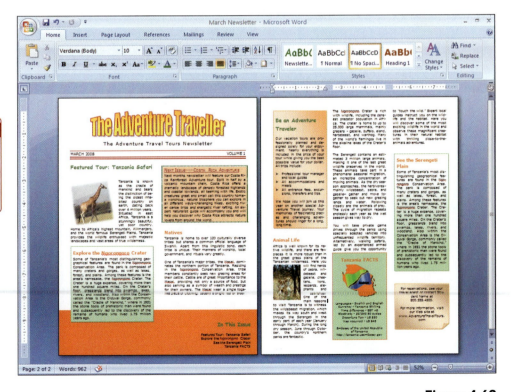

Figure 4.63

The rearrangement of the objects gives the newsletter a more interesting and professional appearance.

Customizing Bullets

As you look at the information on the second page, you decide the three bulleted items in the Be an Adventure Traveler article would stand out more if the bullets were more interesting. In addition to the standard bullets, you can use a unique symbol or a graphic as a bullet. You also can change the size of the indent from the margin and the spacing between the bullet and the text. You will add a custom picture bullet.

1 ● Change the zoom to 100%.

● Select the three bulleted items in the Be an Adventure Traveler article.

● Open the [≣▾] Bullets drop-down list.

● Choose Define New Bullet

● Click [Picture...].

Your screen should be similar to Figure 4.64

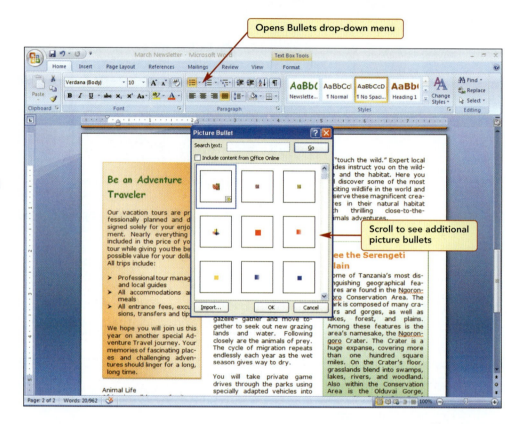

Figure 4.64

From the Picture Bullet dialog box, you select the graphic bullet you want to use. You will use the middle-sized green box bullet.

2 ● Click ▪.

● Click OK twice.

Your screen should be similar to Figure 4.65

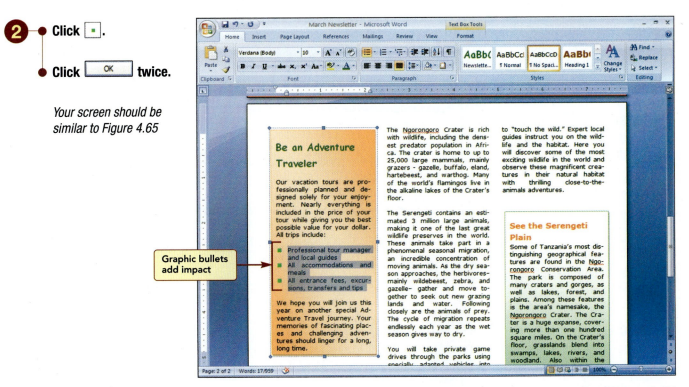

Graphic bullets add impact

Figure 4.65

The graphic bullets add much more impact to the tour features.

Using Special Characters and Symbols

The next change you want to make is to replace the four dashes in the title of the Next Issue box with a single long dash line, called an **em dash.**

1
Select the four dashes in the Next Issue heading on the first page.

Click 【Ω Symbol ▾】 from the Symbols group on the Insert tab.

Choose More Symbols.

Open the Special Characters tab and select Em Dash from the list.

Click 【 Insert 】.

If necessary, move the dialog box to see the Next Issue heading.

Your screen should be similar to Figure 4.66

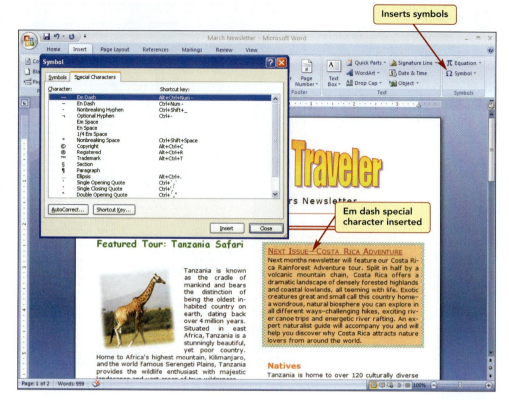

Figure 4.66

The four dashes are replaced with the em dash character, and the Symbol dialog box remains open for you to make additional selections. Those symbols that are frequently used include a shortcut key combination that can be used to insert the symbol automatically for you. You also can specify your own shortcut key combination for any of the characters or have the special character automatically entered whenever a specified character string is typed.

Another change you want to make to customize the newsletter is to place a small symbol at the end of the main article to let the reader know that the article is finished. You will add a symbol at the end of the article on page 2 and change the symbol color to orange.

2 • With the Symbol dialog box still open, move to after the period at the end of the text in the third column on page 2.

• Open the Symbols tab and select Symbol from the Font drop-down list.

• Scroll the list and choose the solid diamond symbol (see Figure 4.67).

Additional Information
The symbol number is 168.

• Click [Insert].

• Click [Close].

• Select the diamond symbol.

• Change the font color to Dark Red.

• Move to the next line to deselect the symbol.

Your screen should be similar to Figure 4.67

Additional Information
You can use the same procedure to change the formatting, such as the color, of bullets and numbering in lists.

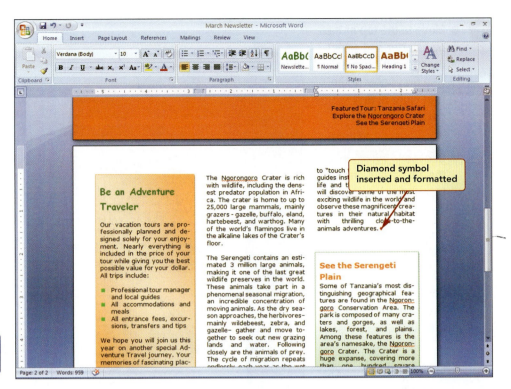

Figure 4.67

Adding a Drop Cap

Finally, you would like to make the first letter of the first paragraph of the newsletter a drop cap. A **drop cap,** used most often with the first character in a paragraph, appears as a large uppercase character with the top part of the letter even with the line and the rest of the letter extending into the paragraph below it. The character is changed to a graphic object in a frame, and the text wraps to the side of the object. The two preset dropped cap options create a drop cap that is three characters high or placed in the margin. You want to create a drop cap that is only two characters high.

1 ● Move to the top of the newsletter and select the "T" in "Tanzania" (the first letter of the first word in first paragraph).

● Choose 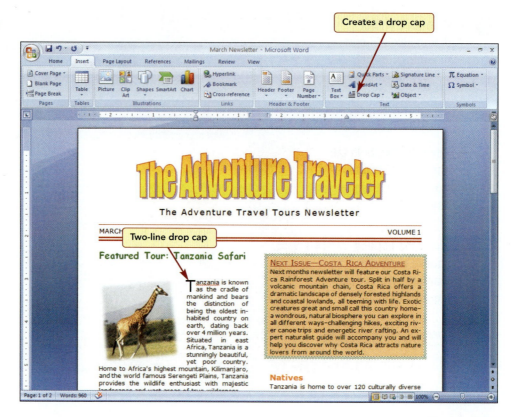 Drop Cap ▾ in the Text group on the Insert tab.

● Choose Drop Cap Options.

● Choose Dropped and decrease the Lines to drop to 2.

● Click OK.

● Position the drop cap graphic appropriately at the beginning of the paragraph.

Your screen should be similar to Figure 4.68

Creates a drop cap

Two-line drop cap

Figure 4.68

The drop-cap effect emphasizes the beginning of the paragraph and makes the columns appear more like those in a magazine.

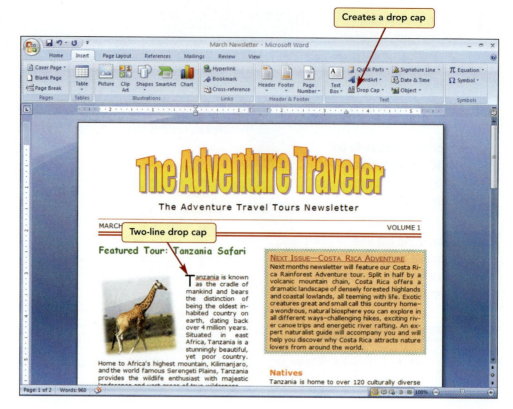

Printing the Newsletter

As a final check before printing, it is a good idea to display the document in the Print Preview window to make sure that elements will print correctly using the specified printer setting.

1 ● Change the zoom to Two Pages and make any final adjustments needed to the layout.

● Save the document again.

● Preview, then print the newsletter.

● Exit Word, closing all open files.

The printed copy of the newsletter should be similar to the document shown in the Case Study at the beginning of the lab.

Focus on Careers

EXPLORE YOUR CAREER OPTIONS

Purchasing Manager

Do you like to shop? Would you like to research products and attend trade shows? Purchasing managers are in charge of obtaining the supplies and property for their employers. They are responsible for researching suppliers and negotiating contracts for the needed merchandise. They also may be responsible for creating the contracts that secure the products. They may create reports for their company and communicate with suppliers and members of the buying department. Purchasing managers must be skilled with a word processing program to accomplish their work. A college degree and experience are usually required. The typical salary range for purchasing managers is between $43,000 and $81,000. Demand for purchasing managers is expected to remain fixed due to technological improvements.

WordArt   (WD4.5)

WordArt is used to enhance your documents by changing the shape of text and adding special effects such as 3-D and shadows.

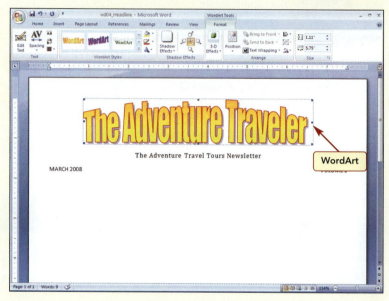

Collect and Paste   (WD4.20)

Collecting and pasting is the capability of the program to store multiple copied items in the Office Clipboard and then paste one or more of them into another document.

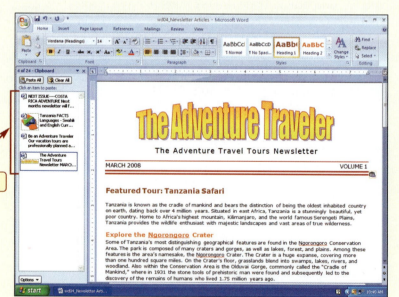

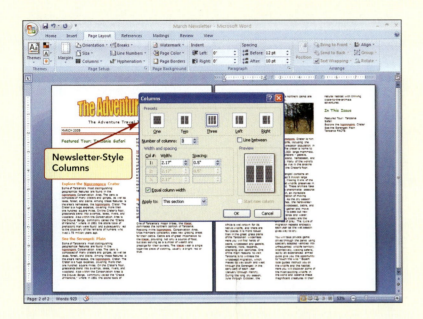

Newsletter-Style Columns (WD4.29)

Newsletter-style columns display text so that it flows from the bottom of one column to the top of the next.

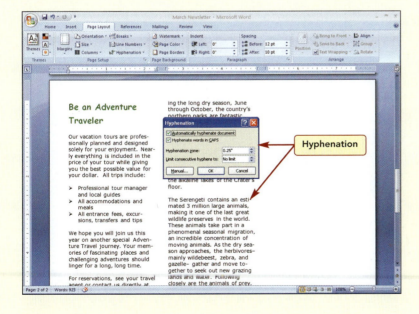

Hyphenation (WD4.33)

The hyphenation feature inserts a hyphen in long words that fall at the end of a line, splitting the word between lines.

Concept Summary

Text Box (WD4.37)

A text box is a graphic object that is a container for text or graphics.

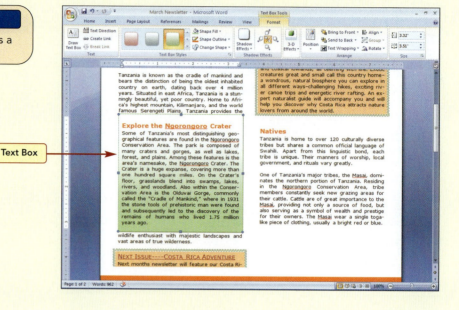

Text Box

Anchor (WD4.53)

Each floating graphic in a document is attached to a particular location, such as to a page or a paragraph by an anchor.

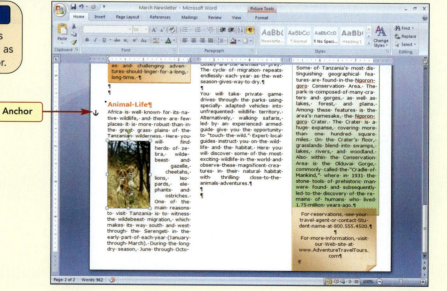

Anchor

Lab Review

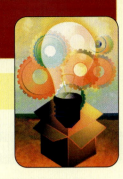

key terms

anchor   WD4.53

bookmark   WD4.25

collect and paste   WD4.20

crop   WD4.49

drop cap   WD4.61

em dash   WD4.59

hyphenation   WD4.33

hyphenation zone   WD4.33

kerning   WD4.11

newsletter-style
columns   WD4.29

optional hyphen   WD4.33

sidebar   WD4.35

story   WD4.37

text box   WD4.37

WordArt   WD4.5

MCAS skills

The Microsoft Certified Applications Specialist (MCAS) certification program is designed to measure your proficiency in performing basic tasks using the Office 2007 applications. Getting certified demonstrates that you have the skills and provides a valuable industry credential for employment. See Reference 2, Microsoft Certified Applications Specialist (MCAS) for a complete list of the skills that were covered in Lab 4.

Lab Review

command summary

Command	Shortcut	Action
Home tab		
Clipboard group		
⬚		Displays the Office Clipboard task pane
Paragraph group		
☰ ▾ Bullets/Define New Bullet/Picture		Applies picture bullets to selected items
⊞ ▾ Border		Customizes the borders for selected text or objects
Styles group		
⬚ More/Save Selection as a New Quick Style		Creates a new style based on formatting of selected text
Editing group		
⬚ Select ▾		Selects text or objects in the document
Insert tab		
Links group		
⬚ Bookmark		Creates, deletes, or goes to a bookmark or assigned name to a specific point in a document
Text group		
⬚ Text Box ▾		Inserts reformatted text boxes
⬚ WordArt ▾		Inserts decorative text into a document
⬚ Drop Cap ▾		Creates a large capital letter at the beginning of a paragraph
Symbols group		
Ω Symbol ▾		Inserts symbols that are not on keyboard into document
Page Layout tab		
Page Setup group		
⬚ Columns ▾		Splits text between two or more columns
⬚ Columns ▾ /More Columns		Sets width and spacing of columns
⬚ Breaks ▾		Adds page, section, or column breaks to the document

command summary

Command	Shortcut	Action
bc² Hyphenation ▾		Turns on hyphenation, allowing words to break lines between the syllables of words.
Review tab		
Proofing group		
🔍 Research		Opens Research task pane to search through reference materials
WordArt Tools Format tab		
Text group		
AV Spacing ▾		Changes the spacing between the letters of text
Arrange group		
Text Wrapping ▾		Changes the way text wraps around a selected object
WordArt Styles group		
A ▾ Change WordArt Shape		Specifies overall shape of WordArt object
🖌 ▾ Shape Fill		Fills selected shape with solid, color, gradient, picture, or texture
✎ ▾ Shape Outline		Specifies color, width, and line style for outline of selected shape
Picture Tools Format tab		
Adjust group		
☀ Brightness ▾		Increases or decreases the brightness of a picture
◑ Contrast ▾		Increases or decrease the contrast of a picture
🖼 Compress Pictures		Compresses pictures in the document to reduce its size
Size group		
Crop		Crops pictures to remove unwanted parts

Lab Exercises

matching

Match the item on the left with the correct description on the right.

1. anchor _____   a. Appears as a large uppercase character that extends into the paragraph below

2. bookmark _____   b. Text that is contained in a single text box or linked text boxes

3. drop cap _____   c. A link that identifies a location or a selection of text

4. hyphenation _____   d. Used to make such things as a list of contributors, addresses, or contact information stand out

5. hyphenation zone _____   e. A feature used to create attractive headlines

6 kerning _____   f. A graphic object that is a container for text or graphics

7. sidebar _____   g. A feature that alters the spacing between particular pairs of letters to improve the appearance of the text

8. story _____   h. Feature that splits words between lines

9. text box _____   i. Attaches a floating graphic to a particular location

10. WordArt _____   j. Controls the amount of white space allowed at the end of a line

multiple choice

Circle the correct response to the questions below.

1. A(n) _____ is a single long dash line.
   a. liner
   b. em dash
   c. horizontal bar
   d. hyphen

2. _____ are graphic objects that are used to contain text or graphics.
   a. Text boxes
   b. List boxes
   c. Phrase boxes
   d. Display boxes

3. Text that flows from the bottom of one column to the top of the next is displayed in _____ column format.
   a. adjusted
   b. fixed
   c. newspaper
   d. newsletter-style

4. _____ adjusts the spacing between particular pairs of letters depending on the font design to improve the appearance of the text.
   a. Floating
   b. Kerning
   c. Anchoring
   d. Locking

5. _____ appear as large uppercase characters that extend into the paragraph below.
   a. Drop caps
   b. Character objects
   c. Enlarged characters
   d. Declining characters

6. Information you want to separate from other articles or information that highlights an article next to it is called a _____.
   a. sidetrack
   b. sidestep
   c. sideline
   d. sidebar

7. You can specify the size of the _____ zone, an unmarked space along the right margin that controls the amount of white space at the end of a line.
   a. tab
   b. border
   c. margin
   d. hyphenation

8. Text that is contained in a single text box or linked text boxes is called a(n) _____.
   a. unibox
   b. graphic object
   c. story
   d. adjusted box

9. _____ is the capability of the program to store multiple copied items and paste one or more into another document.
   a. Gathering and pasting
   b. Collecting and pasting
   c. Hyphenating and adding
   d. Copying and pasting

10. The _____ feature is used to change the shape of text and/or add special effects such as 3-D and shadows.
   a. WordArt
   b. Animation
   c. Format title
   d. Quick Art

true/false

Circle the correct answer to the following questions.

1. When you link text boxes together, large articles automatically flow into the correct text boxes on other pages of a newsletter.   True   False

2. An anchor determines the number of columns in a newsletter.   True   False

3. Kerning adjusts the spacing between paragraphs.   True   False

4. WordArt can be changed using the Review tab.   True   False

5. The last item copied to the Office Clipboard is copied to the system Clipboard.   True   False

6. A drop cap can occur when an object is incorrectly inserted.   True   False

7. Sidebars draw attention to specific information.   True   False

8. The hyphenation feature inserts hyphens in long words that fall at the end of a line.   True   False

9. The Research task pane can be used to locate information on the Web.   True   False

10. You cannot add drawing features to a text box.   True   False

Hands-On Exercises

step-by-step

Water Conservation Newsletter ★

1. The city of Harrisburg has begun a water conservation effort to combat drought conditions. They will send a newsletter that contains water saving tips to all the city residents. You have already compiled the text for the bulletin. You need to gather the text, headline, and photos to complete the document. Your completed newsletter should be similar to that shown here.

   a. Open the files wd04_Water Headline and wd04_Water Tips. Copy the entire wd04_Water Headline document to the first line of the wd04_Water Tips text. Close the wd04_Water Headline document and save the remaining file as Water Newsletter.

   b. Change the WordArt to a two-color gradient fill of your choice. Change the spacing to Tight.

   c. Change the character spacing of the text below the WordArt to expanded by 2 pt.

   d. Create a 1½ pt. blue rule above the date and volume line and a 4½ blue line below it.

   e. Apply a two-column layout to the newsletter text. Specify automatic hyphenation and justify the columns.

   f. Enter your name and today's date at the bottom of the second column.

   g. Replace the bullets under the last section "Watch that Hose!" with a custom bullet of your choice. Set the bullet indent position to 0" and the bullet text positions to the 0.3" position.

   h. Apply borders and shading of your choice to the section that begins "Watch that Hose!" Increase the font of the box table to 12 pt and a color of your choice.

City of Harrisburg Drought Prevention Program

March 2008   **Volume 3**

Recent Rains have ended the severe drought conditions we have experienced for the past six months; all residents should have been alerted that the water restrictions for irrigation and yard maintenance have been lifted. Sadly, reservoir levels are only still only marginally improved.

Water conservation experts hired by the city have determined that with population growth and prevailing weather patterns, Harrisburg may be at risk for additional drought conditions as early as next year. As expert Mark Gault noted, "…water conservation is not an emergency action, it should be practiced all the time."

The city, in cooperation with Mr. Gault, has compiled this list of water saving tips:

Watch that Faucet–Remember to turn off the water as you brush your teeth or shave. Don't waste the water while waiting for hot or cold water, save this water for pets, plants or a cool drink.

Full Load Every Time–Always try to run the dishwasher and laundry with full loads. Also, choose water-saving modes on your machines whenever possible.

Scrimp in the Shower–Installing low-flow shower heads and keeping showers to a minimum goes a long way toward water conservation. Don't fill the bathtub to the top; try bathing with ¼ to ½ of the tub filled.

Rinse vs. Soak–If you hand wash your dishes fill the sink to rinse them instead of letting the water run. Use this method for washing fruit and vegetables as well.

Watch that Hose!
Did you know that a standard water hose can use more than 10 gallons of water a minute?
- Use a nozzle with a cutoff so you can control flow.
- Check your hose and faucet for leaks periodically.
- Don't spray off your driveway; a broom can be great exercise!
- Take your car to a carwash that recycles its water.

All of these tips can save gallons of water outdoors. Remember water conservation isn't just for droughts.

Student Name
2/5/08

i. Insert the image wd04_Water at the beginning of the first column. Change the text wrapping to Square.

j. Apply Heading 2 styles to the four tips as shown in the example.

k. Replace the three dashes following each tip heading with an em dash character.

l. If necessary, resize the photo and make other changes to make the layout of your document similar to the example. Save the newsletter. Print the newsletter.

Lifestyle Newsletter ★

2. The Lifestyle Fitness Club's newsletter for this month will focus on spinning, to highlight the new classes available at the clubs. The newsletter will describe the benefits of taking spinning classes. Your completed newsletter should be similar to that shown here.

a. Open the files wd04_Lifestyle Spinning, wd04_Fitness Club Headline, wd04_Banner, and wd04_Heart Rate Monitors.

b. Copy the contents of the wd04_Fitness Club Headline document, wd04_Banner, and the wd04_Heart Rate Monitors document into the Office Clipboard. Close these three files.

c. From the Office Clipboard, paste the "A Publication for . . . " entry into the wd04_Lifestyle Spinning document above the first heading.

d. Change the title's WordArt style to WordArt style 11. Change the shape fill to Purple, Accent 4, Lighter 40% with a light variation gradient of linear up. Change the shape outline to Black, Text 1. Change the shadow style to Shadow Style 5.

e. Select the subtitle text and format to bold, italic, 14 pt and dark red. Change the character spacing to expanded by 1.5 pt.

f. Save the new newsletter file as Spinning Newsletter.

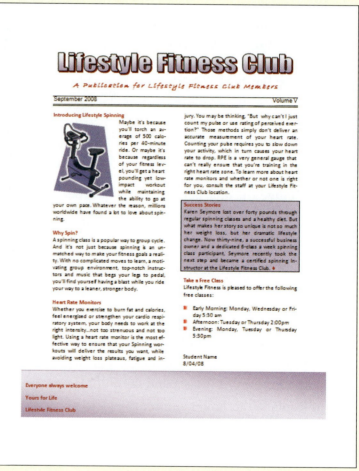

g. From the Office Clipboard, paste the "Heart Rate . . . " entry into the Spinning Newsletter document just above the heading "Success Stories."

h. Set the newsletter text to two columns, automatic hyphenation, and justified.

i. Insert the graphic wd04_Bike at the beginning of the first column. Change the text wrapping to Square. Position the graphic to the left side of the text below the heading.

j. Select the first article heading and format it to bold and dark red. Save the style of this selection as a new Quick Style and apply this new style to all the other headings. Remove any black lines below the headings.

k. Add a black boxed border around the entire Success Stories title and text and fill it with a Purple, Accent 4, Lighter 60% shading.

l. Insert a dark red symbol of your choice at the end of the Success Stories story.

m. Add a custom bullet of your choice before the three items under the "Take a Free Class" topic. Align the bullets with the left column edge. Starting two lines below the last bullet, insert your name and today's date.

n. Insert an Annual Sidebar text box at the bottom of the second column. From the Office Clipboard, paste the "Everyone always . . . " entry into the sidebar. Format the text as bold and Dark Red and apply the Diagonal gradient, Accent 4 Text Box style. Size and position the sidebar and make any other adjustments needed to make the layout of your document similar to the example.

o. Save the changes. Print the newsletter.

Lab Exercises

Cafe Promotion Newsletter ★★

3. The Downtown Internet Cafe would like to use a newsletter to promote its services and products. The newsletter will highlight some of the things people can do at the cafe and describe four coffees the cafe plans to feature each month. Your completed newsletter should be similar to that shown here.

The Downtown Internet Cafe

A Newsletter for Coffee Lovers of the World

Spring 2008   **Volume II**

The Downtown Internet Cafe combines the delicious aromas of a genuine coffeehouse with the convenience of wireless Internet access. The Cafe offers the latest in technology while maintaining the atmosphere of an old time coffeehouse and much more. Enjoy flavored coffees, cappuccino, espresso, lattes, aromatic teas, and tempting desserts, while you enjoy the convenience of easy and fast Internet access.

Buy our Beans!
The Downtown Internet Cafe is celebrating National Coffee Day all month with educational seminars, tastings, and of course a great sale on beans!

Things to Do in the Café
Sit comfortably at one of 30 Pentium - PC stations with access to the Internet via high-speed T1 modem connection. Or connect wirelessly to our high

speed network with you own computer. Our machines are equipped with the latest software for word processing, database, spreadsheets, and graphics software. And don't forget the games!

Our menu includes a fine selection of gourmet coffees, fresh salads, sandwiches, soups, pastries and cookies to get you through the day. You can also purchase our freshly roasted and ground coffee to take home.

Why Choose Free Trade Coffee Beans?
Much has recently been made in the press about Fair Trade Coffee Beans, but we are finding many of our customers are still confused about what it means to buy Fair Trade Coffee.

What is Fair Trade?
Fair Trade is a trade partnership that provides coffee growers a minimum price per pound for their beans.

Why Should I Choose Fair Trade Beans?
When you buy Fair Trade beans you are participating in a system that guarantees the grower will see a profit for his or her hard work. Without this sort of guarantee it is difficult for growers to meet their costs in the face of world food conglomerates. Fair Trade makes it possible for farmers to earn a living wage in their country, for small growers to maintain biodiversity in delicate ecosystems, and for coffee consumers to buy quality beans!

e Reviews

nth in our new-
ve review the
fees we are fea-
n the café
out the month.
fees are rated on
int scale in a
ste test. Stop by
by a cup.

ANS
Lake Toba area of
umatra Province,
a, Indonesia.

7
6
6
8
ste: 6

nent: A solid,
ng-on-classic Su-
rofile: low-toned
, pleasantly pru-
istinct pungency
om bitterness by
ness that grows
r as the coffee

GREAT NORTHERN GOURMET COFFEES
Origin: Lake Biwa region, Aceh Province, northern Sumatra.

Aroma: 6
Acidity: 5
Body: 7
Flavor: 5
Aftertaste: 5

Assessment: Assuming classic and earthy are not mutually exclusive terms, this is a classically earthy Sumatra: a round, muted but full earth taste gently dominates the profile. Apparently the earth taste comes from drying the coffee directly on the ground rather than on tarpaulins. Although the earth tones are wonderfully soft, overall the profile suffers from a slight bitterness.

TIMOTHY'S WORLD COFFEE
Origin: Lake Toba area of North Sumatra Province, Sumatra, Indonesia.

Aroma: 7
Acidity: 7
Body: 8
Flavor: 6
Aftertaste: 6

Assessment: Rich, burgundy-like fullness, gathering under the back edges of the tongue, with just enough acidity to set off dark tickles and echoes. However, a slightly bitter and salty aftertaste gave away this coffee's weakness, which became abundantly clear as the cup cooled.

NEW WORLD COFFEE
Origin: Lake Toba area of North Sumatra Province, Sumatra, Indonesia.

Aroma: 9
Acidity: 5
Body: 6
Flavor: 7
Aftertaste: 6

Assessment: A rather refined profile, lighter and sweeter than most Sumatras, with clean hints of fruit and flowers under the usual Sumatra pungency.

Student Name
2/3/08

a. To create the newsletter, open the file wd04_Coffee. Create a WordArt headline at the top of the document with the words The Downtown Internet Cafe. Choose an appropriate shape and color and adjust the size to fit between the margins.

b. Type, center, and bold "A Newsletter for Coffee Lovers of the World" below the WordArt. Format the line to 14 point and italic. Expand the character spacing of this line by 1 point.

c. Type and bold Spring 2008 and Volume II on the next line. Add a right tab at the right margin and indent "Volume II" to this position. Add appropriately colored rules above and below the date and volume text line.

d. Save the document as Internet Cafe Newsletter.

e. Select the text beginning at the first paragraph and ending just before the heading "Coffee Reviews." Apply two-column format to this selection and insert a page break before the heading "Coffee Reviews."

f. Apply a three-column format to the remaining text with spacing of 0.3 inch and equal columns.

g. Apply automatic hyphenation to all the text in the file.

h. Apply the Heading 2 style to the headings "Buy Our Beans," "Things to Do in the Cafe," and "Coffee Reviews."

i. Apply the Subtitle Reference style to the names of the four featured coffees in the Coffee Reviews article.

j. Create a text box around the Fair Trade story (beginning with the heading "Why Choose Free Trade Coffee Beans" and ending with " . . . buy quality beans!") Add bold to the topic headings in the text box. Reduce to 10 pt the font size of the content below each topic heading. Size the box to fully display the text. Change the text wrapping to Square. Move the text box to the bottom of column two on page one.

k. You want to draw attention to the topics discussed in the text box using a fill effect. Apply a two-color gradient fill effect of your choice to the text box.

l. Insert the picture wd04_City above the first paragraph. Change the text wrapping to Top and Bottom. Increase the picture's brightness and contrast as needed.

m. Insert the clip art wd04_Coffee Beans above the "Coffee Reviews" heading. Increase the picture's brightness and contrast as needed. Change the text wrapping to Square and size it appropriately.

n. At the bottom of column three, insert your name and today's date. Then insert the clip art wd04_Coffee Plant just below today's date. Change the text wrapping to Square and size it appropriately.

o. Adjust the layout of the newsletter as needed to be similar to the layout of the example. Save and print the document.

Animal Angels Newsletter ★ ★ ★

4. Animal Angels, the volunteer group for the Animal Rescue Foundation, sends a monthly newsletter to its members. You are helping to create this month's newsletter, which focuses on Pet Dental Care. Your completed newsletter will be similar to that shown here.

A Newsletter for Animal Rescue Foundation Volunteers

January 2008   Volume I

Pets Need Dental Care, Too!

During National Pet Dental Health Month each February, pet owners are reminded that dogs and cats need good oral care. An educational campaign to consumers, sponsored by the American Veterinary Medical Association and the American Veterinary Dental Society with an educational grant provided by Hill's Pet Nutrition, Inc., helps pet owners understand the importance of regular dental care for their pets.

Particularly at risk are small dog breeds, such as Pekingese and Shihtzu. Experts say these breeds are more likely to develop tooth problems because their teeth are crowded into small mouths. This can create a haven for plaque buildup.

Cervical line lesions (CLL) are the most common dental disease of domestic cats. Studies show that about 28 percent of domestic cats that veterinarians examine have CLL. Because the lesions often begin beneath the gumline, owners usually are unaware that there is a problem until the tooth is seriously damaged.

Prevention

Prevention is the key to helping pets maintain good oral health. The American Veterinary Dental Society recommends that pet owners follow three important steps:

Visit Your Veterinarian

Just as dental visits are the cornerstone of a human dental program, visiting a veterinarian is the key to ensuring the health of your pet's teeth. A veterinarian will conduct a thorough physical examination of your pet as part of the dental evaluation.

Get Regular Veterinary Dental Check-ups

The family veterinarian needs to monitor the progress of your pet's preventive dental care routine much the same way a dentist monitors your teeth. Regular dental check-ups are essential.

Once a pet's teeth display the warning signs -- bad breath, a yellow brown crust of tartar around the gumline, pain or bleeding when the pet eats or when you

gums -- gum disease may already ent. For a professional dental , call your veterinarian today!

isk: Bad Breath Isn't Funny

ught the guest by surprise in the om. He planted a big, breathy on her face. "Ugh! Dog breath!" erupted in laughter.

o funny the next day when Frisco yearly check-up. The 2-½-year-was diagnosed with gum disease, as in danger of losing a tooth if he egin a regular dental care pro-

g to the American Veterinary ciety, Frisco's case is not unique. how that more than 80 percent of age three and 70 percent of cats ree show some signs of gum dis-breath could be an early warn-of the dangerous gum disease

tal Disease

n 85% of dogs and cats that are at ars old have a condition in which attack the soft gum tissue. Peri-disease is the final stage in a process that begins with the development of plaque on your pet's teeth. Plaque is a substance that forms when bacteria multiply on the teeth and gums. Plaque mixes

with saliva, hardens, and becomes the substances known as tartar and calculus. Bacteria, plaque, tartar, and calculus irritate the gums, which become tender, red, and swollen. This stage of dental disease is called gingivitis. Eventually inflamed gums separate from the teeth, creating pockets that can trap more bacteria. These pockets deepen and bacteria may attack the roots of the teeth and the bony tissue of the jaw, causing teeth to loosen, the gums to bleed, mouth odor, and pain when your pet eats. This is full-blown periodontal disease.

Bacteria from the teeth and gums can enter the bloodstream and may travel to major organs and begin infection there. Among organs that are most often affected are the lungs, heart, kidneys, and liver. Parts of the nervous system may be affected as well. Although these infections are usually treatable when caught at an early stage, they can cause serious damage to these organs and, if not caught in time, may cause death.

Start a Dental Care Routine at Home Removing plaque regularly from your pet's teeth should be part of your pet's home dental care routine. Ask your veterinarian about the procedure for brushing your pet's teeth. Dog owners also may feed specially formulated dietary foods that help reduce the accumulation of plaque and tartar from teeth when the pet eats. Your veterinarian can offer more information on dietary options or visit the www.amva.com web site.

Student name
2/5/08

a. To create the newsletter, open the file wd04_Dental Care. Change the document theme to one of your choice. Create and center a WordArt headline at the top of the document containing the words "Animal Angels." Choose a design and colors of your choice to coordinate with your selected theme colors. Adjust the size of the WordArt appropriately.

b. Center and bold "A Newsletter for Animal Rescue Foundation Volunteers" below the WordArt in a font of your choice. Format the line to 12 points and expand the character spacing by 1 point. Enter and bold "January 2008" and "Volume I" on the next line. Add a right tab at the right margin and indent "Volume I" to this position.

c. Add appropriately colored rules above and below the date and volume text line.

d. Insert a blank line below the date and volume text line and a continuous section break below the first paragraph. Change the layout to two columns for the remaining text.

e. Save the document as ARF Newsletter.

f. Open the files wd04_Bad Breath and wd04_Periodontal Disease. Using the Office Clipboard, copy the text in each document. Then, paste the bad breath text and periodontal disease text, in that order, to the bottom of the newsletter. Close the files.

g. Insert the graphic wd04_Paws above the Prevention heading in the first column on page one. Change the wrapping style to Top and Bottom and size and center the graphic. Insert the graphic wd04_Checkup below the Visit Your Veterinarian paragraph. Change the wrapping style to Top and Bottom and size the graphic if necessary. Insert the graphic wd04_Dog with Vet above the Periodontal Disease heading on page two. Change the wrapping style to Top and Bottom.

h. Apply a three-line drop cap to the "D" in "During" at the beginning of the first paragraph. Add color to the drop cap to match the WordArt object. Change the font of the drop cap to one of your choice. (Hint: Select the drop cap and choose the font and font color on the Home tab.)

i. Change the heading styles of all topic headings to Heading 3. Apply the Title heading style to the first heading in the newsletter.

j. Apply automatic hyphenation to and justify all the text in the file.

k. You want to highlight the paragraph on "Start a dental care routine at home" on page one, so you decide to create a text box. Select the whole paragraph including the heading. Create a text box. Move and size it to fill the length and width of the space below the last paragraph on page two.

l. Apply a text box style of your choice.

m. Enter your name and the date below the text box. Adjust the layout of the newsletter as needed to be similar to the layout of the example. Save and print the document.

Lab Exercises

Hiking Newsletter ★★★

5. Adventure Travel Tours publishes a monthly newsletter to highlight upcoming trips and keep clients informed on unique travel opportunities. You are helping to create this month's newsletter, which features information on the Triple Crown hike and explains lightweight backpacking principles. Your completed newsletter will be similar to that shown here.

The Adventure Traveler

The Adventure Travel Tours Newsletter

March 2009   Volume IV

Triple Crown Challenge

Adventure Travel Tours, your premier active adventure vacation planner, is proud to announce three new adventure tours: Lightweight Backpacking Expeditions on the Pacific Coast Trail, Appalachian Trail, and Continental Divide Trail. At over 2000 miles long each, these three trails represent some of the greatest adventures available in the United States!

In order to guarantee your success on these challenging adventures, Adventure Travel Tours is embarking

on several qualifying lightweight backpacking trips to Death Valley, Paria Canyon, Bryce to Zion, Brian Head and Capitol Reef Park. We invite you to join us on these exciting adventures and find out if the Triple Crown is the quest for you!

Why Go Lightweight?

Any hiker will tell you: cutting weight is of utmost importance when you plan on hiking miles in the wilderness with all of your possessions strapped to your back. Accordingly, there are many "tricks of the trade" diehard backpackers use to cut weight from their packs. Some cut the handles from their toothbrushes, others trim the margins from their maps, and other hikers have been known to hike 2000 miles on granola and candy bars to avoid the weight of a cook stove and fuel. Yet most hikers don't flinch when it comes to buying the latest heavyweight hiking boots, pack, or tent.

Most gear is heavy and heavy duty, but all of this durability adds weight to our gear. Backpackers have begun to rethink their actual needs when out in the wilderness with an eye on reducing weight. These adventurers hike in tennis shoes, sleep under the stars, and dehydrate their own high energy food.

Continued on page 2

Impact Adventuring

...ng light doesn't just refer to the ...we carry on our backs, it's also ...reading lightly and treating ...with care and respect. The ...ng tips are designed to lessen ...pact on the natural world when ...out adventuring:

...k it in, Pack it Out! Nothing is ...e discouraging than to ...ounter someone else's garbage ...ng your adventure in the ...ine wilderness. Make sure that ...ything you bring into the wild ...back out with you. Be a Good ...aritan and carry out any refuse ...find during your travels.

...Smarter. Never cut living trees ...for firewood! Always use an existing fire ring in areas where camp fires are allowed. Finally,

absolutely **do not** leave a camp fire untended.

• Leave only footprints, take only photographs! The only thing you should carry out of the wilderness that you didn't bring in with you is the remnants of someone else's high impact campground. Leave the wilderness in the wild!

• Stick to the Trail! When traveling on existing trails please walk single file and stick to the path. These principles protect the ground vegetation near well-traveled paths.

Continued from page 1

The philosophy behind lightweight backpacking is simple: less weight = more miles + more enjoyment. To become a lightweight backpacker you need only to analyze your needs with an eye on carrying the lightest weight, most durable, gear. Once you have scrutinized and evaluated your minimum requirements for comfort and safety, you can begin to look for lightweight gear to meet those needs.

Student Name
2/5/09

a. Start Word 2007 and open the file wd04_Hike Triple Crown.

b. Create a WordArt headline with the text "The Adventure Traveler." Adjust the size to fit between the margins.

c. Enter, center, and bold the text "The Adventure Travel Tours Newsletter" below the WordArt. Increase the character spacing of the line by 2 points.

d. Enter and bold the text "March 2009" and "Volume IV" on the next line. Add a right tab at the right margin and indent "Volume IV" to this position.

e. Add borders of your choice above and below the date and volume line.

f. Insert a blank line and a continuous section break before the first paragraph of the newsletter.

g. Select all the text, excluding the headline, and format it to two columns with 0.3-inch spacing and equal column width.

h. Save the document as ATT Hiking Newsletter.

i. Insert the graphic wd04_Trail at the top of the first column. Change the wrapping style to Square. Crop the left and bottom side of the image. Resize the image to the column width and move it below the first heading.

j. Insert a page break following the end of the text.

k. Create a text box in the second column of page one.

l. Open the files wd04_Lightweight and wd04_Low Impact. Copy the contents of both files into the Office Clipboard. Close both files.

m. Paste the "Why Go Lightweight" article in the text box. Paste the "Low Impact" article to the first column of page two.

n. Create a second text box in the second column of the second page. Link the two text boxes. Add borders and shading of your choice to the boxes. Size the text boxes to match the example with the added right-justified and italic text "Continued on page 2" at the end of the text box on page one and "Continued from page 1" at the top of the text box on page two.

o. Insert the graphic wd04_Forest into the first column of page two. Change the text wrapping style to Square.

p. Replace the bullets with picture bullets of your choice. Decrease the indent of the bullets and insert a blank line between each bulleted item.

q. Add symbols of your choice to the end of the "Why Go Lightweight?" and "Low Impact Adventuring" stories. Add color to the symbols. Insert your name and the date at the end of column two on page two.

r. Increase the brightness and contrast of the photos as needed.

s. Apply a heading style of your choice to all the article topic headings. Change the "A" in the first word of the first paragraph to a three-level drop cap. Adjust the layout of the newsletter as needed to be similar to the example.

t. Save the file and print the document.

Lab Exercises

on your own

Activity Newsletter ★

1. Prepare a two-page newsletter on an activity or club of interest to you. The newsletter should include the following features: drop cap, WordArt, column format, linked text boxes, and clip art and/or pictures. When you are finished, add your name and the current date at the bottom of the last column of the newsletter. Check the layout of your document and make adjustments as necessary. Save the newsletter as Activity Newsletter and print the document.

Creating a Newsletter ★★

2. You are an elementary education major and have written a report on the history of ice cream. Open the file wd04_Ice Cream. Use this file to create a newsletter for students who are learning about the history of products. Use the features you have learned in Word, including drop cap, WordArt, clip art, borders, colors, and text boxes, to create a newsletter that is both informative and visually appealing. When you are finished, add your name and the current date at the bottom of the last column of the newsletter. Check the layout of your document and make adjustments as necessary. Save your file as Ice Cream Newsletter and print the document.

PTA Newsletter ★★★

3. You are a member of the PTA at the local elementary school. The budget for the year has just been released and the parents are trying to accommodate requests from the teachers and staff for equipment and supplies. The parents decide that a fund-raiser will be necessary. In order to fund the purchases, the school has decided to hold an old-fashioned bake sale. You have volunteered to put together a newsletter advertising the event to be distributed to the students. Your completed newsletter should include WordArt, column format, and other graphic features. Add your name and the current date at the bottom of the last column of the newsletter. Save the newsletter as PTA Newsletter and print the document.

Garden Newsletter ★★★

4. The neighborhood that you live in has begun construction of a public garden in a previously vacant lot. You are the chairperson of the committee that raised the funds for the park. You and the other committee members have decided to distribute a newsletter updating the contributors and community on the park's progress. Your newsletter should have great visual appeal. Be sure to include WordArt and other graphic features, as well as photos of the garden. Add your name and the current date at the bottom of the last column of the newsletter. Save the document as Garden Newsletter and print it.

Creating a Personal Newsletter ★★★

5. Create a monthly newsletter with small articles on a topic of your choice. Use the Web or other resources to obtain information on your topic. Use the features you have learned in Word to create a newsletter that is both informative and visually appealing. Include features such as drop cap, WordArt, clip art, borders, colors, and text boxes. When you are finished, add your name and the current date at the bottom of the last column. Check the layout of your document and make adjustments as necessary. Save the document as My Newsletter and print it.

Using Templates and Creating Complex Tables, Charts, and Graphics

LAB 5

Objectives

After completing this lab, you will know how to:

1 Use and modify a template.

2 Group objects.

3 Create and enhance a complex table.

4 Change text and page orientation.

5 Perform calculations in a table.

6 Create and modify a chart.

7 Create a multilevel list.

8 Create a custom template.

9 Create an organization chart.

Adventure Travel Tours

In addition to the four new tours, Adventure Travel Tours offers many established adventure tours. The four most popular tours are the Amazon River Expedition, the Yukon Bicycling Tour, the Australian Outback Adventure, and the Continental Divide Hike. You need to prepare a memo for the regional manager that contains a table showing the sales figures for these four major tours for the past three years. In

addition, you want to include a strategy to increase sales for the four tours.

Your next project is to create a memo to announce the creation of a new department at Adventure Travel Tours. A new group of employees has been created to handle the Adventure Travel Tours Web site. Your memo will include an organization chart to introduce the new department and staff.

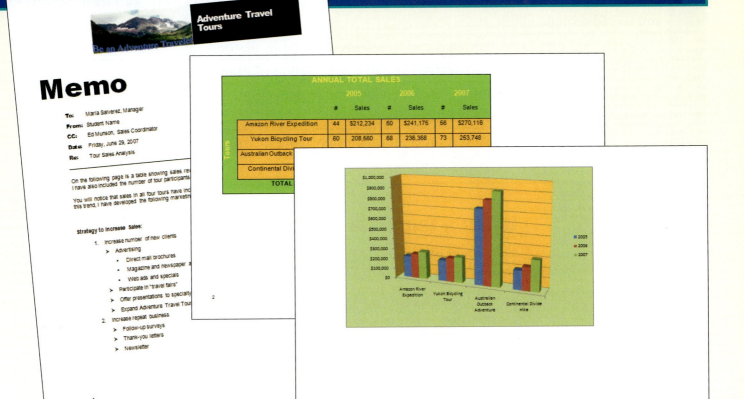

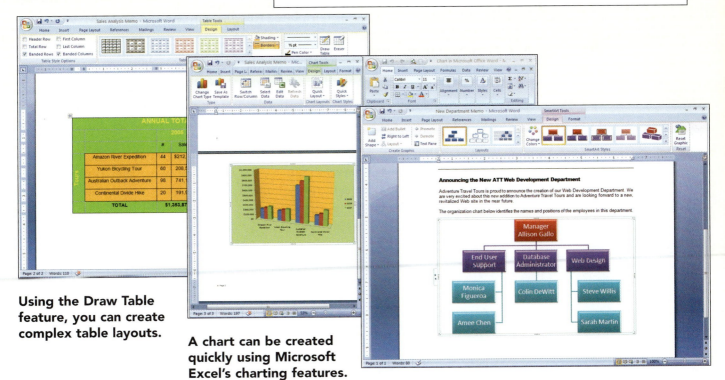

Using the Draw Table feature, you can create complex table layouts.

A chart can be created quickly using Microsoft Excel's charting features.

Organization charts can illustrate any type of concept that consists of a hierarchal organization.

1. **Stacking Order** Stacking order is the order objects are positioned in the drawing layer.

2. **Group** A group is two or more objects that are combined so that you can work with them as you would a single object.

3. **Formulas and Functions** Formulas and functions are used to perform calculations in tables.

4. **Chart** A chart, also called a graph, is a visual representation of numeric data.

5. **SmartArt** The SmartArt graphics feature includes many predesigned diagrams you can add to your document to illustrate textual concepts.

6. **Organization Chart** An organization chart graphically represents the structure of an organization.

Using a Template

You would like to create the sales-figure memo using one of the document templates included with Word. So far you have used the Normal document template to create many different documents. It includes many basic predefined settings. In addition to this template, Word also includes many other templates that are designed specifically to help you create professional-looking business documents such as letters, faxes, memos, reports, brochures, press releases, manuals, newsletters, resumes, invoices, purchase orders, and Web pages. Many of the templates are already installed and are available within Word. Many more are available at the Microsoft Office Online Templates Web page. Unlike global templates, the settings included in these specialized templates are available only to documents based on that template. You also can design and save your own document templates.

All template files have a .dotx file extension and are stored in the Templates folder. The Normal document template, for example, is named Normal.dotx. When you create a new document from a template file a copy of the file is opened and the file type changes to a Word document (.docx). This prevents accidentally overwriting the template file when the file is saved.

You will use one of Word's memo templates that is available at the Microsoft Office Online Web site as the basis for your sales-figure memo. Then you will change different elements in the memo template to give it your own personal style.

1 • Start Office Word 2007.

• Click 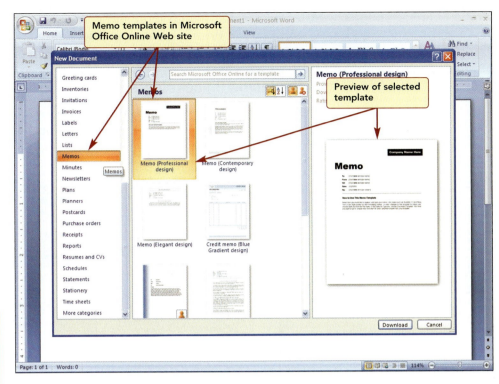 Office Button and choose New to display the New Document dialog box.

Additional Information
Word displays the Blank and recent templates.

• From the Microsoft Office Online section, choose Memos.

Having Trouble?
If you do not have access to Office Online, open the file wd05_Professional Memo from your data file location.

Your screen should be similar to Figure 5.1

Figure 5.1

Word displays a gallery of memo templates in different designs and the Preview area displays how the selected memo template looks. You will use the Professional Memo template to create your memo. Because this memo template is stored on the Office Online Web site, you need to download it to your computer. It will then open automatically for you in Word.

2 • If necessary, select the Memo (Professional design) **template**.

• Click Download .

• If the Microsoft Office Genuine Advantage dialog box appears, click Continue .

• If necessary, click OK to save the file to the Word 2007 file format.

• Change the zoom to Page Width.

Your screen should be similar to Figure 5.2

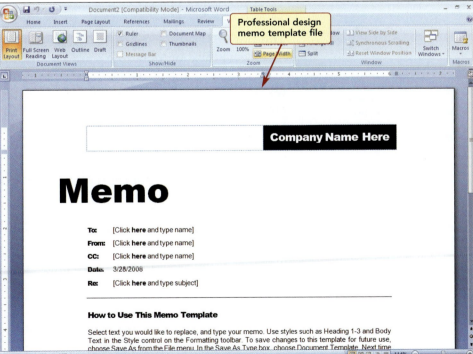

Figure 5.2

Using a Template   **WD5.5**

Word 2007

A copy of the memo template is opened as a new Word document and is displayed in Print Layout view. The template itself is saved to your computer so that you can open and use it again without having to download it again.

Replacing Placeholders

The template uses a single-row table to control the layout of the company letterhead and the Table Tools Design and Layout tabs are displayed. You will replace the placeholder text in the table cell with the company name.

1 • **If the table gridlines are not displayed, click** [☰ View Gridlines] **from the Table group on the Table Tools Layout tab.**

• **Select (highlight) the text Company Name Here.**

• **Type Adventure Travel Tours.**

Your screen should be similar to Figure 5.3

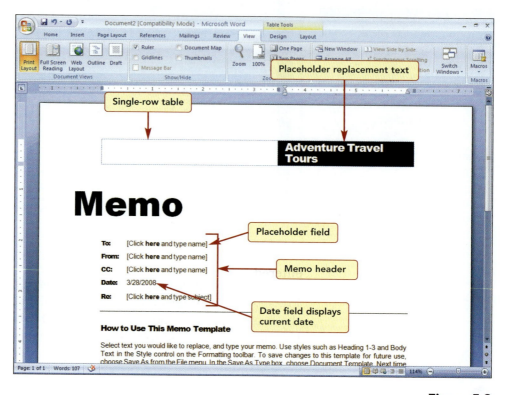

Figure 5.3

The next area in the memo template you need to modify is the memo header, which includes the name of the recipient, the sender's name, a carbon or courtesy (CC) copy recipient, the date, and a subject line. The text in brackets is a placeholder field for the information that needs to be entered at that location. The placeholder displays instructions about the text you are to enter. This feature is found in most templates. Notice that the date is the current system date. This is because the date entry is a date field.

You will enter the appropriate information in the memo header.

Additional Information

You can delete unwanted items from the memo template by selecting the object and pressing [Delete].

2 • Click the **To:** placeholder.

• Type **Maria Salverez, Manager.**

• Replace the remaining four placeholders with the following:

From: **Your Name**

CC: **Ed Munson, Sales Coordinator**

Re: **Tour Sales Analysis**

Your screen should be similar to Figure 5.4

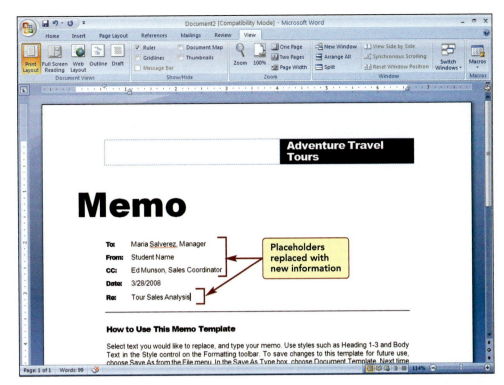

Figure 5.4

The four placeholders are deleted and replaced with the information you entered.

Modifying Field Formats

The date in the memo template is a field that displays the current system date. You want to change the date format to include the day of the week. To do this, you need to edit the field format.

1 • Right-click on the Date field.

• Choose **Edit Field.**

Your screen should be similar to Figure 5.5

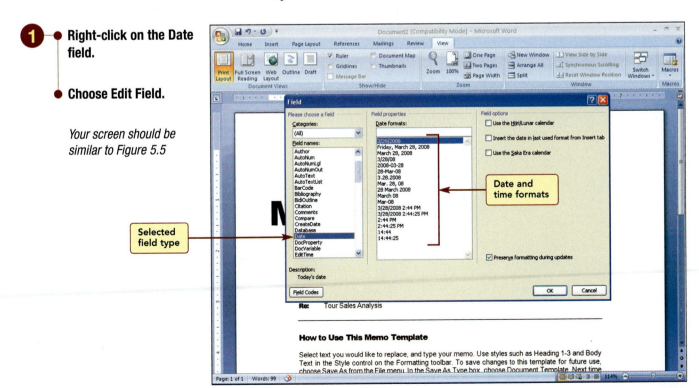

Figure 5.5

The Field dialog box displays a list of field names and formats for the selected field. Because the Date field is selected, the Time category is open and the available formats for date and time are displayed in the Field Properties area.

2 • **From the Date Formats list, select the format that includes the day of the week.**

• **Click** OK .

Your screen should be similar to Figure 5.6

Additional Information

If you type over the Date field with text, you will delete the field code from the document and the date will not update automatically.

Instructions on how to use template

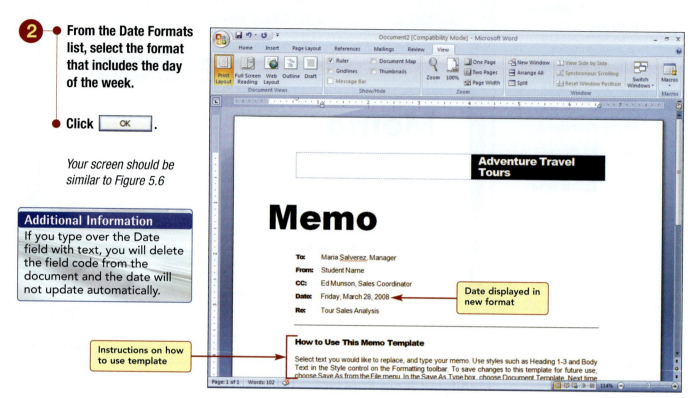

Date displayed in new format

Figure 5.6

Entering Body Text

Next you want to enter the body of the memo. The memo template also includes sample text containing instructions on how to use the template in the body of the memo. You will replace the sample text with the information you want to include in the memo. However, because the sample text is not a field, you first need to select the text to be deleted before typing the replacement text.

1 ● **Select the heading and the instructions paragraph.**

● **Type the following text: On the following page is a table showing sales revenue for the four major tours for the past three years. I have also included the number of tour participants for each year.**

● **Press ←Enter twice.**

● **Click 💾 Save and, if necessary, clear the checkmark from the Maintain compatibility with Word 97-2003 option.**

● **If necessary, click [OK] to continue and save the document as Sales Analysis Memo to your solution file location.**

Your screen should be similar to Figure 5.7

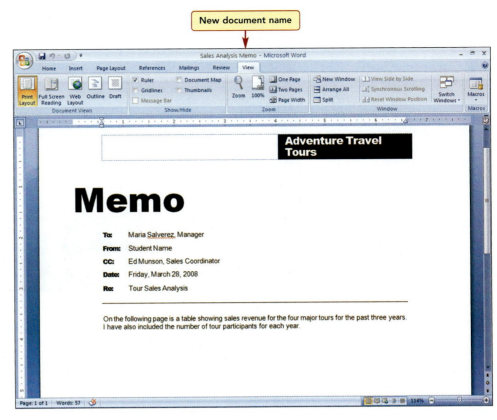

New document name

Figure 5.7

The template instructions are replaced with your own memo text. The memo is automatically saved as a document file with a .docx file extension. The original template file is unchanged on your computer so you can use it again to create another memo.

Creating a Company Logo

Next, you want to create a graphic to use as the company logo to display next to the company name in the letterhead. The logo will consist of a picture of a mountain and a WordArt object of the company slogan, "Be an Adventure Traveler."

Grouping Objects

Additional Information
See Concept 6: Text Wrapping in Lab 3 to review this concept.

You have saved the two graphic objects you will use to create the logo in a file. You will combine the two graphic objects into one object to use as the logo. To do this, you first need to change them from inline objects to floating objects by changing their wrapping style.

1 Open the file
wd05_Logo Elements.

Change the Text
Wrapping style of the
mountain picture to
Square.

*Your screen should be
similar to Figure 5.8*

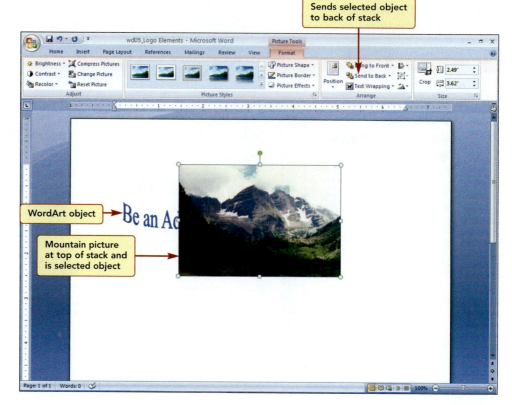

Figure 5.8

The mountain picture has been added to the drawing layer and is a floating object. It appears over the WordArt object, which is also a floating object in the drawing layer. This is because as objects are added to the drawing layer, they automatically stack in individual layers and may overlap.

Concept 1

Stacking Order

1 **Stacking order** is the order objects are positioned in the drawing layer. As each object is added to the drawing layer, it is added to the top layer. Adding objects to separate layers allows each object to be positioned precisely on the page, including in front of and behind other objects, including the text layer. You can cycle between objects in the stack and move objects to different levels within a stack.

Sometimes it is easy to lose an object behind another. If this happens, you can press [Tab⇥] to cycle forward or [⇧Shift] + [Tab⇥] to cycle backward through the stacked objects until the one you want is selected. To actually change the stacking order, you use [Send to Back ▾] or [Bring to Front ▾] on the Picture Tools Format tab. To see how this works, you will move the WordArt object back one position in the stack.

2 ● Click ⟦🖳 Send to Back ▾⟧ in the Arrange group on the Picture Tools Format tab.

● Press ⟦Tab ⇆⟧ to cycle forward through the stack and select the WordArt object.

Your screen should be similar to Figure 5.9

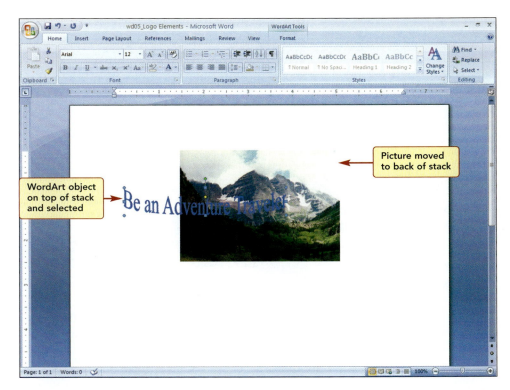

WordArt object on top of stack and selected →

Picture moved to back of stack ←

Be an Adventure Traveler

Figure 5.9

The WordArt object is now the first object in the stack and appears on top of the picture. The WordArt is selected because using ⟦Tab ⇆⟧ cycles forward one object at a time through objects in the stack.

Next, you want to group the two objects to create a single object.

Concept 2

Group

2 A **group** is two or more objects that are combined so that you can work with them as you would a single object. For example, multiple objects in a group can be rotated, flipped, or resized as if they were a single object. You also can change the attributes associated with the grouped object. **Attributes** are features such as line color and fill color that can be changed using drawing tools and menu commands. When an object is grouped, you can change the fill color of all objects in the group at the same time.

Many clip art images are composed of several different pieces that are grouped together. Sometimes you may want to ungroup an object so that the individual parts can be manipulated independently. Other times you may want to combine several objects to create your own graphic object that better suits your needs.

Selected drawing objects (ungrouped)

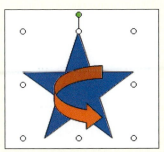

Selected drawing objects (grouped)

Additional Information

Some objects can be selected and grouped without first inserting them into a drawing canvas. To select objects that are stacked, click 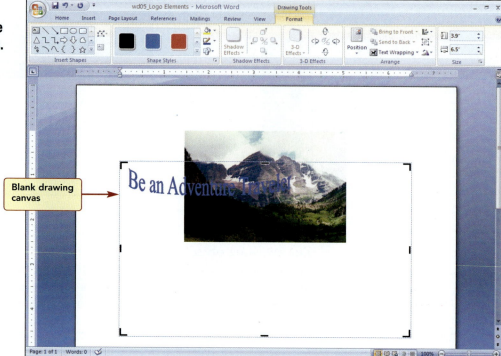 Select ▾ and choose Select objects and then draw a box over the shapes.

Because the objects you want to group include a picture object, you will first need to create a drawing canvas and then insert the objects in the drawing canvas. A drawing canvas acts like a container for graphic objects, keeping them together in a single place, much like a text box.

3 ● Click 🖳 on the **Insert tab and choose New Drawing Canvas.**

Your screen should be similar to Figure 5.10

Blank drawing canvas →

Be an Adventure Traveler

Figure 5.10

A blank drawing canvas box is drawn in the document. Next, you will cut and paste the objects into the canvas box.

4 ● Select and cut the picture.

● Click in the location of the drawing canvas to select it and paste the picture.

● Repeat the process for the WordArt object.

Your screen should be similar to Figure 5.11

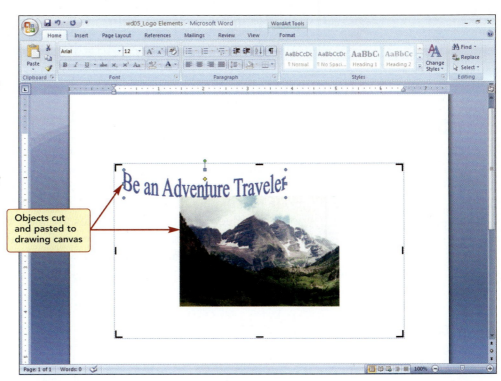

Objects cut and pasted to drawing canvas

Figure 5.11

The two objects have been added to the drawing canvas; however, they are still not grouped. You will position the two objects as you want them to appear and then select and group them next.

5 ● If necessary, click on the WordArt to select it.

● Hold down Ctrl and click on the picture to select it.

● Click ⊞ Align in the Arrange group on the Picture Tools Format tab.

● Choose Align Bottom.

● Click ⊞ Align and choose Align Center.

● Click ⊞ Group and choose Group.

Another Method
You also could select Grouping from the shortcut menu and choose Group.

Your screen should be similar to Figure 5.12

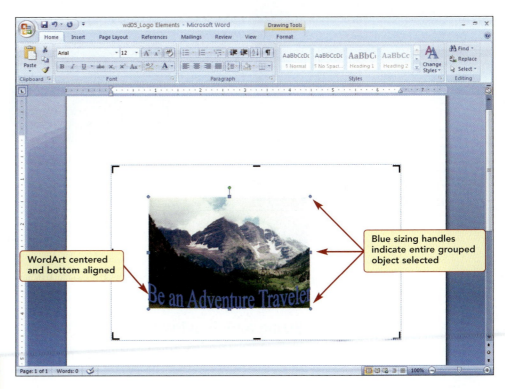

WordArt centered and bottom aligned

Blue sizing handles indicate entire grouped object selected

Figure 5.12

The WordArt is centered and aligned with the bottom of the picture and the two objects are grouped as a single object.

Modifying an Object within a Group

Now that the WordArt is on top of the picture, you decide to make the text color a lighter blue so that it will stand out better. To do this, you can modify the attributes associated with the individual WordArt object while it is still grouped.

Notice the sizing handles are blue 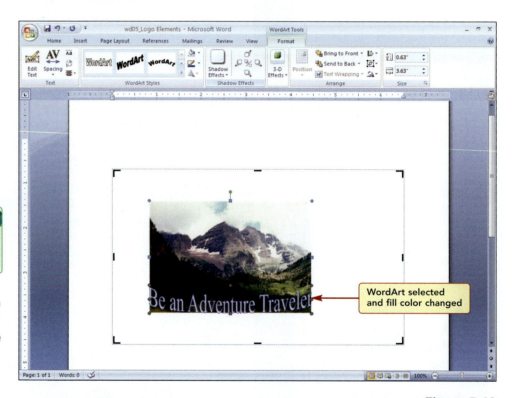 surrounding the object. This indicates that the entire grouped object is selected. When the entire grouped object is selected, you can then modify the grouped object using commands on the Drawing Tools Format tab.

You can select any single object within the group by first selecting the group and then clicking on the individual object. When an object within a group is selected, the sizing handles are gray with an 'X' in the middle. The toolbars and features that are available depend on the type of object within the group that is selected. You will cycle through selecting the different elements of the grouped object, and then you will modify the WordArt object.

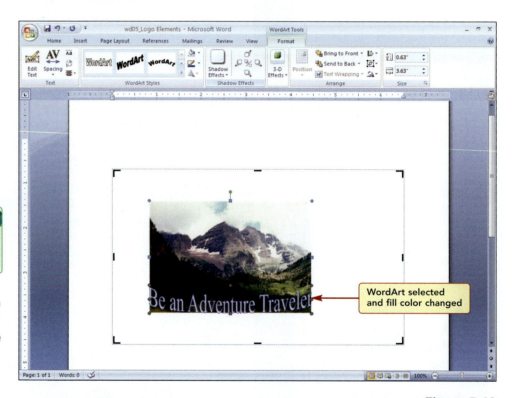

Figure 5.13

The text stands out better on the dark background now that the text color is lighter.

Sizing and Copying a Grouped Object

Next you will reduce the size of the grouped object and copy it to the memo. Because the objects are grouped, when you size and copy the object, it will act as a single object.

Additional Information

In some cases, you may need to ungroup an object before it can be modified. Use Ungroup to break a grouped object into its separate parts and Regroup to group it together again.

---

1 ● Click outside the grouped object to deselect it.

● Click the grouped object to select it.

● Click the WordArt object to select it.

Another Method

You also can press [Tab] to cycle from one object to another in a group.

● Change the fill color to Blue, Accent 1, Lighter 60% using ● Shape Fill on the WordArt Tools Format tab.

Your screen should be similar to Figure 5.13

WordArt selected and fill color changed

1 • Press [Tab ⇥] twice to cycle to select the grouped object.

• Reduce the size of the object to 1 inch high by 2.5 inches wide using the ⬚ 2.51" ⬍ Height and 🖉 ⬚ 3.64" ⬍ Width commands in the Size group of the Drawing Tools Format tab.

• Save the file as Logo Grouped to your solution file location.

Your screen should be similar to Figure 5.14.

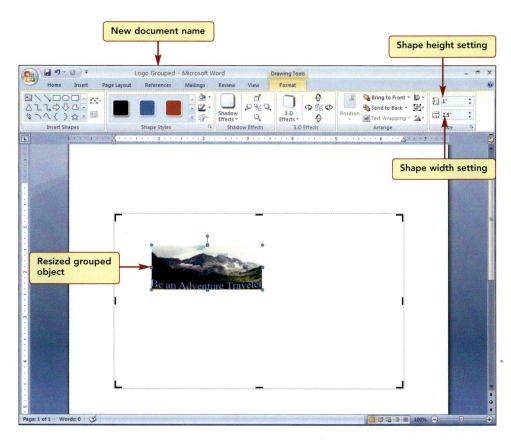

New document name

Shape height setting

Shape width setting

Resized grouped object

Figure 5.14

Now you are ready to copy the grouped object into the table containing the company letterhead of the memo. You also will need to change the text wrapping style of the object from in front of text to square.

2 • Copy the grouped object into the memo.

• Change the wrapping style to Square.

• Drag the object into the left cell of the table and position it next to the company name.

• Right-align the letterhead table as shown in Figure 5.15.

Having Trouble?
Select the table and click 📃 Align Text Right on the Home tab.

• If the table grid is displayed, click 📊 View Gridlines on the Table Tools Layout tab to hide them.

• Save the document.

• Close the file wd05_Logo Elements.

Your screen should be similar to Figure 5.15

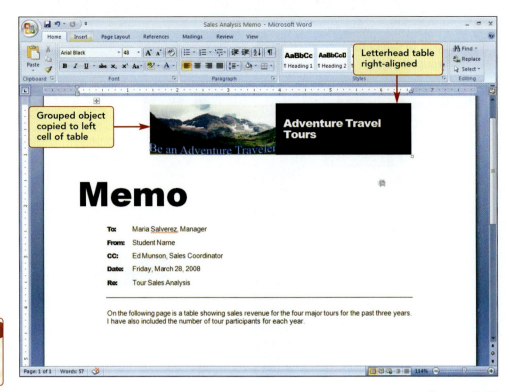

Figure 5.15

You will continue to refine the appearance of the letterhead later. You will continue to work on the memo content next.

Creating a Complex Table

Next, you want to create a table to display the tour sales data below the memo text. The table will display the data vertically (in columns) for the three years and horizontally (in rows) for the four tours and a total. Your completed table will be similar to the one shown on the next page.

Having Trouble?
Refer to Lab 3, Concept 7, to review tables.

ANNUAL TOTAL SALES						
	2005		2006		2007	
	#	Sales	#	Sales	#	Sales
Amazon River Expedition	44	$212,234	50	$241,175	56	$270,116
Yukon Bicycling Tour	60	208,560	68	236,368	73	253,748
Australian Outback Adventure	98	741,125	112	826,198	120	907,498
Continental Divide Hike	20	191,951	24	230,340	32	307,122
TOTAL		$1,353,870		$1,534,081		$1,738,484

Using Draw Table

You will use the Draw Table feature to create this table. The Draw Table feature can be used to create any type of table, but is particularly useful for creating a complex table like this. Using Draw Table to create a table is like using a pen to draw a table. The mouse pointer changes to 🖊 when positioned in the text area, and a dotted line appears to show the boundary or lines you are creating as you drag. First you define the outer table boundaries; then you draw the column and row lines.

1 ● Click [Table] on the Insert tab and choose Draw Table.

● Click below the paragraph and drag downward and to the right to create an outer table boundary of approximately 2$\frac{1}{2}$ inches high by 6 inches wide (refer to Figure 5.16).

Your screen should be similar to Figure 5.16

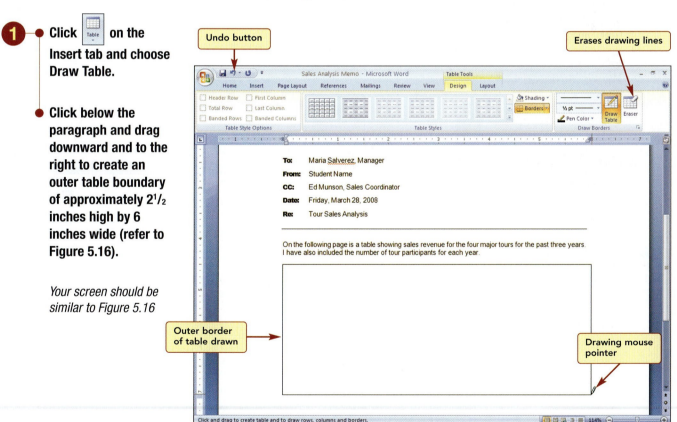

Figure 5.16

The outer border of the table is created. Next, you need to add lines to create the columns and rows. When creating row or column lines, drag from the beginning boundary to the end to extend the line the distance you want. A dotted line appears in the ruler to show your position in the table as you draw. If you make an error, click ↩ Undo or 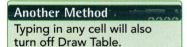 and drag over the line.

As you create the rows and columns in the next step, refer to Figure 5.17 for placement. Do not be concerned if your table does not look exactly like Figure 5.17 when you are done as you will learn all about adjusting table rows and columns in following steps.

2 ● **If necessary, display the ruler.**

● **Add four vertical column lines at positions 0.5, 3, 4, and 5 on the ruler (see Figure 5.17).**

● **Draw seven horizontal lines to create the rows as shown in Figure 5.17. (Lines 4, 5, and 6 begin at the first column.)**

Having Trouble?
Do not be concerned if your rows are not evenly sized, you will adjust them shortly.

● **Click** [Draw Table] **in the Draw Borders group of the Table Tools Design tab to turn off Draw Table.**

Another Method
Typing in any cell will also turn off Draw Table.

Your screen should be similar to Figure 5.17

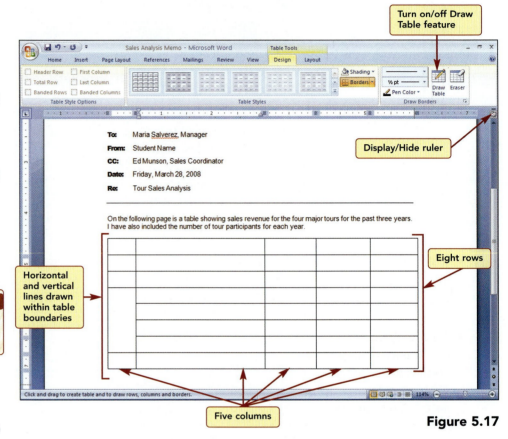

Turn on/off Draw Table feature

Display/Hide ruler

Horizontal and vertical lines drawn within table boundaries

Eight rows

Five columns

Figure 5.17

The table consists of eight rows and five columns. Now you are ready to enter information in the table.

3 Enter the labels and data in the cells as shown in Figure 5.18. (Include $ symbols in row 4 Amazon River Expedition sales values only.)

Your screen should be similar to Figure 5.18

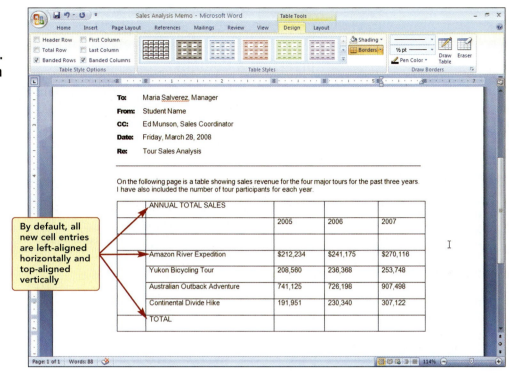

By default, all new cell entries are left-aligned horizontally and top-aligned vertically

Figure 5.18

By default, entries in cells are left-aligned horizontally and top-aligned vertically in the cell space. You want to center the year headings horizontally and right-align the sales values.

4 Select cells C2 through E2, containing the year headings.

• Click ▤ Align Top Center in the Alignment group of the Table Tools Layout tab.

• Select the cells containing the sales values and click ▤ Align Top Right.

• Click in the table to deselect the cells.

• Save the document.

Your screen should be similar to Figure 5.19

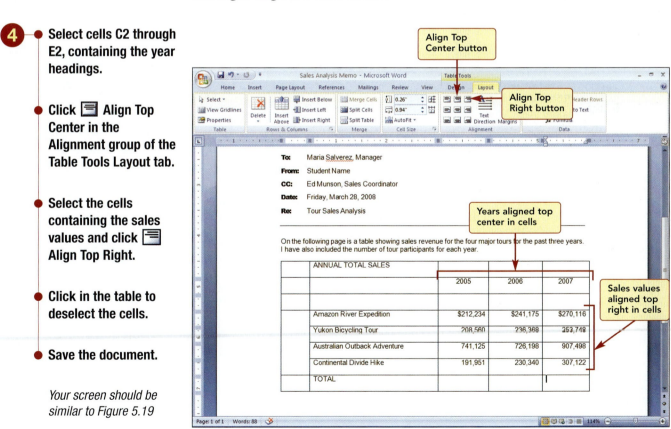

Align Top Center button

Align Top Right button

Years aligned top center in cells

Sales values aligned top right in cells

Figure 5.19

Creating a Complex Table   **WD5.19**

Word 2007

You will continue to add more formatting changes to improve the appearance of the table shortly.

Inserting a Column

You realize that you forgot to include columns for the number of people who took the tours in each year. To add this information, you need to insert three new columns to the left of the sales values. You can do this quickly using the Draw Table feature again.

1 ● Click 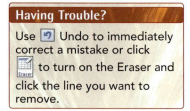 on the Table Tools Design tab.

● Using Figure 5.20 as a reference, drag to add three new columns at the 3.25, 4.25, and 5.25 positions extending from row 3 through row 7.

● Turn off the Draw Table feature.

Having Trouble?

Use ↩ Undo to immediately correct a mistake or click 🗒 to turn on the Eraser and click the line you want to remove.

Your screen should be similar to Figure 5.20

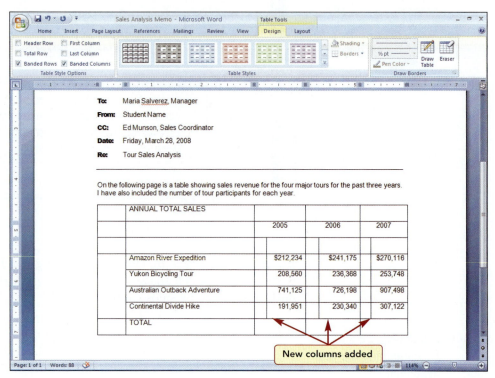

New columns added

Figure 5.20

If the overall table size is too narrow, adding the extra columns may make the sales value rows wider than the other rows in the table. Do not be concerned, as you will learn how to fix these features shortly.

You will enter the heading for the participants columns and the number of participants next. As you add information to the table, the columns will automatically resize to fit the data.

2 • Type **#** in cells C3, E3, and G3.

• Type **Sales** in cells D3, F3, and H3.

• Enter the following values in the cells specified.

	Col C	Col E	Col G
Row 4	44	50	56
Row 5	60	68	73
Row 6	98	112	120
Row 7	20	24	32

Your screen should be similar to Figure 5.21

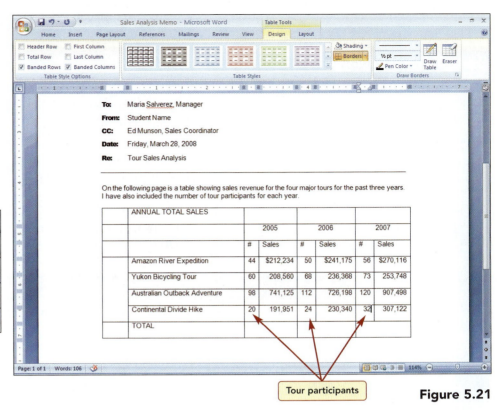

Tour participants

Figure 5.21

Performing Calculations in a Table

Now you want to calculate the sales revenue totals. Rather than adding the values for each column of data and entering them in the Total row, you can enter a formula to make this calculation for you.

3   Formulas and functions are used to perform calculations in tables. A **formula** is an expression that contains any combination of numbers, fields resulting in numbers, table references, and operators. **Operators** specify the type of calculation to perform. The most common operators are + (add), − (subtract), * (multiply), and / (divide).

To use the operators, follow the common arithmetic laws: multiply and divide before adding and subtracting, and calculate whatever is in parentheses first. For example, the formula 125 + D3 * D5 will multiply the value in cell D3 by the value in cell D5 and then add 125. If you want to add 125 to D3 and then multiply the result by D5, put 125 and D3 in parentheses: (125 + D3) * D5.

A **function** is a prewritten formula. One function you may use frequently is the SUM function. SUM calculates the total of a column of numbers. Other functions include

Function	Description
AVERAGE	Calculates the average of a column of numbers
COUNT	Totals the number of cells in the column
MAX	Displays the maximum value in the column
MIN	Displays the minimum value in the column

To reference cells in formulas and functions, use a comma to separate references to individual cells and a colon to separate the first and last cells in a range of cells. For example C1, C5 references the values in cells C1 and C5, whereas C1:C5 references the values in the range of cells C1, C2, C3, C4, and C5.

The calculated result of a formula or function is displayed in the table cell containing the formula or function. The result of the calculation is a field. Therefore, if the data in the referenced cells of the formula or function changes, updating the field quickly recalculates the result.

The formulas and functions in Word let you create simple tables and spreadsheets for your documents. For larger, more complex spreadsheets, use Excel and then paste the spreadsheet into your document.

Calculating a Sum

You will enter a formula to sum the sales revenue values in the 2005 column of data.

1 • Move to the Total cell for the 2005 year.

• Click 🖩 Formula in the Data group of the Table Tools Layout tab.

Your screen should be similar to Figure 5.22

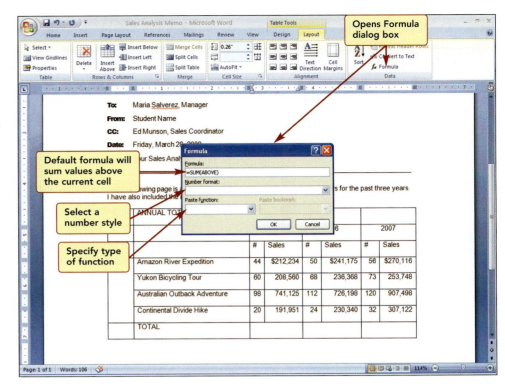

Figure 5.22

In the Formula dialog box, you enter the type of formula and the table cell references for the formula in the Formula text box. The function =SUM(ABOVE) is displayed by default because that is the only location of cells containing values to sum. The range reference ABOVE will calculate a sum for all values directly above the current cell. The Paste Function list box is used to select a different type of function if needed. You also can type the function or formula directly in the Formula text box. From the Number Format drop-down list box, you can select a number style.

You want to sum the values in the range of cells D4 through D7 (D4:D7) and will replace ABOVE with the specific table cell references.

In the Formula text box, replace the word ABOVE in the parentheses with D4:D7.

Having Trouble?
Double-click the word ABOVE to quickly select it.

Additional Information
The cell reference is not case sensitive. You could type D or d.

Click [OK].

Your screen should be similar to Figure 5.23

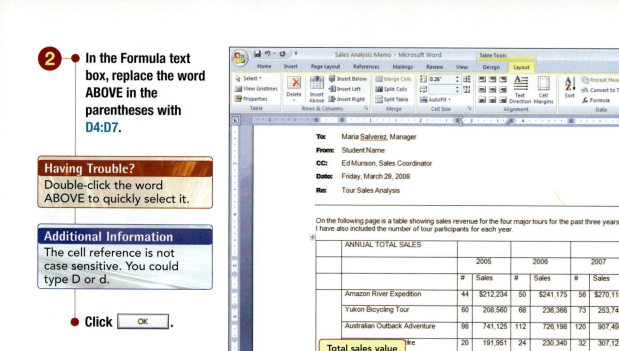

Figure 5.23

Having Trouble?
If your calculation shows a different value, check your entries and make sure you have (,) commas not (.) periods between your numbers.

Using the values in the specified cells of the table, the formula correctly calculates the result of $1,353,870.00. The value is automatically displayed in currency number format style. This is because the first value in the range displays a currency symbol and Word reflects this format by applying the currency number format to the calculated value.

3

In the same manner, enter a formula to calculate the 2006 and 2007 totals.

Having Trouble?
The cell range for 2006 is F4:F7 and for 2007 is H4:H7.

Your screen should be similar to Figure 5.24

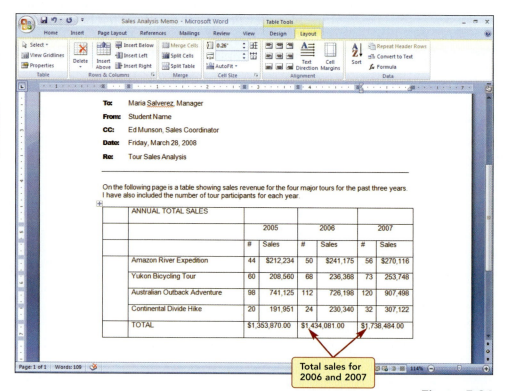

Figure 5.24

Updating a Calculation

As you look at the total, you think it seems a little low and decide to check the values you entered for the year. You see that the Australian Outback Adventure value was entered incorrectly. It should be 826,198. Because the calculated result is a field, after changing the value in the cell, you can quickly update the calculation.

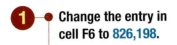

- Change the entry in cell F6 to 826,198.

- Click on the value in the 2006 Total cell and press F9 to update the field.

Another Method

You also can select Update Field from the field's shortcut menu.

Your screen should be similar to Figure 5.25

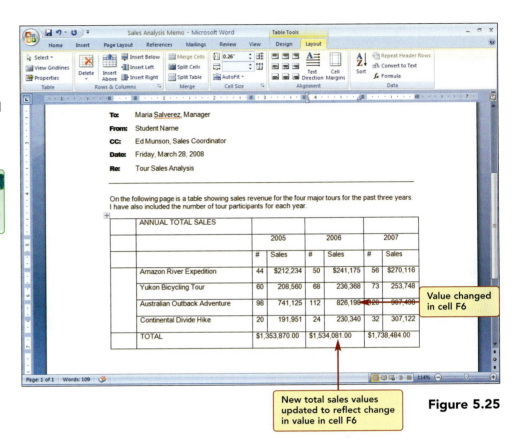

Value changed in cell F6

New total sales values updated to reflect change in value in cell F6

Figure 5.25

The correct calculated value of $1,534,081.00 is displayed in the cell.

Finally, you decide you do not want the two decimal places displayed for the three totals and will delete them.

2 ● Click in the field and delete the decimal and two decimal places from each of the three calculated results.

Having Trouble?
Click to the left of the decimal point and press Delete three times.

● Right-align the TOTAL label and total values.

● Save the document again.

Your screen should be similar to Figure 5.26

Additional Information
Because you did not change the format of the field, the decimal point and two decimal places will reappear if you update the field.

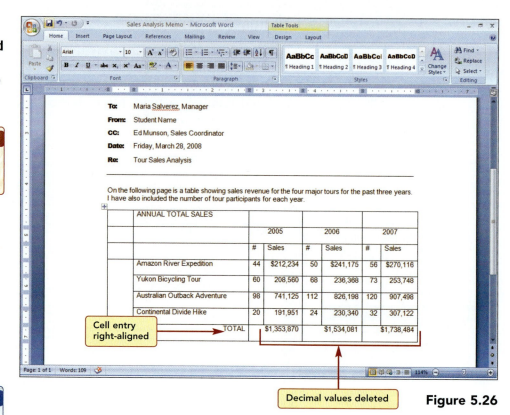

Cell entry right-aligned

Decimal values deleted

Figure 5.26

Enhancing a Complex Table

The table is really taking shape. Now that the content of the table is complete, you want to improve its appearance by enhancing the title, adding color, increasing the text size, and modifying the border lines.

Merging Cells

After looking at the table, you decide to display the title centered over all columns of the table. To do this, you will combine the cells in the first row to create a single cell and then center the label within the cell.

1 • Select row 1.

Having Trouble?
Click at the left edge of the row to select the entire row.

• Click Merge Cells in the Merge group of the Table Tools Layout tab.

• Click Align Top Center.

• Click in the cell to deselect it.

Your screen should be similar to Figure 5.27

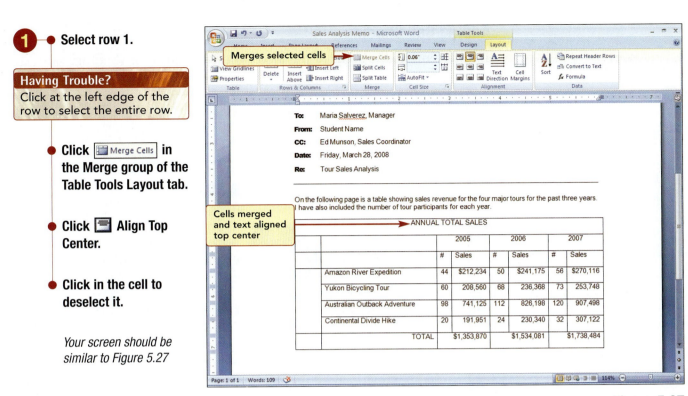

Figure 5.27

MORE ABOUT

To learn how to split cell contents, see 4.3 Modify Tables in the More About appendix.

The four column dividers were eliminated, and the top row is one cell. The entry is centered in the cell space.

Changing Text Orientation

In cell A4, you want to display the heading "Tours." You also want the heading to appear centered and the orientation to be vertical within the cell space.

1 • Enter Tours in cell A4.

• Click Text Direction in the Alignment group twice.

• Click Align Center.

Additional Information
Notice the graphic in the alignment buttons changed to reflect the text orientation of the selection.

Your screen should be similar to Figure 5.28

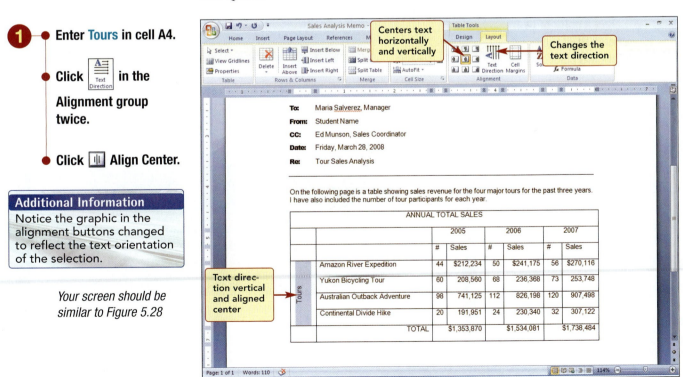

Figure 5.28

Enhancing a Complex Table

Adding Cell Shading

To differentiate the areas of the table, you will add color shading.

1 • Select the entire table.

Having Trouble?

You can click ⊞, or drag, or click 🔲 Select ▾ and choose Select Table to select the entire table.

• Open the 🖌 Shading ▾ drop-down menu in the Table Styles group of the Table Tools Design tab.

• Choose More Colors.

• If necessary, open the Standard tab.

Your screen should be similar to Figure 5.29

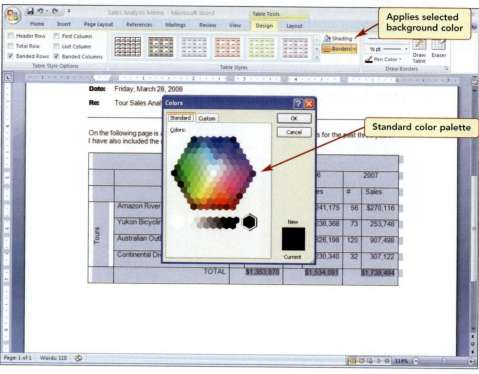

Figure 5.29

From the Colors dialog box, you can select from standard colors or create a custom color. The Standard tab palette includes many shade variations of the same colors that are included in the drop-down color palette list.

2 • Select a color of your choice from the standard color palette.

• Click OK.

• Select the tour names and sales values, and apply another shading color to the cells in this range.

• Deselect the range.

Your screen should be similar to Figure 5.30

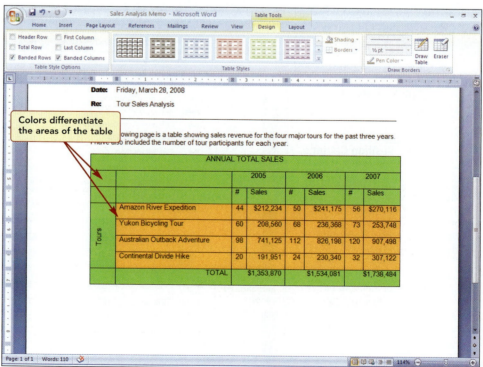

Figure 5.30

Next, you want to enhance the text of the headings and the table data.

3 • Select the table title and increase the font size to 16 points, and add bold with a color of your choice.

• Select the year headings and increase the font size to 14 points; add bold and the same color as the title.

• Apply the same formats to the Tours label.

• Select the remaining text in the table and increase the font size to 12 points.

• Center the # and Sales headings.

• Add bold to the TOTAL label and values.

Your screen should be similar to Figure 5.31

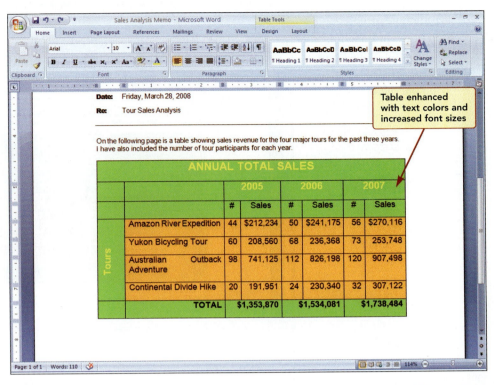

Figure 5.31

Changing Page Orientation

Although the increased point size has made the data in the table easier to read it now appears crowded. To improve the appearance of the table, you decide to make the entire table larger.

1 Select the table.

● Drag the sizing handle to the right to increase the width of the table to the 7-inch position on the ruler.

Your screen should be similar to Figure 5.32

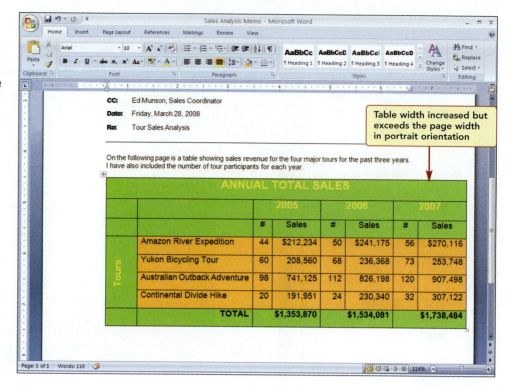

Table width increased but exceeds the page width in portrait orientation

Figure 5.32

MORE ABOUT

You also can change paper size to fit your content. See 1.2 Layout Documents in the More About appendix to learn about this feature.

Now the table is too wide to fit easily within the width of the page. When text is wider than the width of the page, you can change the orientation of the page from **portrait,** in which text is printed across the width of the page, to **landscape,** in which text is printed across the length of the page.

Because the memo will look better in the current orientation of portrait, you decide to display the table on a separate page that will print in landscape orientation. To have different orientations within a document, you need to insert a section break first, and then apply the orientation to the section you want affected.

2 • If necessary, insert a blank line above the table.

• Move to the blank line above the table.

• Click ⊞ Breaks ▾ in the Page Setup group of the Page Layout tab and choose Next page.

• Click ⬛ Orientation ▾ and choose Landscape.

• Change the zoom to Two Pages.

Your screen should be similar to Figure 5.33

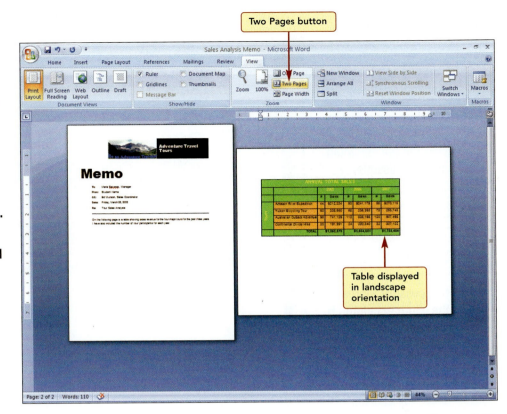

Two Pages button

Table displayed in landscape orientation

Figure 5.33

The entire table now easily fits within the width of the page.

Sizing Rows and Columns

Next, you want to decrease the width of column A. To change the width of a column or row, point to the column divider line and drag it to the right or left to increase or decrease the column width, or up or down to increase or decrease the row height. A temporary dotted line appears to show your new setting.

1 • Return the zoom to Page Width.

• Point to the right border of column A and drag to the left to decrease the column width to the minimum amount possible.

Additional Information
The mouse pointer appears as ‖ when you can drag to size a row or column.

• If necessary, increase the width of column B to display the tour names on a single line.

Your screen should be similar to Figure 5.34

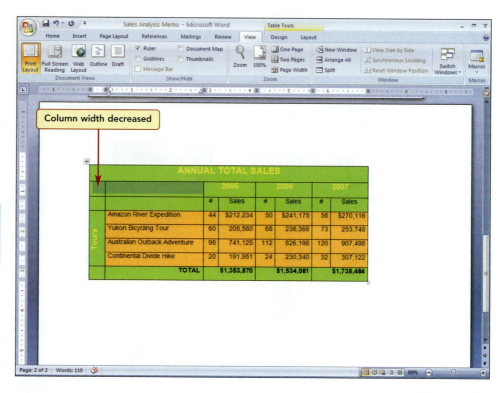

Figure 5.34

Next, you want to adjust the height of the rows to be equally sized.

2 • Select the entire table.

• Click ⊞ Distribute Rows in the Cell Size group of the Table Tools Layout tab.

• Click any cell in the table to deselect the table.

Your screen should be similar to Figure 5.35

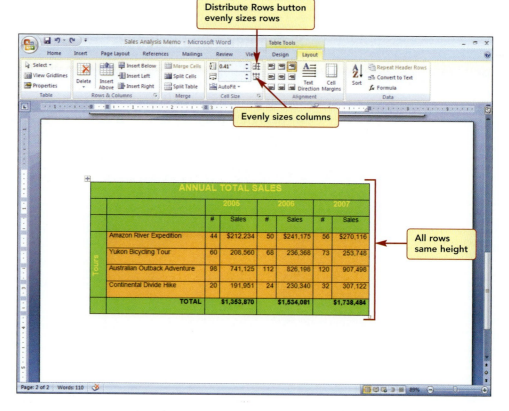

Figure 5.35

You also want the widths of the # columns to be the same and the widths of the Sales columns to be the same. However, because these columns are not adjacent, you cannot use the ▦ Distribute Columns command. Instead, you need to adjust each column individually.

3 ● Select the entire table.

● Point to the right column border of the 2005 # column until the pointer changes shape to +‖+.

● Drag the right column border line to adjust the column width to approximately 0.5 inch as shown in Figure 5.36.

● In a similar manner, increase the column width of the 2005 Sales column to approximately 1 inch.

Having trouble?
The total 2005 column width will be 1.5 inches.

Your screen should be similar to Figure 5.36

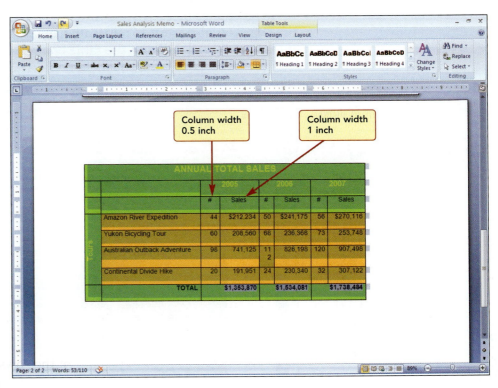

Figure 5.36

You want to make the same change to the other columns.

4 ● In a similar manner, change the column width for 2006 and 2007.

● Click any cell in the table to deselect the table.

Your screen should be similar to Figure 5.37

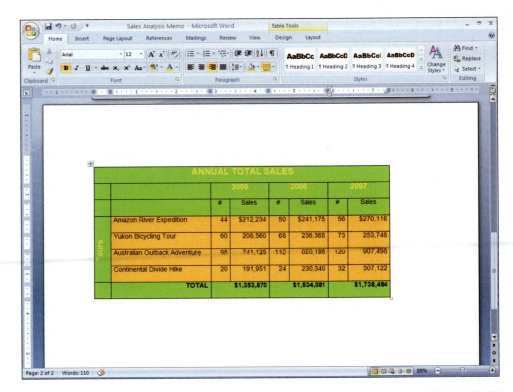

Figure 5.37

Changing Cell Margins and Centering Vertically

Although you have adjusted the size of the columns and rows, the table content still looks a little crowded. You will increase the cell margin space to increase the space between the boundary of the cell and the text inside the cell. You also want to vertically center the data in the table to further improve the readability of the table content.

1
- Select the entire table.

- Click [Cell Margins] in the Alignment group on the Table Tools Layout tab.

- Increase the Right margin setting to 0.15.

- Click [OK].

- Click [≡] Align Center.

- If necessary, adjust column widths as needed to display cell contents on a single line.

- Click in the table to deselect it.

Your screen should be similar to Figure 5.38

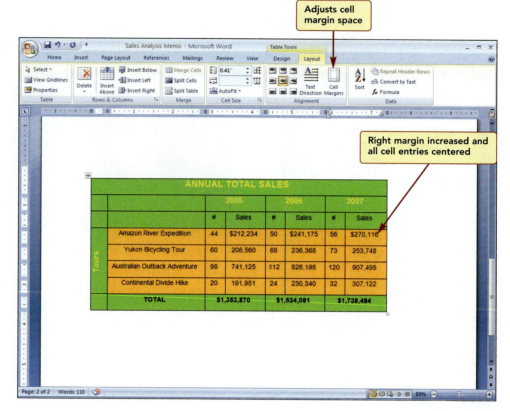

Figure 5.38

The extra margin padding on the right side of the cell makes the data much easier to read.

Removing Border Lines

When a table is created, single, black, 0.5-point solid-line borders are added by default around each cell. Once color and other formatting have been added to a table, you may no longer need all the border lines to define the spaces. You will remove the border line below row 1 first.

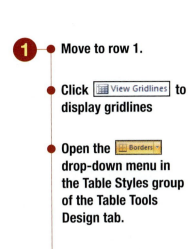

1 Move to row 1.

Click ![View Gridlines] to display gridlines

Open the ![Borders] drop-down menu in the Table Styles group of the Table Tools Design tab.

Click Bottom Border to clear the border line.

Additional Information
The Border drop-down menu identifies the border lines that are used in a selected cell by highlighting them.

Your screen should be similar to Figure 5.39

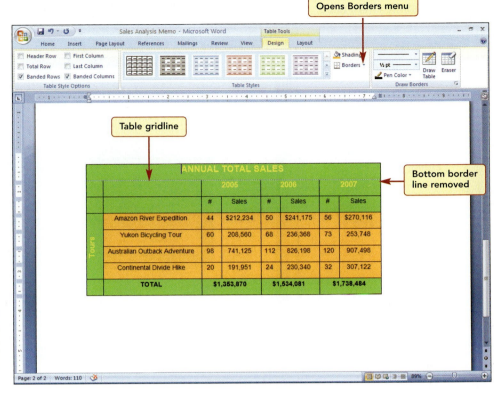

Figure 5.39

The border line is removed, but a gray gridline is still displayed. Gridlines are used to help you see the cell boundaries; however, they are not printed.

2 Remove the border lines from the cells as shown in Figure 5.40.

Additional Information
The Inside Border option quickly removes all inside border lines from a selection.

Your screen should be similar to Figure 5.40

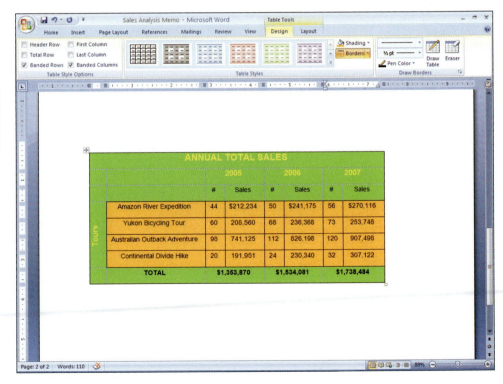

Figure 5.40

Finally, you want the table centered on the page.

3 ● Select the entire table.

● Click ▤ Center on the Home tab.

● Deselect the table.

● Save the document again.

Your screen should be similar to Figure 5.41

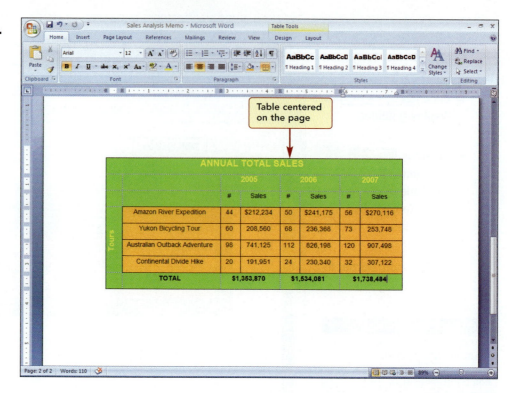

Figure 5.41

Note: If you are running short on time, this is an appropriate place to end this session.

Creating a Chart

Note: To complete this section, you will need to have Microsoft Excel 2007 installed on your computer.

As you look at the data in the table, you decide to include a chart of the data below the table, to illustrate the trends in sales.

Concept 4

Chart

4 A **chart**, also called a graph, is a visual representation of numeric data. Presenting data as a chart provides more impact than the data alone and makes it easier to see trends and comparisons. Office Word 2007 uses the Excel 2007 chart tools to create and modify charts. Charts that you create are embedded in the Word document and the chart data is stored in an Excel worksheet that is incorporated in the Word file. If Microsoft Excel 2007 is not installed, Microsoft Graft opens and is used to create charts.

Each type of chart represents the data differently and has a different purpose. It is important to select the type of chart that will provide the right emphasis to support the data. The basic chart types are described below.

Type of Chart		Description
	Column	Similar to a bar chart, except categories are organized horizontally and values vertically.
	Line	Shows changes in data over time, emphasizing time and rate of change rather than the amount of change.
	Bar	Displays categories vertically and values horizontally, placing more emphasis on comparisons and less on time. Stacked-bar charts show the relationship of individual items to a whole by stacking bars on top of one another.
	Area	Shows the relative importance of a value over time by emphasizing the area under the curve created by each data series.
	Pie	Shows the relationship of each value in a data series to the series as a whole. Each slice of the pie represents a single value in a data series.

Most charts are made up of several basic parts, as described in the following table.

Part	Description
X axis	The bottom boundary of the chart, also called the category axis, is used to label the data being charted; the label may be, for example, a point in time or a category.
Y axis	The left boundary of the chart, also called the value axis, is a numbered scale whose numbers are determined by the data used in the chart. Each line or bar in a chart represents a data value. In pie charts, there are no axes. Instead, the data that is charted is displayed as slices in a circle or pie.
Legend	A box containing a brief description identifying the patterns or colors assigned to the data series in a chart.
Titles	Descriptive text used to explain the contents of the chart.

Selecting the Chart Type

You decide a basic column chart will illustrate the sales data appropriately.

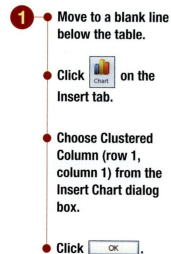

1. Move to a blank line below the table.

- Click **Chart** on the Insert tab.

- Choose Clustered Column (row 1, column 1) from the Insert Chart dialog box.

- Click **OK**.

Your screen should be similar to Figure 5.42

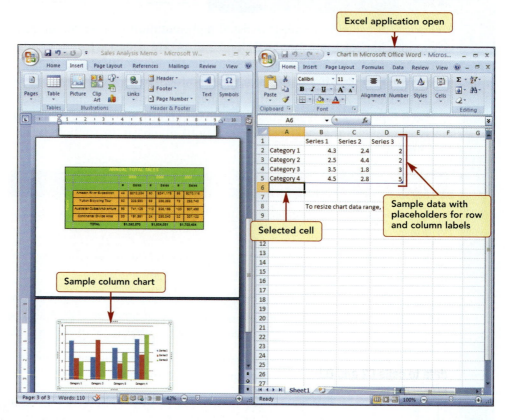

Figure 5.42

The Excel 2007 application is opened and displayed in a split window. A sample column chart was inserted into the Word document using sample data from the Excel worksheet. A worksheet is similar to a table in that it consists of intersecting rows and columns that create cells for holding data. The cell that is surrounded by the border is the selected cell and is the cell you can work in.

In addition to displaying sample data, the worksheet also contains placeholders for the row labels, which are used as the legend in the chart, and for the column labels, which are used as X-axis labels.

Specifying the Chart Data

Your first step is to replace the sample data in the worksheet with the data from the table. Rather than retype the data that is in the table, you will copy it into the Excel worksheet.

To specify the data in the table to use in the chart, you will copy the sales labels in row 3, the four tour names in column B, and the sales values for the three years in columns D, F, and H.

1 • **Select cells B4 through B7 in the table.**

• **Click** [icon] **Copy or press** Ctrl **+ C.**

• **Click on cell A2 in the worksheet to make it active and click** [icon Paste] **in the Excel Home tab or press** Ctrl **+ V.**

• **Copy the 2005 sales data in the table and paste it to cell B2 in the worksheet.**

• **In a similar manner, copy and paste the 2006 and 2007 sales data to cells C2 and D2 respectively.**

• **In the worksheet, drag the right border line of each column heading to the right to increase the size of the columns to fully display the data.**

Your screen should be similar to Figure 5.43

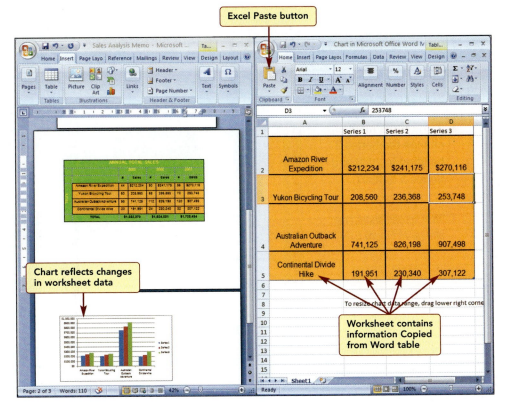

Excel Paste button

Chart reflects changes in worksheet data

To resize chart data range, drag lower right corne[r]

Worksheet contains information Copied from Word table

Figure 5.43

The data in the worksheet is updated to include the same data that is in the table, and the chart reflects the change in data. Next, you need to change the three remaining Series column headings to reflect the three years.

2 ● Click on cell B1 in the worksheet and type **2005** and press ⏎Enter to replace the Series 1 label.

● In the same manner, change the Series 2 heading to **2006** and Series 3 to **2007.**

Your screen should be similar to Figure 5.44

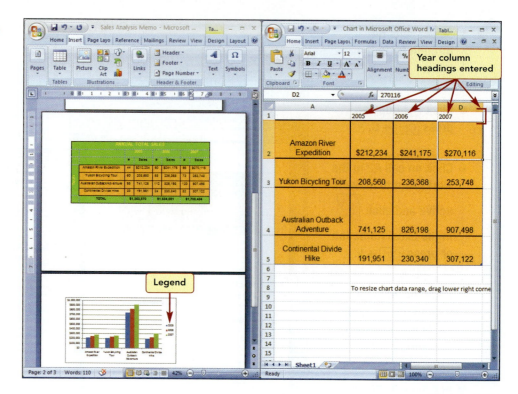

Figure 5.44

The legend in the chart in the document is updated immediately. Each group of related data that is plotted in the chart is a data series. Each data series has a unique color or pattern assigned to it so that you can identify the different series. The legend identifies the color or pattern associated with each data series. As you can see, the values and text in the chart are directly linked to the datasheet, and any changes you make in the datasheet are automatically reflected in the chart.

Sizing the Chart

Now that the data is specified, you can close the worksheet. Then you will increase the size of the chart.

1 • Close the Excel 2007 window.

• Move to page three of the memo to display the chart.

• Select the chart object and drag the lower right-corner sizing handle to increase the height and width of the chart.

Your screen should be similar to Figure 5.45

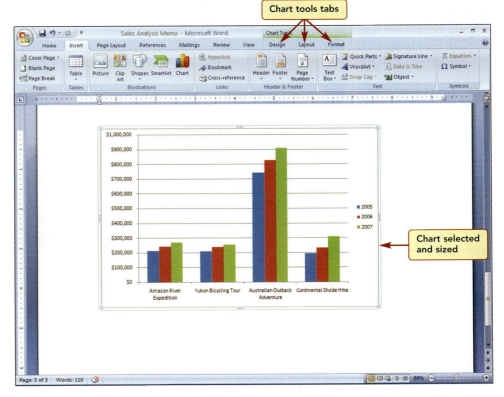

Figure 5.45

Modifying the Chart

As you look at the chart, you decide you want to change the default colors to colors that coordinate better with the table in the memo. You also want to add a 3-D effect to the chart. The three Chart tools tabs contain commands to help you format a chart.

First, you will change the background color of the plot area. To format different areas of the chart, you click on them to select them. The selected area is surrounded with selection handles and the name of the selected area appears in the Chart Elements text box.

Another Method

You also can select a chart area from the Chart Elements drop-down list.

1 • Click on the area behind the columns of data to select the plot area.

Additional Information
The mouse pointer ScreenTip displays the name of the chart element as you point to it.

• Click 🔲 Format Selection in the Current Selection group of the Chart Tools Format tab.

Another Method
You also can choose Format Plot Area from the selection's shortcut menu.

• Choose Solid Fill and open the Fill color palette and select a color of your choice.

• Click ⬜ Close .

Your screen should be similar to Figure 5.46

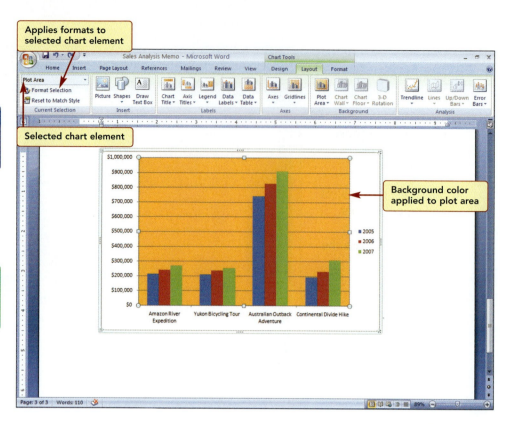

Applies formats to selected chart element

Selected chart element

Background color applied to plot area

Figure 5.46

You also want to change the background color of the chart area.

2 • Right-click on the white background of the chart.

• Choose Format Chart Area.

• Open the Fill color palette and select a color of your choice.

• Click ⬜ Close .

Your screen should be similar to Figure 5.47

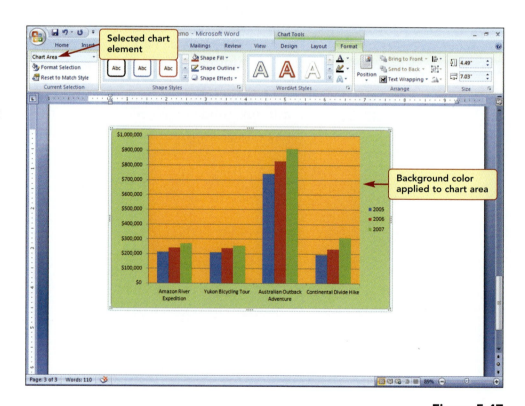

Selected chart element

Background color applied to chart area

Figure 5.47

Next, you want to change the type of column chart to display three-dimensional columns rather than flat columns.

3 • Click 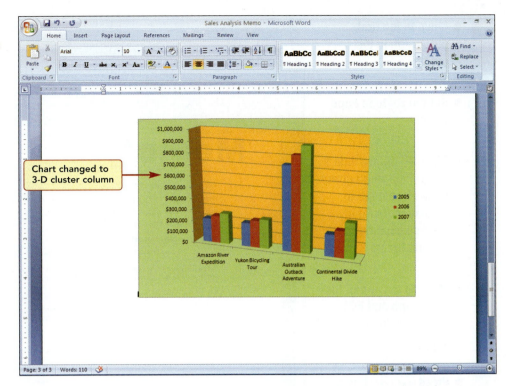 in the Type group of the Chart Tools Design tab.

• Choose 3-D Clustered Column (row 1, column 4).

• Click OK.

• Click ≣ Center on the Home tab.

• Deselect the chart object.

• Save the document again.

Your screen should be similar to Figure 5.48

Figure 5.48

The 3-D effect has been added to the columns. The changes you made to the chart greatly improve its appearance.

Creating a Multilevel List

Now that you have created the table and chart, you want to include in the memo a strategy on how to increase sales for the four major tours. On the first page, before the section break, you will add a lead-in paragraph and then you will enter the proposed strategy to increase sales.

1 ● Move to the first paragraph in the memo.

● Set the zoom to Page Width.

● Click ¶ Show/Hide ¶ in the Paragraph group on the Home tab to display paragraph marks including the section break.

● Move to the end of the paragraph and just before the section break.

● Press ⏎ Enter twice.

● Type: **You will notice that sales in all four tours have increased steadily over the past three years. To maintain this trend, I have developed the following marketing strategy.**

● Press ⏎ Enter three times.

● Type **Strategy to Increase Sales:.**

● Press ⏎ Enter.

Your screen should be similar to Figure 5.49

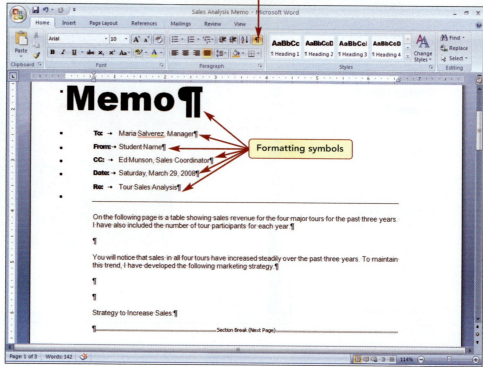

Button shows/hides hidden formatting symbols

Formatting symbols

Figure 5.49

The strategy consists of several main points and corresponding subpoints. The best way to add this information to your memo is to use a **multilevel list**, which applies a hierarchical structure to a list, similar to creating an outline. Unlike an outline, built-in heading styles are not applied to the items in the list. A multilevel list can be either numbered or bulleted or a mix of letters, numbers, and bullets with up to nine levels.

② ● Click ¶ to turn off paragraph marks.

● Click ⃞ Mulitlevel List in the Paragraph group.

● Point to the first list style to the right of None in the List Library.

Your screen should be similar to Figure 5.50

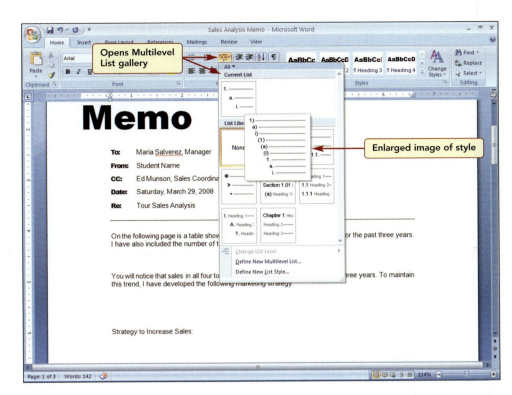

Figure 5.50

Additional Information
You also can create your own custom multilevel list style using Define New List Style and setting the characteristics for each level.

The List Library section of the Multilevel List gallery displays seven outline numbered-list styles. The styles include different variations of letters, numbers, bullets, and roman numerals. Because the document does not include a multilevel list, the None option is selected. Using None will remove an existing multilevel list style. Pointing to a style displays an enlarged image. You think the style you are currently previewing looks good and will use this style.

③ ● Click on the enlarged preview.

● Type **Increase number of new clients**.

● Press ⏎Enter.

Your screen should be similar to Figure 5.51

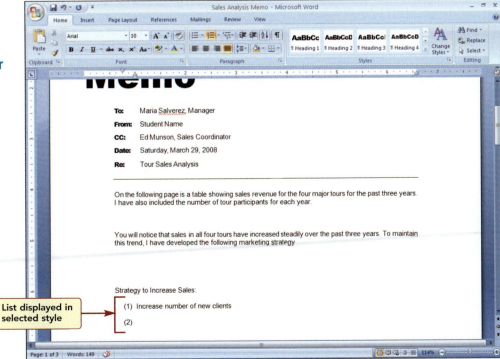

Figure 5.51

Changing the Level

The number (1) in the selected style is inserted for the first line, and the text following the number is automatically indented to the 0.25-inch position. The next line is automatically numbered (2) for the second entry at the same outline level. Next, however, you want to add the list of strategies as subtopics under the first level. They will be entered at a level two. To decrease the list level, you press [Tab⇥] or click 🔲 Increase Indent.

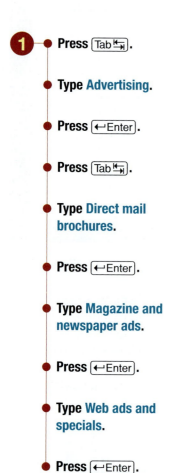

1 ● Press [Tab⇥].

● Type **Advertising**.

● Press [←Enter].

● Press [Tab⇥].

● Type **Direct mail brochures**.

● Press [←Enter].

● Type **Magazine and newspaper ads**.

● Press [←Enter].

● Type **Web ads and specials**.

● Press [←Enter].

Your screen should be similar to Figure 5.52

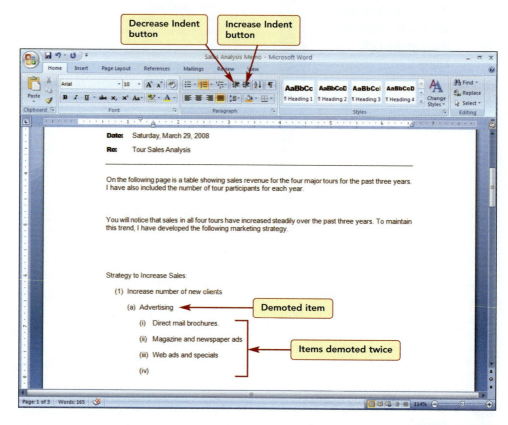

Figure 5.52

Each time you press [Tab⇥] to indent a line, the next line indents to the 0.25-inch position and the list level is demoted to the next lower level. That completes the first category. To add the second and third categories, you need to promote the list level by decreasing the indent by pressing [⇧Shift] + [Tab⇥] or 🔲 Decrease Indent. You also can press [←Enter] multiple times to decrease the indent level one step at a time.

2
- Press ⇧Shift + Tab⇥.

- Enter the following three items at the levels shown:

  (b) Participate in "travel fairs"

  (c) Offer presentations to specialty groups (biking, hiking, etc.)

  (d) Expand Adventure Travel Tours Web site

- Press ↵Enter.

- Click ⯐ Decrease Indent.

Your screen should be similar to Figure 5.53

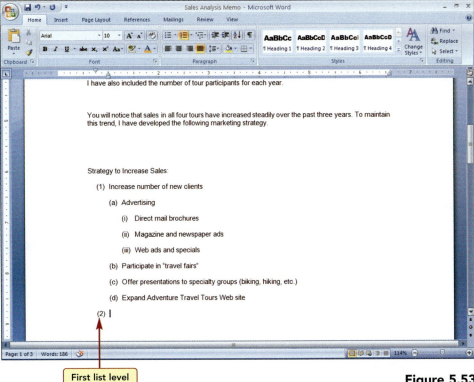

First list level

Figure 5.53

The level is back at the first level, and you are ready to enter the second main sales strategy.

3 Complete the memo by entering the following topics at the levels shown:

(2) **Increase repeat business**

(a) **Follow-up surveys**

(b) **Thank-you letters**

(c) **Newsletter**

● Press ⏎Enter 2 times to return the level to the first level.

● Press ⏎Enter 4 more times to back up through all the levels and finally to turn off the list feature.

Another Method

You also can click  Numbering to turn off the multilevel list feature.

● If necessary, correct any typing or spelling errors.

Your screen should be similar to Figure 5.54

Additional Information

Some list styles do not use indentation to indicate list level. Instead, they may use different formatting effects, such as font size, bold, and italics.

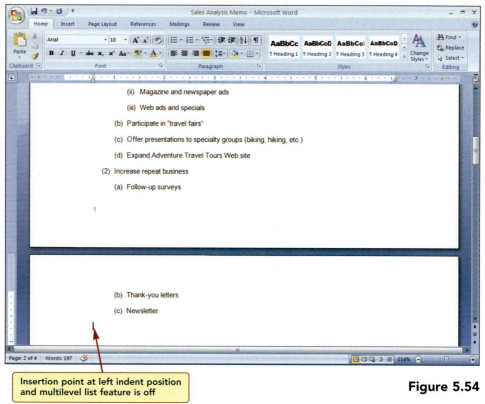

Insertion point at left indent position and multilevel list feature is off

Figure 5.54

Each time you pressed ⏎Enter, the list level increased to the next higher level. Finally, when the left page margin was reached and the highest level reached, the multilevel list feature was turned off and the insertion point is displayed at the document's left indent location.

Selecting and Changing List Levels

Because the memo template has the left indent set at 0.58 inch, when the multilevel list was started, it began the list level at the level associated with this indent setting (1) instead of 1) the highest level.

To fix this, you need to decrease the indent for the entire list until it is positioned at the left margin. This will move the outline number level to the highest level. Then you will indent the list from the right again without affecting the list levels.

First, you will select the second level list items and format them to include a font color. Because a multilevel list is essentially a single-level list within another list, each list level can be selected and formatted independently.

1 • Click the letter in front of any second-level item.

• Click 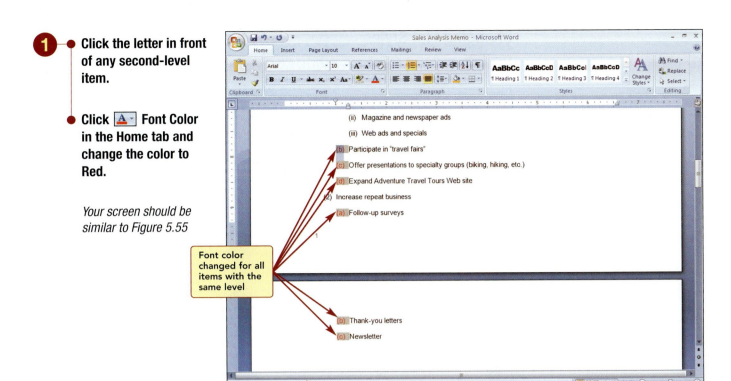 Font Color in the Home tab and change the color to Red.

Your screen should be similar to Figure 5.55

Figure color changed for all items with the same level

Figure 5.55

Only the letters at the selected level are highlighted and affected by the font color change. In complicated lists with many levels, this feature is particularly useful for easily identifying levels.

Next, you will move the entire list to the left margin to quickly readjust the list levels.

2 • Drag to select all the items in the list.

• Click 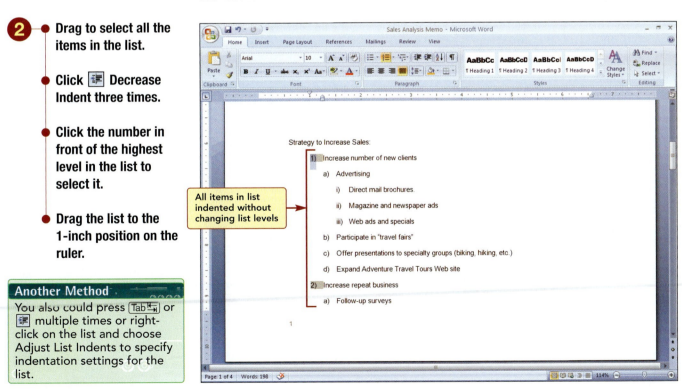 Decrease Indent three times.

• Click the number in front of the highest level in the list to select it.

• Drag the list to the 1-inch position on the ruler.

Another Method

You also could press [Tab] or ▤ multiple times or right-click on the list and choose Adjust List Indents to specify indentation settings for the list.

All items in list indented without changing list levels

Your screen should be similar to Figure 5.56

Figure 5.56

The list level number did not change when the list was indented.

Changing List Styles

Next, you want to see how another list style would look.

1 ● Click anywhere on the list.

● Click 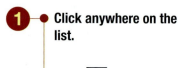 Multilevel List and select the bullet style list (second row, first column).

Your screen should be similar to Figure 5.57

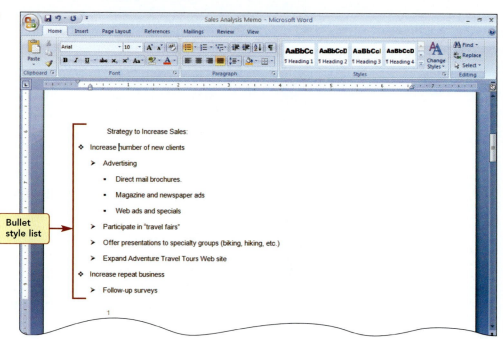

Figure 5.57

The entire list is quickly updated to the new style and reset to the left margin. Although you like how the bullets look at all the lower list levels, you want to change the first level back to a number.

2 ● Select the first-level bullets.

● Click 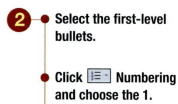 Numbering and choose the 1. number style.

● Drag the list back to the 1-inch position.

Your screen should be similar to Figure 5.58

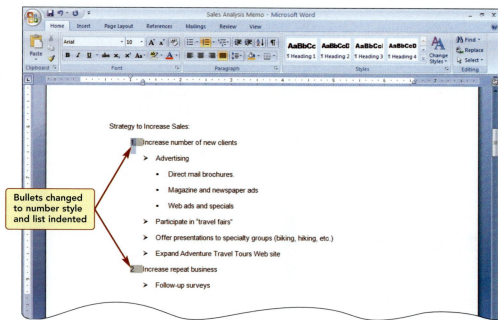

Figure 5.58

The multilevel list now consists of a combination of numbers and bullets.

Lab 5: Using Templates and Creating Complex Tables, Charts, and Graphics

www.mhhe.com/oleary

MORE ABOUT

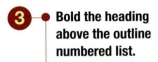

▶ To learn how to change bullet options, see 4.2 Use Tables and Lists to Organize Content in the More About appendix.

The final changes you want to make to the list are to bold the list heading and to reduce the spacing between lines.

3 ● Bold the heading above the outline numbered list.

● Select the entire list and reduce the spacing after paragraphs to 6 pt.

● Delete the blank line between the paragraphs and one blank line above the list.

Your screen should be similar to Figure 5.59

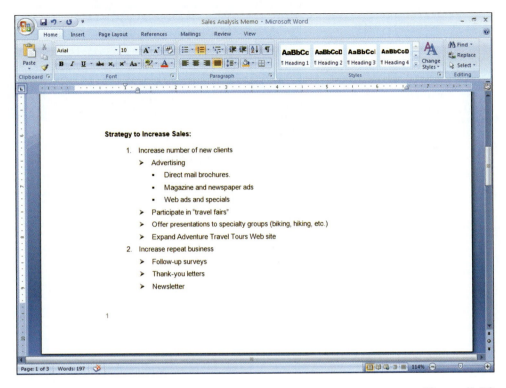

Figure 5.59

4 ● Preview and then print the memo.

● Hide the table gridlines.

● Save the file.

Your completed memo should be three pages long and should look like the memo shown in the Case Study at the beginning of the lab.

Creating a Custom Template

The next memo you will work on will be an announcement about the creation of a new department at Adventure Travel Tours. You want to use the same Memo template you used to create the Sales Analysis memo. A copy of the Memo template was saved to the templates folder on your computer when it was downloaded. Since you plan to use this template frequently, you decide to create a custom template that includes the company logo.

Modifying the Template

You will open the Memo template file and copy the letterhead from the Sales Analysis memo to the template file. Then you will make several additional changes to customize the template for your own use.

1 • **Click** 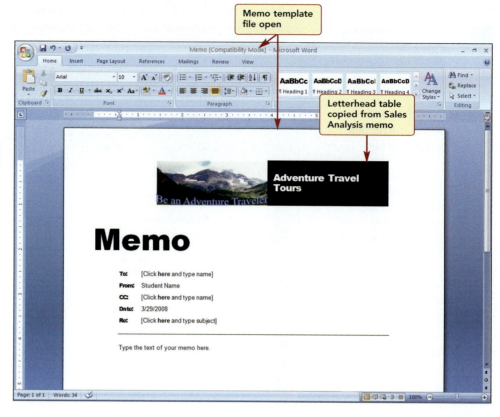 **Office button and choose Open.**

• **Choose Trusted Templates from the Navigation pane.**

Having Trouble?
If you are using Windows Vista, Templates is the name of the location in the Navigation pane.

• **Choose Memo and click** Open .

• **Select the blank letterhead table at the top of the memo.**

• **Click** Delete **in the Rows & Columns group of the Table Tools Layout tab and choose Delete Table.**

• **Copy the letterhead table from the Sales Analysis memo to the top of the template memo as shown in Figure 5.60.**

• **Type your name in place of the From placeholder.**

• **Replace the template instructions with Type the text of your memo here..**

• **Press** ←Enter .

Your screen should be similar to Figure 5.60

Figure 5.60

Rather than opening up a copy of itself, the template itself opens and the template file name is displayed in the title bar. You are actually modifying the template file with the changes you want to be available each time you use the template to create a new memo.

Saving the Template

Now that the memo template is the way you want it to appear when it is opened, you will save it as a template file. If you save the changes they will automatically be saved to the Memo template file in the Templates folder on your computer. You want to keep the original template and save the revised template with a new file name to your solution file location.

1 ● **Click** 🔵 **Office Button select Save As and choose Word Template.**

● **Select your solution file location as the Save in location.**

● **Enter** ATT Memo **as the file name.**

Your screen should be similar to Figure 5.61

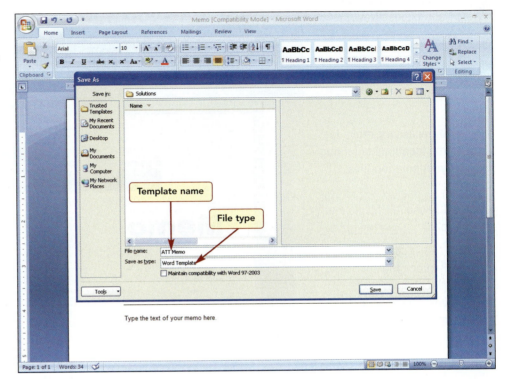

Figure 5.61

Templates are saved by default to the Templates folder on your computer. You also can save templates to other locations just like any other document.

2 ● **Click** [Save] .

● **If necessary, click** [OK] **to update the document to Word 2007 format.**

● **Close all open Word files.**

Using the Template

Now you will use the new ATT Memo template to create the memo announcing the new Web Development Department at Adventure Travel Tours. Custom templates appear by default in the General tab of the Templates dialog box.

1 ● Click 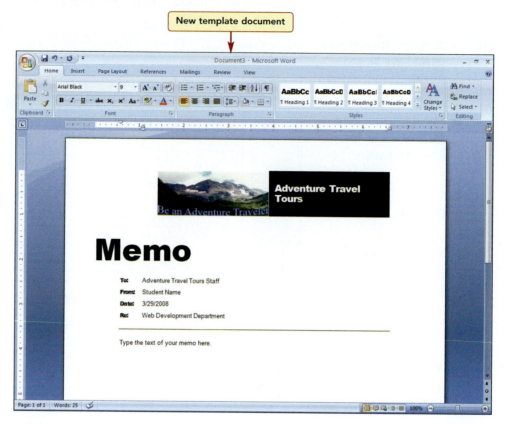 Office Button and choose New.

● Choose New from existing from the Templates list.

● If necessary, move to the location containing your solution files.

● Choose ATT Memo and click **Create New**.

● Replace the placeholder text with the following information:

To: Adventure Travel Tours Staff

Re: Web Development Department

● Delete the CC line in the header.

Your screen should be similar to Figure 5.62

New template document

Figure 5.62

A copy of your custom template file is open and works just like the Professional Memo template you used earlier. Now, however, because you have added the logo and your name in the memo header, it saves even more time.

The body of the memo will explain the new department and introduce the employees in the department.

2

- Replace the template directions with the following text: **Announcing the New ATT Web Development Department.**

- Press ⏎Enter and type the following text: **Adventure Travel Tours is proud to announce the creation of our Web Development Department. We are very excited about this new addition to Adventure Travel Tours and are looking forward to a new, revitalized Web site in the near future.**

- Apply a Heading 1 style to the first line.

- Save this memo to your solution file location as New Department Memo.

Your screen should be similar to Figure 5.63

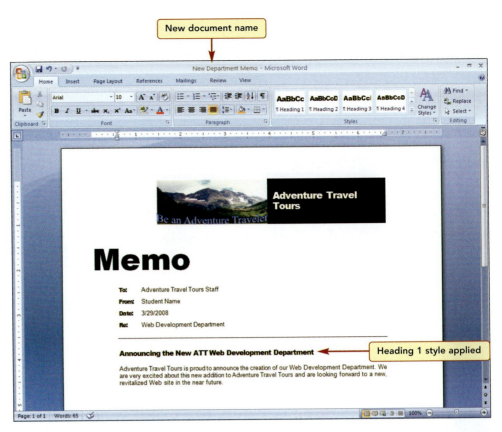

New document name

Heading 1 style applied

Figure 5.63

The ATT Memo template is unchanged and can be used again to create a new memo.

Creating an Organization Chart

Now you are ready to create a diagram showing the organization of the new department and staff. A **diagram** is a graphic object that can be used to illustrate concepts and enhance your documents. Unlike charts, diagrams are based on text rather than numeric information. The Microsoft Office SmartArt graphics tool is used to quickly create many different types of diagrams.

Concept 5

SmartArt

5 The **SmartArt** graphics feature includes many predesigned diagrams you can add to your document to illustrate textual concepts. The type of SmartArt graphic you choose depends on the purpose of the diagram and the type of concept you want to illustrate. The table below describes the SmartArt graphic types and uses.

Type	Use
List	Shows nonsequential information
Process	Shows steps in a process
Cycle	Shows a process that has a continuous cycle
Hierarchy	Creates an organization chart or decision tree that shows hierarchical-based relationships
Relationship	Illustrates connections
Matrix	Shows relationships of elements to a core element
Pyramid	Shows foundation-based relationships

You also want to consider the amount of text you want to include in the diagram and the number of shapes you will need when selecting the layout. In general, it is best to keep the number of shapes and the amount of text to key points. Larger amounts of text can distract from the visual appeal of the graphic and make it harder to convey the message.

Selecting a SmartArt Graphic

You will enter an introductory paragraph about the new department and then create an organization chart diagram to display the department organization. The completed diagram you will create is shown below.

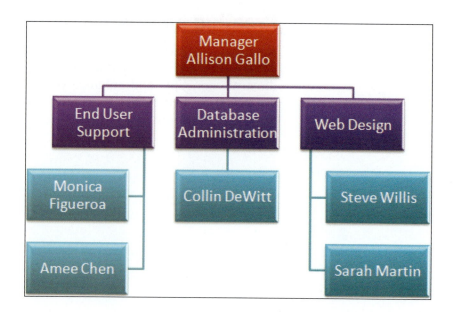

1 Move to the end of the paragraph and press ↵Enter.

Type: **The organization chart below identifies the names and positions of the employees in this department.**

Press ↵Enter.

Click  on the Insert tab.

Your screen should be similar to Figure 5.64

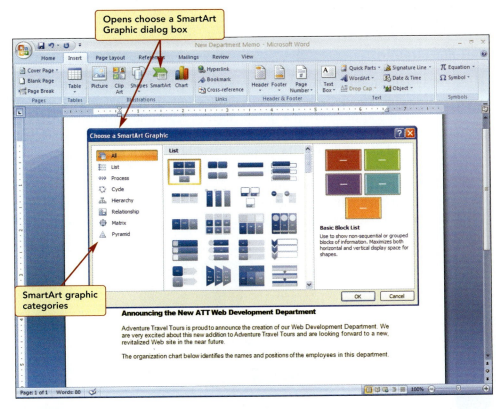

Figure 5.64

From the Choose a SmartArt Graphic dialog box, you select the category and then the specific type of diagram within the category that you want to create. The best type of diagram to represent the new department is an organization chart.

Concept 6

Organization Chart

6 An **organization chart** graphically represents the structure of an organization. Traditionally, it includes names and job titles, but also can include any items that have a **hierarchical relationship**. A **hierarchy** shows ranking of items in a group, such as reporting structures within a department in a business.

There are several different styles of organization charts from which you can choose, depending on how you would like to display the hierarchy and how much room you have on your page. A basic organization chart is shown below. All organization charts consist of different levels that represent the hierarchy. A level is all the boxes at the same hierarchical position regardless of the boxes each reports to. The topmost box in the organization chart is at level 1. All boxes that report directly to it are at level 2. Those boxes reporting to a level 2 box are at level 3, and so forth. An organization chart can have up to 50 levels.

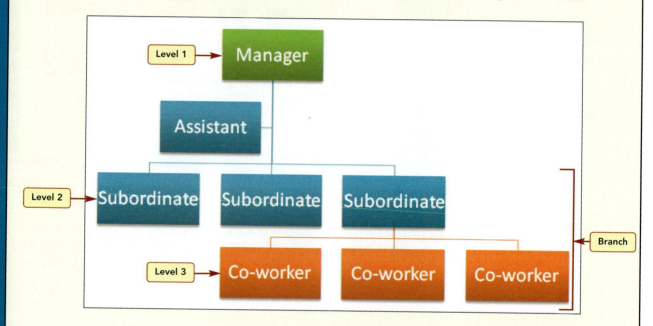

The **manager box** is the top-level box of a group. Subordinate boxes report to the manager box. Co-worker boxes are boxes that have the same manager. Co-workers form a group. A **group** consists of all the boxes reporting to the same manager, excluding assistant boxes. **Assistant boxes** represent administrative or managerial assistants to a manager. A **branch** is a box and all the boxes that report to it. A level is all the boxes at the same level regardless of the boxes each reports to.

Organization chart diagrams are in the Hierarchy SmartArt category. Within each category are different layouts. As you select a layout, the dialog box displays an enlarged version of the graphic and a brief description of its use.

2 • Choose the Hierarchy category.

• Choose each of the organization chart layouts and read the description.

• Choose 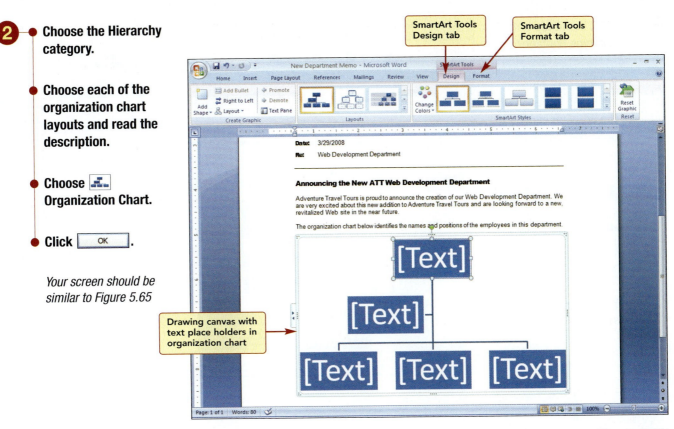 Organization Chart.

• Click [OK].

Your screen should be similar to Figure 5.65

Figure 5.65

An organization chart consisting of five boxes containing placeholder text is displayed. A drawing canvas surrounds the entire chart and keeps all pieces of the chart together as a unit. Additionally, the SmartArt Tools tabs are automatically opened to help you add shapes, modify the layout, and enhance the graphic.

Adding Text to the Organization Chart

To enter text into the organization chart, you can type or copy the information directly in the shapes. Alternatively, you can use the Text pane. You will use both methods.

1 • Click in the top box and type **Manager**.

• If necessary, click ⌷ along the left edge of the drawing canvas to open the Text pane.

Another Method

You also can click ▣ Text Pane in the Create Graphics group of the SmartArt Tools Design tab to display and hide the Text pane.

Your screen should be similar to Figure 5.66

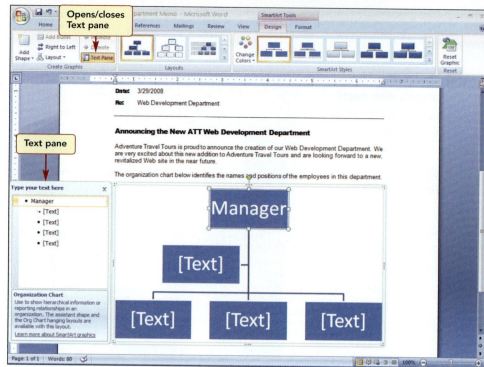

Figure 5.66

The Text pane appears along the left edge of the drawing canvas. Each bullet in the Text pane represents one of the shapes in the graphic. The currently selected box is highlighted and contains the insertion point. A bullet with a line attached indicates an Assistant shape.

2 • Click at the end of "Manager" in the top box of the text pane, enter a blank space, and type **Allison Gallo**.

• Click in the third bullet and type **End User Support**.

• In the fourth bullet, type **Database Administration**.

• In the fifth bullet, type **Web Design**.

• If necessary, scroll down to display the organization chart.

Your screen should be similar to Figure 5.67

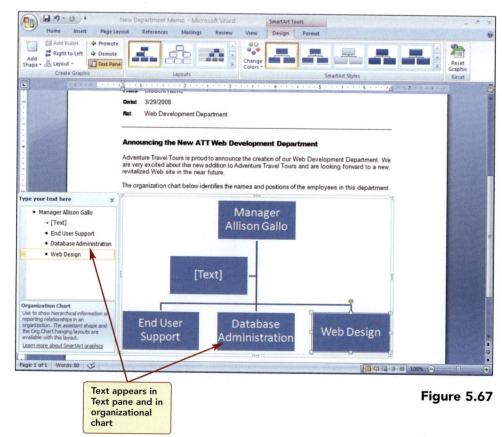

Figure 5.67

The text appears in the existing graphic shapes as you type in the Text pane. The font size adjusts automatically as more text is added.

Adding and Deleting Shapes

Next you need to delete the Assistant shape below the Manager box and add subordinate shapes below the End User Support shape to contain the names of the employees. As you add and delete shapes, the graphic will automatically resize to fit the drawing canvas.

To add a shape, you first select an existing shape that is located closest to where you want to add the new shape. Then you add the new shape relative to the location of the selected shape. In this case, you want to add shapes below the End User Support shape.

In the Text pane, adding a shape is accomplished by selecting the bullet that represents the shape closest to where you want the new shape inserted and pressing ⏎Enter.

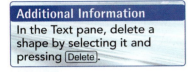

Additional Information

In the Text pane, delete a shape by selecting it and pressing Delete.

1 ● **Click at the end of the End User Support bullet and press** ⏎Enter**.**

Your screen should be similar to Figure 5.68

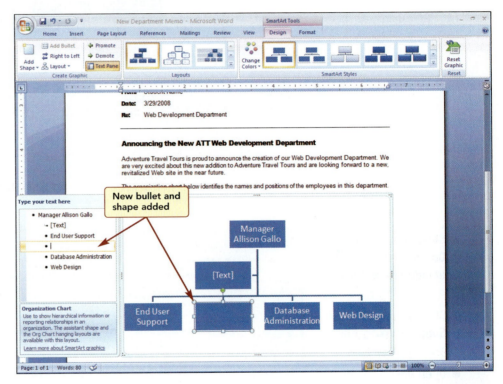

Figure 5.68

A new bullet and shape are added at the same level as the selected shape. Because you want the shape to be subordinate to the End User Support shape, you need to decrease the level to make it subordinate.

2 • Click **➡ Demote** in the Create Graphic group.

• Type **Monica Figueroa**.

Your screen should be similar to figure 5.69

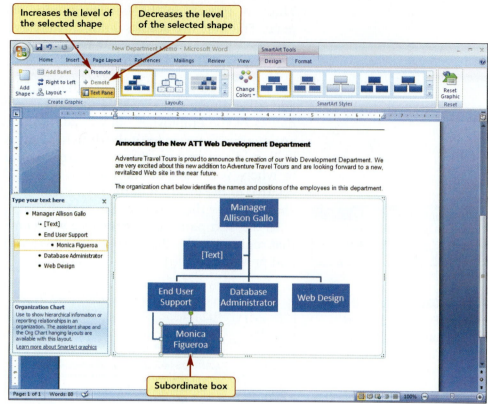

Figure 5.69

You have one more subordinate box you need to add below the End User Support box. You will add this shape directly in the graphic.

3 • Click **Text Pane** in the Create Graphic group to hide the Text pane.

• Click on the End User Support box.

• Open the **Add Shape** drop-down menu in the Create Graphic group and choose Add Shape Below.

• Enter **Amee Chen** in the second subordinate shape.

Your screen should be similar to figure 5.70.

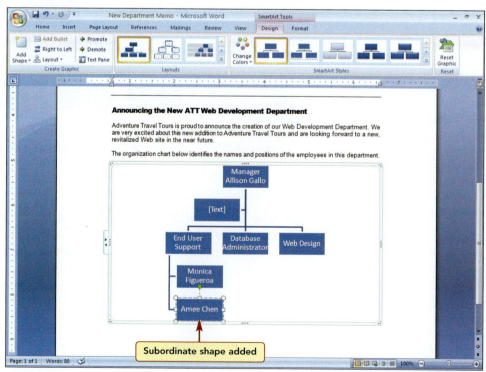

Figure 5.70

Lab 5: Using Templates and Creating Complex Tables, Charts, and Graphics

www.mhhe.com/oleary

Changing the Diagram Layout

The two new shapes are added in a horizontal line subordinate to the selected shape. You decide to change the layout of this grouping so the subordinate shapes line up in a column below the superior shape. The four types of layouts are described in the following table.

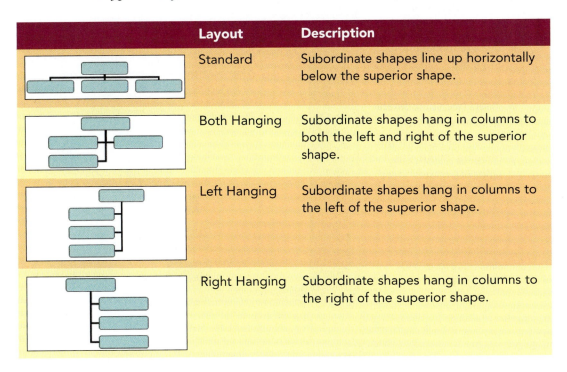

	Layout	Description
	Standard	Subordinate shapes line up horizontally below the superior shape.
	Both Hanging	Subordinate shapes hang in columns to both the left and right of the superior shape.
	Left Hanging	Subordinate shapes hang in columns to the left of the superior shape.
	Right Hanging	Subordinate shapes hang in columns to the right of the superior shape.

When changing the layout, the superior shape above the shapes whose layout you want to change must be selected.

1 ● If necessary, click on the End User Support box.

● Click 🔲 Layout ▾ in the Create Graphic group and choose Left Hanging.

Your screen should be similar to Figure 5.71

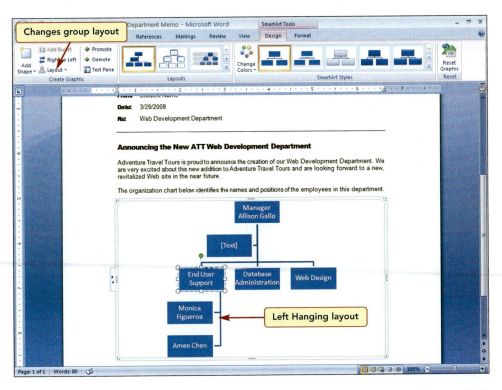

Figure 5.71

Now you will add subordinate shapes for the other two areas.

2 ● Add a subordinate shape below Database Administrator and enter Collin DeWitt.

● Change the layout to Standard.

● Insert two subordinate shapes below Web Design using the Right Hanging layout, and enter the names Steve Willis and Sarah Martin.

Your screen should be similar to Figure 5.72

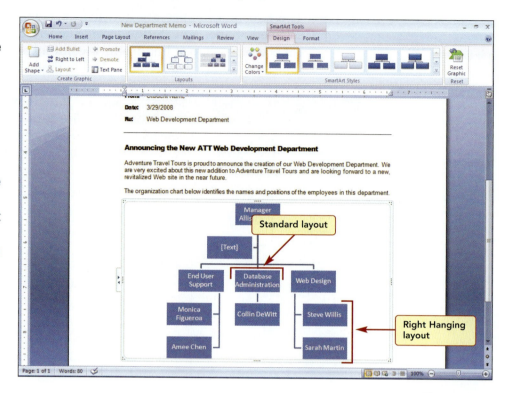

Figure 5.72

As more subordinate shapes were added to the chart, the boxes resized to fit within the drawing canvas and the font size within the boxes decreased as well.

Finally, you need to delete the Assistant text box below the Manager shape.

3 ● Select the blank shape below the Manager shape and press Delete.

Your screen should be similar to Figure 5.73

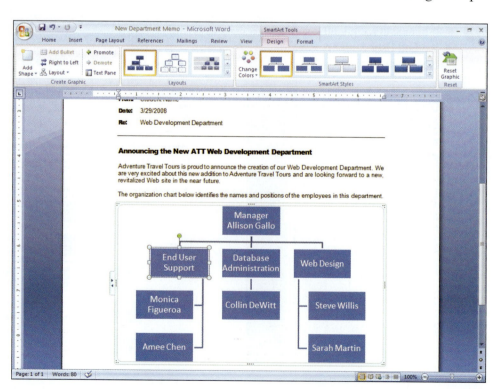

Figure 5.73

Again, the shapes resized to fit the drawing canvas. If you did not want the graphic to resize, you would need to expand the drawing canvas before adding shapes by dragging the drawing canvas handles.

Enhancing the Organization Chart

To make the organization chart more interesting, you want to enhance its appearance. You could select each element and add color and format each individually, but this would take quite a bit of time. Instead, you can use one of the prepackaged styles in the SmartArt Styles group. A SmartArt style is a combination of different formatting options such as edges, gradients, line styles, shadows, and three-dimensional effects that can be quickly applied to the entire graphic in one easy step. You also can choose different color combinations. As you point to the design choices, Live Preview shows how the graphic will look.

1 ● Click [Change Colors] in the SmartArt Styles group.

● Choose Colorful Range - Accent Colors 3 to 4 (second row, third design) in the Colorful category.

● Click ⯆ More in the SmartArt Styles group.

● Choose Polished in the 3-D category.

● Click outside the graphic to deselect it.

Your screen should be similar to Figure 5.74

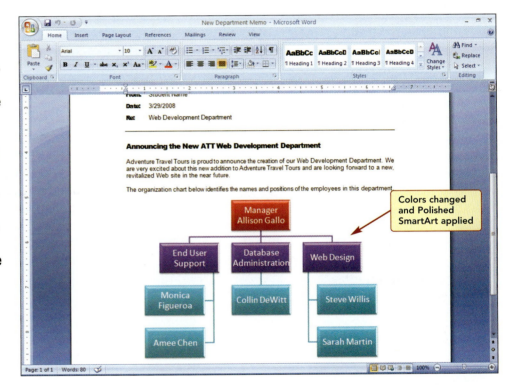

Figure 5.74

Additional Information
If, after making many formatting changes to a SmartArt graphic, you want to return to the original graphic design, use [Reset Graphic] .

The selected SmartArt colors and style features were quickly applied to all the shapes in the organization chart. These changes greatly improve the appearance of the graphic.

2 ● Save, preview, and print the memo.

● Exit Word.

Your completed memo should be similar to that shown in the Case Study at the beginning of the lab.

Focus on Careers

EXPLORE YOUR CAREER OPTIONS

Landscape Architect

Have you ever wondered who designs parks, walkways, and residential common areas? Do you admire the shrubs, flowers, and trees that line the roadways? Landscape architects are responsible for the design and installation of landscaping. They also may help restore endangered environments such as forests or wetlands. Landscape architects are responsible for project design, but additionally they communicate with clients and contractors. They must produce detailed written reports, land use studies, cost estimates, and many other documents. Landscape architects must be skilled computer users with experience in word processing. A college degree and experience is usually required, and many states require a license. The typical salary is between $40,900 and $70,400. Demand for landscape architects is expected to increase as the cost of land increases and good site planning becomes more important.

Using Templates and Creating Complex Tables, Charts, and Graphics

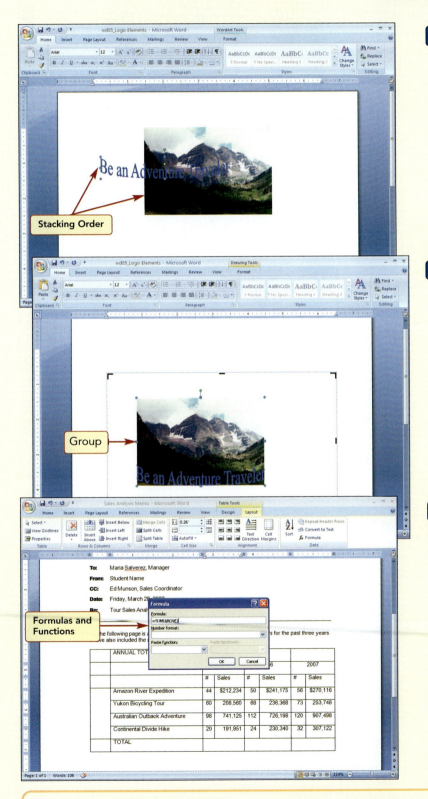

Stacking Order (WD5.10)

Stacking order is the order objects are positioned in the drawing layer.

Stacking Order

Group (WD5.11)

A group is two or more objects that are combined so that you can work with them as you would a single object.

Group

Formulas and Functions (WD5.22)

Formulas and functions are used to perform calculations in tables.

Formulas and Functions

Concept Summary

Chart (WD5.37)

A chart, also called a graph, is a visual representation of numeric data.

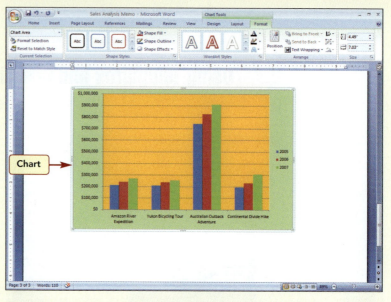

SmartArt (WD5.56)

The SmartArt graphics feature includes many predesigned diagrams you can add to your document to illustrate textual concepts.

Organization Chart (WD5.58)

An organization chart graphically represents the structure of an organization.

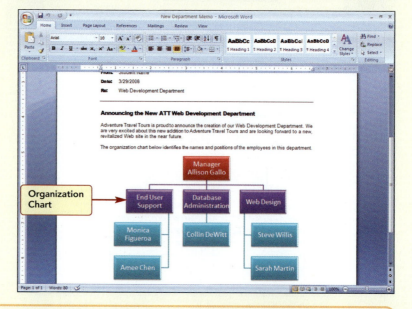

Lab Review

LAB 5

Using Templates and Creating Complex Tables, Charts, and Graphics

key terms

assistant box WD5.58

attribute WD5.11

branch WD5.58

chart WD5.37

co-worker box WD5.58

diagram WD5.55

formula WD5.22

function WD5.22

group WD5.11, WD5.58

hierarchical relationship WD5.58

hierarchy WD5.58

landscape WD5.30

legend WD5.37

manager box WD5.58

multilevel list WD5.44

operator WD5.22

organization chart WD5.58

portrait WD5.30

SmartArt WD5.56

stacking order WD5.10

title WD5.37

X axis WD5.37

Y axis WD5.37

MCAS skills

The Microsoft Certified Applications Specialist (MCAS) certification program is designed to measure your proficiency in performing basic tasks using the Office 2007 applications. Getting certified demonstrates that you have the skills and provides a valuable industry credential for employment. See Reference 2, Microsoft Certified Applications Specialist (MCAS) for a complete list of the skills that were covered in Lab 5.

Lab Review

command summary

Command	Action
Office Button	
New/Memos	Provides memo templates from Microsoft Office Online
Open/Trusted Templates	Opens location of custom templates
Save As/Word Template	Saves document as a template
Home tab	
Paragraph group	
Multilevel List	Presents alternative listing formats
Insert tab	
Tables group	
/Draw Table	Draws table borders
Illustrations group	
/New Drawing Canvas	Open drawing canvas to create and manipulate objects
SmartArt	Opens list of alternative SmartArt graphics
/Hierarchy/Organization Chart	Opens Organization Chart SmartArt graphic
Chart	Inserts a variety of charts
Page Layout tab	
Page Setup group	
Orientation	Switches between portrait and landscape layouts
Table Tools Design tab	
Table Styles group	
Shading	Colors cell background
Borders	Customizes cell borders
Draw Borders group	
Draw Table	Draws table borders
Eraser	Erases table borders

command summary

Command	Action
Table Tools Layout tab	
Table group	
▦ View Gridlines	Shows or hides table gridlines
Rows & Columns group	
Delete	Deletes rows, columns, cells, or entire table
Merge group	
▦ Merge Cells	Merges cells in a table
Cell Size group	
▦ Distribute Rows	Equally distributes row heights
Alignment group	
▦ Align Top Center	Centers text and aligns to top of cell
▥ Align Center	Centers text horizontally and vertically within cell
Text Direction	Changes text direction within cell
Cell Margins	Customizes cell margins and spacing between cells
Data group	
fx Formula	Adds formula to cell
Picture Tools Format tab	
Arrange group	
Send to Back ▾	Sends object back in the stack
Bring to Front ▾	Brings object to front of stack
Align	Aligns edges or centers objects
Group	Groups objects to be treated like a single object
Chart Tools Design tab	
Type group	
Change Chart Type	Changes current chart to another type

Lab Review

command summary

Command	Action
Chart Tools Format tab	
Current Selection group	
Format Selection	Formats selected chart elements
SmartArt Tools Design tab	
Create Graphic group	
Add Shape	Adds a shape to SmartArt graphic
Layout	Changes the branch layout of SmartArt graphic
Demote	Decreases level of selected shape
Text Pane	Displays or hides text pane
SmartArt Styles group	
Change Colors	Changes color variations in SmartArt graphic
More	Presents alternative visual styles for SmartArt graphic

Lab Exercises

matching

Match the item on the left with the correct description on the right.

1. attributes _____ a. A prewritten formula

2. datasheet _____ b. Features such as line color and fill color

3. diagram _____ c. Expression containing combinations of numbers, fields, table references, and operators.

4. formula _____ d. Specify the type of calculation to perform

5. function _____ e. Page orientation with text printed across the width

6. group _____ f. Table containing sample data used in a graph object

7. operators _____ g. Graphic object used to illustrate concepts

8. portrait _____ h. Placed below and connected to a superior shape

9. stacking order _____ i. Order objects are positioned in the drawing layer

10. subordinate _____ j. Two or more objects combined as a single object

multiple choice

Circle the correct response to the questions below.

1. An outline numbered list applies a _____ structure to a list.
   a. sequential
   b. linear
   c. circular
   d. hierarchical

2. A graphic object that is used to illustrate concepts is called a _____.
   a. table
   b. diagram
   c. template
   d. chart

3. The bottom boundary of the chart, often called the category axis, is called the _____.
    a. X axis
    b. Y axis
    c. legend
    d. title

4. In an organization chart, a shape that's placed next to another shape and is connected to the same superior shape is a _____ shape.
    a. superior
    b. assistant
    c. co-worker
    d. subordinate

5. _____ and functions are used to perform calculations in tables.
    a. Operators
    b. Cell references
    c. Fields
    d. Formulas

6. A _____, also called a graph, is a visual representation of numeric data.
    a. chart
    b. legend
    c. placeholder
    d. portrait

7. _____ is/are the order objects are positioned in the drawing layer.
    a. Attributes
    b. Layers
    c. Diagram
    d. Stacking order

8. _____ are prewritten formulas.
    a. Legends
    b. Functions
    c. Data fields
    d. Records

9. _____ list applies a hierarchal structure to a list, similar to creating an outline.
   a. Ordered
   b. Top-down
   c. Directed
   d. Multilevel
10. Page orientation with text printed across the length of the page is called _____.
   a. portrait
   b. legend
   c. placeholder
   d. landscape

true/false

Circle the correct answer to the following questions.

1.	Text in a placeholder tells the user what information to enter.	True	False
2.	A multilevel list can be either numbered or bulleted or a mix of letters, numbers, and bullets with up to nine levels.	True	False
3.	You cannot cycle between objects in a stack.	True	False
4.	Many clip art images are groups.	True	False
5.	A function is an expression that combines numbers and operators.	True	False
6.	List, Cycle, and Hierarchy are types of SmartArt graphics.	True	False
7.	A formula is an expression that contains numbers only.	True	False
8.	Global templates contain settings available to all documents.	True	False
9.	In landscape orientation, text is printed across the width of the page.	True	False
10.	The Y axis is the bottom boundary of a chart.	True	False

Hands-On Exercises

rating system

★ Easy

★★ Moderate

★★★ Difficult

step-by-step

Café Sales Memo ★★

1. You work for the Downtown Internet Café in the purchasing department. One of your responsibilities is to bring new products you think will be successful into the shop. You have recently heard about a new product you think will sell well and have decided to brief the owner about the product and cost analysis. Your completed memo is shown here.

   a. Create a new document using the Memo (Elegant design) template. (If you do not have access to Office Online, open the file wd05_Elegant Design Memo from your data file location.)

   b. Delete the placeholder title and replace the sample text with the following:

To:	**EVAN**
From:	**[Your Name]**
Subject:	**GREEN TEA SALES ANALYSIS**
CC:	**JAMES LAMAR**

   c. Change the date field format to the dddd, MMMM dd, yyyy format.

   d. Replace the sample text with the following:

   The local press is preparing to highlight the current "Green Tea" fad in the upcoming Spring Style edition of the Life section. This tea drink that was once hidden in health food shops has gone distinctly mass market.

   The most popular green tea product appears to be a blended ice drink. These drinks typically retail between $3.50 and $4.00 for 16 ounces. According to the National Coffee and Tea Association, successful operations can sell up to 150 units per day.

   I have prepared the following cost analysis to aid you in your decision on this opportunity.

INTEROFFICE MEMORANDUM

TO:	EVAN
FROM:	STUDENT NAME
SUBJECT:	GREEN TEA SALES ANALYSIS
DATE:	SATURDAY, MARCH 29, 2008
CC:	JAMES LAMAR

The local press is preparing to highlight the current "Green Tea" fad in the upcoming Spring Style edition of the Life section. This tea drink that was once hidden in health food shops has gone distinctly mass market.

The most popular green tea product appears to a blended ice drink. These drinks typically retail between $3.50 and $4.00 for 16 ounces. According to the National Coffee and Tea Association, successful operations can sell up to 150 units per day.

I have prepared the following cost analysis to aid you in your decision on this opportunity.

Supply	Quantity	Cost
Tea Straws	45	$1.99
16 oz. plastic cups	100	$13.95
Plastic oval lids	100	$8.95
Whip Cream	9.0 oz. (approximately 20 servings)	$3.95
Flavored Syrup	20.2 oz. (approximately 90 servings)	$7.95
Green Tea in Filter Bags	20-1oz. bags (each bag makes 1 quart)	$9.95

e. Increase the font size for the entire memo body to 14 pt.

f. Create a table to contain the following information below the paragraph:

Supply	Quantity
Tea Straws	45
16 oz. plastic cups	100
Plastic oval lids	100
Whip Cream	9.0 oz. (approximately 20 servings)
Flavored Syrup	20.2 oz. (approximately 90 servings)
Green Tea in Filter Bags	20 1 oz. bags (each bag makes 1 quart)

g. Add cell shading and font colors of your choice to the table.

h. Add a new column to the end of the table. Include the following information in the new column:

Cost
$1.99
$13.95
$8.95
$3.95
$7.95
$9.95

i. Set the font size of the table to 11 pt. Bold and change the font size of the text in row 1 to 14 pt.

j. Vertically center columns A and B. Vertically center and right-align column C.

k. Appropriately size the rows and columns of the table. Center the table in the document.

l. Save the document as Green Tea Memo. Print the memo.

Lab Exercises

Yoga Memo ★

2. The CEO of Adventure Travel Tours has asked you to do some research in response to client requests for Body/Mind Restoration retreats. She has asked you to gather information on Body/Mind Restoration packages the agency could offer. You did some research and found several resorts that offer such packages. You would like to send a memo to Carol Cooper, the CEO, with an update on your progress. Your completed memo should be similar to that shown here:

a. Create a new document using the Memo (Contemporary design) template. (If you do not have access to Office Online, open the file wd05_ Contemporary Design Memo from your data file location.)

b. Replace the placeholders with the following information:

To:	**Carol Cooper**
CC:	**Jill Willis**
From:	**[Your Name]**
Re:	**Body/Mind Restoration Retreats**

c. Change the Date field format to the M/d/yyyy h:mm am/pm format.

d. Delete the placeholder title and replace the sample text with the following:

I researched several Body/Mind Restoration retreats that meet our client requests. The Body Mind Restoration Spa has agreed to offer exclusive opportunities to Adventure Travel Tours guests. I am now working on a document that will provide our agents with the information they will need to sell the packages. I plan to format the document as shown below. If you have any questions or would like me to provide additional information about the retreats please let me know.

Body Mind Restoration Spa

Our health retreats are designed to heal and rejuvenate the body and mind. This is not just a spa experience; it is a comprehensive program that introduces a way of living that leads to sustainable good health. Come experience what health feels like at a serene 60-acre facility.

e. Set the font size of all the text in the memo (including the memo header) to 12 points.

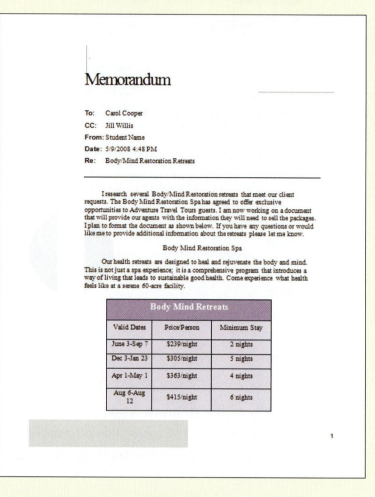

f. Draw a table with the appropriate number of columns and rows to hold the following data. Place the table below the descriptive paragraph.

Body Mind Retreats		
Valid Dates	**Price/Person**	**Minimum Stay**
June 3–Sep 7	$239/night	2 nights
Dec 3–Jan 23	$305/night	5 nights
Apr 1–May 1	$363/night	4 nights
Aug 6–Aug 12	$415/night	6 nights

g. For row 1: merge and center the cells; apply the shading Purple, Accent 4, lighter 40%; increase the font size to 16 pt; bold the text; and set the font color to white.

h. For rows 2 through 6: center the cell contents of cells; apply the shading Purple, Accent 4, lighter 80%; and adjust the row and column size as necessary.

i. Center the table in the memo. Save the document as Body Mind Memo. Print the document.

Rock Climbing Classes ★★

3. You work in program development at Lifestyle Fitness Club. The company has recently added a rock climbing wall in several club locations and has offered Friday Cardio Climbing Classes. Response to the new feature and to the classes has been very positive. You have been asked to consult the climbing instructors and gather data that will help determine if it is necessary to add additional classes. Your completed memo should be similar to that shown here.

a. Create a new document using the Memo (Professional design) template. (If you do not have access to Office Online, open the file wd05_Professional Design Memo from your data file location.)

b. Replace the Company Name placeholder with **Lifestyle Fitness Club.**

c. Open the file wd05_LFC Logo and arrange the graphics as shown in the completed memo. Group the graphics. Reduce the size of the grouped object to approximately 1″ by 2.5″. Copy the graphic to the memo. Change the wrapping style to Square. Insert the graphic in the left cell of the table in the memo letterhead. Increase the font size of the company name to 18 pt. Adjust the letterhead as shown in the completed memo.

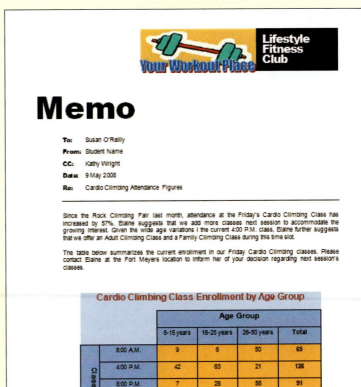

d. Delete the placeholder title and replace the sample text with the following:

To: **Susan O'Reilly**

From: **[Your Name]**

CC: **Kathy Wright**

Re: **Cardio Climbing Attendance Figures**

e. Change the date field format to d MMMM yyyy.

f. Replace the sample body text with the following:

Since the Rock Climbing Fair last month, attendance at the Friday's Cardio Climbing Class has increased by 57%. Elaine suggests that we add more classes next session to accommodate the growing interest. Given the wide age variations in the current 4:00 P.M. class, Elaine further suggests that we offer an Adult Climbing Class and a Family Climbing Class during this time slot.

The table below summarizes the current enrollment in our Friday Cardio Climbing classes. Please contact Elaine at the Fort Meyers location to inform her of your decision regarding next session's classes.

g. Create a table with five rows and five columns. Insert the following information:

Cardio Climbing Class Enrollment by Age Group				
		Age Group		
		6–15 years	16–25 years	26–50 years
Class	8:00 A.M.	9	6	50
	4:00 P.M.	42	63	21
	8:00 P.M.	7	26	58

h. Add the title "Cardio Climbing Class Enrollment by Age Group" just above the table centered across columns A through F. Change the font to bold and a color of your choice.

i. Add a row at the bottom of the table and a column at the left of the table to total the row and column values. Enter appropriate formulas to sum the enrollment by age group and by class time. Add the appropriate row and column labels.

j. Center the "Age Group" label across columns C through F. Change the text direction for the "Class" label to vertical and center across rows 4 through 7. Set the font of both labels to bold and with font size of 12.

k. Center the contents of cells C2:F7. Bold the Total row and the Total column.

l. Delete the appropriate border lines, size and center the table, and add cell shadings so that your solution is similar to the completed memo above.

m. Save the document as Rock Climbing Memo and print.

Lab 5: Using Templates and Creating Complex Tables, Charts, and Graphics

www.mhhe.com/oleary

Adoption Statistics Memo ★★★

4. Annabelle works in the fund-raising division at Animal Rescue Foundation. She has been very busy this month preparing for upcoming charity events and the annual silent auction. The director of the foundation has asked her to compile the adoption rates for the past three years for use in the auction brochure and send them to his office. The completed memo is shown here.

   a. Create a new document using the Memo (Elegant design) template. (If you do not have access to Office Online, open the file wd05_Elegant Design Memo from your data file location.)

   b. Replace the text "Interoffice Memorandum" with **Animal Rescue Foundation.**

   c. Replace the placeholders with the following information:

      To: **Sam Johnson**

      From: **[Your Name]**

      Subject: **Animal Adoption Statistics**

      CC: **Mary Munson, Fred Samuels, Sara Joseph**

   d. Change the date field to the MMMM d, yyyyy format.

   e. Replace the sample title text with **Animal Adoption Rates**.

   f. Replace the sample body text with the following:

      I have finished compiling the adoption statistics for use in our upcoming fundraising events. Below you will find the quarterly adoption rates for the past four years. Please note that the zero adoptions value in 2006 corresponds with the renovation of the kennel area.

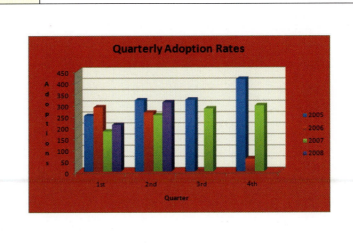

ANIMAL RESCUE FOUNDATION

TO:	SAM JOHNSON
FROM:	STUDENT NAME
SUBJECT:	ANIMAL ADOPTION STATISTICS
DATE:	MAY 9, 2008
CC:	MARY MUNSON, FRED SAMUELS, SARA JOSEPH

ANIMAL ADOPTION RATES

I have finished compiling the adoption statistics for use in our upcoming fundraising events. Below you will find the quarterly adoption rates for the past four years. Please note that the zero adoptions value in 2006 corresponds with the renovation of the kennel area.

Animal Adoption Rates

Quarter	2005	2006	2007	2008
1st	250	289	180	209
2nd	320	265	253	311
3rd	323	0	283	
4th	415	57	297	
Total	1308	611	1013	520

g. Below the paragraph, insert the following information in an appropriately sized table:

Animal Adoption Rates			
	2005	2006	2007
1st	250	289	180
2nd	320	265	253
3rd	323	0	283
4th	415	57	297

h. Insert a new column for the year 2008. Enter **209** for the 1st quarter and **311** for the 2nd quarter. Add a row to the bottom of the table and enter formulas to calculate the yearly totals. Add an appropriate row label.

i. Merge the cells in the title row. Increase the title text to 16 and center the title. Center the labels in row 2, set the font size to 14, and bold.

j. Add the label **Quarter** to the cell to the left of the cell containing 1st. Change the text direction for the "Quarter" label to vertical, center across rows 3 through 6, set the font size to 14, and bold. Increase the font to 12, bold, and center the four quarter labels in the second column.

k. Center the data in cells C3:F6. Equally size all rows. Equally size the four columns of data.

l. Bold the data in the last row. Delete the appropriate border lines, size and center the table, and add cell shadings so that your table is similar to the table in the completed memo above.

m. Create a 3-D clustered-column chart using the data from the table. Enter the chart title and axis labels (see solution above; use the Labels group on the Chart Tools Layout tab). Add formatting of your choice to the chart.

n. Save the document as Animal Adoption Memo and print it.

Children's Theater Memo ★★★

5. You work for the board of directors at Children's Theater Company. The board will be making a decision on the spring production and has asked you to research the most popular productions. They also would like to have statistics on attendance by young people. The foundation is dedicated to increasing attendance and would like you to make some suggestions on improving customer service. Your completed memo should be similar to that shown here:

Children's Theater Company

Memo

To: Spring Planning Board
From: Student Name
CC: Danielle Delgado
Date: May 9, 2008
Re: Spring Production

I have finished researching the most popular US children's productions in the [past] ten years. As we suspected, Dr. Seuss' How the Grinch Stole Christmas and the [BFG] (Big Friendly Giant) are in the top five productions in the US as shown in the ta[ble] below. Since we sponsored Huck Finn last years, perhaps we should consider on[e of] the other top five productions.

Top Five Works Over Past Ten Seasons		
Production	**Script/Adopted By**	**Number of US Productions**
Dr/ Seuss' How the Grinch Stole Christmas	Timothy Mason	182
Huck Finn	Greg Banks	180
The BFG (Big Friendly Giant)	David Wood	160
The Sorcerer's Apprentice	OyamO	156
Goodnight Moon	Chad Henry	146
Total Number of Productions		**824**

1

Our customer service research has yielded some encouraging results. Over 75 percent of our current customers state that they are looking forward to coming back again! As we all know, the best way to keep our audience is to provide excellent customer service. Here are some tips to improve that service.

Improving Customer Service

1) Have a written customer service policy.
   a) Make sure employees know that customer service is the paramount goal of the company.
   b) Publicize your customer service policy; let customers know that it is your priority.
2) View the experience through the customer's eyes.
   a) Have a friend attend a performance and make suggestions about improving your customer service.
   b) Send employees to attend another company's performance and give examples of good and bad customer service they received.
3) Have a procedure in place to deal with customer complaints.
   a) Determine who handles complaints.
   b) Track customer complaints and resolutions.

I have also compiled some data on attendance from a survey we conducted in 2006 and 2007. Please note the encouraging statistics for the 6-12 age group!

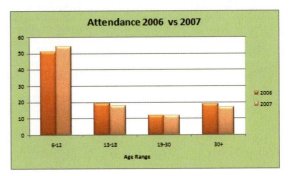

● Page 2

a. Create a new document using the Memo (Professional design) template. (If you do not have access to Office Online, open the file wd05_Professional Design Memo from your data file location.) Replace the company name placeholder with **Children's Theater Company**. Resize the cell so that the company name appears on a single line. Change the date field format to dddd, MMMM dd, yyyy. Replace the remaining placeholders with the following information:

To: **Spring Planning Board**

From: **[Your Name]**

CC: **Danielle Delgado**

Re: **Spring Production**

b. Delete the placeholder title, change the font size of the body text to 12, and replace the sample text with the following:

I have finished researching the most popular US children's productions. As we suspected, Dr. Seuss' How the Grinch Stole Christmas and The BFG (Big Friendly Giant) are in the top five productions in the US as shown in the table below. Since we sponsored Huck Finn last year, perhaps we should consider one of the other top five productions.

c. Open the file wd05_Theater. Arrange the graphics as shown in the example. Group the graphics. Change the size of the object to approximately 1.0″ by 2.5″. Copy the graphic to the memo. Change the wrapping style of the grouped object to Square. Move the graphic into the left cell of the table. Adjust the letterhead table as shown in the example.

d. Create a table with the following information below the paragraph.

Top Five Works Over Past Ten Seasons	
Production	**Script/Adopted By**
Dr. Seuss' How the Grinch Stole Christmas	**Timothy Mason**
Huck Finn	**Greg Banks**
The BFG (Big Friendly Giant)	**David Wood**
The Sorcerer's Apprentice	**OyamO**
Goodnight Moon	**Chad Henry**

e. Insert a column at the end of the table with the following information:

Number of US Productions

182

180

160

156

146

f. Insert a row at the bottom of the table. Enter **Total Number of Productions** in cell A8, bold the text, and right-center-align over columns A and B. Insert a formula in cell C8 that calculates the total number of productions of the top five operas and bold the resulting number.

g. In row 1, merge the cells and center the title across the columns. Set the title font to bold and 16. Center the labels in row 2 and set the font to bold and 14. Center the data in column C.

h. Add cell shading, font color, and other formats of your choice to the table. Adjust the size of the table rows and columns as necessary. Center the table in the memo.

i. Enter the following as a new paragraph below the table:

Our customer service research has yielded some encouraging results. Over 75 percent of our current customers state that they are looking forward to coming back again! As we all know, the best way to keep our audience is excellent customer service. Here are some tips to improve that service.

j. Enter **Improving Customer Service** in a heading 1 style below the paragraph. Enter the following as an outline numbered style list:

1) Have a written customer service policy.

   a) Make sure employees know that customer service is the paramount goal of the company.

   b) Publicize your customer service policy; let customers know that it is your priority.

2) View the experience through the customer's eyes.

   a) Have a friend attend a performance and make suggestions about improving your customer service.

   b) Send employees to attend another company's performance and give examples of good and bad customer service they received.

3) Have a procedure in place to deal with customer complaints.

   a) Determine who handles complaints.

   b) Track customer complaints and resolutions.

k. Change the spacing after paragraphs in the list to 6pt.

l. Enter the following as a new paragraph below the outline list in a font size of 12 pt.

I have also compiled some data on attendance from surveys we conducted in 2006 and 2007. Please note the encouraging statistics for the 6–12 age group!

Lab Exercises

m. Create a clustered-column chart using the data in the following table. Enter a chart title and label the X axis (see solution above; use the Labels group on the Chart Tools Layout tab). Add formatting of your choice to the chart.

Age Range	2006	2007
6–12	50.7	54.0
13–18	18.9	17.6
19–30	11.7	11.8
30+	18.7	16.6

n. Save the document as Theater Memo and print.

on your own

Movie Data Research ★

1. For your marketing class, your project group has been asked to create a report on historical movie promotions. You have started researching the top domestic grossing movies from 1997 to 2006. Your findings are shown below.

Rank	Title	Studio	Domestic Gross	Year
1	Titanic	Paramount	$600,788,188	1997
2	Star Wars	Fox	$460,998,007	1977
3	Shrek 2	DreamWorks	$441,226,247	2004
4	E.T.: The Extra-Terrestrial	Universal	$435,110,554	1982
5	Star Wars: Episode I – The Phantom Menace	Fox	$431,088,301	1999
6	Pirates of the Caribbean: Dead Man's Chest	Buena Vista	$418,786,083	2006
7	Spider-Man	Sony	$403,706,375	2002
8	Star Wars: Episode III – Revenge of the Sith	Fox	$380,270,577	2005
9	The Lord of the Rings: The Return of the King	New Line	$377,027,325	2003
10	Spider-Man 2	Sony	$373,585,825	2004

To share your research with the rest of your group, create a memo using a memo template of your choice. Address the memo to your project group, from you, with a copy to Professor Grant, your instructor, and enter an appropriate subject for the memo. In the body of the memo, enter a short introductory paragraph followed by a table presenting your research. This table should include a title along with appropriate labels and the data presented above. Format the table with shading and fonts of your choice. Save the document as Movie Data and print the memo.

Language Data Memo ★★

2. You work for the Languages and Literature department at the local community college. You are preparing some information for the faculty regarding the world's most widely used languages. Use a memo template of your choice and create a table using the data below. Your completed memo should include your name as the sender of the memo, appropriate labels, cell shading, modified date field, and merged title cells. Save the memo as Language Memo and print it.

Most Widely Spoken Languages in the World	
Language	Approx. number of speakers
1. Mandarin	1 billion+
2. English	508 million
3. Hindustani	497 million
4. Spanish	392 million
5. Russian	277 million
6. Arabic	246 million
7. Bengali	211 million
8. Portuguese	191 million
9. Malay-Indonesian	159 million
10. French	129 million

Lab Exercises

Household Pet Ownership Memo ★★

3. You work in the public relations department of the Animal Rescue Foundation. You have been asked to compile some information on pet ownership in the United States for the annual report. Create a memo using a template of your choice. Change the date field format to one of your choice. Use the information below to create a table. Your table should have a title in a row with merged cells. Use a formula to total the total expenditures on pets in a new column. Add cell shading of your choice to the table. Size the table appropriately. Create a pie chart comparing the percent of households owing dogs, cats, birds, and horses. Title the pie chart "Percent of all households." Enter your name as the sender of the memo; enter an appropriate introductory paragraph followed by the table. Conclude the memo by entering a paragraph citing the source of the data. Save the memo as Pet Ownership Memo and print it.

	Dog	Cat	Pet bird	Horse
Households owning companion pets (millions)	31.20	27.00	4.60	1.50
Percent of all households	31.60%	27.30%	4.60%	1.50%
Average number owned	1.70	2.20	2.70	2.70
Total companion pet population (millions)	52.90	59.10	12.60	4.00
Households obtaining veterinary care	88.70%	72.90%	15.80%	66.30%
Average visits per household per year	2.60	1.90	0.20	2.30
Average annual costs per household	$186.80	$112.24	$10.95	$226.26
Total expenditures (millions)	$5,828.00	$3,030.00	$50.00	$339.00

Source: American Veterinary Medical Association, Schaumburg, Ill., U.S. Pet Ownership and Demographics Sourcebook.

Worldwide Internet Usage Memo ★★★

4. As part of your study of the Internet for a sociology course, your project team has been asked to research Internet usage worldwide. Using the Memo (Professional design) template, create a memo. Replace the Company Name Here placeholder with **Sociology Group Three**. Create a logo from a grouped graphic for your group and display it adjacent to your group's name. Address the memo to your group members, from you, displaying a date in a format of your choice, and regarding "Worldwide Internet Use". Use the data you gathered shown in the table below to create a table in the memo. Your completed table should have merged cells for the title and perform calculations for the total usage worldwide. Change the table orientation as needed. Add cell shading of your choice to the table and size the rows and columns appropriately. Remove the border lines in the Total row. Create a chart using the table data. Format the chart using features you learned in the lab. Insert an introductory paragraph at the beginning of the memo followed by the table and then the chart. Save the memo as World Internet Use and print it.

How many people online?

Top 15 Online Populations by Country, Among Visitors Age 15+ March 2006 Total Worldwide – All Locations Unique Visitors (000) Source: comScore World Metrix	
Unique Visitors (000)	
Worldwide Total	**694,260**
United States	152,046
China	74,727
Japan	52,100
Germany	31,813
United Kingdom	30,190
South Korea	24,645
France	23,884
Canada	18,996
Italy	16,834
India	16,713
Brazil	13,186
Spain	12,452
Netherlands	10,969
Russia	10,833
Australia	9,735

Top 10 Cars Memo ★★★

5. You work for a local newspaper in the Research department. You have been asked to compile information about the top 10 cars for students. Use a memo template of your choice to compose a memo to send to the Features Development Editor. Modify the date field format to one of your choice. Create a grouped graphic using an image of your choice and a WordArt object. Create a table using information you find on the Internet. The table should show the type of vehicle and the manufacturer's suggested selling price ranges (lowest–highest). Add a title in a new row at the top of your table. Merge the cells in the new row. Adjust the table, row, and column size as needed. Insert a new column at the end of the table. Average the price of each vehicle in the new column using a formula. Add cell shading of your choice to the table. Remove the extra border lines in the bottom row. Create a chart using the table data. Enhance the table using the features you learned in the lab. Add an outline-style numbered list to the memo that lists tips on buying a new car. Save the memo as Cars Memo and then print it.

Creating Forms, Using Mail Merge, and Reviewing Documents

LAB 6

Objectives

After completing this lab, you will know how to:

1 Create a form.

2 Add content controls.

3 Prepare a document for distribution.

4 Use the Track Changes feature.

5 Add, modify, and delete comments.

6 E-mail a document for review.

7 Compare and merge reviewed documents.

8 Accept and reject tracked changes.

9 Use the Mail Merge feature to create form letters.

10 Create mailing labels and envelopes.

Case Study

Adventure Travel Tours

Today you are working on several different projects that are already underway and that you want to complete. The first is a catalog request form. This form will be printed and sent to clients along with the letter about the new tours and presentations. It also will be sent via e-mail and made available on the company Web site for customers to complete using Word 2007.

The second project is to review a document about the Africa Safari tour that a co-worker wrote for the new Africa Adventures catalog. Then you will look at the comments and tracked changes made by others to a document about the Mt. Everest tour that you sent to them to review. Writing documents such as travel brochures and newsletters is often not a solo effort. One person is typically

responsible for assembling the document, but several people may be involved in writing and/or reviewing the text. You will learn about the collaboration features in Office Word 2007 that make it easy to work on a group project.

The last project is to prepare the letter you wrote about the new tours and presentations to be sent to clients by including an inside address for each client and using his or her first name in the salutation. To do this, you will create a form letter. Form letters are common business documents used when the same information needs to be communicated to many different people. You will also create mailing labels for the letter and learn how to quickly address a single envelope.

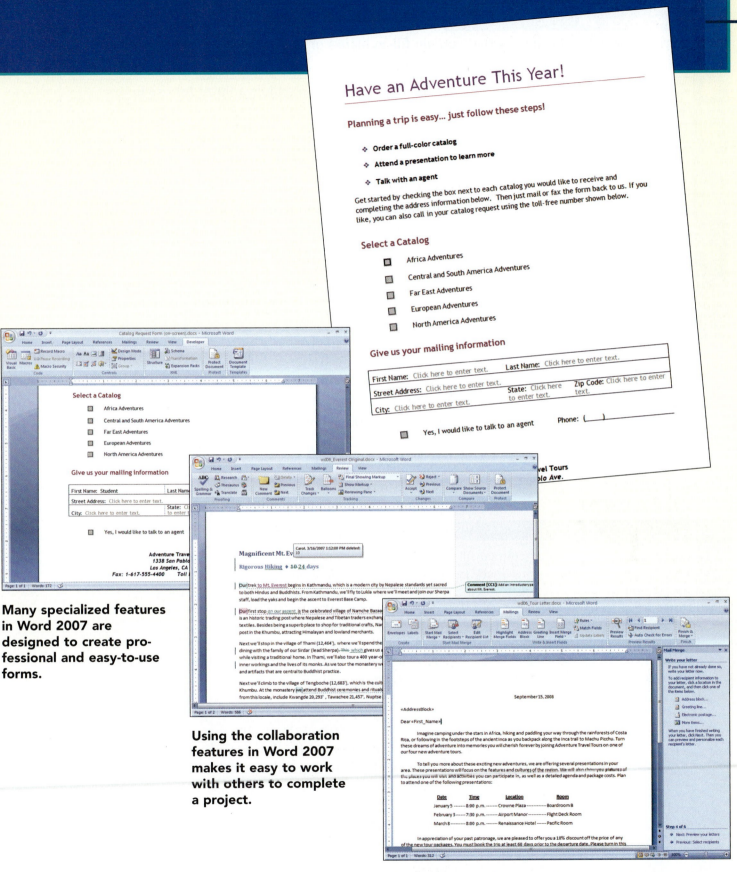

Many specialized features in Word 2007 are designed to create professional and easy-to-use forms.

Using the collaboration features in Word 2007 makes it easy to work with others to complete a project.

The Mail Merge feature helps you quickly genearate form letters.

① Forms Forms are documents that contain fill-in blanks or spaces reserved for entering information.

② Controls Controls are graphical objects that you can add to and customize for use in templates, forms and documents.

③ Protection The protection feature controls what information can be changed in a document.

④ Tracked Changes and Comments To make online reviewing of documents easier, you can add tracked changes and comments to a document.

⑤ Mail Merge The Mail Merge feature combines a list of data (typically a file of names and addresses) with a document (commonly a form letter) to create a new document.

⑥ Data Source The data source is a table of information that contains the data that varies in each copy of a merged document.

⑦ Field Name Field names are used to label the different data fields in the recipient list in a mail merge.

Creating a Form

The first project you are working on is to create a form for clients to use to order a catalog.

Concept 1

Forms

1 Forms are documents that contain fill-in blanks or spaces reserved for entering information. They are used to get information or feedback from users or to provide information. There are two basic types of forms: printed and on-screen. Printed forms are designed to be filled in on paper by the user. On-screen forms are interactive and designed to be completed using Word 2007 and returned by the user as an electronic document. These forms can be distributed by e-mail and online.

When creating a form, you need to first decide the purpose of the form and what information you need to collect to meet that purpose. Then, it is a good idea to sketch a layout of what you want the form to look like before creating it in Word 2007.

The purpose of this form is to identify the catalog a client would like to receive and to provide the mailing information where the requested materials should be sent. After considering the information you need, you have sketched out a layout for the form shown below.

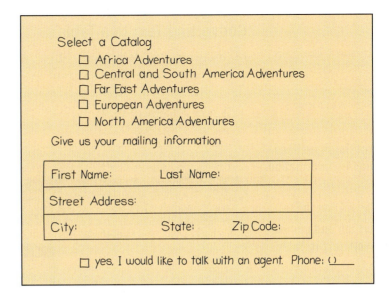

Many different features can be used to create a form. Commonly, forms are based on a grid and use a table to help align the entry areas. Most also use graphical objects such as check boxes and text boxes where information is entered that make the form easier to use. Additionally, lines can be used to identify areas to fill in information.

You have already started working on the content for the form. It includes a heading and introductory text with information about how to complete the form.

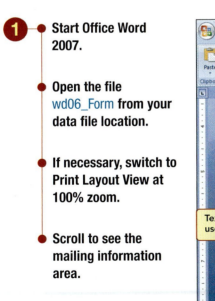

1 Start Office Word 2007.

Open the file wd06_Form from your data file location.

If necessary, switch to Print Layout View at 100% zoom.

Scroll to see the mailing information area.

Your screen should be similar to Figure 6.1

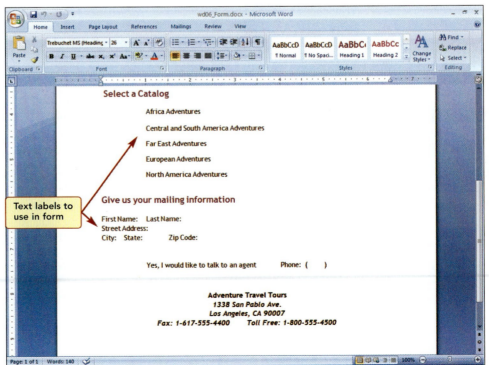

Figure 6.1

The document includes text labels identifying the mailing information you want the user to complete. You will use a table to help align the mailing information in the form.

Converting Text to a Table

MORE ABOUT

You also can convert the contents of a table to regular text. To learn about this feature, see 4.2 Use Tables and Lists to Organize Content in the More About appendix.

Many times, a document already contains text that is appropriate for display in a table. Rather than creating the table and entering the text in the cells, you can save time by converting existing text to a table format. You will use this feature to display the mailing information.

1 ● **Select the three lines of mailing information.**

● **Click** [Table] **on the Insert tab and choose Convert Text to Table.**

Your screen should be similar to Figure 6.2

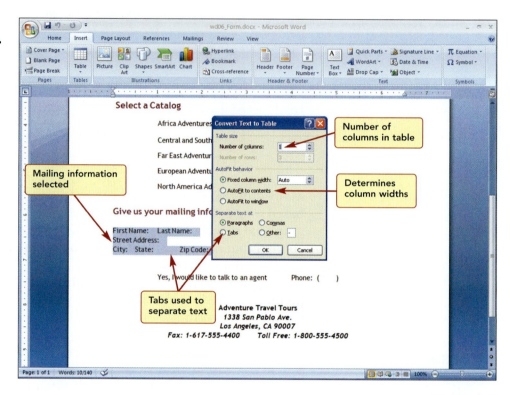

Figure 6.2

From the Convert Text to Table dialog box, you need to specify the number of columns and rows you want in the table, how the column widths are to be determined, and what means the program will use to separate text into columns. Common separators are a comma and a tab.

Additional Information

A paragraph mark indicates where a new row starts.

This table will have three columns and three rows. You will use the default selection of a fixed column width for the columns, which is automatically determined by the program. Finally, because the text in the document used tabs to separate the labels, the separator setting of Tabs will be used. Word attempts to determine these settings for you automatically from the selected text and displays the most likely selections.

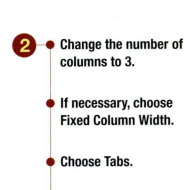

2 • Change the number of columns to 3.

• If necessary, choose Fixed Column Width.

• Choose Tabs.

• Click ⬚ OK ⬚.

• Click outside the table to deselect it.

Your screen should be similar to Figure 6.3

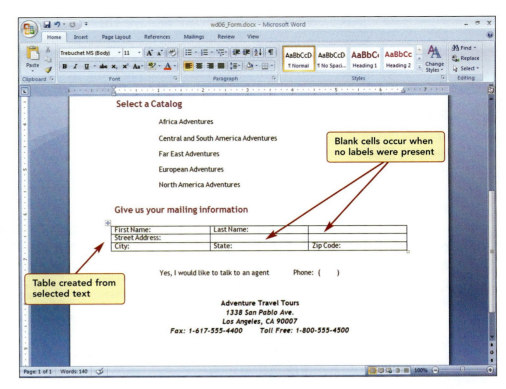

Figure 6.3

Each text label appears in a separate cell of the table. Blank cells appear when there was only one or two labels on the line that was converted. Next, you need to modify the table by merging cells and changing column widths.

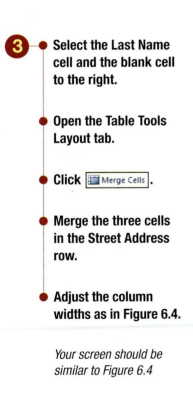

3 • Select the Last Name cell and the blank cell to the right.

• Open the Table Tools Layout tab.

• Click ⬚ Merge Cells ⬚.

• Merge the three cells in the Street Address row.

• Adjust the column widths as in Figure 6.4.

Your screen should be similar to Figure 6.4

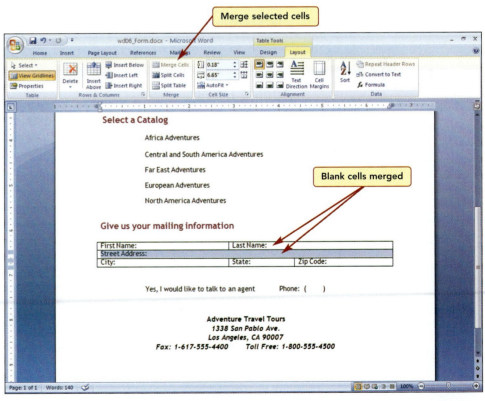

Figure 6.4

Next, you want to remove the interior table vertical border lines and increase the height of the row space by increasing the line spacing. You also want to change the alignment of text in the cell from the default of top-left-aligned to bottom-left-aligned.

4 ● Select the entire table.

● Open the [Borders] drop-down menu on the Table Tools Design tab.

● Choose Inside Vertical Border to remove the interior vertical border lines.

● Open the Table Tools Layout tab and use [0.19"] Table Row Height to increase the row height to 0.3.

● Click [≣] Align Bottom Left in the Alignment group.

● Deselect the table.

Your screen should be similar to Figure 6.5

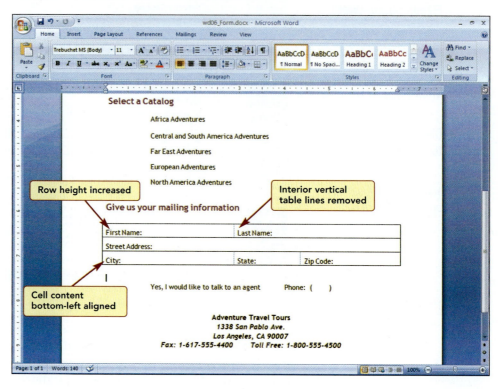

Figure 6.5

The table is now formatted how you want it to look.

Adding Lines

Next to the Phone: label you want to display a line to show where the user should enter the information. You will create this line using the Line tool in the [Shapes] gallery.

1 Click [Shapes] on the Insert tab and choose ⬊ Line from the Line category.

- Click below the left parenthesis in the phone number area and drag to the right to create a line approximately 2 inches long.

Another Method
You also could use the underline character to create a solid line.

- Save the document as Catalog Request Form to your solution file location.

Your screen should be similar to Figure 6.6

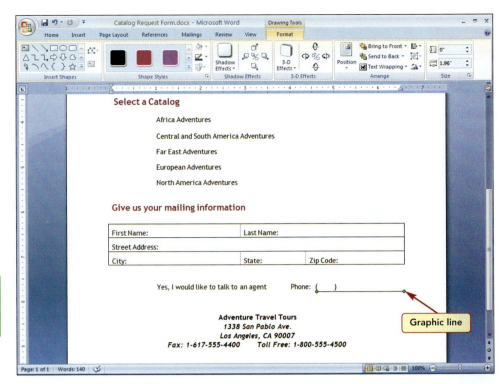

Figure 6.6

Adding Form Controls

You will create two versions of the form. One will be printed and mailed with the letter. Another version will be sent via e-mail to be completed by users in Word 2007. This version also will be provided online on the company Web site.

First you will work on the printed from. Because forms are designed to be filled in, Word 2007 includes many special form controls that are designed just for this purpose.

Concept 2

Controls

2   **Controls** are graphical objects that you can add to and customize for use in templates, forms, and documents. Many controls are interactive controls that display data choices and perform actions such as displaying a drop-down list of choices. These controls are commonly used in e-mail and Web forms.

Word 2007 includes six **content controls** that are only available in a Word 2007 document. In addition, you also can use legacy controls, called **form field controls**, in a Word 2007 document. These controls are similar to content controls but were designed for use in earlier versions of Word. The content controls are described below.

Content Control	Description
Rich Text	Use for text entries that include formatting
Text	Use for plain text entries
Picture	Use for a drawing, shape, chart, table, clip art, or SmartArt graphic
Drop-Down List	Use to provide a set of choices
Date Picker	Use to help enter a date
Building Blocks Gallery	Use to add preformatted design choices to a control

All controls include a set of properties that affect the control's appearance and behavior. Modifying the control properties allows you to customize how the control operates and provides much flexibility in the design of your form.

To access controls, you need to use the Developer tab. If this tab is not displayed on your Ribbon, you will need to add it as directed in step 1. Otherwise, skip to step 2.

1 • Click 🗔 Office Button and click 🔲 Word Options .

• From the Popular group, choose Show Developer tab in the Ribbon.

• Click ⬜ OK .

Your screen should be similar to Figure 6.7

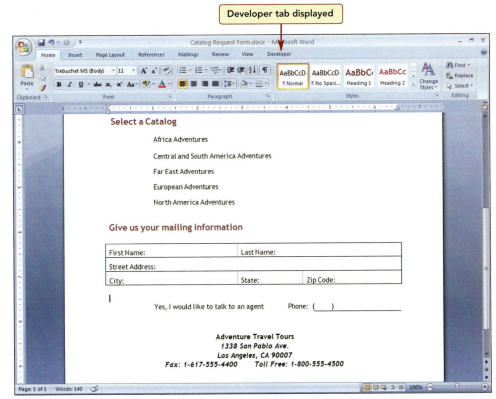

Developer tab displayed

Figure 6.7

You want to add a graphic box in front of each catalog name that the clients will check to identify which catalogs they want to receive.

2 • Open the Developer tab.

• Move to the 0.5-inch tab stop in front of the Africa Adventures catalog item.

• Click 🗔 Legacy Tools in the Controls group and choose ☑ Check Box Form Field in the Legacy Forms section of the gallery.

Your screen should be similar to Figure 6.8

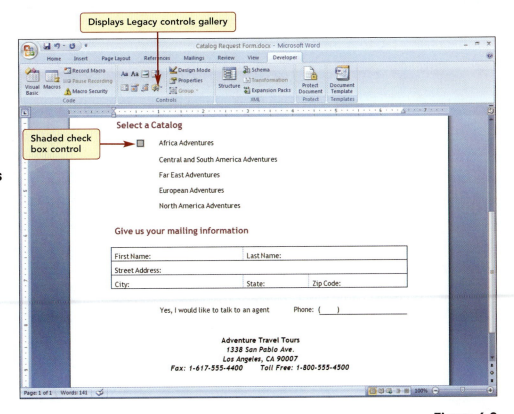

Displays Legacy controls gallery

Shaded check box control

Figure 6.8

Another Method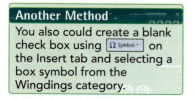

You also could create a blank check box using ⌨ Symbol ▾ on the Insert tab and selecting a box symbol from the Wingdings category.

3 ● Double-click on the control to access the properties.

Another Method

You also could click 🔲 Properties in the Controls group of the Developer tab.

Your screen should be similar to Figure 6.9

This type of check box control will display a check mark in the box when it is selected. This is the default property setting for the control. In the printed form document, you do not want the check box to actually allow someone to select the option, so you will turn off this feature. You also do not want the shading to appear in the check box.

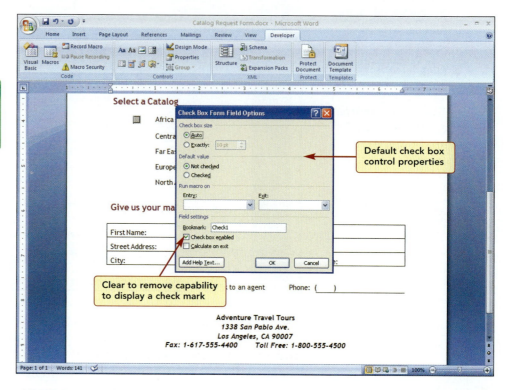

Figure 6.9

The default check box properties include automatically sizing the check box, not displaying a check mark in the control, and displaying a check mark when the control is selected. You can change the default size to an exact size you specify and add a check mark as the default value. You also can associate a macro with the control. A **macro** is a stored series of commands or actions that will be executed when the control is selected. Finally, in the field settings section, you can remove the capability to display a check mark when the check box is selected, which affects the behavior of the control.

4 • Choose the Check box enabled option to clear it.

• Click OK .

• Click 🖳▾ Legacy Tools and choose 🄰 Form Field Shading to remove shading from all controls.

• Click outside the control to deselect it.

Your screen should be similar to Figure 6.10

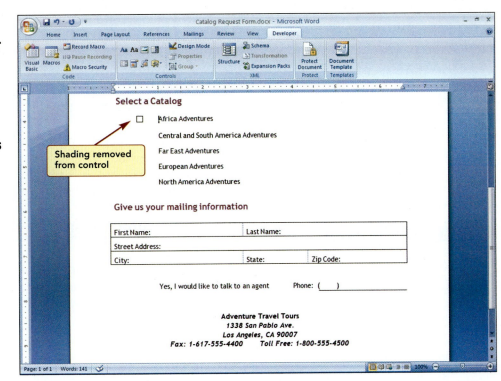

Figure 6.10

Next, you need to add the same control to the other four catalog choices and to before the "Yes, I would like to talk to an agent" text. Like any other type of graphic objects, content controls can be copied.

5 • Select and copy the check box control to the four catalog choices.

• Copy the check box control to before the "Yes, I would like to talk to an agent" text.

• Save the document as Catalog Request Form (printed) in your solution file location.

Your screen should be similar to Figure 6.11

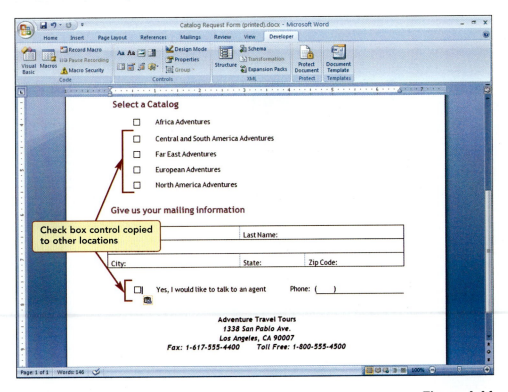

Figure 6.11

Copying the control also included the properties and settings associated with it. This was a lot quicker than creating and setting the properties for each control individually.

The printed version of the form is complete.

Preparing the Form for Use

Because the printed form document file will be distributed for use to all ATT offices, you need to take several steps to prepare it for use. These steps include removing private information, marking the document as final, adding a digital signature and protecting the document.

Checking for Private Information

Additional Information

It is a good idea to save a backup copy of a document before using Document Inspector, as it is not always possible to restore data that was removed by this feature.

Before you give a file to another user, it is a good idea to check the document for hidden data or personal information that may be stored in the computer itself or in the document's properties that you may not want to share. To help locate and remove this information, you can use the Document Inspector.

1 ● Click 📄 Office Button, select Prepare, and choose Inspect Document.

Your screen should be similar to Figure 6.12

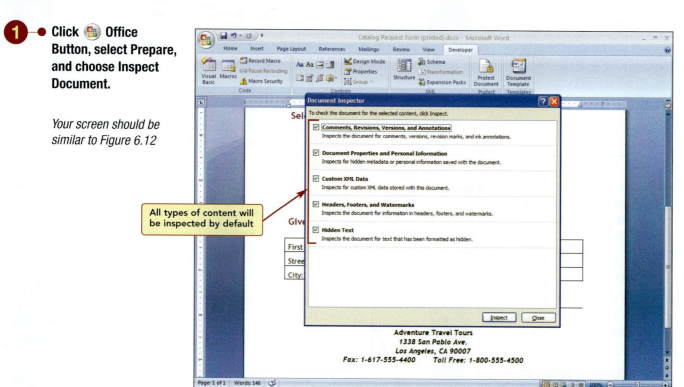

All types of content will be inspected by default

Figure 6.12

Using the Document Inspector dialog box, you can specify the type of content you want inspected by checking each of the types described in the following table.

Type	Removes
Comments, Revisions, Versions, and Annotations	Comments, tracked changes revision marks, document version information, and ink annotations
Document Properties and Personal Information	All document properties, including statistical information, e-mail headers, routing slips, send-to-review information, document server properties, content type information, user name, template name
Custom XML Data	All custom XML data that was stored within the document
Headers, Footers, and Watermarks	All information in headers and footers as well as watermarks
Hidden text	Any text that was formatted as hidden

You will inspect the document for all types of information.

2 • **If necessary, select all five types of content to check.**

• **Click Inspect .**

Your screen should be similar to Figure 6.13

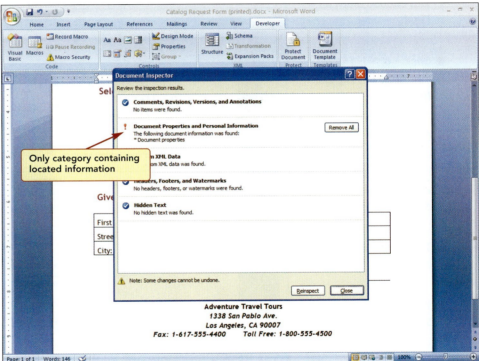

Figure 6.13

The Inspector results show that only Document Properties and Personal Information were located. For any located items, you have the option of removing the information. To remove any located information, you would click Remove All next to each item in the list; otherwise, the information is maintained. You will remove all document properties.

3 • Click [Remove All] and click [Close].

Now, if you were to open the Document Information Panel, it would be blank and all past statistical data maintained with the document would be cleared and started fresh. However, they continue to be maintained as you work with the file.

Marking a Document as Final

Another feature you can use when sharing a workbook with others is to mark it as final. This feature makes the document read-only and thereby prevents changes to the document. However, this feature is not a security feature, as anyone using the file can easily remove the Mark as Final status from the file. You will try out this feature to see how it works as it may be useful in other situations. Then you will turn the feature off.

1 • Click 🅑 Office Button, select Prepare, and choose Mark as Final.

• Click [OK] to authorize saving the file.

• Click [OK] in response to the informational message about marking the document as final.

• Try to edit the document.

Your screen should be similar to Figure 6.14

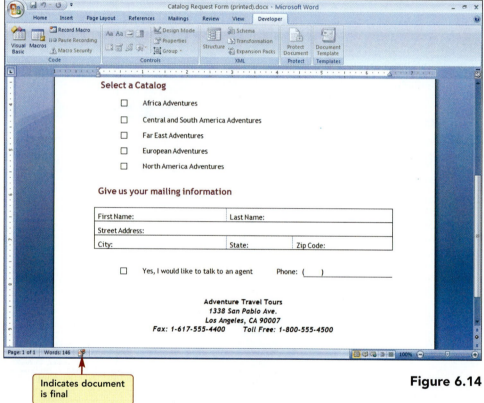

Indicates document is final

Figure 6.14

The 🔖 Mark as Final icon appears in the status bar to show that this feature is on and that the file cannot be edited. Since you may still want to make changes to the document, you will turn off this feature.

2 • Click 🅑 Office Button, select Prepare, and choose Mark as Final.

The read-only restriction is removed from the file and the 🔖 Mark as Final icon is no longer displayed in the status bar.

Adding a Digital Signature

Another feature that can be used when giving someone else a file to look at is a digital signature. This feature authenticates that the people and products are who and what they claim to be through the use of a digital signature. A **digital signature** is an electronic encryption-based stamp of authentication that confirms the document originated from the signer and has not been changed. For the signature to be valid, it must by issued by a certificate authority (CA), a commercial organization that issues digital signatures.

Digital signatures can be visible in a document or invisible. A visible digital signature is displayed on a signature line in the document. An invisible signature is stored in the document file and recipients can verify that the document was digitally signed by viewing the document's digital signature or by looking at the Signatures button in the status bar. You will add and then remove an invisible digital signature.

MORE ABOUT

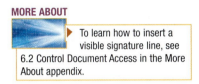

To learn how to insert a visible signature line, see 6.2 Control Document Access in the More About appendix.

1 ● Click ⊞ Office Button, select Prepare, and choose Add a Digital Signature.

● Read the information message and click ⟨ OK ⟩.

Having Trouble?
If necessary, choose Create your own digital signature and click ⟨ OK ⟩. Then enter your name in the Name box and click ⟨ Create ⟩.

● Click ⟨ Sign ⟩ to add your digital signature.

Additional Information
The default signature is the user name on your computer.

● Click ⟨ OK ⟩ in response to the Signature Confirmation message.

Your screen should be similar to Figure 6.15

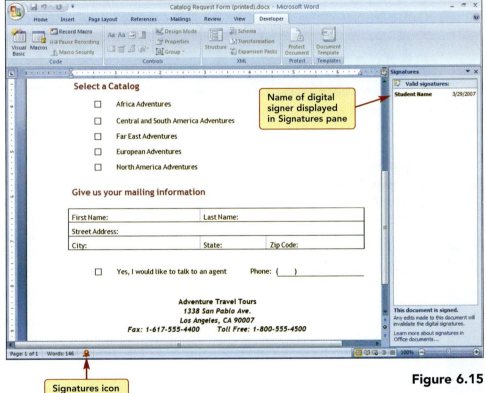

Figure 6.15

The file is saved as a read-only file and the status bar displays the Signatures icon. Clicking on this button hides and displays the Signatures pane. The Signatures pane displays the names of the digital signers. Again, because you want to be able to make changes to the worksheet, you will turn off this feature.

2 ● Point to the digital signature name in the Signatures pane and open the drop-down menu.

● Choose Remove Signature.

● Click [Yes] to permanently remove the signature.

● Click [OK] to acknowledge that the signature was removed.

● Close the Signatures task pane.

The Read-Only restriction is removed and the [🧑] Signatures icon is no longer displayed in the status bar.

Protecting the Form

Now that the form is how you want it to appear, you want to prevent unwanted changes to it by others. To do this, you can protect the document.

Concept 3

Protection

3 The **protection** feature controls what information can be changed in a document. Word allows you to add protection to individual controls or to a group of controls in a template or form to help prevent users from deleting or changing them. You also can protect the entire document.

To protect specific controls, you select them and then specify the type of protection. Controls can be protected to prevent changes to content if they contain text and/or to prevent them from being deleted.

Document level protection prevents changes to an entire document. Again, you can specify the degree of protection you want. You can protect a document from all changes, which makes the document read-only. You can restrict changes to specific types of editing or formatting changes. You also can specify which areas in the document can be changed. Further, you can give permission to allow specific people only to change the unrestricted parts of the document.

In addition, you can include a **password** that prevents any unauthorized person from either viewing or saving changes to the document. Two separate passwords can be used: one to open and view the file and another to edit and save the file. Strong passwords combine uppercase and lowercase letters, numbers, and symbols and are at least eight characters in length. If you use a password, you must remember the password in order to use the workbook or worksheet or to turn protection off in the future. Because passwords cannot be retrieved, it is recommended that you write down and store your passwords in a secure place away from the information they protect or use a strong password that you can remember.

You will protect the entire document.

1 • Click  in the Protect group of the Developer tab.

• Choose **Allow only this type of editing in the document** from the Restrict Formatting and Editing task pane.

MORE ABOUT

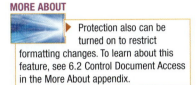 ▶ Protection also can be turned on to restrict formatting changes. To learn about this feature, see 6.2 Control Document Access in the More About appendix.

Your screen should be similar to Figure 6.16

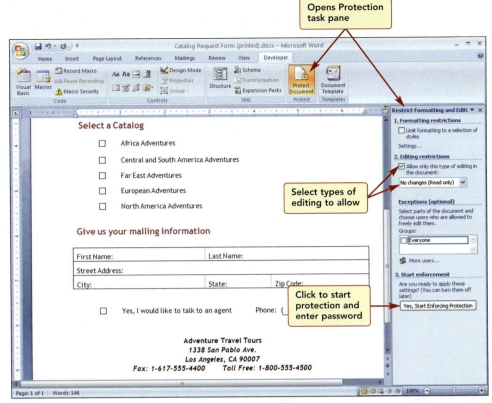

Figure 6.16

Next, you need to specify the type of editing that can be made to the document. In this case, you want to prevent all changes to the document. This is the default setting. Then you need to start protection and enter a password so that only users who know the password can remove protection.

2 • Click | Yes, Start Enforcing Protection |.

• Enter your name as the password.

• Enter your name again exactly as you just entered it to confirm the password.

• Click | OK |.

Your screen should be similar to Figure 6.17

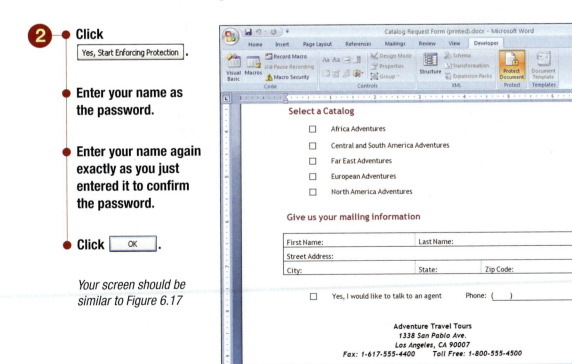

Figure 6.17

Now, the only changes that will be allowed in the document are to complete the form. If you wanted to revise the form, you would need to turn off protection by clicking Stop Protection and entering your password.

3 ● Close the task pane.

● Save and close the document.

Adding Text Content Controls

Next you will create a second form that is designed for clients to fill in the information using Word 2007. This form will be available for download from the company's Web site and sent to registered clients via e-mail with the letter. Although the form content will be the same, several different content controls will be used so that the form can be filled in using Word 2007.

First you will add check box controls to the form. You will leave the default property setting of enabled so that it will display a check mark when selected by the user. You also will keep the shading effect.

1 ● Open the Catalog Request Form file you saved earlier.

● Add the five catalog check boxes to the form at the 0.5-inch tab stop position.

● Add a check box before the Yes, I would like to talk to an agent text.

Your screen should be similar to Figure 6.18

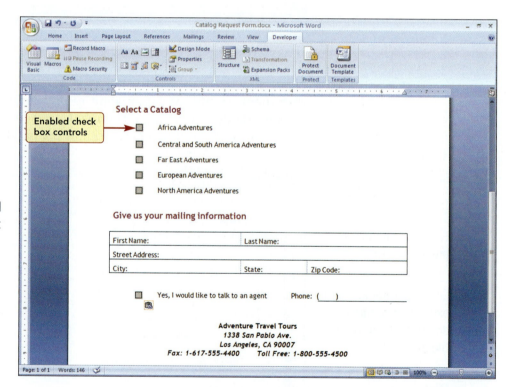

Figure 6.18

Now you are ready to add text controls where users are to enter their mailing information.

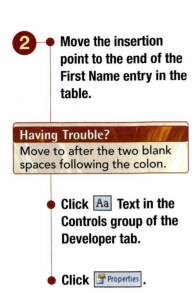

2 ● **Move the insertion point to the end of the First Name entry in the table.**

Having Trouble?
Move to after the two blank spaces following the colon.

● **Click** Aa **Text in the Controls group of the Developer tab.**

● **Click** Properties.

Your screen should be similar to Figure 6.19

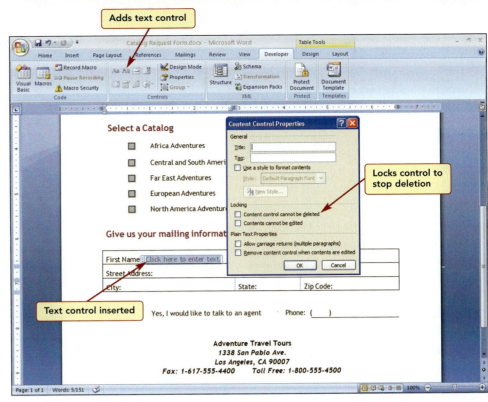

Adds text control

Locks control to stop deletion

Text control inserted

Figure 6.19

A different set of properties is associated with the text control then were associated with the Check Box control. You will select the option to lock the control so that it cannot be deleted.

3 ● **Choose Content control cannot be deleted from the Locking area.**

● **Click** OK.

● **Click outside the control to deselect it.**

Your screen should be similar to Figure 6.20

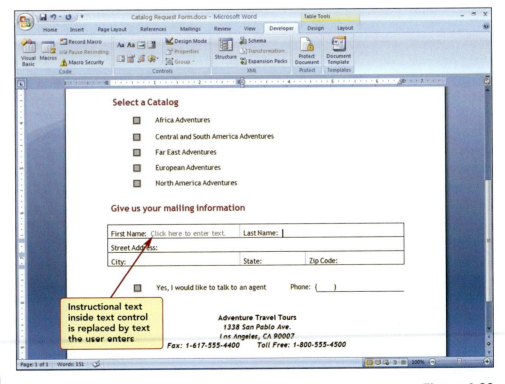

Instructional text inside text control is replaced by text the user enters

Figure 6.20

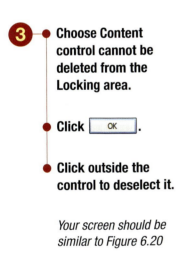

Additional Information
You can change the default instructional text to your own text by clicking Design Mode and typing the text you want to appear in the control.

The text control includes instructional text that will be replaced by the text the user enters. The contents of the text control can be edited; however, the control cannot be deleted.

4 ● Select and copy the text control to after the text in the other five table cells.

Having Trouble?
Click on the control and click ⋮ on the upper-left corner to select it.

● Save the form as Catalog Request Form (on-screen) in your solution file location.

● Click in the First Name text control and type your first name.

● Click on a catalog check box to try to select it.

Your screen should be similar to Figure 6.21

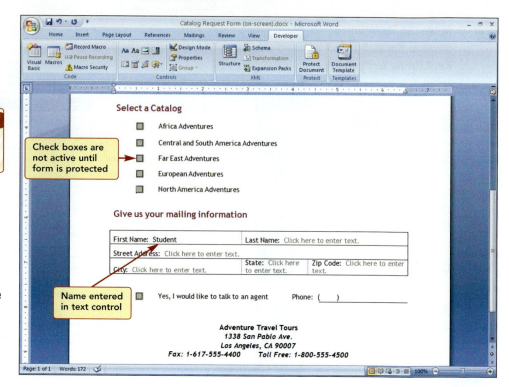

Figure 6.21

Your name appears in place of the text control in the table. However, you were not able to select the check box. To actually use a check box to check off items in the form, you first need to lock the form by protecting it. You will learn about protecting an online form next and then you will test the form.

Protecting and Testing the On-screen Form

This document contains both legacy and content controls. To lock the legacy controls, you need to protect the document. However, this will inactivate the content controls. To resolve this problem, you will divide the document into three sections and then apply protection only to those sections containing the legacy controls. Since clients will fill in information, you need to limit the protection restriction to allow this type of change.

1 • Click 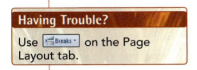 to remove your name from the table cell.

• Move to the blank line above the table and insert a continuous section break at that location.

Having Trouble?

Use ⌗Breaks ▾ on the Page Layout tab.

• Insert a second continuous section break at the blank line below the table.

• Click 📄 Protect Document in the Protect group of the Developer tab.

• Choose Allow only this type of editing in the document.

• Open the drop down menu and choose Filling in Forms as the type of editing that is allowed.

• Choose Select sections.

Your screen should be similar to Figure 6.22

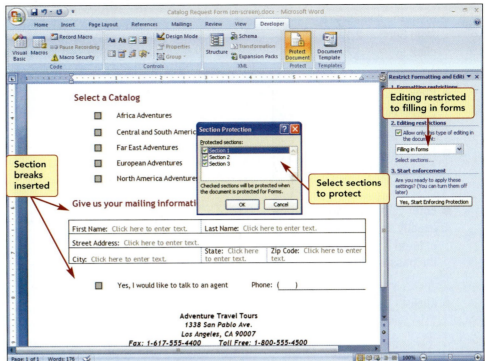

Figure 6.22

Next, you need to select the sections that you want protected. You will not protect section two containing the table with the content controls.

2

- Clear the checkmark from Section 2 and click OK .

- Click Yes, Start Enforcing Protection .

- Enter your name as the password.

- Enter your name again exactly as you just entered it to confirm the password.

- Click OK .

Your screen should be similar to Figure 6.23

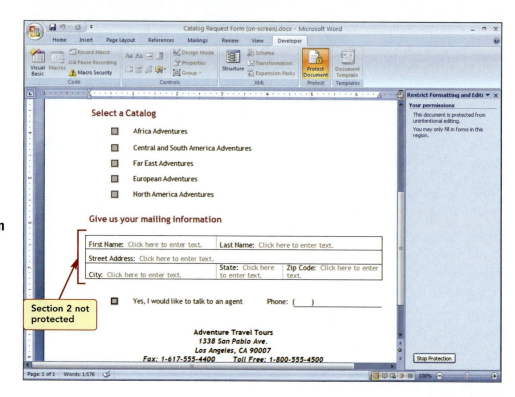

Section 2 not protected

Figure 6.23

Now you will test the form to confirm that protection is working and that the content controls are still operational.

3

- Close the task pane and save the document.

- Try clicking anywhere in section one of the form other than on the check box.

- Click on a catalog check box to select it.

- Click in the First Name text control in the table and enter your first name.

- Double-click on the word First in the table and press Delete .

Your screen should be similar to Figure 6.24

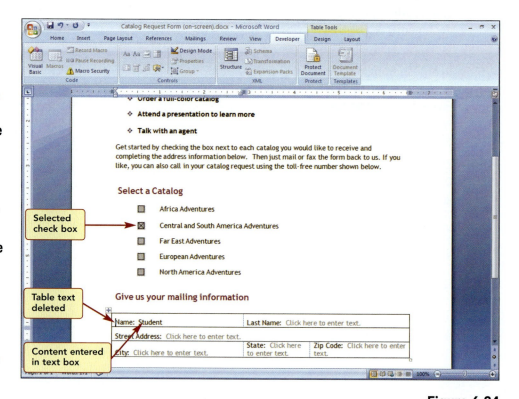

Selected check box

Table text deleted

Content entered in text box

Figure 6.24

In the protected areas of the form, you were not able to make any changes to the form other than to select the check box. In the unprotected section, you were able to enter content in the text control and change text in the table.

You also do not want the text in the table to be able to be edited. To fix this, you need to remove protection and place the table in a rich-text content control. You will set the properties for the rich text control to prevent editing and deletion. This will protect the regular text in the table against editing but will not affect the operation of the embedded content controls.

4 ● Click ⟲ twice to undo the changes to the document.

● Clear the check in the check box.

● Click [Protect Document], click [Stop Protection], and enter your password.

● Select the table.

● Click [Aa] Rich Text Control and click [Properties].

● Choose Content control cannot be deleted.

● Choose Contents cannot be edited.

● Click [OK].

Your screen should be similar to Figure 6.25

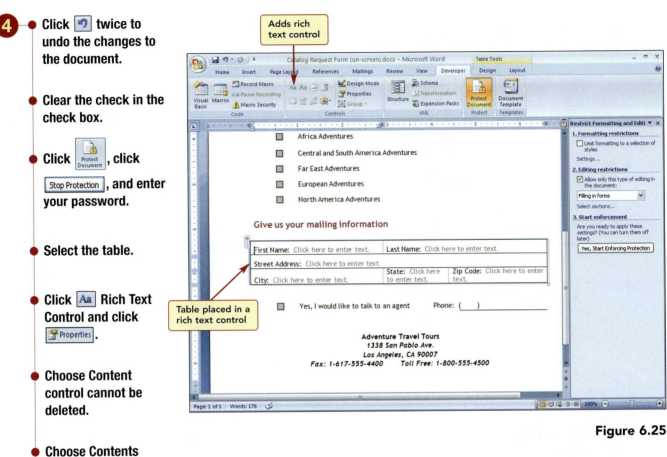

Adds rich text control

Table placed in a rich text control

Figure 6.25

The table is now enclosed in a rich text control that cannot be deleted or edited. The text controls inside the rich text control, however, can still be edited. You will reapply protection and save the form as a template. Then you will use the template to complete the form.

5 ● Reapply protection and close the task pane.

● Save the document as a Word template file in the Trusted Templates folder using the same file name.

Having Trouble?
If a file exists with that name already, click Yes to replace it.

● Close the document.

● Click 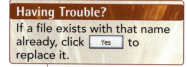 Office Button and choose New/My Templates.

● Select Catalog Request Form (on-screen) and click OK to open the template.

● Select a catalog.

● Enter your first and last names in the appropriate text controls in the table.

Additional Information
You can press Tab to move from one content control to the next.

● Try to delete the word First in the table.

Your screen should be similar to Figure 6.26

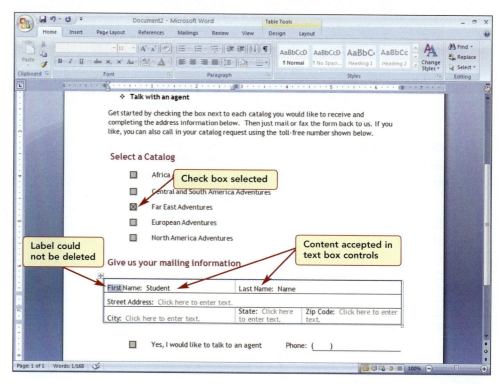

Figure 6.26

The form is working correctly now.

6 ● Preview and print the completed form.

● Save and replace the Catalog Request Form (on-screen) **Word document in your solution file location with the completed form.**

● Turn off the display of the Developer tab.

Having Trouble
Clear the Show Developer tab in Ribbon option in the Popular category of the Word Options dialog box.

● Close the document.

Your completed form should be similar to that shown in the Case Study at the beginning of the lab.

Using Collaboration Features

Your next project is to review a document about the Africa Safari tour that a co-worker wrote for the new Africa Adventures catalog. Writing documents such as travel brochures and newsletters is often not a solo effort. One person is typically responsible for assembling the document, but several people may be involved in writing and/or reviewing the text. Office Word 2007 includes many features that make it easy to collaborate or work with others to complete a project. These features include the capability to circulate documents for review, to insert, view, and edit comments, and to track and accept or reject proposed changes.

Tracking Changes to a Document

You have a copy of the text file and want to enter your suggested changes and return it to the author. To show the author what changes you are suggesting, you will use the Track Changes feature and add comments.

Concept 4

Tracked Changes and Comments

4 To make reviewing of documents easier, you can add tracked changes and comments to a document. **Tracked changes** identify any insertion, deletion, move, or formatting change that is made to the document. Notes or annotations called **comments** also can be added to a document without changing the document text.

Tracked changes and comments are displayed using markup. **Markup** elements include colored and underlined text and balloons. **Balloons** show text that has been deleted and the text of comments. They appear in the right margin so that they are easily visible and to preserve the layout of the original document.

Typically, a document is sent out for review by several people. When it is returned to the author, a document that has been edited using tracked changes can then be quickly reviewed to evaluate the suggested changes. As the author reviews tracked changes and comments, each change can be accepted or rejected as appropriate. Comments can be deleted when they are no longer needed.

You will open the document file you want to review and turn on the Track Changes feature before making any changes.

1 ● Open the wd06_Camping Safari file.

● Hide the spelling and grammar errors.

● Click 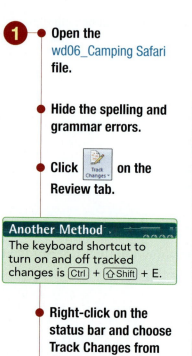 on the Review tab.

Another Method
The keyboard shortcut to turn on and off tracked changes is [Ctrl] + [⇧ Shift] + E.

● Right-click on the status bar and choose Track Changes from the shortcut menu.

● Click outside the menu to clear it.

Your screen should be similar to Figure 6.27

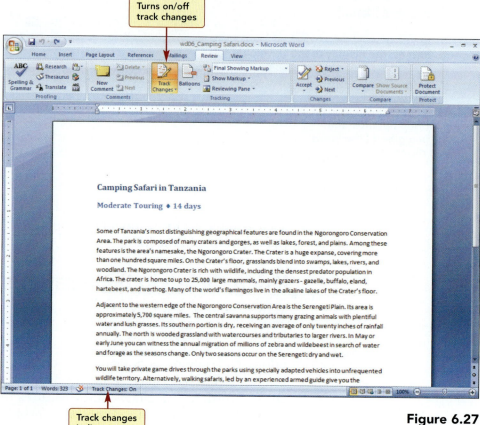

Turns on/off track changes

Track changes indicator

Figure 6.27

The change tracking feature is on and now, when changes are made, the document will display markup of the tracked changes. Additionally, because you turned on the track changes indicator in the status bar, you can quickly tell when this feature is on or off.

First, you want to delete some text in the first paragraph and replace it with new text.

2 • Move to the end of the third sentence, after the word "Crater" and before the period.

• Select the text to the right through the end of the word "covering."

• Press [Delete].

• Type **, which covers.**

Your screen should be similar to Figure 6.28

Having Trouble?
If revision marks are not displayed, click 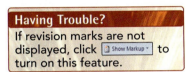 to turn on this feature.

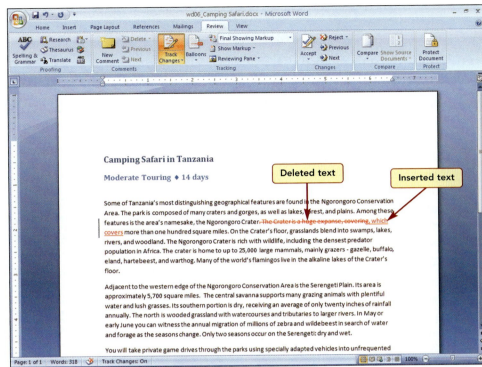

Figure 6.28

The deleted text is identified with markup of red text color with a red strikeout line through it and the inserted text is also in red and underlined.

The next change you want to make is to change the word "Crater" to all lowercase characters when it does not follow the name Ngorongoro.

3 • Use Find and Replace to locate all occurrences of "Crater" and replace them with **crater** when they are not following Ngorongoro. Do not replace the word in the deleted text.

Having Trouble?
Use the Match case Search option while using Find and Replace.

• When you are finished, close the Find and Replace dialog box.

• Point to any markup for the word "crater."

Your screen should be similar to Figure 6.29

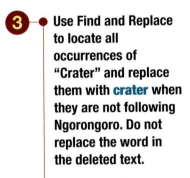

Figure 6.29

The inserted changes are identified and a ScreenTip with information about who made the change and when the change was made is displayed. The lines of the document that have been changed are identified with a vertical rule along the left margin. The different markup elements help preserve the layout of the document while changes are being tracked.

In the second paragraph, you have several changes to make, including moving a sentence.

4 ● At the end of the first sentence of the second paragraph, delete the period and "Its area is" and replace it with **covering**.

● At the beginning of the third sentence, change "Its" to **In contrast, the**.

● Move the last sentence by dragging it to before the sentence preceding it.

Your screen should be similar to Figure 6.30

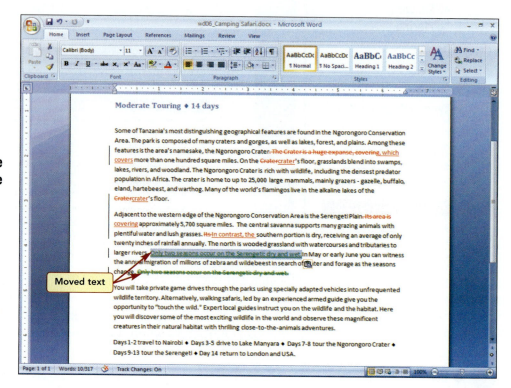

Figure 6.30

The moved sentence is marked in green with a double underline at the new location and in green with a double strikethrough at the original location.

Adding Comments

As you read the final paragraph, you decide it does not contain enough information about the activities and camping experiences that will be encountered on the safari. Rather than making these changes, you decide to add a comment about this to the author.

1 Move to the beginning of the third paragraph.

Click 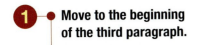 in the Comments group of the Review tab.

Your screen should be similar to Figure 6.31

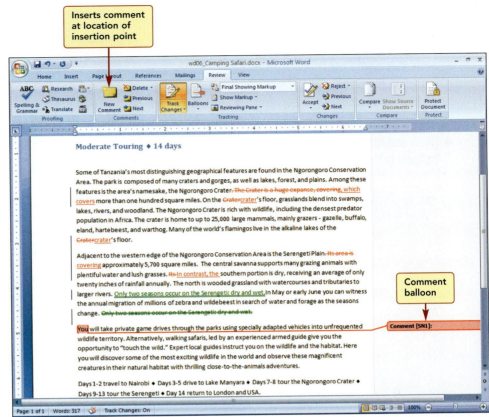

Figure 6.31

Additional Information
Balloons appear only in Print Layout and Web Layout view.

A blank comment balloon is displayed in a markup area on the right side of the document. A line connects it to the location where you inserted the comment. The font size of the text has been reduced to allow the comment balloon to be displayed in a larger margin space. The comment balloon displays the initials of the person who added the comment followed by a comment number. Comments are numbered sequentially in a document much like footnotes. Next, you need to add the text of the comment.

2 • Type **Add more information to this paragraph about the activities and camping experiences on this tour.**

• Click outside the balloon to deselect it.

Your screen should be similar to Figure 6.32

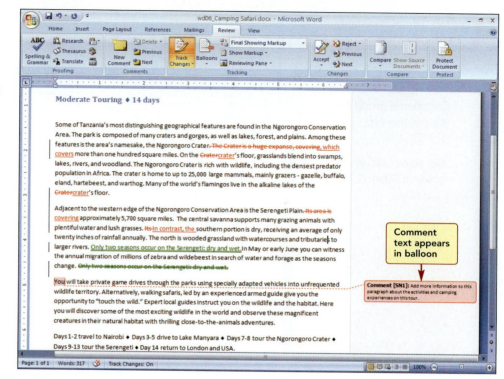

Figure 6.32

The comment text appears in the balloon. You decide the comment is too long and want to revise it.

3 • Click in the comment balloon to select it.

• Delete the word "more."

• Delete the words "to this paragraph."

• Delete the words "on this tour."

Your screen should be similar to Figure 6.33

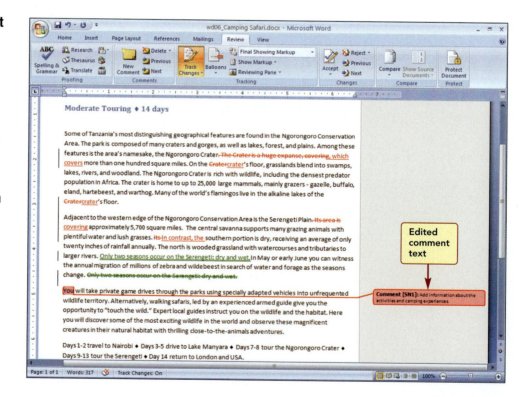

Figure 6.33

Finally, you will make a formatting change to the title. Then you will change the display to show all revisions in balloons.

4 ● Format the title line to 16 points with a dark red color.

● Format the subtitle line to 14 points, olive green color.

● Click on the selection to clear it.

● Click [Balloons] in the Review tab and choose Show Revisions in Balloons.

Your screen should be similar to Figure 6.34

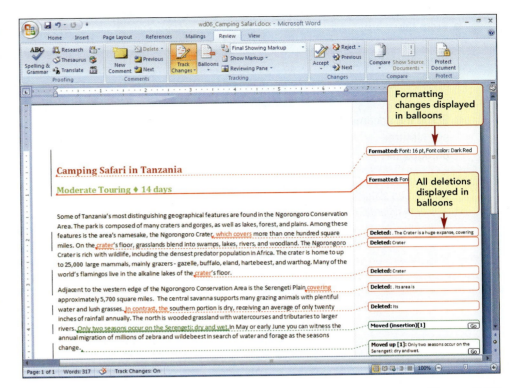

Figure 6.34

Now any text that was deleted is removed from the document and displayed in the balloon. This makes it easier to focus on the insertions rather than the deletions.

Viewing Changes

As a final check, before returning the marked-up document to the author, you want to view the document without the markup showing. There are four different views, described below, that are used to specify the type of changes you want to see in a document that contains tracked changes.

Option	Effect
Final Showing Markup	Displays the final document with the insertions underlined and the deletions indicated in the revision balloons.
Final	Displays how the document would appear if you accepted all the changes.
Original Showing Markup	Displays the original document with the deletions underlined and the insertions indicated in the revision balloons.
Original	Displays the original unchanged document so you can see how the document would look if you rejected all the changes.

You want to read the document as it will appear with the changes, but without the markup.

1 From the

drop-down list, choose Final.

● Scroll the document to see all three paragraphs.

Your screen should be similar to Figure 6.35

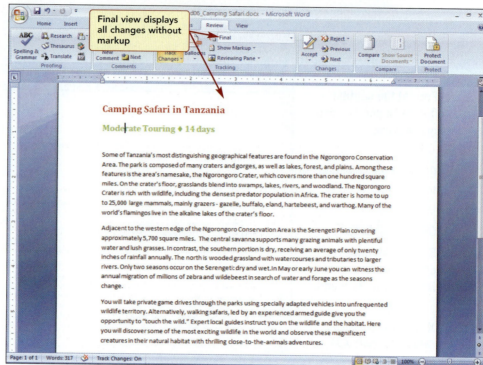

Figure 6.35

The document appears as it would look if all changes were made. Next you want to see the original document before the changes were made.

2 From the

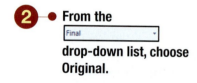

drop-down list, choose Original.

Your screen should be similar to Figure 6.36

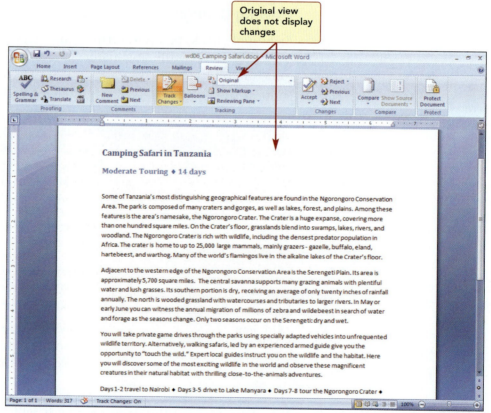

Figure 6.36

The original document appears without the revisions. You can quickly switch between the document views to check the changes. You will display the final document with markups again with comments and formatting in balloons.

3 ● Change the tracked changes view back to Final Showing Markup.

● Click [Balloons] and choose Show Only Comments and Formatting in Balloons.

Changing Tracking Options

You also can change other options associated with tracking changes, including the color and style of markup, how formatting and moves are identified, and the appearance of balloons.

You will change several of these options to see how they affect the existing markup of tracked changes.

1 ● Open the [Track Changes] drop-down menu and choose Change Tracking Options.

Your screen should be similar to Figure 6.37

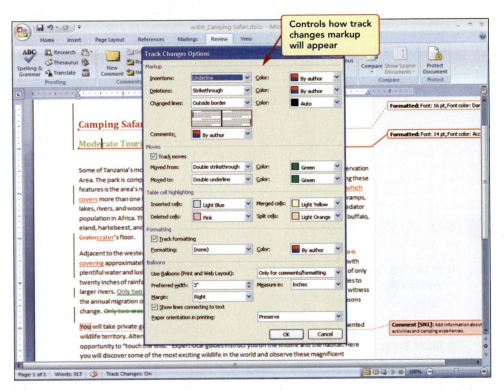

Figure 6.37

The Track Changes Options dialog box is divided into five categories that each contains options to control how tracked changes will appear for the item in the selected category. The By Author color option lets Word choose which colors go with which authors and assures that each reviewer's changes are in a different color. However, the colors on one computer are often different from the colors on another computer. You can select a specific color for your track changes, but then another reviewer's markup may be in the same colors. You cannot control which color is assigned to any reviewer and the colors may change each time a document is opened.

2 • In the Markup category, change Insertions to Bold and Bright green.

• Change Deletions to Italic and blue.

• Clear the Track Moves option.

• Clear the Track Formatting option.

• Change the balloon width to 2.5 inches.

Your screen should be similar to Figure 6.38

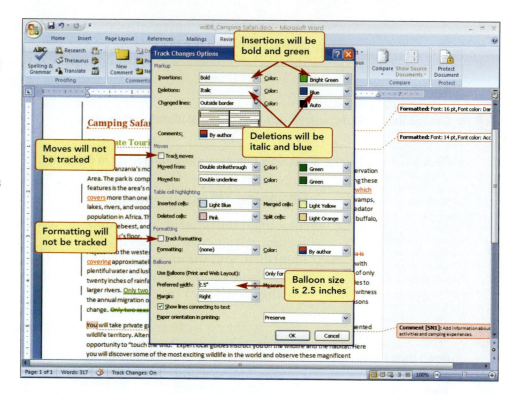

Figure 6.38

The changes you have made to the markup settings will be immediately applied to the document. To see the effects of the changes to the moving and formatting markup, you will move and format some text to verify that these settings were changed.

3 • Click .

• In the first sentence, add bold to the word "distinguishing."

• Move the word "distinguishing" by dragging it two words to the right.

Your screen should be similar to Figure 6.39

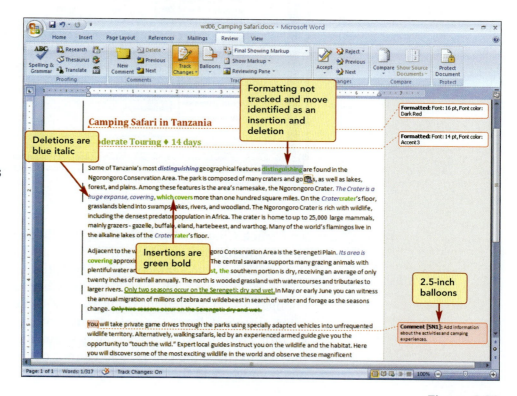

Figure 6.39

Lab 6: Creating Forms, Using Mail Merge, and Reviewing Documents

Deletions are italic and blue, insertions are bold and bright green, and balloons are 2.5 inches. The formatting and move changes were not marked. The move was instead identified as a deletion and an insertion.

You will undo the two changes you just made and reset the tracking options back to the defaults. Then you will turn off tracking changes.

4 • Undo both changes.

• Open the  drop-down menu and choose Change Tracking Options.

• Change Insertions to Underline and color to By Author.

• Change Deletions to Strikethrough and color to By Author.

• Enable Track moves and Track formatting.

• Change the balloon width back to 3 inches.

• Click OK .

• Click Track Changes in the status bar to turn off this feature.

Another Method
You also can click Track Changes to turn this feature off.

*Your screen should be
similar to Figure 6.40*

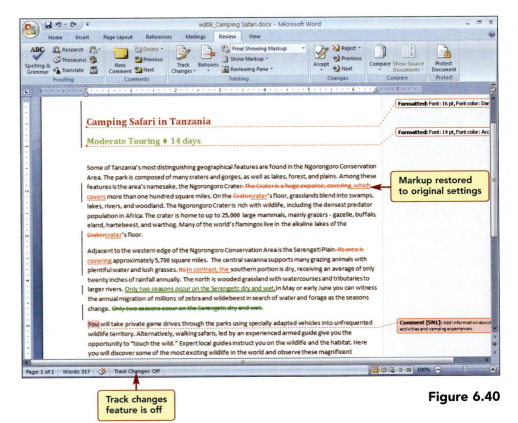

Figure 6.40

The markup tracking options are restored to the defaults and the tracked changes indicator now displays off.

5 ● **Save the document as** Camping Safari Reviewed **to your solution file location.**

● **Print the document showing markup.**

Having Trouble?
The Print What option in the Print dialog box will automatically display "Document Showing Markup" whenever you print a document with markup showing.

● **Turn off the display of the Tracked Changes indicator in the status bar.**

The program automatically sets the zoom level and page orientation needed to best display the tracked changes in the printed document.

E-mailing a Document

Next, you will return the document with your suggested changes to the author. You will return the document via e-mail with the document as an attachment. An **attachment** is a file that is sent with the e-mail message but is not part of the e-mail text. You open the attachment with the application in which it was created.

Note: Skip this section if you do not have an e-mail program installed on your system and an Internet connection.

1 ● **Choose** 🔵 **Office Button, select Send, and choose E-mail.**

Your screen should be similar to Figure 6.41

Having Trouble?
Your e-mail message window may look different than that shown in Figure 6.41 depending on the e-mail program on your computer.

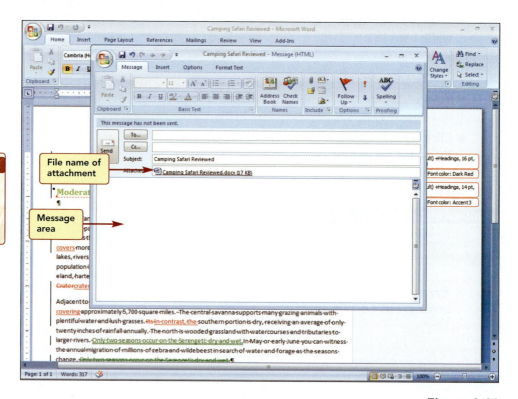

File name of attachment

Message area

Figure 6.41

An e-mail window is displayed in which you can address your e-mail message. Notice that the Subject and the Attach fields display the file name of the attached document. The extension indicates the application in which the file will open, which is helpful to know.

2 In the To field, type your e-mail address.

In the message area, type **I reviewed the Camping Safari document and made my suggested changes using the Track Changes feature.**.

Your screen should be similar to Figure 6.42

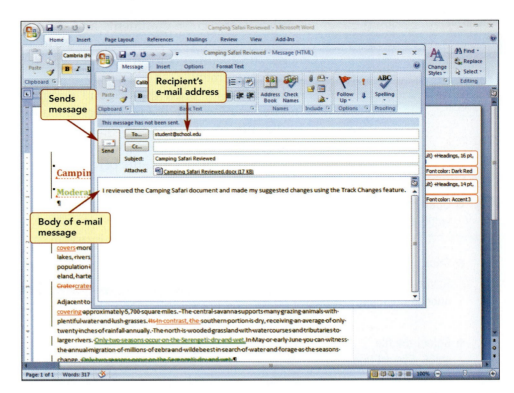

Figure 6.42

Now you are ready to send the message. If you have access to the Internet, you will send the message; otherwise, you will save it to be sent at a later time.

3 If you have Internet access, click .

Having Trouble?
The Send button on your e-mail program may be different than the one shown here.

If you do not have Internet access, close the new message window and save the message as Camping Safari E-mail when prompted.

Close the e-mail window.

Close the Word document.

MORE ABOUT

Depending on your Word 2007 settings, Word document attachments may open in regular mode or in reading mode. To learn about this feature, see Personalize Word in the More About appendix.

The recipient of the e-mail message will be able to open the attached file in Word and view and make changes to it like any other document.

Comparing and Merging Documents

While checking your e-mail for new messages, you see that two co-workers have returned a document you sent to them to review with their comments and tracked changes. You have saved the two attachments on your computer and now you want to review the suggested changes.

MORE ABOUT

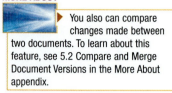

You also can compare changes made between two documents. To learn about this feature, see 5.2 Compare and Merge Document Versions in the More About appendix.

When you receive comments and changes from multiple reviewers for the same document, the easiest way to review them is to combine or merge the documents together. This way you can review the changes from a single document.

You will first open the original document you sent to the reviewers. Then you will merge the reviewers' documents with the original. You can display the results of the merge in the currently open document, in the next document you open, or in a new document. You will merge the reviewed documents into the original document.

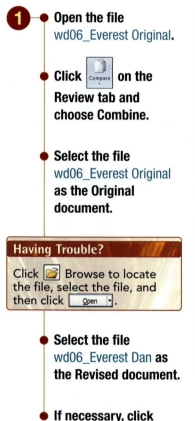

1 • Open the file wd06_Everest Original.

• Click [Compare] on the Review tab and choose Combine.

• Select the file wd06_Everest Original as the Original document.

Having Trouble?

Click [📁] Browse to locate the file, select the file, and then click [Open ▾].

• Select the file wd06_Everest Dan as the Revised document.

• If necessary, click [More >>] to display additional options.

Your screen should be similar to Figure 6.43

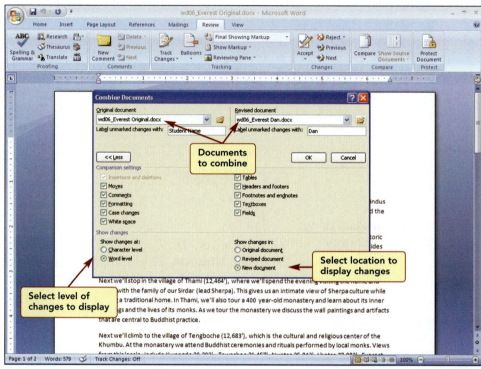

Figure 6.43

From the Comparison settings section of the dialog box, you can specify the types of changes you want displayed in the combined document. The Insertions and Deletions option is checked and dimmed because this setting is required.

The Show Changes area lets you specify the level and location where you want changes displayed. Changes can be displayed at the character or word level. Word level is the default and shows that the entire word was changed, even though only a part of the word may actually have been changed. For example, a change from the word "view" to "views" will show the entire word as changed, not simply the character "s".

The location where you want the changes displayed is specified in the Show Changes in section. Changes can be displayed in the original document, the revised document, or a new document. You will keep all the default settings, except you will change the Show changes in setting to Original document if needed.

MORE ABOUT

To learn about merging documents to a new document, see 5.2 Compare and Merge Document Versions in the More About appendix.

2

If necessary, choose Original document.

Additional Information

Any options you select will be the default options for comparison the next time you combine documents.

● **Click** OK **.**

Having Trouble?

If your screen displays additional document windows, click 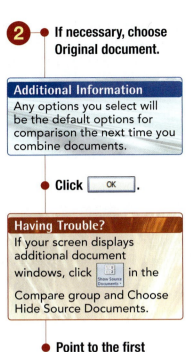 in the Compare group and Choose Hide Source Documents.

● **Point to the first markup to see the ScreenTip.**

Your screen should be similar to Figure 6.44

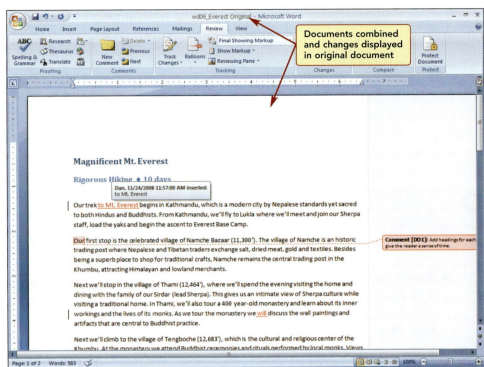

Figure 6.44

This reviewer, Dan, inserted only one comment and made two editing changes. Now you will merge the document containing changes made by the second reviewer with this document.

3

● **Click** Compare **and choose Combine.**

● **Select the file wd06_Everest Original as the Original document.**

● **Select the file wd06_Everest Carol as the Revised document.**

● **Click** << Less **.**

● **Click** OK **.**

● **Point to the first markup change to see the ScreenTip.**

Your screen should be similar to Figure 6.45

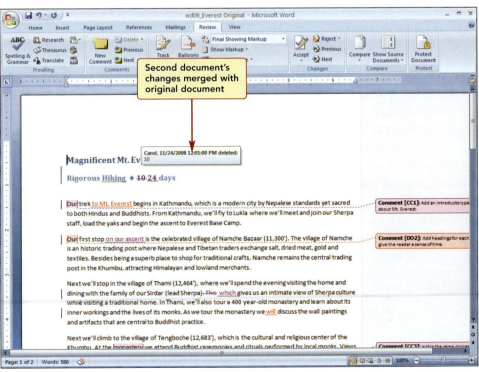

Figure 6.45

Having Trouble?

The colors used to identify the tracked changes may be different on your screen.

The markup from both reviewed documents is displayed in the original document. Word automatically assigned unique colors to the comments and tracked changes made by each reviewer.

Accepting and Rejecting Changes

Now you are ready to review the changes and comments and decide whether to accept or reject them. You will review each item in sequence to evaluate the suggestion. To help clarify the changes, you will display the Reviewing pane.

1 • If necessary, move to the beginning of the document.

• Open the 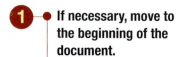 drop-down menu and choose Reviewing Pane Horizontal.

Additional Information

Clicking Reviewing Pane will display the Reviewing pane in the last-used location.

• Click Next in the Changes group of the Review tab.

Your screen should be similar to Figure 6.46

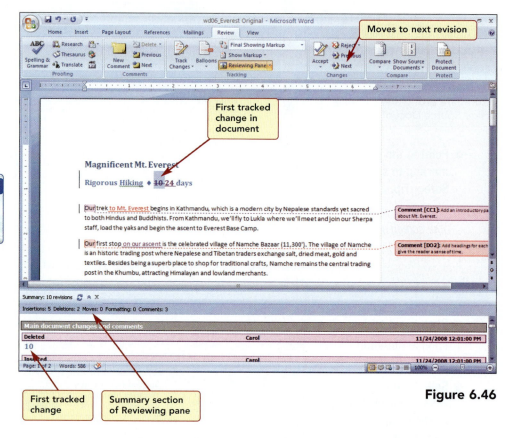

Figure 6.46

The summary section at the top of the reviewing pane displays the number and type of visible tracked changes and comments in the document. Below the summary section, the tracked changes and comments are displayed. The reviewing pane is useful for reading long comments that do not fit within a bubble rather than for actually making the editorial changes.

The first tracked change made by Carol is to delete the number 10 and replace it with the number 24. Each part of an insertion and deletion is considered a separate change and needs to be accepted or rejected individually. Since this tour is 24 days in length, you want to accept the change to delete the 10.

Additional Information

During the compare and merge process, even if changes were made to a document without tracked changes on, Word detects those changes and displays them as tracked changes.

2 Click .

*Your screen should be
similar to Figure 6.47*

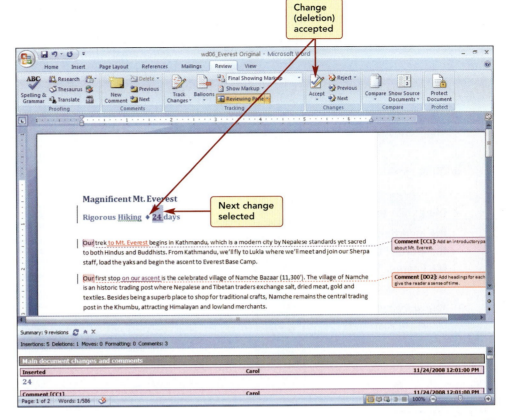

Figure 6.47

The number 10 is deleted along with the revision mark. The next suggested change, to insert the number 24, is selected. Again, this is correct and you want to accept the change.

3 Click .

*Your screen should be
similar to Figure 6.48*

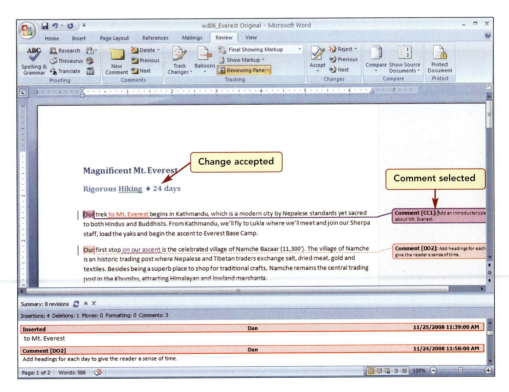

Figure 6.48

The next change is a comment. You decide you do not want to consider the comments at this time and will hide them. This way you will focus mainly on the insertions and deletions. You will address the comments after you review the editing changes.

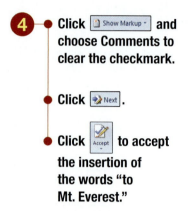

4 ● **Click** [Show Markup ▾] **and choose Comments to clear the checkmark.**

● **Click** [Next].

● **Click** [Accept] **to accept the insertion of the words "to Mt. Everest."**

Your screen should be similar to Figure 6.49

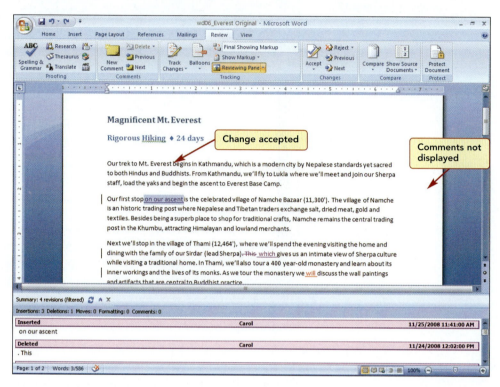

Figure 6.49

With the comments hidden, you can move directly to editing changes and respond to them accordingly. The next change is to insert "on our ascent." You feel this change is unnecessary and you will reject it.

Having Trouble?

You can use ↺ to undo the last acceptance or rejection of a tracked change.

● **Insert a space between the words "stop" and "is."**

● **Scroll the document to see the markup in the remainder of the document.**

● **Display the third paragraph.**

Your screen should be similar to Figure 6.50

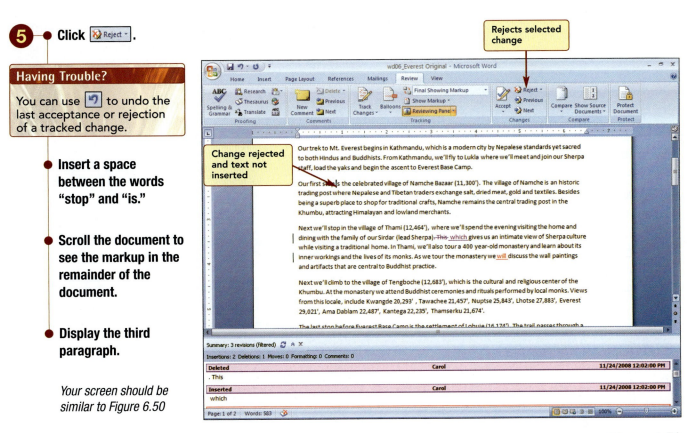

Rejects selected change

Change rejected and text not inserted

Figure 6.50

The inserted text was removed. As you look at the other editing changes in the document, you decide they are all acceptable. Rather than moving to each one independently and accepting it, you can quickly accept all changes.

⑥ ● **From the [Accept] drop-down list, choose Accept All Changes in Document.**

Your screen should be similar to Figure 6.51

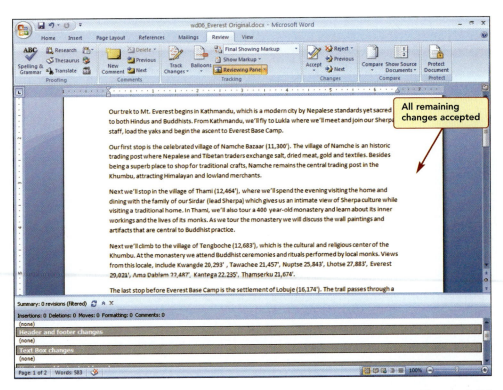

All remaining changes accepted

Figure 6.51

All the remaining changes have been accepted and the original document contents deleted. Now, you want to review the comments.

Reviewing Comments

You will show the comments in the document again and then move to the first comment to consider the suggestion.

1 ● Click [Show Markup ▾] and choose Comments to display the checkmark.

● Click [Previous] twice to move to the first comment.

Your screen should be similar to Figure 6.52

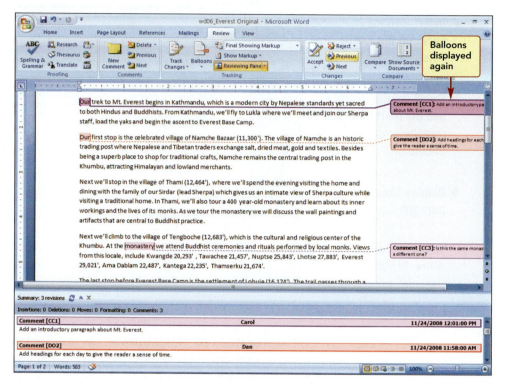

Figure 6.52

In the first comment, the reviewer wants you to add an introductory paragraph about Mt. Everest. This sounds like a good suggestion. In fact, you already have a paragraph you had written and saved in a separate file that you can add to the document that will take care of this.

 **Click** [Delete ▾] **in the Comments group.**

Your screen should be similar to Figure 6.53

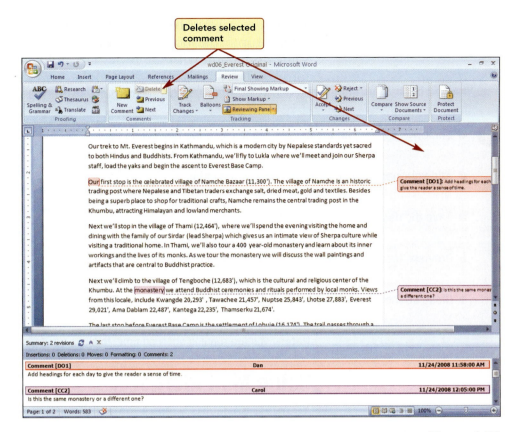

Deletes selected comment

Figure 6.53

The comment is deleted and you are ready to add the paragraph. Rather than opening the file and copying the paragraph into the document, you can insert the contents of a file directly into an open document.

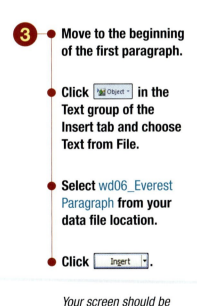 **3** ● **Move to the beginning of the first paragraph.**

● **Click** [Object ▾] **in the Text group of the Insert tab and choose Text from File.**

● **Select** wd06_Everest Paragraph **from your data file location.**

● **Click** [Insert ▾].

Your screen should be similar to Figure 6.54

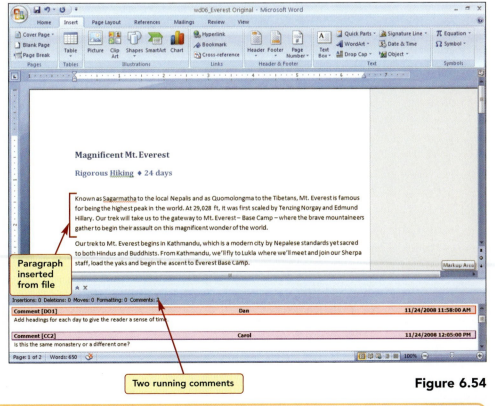

Paragraph inserted from file

Two running comments

Figure 6.54

The entire content from the file, in this case one paragraph, was quickly inserted into the document. You feel the remaining comments require some discussion with the reviewers and will leave them in the document for now. The summary section of the reviewing pane shows that there are two comments remaining in the document.

4 ● Click [Reviewing Pane ▾] on the Review tab to close the Reviewing pane.

● Add your name and the current date in a header.

● Save the document as Everest Revised.

● Preview, then print the document on a single page with markup showing.

● Close all the open documents.

Note: If you are running short on time, this is a good place to end this session.

Using Mail Merge

Your last project is to personalize the letter you wrote about the new tours and presentations by including each client's name and address information in the inside address and his or her first name in the salutation. To do this, you will use the Mail Merge feature to create a personalized form letter and mailing labels to be sent to all clients.

5   The **Mail Merge** feature combines a list of data (typically a file of names and addresses) with a document (commonly a form letter) to create a new document. The names and addresses are entered (merged) into the form letter in the blank spaces provided. The result is a personalized form letter.

Main Document

Data Source

Data Source	☑	Last Name ▼	First Name ▼	Address Line 1 ▼	City ▼	State ▼	ZIP Code ▼
Client List.mdb	☑	Micela	Joe	2334 Montrose St.	Los Angeles	CA	90012-2330
Client List.mdb	☑	Martinez	Cecelia	290 N. Hampton Ave.	Claremont	CA	91711-6430
Client List.mdb	☑	Name	Student	89 Any St.	Any Town	CA	99999-9999

Merged Documents

Mail Merge usually requires the use of two files: a main document and a data source. The **main document** contains the basic form letter. It directs the merge process through the use of merge fields. A **merge field** is a field code that controls what information is used from the data source and where it is entered in the main document. The **data source** contains the information needed to complete the letter in the main document. It is also called an **address list** because it commonly contains name and address data.

To complete the process of performing a mail merge, you follow these four steps:

1. Open or create a main document.
2. Open or create a data source with individual recipient information.
3. Add or customize merge fields in the main document.
4. Merge data from the data source into the main document to create a new, merged document.

You will open the tour letter as the main document and create the data source of clients' names and addresses. Then you will add the merge fields to the main document. When you perform the merge, Word takes the data field information from the data source and combines or merges it into the main document.

Creating the Main Document

You are going to use an existing letter as the main document. This letter is similar to the tour letter you saved in Lab 2.

1 ● **Open the file wd06_Tour Letter.**

● **Change the name in the closing to your name.**

● **Move to the center blank line above the salutation.**

● **Click**  **on the Mailings tab and choose Step by Step Mail Merge Wizard.**

Your screen should be similar to Figure 6.55

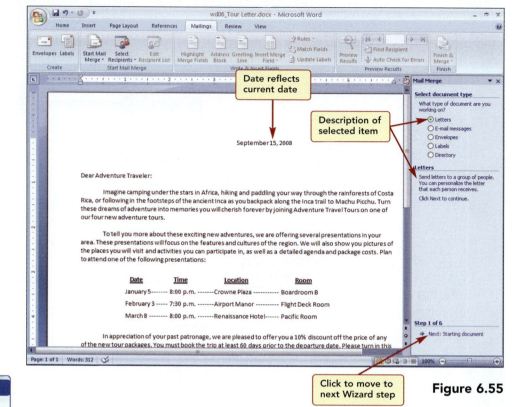

Figure 6.55

Additional Information

Notice that the date in the letter on your screen is automatically updated to the current system date. This is because a Date field was used in the document.

Another Method

You also can use the buttons on the Mailings tab instead of the Mail Merge task pane to create a merge document.

The Mail Merge task pane opened. Unlike most task panes, this task pane uses a **wizard** that asks questions and then creates the item based upon your responses. There are several different wizards that are designed to help you quickly create many types of documents such as a memo, a form, or a Web page. The Mail Merge task pane will guide you through the four steps in the mail merge process.

The first step is to specify the type of document you want to create: letters, mailing labels, envelopes, directories, and mass e-mail and fax distributions. An explanation of the selected document type is displayed below the list of options.

2 ● **If necessary, choose Letters.**

● **Click Next: Starting document.**

Your screen should be similar to Figure 6.56

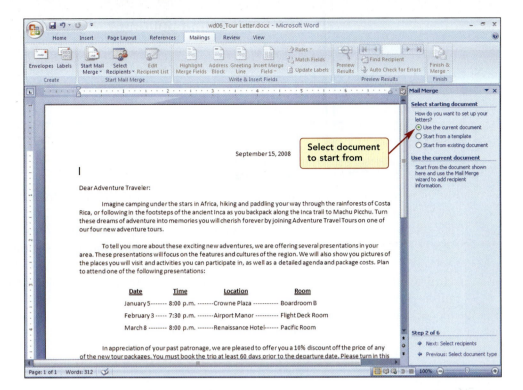

Select document to start from

Figure 6.56

In the next step, you identify the starting document. Since the document you want to use is already open, you will use the "Use the current document" option.

3 ● **If necessary, choose Use the current document.**

● **Click Next: Select recipients.**

Your screen should be similar to Figure 6.57

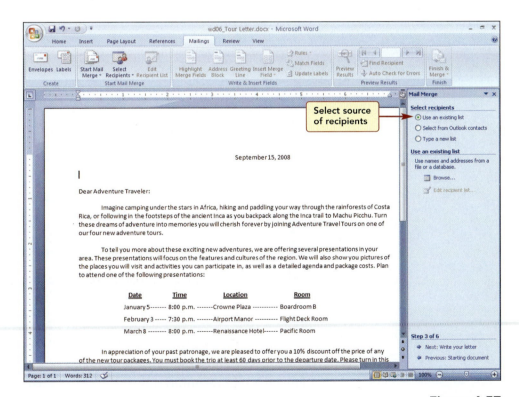

Select source of recipients

Figure 6.57

Creating the Data Source

Next, you select the recipients to use as the data source for the mail merged document. You can use an existing list, select from your Outlook contacts, or type a new address list.

Concept 6

Data Source

6 The **data source** is a table of information that contains the data that varies in each copy of a merged document. Each column in the table is a **data field** or a category of information. For example, a client's first name is a data field; the last name is a data field; the street address is another data field; the city, a fourth data field; and so on. The first row of the table, called the **header row**, contains the names of each data field. All following rows in the table contain data records. A **data record** contains a complete set of related information for one person (or other entity); for example, the client's first name, last name, and so forth. Commonly, a database table created using a database application is used for the data source. However, the data source also can be created using Word. It is called an Office Address List and is best for small, simple lists that are not used frequently.

You are going to create a new Office Address List using Word.

1 ● **Choose Type a new list.**

● **Click Create.**

Your screen should be similar to Figure 6.58

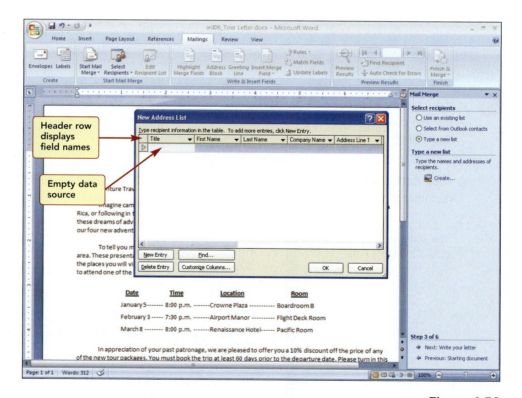

Figure 6.58

The New Address List dialog box is used to specify the field names for the data that will be entered in the recipient list.

Lab 6: Creating Forms, Using Mail Merge, and Reviewing Documents

www.mhhe.com/oleary

7 **Field names** are used to label the different data fields in the recipient list. A field name can contain only letters, numbers, or the underline character. It can be a maximum of 40 characters and cannot contain spaces. The first character of a field name must be a letter. Field names should describe the contents of the data field.

The New Address List list box displays the empty data source table. The header row displays the names of commonly used form-letter field names. You can remove any field names that you do not need in your letter, or you can add new field names or rename existing field names. In this case, you will remove several field names from the header row.

2 ● Click .

Your screen should be similar to Figure 6.59

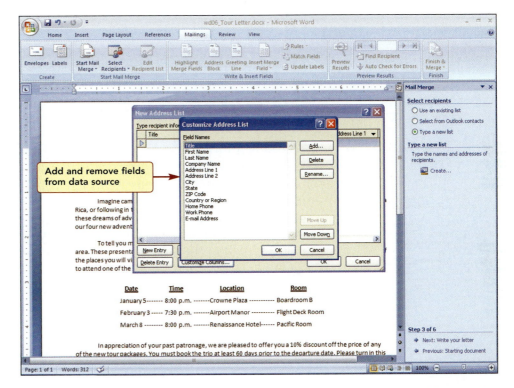

Figure 6.59

Because you only need basic address information, you will remove any extra field names. You will delete the title field name first since it is already selected.

3 • Click [Delete] to remove the Title field from the list.

• Click [Yes] to confirm the deletion.

• Select and remove the following field names: Company Name, Address Line 2, Country or Region, Home Phone, Work Phone, and E-mail Address.

Additional Information

The [Move Up] and [Move Down] buttons let you rearrange the order of the fields.

• Click [OK].

Your screen should be similar to Figure 6.60

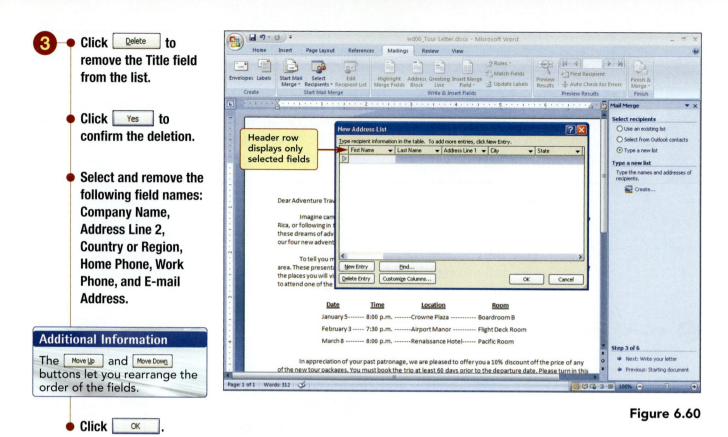

Figure 6.60

The New Address List dialog box now displays in the header row only the six field names you want to use in the letter. Below the header row is a blank row containing cells in which you enter the information for each data record. The information must be entered exactly as you want it to appear in the letter. If you do not have the information you need to complete a field, you can leave it blank. You will enter the information for the first field of the first data record, the client's first name.

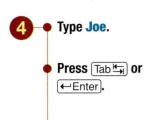**4** ● Type **Joe**.

● Press **Tab⇥** or **↵Enter**.

● Enter the following information for the remaining fields of this record:

Last Name:	**Micela**
Address Line 1:	**2334 Montrose St.**
City:	**Los Angeles**
State:	**CA**
ZIP Code:	**90012-2330**

● If you see any errors in the field data, move back to the entry and edit it.

Your screen should be similar to Figure 6.61

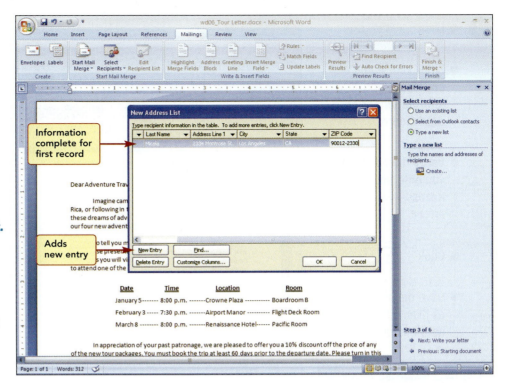

Figure 6.61

Now you are ready to add a second record to the data source file.

**5** ● Click **New Entry**.

● Enter the field information for the second data record using the information:

First Name:	**Cecelia**
Last Name:	**Martinez**
Address Line 1:	**29 N. Hampton Ave.**
City:	**Claremont**
State:	**CA**
ZIP Code:	**91711-6430**

Your screen should be similar to Figure 6.62

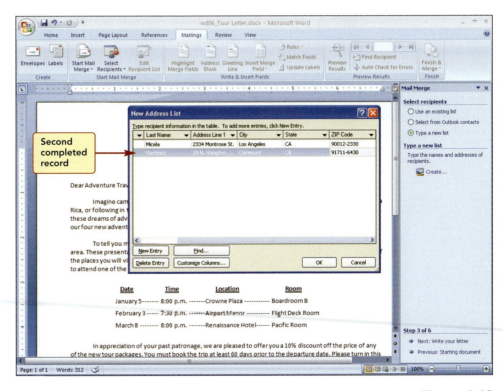

Figure 6.62

Finally, you will add a third record with your information.

6 • Click New Entry .

• Enter your name and address as the information for third data record.

• Verify the information you entered. If necessary, correct any errors.

• Click OK .

• Save the address list as Client List to your data file location.

Additional Information

The address list is saved as an .mdb file, which is a Microsoft Office Address List.

Your screen should be similar to Figure 6.63

Additional Information

The number of data records you enter in the data source file is limited only by your disk space. At any time, you can click [Edit Recipient List] to display the address list and add, delete, or edit records.

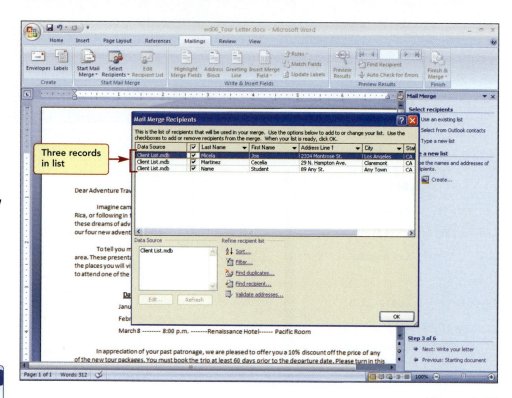

Figure 6.63

The Mail Merge Recipients dialog box displays all the data you entered in a table format. This dialog box is used to select the records you want included in the merge. You can sort the list or edit the data before you perform the merge. As you look at the three records, you see that you entered the address for the second record incorrectly. You will edit the record to correct it.

7 • Click Client List.mdb in the Data Source list box.

• Click Edit...

• Click in the Address Line 1 cell for Martinez and change the address to 290 N. Hampton Ave..

• Click OK and click Yes to update and save the list.

Your screen should be similar to Figure 6.64

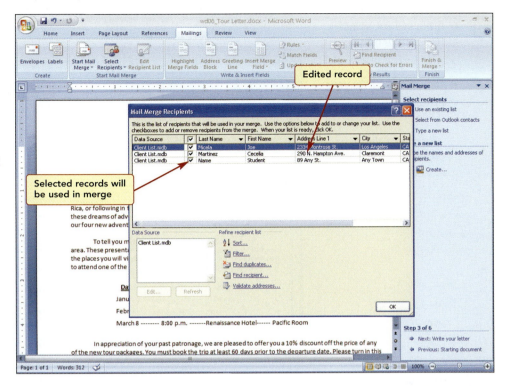

Figure 6.64

Next, you will select those records you want to use in the merge. To test out the merge, you will use your record only.

8 • Clear the checkmarks from all records except the record displaying your information.

• Click OK.

Your screen should be similar to Figure 6.65

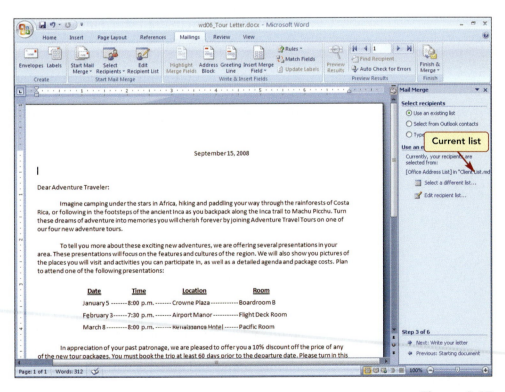

Figure 6.65

Now the name of the address list file you created appears in the Use an existing list section in the task pane. You will use this address list and advance to the next step.

9 • If necessary, select Use an existing list.

• Click Next: Write your letter.

Your screen should be similar to Figure 6.66

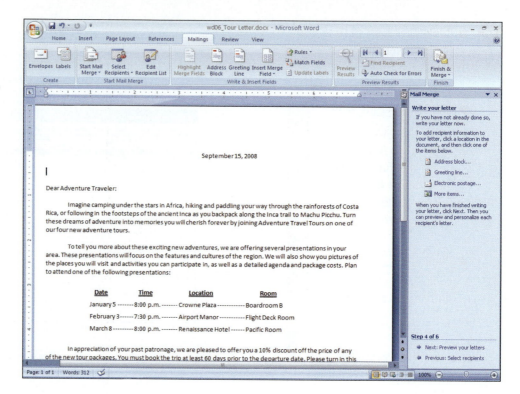

Figure 6.66

Entering Merge Fields in the Main Document

The next step is to create your letter, if you have not done so already, and to include the recipient information in it. How will Word know where to enter the client's name and other source data in the main document? Word uses merge fields to do this. Merge fields direct the program to accept information from the data source at the specified location in the main document. To prepare the letter to accept the fields of information from the data source, you need to add merge fields to the letter.

The letter needs to be modified to allow entry of the name and address information for each client from the data source. The inside address will hold the following three lines of information, which are the components of the address block:

First Name Last Name
Address Line 1
City, State Zip Code

The first line of the inside address, which will hold the client's full name, will be entered as line 5 of the tour letter. A merge field needs to be entered in the main document for each field of data you want copied from the data source. The location of the merge field indicates where to enter the field data. First you need to position the insertion point on the line where the client's name and address will appear.

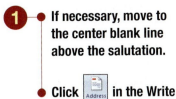

1 • If necessary, move to the center blank line above the salutation.

• Click [Address Block] in the Write & Insert Fields group.

Another Method

You also could click Address block in the Mail Merge pane.

Your screen should be similar to Figure 6.67

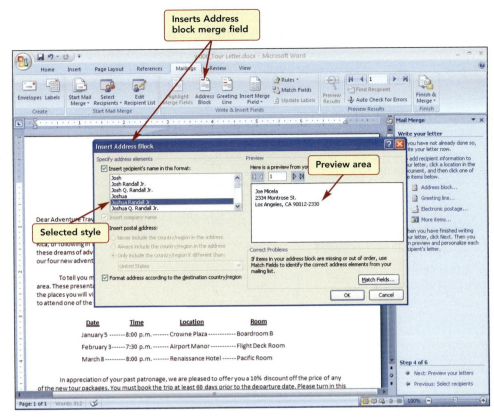

Figure 6.67

The Insert Address Block dialog box has many options for customizing the appearance of the fields. The Preview area displays how the Address Block will appear in the letter.

2 • Choose the example "Joshua Randall Jr." as the format for the recipient's name.

• Click [OK].

Having Trouble?

You also can click [Insert Merge Fields] and insert the merge fields one at a time.

Your screen should be similar to Figure 6.68

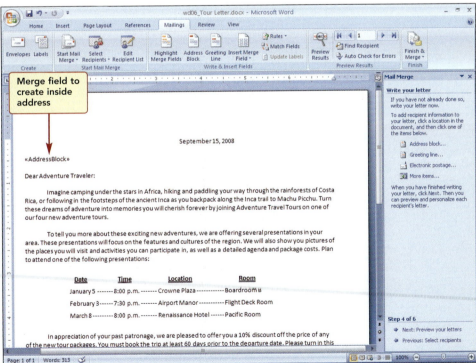

Figure 6.68

The merge field is displayed at the insertion point in the main document. It is a field code that instructs Word to insert the information from the data fields (from the data source) at this location in the main document when the merge is performed.

3 • Select "Adventure Traveler" in the salutation.

• Open the 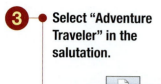 drop-down menu and choose the First_Name merge field.

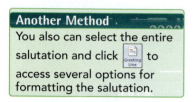

Another Method

You also can select the entire salutation and click 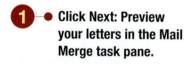 to access several options for formatting the salutation.

Additional Information

The same merge field can be used more than once in the main document.

Your screen should be similar to Figure 6.69

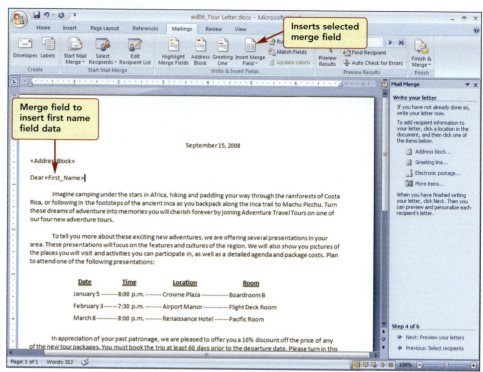

Figure 6.69

Previewing the Merged Letter

The next step is to see how the form letter appears with the merged data.

1 • Click Next: Preview your letters in the Mail Merge task pane.

Another Method

You also could click 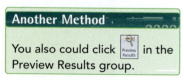 in the Preview Results group.

Your screen should be similar to Figure 6.70

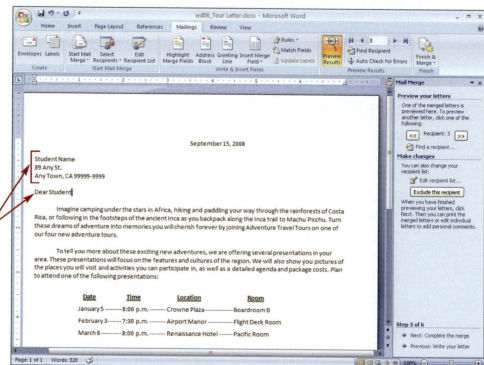

Figure 6.70

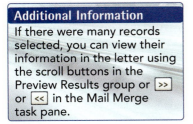

Additional Information

If there were many records selected, you can view their information in the letter using the scroll buttons in the Preview Results group or ➤➤ or ◄◄ in the Mail Merge task pane.

The data from the selected record in the address list is displayed in place of the merge fields.

2 ● Click [Preview Results] in the Preview Results group to show the field codes again.

● Save the letter as Tour Letter Main Document to your solution file location.

The Tour Letter Main Document file contains the merge field codes that are needed to direct the mail merge process. Each merge field code includes links to the appropriate fields in the data source file that are needed to create the individualized form letters.

Printing the Merged Letter

Now that you have created the main document and data source file, you are ready to complete the merge and print the new personalized tour letter.

1 ● Click Next: Complete the merge in the Mail Merge task pane.

● Choose Print in the task pane.

Another Method

You also can click [Finish & Merge] on the Mailing tab and then choose Print Documents.

Your screen should be similar to Figure 6.71

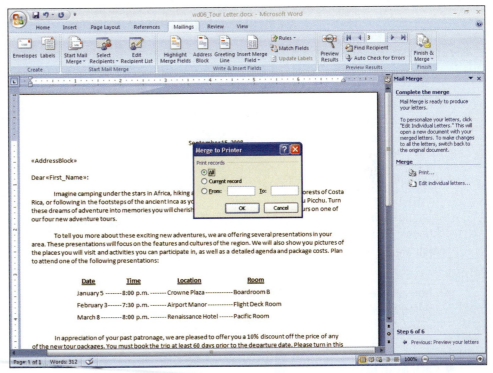

Figure 6.71

From the Mail Merge task pane, you can print the merged letters immediately or you can further edit the letters before you print them. If you want to edit the letters, Word opens a new document that contains all the individual letters. Then you can modify the letters, save the file, and print the document just as you would any regular Word document. You also can direct the merge to output the form letters to e-mail or a fax if your system is set up to include these features.

Finally, if you do not want every selected record in your data source to receive a copy of the form letter, you can specify a range of records to merge or the currently displayed record only. In this case, because there is only one selected record in the data source, you can simply use the All option.

2 ● Click 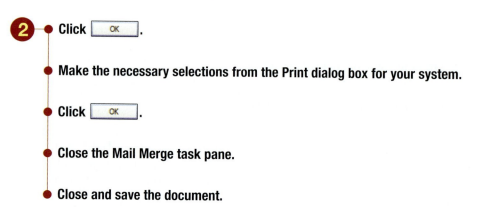 OK .

● Make the necessary selections from the Print dialog box for your system.

● Click OK .

● Close the Mail Merge task pane.

● Close and save the document.

Now each time you need to send tour letters, all you need to do is open the Tour Letter Main Document file, use the Mail Merge command, edit the client data source file, select the records you want to merge, and print the letters.

Printing Mailing Labels

Now that the form letter is ready to be sent to clients, you want to create mailing labels for the envelopes. To create mailing labels for your form letter, you will use the Mailing Label Wizard.

1 ● Display or open a new blank document.

● Open the Start Mail Merge drop-down menu on the Mailings tab and choose Step by Step Mail Merge Wizard.

● Choose Labels from the Mail Merge task pane.

● Click Next: Starting Document.

● Choose Label options.

Your screen should be similar to Figure 6.72

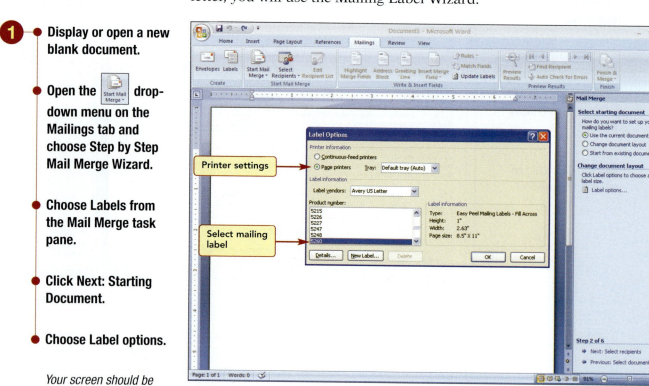

Figure 6.72

Lab 6: Creating Forms, Using Mail Merge, and Reviewing Documents

You have selected the default option to change the layout of the current document for the setup of the mailing labels. Next, you need to select the type of printer and the manufacturer of mailing labels from the Label Options dialog box. The Product Number list shows all the types of labels for the selected manufacturer.

2 ● **Choose Avery US Letter from the Label Vendors list.**

● **Select 5260-Easy Peel Mailing Labels**

● **Click OK .**

Your screen should be similar to Figure 6.73

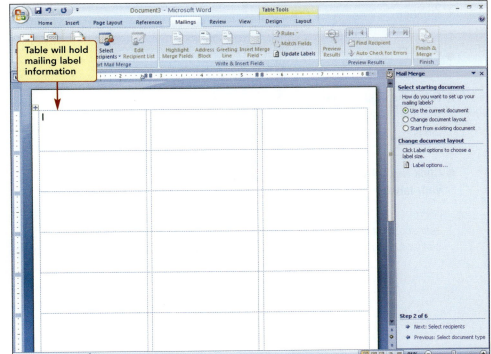

Figure 6.73

The document displays a three-column table that will be used to hold the mailing label information. You will use the Client List, which is the same data source you used for the merged letter, as the source for the mailing label information.

3 • Click **Next: Select recipients.**

• Click **Browse** and choose **Client List** from your solution file location.

• Click [Open].

• From the Mail Merge Recipients dialog box, click [OK].

• Click **Next: Arrange your labels.**

Your screen should be similar to Figure 6.74

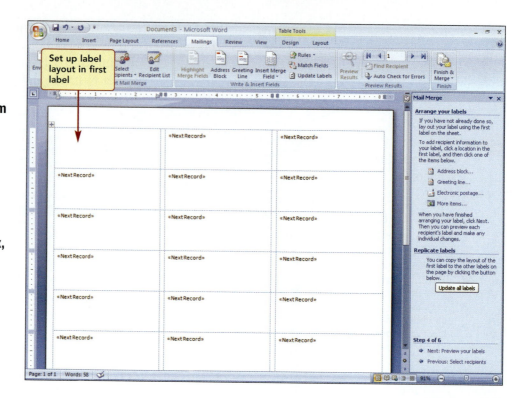

Figure 6.74

Next, you set up the first label on the sheet and replicate that setup to the rest of the labels.

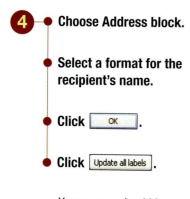

4 • Choose **Address block.**

• Select a format for the recipient's name.

• Click [OK].

• Click [Update all labels].

Your screen should be similar to Figure 6.75

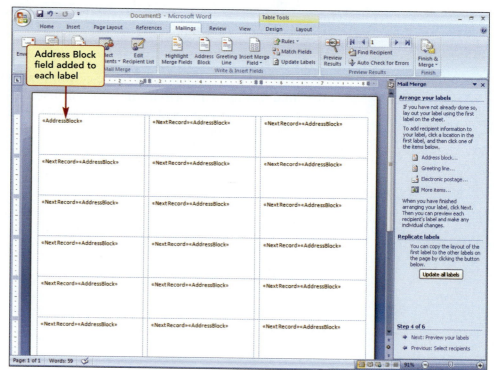

Figure 6.75

Next you will preview the labels before you perform the merge.

5 ● **Click Next: Preview your labels.**

Your screen should be similar to Figure 6.76

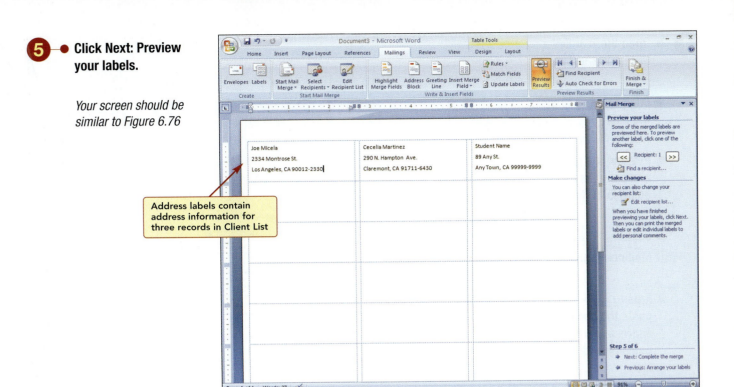

Address labels contain address information for three records in Client List

Figure 6.76

The labels look good, so you can complete the merge and, if you wanted, print the labels. Instead, you will save the merged label file. Now, when you send the tour letters, you can create mailing labels using the same data source as the letter.

6 ● **Click Next: Complete the merge.**

● **Save the document as ATT Mailing Labels.**

● **Close the Mail Merge task pane and close the document.**

Preparing and Printing Envelopes

Sometimes you may want to quickly address a single envelope. To see how this feature works, you will address an envelope for a letter in the Tour Letter Main Document file.

1 ● **Open the** Tour Letter Main Document **file.**

● **Click** [Yes] **to insert the data.**

● **Preview the results and copy the inside address of the letter.**

● **Click** [Envelopes] **from the Mailings tab.**

● **Press** [Ctrl] **+ V to paste the copied address into the Delivery Address text box.**

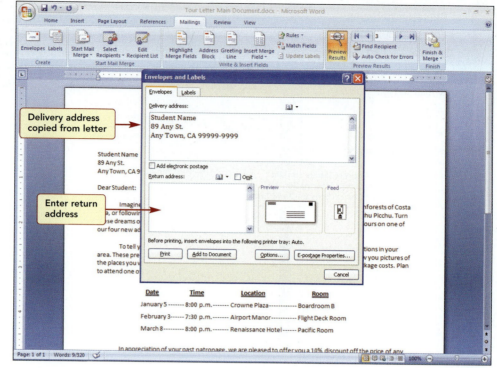

Figure 6.77

Additional Information
You also can type an address directly in the Delivery Address text box.

Additional Information
The Labels tab is used to create a mailing label rather than to print the address directly on the envelope. This feature is accessed by clicking [Labels].

Your screen should be similar to Figure 6.77

To complete the information for the envelope, you need to add the return address. Then you will check the options for printing and formatting the envelope.

2 — Enter your school's address in the Return Address text box.

- Click Options... .

- If necessary, open the Envelope Options tab.

Your screen should be similar to Figure 6.78

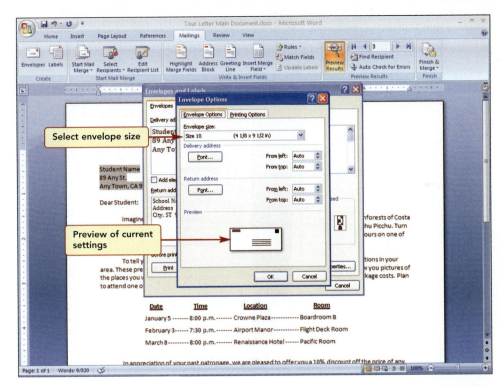

Select envelope size

Preview of current settings

Figure 6.78

Additional Information
You can select other envelope sizes from the Envelope Size drop-down list.

Using the Envelope Options dialog box, you can change the envelope size and the font and placement of the delivery and return addresses. The Preview area shows how the envelope will appear when printed using the current settings.

The default envelope size 10 is for standard 8½-by-11-inch letter paper. This is the appropriate size for the letter. Next, you will check the print options.

3 ● **Open the Printing Options tab.**

Your screen should be similar to Figure 6.79

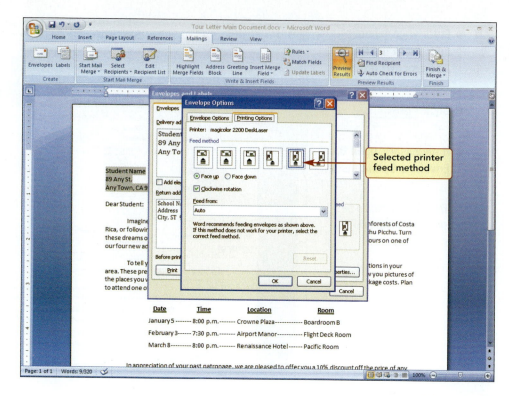

Selected printer feed method

Figure 6.79

The options in this tab are used to specify how the envelope is fed into the printer. Word automatically selects the best option for the selected printer. You do not need to change any of the envelope options. If you were printing an actual envelope, you would need to insert the correct-size envelope in the printer at this time. However, you will simply print it on a sheet of paper.

4 ● **Close the Envelope Options dialog box.**

Additional Information

Use [Add to Document] to add the envelope to the beginning of the active document so that you can print the envelope at the same time you print the document.

● **Click** [Print].

● **Click** [No] **in response to the prompt to save the return address as the default.**

Additional Information

Responding [Yes] displays that address automatically whenever envelopes are printed.

● **Close the** Tour Letter Main Document **file without saving it.**

● **Exit Word 2007.**

Focus on Careers

EXPLORE YOUR CAREER OPTIONS

Forensic Science Technician

Do you like murder mysteries? Are you fascinated by court dramas? Forensic science technicians are involved in the investigation of crimes and are often called to testify in court to explain their findings to the jury. Most forensic science technicians specialize in one area of the field, such as DNA analysis or firearms. They must prepare reports that clarify their findings and explain the techniques used in the laboratory. Most positions require relevant experience and at least an associate degree in applied science; however, a bachelor's degree in forensic technology may be preferred. The median hourly earnings for forensic science technicians is $21.16 per hour or $43,600 annually based on a 40-hour work week (as of 2004, the most recent year for which this information is available.)

Creating Forms, Using Mail Merge, and Reviewing Documents

Forms (WD6.4)

Forms are documents that contain fill-in blanks or spaces reserved for entering information.

Controls (WD6.10)

Controls are graphical objects that you can add to and customize for use in templates, forms, and documents.

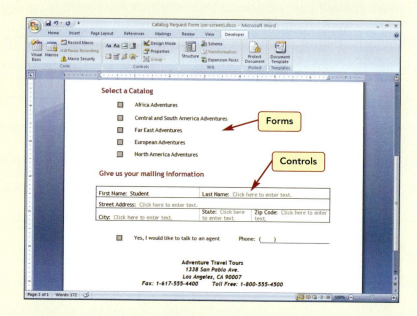

Protection (WD6.18)

The protection feature controls what information can be changed in a document.

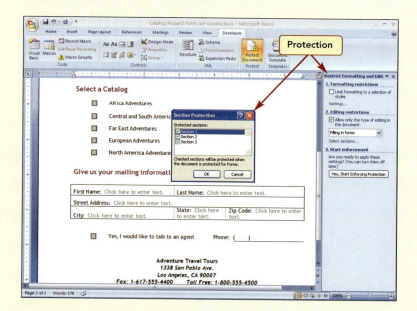

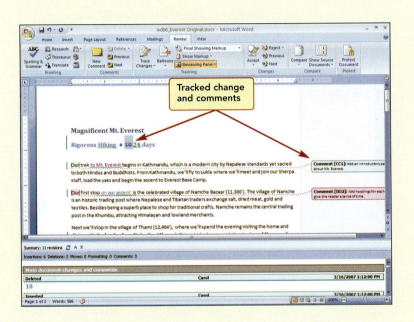

Tracked Changes and Comments (WD6.27)

To make online reviewing of documents easier, you can add tracked changes and comments to a document.

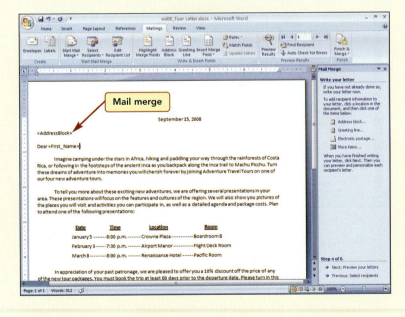

Mail Merge (WD6.49)

The mail merge feature combines a list of data (typically a file of names and addresses) with a document (commonly a form letter) to create a new document.

Data Source   (WD6.52)

The data source is a table of information that contains the data that varies in each copy of a merged document.

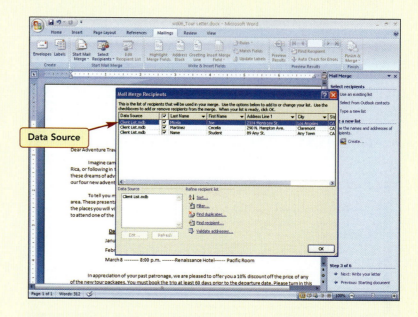

Field Names   (WD6.53)

Field names are used to label the different data fields in the recipient list in a mail merge.

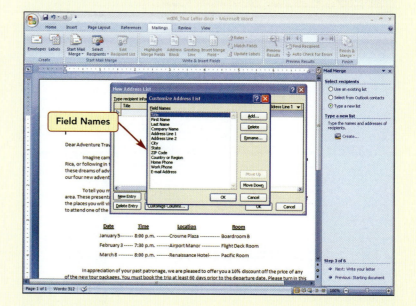

Lab Review

LAB **6**

Creating Forms, Using Mail Merge, and Reviewing Documents

key terms

address list WD6.49
attachment WD6.38
balloon WD6.27
comment WD6.27
content control WD6.10
control WD6.10
data field WD6.52
data record WD6.52

data source WD6.49, WD6.52
digital signature WD6.17
field name WD6.53
form WD6.4
form field control WD6.10
header row WD6.52
macro WD6.12
Mail Merge WD6.49

main document WD6.49
markup WD6.27
merge field WD6.49
password WD6.18
protection WD6.18
tracked changes WD6.27
wizard WD6.50

MCAS skills

The Microsoft Certified Applications Specialist (MCAS) certification program is designed to measure your proficiency in performing basic tasks using the Office 2007 applications. Getting certified demonstrates that you have the skills and provides a valuable industry credential for employment. See Reference 2, Microsoft Certified Applications Specialist (MCAS) for a complete list of the skills that were covered in Lab 6.

Lab Review

command summary

Command	Shortcut	Action
🔵 Office Button		
Prepare/Inspect Document		Starts Document Inspector to check document for hidden data or personal information
Prepare/Mark as Final		Lets readers know document is final and makes it read-only
Prepare/Add a Digital Signature		Ensures integrity of document by adding an invisible digital signature
Send/E-mail		Sends document as an attachment by e-mail
[Word Options]/Popular/Show Developer tab in Ribbon		Displays or hides Developer tab in Ribbon
Insert tab		
Tables group		
[Table]/Convert Text to Table		Changes existing text in a document to text displayed in a table
Text group		
[Object ▾]/Text from File		Inserts contents of an entire file
Mailings tab		
Create group		
[Envelopes]		Prints delivery and return addresses on envelopes
[Labels]		Creates mailing labels for envelopes
Start Mail Merge group		
[Start Mail Merge ▾]/Step by Step Mail Merge Wizard		Starts Mail Merge Wizard
[Select Recipients ▾]		Select recipients from client list to mail document to
[Edit Recipient List]		Edits records in recipient list
Write & Insert Fields group		
[Greeting Line]		Inserts greeting line in main document
[Insert Merge Field ▾]		Inserts merge fields in main document

command summary

Command	Shortcut	Action
Preview Results group		
Preview Results		Replaces merge fields with actual data from recipient list to see how merged document will look
Review tab		
Comments group		
New Comment		Inserts a comment
Delete ▾		Deletes selected comment
Tracking group		
Track Changes ▾	Ctrl + ⇧Shift + E	Turns on/off tracked changes feature
Balloons ▾		Sets revision balloon
Final Showing Markup ▾		Changes how to view proposed changes to document
Show Markup ▾		Choose what type of markup to show
Reviewing Pane ▾		Displays/hides Reviewing pane
Changes group		
Accept ▾		Accepts change and moves to next change
Reject ▾		Rejects change and moves to next change
Previous		Moves to previous change
Next		Moves to next change
Compare group		
Compare ▾ /Combine		Combines documents and identifies differences
Protect group		
Protect Document		Restricts access and changes to document by adding protection and a password

command summary

Command	Shortcut	Action
Developer tab		
Controls group		
Aa Text		Inserts plain text control
Drop-Down List		Inserts drop-down list control
Legacy Tools		Displays Legacy controls
Properties		Accesses Properties for selected control
Protect group		
Protect Document		Turns on/off document protection

Lab Exercises

matching

Match the item on the left with the correct description on the right.

1. markup _____
2. forms _____
3. field name _____
4. comment _____
5. data source _____
6. balloon _____
7. Mail Merge _____
8. Track Changes _____
9. Rich Text _____
10. Document Inspector _____

a. Checks document for hidden data or personal information
b. Elements used to display tracked changes
c. Element that displays comments in reviewed documents
d. Combines a list of data with a document
e. Documents with blanks for entering information
f. Table of information that contains data fields
g. Feature that monitors changes to a document
h. A note added to a document without changing the document text
i. A content control used for formatted text entries
j. Used to label different data fields in the data source

multiple choice

Circle the correct response to the questions below.

1. The mark as final feature makes a document _____ to prevent changes to the document.
   a. protected
   b. read-only
   c. access-restricted
   d. edit-restricted

2. A _____ guides you step by step through a process.
   a. template
   b. placeholder
   c. wizard
   d. merge

3. The _____ document contains the text that will become the basis of a form letter.
   a. letter
   b. data source
   c. address file
   d. main

4. _____ names are used to label each data field in the data source.
   a. Row
   b. Record
   c. Field
   d. File

5. The _____ feature controls what information can be changed in a document.
   a. protection
   b. password
   c. digital signature
   d. mark as final

6. A _____ is used in the main document for each field of data that is inserted from the data source.
   a. merge field
   b. data record
   c. row
   d. data field

7. A(n) _____ is a note inserted in a document that does not change the text.
   a. comment
   b. balloon
   c. tracked change
   d. attachment

8. The data source is also commonly called the _____.
   a. main document
   b. address file
   c. balloon
   d. data field

9. A(n) _____ is an electronic encryption-based stamp of authentication.
   a. signature stamp
   b. authenticity certificate
   c. certificate of authority
   d. digital signature

10. The first row of the data source table is called the _____.
    a. field name row
    b. category name row
    c. data record row
    d. header row

true/false

Circle the correct answer to the following questions.

1. Legacy controls are only available in Word 2007.	True	False
2. A password is required when adding protection to a document.	True	False
3. A data source is also known as the main document.	True	False
4. A wizard commonly contains data fields and addresses.	True	False
5. Field names can be letters, numbers, and the underline character.	True	False
6. A text content control can include formatted text.	True	False
7. Markup includes balloons, underlines, and strikethroughs.	True	False
8. Comment balloons are displayed in the markup area.	True	False
9. A digital signature cannot be invisible.	True	False
10. Even if Track Changes was not on, Word always detects changes in a merge document.	True	False

Hands-On Exercises

rating system

★ Easy
★★ Moderate
★★★ Difficult

step-by-step

Lifestyle Fitness Printed Form ★

1. You work at Lifestyle Fitness Club headquarters in the marketing and public relations department. Each year you conduct a brief member survey to make management aware of problems and ways to improve the club. You started creating the form by entering the questions you want to ask and now need to format the form. The form will be given to members at the service desk to complete and return. Your completed form will be similar to that shown here.

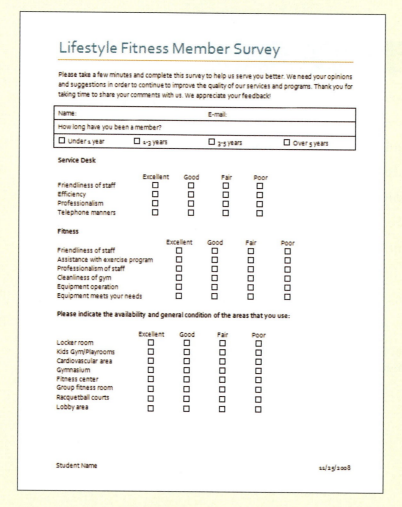

a. Open the file wd06_Fitness Member Survey.

b. Convert the name, e-mail, and membership length lines to a table with four columns. Merge cells and remove the interior vertical border line. Increase the row height to 0.3. Left-center-align the contents.

c. Add check box controls that have the check box enabled property turned off and no shading to before each of the four membership time categories. Adjust spacing appropriately.

d. Save the document as Fitness Member Survey.

e. Convert the survey information in the Fitness area to a table. Appropriately size the table cells. Increase row height to 0.2. Add disabled check boxes without shading in the four rating category cells for each row. Center-align the table, excluding the first column. Do not display any border lines.

f. In the same manner, format the remaining two survey areas as a table with check boxes.

g. Add your name and the date in a footer.

h. Check the form for private information and remove all except in the footer.

i. Protect the form and use a password.

j. Print the form and close the file.

Lifestyle Fitness On-screen Form ★★

2. After completing the printed form for the member survey for the Lifestyle Fitness Club (Step-by-Step 1), your manager has asked you to make the form available for members to complete on-screen. They plan to send the form via e-mail to all members to ensure that they get as many responses as possible. Your completed on-screen form will be similar to that shown here.

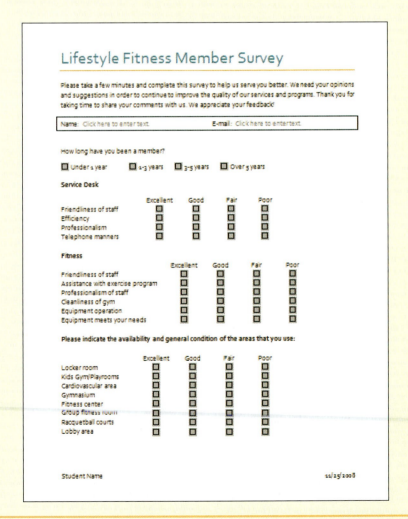

a. Open the file wd06_Fitness Member Survey.

b. Make the name and e-mail lines a table with two columns. Merge cells and remove the interior vertical border line. Increase the row height to 0.3. Left-center-align the contents.

c. Add text content controls to each cell. Lock the controls so they cannot be deleted. Adjust spacing appropriately.

d. Save the document as Fitness Member Survey On-screen.

e. Convert the survey information in the Fitness area to a table. Appropriately size the table cells. Increase row height to 0.2. Add enabled check boxes with shading in the four rating category cells for each row. Center-align the table, excluding the first column. Do not display any border lines.

f. In the same manner, format the remaining two survey areas as a table with check boxes.

g. Add your name and the date in a footer. Save and print the form.

h. Check the form for private information and remove all, except in the footer.

i. Protect the form and use a password.

j. Save the form using the same file name as a template.

Downtown Internet Café Form ★★

3. Jennifer is working on the upcoming month's schedule of events for the Downtown Internet Café. She has created a rough draft of the schedule and provided a copy to Evan and Melissa, the owners, for review. They have several suggestions for the document. After looking at their comments and making the suggested changes, the completed document will be similar to that shown here.

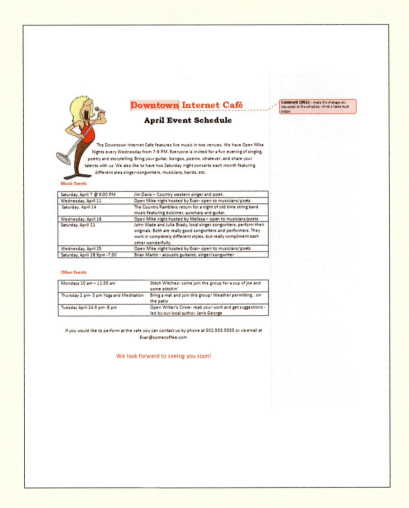

a. Open the file wd06_Cafe Schedule. Combine wd06_Cafe Schedule Evan and wd06_Cafe Schedule Melissa with the open file.

b. Read the comments from Evan and Melissa. In response to the first two comments, locate a graphic in the online ClipArt gallery (or use wd06_Mike Night) and add it to the top of the schedule. Size and format it appropriately. Add a complementary font color to the title. Delete the two comments.

c. As directed in the next comment, insert the contents of the file wd06_Cafe Schedule Paragraph. Delete the comment.

d. Do not show the remaining comments. Accept all marked changes.

e. Redisplay comments. As directed in the first comment, convert the schedule to a table. Hide the inside vertical border lines.

f. Convert the Other Events items to a table. Do not display interior vertical border lines. Adjust the table as needed. Add formatting to the Other Events heading. Delete the comment. Add a blank line below the table if needed.

g. Add the heading **Music Events** above the first table and format the same as the Other Events heading. Format the last line using the same font color as the title.

h. Add your name and the current date in a footer.

i. At the top of the document, add the comment **I made the changes you requested to the schedule. I think it looks much better!**.

j. Save the document as April Cafe Schedule. Send the document as an attachment to your instructor. Print the document with your comment and close the file.

Animal Rescue Foundation ★★

4. The Animal Angels volunteer group of the Animal Rescue Foundation is sending a letter to all the veterinarians and pet stores in the local area to enlist their help in finding and caring for homeless pets. You have been asked to compose the new letter and create a form the recipient can return for more information on donation programs. You have begun working on the letter but need to complete the form and mail merge. Your completed letter should be similar to that shown here.

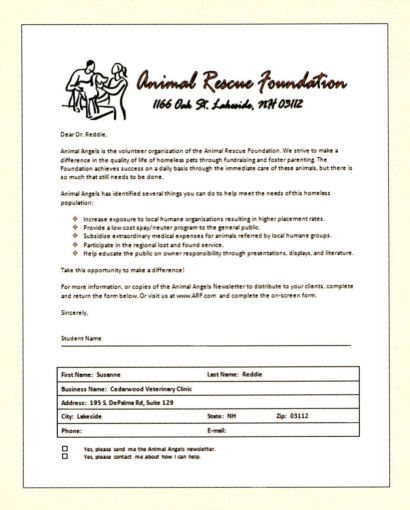

   a. Open the file wd06_Animal Rescue Volunteer Letter.

   b. Replace Student Name in the closing with your name.

   c. Add a horizontal line below your name the width of the text area.

   d. Convert the five lines of text below the line to a table. Merge cells where appropriate and remove the interior vertical border lines. Increase the row height to 0.3. Center-left-align the text. Your table should be similar to the example.

   e. Add unshaded check boxes before the last two lines of the letter.

f. Using the Mail Merge wizard, choose Letters as the document type and the current document as the starting document.

g. Create a new recipient list and enter the following information in the appropriate fields.

Dr. Suzanne Reddie
Cedarwood Veterinary Clinic
195 S. DePalma Rd., Suite 129
Lakeside, NH 03112

Pet Place
622 E. Kennedy Loop
Lakeside, NH 03112

Dr. Michael Miniri
Armstrong Animal Hospital
233 W. Armstrong Rd.
Lakeside, NH 03112

h. Save the address list as ARF Volunteer Recruitment List to your solution file location.

i. In the main document, replace the salutation with the preformatted greeting line.

j. Enter the appropriate merge fields to complete the fields of the return form. (Hint: Use on the Mailings tab.)

k. Preview your letters. Edit the letter as needed to fix spacing or other items.

l. Edit the recipient list to select only one of the three records.

m. Use Print Preview and shrink the letter to fit on one page.

n. Complete the merge and print the letter.

o. Save the merge letters as ARF Volunteer Letter.

p. Create mailing labels for the letters using the same data source file. Use the Avery 5262 style label. Save the mailing labels as ARF Labels.

q. Create and print an envelope for the Pet Place. Use your name in the return address.

Summer Movie Promotion Flyer ★★★

5. Every summer, the local theater hosts a "Kids Rule" series of movies geared to kids and families. You have been asked by the movie theater manager, Max, to create a flyer to be included in the town's summer program activities booklet to advertise the series. The flyer also will be sent to Kids Rule Movie Club members. You sent a copy of your first draft to Max to review and now need to review and incorporate the changes. Then you will use the Mail Merge feature to customize the flyer to be sent to club members. Your completed flyer will be similar to that shown here.

Come join the **Kids Rule** summer movie program at Preview Cine

Movies will show each Wednesday and Thursday at 10am starting o 23rd. All seats are $2.50.

Turn in the coupon below for one free large popcorn with your admis Over the Hedge.

June 23 & 24	Over the Hedge
June 30 & July 1	The Pink Panther
July 8 & 9	Shreck 1
July 15 & 16	Garfield's A Tale of Two Kitties
July 22 & 23	Nanny McPhee
July 29 & 30	Shreck 2
Aug 5 & 6	Ice Age: The Meltdown
Aug 12 & 13	Monster House

First Name:	Last Name:
Address:	
Phone:	E-mail:

Come join the **Kids Rule** summer movie program at Preview Cinema!!

Movies will show each Wednesday and Thursday at 10am starting on June 23rd. All seats are $2.50.

Turn in the coupon below for one free large popcorn with your admission to Over the Hedge.

June 23 & 24	Over the Hedge
June 30 & July 1	The Pink Panther
July 8 & 9	Shreck
July 15 & 16	Garfield's A Tale of Two Kitties
July 22 & 23	Nanny McPhee
July 29 & 30	Shreck 2
Aug 5 & 6	Ice Age: The Meltdown
Aug 12 & 13	Monster House

First Name: Student		Last Name: Name
Address: 89 Any St., Any Town, NM 87505		
Phone: 555-555-5555	E-mail: SN@School.edu	

a. Open the file wd06_Kids Rule Summer Movies. Compare and combine with the reviewed document wd06_Kids Rule Summer Movies Reviewed. In response to the dialog box, select The other document to keep formatting changes from the other document before you continue with the Merge.

b. Do not show comment markup. Review and accept all the tracked changes.

c. Show comments and make the suggested changes in each comment.

- Format the Kids Rule text using formatting of your choice.

- Convert the movie schedule to a table. Size and format it appropriately.

- Insert the following text below the table: Yes, I want to join the Kids Rule Movie Club.. Add an unshaded check box to the beginning of the sentence.

d. Delete the comments when you are done.

e. Format the coupon information as a table. Merge cells where appropriate and remove the interior vertical border lines. Increase the row height to 0.3. Center-left-align the text. Your table should be similar to the example.

f. Save the document as Kids Rule Summer Movie Flyer.

g. Next, you will modify the flyer to be sent to current Kids Rule club members. Start the Mail Merge Wizard. Select Letter as the document type, and use the current document.

h. You will create a new list of recipients. Create a list with the following fields:

First Name
Last Name
Address Line 1
City
State
ZIP Code
Home Phone
E-Mail Address

i. Enter the following names in the list:

[Your Name]
2337 W. Skylark Lane
Santa Fe, NM 87505
(505) 555-9834
[your e-mail address]

Sandy Mosiman
78007 La Puente Avenue
Santa Fe, NM 87505
(505) 555-8744
mosiman@mail.com

Manuel Rojero
68805 N. Saddleback Place
Santa Fe, NM 87505
(505) 555-8321
rojero@mail.org

j. Save the data list as Kids Rule List. Insert the merge fields into the table you created. (Hint: Use ⊞ Insert Merge Field ▾ on the Mailings tab.)

k. Preview the document and shrink it to fit on one page. Perform the merge. Save the file as Kids Rule Movie Merge Letter. Print the letter displaying your name in the table.

l. Create and print mailing labels using the Kids Rule list.

Lab Exercises

on your own

Zoo Survey Printed Form ★

1. Your job with the local zoo is to plan features and activities for the future. To help plan, you decided to conduct a survey asking visitors to evaluate their time at the zoo. Use the features you learned in this lab to create a printed form that will be given to visitors as they enter. Use the survey information provided in the file wd06_Zoo Survey to create the form. Many of the responses will be Yes/No answers. Others require spaces to enter information. Add a formatted title, with a Zoo name of your choice. Include an introductory paragraph and thanks for completing the form. Include your name in the footer. Protect the form. When you are finished, save the document as Zoo Survey Printed. Print the survey.

Zoo Survey On-Screen Form ★★

2. Your job with the local zoo is to plan features and activities for the future. To help plan, you decided to conduct a survey asking visitors to evaluate their time at the zoo. Use the features you learned in this lab to create an on-screen form that will sent via e-mail to zoo members. Use the survey information provided in the file wd06_Zoo Survey to create the form. Many of the responses will be Yes/No answers. Others require spaces to enter information. Add a formatted title, with a Zoo name of your choice. Include an introductory paragraph and thanks for completing the form. Include your name in the footer. When you are finished, save the document as Zoo Survey On-screen. Print the survey.

Historical Society Letter ★★

3. Janet Bowers works for the local historical society. She leads tours of historical homes in her area and coordinates fundraising for restoration. She has composed a letter to send to society members regarding membership in the society. Janet's co-chair has reviewed the document and returned it to her. Use the file wd06_Historical Society to create the merge document Janet will send to members. Respond to the comments, making the suggested changes. Use at least three addresses in your recipient list. Save the document as Historical Society Letter. Send your completed document to your instructor as an attachment.

Safari Park Membership Letter ★★★

4. Nigel Peterson works for the Safari Park, a preserve for elephants. He has created a letter to attract new donations for the park and the preservation of habitat. Nigel sent a draft of the letter to his media relations director for review and will now complete the letter and create the merge document. Open the file wd06_Safari Park, review the comments, and make the suggested changes. Create a merge document with at least three addresses. Save the document as Safari Park Letter. Send the file to your instructor as an attachment.

Rewards Program Letter ★★★

5. You work for National Hotels Incorporated. You have been asked to create a merge letter that will inform customers about the company's reward program. Create a draft of a letter informing customers about the rewards program. Add comments to the document that inquire about the types of free gifts offered, and whether you should be specific about the gifts in the letter or not. After completing your draft, send a copy to a classmate for review and comment. Review the comments and keep any relevant suggestions. Your completed document should have a table, check boxes, and lines. Create a merge document with at least three addresses. Print the letters. Save the document as Hotel Rewards Letter. Send the file to your instructor as an attachment.

Working Together 2: Copying, Linking, and Embedding Between Applications

Case Study

Adventure Travel Tours

You recently prepared a memo to the regional manager that contained a table showing the sales figures for the four major tours for the past three years. You realize that this information will be updated each year with the previous year's sales figures. Rather than create the table each year for the sales information, you decide it would be easier to create an Excel worksheet of this data and then copy the Excel information into the Word memo when requested. Because you have done a lot of work creating the table in Word already, to save time you will copy the information from the Word table into an Excel workbook.

A second project you are working on is to provide a monthly status report to the regional manager showing the bookings for the four new tours. You maintain this information in an Excel worksheet and want to include the worksheet of the tour status in a memo each month. You will link the worksheet data to the memo.

The last thing you need to do is to create a memo to the regional manager that shows the sales from the four new tours. Because the manager also wants a copy of the file, you will embed the worksheet data in the memo.

You will learn how to share information between applications as you create the Excel worksheet and the memos.

Note: This lab assumes that you already know how to use Excel 2007 and that you have completed Labs 2 and 3 of Excel.

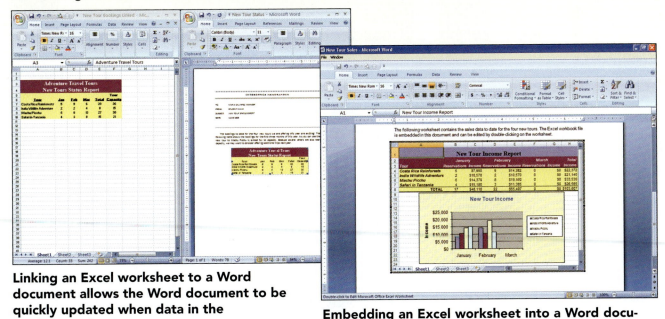

Linking an Excel worksheet to a Word document allows the Word document to be quickly updated when data in the worksheet changes.

Embedding an Excel worksheet into a Word document allows the worksheet to be used from within the Word document.

Copying Between Applications

All Microsoft Office 2007 applications have a common user interface such as similar Ribbons and commands. In addition to these obvious features, they have been designed to work together, making it easy to share and exchange information between applications. For example, the same procedures that are used to copy information within a Word 2007 document are used to copy information to other Office applications such as Excel 2007. The information is pasted in a format the application can edit, if possible. Information also can be copied as a linked object or an embedded object. You will use each of these three methods to copy information between Word 2007 and Excel 2007.

First you will copy sales data for the four major tours that you entered in a table in a Word 2007 document to Excel. You will open the file and copy the table to the Clipboard.

1 ● **Start Office Word 2007 and open the document** wdwt2_Annual Tour Sales**.**

● **Select the cells of the table that include the years and tour names through the last row of tour data (excluding the totals).**

● **Click** ▤ **Copy.**

Your screen should be similar to Figure 1

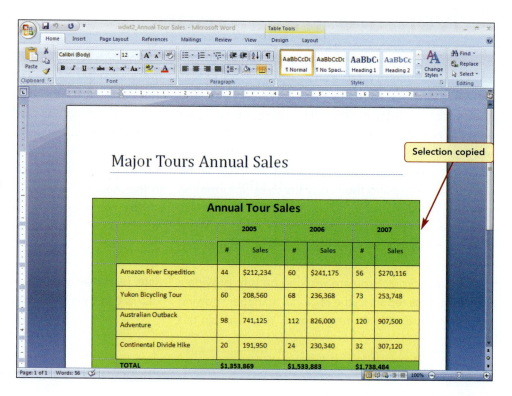

Figure 1

Now you are ready to paste the information into a new Excel workbook file.

2 • **Start Office Excel 2007.**

• **If necessary, maximize the workbook and sheet window.**

• **Click on cell A4 of the worksheet.**

Your screen should be similar to Figure 2

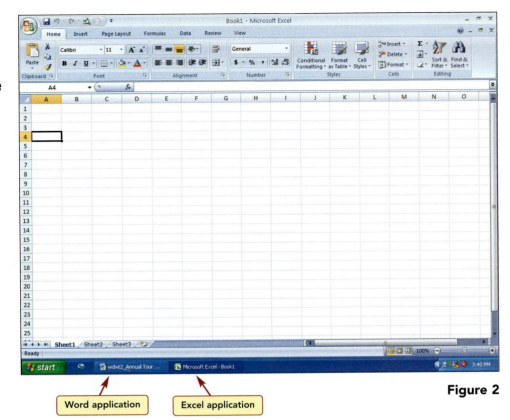

Word application

Excel application

Figure 2

There are now two open applications, Word and Excel, and both application buttons are displayed in the taskbar. You are now ready to paste the table into the worksheet. While using Word, you have learned how to use cut, copy, and paste to move or copy information within and between documents. You also can perform these operations between files in the same application and between files in different Office applications.

3 • **Click [Paste] to copy the contents from the Clipboard into the worksheet.**

Your screen should be similar to Figure 3

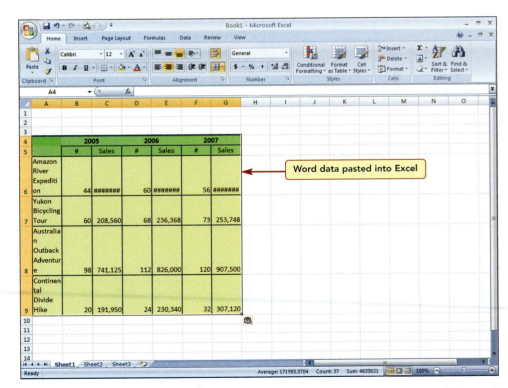

Word data pasted into Excel

Figure 3

The content from each cell of the copied table has been inserted into individual cells of the Excel worksheet. The data can now be edited and formatted using Excel commands. You will make a few quick changes to improve the appearance of the worksheet and total the worksheet values.

4 ● Size the column widths and row heights appropriately.

● Enter the label **TOTAL** in cell A10.

● Drag to select cells B6 through G10.

● Click **Σ ▾** Sum in the Editing group on the Home tab.

● Format cell A10 to Bold and the same color green as in row 4.

● Apply the same color to cells B10:G10.

● Add an outside border around the worksheet data.

● Click on cell A2.

Your screen should be similar to Figure 4

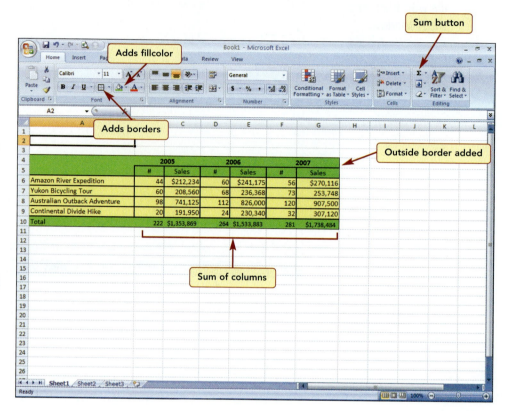

Figure 4

The total values were quickly calculated. It is much easier to use Excel to perform calculations than Word. Finally, you will copy the title from the Word document to above the worksheet.

5 ● **Switch to the Word document.**

Having Trouble?
Click on the taskbar button to switch to the Word window.

● **Select the document's title text.**

● **Click** 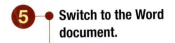 **Copy.**

● **Switch to Excel.**

● **Paste the title into cell A2 keeping the source formatting.**

● **Enter your name in cell A12.**

● **Save the Excel file as** Major Tour Sales.

● **Print the worksheet.**

Your screen should be similar to Figure 5

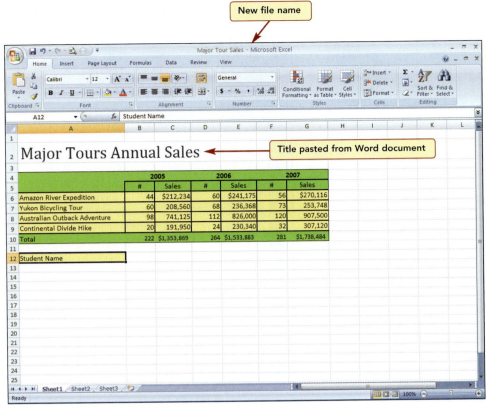

Figure 5

Copying the information from the Word table into an Excel worksheet was much quicker than entering all the data over again.

Linking Between Applications

Your second project is to create a memo to the manager each month to keep her apprised of the reservation status for the four new tours. This information is maintained in an Excel worksheet. You have already started the memo and need to add the Excel worksheet data to the memo.

1
- **Switch to Word and close the** wdwt2_ Annual Tour Sales **file.**

- **Open the file** wdwt2_New Tour Status**.**

- **In the memo header, replace "Student Name" with your name.**

- **Save the file as** New Tour Status**.**

Your screen should be similar to Figure 6

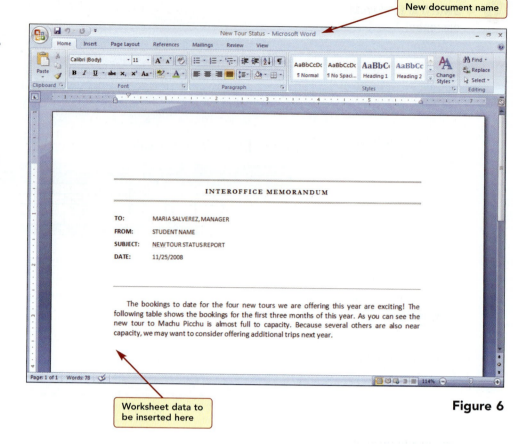

New document name

INTEROFFICE MEMORANDUM

TO: MARIA SALVEREZ, MANAGER
FROM: STUDENT NAME
SUBJECT: NEW TOUR STATUS REPORT
DATE: 11/25/2008

The bookings to date for the four new tours we are offering this year are exciting! The following table shows the bookings for the first three months of this year. As you can see the new tour to Machu Picchu is almost full to capacity. Because several others are also near capacity, we may want to consider offering additional trips next year.

Worksheet data to be inserted here

Figure 6

You will insert the worksheet data below the paragraph. To insert the information from the Excel workbook file into the Word memo, you need to open the workbook file and copy the worksheet range. You will then tile the two open application windows to make it easier to see and work with both files.

2

- Switch to Excel and close the Major Tour Sales file.

- Open the workbook file wdwt2_New Tour Bookings.

- Save the file as New Tour Bookings Linked.

- Change the zoom to 75%.

- Tile the two open windows vertically.

Having Trouble?
Choose Tile Windows Vertically from the Taskbar shortcut menu.

- Click in the Excel window to make it active.

- Select the worksheet range A3 through F10.

- Click 📋 Copy.

Your screen should be similar to Figure 7

Another Method
You also can insert an object as an embedded object, which stores the entire source file in the document in which it is inserted. Opening the embedded object opens the program in which it was created.

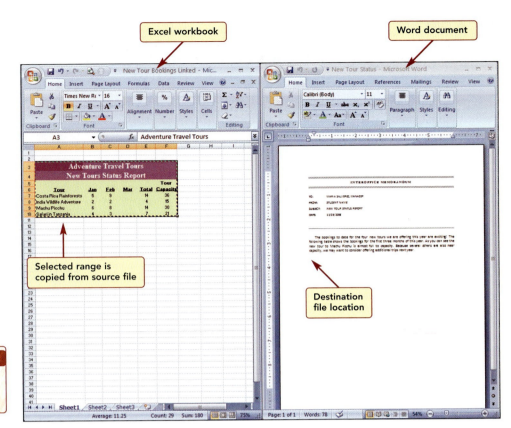

Figure 7

You will insert the worksheet into the memo as a **linked object.** A linked object is information created in one application that is inserted into a document created by another application while maintaining a link between the files. When an object is linked, the data is stored in the **source file** (the document it was created in). A graphic representation or picture of the data is displayed in the **destination file** (the document in which the object is inserted). A connection between the information in the destination file and the source file is established by the creation of a link. The link contains references to the location of the source file and the selection within the document that is linked to the destination file.

When changes are made in the source file that affect the linked object, the changes are automatically reflected in the destination file when it is opened. This is called a **live link.** When you create linked objects, the date and time on your machine should be accurate. This is because the program refers to the date of the source file to determine whether updates are needed when you open the destination file.

You will make the worksheet a linked object, so it will be automatically updated when you update the data in the worksheet.

3 • Click on the Word document window to make it active.

• Move to the blank space below the paragraph.

• Open the [Paste] drop-down menu and choose Paste Special.

• Choose Paste Link.

Your screen should be similar to Figure 8

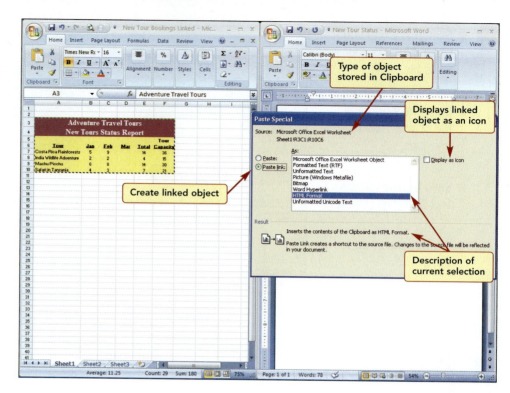

Figure 8

Additional Information

Using Paste inserts the worksheet in Word as a table that can be manipulated within Word.

The Paste Special dialog box displays the type of object contained in the Clipboard and its location in the Source area. From the As list box, you select the type of format in which you want the object inserted into the destination file. There are many different object types from which you can select. It is important to select the appropriate object format so that the link works correctly when inserted in the destination.

The Result area describes the effect of your selections. In this case, you want to insert the object as an Excel Worksheet Object, and a link will be created to the worksheet in the source file. Selecting the Display as Icon option changes the display of the object from a picture to an icon. Then, to open or edit the object, you would double-click the icon. You need to change the type of format only.

4 ● Select Microsoft Office Excel Worksheet Object.

● Click ▢ OK ▢.

● Click ▤ Center in the Paragraph group on the Home tab.

Your screen should be similar to Figure 9

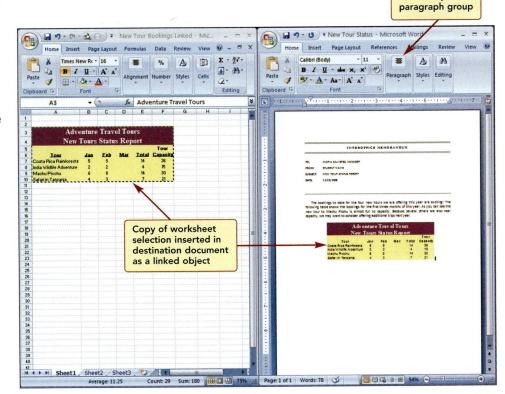

Click to open paragraph group

Copy of worksheet selection inserted in destination document as a linked object

Figure 9

Updating a Linked Object

While preparing the memo, you received the tour bookings for March and will enter this information into the worksheet. To make these changes, you need to switch back to Excel. Double-clicking on a linked object quickly switches to the open source file. If the source file is not open, it opens the file for you. If the application is not open, it opens both the application and the source file. Because the Excel application and worksheet file are already open, you will just switch to the Excel window.

1 • Click in the Excel window.

• Enter the values for March in the cells specified.

D7	6
D8	4
D9	13
D10	8

• Press ⏎Enter.

• Click on the linked object in the Word document to select it and press F9 to update the link.

Another Method
You also could choose Update Link from the object's shortcut menu.

Your screen should be similar to Figure 10

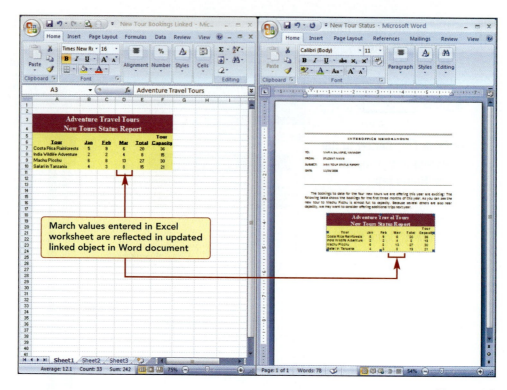

March values entered in Excel worksheet are reflected in updated linked object in Word document

Figure 10

The worksheet in the memo reflects the changes in data. This is because any changes you make to the worksheet in Excel will be automatically reflected in the linked worksheet in the Word document.

Editing Links

Whenever a document is opened that contains links, the application looks for the source file and automatically updates the linked objects. If there are many links, updating can take a lot of time. Additionally, if you move the source file to another location or perform other operations that may interfere with the link, your link will not work. To help with situations like these, you can edit the settings associated with links. You will look at the links to the worksheet data created in the Word document.

1 If necessary, switch to the Word document.

● Right-click on the linked object, select Linked Worksheet Object, and choose Links.

Your screen should be similar to Figure 11

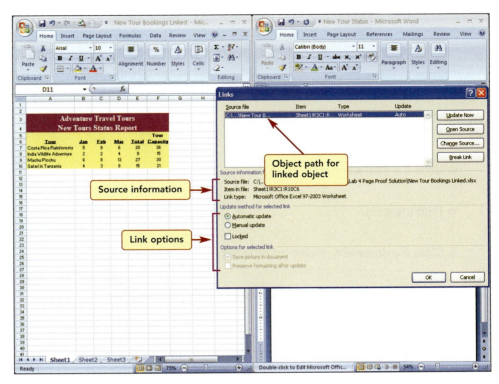

Figure 11

The Links dialog box displays in the list box the object path for all links in the document. The field code specifies the path and name of the source file, the range of linked cells or object name, the type of file, and the update status. Below the list box, the details for the selected link are displayed.

The other options in this dialog box are described in the table below.

Option	Effect
Automatic update	Updates the linked object whenever the destination document is opened or the source file changes. This is the default.
Manual update	The destination document is not automatically updated and you must use the Update Now command button to update the link.
Locked	Prevents a linked object from being updated.
Open Source	Opens the source document for the selected link.
Change Source...	Used to modify the path to the source document.
Break Link	Breaks the connection between the source document and the active document.

As you can see, the link in the Word document is to the New Tour Bookings Linked workbook file and the link is set to update automatically. You do not need to make any changes to these settings. Now that the memo is complete, you will untile the windows and save the documents.

2 ● Click [Cancel] .

● Undo the tiled windows.

● Print the memo.

● Close the document, saving the changes.

● Switch to Excel and close the worksheet, saving the changes.

Linking documents is a very handy feature, particularly in documents whose information is updated frequently. If you include a linked object in a document that you are giving to another person, make sure the user has access to the source file and application. Otherwise the links will not operate correctly.

Embedding an Object in Another Application

The last thing you need to do is to create a memo to the regional manager that shows the sales from the four new tours. Because the manager also wants a copy of the file, you will embed the worksheet data in the memo. An object that is embedded is stored in the destination file and becomes part of that document. The entire file, not just the selection that is displayed in the destination file, becomes part of the document. This means that you can modify it without affecting the source document where the original object resided.

1
- Open the Word document wdwt2_New Tour Sales.

- In the memo header, replace "Student Name" with your name.

- Save the document as New Tour Sales.

- Switch to Excel and open the workbook file wdwt2_New Tour Income.

Your screen should be similar to Figure 12

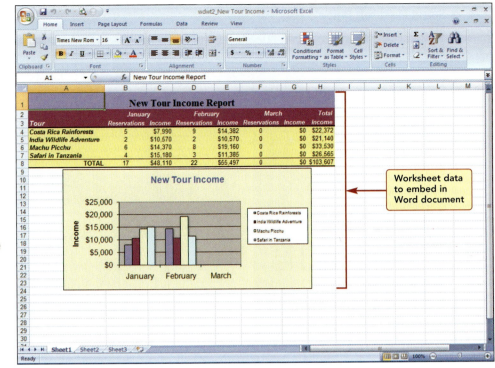

Worksheet data to embed in Word document

Figure 12

You will embed the worksheet in the Word document.

2
- Copy the range A1 through H24.

- Switch to the Word document window.

- Move to the second blank line below the first paragraph of the memo.

- Open the Paste drop-down menu and choose Paste Special.

Your screen should be similar to Figure 13

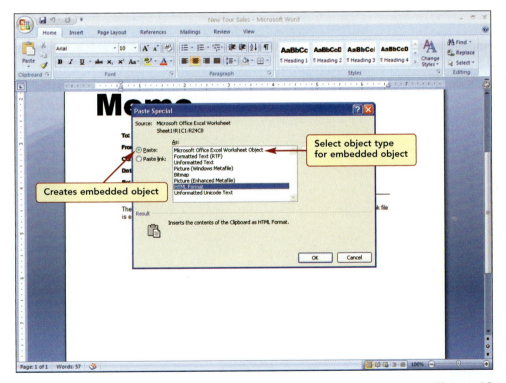

Select object type for embedded object

Creates embedded object

Figure 13

The Paste option inserts or embeds the Clipboard contents in the format you specify from the As list box. In this case, you are embedding a Microsoft Office Excel Worksheet Object.

3 ● Select Microsoft Office Excel Worksheet Object.

● Click [OK].

● Click on the worksheet object to select it.

● Reduce the size of the worksheet object to fit on the first page below the memo text.

Your screen should be similar to Figure 14

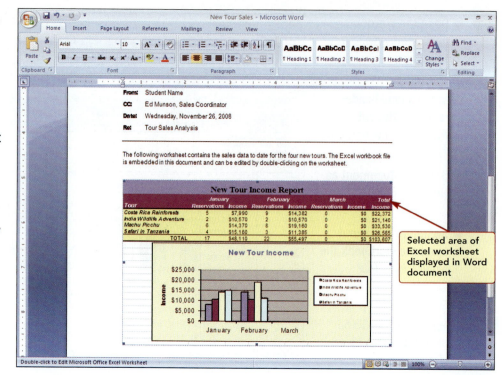

Selected area of Excel worksheet displayed in Word document

Figure 14

The selected portion of the worksheet is displayed in the memo at the location of the insertion point.

Updating an Embedded Object

You want to add the March reservations to the worksheet. Because the worksheet is embedded, you can do this from within the Word document. To open Excel from within the document, double-click the embedded object.

1 ● Double-click the worksheet object in Word.

Your screen should be similar to Figure 15

Having Trouble?

If the worksheet does not fully display the numbers, click outside the worksheet to close Excel. Select the worksheet object again, increase the width of the object, and then double-click on the object to open Excel again.

Additional Information

To open an embedded object, the user must have the appropriate application on his or her system to be able to open and edit the embedded object.

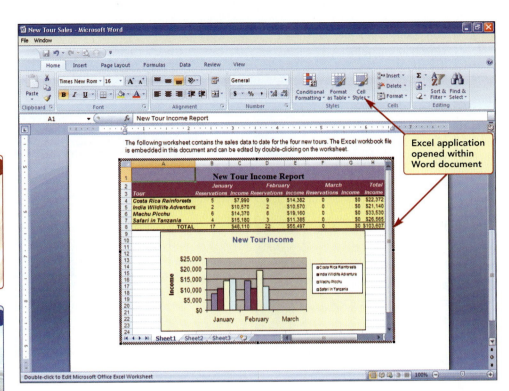

Figure 15

The associated application, in this case Excel, is opened. The Excel menus and toolbars replace the menus and toolbars in the Word application window. The selected portion of the embedded object is displayed in an editing worksheet window. Now you can use the Excel commands to edit the object.

2 ● Enter the values for March in the cells specified.

F4	6
F5	4
F6	13
F7	8

● Press ⏎Enter.

● Close the embedded application by clicking anywhere outside the object.

● Scroll the window to display the entire worksheet object.

● Preview, print, and save the document.

Your screen should be similar to Figure 16

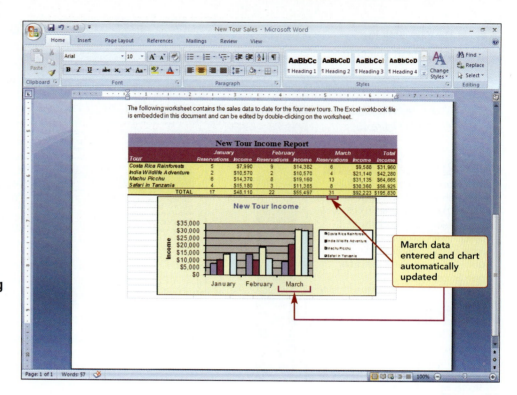

The following worksheet contains the sales data to date for the four new tours. The Excel workbook file is embedded in this document and can be edited by double-clicking on the worksheet.

New Tour Income Report

Tour	January Reservations	Income	February Reservations	Income	March Reservations	Income	Total Income
Costa Rica Rainforests	5	$7,990	9	$14,382	6	$9,588	$31,960
India Wildlife Adventure	2	$10,570	2	$10,570	4	$21,140	$42,280
Machu Picchu	6	$14,370	8	$19,160	13	$31,135	$64,665
Safari in Tanzania	4	$15,180	3	$11,385	8	$30,360	$56,925
TOTAL	17	$48,110	22	$55,497	31	$92,223	$195,830

March data entered and chart automatically updated

Figure 16

The embedded object in the memo is updated to reflect the changes you made. Notice the chart also updated to reflect the addition of the March data.

3 ● **Switch to the Excel window.**

Your screen should be similar to Figure 17

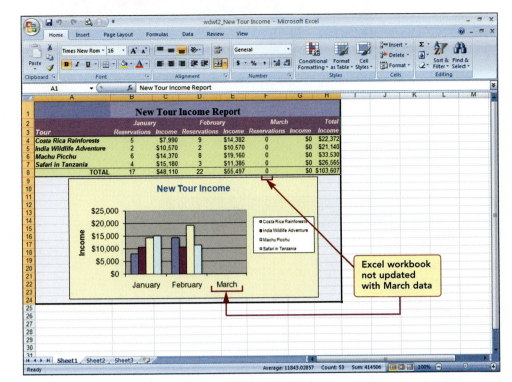

Excel workbook not updated with March data

Figure 17

The data in the Excel worksheet is unchanged. This is because it is not linked to the Word document and is a separate file.

4 ● **Enter the March reservation data as you did in the memo.**

● **Save the workbook as** New Tour Income **and exit Excel.**

● **Exit Word.**

Lab Review

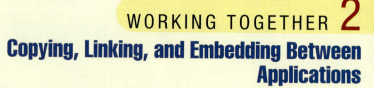

key terms

destination file   WDWT2.7
linked object   WDWT2.7
live link   WDWT2.7
source file   WDWT2.7

MCAS skills

The Microsoft Certified Applications Specialist (MCAS) certification program is designed to measure your proficiency in performing basic tasks using the Office 2007 applications. Getting certified demonstrates that you have the skills and provides a valuable industry credential for employment. See Reference 2, Microsoft Certified Applications Specialist (MCAS) for a complete list of the skills that were covered in Working Together 2

command summary

Command	Shortcut	Action
Home tab		
Clipboard group		
/Paste Special/Paste link		Pastes contents of Clipboard as a linked object
/Paste Special/Paste		Embeds contents of Clipboard as selected type of object

Hands-On Exercises

step-by-step

Sales Analysis Memo ★

1. Tamira Jones manages the Animal Rescue Foundation's new retail store. The Foundation director has requested a summary of the sales and expenses for the board of directors. She has completed the memo and worksheet and will now complete the assignment. The completed memo should be similar to that shown here.

   a. Start Word and open the document wdwt2_Animal Angels Sales.

   b. In the memo header, replace the From placeholder with your name.

   c. Start Excel and open the workbook file wdwt2_AA Sales. Copy the worksheet data and paste it just below the paragraph in the Word memo. Size and format the table using a table design style of your choice.

   d. Save the Word document as AA Sales Memo. Preview and print the document.

   e. Exit Word and Excel.

Memo

To: Sam Johnson
From: [Click here and type name]
CC: Sally Lamy
Date: July 14, 2008
Re: Animal Angel's Retail Sales Figures

Biannual Sales Review

I have concluded my survey of the first six months of sales at the retail outlet. Expenses have been trimmed, and profits have been greater than anticipated. I have talked to Mary Munson about using the profits to the fullest advantage. Below I have included the sales details for the first six months of operations.

	JAN	FEB	MAR	APR	MAY	JUN	TOTAL
Total Income	$7,419.96	$7,477.64	$7,548.97	$8,445.82	$9,007.62	$9,059.33	$48,959.36
Total Expenses	$3,320.58	$3,690.20	$4,100.47	$3,987.66	$3,898.42	$4,177.60	$23,174.93

Lab Exercises

Payroll Department Memo ★★

2. Karen works for a large hotel chain in the payroll department. She has recently created a new time sheet to be used to track hours worked and wants to send a memo informing department managers of the new procedure. She also wants to include a copy of the time sheet from Excel in the memo. The completed memo should be similar to that shown here.

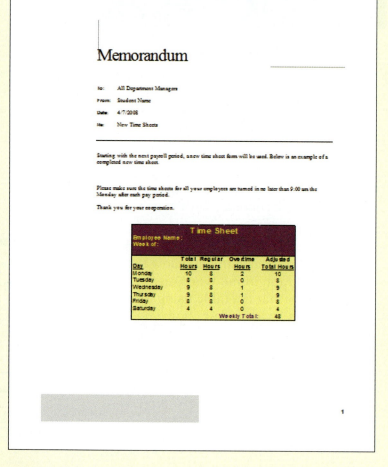

   a. Start Word and open the document wdwt2_Time Sheet Memo.

   b. In the memo header, replace the From placeholder with your name.

   c. Start Excel and open the workbook file wdwt2_Time Sheet. Copy the range containing the time sheet and paste it as a linked object just below the first paragraph in the Word memo. Center the time sheet in the memo.

   d. You still need to complete the sample by entering the hours worked on Saturday. In the Excel Worksheet, enter **4** as the Total Hours and Regular Hours worked on Saturday.

   e. Save the Excel workbook as Time Sheet. Exit Excel.

f. Update the linked worksheet object in the Word document.

g. Save the Word document as Time Sheet Linked. Preview and print the document. Exit Word.

Opera Donors Memo ★★★

3. The City Opera Foundation has decided to hold a spring fund-raising event. They would like to extend invitations to the top donors and have asked you to provide the appropriate donor records to the board. You have compiled the records in a worksheet and started the memo. Your completed memo should be similar to that shown here.

   a. Start Word and open the document wdwt2_Opera Donors.

   b. In the memo header, replace the From placeholder with your name.

   c. Start Excel and open the workbook wdwt2_COF Donors.

   d. Copy the range containing the donations and paste it as an embedded object in the Word document just below the text in the memo. Center the worksheet in the memo.

   e. You received a memo that contains anticipated donation information that has not yet been entered in the Excel worksheet. Include the following text at the end of the memo: **Please note that the 2008 donation listed for Palmquist Equipment has not been finalized, but Mary assures me that this donation has been promised and "is in the works."**

   f. From the Word document, open the embedded Excel worksheet and enter **12400** as the Palmquist Equipment 2008 donation.

   g. Save the Word document as Opera Donors2. Preview and print the document. Exit Word. Exit Excel.

City Opera Foundation

Memo

To: City Opera Foundation Board

From: Student Name

Date: January 14, 2009

Re: Top Donors

I have finished reviewing the foundation donation records. I am including the list of corporations and individuals that have contributed over $50,000 in the table below.

	2005	2006	2007	2008	Total Donations
T.W.B Foundation	$24,588	$25,994	$22,198	$28,005	$ 100,785
Red Finch Antiques	$10,384	$15,832	$14,892	$13,855	$ 54,963
Café Trocadero	$13,765	$14,893	$12,854	$12,844	$ 54,356
Fulton Farms	$16,834	$17,455	$18,933	$15,693	$ 68,915
Palmquist Equipment	$15,330	$14,832	$17,005	$12,400	$ 59,567
Total	$80,901	$89,006	$85,882	$82,797	$ 338,586

Please note that the 2008 donation listed for Palmquist Equipment has not been finalized, but Mary assures me that this donation has been promised and "is in the works."

Word 2007 Command Summary

Command	Shortcut	Action
Office Button		**Opens File menu**
New	Ctrl + N	Opens new document
New/Memos		Provides memo templates from Microsoft Office Online
Open	Ctrl + O	Opens existing document file
Open/Trusted Templates		Opens location of custom templates
Save	Ctrl + S, 💾	Saves document using same file name
Save As	F12	Saves document using a new file name, type, and/or location
Save As/Word Template		Saves document as a template
Save As/Save As type/ Web Page		Saves file as a Web page document
Print	Ctrl + P	Specify print settings before printing document
Print/Quick Print		Prints document using default printer settings
Print/Print Preview		Displays document as it will appear when printed
Prepare/Properties		Opens Document Information Panel
Prepare/Inspect Document		Starts Document Inspector to check document for hidden data or personal information
Prepare/Add a Digital Signature		Ensures integrity of document by adding an invisible digital signature
Prepare/Mark as Final		Lets readers know document is final and makes it read-only
Send/E-mail		Sends document as an attachment by e-mail
Close	Ctrl + F4	Closes document
Word Options /Popular/ Show Developer tab in Ribbon		Displays or hides Developer tab in Ribbon
Word Options /Proofing		Changes settings associated with Spelling and Grammar checking
Word Options /Advanced/ Mark formatting inconsistencies		Checks for formatting inconsistencies
X Exit Word	Alt + F4, 🗙	Closes the Word application

Command	Shortcut	Action
Quick Access Toolbar		
🖫 Save		Saves document using same file name
↩ ▾ Undo	Ctrl + Z	Restores last editing change
↪ Redo	Ctrl + Y	Restores last Undo or repeats last command or action
Home tab		
Clipboard group		
Paste	Ctrl + V	Pastes item from Clipboard
Paste /Paste Special/Paste		Embeds contents of Clipboard as selected type of object
Paste /Paste Special/Paste Link		Pastes contents of Clipboard as a linked object
✂ Cut	Ctrl + X	Cuts selection to Clipboard
📋 Copy	Ctrl + C	Copies selection to Clipboard
🖌 Format Painter		Copies format to selection
⤵		Displays the Office Clipboard task pane
Font group		
Calibri (Body) ▾ Font		Changes typeface
11 ▾ Size		Changes font size
A˄ Grow Font		Increases font size
A̳ Clear Formatting		Clears all formatting from selected text, leaving plain text
B Bold	Ctrl + B	Makes selected text bold
I Italic	Ctrl + I	Applies italic effect to selected text
U̲ ▾ Underline	Ctrl + U	Adds underline below selected text
Aa▾ Change Case		Changes case of selected text
abₑ ▾ Text Highlight Color		Applies highlight color to selection
A ▾ Font Color		Changes text to selected color
Paragraph group		
☰ ▾ Bullets		Creates a bulleted list
☰ ▾ Bullets/ Define New Bullet/Picture		Applies picture bullets to selected items
☰ ▾ Numbering		Creates a numbered list
☰ ▾ Multilevel List		Creates a multilevel list
☰ Decrease Indent	⇧ Shift + Tab ⇥	Decreases indent level of paragraph
☰ Increase Indent	Tab ⇥	Increases indent level of paragraph

Command	Shortcut	Action
↕↓ Sort		Rearranges items in a selection into ascending alphabetical/numerical order
¶ Show/Hide	Ctrl + → + *	Displays or hides formatting marks
▤ Align Text Left	Ctrl + L	Aligns text to left margin
▤ Center	Ctrl + E	Centers text between left and right margins
▤ Align Text Right	Ctrl + R	Aligns text to right margin
▤ Justify	Ctrl + J	Aligns text equally between left and right margins
▤▾ Line Spacing	Ctrl + #	Changes amount of white space between lines
▨▾ Shading		Colors the background behind selected text or paragraph
▦▾ Border		Customizes the borders for selected text or objects
Styles group ▾ More		Opens Quick Styles gallery
▾ More/Save Selection as a New Quick Style		Creates a new style based on formatting of selected text
Editing Group 🔍 Find ▾	Ctrl + F	Locates specified text
🔄 Replace	Ctrl + H	Locates and replaces specified text
▷ Select ▾		Selects text or objects in the document

Insert tab

Command	Shortcut	Action
Pages group 📄 Cover Page ▾		Inserts a preformatted cover page
📄 Blank Page		Inserts a blank page
📄 Page Break	Ctrl + ↵Enter	Inserts a hard page break
Tables group ▦ Table ▾		Inserts a table
▦ Table ▾ /Draw Table		Draws table borders
▦ Table ▾ /Convert Text to Table		Changes selected text in a document to text displayed in a table
Illustrations group 🖼 Picture		Inserts a picture from file

Command	Shortcut	Action
Clip Art		Inserts clip art, drawings, movies, sound
Shapes		Inserts ready-made shapes
Shapes /New Drawing Canvas		Inserts drawing canvas to create and manipulate objects
SmartArt		Inserts selected SmartArt graphic shape
SmartArt /Hierarchy/ Organization Chart		Opens Organization Chart SmartArt graphic
Chart		Inserts selected chart type and opens Excel 2007
Links group		
Hyperlink	Ctrl + K	Inserts hyperlink
Bookmark		Creates, deletes, or goes to a bookmark or assigned name to a specific point in a document
Header & Footer group		
Header		Inserts predesigned header style
Footer		Inserts predesigned footer style
Page Number		Inserts page number in document
Text group		
Text Box		Inserts preformatted text boxes
Quick Parts		Inserts reusable pieces of content
WordArt		Inserts decorative text into document
Drop Cap		Creates a large capital letter at the beginning of a paragraph
Date & Time		Inserts current date or time, maintained by computer system, in selected format
Object /Text from File		Inserts contents of an entire file
Symbols group		
Symbol		Inserts symbols that are not on keyboard into document

Command	Shortcut	Action
Page Layout tab		
Themes group		
Themes		Applies selected theme to document
		Changes colors for current theme
		Changes fonts for current theme
Page Setup group		
Margins		Sets document or section margin sizes
Orientation		Switches between portrait and landscape layouts
Columns		Splits text between two or more columns
Columns /More Columns		Sets width and spacing of columns
Breaks	Ctrl + E	Adds page, section, or column breaks to the document
Breaks /Text Wrapping		Stops text from wrapping around objects on Web page
Hyphenation		Turns on hyphenation, allowing Word to break lines between the syllables of words
Page Background group		
Watermark		Inserts ghosted text behind page content
Page Color		Adds selected color to page background
Page Color /Fill Effects		Adds selected color effect to page background
Page Borders		Adds a border around page
Arrange group		
Text Wrapping		Controls how text wraps around a graphic
References tab		
Table of Contents group		
Table of Contents		Generates a table of contents
Add Text		Adds selected text as an entry in table of contents
Update Table	F9	Updates the table of contents field
Footnotes group		
Insert Footnote	Alt + Ctrl + F	Inserts footnote reference at insertion point

Command	Shortcut	Action
Citations & Bibliography group		
Insert Citation ▾		Creates a citation for a reference source
Manage Sources		Displays list of all sources cited
Style: APA ▾		Sets the style of citation to use in document
Bibliography ▾		Creates a bibliography list of sources cited in document
Captions group		
Insert Caption		Adds a figure caption
Insert Table of Figures		Inserts a table of figures
Cross-reference		Creates figure cross-references
Mailings tab		
Create group		
Envelopes		Prints delivery and return addresses on envelopes
Labels		Creates mailing labels for envelopes
Start Mail Merge group		
Start Mail Merge ▾ /Step by Step Mail Merge Wizard		Starts Mail Merge Wizard to create a form letter, envelopes, and labels
Select Recipients ▾		Select recipients from client list to send document to
Edit Recipient List		Edits records in recipient list
Write & Insert Fields group		
Greeting Line		Inserts greeting line in main document
Insert Merge Field ▾		Inserts merge fields in main document
Preview Results group		
Preview Results		Replaces merge fields with actual data from recipient list to see how merged document will look
Review tab		
Proofing group		
ABC Spelling & Grammar	F7	Starts Spelling and Grammar Checker
Thesaurus	⇧ Shift + F7	Starts Thesaurus tool

Command	Shortcut	Action
Research		Opens Research task pane to search through reference materials
Comments group		
New Comment		Inserts a comment
Delete ▾		Deletes selected comment
Tracking group		
Track Changes ▾	Ctrl + ⇧Shift + E	Turns on/off Track Change feature
Balloons ▾		Choose how to show revision: balloons or inline
Final Showing Markup ▾		Changes how to view proposed changes to document
Show Markup ▾		Choose what type of markup to show
Reviewing Pane ▾		Displays/hides Reviewing pane
Changes group		
Accept ▾		Accepts change and moves to next change
Reject ▾		Rejects change and moves to next change
Previous		Moves to previous change
Next		Moves to next change
Compare group		
Compare /Combine		Combines documents and identifies differences
Protect group		
Protect Document		Restricts access and changes to document by adding protection and a password

View tab

Command	Shortcut	Action
Document Views group		
Print Layout		Shows how text and objects will appear on printed page
Web Layout		Shows document as it will appear when viewed in a Web browser
Outline		Shows outline structure of document

Command	Shortcut	Action
Draft		Shows text formatting and simple layout of page
Show/Hide group		
☑ Ruler	▣	Displays/hides horizontal ruler bar
☐ Document Map		Displays or hides Document Map pane
☐ Thumbnails		Displays or hides Thumbnails pane
Zoom group		
Zoom		Opens the Zoom dialog box to specify zoom level
100%		Zooms document to 100% of normal size
One Page		Zooms document so an entire page fits in window
Two Pages		Zooms document so that two pages fit in window
Page Width		Zooms document so width of page matches width of window
Window group		
Arrange All		Arranges all open windows horizontally on screen
Split		Divides a document into two horizontal sections
View Side by Side		Displays two document windows side by side to make it easy to compare content
Synchronous Scrolling		Turns on/off synchronized scrolling
Switch Windows		Switches between open document windows

Developer tab

Command	Shortcut	Action
Controls group		
Aa Rich Text		Inserts rich text control
Aa Text		Inserts plain text control
Drop-Down List		Inserts drop-down list control
Legacy Tools		Displays Legacy controls
Design Mode		Changes to Design mode
Properties		Displays properties for selected control
Protect group		
Protect Document		Turns on/off document protection

Command	Shortcut	Action
Chart Tools Design tab		
Type group		
Change Chart Type		Changes current chart to another type
Chart Tools Format tab		
Current Selection group		
Format Selection		Formats selected chart elements
Picture Tools Format tab		
Adjust group		
Brightness		Increases or decreases the brightness of a picture
Contrast		Increases or decreases the contrast of a picture
Compress Pictures		Compresses pictures in the document to reduce its size
Picture Styles group		
More		Opens Picture Styles gallery
Picture Shape		Changes shape of picture
Picture Border		Adds specified outline style border around picture
Picture Effects		Adds selected visual effects to picture such as shadow and glow
Arrange group		
Bring to Front		Brings object to front of stack
Send to Back		Sends object back in the stack
Text Wrapping		Specifies how text will wrap around picture
Align		Aligns edges or centers objects
Group		Groups objects to be treated like a single object
Size group		
Crop		Crops pictures to remove unwanted parts
SmartArt Tools Design tab		
Create Graphic group		
Add Shape		Adds a shape to SmartArt graphic
Layout		Changes the branch layout of SmartArt graphic
Demote		Decreases level of selected shape
Text Pane		Displays or hides text pane

Command	Shortcut	Action
SmartArt Styles group		
Change Colors		Changes color variations in SmartArt graphic styles
More		Opens gallary of visual styles for SmartArt graphic
Table Tools Design tab		
Table Style Options group		
☑ Header Row		Turns on/off formats for header row
☑ First Column		Turns on/off formats for first column
☑ Last Column		Turns on/off formats for last column
Table Styles group		
More		Opens gallery of predesigned table formats
Shading		Colors cell background
Borders		Customizes cell borders
Draw Borders group		
Draw Table		Draws table borders
Eraser		Erases table borders
Table Tools Layout tab		
Table group		
View Gridlines		Shows or hides table gridlines
Rows & Columns group		
Delete		Deletes rows, columns, cells, or entire table
Insert Above		Inserts a new row in table above selected row
Merge group		
Merge Cells		Merges cells in a table
Split Cells		Returns merged cells to individual cells
Cell Size group		
Distribute Rows		Equally distributes row heights
Distribute Columns		Equally distributes column widths
Alignment group		
Align Top Center		Aligns text at top center of cell space
Align Center		Centers text horizontally and vertically within cell

Command	Shortcut	Action
Text Direction		Changes text direction within cell
Cell Margins		Customizes cell margins and spacing between cells
Data group		
Convert to Text		Converts text in table to normal text
Formula		Adds formula to cell

WordArt Tools Format tab

Command	Shortcut	Action
Text group		
Spacing		Changes the spacing between the letters of the text
Arrange group		
Text Wrapping		Changes the way text wraps around a selected object
WordArt Styles group		
More		Opens WordArt Styles gallery
Change WordArt Shape		Specifies overall shape of WordArt object
Shape Fill		Fills selected shape with solid, color, gradient, picture, or texture
Shape Outline		Specifies color, width, and line style for outline of selected shape

Header & Footer Tools Design tab

Command	Shortcut	Action
Header & Footer Group		
Page Number		Inserts page number in header or footer
Insert group		
Date & Time		Inserts current date or time in header or footer
Quick Parts /Document Property		Inserts selected document property
Quick Parts /Field		Inserts selected Quick Part
Navigation group		
Go to Header		Switches to header area
Go to Footer		Switches to footer area
Previous Section		Navigates to previous section's header/footer

Command	Shortcut	Action
Next Section		Navigates to next section's header/footer
Link to Previous		Turns on/off link to header or footer in previous section
Options group		
Different First Page		Specify a unique header and footer for the first page
Position group		
Insert Alignment Tab		Inserts a tab stop to align content in header/footer
Close group		
Close Header and Footer		Closes header/footer area

Outlining tab

Command	Shortcut	Action
Outline Tools group		
Promote to Heading 1		Promotes selected item to Heading 1 level
Promote	Alt + ⇧ Shift + ←	Promotes selected item one level
Body Text — Outline Level		Choose outline level for selected item
Demote	Alt + ⇧ Shift + →	Demotes selected item one level
Demote to body text		Demotes selected item to body text
Move Up	Alt + ⇧ Shift + ↑	Moves selected item up in outline
Move Down	Alt + ⇧ Shift + ↓	Moves selected item down in outline
Expand	Alt + ⇧ Shift + +	Expand selected item
Collapse	Alt + ⇧ Shift + −	Collapse selected item
Show Level: All Levels		Shows only specified outline levels
Show Text Formatting		Shows outline as formatted text
Show First Line Only		Shows only first line of each item
Close group		
Close Outline View		Closes outline view and displays last used view

Glossary of Key Terms

active window The window containing the insertion point and that will be affected by any changes you make.

address list The data source file used in a merge; it typically contains name and address data to be combined with the main document.

alignment How text is positioned on a line between the margins or indents. There are four types of paragraph alignment: left, centered, right, and justified.

anchor Method used to attach floating graphics to a particular location in a document such as to a page or a paragraph.

antonym A word with the opposite meaning.

assistant box The box below the manager box in an organization chart that represents an administrative or managerial assistant.

attachment A file that is sent along with an e-mail message but is not part of the e-mail text.

attribute A feature such as line color or fill color that can be changed using drawing tools and menu commands.

author The process of creating a Web page.

AutoCorrect A feature that makes basic assumptions about the text you are typing and automatically corrects the entry.

balloon A box that displays markup elements such as comments and tracked changes in the margin of the document.

bibliography A listing of source references that appears at the end of the document.

bookmark A link that identifies a location or a selection of text that you name allowing you to quickly move to that location in the document by selecting the bookmark.

branch In an organization chart, a box and all boxes that report to it.

browser A program that connects you to remote computers and displays the Web pages you request.

building blocks Document fragments that include text and formatting and can be easily inserted into a document.

bulleted list Displays items that logically fall out from a paragraph into a list, with items preceded by bullets.

caption A title or explanation for a table, picture, or graph.

case sensitive The capability to distinguish between uppercase and lowercase characters.

cell The intersection of a column and row where data are entered in a table.

character formatting Formatting features such as bold and color that affect the selected characters only.

chart A visual representation of numeric data. Also called a graph.

citations Parenthetical source references that give credit for specific information included in a document.

Click and Type A feature available in Print Layout and Web Layout views that is used to quickly insert text, graphics, and other items in a blank area of a document, avoiding the need to enter blank lines.

clip art Professionally drawn graphics.

collect and paste The capability of the program to store multiple copied items in the Office Clipboard and then paste one or more of the items.

comment A note that can be added to a document without changing the document text.

comment balloon A graphic element typically appearing in the markup area of a document that contains the text of person commenting on the document.

content control Graphical objects that can be added to and customized for use in templates, forms, and documents.

control (1) A graphic element that is a container for information or objects. (2) Graphic object that you can add to and customize for use in templates, forms, and documents.

co-worker boxes Boxes in an organization chart at the same level that have the same manager. Co-worker boxes form a group.

crop To trim vertical or horizontal edges of a picture.

cross-reference A reference in one part of a document related to information in another part.

cursor The blinking vertical bar that shows you where the next character you type will appear. Also called the insertion point.

custom dictionary A dictionary of terms you have entered that are not in the main dictionary of the spelling checker.

data field Each category of information in the data source.

data record All the fields of data that are needed to complete the main document for one entity in a merge operation.

data series Each group of related data that is plotted in the chart. Each data series has a unique color or pattern assigned to it so that you can identify the different series.

data source The file that supplies the data in a mail merge.

datasheet The data validation restrictions you place on a field.

default The initial Word document settings that can be changed to customize documents.

destination The location to which text is moved or copied.

destination file A document in which a linked object is inserted.

diagram A graphic object that can be used to illustrate concepts and to enhance documents.

digital signature An electronic encryption-based stamp of authentication that confirms the document originated from the signer and has not been changed.

Document Map A feature that displays the headings in the document in the navigation window.

document properties Details about a document that describe or identify it and are saved with the document content.

document theme A predefined set of formatting choices that can be applied to an entire document in one simple step.

document window The area of the application window that displays the contents of the open document.

drag and drop A mouse procedure that moves or copies a selection to a new location.

drawing layer The layer above or below the text layer where floating objects are inserted.

drawing object A simple object consisting of shapes such as lines and boxes.

drop cap A large, uppercase character with the top part of the letter even with the line and the rest of the letter extending into the paragraph below it.

edit The process of changing and correcting existing text in a document.

em dash A single long dash line.

embedded object An object such as a picture graphic that becomes part of the Word document and that can be opened and edited using the program in which it was created.

end-of-file marker The horizontal line that marks the end of a file.

endnote A reference note displayed at the end of the document.

field A placeholder that instructs Word to insert information in a document.

field code The code containing the instructions about the type of information to insert in a field.

field name A name used to label each data field in the data source.

field result The results displayed in a field according to the instructions in the field code.

floating object A graphic object that is inserted into the drawing layer and can be positioned anywhere on the page.

font A set of characters with a specific design. Also called a typeface.

font size The height and width of a character, commonly measured in points.

form Document that contains fill-in blanks or spaces reserved for entering information.

form field control Legacy controls that were designed for use in earlier versions of Word.

footer The line or several lines of text at the bottom of every page just below the bottom margin line.

footnote A reference note displayed at the bottom of the page on which the reference occurs.

format   To enhance the appearance of the document to make it more readable or attractive.

Format Painter   The feature that applies formats associated with the current selection to new selections.

formula   Table entry that performs arithmetic calculations on values in cells.

function   A prewritten formula that performs a calculation automatically in a table.

global template   The normal document template whose settings are available to all documents.

gradient   A gradual progression of colors and shades, usually from one color to another, or from one shade to another of the same color.

grammar checker   The feature that advises you of incorrect grammar as you create and edit a document, and proposes possible corrections.

graphic   A nontext element in a document.

group   (1) Two or more objects that are combined so that you can work with them as you would a single object. (2) In an organization chart, all boxes that report to the same manager.

hard page break   A manually inserted page break that instructs Word to begin a new page regardless of the amount of text on the previous page.

header   The line or several lines of text at the top of each page just above the top margin line.

header row   The first row in the data source that displays the field names.

heading style   A style that is designed to identify different levels of headings in a document.

hierarchical relationship   A relationship that shows ranking such as reporting structures within a department in a business that is commonly represented in an organization chart.

hierarchy   Ranking of items in a group.

HTML (HyperText Markup Language)   The programming language used to create Web pages.

hyperlink   A connection to locations in the current document, other documents, or Web pages. Clicking a hyperlink jumps to the specified location.

hyphenation   Inserts a hyphen (-) in long words that fall at the end of a line to split the word between lines.

hyphenation zone   An unmarked space along the right margin that controls the amount of white space in addition to the margin that is allowed at the end of a line.

indent   To set in a paragraph from the margins. There are four types of indents: left, right, first line, and hanging.

inline object   An object that is inserted directly in the text at the position of the insertion point, becoming part of the paragraph.

Insert mode   Method of text entry in which new characters are inserted into existing text, which moves to the right to make space for the new characters; the text on the line is reformatted as necessary.

insertion point   The blinking vertical bar that shows you where the next character you type will appear on the line. Also called the cursor.

kerning   Adjusting the spacing between particular pairs of letters, depending on the font design.

landscape   Orientation in which text is printed across the length of the page.

leader characters   Solid, dotted, or dashed lines that fill the blank space between tab stops.

legend   A box containing a brief description that identifies the patterns or colors assigned to the data series in a chart.

line spacing   The vertical space between lines of text.

linked object   Information created in a source file from one application and inserted into a destination file of another application while maintaining a link between files.

live link   A linked object that automatically reflects in the destination document any changes made in the source document when the destination document is opened.

Live Preview   A feature that allows you to preview in your document the results of applying formatting changes as you select different format options.

macro   A stored series of commands or actions that will execute when the control is selected.

Mail Merge   A feature that combines a text document with a data document or file containing names and addresses to produce a merged document or form letter.

main dictionary   The dictionary of terms that comes with Word 2007.

main document The document that contains the basic form letter with merge fields in a merge operation.

manager box The top-level box of a group in an organization chart.

markup Elements used to identify changes made to a document when Track Changes is on.

merge field A field code that controls what information is used from the data source and where it is entered in the main document.

multilevel list A list of items that is organized in a hierarchical structure, similar to an outline.

navigation window A separate window that displays the Document Map and thumbnails.

newsletter-style columns The arrangement of text in a document so that it flows from the bottom of one column to the top of the next column.

Normal template The document template that is opened when you start Word.

note pane Lower portion of the window that displays footnotes.

note reference mark A superscript number or character appearing in the document at the end of the material being referenced.

note separator The horizontal line separating footnote text from the main document text.

note text The text in a footnote.

numbered list Displays items that convey a sequence of events in a particular order, with items preceded by numbers or letters.

object An item that can be sized, moved, and manipulated.

Office Clipboard A temporary Windows storage area in memory.

operator Specifies the type of calculation to perform. The most common operators are + (add), - (subtract), * (multiply), and / (divide).

optional hyphen A hyphen that is inserted automatically when a word is broken between two lines because the full word did not fit.

organization chart A graphic representation of the structure of an organization.

outline numbered list Displays items in multiple outline levels that show a hierarchical structure of the items in the list.

page break Marks the point at which one page ends and another begins.

page margin The blank space around the edge of the page.

paragraph formatting Formatting features such as alignment, indentation, and line spacing that affect an entire paragraph.

password A combination of letters, numbers, and symbols that is stored with the document and prevents unauthorized users from either viewing or saving changes to the document.

picture An illustration such as a scanned photograph.

placeholder (1) A graphic element that is designed to contain specific types of information. (2) Text in a template that marks the space and provides instructions for the text that should be entered at that location.

portrait Orientation of the page in which text is printed across the width of the page.

protection A feature that controls what information can be changed in a document.

protocol The rules that control how hardware and software on a network communicate.

quick styles A gallery of predefined sets of formatting characteristics that allows you to quickly apply a whole group of formats in one simple step to a selection.

ruler The ruler located below the Formatting toolbar that shows the line length in inches.

sans serif font A font such as Arial or Helvetica that does not have a flair at the base of each letter.

section A division into which a document can be divided that can be formatted separately from the rest of the document.

section break Marks the point at which one section ends and another begins.

selection rectangle The rectangular outline around an object that indicates it is selected.

serif font A font such as Times New Roman that has a flair at the base of each letter.

sidebar An article set off from other articles or information that highlights an article next to it.

sizing handles Black squares around a selected object that can be used to size the object.

SmartArt A graphic feature that includes many predesigned diagrams you can add to your document to illustrate textual concepts.

soft page break A page break automatically inserted by Word to start a new page when the previous page has been filled with text or graphics.

soft space   A space between words automatically entered by Word to justify text on a line.

sort   To arrange alphabetically or numerically in ascending or descending order.

source   The location from which text is moved or copied.

source file   The document in which the linked item was created.

source program   The program in which an object was created.

spelling checker   The feature that advises you of misspelled words as you create and edit a document, and proposes possible corrections.

split window   A division of the document window into two horizontal sections making it easier to view different parts of a document.

stacking order   The order in which objects are positioned in the drawing layer.

story   Text that is contained in a single text box or linked text boxes.

synchronized   Documents in multiple open windows that move together when you scroll the window.

synonym   A word with a similar meaning.

system Clipboard   Where a selection that has been cut or copied is stored.

tab stop   A marked location on the horizontal ruler that indicates how far to indent text when the ⌷Tab⇆ key is pressed.

table   Displays information in horizontal rows and vertical columns.

table of contents   A listing of topic headings and associated page numbers in a document.

table of figures   A listing of figures and associated page numbers in a document.

table reference   The letter and number (for example, A1) that identify a cell in a table.

tag   Embedded codes that supply information about a Web page's structure, appearance, and contents.

template   A document that includes predefined settings and content that is used as the basis for a new document.

text box   A container for text and other graphic objects.

text wrapping   Controls how text appears around a graphic.

thesaurus   Word feature that provides synonyms and antonyms for words.

thumbnail   A miniature representation of a picture.

title   Descriptive text used to explain the contents of the chart.

tracked changes   Insertions, deletions, and formatting changes that are made to a document while the Track Changes feature is on.

TrueType   A font that is automatically installed when you install Windows.

typeface   A set of characters with a specific design. Also called a font.

URL   The address that indicates the location of a document on the World Wide Web. URL stands for Uniform Resource Locator.

watermark   Text or pictures that appear behind document text.

Web page   A document that can be used on the World Wide Web and viewed in a browser.

wizard   A guided approach to creating special types of documents, such as merge documents, consisting of a series of steps in which you specify settings. The wizard creates a document based on your selections.

word wrap   A feature that automatically determines where to end a line and wrap text to the next line based on the margin settings.

WordArt   A graphic feature that is used to enhance a document by changing the shape of text, adding 3-D effects, and changing the alignment of text on a line.

X axis   The bottom boundary of the chart, also called the category axis, is used to label the data being charted; the label may be, for example, a point in time or a category.

Y axis   The left boundary of the chart, also called the value axis, is a numbered scale whose numbers are determined by the data used in the chart.

Appendix

1. CREATING AND CUSTOMIZING DOCUMENTS

1.1 CREATE AND FORMAT DOCUMENTS

SET THEMES AS DEFAULT

Whenever you start Microsoft Office Word 2007, the Normal.dotm template opens. It includes default settings such as margins, page size, and theme that determine the basic look of a document. You can change the settings in the Normal.dotm template so that whenever a new document is opened, the settings you specified are used in all new documents you create. To change the default theme from the Office theme to another, follow these steps:

- Click Office Button.
- Choose Open.

Do one of the following:
In Microsoft Windows Vista:

- Choose Templates, and then double-click the Normal.dotm file to open it.

In Microsoft Windows XP or Microsoft Windows Server 2003:

- Click Templates next to File name.
- Double-click Normal.dotm to open it.

The default document template file is opened and Normal.dotm appears in the Word title bar. This file can be modified like any other file. Next, to change the theme associated with the default document template,

- Open the Page Layout tab.
- Click and select a built-in theme of your choice or create your own custom theme.

Having Trouble?
If no templates are listed in the Open dialog box, open the Files of type list box, and then choose All Word Templates.

If you wanted, you also could make changes to the fonts, margins, spacing, and other settings. Once you are done and the file contains the settings you want the Normal.dotm to include, you save the changes you have made to the template.

- Click Office Button and choose Save.
- Save the document as Normal.dotm to replace the contents of the template file with the new settings you specified.

Next time you open a new blank document, the new settings you specified will be the default document settings.

RESTORE TEMPLATE THEMES

Many times after applying a different theme or customizing a theme, you may decide you want to restore the default document theme. Use the following steps to restore the theme associated with the template you are using:

- Open the Page Layout tab.
- Click and choose Reset to Theme from Template in the Themes menu.

The theme associated with the template file you are using is reapplied to the entire document.

CHANGE THEME COLORS

Each theme has a color scheme that consists of a set of 12 theme colors that are applied to different elements of the theme. To customize a theme, you can apply a different built-in color scheme to your selected theme or customize the theme's color scheme by changing the colors associated with the different elements. The new color scheme can then be saved as a Custom Theme Color and can then be quickly applied to other themes. Follow these steps to change theme colors:

- Open the Page Layout tab.

- Click ⬜ and choose a theme of your choice.

- Click ⬜ Theme Colors.

- Choose Create New Theme Colors.

The Theme Colors dialog box identifies the colors associated with the different elements. The Sample box shows where the selected colors are used in a document. Theme colors contain four text and background colors, six accent colors, and two hyperlink colors.

- Click the button of the theme color element that you want to change.

- Choose the color that you want to use.

- In the same manner, select and change colors for all of the theme color elements that you want to change.

The Sample box reflects the new colors you selected so you can see the effect of the changes that you make. Once you are satisfied with your selections, you save the color scheme.

- In the Name text box, type a name that will identify the color scheme.

- Click ⬜ Save ⬜ .

The custom theme color name appears at the top of the Theme Colors menu so you can quickly select and apply it to other themes.

CHANGE THEME EFFECTS

Each theme includes a set of lines and fill effects. Although you cannot create your own set of theme effects, you can apply a different built-in theme effect from another theme to your own document theme. To do this, follow these steps:

- Open the Page Layout tab.
- Click ⬜ Theme Effects in the Themes group.

The lines and fill effects that are used for each set of theme effects appear in the graphic that is displayed next to the theme effects name.

- Select the effect that you want to use.

The effects for the current theme have been changed to the selected theme effects.

1.2 LAY OUT DOCUMENTS

CHANGE PAPER SIZE

Many specialty types of documents, such as legal documents and manuscripts, require different sizes of paper. To change the paper size from the default letter size, follow these steps:

- Click ⬜ Size ⬜ in the Page Setup group of the Page Layout tab.
- Select the paper size that suits your needs.

Additional Information

To return all theme color elements to their original theme colors, you can click Reset before you click Save.

ADD PAGE NUMBERS

In addition to adding page numbers in headers and footers, you can insert page numbers within the text of the document. To do this, follow these steps:

- Move to the location in the text where you want the number to appear.
- Click [Quick Parts ▾] in the Text group of the Insert tab.
- Choose Field.
- Choose the Numbering category.
- Select Page from the field list.
- Select a format of your choice.
- Click [OK].

The number of the current page is inserted in the document at the location of the insertion point. It is a field that can be updated if the page number changes.

1.3 MAKE DOCUMENTS AND CONTENT EASIER TO FIND

ADD TEXT TO TABLE OF CONTENTS

You also can add static text (not a field) to a table of contents. For example, in the table of contents you created in Lab 3, you might want to add the continents above each country. To insert text in a table of contents, follow these steps:

- Click in the table of contents to select it.
- Move the insertion point to the location where you want to enter text.
- If you want the text on a new line, press [←Enter] to insert a new line.
- Type the text you want to include.

Because the text you entered is static, if you regenerate the table of contents list, the text is lost and would need to be entered again. If you simply update the page numbers of the table of contents, the text remains.

MARK AN ENTRY FOR INDEXING

An index is a list of the terms and topics that are discussed in a document, along with the pages that they appear on. An index generally appears at the end of the document and makes it easy for readers to locate information in the document.

To create an index, you first mark the index entries by providing the name of the main entry and the cross-reference in your document. Then you select an index design and build the index.

To identify the text you want to appear in the index, select the text and mark it as an index entry. Word then adds a special XE (Index Entry) field that includes the marked main entry and any cross-reference information that you choose to include.

You can create an index entry for an individual word, phrase, or symbol; a selection; or for a cross-reference that refers to another entry.

To mark existing words or phrases as index entries:

- Select the text.
- Click [Mark Entry] in the Index group of the References tab.
- Click [Mark].

To enter your own text as an index entry:

- Click where you want to insert the index entry.
- Click [Mark Entry] in the Index group of the References tab.
- Type or edit the text in the Main entry box.
- Click [Mark].

To mark entries that span a range of pages:

- Select the range of text that you want the index entry to refer to.
- Click [Bookmark] in the Links group of the Insert tab.
- In the Bookmark name box, type a name and then click [Add].
- In the document, click at the end of the text that you marked with a bookmark.
- Click [Mark Entry] in the Index group of the References tab.
- In the Main entry box, type the index entry for the marked text.
- Under Options, choose Page range.
- In the Bookmark box, type or select the bookmark name that you typed.
- Click [Mark].
- Click [Close] to end marking entries.

If you want, you can customize the entry by creating a subentry, a third-level entry, or a cross-reference to another entry. You also can format the page numbers that will appear in the index using bold or italic.

CREATE THE INDEX

After you mark all the index entries, you choose an index design and build the finished index. Word collects the index entries, sorts them alphabetically, references their page numbers, finds and removes duplicate entries from the same page, and displays the index in the document.

- Click where you want to add the index.
- Click [Insert Index] in the Index group of the References tab.
- Select a design in the Formats box or click [Modify...] to design a custom index layout by modifying a built-in design.
- Select any other index options that you want, such a number of columns and page number alignment.
- Click [OK] to complete the command.

MODIFY AND UPDATE THE INDEX

An index, like a table of contents, is a field that can easily be updated if you add, edit, format, or delete index entries after the index is generated.
To edit or format an existing index entry:

- Locate and click on the index entry in the text (each index entry is enclosed in a special XE (Index Entry) field).
- Change the text inside the quotation marks or apply formatting.

To delete an index entry

- Select the entire index entry field, including the braces ({}), and then press [Delete].

After modifying the index entries, you update the index.

- Click the index and press [F9] or click [Update Index] in the Index group on the References tab.

The index is updated using the same index design settings. If you want to both change the design and update the index, you can regenerate the entire index again.

- Click the index and click [Insert Index] in the Index group of the References tab.
- Select a design in the Formats box or click [Modify...] to design a custom index layout by modifying a built-in design.

- Select any other index options that you want, such as number of columns and page number alignment.
- Click [OK] twice to complete the command and replace the existing index.

CUSTOMIZE AUTOCORRECT OPTIONS

Word includes many default program settings that you can change to personalize how Word works for you. The AutoCorrect settings make corrections to text automatically as you type. To change these settings:

- Click [Office Button] Office Button and click [Word Options].
- Choose the Proofing group.
- Click [AutoCorrect Options...].
- On the AutoCorrect tab, select or clear any of the following check boxes:

  Correct TWo INitial CApitals

  Capitalize first letter of sentences

  Capitalize first letter of table cells

  Capitalize names of days

  Correct accidental use of cAPS LOCK key

  Replace text as you type

  Automatically use suggestions from the spelling checker
- Click [OK].

The changes you make to the AutoCorrect settings will remain in effect until you change them again.

CUSTOMIZE THE QUICK ACCESS TOOLBAR

The Quick Access Toolbar includes three buttons initially: Save, Undo, and Redo. You can customize the Quick Access Toolbar to personalize it for your own use by adding and removing any commands that you want. The first method you can use to do this is to select the commands from a list.

- Click [Office Button] Office Button and click [Word Options].
- Open the Customize group.
- Open the Choose commands from drop-down list and choose the command category that you want.
- In the list of commands in the selected category, click the command that you want to add to the Quick Access Toolbar and then click [Add].
- Alternatively, to remove commands from the Quick Access Toolbar, select the command that you want to remove from the Quick Access Toolbar list and click [Remove].
- After you finish adding/removing any commands that you want, click [OK].

You also can add a command to the Quick Access Toolbar directly from commands that are displayed on the Ribbon. Only commands can be added to the Quick Access Toolbar. The contents of most lists, such as indent and spacing values and individual styles, which also appear on the Ribbon, cannot be added to the Quick Access Toolbar.

- On the Ribbon, click the appropriate tab or group to display the command that you want to add to the Quick Access Toolbar.
- Right-click the command and then choose Add to Quick Access Toolbar from the shortcut menu.

SET THE DEFAULT SAVE LOCATION

Word includes many default program settings that you can change to personalize how Word works for you. Among these settings are the default document format (.docx), the time interval to perform automatic backup for recovery, and locations to save files and recovered files. The default location to save a file is in the current user's My Document folder. To change the default location to save a file:

- Click [Office Button] Office Button and click [Word Options].
- Open the Save group.
- Click [Browse...] next to the Default Save Location text box.
- Find the location where you want your files saved and click [OK].
- Click [OK] to complete the change.

DISABLE OPEN E-MAIL ATTACHMENTS IN READING MODE

Depending on your Word 2007 settings, Word document attachments may open in Print Layout view or in Full-Screen Reading view. The setting that controls the view that will appear when a Word document attachment is opened is controlled by the Word 2007 application settings. To prevent Full-Screen Reading view from opening automatically when you receive a Microsoft Office Word document in e-mail, follow these steps:

- Click [Office Button] Office Button and click [Word Options].
- In the Popular category, deselect the Open e-mail attachments in Full Screen Reading view option to display attachments in Print Layout view.

PERSONALIZE USER NAME AND INITIALS

Word includes many default program settings that you can change to personalize how Word works for you. You can personalize your copy by adding your user name and initials to the program settings so that this information is automatically recorded in a file's document properties.

- Click [Office Button] Office Button and click [Word Options].
- Open the Popular group.
- Enter your name in the User Name text box.
- Enter your initials in the Initials text box.
- Click [OK] to complete the change.

CHANGE RESEARCH OPTIONS

When using the Research task pane to research information, it is often helpful to customize the list of services and reference books that appear in the task pane. You can do this by selecting or excluding specific reference books and research sites and adding research services of your choice. You also can add parental control to this feature to restrict access. Follow these steps to customize the Research task pane:

- Click [Research] in the Proofing group of the Review tab.
- Click Research options in the Research task pane.
- Select or clear the checkmark from the reference book or service that you want included or excluded.
- Add additional features by clicking one of the following options.

Add Services	Enter the URL of the provider of the service you want to add to the list
Update/Remove	Update or remove currently provided services
Parental Control	Turn on content filtering and add a password to prevent turning off this feature

- Click [OK].

2. FORMATTING CONTENT

2.1 FORMAT TEXT AND PARAGRAPHS

CHANGE ALL TEXT FORMATTED WITH ONE STYLE TO ANOTHER STYLE

Sometimes, you may have applied a Quick Style such as a heading to many areas in a document and then you decide to change the style to another for all those entries. To quickly change all text that is formatted in one style to another throughout the document, follow these steps:

- Select the text that is formatted using the Quick Style you want to change.
- Right-click on the selection and choose Styles/Select text with similar formatting.
- Choose another Quick Style.

All text that is formatted in the original Quick Style is updated to the newly selected style.

FORMAT QUOTED MATERIAL

Quoted material can be made to stand out more from surrounding text by applying a predesigned quote style to the selected text. To format quoted material, follow these steps:

- Select the quoted text.
- Choose Quote or Intense Quote from the Quick Styles gallery (Styles group of the Home tab).

The text is formatted using the settings associated with the selected Quick Style.

2.2 MANIPULATE TEXT

USING PASTE ALL

When using the Office Clipboard, if you want to add all the items listed in the Clipboard task pane to the document, follow these steps.

- Click ▣ in the Clipboard group of the Home tab to display the Office Clipboard task pane.
- Copy or cut items to add to the Office Clipboard.
- Click [Paste All] to insert all the items that are listed in the Clipboard task pane into the document.

The items are pasted in the document at the location of the insertion point in the same order in which they were added to the Office Clipboard.

2.3 CONTROL PAGINATION

SECTION BREAKS

Section breaks, like hard page breaks, can easily be removed. When deleting section breaks, however, all formatting that was associated with that section before the break is removed and the text assumes the formatting of the following section.

- Switch to Draft view or display paragraph marks in Print Layout view so that you can see the double-dotted-line section break line.
- Select the section break that you want to delete.
- Press [Delete].

3. WORKING WITH VISUAL CONTENT

3.2 FORMAT ILLUSTRATIONS

SCALING A GRAPHIC

In addition to sizing a graphic object by dragging its sizing handles or by entering exact height and width measurements, you can adjust the size of an

Additional Information

Choose Lock Aspect Ratio if you want both the height and width scales to change together.

object by scaling it. Scaling increases or reduces the height or width of an object by a percentage of the current size. To scale a graphic, follow these steps:

- Select the graphic object whose size you want to change.
- Click ⬜ in the Size group of the Picture Tools Format tab to open the Size dialog box.
- Specify the Height and Width scaling percentages.
- Click OK .

RECOLOR A PICTURE

In addition to adjusting the contrast and brightness of a picture object, you also can change the coloration. Follow these steps to change color effects:

- Select the picture object you want to change.
- Click Recolor in the Adjust group of the Picture Tools Format tab.
- Select from the following options:

Automatic	Applies the default colors associated with the picture
Grayscale	Converts colors to shades of gray
Black and White	Converts colors to black and white
Washout	Changes colors to lighter shades so graphic appears washed out
Transparency	Converts selected color areas to transparent to make underlying information visible

3.3 FORMAT TEXT GRAPHICALLY

INSERT PULL QUOTES

A pull quote is a quote or excerpt from an article that is placed in a larger typeface on the same page, serving to lead readers into an article and to highlight a key topic. Word includes several built-in pull quote text box designs (quick parts) that help you quickly add a pull quote to your document. To format text as a pull quote, follow these steps:

- Click Quick Parts in the Text group of the Insert tab.
- Choose Building Blocks Organizer.
- In the Text Boxes category of the Building Blocks Organizer dialog box, select any of the built-in quote designs (the design name includes the word Quote).
- Enter the text you want displayed in the pull quote text box and move and size it appropriately.

4. ORGANIZING CONTENT

4.1 STRUCTURE CONTENT USING QUICK PARTS

INSERT, EDIT, AND SORT BUILDING BLOCKS

As you learned, building blocks are predesigned pieces of content, such as cover pages, that give you a head start in creating many common types of content. A feature, called the Building Block Organizer, allows you to view, organize, edit properties of, and insert building block elements.

- Click where you want to insert a building block in the document.
- Click Quick Parts in the Text group of the Insert tab.
- Choose Building Blocks Organizer.
- If you know the name, gallery, or category of the building block you want to use or modify, click the column header button to sort the building blocks by the information in the column.

- Select the building block you want to use. (A preview and description of the selected item are displayed.)
- To edit the properties of the selected item, click [Edit Properties...] and make any changes to the properties, such as the category or description of the building block.
- Click [OK] and click [Yes] to update the existing building block with the property changes you made.
- Click [Insert] to insert the building block in the document.

SAVE COMPANY CONTACT INFORMATION AS BUILDING BLOCKS

In Lab 2, you created a building block for a closing. In a similar manner, you could create a building block to save company contact information. To do this, follow these steps:

- Enter the text for the company contact information as you want it to appear when inserted in the document.
- Select the text.
- Click [Quick Parts ▾] in the Text group of the Insert tab.
- Choose Save Selection to Quick Part Gallery.
- Enter a name and other information that is needed to identify and use the building block in the Create New Building Blocks dialog box and click [OK].

MODIFY AND SAVE BUILDING BLOCKS

You also can modify an existing building block and use the same name. For example, you may have created a building block for the company contact information but have forgotten to include the telephone number. To do this, follow these steps:

- Insert the existing building block in the document.
- Edit the building block as needed.
- Select the text to include in the building block.
- Click [Quick Parts ▾] in the Text group of the Insert tab.
- Choose Save Selection to Quick Part Gallery.
- Enter the same name to identify the building block in the Create New Building Blocks dialog box and click [OK].
- Click [Yes] to redefine the existing building block.

INSERT HEADERS FROM QUICK PARTS AND EDIT DOCUMENT TITLES

Another way you can add information in a header or footer is to use the Quick Parts Organizer and select the header or footer building block you want to use. To do this, follow these steps:

- Click [Quick Parts ▾] in the Text group of the Insert tab.
- Choose Building Blocks Organizer.
- Double-click the Gallery heading to sort the building blocks by gallery.
- Select the header building block you want to use. (A preview and description of the selected item are displayed.)
- Click [Insert].

The selected header building block is inserted in the document and the header area is active, ready for you to complete or modify the placeholder information.

4.2 USE TABLES AND LISTS TO ORGANIZE CONTENT

CONVERT TABLE CONTENT TO TEXT

Information that is displayed in a table can be quickly converted to regular text. You can convert an entire table or selected rows of the table. To do this, follow these steps:

- Select the rows or table that you want to convert to paragraphs.
- Click ⊞≣ Convert to Text in the Data group of the Table Tools Layout tab.
- In the Convert Table to Text dialog box, select the type of separator character that you want to use in place of the column boundaries.
- Click OK.

Selecting Paragraphs as the separator displays the contents of each table cell on a separate line. Selecting Tabs as the separator displays the content of each table cell on a single line, separated by tab spaces; the table rows are separated with paragraph marks.

4.3 MODIFY TABLES

SPLIT CELLS

In opposition to merging cells, the contents of table cells can be split into multiple cells. To split table cells, follow these steps:

- Click in a cell, or select multiple cells that you want to split.
- Click ⊞ Split Cells in the Merge group of the Table Tools Layout tab.
- Enter the number of columns or rows that you want to split the selected cells into.
- Click OK.

4.4 INSERT AND FORMAT REFERENCES AND CAPTIONS

CREATE, MODIFY, AND UPDATE A TABLE OF AUTHORITIES

A table of authorities is a list of the references in a legal document, such as to cases, statutes, and rules, along with the numbers of the pages the references appear on. The process of creating a table of authorities is similar to creating a bibliography.

First, you identify the citations by marking them. As you mark citations, you specify the category you want the citation to appear in, such as cases or statutes. You also can change or add categories of citations. To do this, follow these steps:

- Select the legal citation text that has already been entered in the document.
- Click ⧉ Mark Citation in the Table of Authorities group of the References tab.
- Select the category for the citation and click Mark. Use Mark All to locate and mark identical citations in the document.
- Click Close when you are finished.
- Continue to mark all citations in the document in the same manner.

Next, you build the table of authorities. When you build a table of authorities, Word searches for the marked citations, organizes them by category, references their page numbers, and displays the table of authorities in the document. To do this, follow these steps:

- Move to the location in the document where you want the table of authorities inserted.
- Click 🗒 Insert Table of Authorities in the Table of Authorities group of the References tab.

- Select All from the Categories list if you want to display citations in all categories, or select only the category you want generated.
- Select a design from the Format list or click [Modify...] to design a custom format by modifying the built-in template design.
- Select any other options for the table of authorities that you want to use, such a tab leaders.
- Click [OK].

The table of authorities is generated. Citations appear listed in the categories that they were assigned along with the page number the citation is on. The table of authorities is a field that can be updated, just like updating a table of figures. To do this, follow these steps:

- Click the table of authorities and press [F9] or click [🔳] Update Table of Authorities in the Table of Authorities group on the References tab.

The table of authorities is updated using the same format settings. If you want to both change the format and update the table, you can regenerate the entire table of authorities again.

- Click the table of authorities and click [🔳] Insert Table of Authorities in the Table of Authorities group of the References tab.
- Select the category and format and any other options that you want.
- Click [OK] to complete the command and click [Yes] to replace the existing table of authorities.

5. REVIEWING DOCUMENTS

5.2 COMPARE AND MERGE DOCUMENT VERSIONS

COMPARE DOCUMENT VERSIONS

You can compare changes made to two versions of the same document using the legal blackline feature. This feature compares two documents and displays only what changed between them. The documents that are being compared are not changed. To use this feature, follow these steps:

- Click [Compare] in the Compare group of the Review tab and choose Compare.
- Select the original document and the revised document in the Compare Documents dialog box.
- Click [More >>] and choose the comparison settings you want to compare in the documents. Under Show changes, choose whether you want to show character- or word-level changes. Under Show changes in, choose which document you want the changes to appear in. The default is in a new third document.
- Click [OK].

A new third document is displayed in which tracked changes in the original document are accepted, and changes in the revised document are shown as tracked changes. The source documents that are being compared are not changed.

SELECT REVIEWERS

In a merged document with tracked changes from several reviewers, it is often helpful to display tracked changes and comments only from selected reviewers at any one time. To select reviewers, follow these steps:

- Open the [Show Markup ▾] drop-down list in the Tracking group of the Review tab.
- Select Reviewers and clear all check boxes except for the ones next to the names of the reviewers you want to see.

MERGE INTO NEW DOCUMENT

Generally, when merging documents, you merge changes into the original document. However, you can choose to merge the changes into a new, third document. To do this, follow these steps:

- Click [Compare] on the Review tab and choose Combine.
- In the Combine dialog box, select the files to combine.
- Specify the comparison settings.
- Under Show changes in, choose New document as where you want the changes to appear.
- Click [OK].

6. SHARING AND SECURING CONTENT

6.1 PREPARE DOCUMENTS FOR SHARING

SAVE TO APPROPRIATE FORMATS

Word 2007 uses a new file format based on the Office Open XML format (XML is short for Extensible Markup Language). This new format makes your documents safer by separating files that contain scripts or macros to make it easier to identify and block unwanted code or macros that could be dangerous to your computer. It also makes file sizes smaller and makes files less susceptible to damage. The file extensions shown in the table below are used to identify the different types of Word document files.

FILE EXTENSION	DESCRIPTION
.docx	Word 2007 document without macros or code
.dotx	Word 2007 template without macros or code
.docm	Word 2007 document that could contain macros or code
.xps	Word 2007 shared document (see note below)
.doc	Word 95–2003 document

Note: The XPS format is a fixed-layout electronic file format that preserves document formatting and enables file sharing. The XPS format ensures that when the file is viewed online or printed, it retains exactly the format, that you intended and that data in the file cannot be easily changed. To save as an XPS file format, you must have installed the free add-in.

There are several ways to save a Word document as any of these types:

- Click Office Button and choose Save As.
- Choose Word Document or Other Formats to open the Save As dialog box.
- Open the Save as Type drop-down list and select the file type.
- Specify a name for the file and location to save it.
- Click [Save].

OR

- Click Office Button and choose Save As.
- Select Word Document, Word Template, or Word 97-2003 Document. (The default file type in the Save as Type drop-down list will reflect the file type of your selection. You could still change it to any other type.)

- Specify a name for the file and location to save it.
- Click [Save].

If you open a file in Word 2007 that was created in an earlier version, the automatic option in the Save As dialog box is to save it as the previous version type (.doc).

USE THE COMPATIBILITY CHECKER

In Word 2007, you can open files created in previous versions of Word, from Word 95 to Word 2003. You also can create a file in Word 2007 format and then save it as the previous version (.doc). If any 2007 features are not compatible with the previous version, the Compatibility Checker tells you so and any new features will not work. The Compatibility Checker runs automatically; however, you can run it manually if you want to find out what features in a document you are creating will be incompatible. The Compatibility Checker identifies those features that are incompatible and the number of occurrences in the document.

Follow these steps to run the Compatibility Checker:

- Click 🔵 Office Button and choose Prepare.
- Choose Run Compatibility Checker.
- Click [OK] after looking at the features that were identified and the number of occurrences.

6.2 CONTROL DOCUMENT ACCESS

RESTRICT FORMATTING IN PROTECTED DOCUMENTS

In addition to protecting a document from editing changes, a document also can be protected against formatting changes. You can stop users from making formatting changes to selected portions of the document or the entire document. You also can restrict the styles that can be used to those you select. To restrict formatting, follow these steps:

- Click 🔲 in the Styles group of the Home tab to open the Styles dialog box.

- In the Styles task pane, click 📝 Manage Styles.

- Open the Restrict tab and make the following selections as needed.

- In the Sort order list, select the sort order that you want to use to view the styles.

- Click the individual styles that you want to restrict, or select groups of styles by clicking one of the following options.

Select Visible	Highlights the styles that appear by default in the recommended list. To see the list of recommended styles, open the Recommend tab
Select Built-in	Selects all of the styles that are included in Word 2007 but not any custom styles that you created
Select All	Selects all of the styles that are included in Word 2007 including custom styles

- Select one or more of the following:

Limit formatting to permitted styles	Allow reviewers to change formatting using only permitted styles. Reviewers won't be able to format text directly or use styles that are restricted.
Allow AutoFormat to override formatting	Allow reviewers to use restricted styles when automatically formatting text such as hyperlinks or automatic bullets. This option is available only if Limit formatting to permitted styles is selected.

| Block Theme or Scheme switching | Prevent reviewers from changing the themes that are used in the document. |
| Block Quick Style Set switching | Prevent reviewers from changing the current style set. |

- Click [Restrict].
- Click [OK].
- Add a password so that only people who know the password can remove the restriction.

Additional Information

A lock icon 🔒 appears next to any styles that are restricted.

ADD A SIGNATURE LINE FOR DIGITAL SIGNATURES

A visible digital signature is displayed on a signature line in the document. A signature line looks like a typical signature placeholder that might appear in a print document, but it works differently. When a signature line is inserted into an Office document, the document author can specify information about the intended signer, as well as instructions for the signer.

To create a signature line for a digital signature, follow these steps:

- Move to the location in your document where you want to add a signature line.
- Click [Signature Line ▾] in the Text group of the Insert tab.
- In the Signature Setup dialog box, type information about the person (name, position, e-mail address) who will be digitally signing on this signature line. This information is displayed directly beneath the signature line in the document.

X
_____
Linda
Author

- If you want to provide the signer with any instructions, type these instructions in the Instructions to signer box. These instructions are displayed in the Signature dialog box that the signer uses to sign the document. If you want the signer to be able to add comments along with the signature, select the Allow the signer to add comments in the Sign dialog check box. If you want to show the date when the signature is added in the signature line, select the Show sign date in signature line check box.
- Click [OK].

When an electronic copy of the document is sent to the intended signer, this person sees the signature line and a notification that his or her signature is requested. The signer can click the signature line to digitally sign the document. The signer can then either type a signature, select a digital image of his or her signature, or write a signature by using the inking feature of the Tablet PC.

When the signer adds a visible representation of his or her signature to the document, a digital signature is added simultaneously to authenticate the identity of the signer. After a document is digitally signed, it will become read-only to prevent modifications to its content.

Data File List

Use	Create
Lab 1	
wd01_Flyer1.docx	
wd01_Lions.wmf	Flyer.docx
wd01_Parrot.wmf	Flyer1.docx
Step-by-Step	
1.	Web Site Memo.docx
2. wd01_Child on Bike.wmf	Bike Event.docx
3. wd01_Coffee.wmf	Grand Re-Opening.docx
4. wd01_Note Taking Skills.docx	Note Taking Skills.docx
5. wd01_History of Ice Cream.docx	Ice Cream History.docx
wd01_Ice Cream.wmf	
On Your Own	
1.	Mexico Adventure.docx
2.	Pool Rules.docx
3.	Astronomy Basics.docx
4.	Volunteer Opportunities.docx
5.	Career Report.docx
Lab 2	
wd02_Tour Letter.docx	Tour Letter2
wd02_Flyer2.docx	
Step-by-Step	
1. wd02_Note Taking Tips.docx	Note Taking Skills2.docx
Note Taking Skills.docx (Lab 1)	
2. wd02_Water Conservation.docx	Water Conservation Column.docx
wd02_Conservation Tips.docx	
wd02_Water Hose	
3. wd02_Fitness Fun.docx	Fitness Fun Flyer.docx
4.	Conference Volunteers.docx
5. wd02_Coffee Flyer.docx	Weekly Specials.docx
On Your Own	
1.	Reterence Letter.docx
2.	Cell Phone Rates.docx
3.	Yard Sale Flyer.docx
4.	Wyoming Facts.docx
5.	Ethics Report.docx

Use	Create
Lab 3	
wd03_Tour Research.docx	Research Outline.docx
wd03_Giraffe.wmf	Tour Research.docx
wd03_Parrots.wmf	
Step-by-Step	
1.	Spam Outline.docx
2.	ARS Department Contacts.docx
3. wd03_Digital Cameras.docx	Digital Cameras.docx
wd03_Camera.wmf	
wd03_Computer.wmf	
4. wd03_ATT Brochure.docx	ATT Brochure.docx
wd03_ATT.wmf	
wd03_Hiking.wmf	
wd03_Kayaking.wmf	
wd03_Tracey.wmf	
wd03_Train.wmf	
5. wd03_Yoga Guide.docx	Yoga Guide.docx
wd03_History.wmf	
wd03_Yoga Pose.wmf	
On Your Own	
1. wd03_Kayaking flyer.docx	Kayaking Flyer.docx
wd03_Kayaking.wmf	
2. wd03_Coffee Outline.docx	Coffee Report.docx
3.	Job Search.docx
4.	Research.docx
5.	Computer Viruses.docx
Working Together 1	
wdwt_Presentations.docx	New Tour Presentations.html
wdwt_Locations.docx	Tour Locations.html
Step-by-Step	
1. wdwt_LosAngeles.docx	LosAngeles.html
Tour Locations (Lab WT1)	
2. Bike Event.docx (Lab 1)	Celebrate Bicycling.html
3. Grand Re-Opening.docx (Lab 1)	Café Locations.html
	Cafe Flyer.html
wdwt_Coffee.wmf	
wdwt_Café Locations.docx	
Lab 4	
wd04_Headline	Newsletter Headline
wd04_Tanzania Facts	Tanzania Facts
wd04_Be An Adventure Traveler	March Newsletter
wd04_Costa Rica Adventure	
wd04_Newsletter Articles	
wd04_Giraffe.jpg	

Use	Create
Supplied/Used File	**Created/Saved As**
Step-by-Step	

1. wd04_Water Headline
   wd04_Water Tips
   wd04_Water.jpg
	Water Newsletter

2. wd04_Lifestyle Spinning
   wd04_Fitness Club Headline
   wd04_Banner
   wd04_Heart Rate Monitors
   wd04_Bike.wmf
	Spinning Newsletter

3. wd04_Coffee
   wd04_City.jpg
   wd04_Coffee Beans.gif
   wd04_Coffee Plant.gif
	Internet Cafe Newsletter

4. wd04_Dental Care
   wd04_Bad Breath
   wd04_Periodontal Disease
   wd04_Paws.wmf
   wd04_Dog with Vet.jpg
   wd04_Checkup.wmf
	ARF Newsletter

5. wd04_Hike Triple Crown
   wd04_Trail.jpg
   wd04_Lightweight
   wd04_Low Impact
   wd04_Forest.jpg
	ATT Hiking Newsletter

On Your Own	
1.	Activity Newsletter
2. wd04_Ice Cream	Ice Cream Newsletter
3.	PTA Newsletter
4.	Garden Newsletter
5.	My Newsletter
Lab 5	
wd05_Professional Memo	Sales Analysis Memo ATT Memo New Department Memo
wd05_Logo Elements	Logo Grouped
Step-by-Step	
1. wd05_Elegant Design Memo	Green Tea Memo
2. wd05_Contemporary Design Memo	Body Mind Memo
3. wd05_Professional Design Memo wd05_LFC Logo	Rock Climbing Memo LFC Logo Grouped
4. wd05_Elegant Design Memo	Animal Adoption Memo
5. wd05_Professional Design Memo wd05_Theater	Theater Memo
On Your Own	
1.	Movie Data
2.	Language Memo

Reference 1

Use	Create
3.	Pet Ownership Memo
4.	World Internet Use
5.	Cars Memo

Lab 6

Use	Create
wd06_Form	Catalog Request Form
	Catalog Request Form (printed)
	Catalog Request Form (on-screen)
wd06_Camping Safari	Camping Safari Reviewed
wd06_Everest Original	Camping Safari E-mail
wd06_Everest Dan	Everest Revised
wd06_Everest Carol	
wd06_Everest Paragraph	
wd06_Tour Letter	Tour Letter Main Document
	Client List (.mdb file)
	ATT Mailing Labels

Step-by-Step

Use	Create
1. wd06_Fitness Member Survey	Fitness Member Survey
2. wd06_Fitness Member Survey	Fitness Member Survey On-screen
3. wd06_Cafe Schedule	April Café Schedule
wd06_Cafe Schedule Evan	
wd06_Cafe Schedule Melissa	
wd06_Cafe Schedule Paragraph	
wd06_Mike Night.wmf	
4. wd06_Animal Rescue Volunteer Letter	ARF Volunteer Letter
	ARF Volunteer Recruitment List
	ARF Labels
5. wd06_Kids Rule Summer Movies	Kids Rule Summer Movie Flyer
wd06_Kids Rule Summer Movies Reviewed Kids Rule List	
	Kids Rule Movie Merge Letter

On Your Own

Use	Create
1. wd06_Zoo Survey	Zoo Survey Printed
2. wd06_Zoo Survey	Zoo Survey On-screen
3. wd06_Historical Society	Historical Society Letter
4. wd06_Safari Park	Safari Park Letter
5.	Hotel Rewards Letter

Working Together 2

Use	Create
wdwt2_Annual Tour Sales	Major Tour Sales.xls
wdwt2_New Tour Status	New Tour Status
wdwt2_New Tour Bookings.xlsx	New Tour Bookings Linked
wdwt2_New Tour Sales	New Tour Sales
wdwt2_New Tour Income.xlsx	New Tour Income

Step-by-Step

Use	Create
1. wdwt2_Animal Angels Sales	AA Sales Memo
wdwt2_AA Sales.xlsx	
wdwt2_Time Sheet Memo	Time Sheet Linked
wdwt2_Time Sheet.xlsx	Time Sheet
2. wdwt2_Opera Donors	Opera Donors2
wdwt2_COF Donors.xlsx	

Microsoft Certified Applications Specialist (MCAS)

Microsoft Office Word 2007

The Microsoft Certified Applications Specialist (MCAS) certification program is designed to measure your proficiency in performing basic tasks using the Office 2007 applications. Getting certified demonstrates that you have the skills and provides a valuable industry credential for employment.

After completing the labs in the Microsoft Office Word 2007 Introductory edition, you have learned the following MCAS skills:

Description	Lab
1. Creating and Customizing Documents	
1.1 Creating and Formatting Documents	
Work with templates	Labs 1, 5, 6
Apply Quick Styles to documents	Lab 3
Format documents by using themes	Lab 3, More About
Customize themes	Lab 3, More About
Format document backgrounds	Lab 1, Working Together 1
Insert blank pages or cover pages	Lab 3
1.2 Lay Out Documents	
Format Pages	Labs 1, 2, 3, 5, More About
Create and modify headers and footers	Lab 3
Create and format columns	Lab 4
1.3 Make Documents and Content Easier to Find	
Create, modify, and update tables of contents	Lab 3, More About
Create, modify, and update indexes	More About
Modify document properties	Lab 1
Insert document navigation tools	Labs 3, 4, Working Together 1
1.4 Personalize Office Word 2007	
Customize Word options	Common Features, Lab 1, More About
Change research options	More About
2. Formatting Content	
2.1 Format text and paragraphs	
Apply styles	Labs 2, 3, More About

Description	Lab
Create and modify styles	Labs 3, 4
Format characters	Labs 1, 2, 4
Format paragraphs	Labs 1, 2, 4, More About
Set and clear tabs	Lab 2
2.2 Manipulate text	
Cut, copy, and paste text	Labs 2, 4, Working Together 2, More About
Find and replace text	Labs 2, 6
2.3 Control pagination	
Insert and delete page breaks	Labs 2, 3, 4
Create and modify sections	Labs 3, 4, 5, 6

3. Working with Visual Content

Description	Lab
3.1 Insert illustrations	
Insert SmartArt graphics	Lab 5
Insert pictures from files and clip art	Labs 1, 3, 5
Insert Shapes	Lab 2
3.2 Format illustrations	
Format text wrapping	Labs 3, 4, 5, Working Together 1
Format by sizing, cropping, scaling, and rotating	Labs 1, 4, 5, More About
Apply Quick Styles	Lab 5
Set contrast, brightness, and coloration	Lab 4, More About
Add text to SmartArt graphics and shapes	Labs 2, 5
Compress pictures	Lab 4
3.3 Format text graphically	
Insert and modify WordArt	Lab 4
Insert Pull Quotes	More About
Insert and modify drop caps	Lab 4
3.4 Insert and modify text boxes	
Insert text boxes	Lab 4
Format text boxes	Lab 4
Link text boxes	Lab 4

4. Organizing Content

Description	Lab
4.1 Structure content by using Quick Parts	
Insert building blocks in document	Labs 2, 4, More About
Save frequently used data as building blocks	Lab 2, More About
Insert formatted headers and footers from Quick Parts	Lab 3, More About
Insert fields from Quick Parts	Lab 3
4.2 Use tables and lists to organize content	
Create tables and lists	Labs 2, 3, 6, More About

Reference 2: Microsoft Certified Applications
Specialist (MCAS)

www.mhhe.com/oleary

Description	Lab
Sort content	Labs 2, 3
Modify list formats	Labs 2, 5
4.3 Modify tables	
Apply Quick Styles to tables	Lab 3
Modify table properties and options	Labs 3, 5
Merge and split table cells	Labs 3, 5, More About
Perform calculations in tables	Lab 5
Change the position and direction of cell contents	Lab 5
4.4 Insert and format references and captions	
Create and modify sources	Lab 3
Insert citations and captions	Lab 3
Insert and modify bibliographies	Lab 3
Select reference styles	Lab 3
Create, modify, and update tables of figures	Lab 3
Create, modify, and update tables of authorities	More About
4.5 Merge documents and data sources	
Create merged documents	Lab 6
Merge data into form letters	Lab 6
Create envelopes and labels	Lab 6
5. Reviewing Documents	
5.1 Navigate documents	
Move quickly using the Find and GoTo commands	Labs 2, 3, 4
Change window views	Labs 1, 2, 3, Working Together 1
5.2 Compare and merge document versions	
Compare document versions	More About
Merge document versions	Lab 6, More About
5.3 Manage track changes	
Display markup	Lab 6
Enable, disable, accept, and reject tracked changes	Lab 6
Change tracking options	Lab 6, More About
5.4 Insert, modify, and delete comments	Lab 6
6. Sharing and Securing Content	
6.1 Prepare documents for sharing	
Save to appropriate formats	Lab 1, Working Together 1
Identify document features not supported by previous versions	More About
Remove inappropriate or private information	Lab 6

Description	Lab
6.2 Control document access	
Restrict permissions to documents	Lab 6
Mark documents as final	Lab 6
Set passwords	Lab 6
Protect documents	Lab 6, More About
6.3 Attach digital signatures	
Authenticate documents by using digital signatures	Lab 6
Insert a line for a digital signature	More About

Reference 2: Microsoft Certified Applications
Specialist (MCAS)

Index

Credits

WordLab1   (c) Brand X Pictures/PunchStock
WordLab2   Javier Pierini/Getty Images
WordLab3   Corbis
WordLab4   Photodisc/Getty Images
WordLab5   Bruno Herdt/Getty Images
WordLab6   RF/Corbis